An Anthology of the Cambridge Platonists

Notwithstanding their neglect in many histories of ideas in the West, the Cambridge Platonists constitute the most significant and influential group of thinkers in the Platonic tradition between the Florentine Renaissance and the Romantic Age. This anthology offers readers a unique, thematically structured compendium of their key texts, along with an extensive introduction and a detailed account of their legacy. The volume draws upon a resurgence of interest in thinkers such as Benjamin Whichcote, 1609–1683; Ralph Cudworth, 1618–1688; Henry More, 1614–1687; John Smith, 1618–1652, and Anne Conway 1631–1679, and includes hitherto neglected extracts and some works of less familiar authors within the group, like George Rust 1627?–1670; Joseph Glanvill, 1636–1680, and John Norris 1657–1712. It also highlights the Cambridge Platonists' important role in the history of philosophy and theology, influencing luminaries such as Shaftesbury, Berkeley, Leibniz, Joseph de Maistre, S.T. Coleridge, and W.R. Emerson. *An Anthology of the Cambridge Platonists* is an indispensable guide to the serious study of a pivotal group of Western metaphysicians and is of great value for both students and scholars of philosophy, literature, history, and theology.

Key Features

- The only systematic anthology to the Cambridge Platonists available, facilitating quick comprehension of key themes and ideas
- Uses new translations of the Latin works, vastly improving upon faulty and misleading earlier translations
- Offers a wide range of new perspectives on the Cambridge Platonists, showing the extent of their influence in early modern philosophy and beyond.

Douglas Hedley is Professor of the Philosophy of Religion in the Faculty of Divinity at the University of Cambridge and Fellow of Clare College. He is the author of *Coleridge, Philosophy and Religion* (2000) and a trilogy on the Religious Imagination, and has edited various volumes including *Revisioning Cambridge Platonism* (2019). He was the Principal Investigator of an AHRC grant, "The Cambridge Platonists at the Origins of Enlightenment, 2016–2019."

Christian Hengstermann is Associate Lecturer in Classics at Wuppertal University in Germany and Member of the Cambridge Centre of the Study of Platonism. He is the author of *Origenes und der Ursprung der Freiheitsmetaphysik* (2016) and has edited various volumes, including *"That Miracle of the Christian World": Origenism and Christian Platonism in Henry More* (2020) and *The History of the Religious Imagination in Christian Platonism* (2021).

An Anthology of the Cambridge Platonists

Sources and Commentary

Edited by Douglas Hedley and
Christian Hengstermann

NEW YORK AND LONDON

Designed cover image: Courtesy of the British Museum

First published 2024
by Routledge
605 Third Avenue, New York, NY 10158

and by Routledge
4 Park Square, Milton Park, Abingdon, Oxon, OX14 4RN

Routledge is an imprint of the Taylor & Francis Group, an informa business

© 2024 selection and editorial matter, Douglas Hedley and Christian Hengstermann; individual chapters, the contributors

The right of Douglas Hedley and Christian Hengstermann to be identified as the authors of the editorial material, and of the authors for their individual chapters, has been asserted in accordance with sections 77 and 78 of the Copyright, Designs and Patents Act 1988.

All rights reserved. No part of this book may be reprinted or reproduced or utilised in any form or by any electronic, mechanical, or other means, now known or hereafter invented, including photocopying and recording, or in any information storage or retrieval system, without permission in writing from the publishers.

Trademark notice: Product or corporate names may be trademarks or registered trademarks, and are used only for identification and explanation without intent to infringe.

ISBN: 978-1-032-02383-0 (hbk)
ISBN: 978-1-032-02384-7 (pbk)
ISBN: 978-1-003-18315-0 (ebk)

DOI: 10.4324/9781003183150

Typeset in Bembo
by Apex CoVantage, LLC

Contents

Acknowledgements   *viii*

PART I
Cambridge Platonism at the Origins of the Enlightenment   **1**

1 Cambridge Platonism: A Philosophical Introduction   3
   DOUGLAS HEDLEY

2 The Cambridge Platonists: A Very Brief History   21
   MARILYN A. LEWIS

3 From the Latitude Men to the Cambridge Enlightenment: Changing Nomenclatures   29
   CHRISTIAN HENGSTERMANN

4 From Campagnac to Taliaferro and Teply: Cambridge Platonist Anthologies Old and New   33
   CHRISTIAN HENGSTERMANN

PART II
Historical Context and Philosophical Programme   **39**

5 Conversion and Original Insight   45
   CHRISTIAN HENGSTERMANN

6 Political Platonism and Early Sermons on Rational Theology   53
   CHRISTIAN HENGSTERMANN

7 The New Sect of Latitude Men: Religious Toleration and Moderation in Revolutionary and Restoration England   60
   MARILYN A. LEWIS

8 True Theism and the Philosophy of Religion   65
   CHRISTIAN HENGSTERMANN

PART III
Cambridge Platonism in Early Modern Thought 71
CHRISTIAN HENGSTERMANN

9	The Critique of John Calvin: Divine Fate Immoral	93
10	The Critique of Thomas Hobbes: Mechanistic Fate	107
11	The Critique of René Descartes: Infinity and Nullibism	121
12	The Critique of Jacob Böhme: The Critiques of Enthusiasm and Alchemistic Pantheism	156
13	The Critique of Baruch de Spinoza: Atheism and Hylozoism	167

PART IV
Ontology and Metaphysics 197
DOUGLAS HEDLEY

14	The Character of Metaphysics	199
15	The Existence and Nature of God	201
16	Space	210
17	Nature	218
18	Body and Spirit	224

PART V
Epistemology and Ethics 241
CHRISTIAN HENGSTERMANN

19	Intuitive Vision and the First Principle of Divine Goodness	243
20	Libertarian Freedom	251
21	Theoretical Reason and Knowledge	258
22	Practical Reason and Virtue	260
23	The Sources of Political Power	266

PART VI
Rational Theology 273

24	Faith and Reason DOUGLAS HEDLEY	281
25	The Fall of the Soul and the Resurrection of the Body MARILYN A. LEWIS	290

26	**Soul-Making Theodicy** CHRISTIAN HENGSTERMANN	295
27	**Christ's Sacrifice** DOUGLAS HEDLEY	302
28	**The Conflagration and Restitution of All Things** CHRISTIAN HENGSTERMANN	306

PART VII
Epilogue 319
DOUGLAS HEDLEY

29	The Reception History of the Cambridge Platonists	321

Suggested Further Reading   *336*
A Brief Cambridge Platonist Prosopography   *340*
MARILYN A. LEWIS

Name Index   *344*
Subject Index   *347*

Acknowledgements

One of the explicit aims of our anthology is to repudiate decisively the widespread error that the Cambridge Platonists were an insular phenomenon. It is fitting to note that the present work is the product of a modern republic of letters. The editors have a deep debt to Marilyn Lewis. Marilyn is a decisive collaborator for the Anthology: her historical knowledge and unstinting support has been an invaluable element in the project. Ben Davidson's enthusiasm, critical acumen and scholarly judgement have been indispensable.

The present work is the product of several research projects. One is a decade of collaboration between the University of Cambridge and the Westphalian Wilhelms-Universität of Münster, especially the Origen Research Centre (Forschungstelle Origines) (2010–2016) led by Alfons Fürst. Since 2017, there has been regular co-operation on themes of religious philosophy in relation to the Cambridge Platonists with Klaus Müller, Benedikt Göcke and Thomas Hanke at the universities of Bochum and Münster. 2022 saw the Foundation or the Cambridge Platonist Research Caucus in Cambridge.

The current book also draws upon the work of an AHRC major grant The Cambridge Platonists at the origins of Enlightenment (2016–2019) at the Universities of Cambridge and Bristol. Foremost among those deserving thanks is Sarah Hutton for her pioneering and inspiring work on the Cambridge Platonists, but also David Leech, Mark Burden, James Bryson as other members of the research team for the Cambridge Platonist Sourcebook. Adrian Mihai's British Academy grant on Ralph Cudworth's *True Intellectual System of the Universe* was of fundamental significance for the development of the research on Cudworth.

In 2018 The Cambridge Centre for the Study of Platonism co-hosted the 'Metaphysics of Conversion from Late Antiquity to Early Modernity' Research Seminar with members of McGill University's conversion project in Montreal, Canada, sponsored by the Social Science and Humanities Research Council of Canada. Moreover, much further research was stimulated by the 2020–2023 Grant awarded from the Social Sciences and Humanities Research Council of Canada (SSHRC) The Reception of German Mysticism in Early Modern England, hosted by Torrance Kirby at McGill University together with co-investigators Garth Green and Douglas Hedley.

The present work would not have been possible without the support, encouragement and judicious critique of scholars of the Cambridge Platonists, and more broadly The British Society for the History of Philosophy. Jasper Reid has provided invaluable suggestions and criticisms. Daniel Tolan, Stephen Gersh, Stephen Clark, Jon Thompson, Andreea Maria Lemnaru-Carrez, Bogdan Deznan, Anna Corrias, Dragos Calma, Maria Rosa Antognazza, Karen Felter Vaucanson and Jonathan Lyonhart have all made significant contributions. All errors and failings, however, are entirely down to the editors.

The Cambridge Platonists were divines as well as philosophers, and it has always seemed appropriate that the legacy of one of the great schools of British philosophy should be housed in the Faculty of Divinity, the home of later Platonic Divines such as B.F. Westcott or W.R. Inge. The editors are grateful for the generous financial and logistical support of the Faculty of Divinity, not least for hosting a special seminar on the texts chosen for this Anthology.

Clare College, once the stamping ground of Ralph Cudworth, Thomas Burnet and John Tillotson, has often provided the venue for numerous workshops, and the generous support of the Master and Fellows is gratefully acknowledged.

Douglas Hedley and Christian Hengstermann
September 2022

Part I

Cambridge Platonism at the Origins of the Enlightenment

Chapter 1

Cambridge Platonism
A Philosophical Introduction

Douglas Hedley

Again, Plato may be regarded as the 'captain' (ἀρχηγὸς) or leader of a goodly band of followers; for in the Republic is to be found the original of Cicero's De Republica, of St. Augustine's City of God, of the Utopia of Sir Thomas More, and of the numerous other imaginary States which are framed upon the same model. The extent to which Aristotle or the Aristotelian school were indebted to him in the Politics has been little recognised, and the recognition is the more necessary because it is not made by Aristotle himself. The two philosophers had more in common than they were conscious of; and probably some elements of Plato remain still undetected in Aristotle. In English philosophy too, many affinities may be traced, not only in the works of the Cambridge Platonists, but in great original writers like Berkeley or Coleridge, to Plato and his ideas.

Benjamin Jowett[1]

The seventeenth century is often referred to as the age of genius. It was the era of a group of philosophers and divines whom we know as 'the Cambridge Platonists'. There has been a remarkable resurgence of work on the Cambridge Platonists in the last couple of decades. Charles Taliaferro produced an introduction to the philosophy of religion, *Evidence and Faith: Philosophy and Religion since the Seventeenth Century* (Cambridge, UK: Cambridge University Press, 2005), that began with them. Individual Cambridge Platonists have been the subject of major monographs, including most recently Jasper Reid's *The Metaphysics of Henry More* (Springer, 2012); David Leech's *The Hammer of the Cartesians: Henry More's Philosophy of Spirit and the Origins of Modern Atheism* (Leuven: Peeters, 2015); and Lutz Bergemann's *Ralph Cudworth, System aus Transformation: Zur Naturphilosophie der Cambridge Platonists und ihrer Methode* (Berlin: De Gruyter, 2017). There have also been collections dedicated to Cambridge Platonism, such as a 2017 issue of the *British Journal for the History of Philosophy* edited by Sarah Hutton; and *Revisioning Cambridge Platonism*, edited by Douglas Hedley and David Leech (Springer, 2020). The Cambridge Platonist Research Group was set up in 2012 with the aim of reviving interest in these thinkers and of initiating new research into their thought and legacy. In 2016, the group acquired AHRC funding for a three-year project with the title 'The Cambridge Platonists at the Origins of the Enlightenment'. The principal output of this project was an online sourcebook of primary texts from Cambridge Platonists, their defenders and their detractors.[2] In 2017, the Cambridge Centre for the Study of Platonism was established, and it has since hosted an array of workshops and conferences on the Cambridge Platonists. In 2022, the Cambridge Platonist Research Caucus was founded. All this has coincided with an increasing awareness of the limitations of the well-established curriculum of Descartes-Locke-Berkeley-Hume as a problem-orientated prelude to contemporary issues in philosophy of mind and epistemology. The current volume is in part an endeavour to remedy such restrictions.

It may seem odd that there was a resurgence of Platonism in the heyday of the new science, a time of relentless conflict and controversy about government, sovereignty and tolerance. Yet this epoch of Hobbes' "war of all against all", the site of the revival of radical materialism, was also the "spiritual Platonic old England" so admired by Samuel Taylor Coleridge (Notebooks II, 2598). Indeed, the Cambridge Platonists are foundational figures in the development of philosophy in the English language: familiar terms, such as 'materialism', 'consciousness', 'Cartesianism', 'Gnosticism' and even 'Philosophy of Religion' itself, were coined by these writers. In an age of turmoil and tumult, the scholastic orthodoxy of the university curriculum was under threat; yet not just from reductionists and materialists like Hobbes. There was a conscious renewal of the legacy of the Athenian sage, his late antique interpreters and the Platonising fathers of the early church in Benjamin Whichcote, Ralph Cudworth, Henry More and their circle. Theirs was a Platonism shaped by the interests and obsessions of these genial minds, a system of Neoplatonism developed in dialogue with the philosophy of Descartes and the physiology of Harvey.[3] The Cambridge Platonists, like their better-known contemporaries, rejected the substantial forms and intentional species of the late scholastic world; they also accepted the distinction between primary and secondary qualities. But for the Cambridge Platonists, primary qualities cannot explain consciousness; neither can nature be reduced to matter in motion, nor the human being be understood in stark Cartesian terms. Thus, theirs was a philosophy that sought variously to qualify and counter the dualism of Descartes, the materialism of Hobbes and the pantheism of Spinoza and to promote instead a metaphysics of spirit.

The reasons for the relative neglect of the Cambridge Platonists are various. One is the influential interpretation of Ernst Cassirer in *Die Platonische Renaissance in England* (Leipzig: B.G. Teubner, 1932), in which the Cambridge Platonists are seen as admirable humanists who are nevertheless essentially antiquarian and backward-looking. Yet the work of eminent historians of thought like Frederick Beiser in *The Sovereignty of Reason* (Princeton, NJ: Princeton University Press, 1996) has shown how the Cambridge Platonists played a central role in the emergence of reason as the sovereign model of truth in politics and religion. Stephen Darwall in his seminal work, *The British Moralists and the Internal Ought 1640–1740* (Cambridge, UK: Cambridge University Press, 1995), has shown convincingly that Cudworth, Shaftesbury and Butler developed a theory of ethical obligation as requiring self-determination, a view at odds with a more empirical or naturalistic approach. It is also often assumed that the legacy of the Cambridge Platonists was limited to the national context, and short-lived on account of the pre-eminence, by the end of the seventeenth century, of Newton and Locke. Yet More's letters to Descartes were debated throughout Europe, and Cudworth was discussed by Leibniz, Bayle and Le Clerk. Finally, it is often assumed that the philosophy of the Cambridge Platonists is devoid of original power, and that they were unworldly and obscure mystics. The structure of this anthology should illustrate the systematic nature of the shared intellectual vision of these thinkers.

The Cambridge Platonists constitute, in fact, the most important Platonic school between the Renaissance and the Romantic era. The German historian Johann Jacob Brucker, writing in his *Kurtze Fragen aus der Philosophischen Historie* of 1735, described the Cambridge Platonists as constituting an 'Alexandrian' form of Platonism.[4] This is a useful way of describing the figures under debate. Their Platonism is eclectic in the mode characteristic of the Alexandrian school, and religious, in this case Christian. Plotinus and Origen are the most notable sources for their thought, though one can also trace sources in medieval mysticism and the Renaissance, especially Ficino and Erasmus. But the term 'Alexandrian' deserves some further exposition.

Philosophy and Religion

The eminent Victorian and translator of Plato, Benjamin Jowett, in the quotation given at the beginning of this chapter, presents the ancient Athenian philosopher as "a leader of a goodly band of followers" which includes Cicero, St. Augustine, the Cambridge Platonists, Berkeley and Coleridge. The history of philosophy has devoted many pages to the interpretation of Plato's thought. His profound influence upon philosophy up to the contemporary is without doubt. Frege, Whitehead, Bergson and Heidegger would be examples of modern philosophers who bear the deep stamp of Platonism, albeit in differing, and sometimes oblique, ways. The Platonic influence upon the Cambridge Platonists is rather less obscure. The extent of their indebtedness to Platonism was by some considered excessive: Anthony Tuckney (1599–1670) noted that the Cambridge Platonists were "learned and ingenious men" who "studied . . . Plato and his schollars . . . more than scriptures".[5] Tuckney accused Whichcote of a "Platonique faith" and a "moral divinitie", and he was critical of these "high flowen" Platonists.[6] What is evident from Tuckney's critique of Whichcote is that the Puritan considered his friend as having departed far from a robustly scriptural Christianity and that he saw him as relying far too much upon pagan philosophical sources for his thought. Yet in the Platonic 'school' throughout the centuries, philosophy and theology—including Christian theology—have had a particularly intimate relationship.

The pith and kernel of Plato's religious thought is neglected by much contemporary scholarship on his philosophy. Dominant recent perspectives on Plato have been shaped by conflicting presentations of his oeuvre, between those who view the dialogues as a series of inconclusive and mutually inconsistent thought experiments, to those who, based on the reports of Aristotle and other contemporaries, regard them as the public face of a philosophical system of unwritten doctrines that was taught by Plato himself within the Athenian Academy. The Cambridge Platonists were unperturbed by such questions of Plato interpretation. Their 'Platonism' was crucially shaped by Middle Platonism and Neoplatonism— that is, the form in which Plato's thought came to be interpreted in late antiquity, the form in which it shaped medieval thought, and the form which emerged afresh in the Renaissance, especially through Marsilio Ficino. The key aspects of this version of Platonism are: 1) the identification of the Good in Plato's *Republic* with God; 2) the location of the Platonic ideas within the mind of God; and 3) the contrast between the temporal world of flux and the unchanging world of the divine mind, according to which the visible transient world is a reflection of the invisible and eternal.

These three aspects of Middle and Neo-Platonism clearly have powerful theological implications, and as such Platonic philosophy came to have immense influence in religious and theological thought, with which it often went hand-in-hand. While Jowett was surely correct to insist upon the living tradition of thought derived from Plato's works, one might also note that most of the authors he mentions have profound *theological* interests. Much of the theological dimension of the Cambridge Platonists seems perplexing and obsolete today. I will designate this the 'Alexandrian' dimension. This Alexandrian legacy is linked to Plotinus, whose shaping influence upon the subsequent tradition was so momentous that H.G. Gadamer could even speak of the 'platonisch-plotinische Wirkungseinheit'—the 'Platonic-Plotinian unitary legacy'.[7]

As Lloyd Gerson argued in *From Plato to Platonism* (Ithaca, NY: Cornell University Press, 2017), it was widely assumed in Antiquity that Plato was not the beginning of 'Platonism': for example, Aristotle in the *Metaphysics* says that Plato was reliant upon the Pythagoreans.[8] We find a similar view persisting amongst the Cambridge philosophers: Cudworth went so far as to describe Pythagoras "the most eminent of all the ancient philosophers". Pythagoras had the status of a magisterial mystagogue in Antiquity, known for his travels throughout the Mediterranean; by the time of the late Renaissance and particularly through Johannes Reuchlin, the philosopher of Samos was understood to have been a Kabbalist: in his dialogue *De verbo mirifico* (1494), Reuchlin discussed the ineffable divine name YHWH of Exodus 3.14, in which the four letters of tetragrammaton are identified with the Pythagorean tetractys.

"Plato's school . . .
  well agrees with learned Pythagore, Egyptian Trismegist, and th' antique roll
  Of Chaldee wisdome, all which time hath tore But Plato and deep Plotin do restore"

In these lines, taken from the fourth stanza of the first canto of Henry More's philosophic poem *Psychozoia*, it is apparent that More like Cudworth, views Plato as the eloquent beneficiary of an older tradition of thought. However, as also indicated here, the key figure in the formulation of the idea of Platonism is Plotinus. Plotinus synthesised the arguments of Plato's dialogues and much of the philosophical debate which, from Aristotle on, followed in their wake, into a comprehensive and coherent system of thought. He is therefore the so-called 'founder of Neoplatonism', but he did not conceive himself as such, viewing his own philosophy as merely the true interpretation of Plato. Though Plotinus' system is often regarded by contemporary scholars of Plato as an anachronistic distortion, the great twentieth century metaphysician and Platonist John Findlay took a rather different view. According to Findlay, the metaphysics of Plotinus is

> simply what one arrives at if one meditates on the major speculative passages in Plato's written work with a willingness to carry eidetic thinking to the limit, a willingness which has not been present in many of the empiricists, pluralists, nominalists, sceptics, formal logicians, anti-mystics and pure scholars who have ventured to interpret Plato.[9]

The speculative willingness that Findlay finds lacking in contemporary scholarship but present in Plotinus can also be found abundantly in the Cambridge Platonists. For them too, there was little or no interest in the aporetic, suggestive, or dramatic dimension of Plato's thought. Plato was 'the divine Plato', 'the Attic Moses' lauded by Plotinus' Middle Platonic predecessor Numenius. For the Cambridge Platonists, the Athenian sage was not merely a great thinker but a divine prophet; but unlike for Numenius and Plotinus, they found in Plato's works prophecies of the Christian gospel. Such interpretations were not new: Plato's portrayal of the execution of Socrates was thought by early Christian theologians to have parallels with the prophecy of the Suffering Servant in Isaiah 52–53, while Glaucon's reference in *Republic* 361A–362B to "the most just man" who will suffer crucifixion was taken by the church fathers to be another instance of Plato's prophetic powers.[10] Though such a reading of the Platonic corpus doubtless seems rather fanciful to the modern reader, it came naturally to the fathers of the early church who, whatever their rhetoric against the supposed deceit of pagan philosophy, welcomed and shared in the basic tenets of Platonic metaphysics according to which the sensible world is the image, the lower manifestation, of a higher and in some sense divine, intelligible dimension.

Platonic metaphysics thrived in the Hellenistic Egyptian city of Alexandria, where it was taken up by figures of various religious persuasions. When Plotinus studied here for ten or eleven years in the third century, it was already a vibrant intellectual centre. It had been home, in previous centuries, to the Jewish philosopher Aristobulus, who was amongst those (many of them pagan) who, like Reuchlin many centuries later, believed the essentials of Platonism could be found in the Hebrew scriptures and indeed that Plato's wisdom was derived from them; and Philo, a Hellenistic Jew who interpreted those Hebrew scriptures in a robustly Middle Platonic fashion, composing pioneering commentaries on the Books of Moses and on Plato's *Timaeus*. Philo probably reinforced the religious dimension of Platonism in Alexandria, so that the Platonism of Plotinus has strong monotheistic elements. This Alexandrian context, with its literary institutions and its position as a meeting point of East and West, would be decisive for Christianity. Plotinus's older contemporary and possible fellow-student under the tutelage of Ammonius Saccas, Origen, was also the product of the rich milieu of ancient Alexandria,[11] as was Clement of Alexandria before him, amongst other Christian philosophical and theological luminaries. As Christianity rose to dominance in late antiquity, Origen's Christian Platonism would prove key to the religion's theological maturation in the great Christological and trinitarian disputes of the period.

The Platonism of the Cambridge Platonists was partly the result of the critical integration of Platonic ideas, especially Plotinus, into patristic theology, both by Alexandrian Christians, and by those who read and learned from them, from the Cappadocians in the East to Marius Victorinus and Augustine in the West; and partly the result of the later revival of Christian Platonism in the Renaissance through Marsilio Ficino and Erasmus. As we have noted, Johann Jacob Brucker views the Cambridge Platonists as revivers of Alexandrian philosophy, which he also calls "eclectic". There is no tension between Athens and Jerusalem, between philosophy and reason on the one side and theology and faith on the other, according to this paradigm of Alexandrian Platonism. On the contrary, the thought of the Cambridge Platonists is, like that of Clement and Origen, deeply syncretistic. Indeed, the Cambridge men readily deploy Philo in interpreting the Old Testament, while the key church father is Origen himself. Origen is understood by them to have been the fellow student of Plotinus, and Plotinus' philosophy was hugely important for the Cambridge Platonists as well, its pagan dimension going largely unheeded. The Cambridge Platonists also tended to see contemporary thinkers and debates in the light of ancient ones, thus Descartes was viewed by the Cambridge men as reviving a genuine atomism that could be traced back to Moses, unlike atomism of the Democritean (atheistic) kind, which they found represented in their own day by Hobbes.

However, sympathy for this Alexandrian philosophical syncretism has not been universal. As we have already seen with Tuckney, there are doubts over the extent to which Christianity and Platonism can or ought to be allied, and many scholars throughout the centuries have objected that even open affinity between the early church fathers and Platonic themes does not warrant the designation of their Christianity as 'Platonic'. The Cambridge Platonists encountered this line of critique in their own day in the anti-Platonic polemics of Samuel Parker, bishop of Oxford.[12] The contemporary philosopher of religion William Lane Craig claims that Platonism, with its doctrine of uncreated eternal and immutable verities, is more threatening to Christianity than the problem of evil. His argument is that the doctrine of ideas conflicts with the principle of divine aseity, according to which God is the *sole* ultimate reality.[13] Meanwhile, Heinrich Dörrie has remarked that Christian Platonism is an oxymoron because of the strident and unavoidable opposition of Christianity to the pagan philosophical schools of antiquity.[14] It is the case that, in late antiquity, Platonism was the major ideological opponent of the Christian religion until the closure of the Platonic Academy by the Christian Emperor Justinian in 529. Porphyry, the pupil of Plotinus, wrote explicitly against the Christians, and a later pagan figure like Proclus had to be prudent in any critique of the new religion of the empire when paganism was under siege. Marinus of Samaria in his *Life of Proclus* recounts that Proclus dreamt the goddess Athena intended to *move* her house after the removal of her statue from the Parthenon. Mark Edwards meanwhile has argued for a distinctly *Christian* philosophy which was never identified with the ancient schools, Platonism included. On his view, any philosophy constructed by Christians was a preliminary to theology.[15]

The positions of writers such as Dörrie and Edwards have not been uncontested. The work of Werner Beierwaltes, and especially his seminal volume *Platonismus und Christentum* (Frankfurt: Vittorio Klostermann, 2013), argues that notwithstanding the shift effected by Christian revelation, Platonic, and indeed, Neoplatonic themes and arguments remained constitutive for the reflexive structure of Christian theology.[16] He uses various philosophers, such as Pseudo-Dionysius the Areopagite, Boethius, Eriugena, the school of Chartres, Bonaventure, Nicolas of Cusa, Marsilio Ficino and Pico della Mirandola as paradigms to assert this link. The analysis of these thinkers in the work of Beierwaltes is part of a larger strategy to exhibit the profound influence of Platonic-Neoplatonic structures of thought upon Christian theology culminating in the model of God as a divine unity—or tri-unity—whereby the deity thinking himself as *Sapientia* or *Logos*, comprises *Ipsum Esse*, Being Itself.

We need not, however, adjudicate here between these opposing views about the validity of the term 'Christian Platonism'. The Cambridge Platonists Benjamin Whichcote, Ralph Cudworth, John Smith and Henry More were university men, and they were profoundly learned in classical philosophy, patristic thought and rabbinic literature. At Cambridge in the mid-seventeenth century the dominant philosophy of the university was still scholasticism, generally in a late form shaped by Suarez and his successors, but the scientific revolution in the wake of Galileo and Descartes had changed the thought of their world to a degree similar to the impact of Darwin in the nineteenth century. For Henry More, the "infinity of worlds" became proof of an infinite omnipresent Deity,[17] just as later divines, such as Charles Kingsley and the authors of *Lux Mundi*, endeavoured to integrate Darwin's theory of evolution into a metaphysical theology. But notwithstanding their interest in contemporary science, the Cambridge Platonists' is still a world in which philosophy and theology are closely intertwined. If it is not forgotten that even philosophers such as Hobbes and Locke made various references to the Christian scriptures and theological matters, it is unsurprising that Cudworth was both a leading philosophical thinker and the regius professor of Hebrew who published sermons as well as his magnum opus, *The True Intellectual System of the Universe*, or that More wrote both letters to Descartes and a number of biblical commentaries, especially on the book of Revelation.

Ficino and Erasmus

Henry More is quite explicit about his own immersion in the Platonic tradition as mediated by Ficino and Plotinus:

> For it made me seriously at last begin to think with myself; whether the Knowledge of things was really that Supreme Felicity of Man; or something Greater and more Divine was: Or, supposing it to be so, whether it was to be acquir'd by such an Eagerness and Intentness in the reading of Authors and contemplating of Things; or by the Purging of the Mind from all sorts of Vices whatsoever: Especially having begun to read now the Platonick Writers, Marsilius Ficinus, Plotinus himself, Mercurius Trismegistus; and the Mystical Divines; among whom there was frequent mention made of the Purification of the Soul, and of the Purgative Course that is previous to the Illuminative; as if the Person that expected to have his Mind illuminated of God, was to endeavour after the Highest Purity.[18]

More makes it clear in this passage that the source of happiness in human life is contemplation of the divine and what he describes as a process of purgation and illumination. This is a process of contemplative ascent to the divine as described in the *Enneads* of Plotinus and in the works and commentaries of Ficino. The plan of More's first published work, *Psychodia Platonica*, as C.A. Staudenbaur has convincingly established,[19] was influenced by Marsilio Ficino's *Theologia Platonica de immortalitate animorum*, and early modern Platonism in Western thought generally is inconceivable without the mediating work of Ficino (1433–1499), since later scholars had access to the works of Plato and Plotinus principally through Ficino's texts, translations and commentaries. Ficino's paramount significance lay in his erudite transmission of the elements of pagan Platonic thought in a baptised form as part of a systematic Christian Platonism. Yet whilst Cassirer and others are correct to stress the Renaissance inheritance of the Cambridge Platonists, they were not uncritical antiquarians. The Cambridge Platonists were Christian humanists who worked out their philosophy and theology in the wake of the great Dutch humanist, and sometime Cantabrigian, Erasmus. In this sense Erasmus was a paradigmatic figure for them, since Erasmus was a staunch admirer of OrigenLeibniz stated that

"M. Morus était Platonicien et Origeniste"[20]—and Erasmus transmitted his enthusiasm for Origen to the Cambridge Platonists. As a result of this Erasmian philosophia Christi and the Origenian influence, there is a significant difference between the Christian Platonism of More, Cudworth and the Cambridge Platonists and that of Ficino and other medieval and early renaissance thinkers.

For Ficino, the supreme theological authority was Dionysius, or Denys, the Areopagite, not least because of his almost apostolic status. The author of the works now described as 'the Corpus of Pseudo-Denys' was taken to have been a philosophical contemporary of St. Paul—indeed the Dionysius mentioned in the Acts of the Apostles as converted to Christianity by Paul's preaching at the Areopagus at Athens (Acts 17:22–34). The fact that, in reality, these writings were the works of a sixth century Syrian Christian and disciple of the pagan Neoplatonist Proclus, meant that through them a particular form of Christian Neoplatonism exerted an enormous influence on subsequent Christian thought. Ficino's metaphysical theology could be described as a mixture of Plotinus and Denys. By the time of the Cambridge Platonists, however, Denys had been exposed as a fake. His authenticity was first queried by Lorenzo Valla in 1457 and then by John Grocyn in 1501, but this sceptical perspective on Denys was forcibly propagated by Erasmus from 1504 onwards. Erasmus contributed significantly to the discrediting of the status of Denys as an apostolic author. Though it was not until the nineteenth century that parallels between Dionysius and Proclus established the certainty of the pseudonym, the damage to Denys the Areopagite's theology as authoritative had been done much earlier. A simple indication of this erosion of authority can be seen in the fact that Cudworth mentions the Areopagite only once in his enormous *True Intellectual System of the Universe* of 1678.

The discrediting of Denys had two significant results. One was the rejection of the strongly ecclesiastical aspect of Pseudo-Dionysius the Areopagite. Whilst the universe of Denys is one of a sacred hierarchy uniquely mediated by the ecclesial-sacred structures. The Cambridge Platonists—'men of latitude'—were open to the encounter with the divine both within and without the Church. John Smith writes: "God made the universe and all the creatures contained therein as so many glasses wherein He might reflect his own glory. He hath copied forth Himself in the Creation".[21] This is akin to the medieval Christian Neoplatonist Eriugena, for whom "every visible and invisible creature is a theophany".[22]

The second result of the Cambridge Platonists' turning away from the Dionysian Corpus was their rejection of the negative theology of Denys the Areopagite. By 'negative theology' we mean the process of denial rather than affirmation of predicates about God, indeed the corollary of absolute divine transcendence. Denys represents in radical form the view of God as 'super-essential': God the creator of things is not any thing, nor in any way to be counted among them, but is beyond all that is—beyond Being. As such, God as the absolute first principle cannot properly be named with any label we apply to created things, nor known according to any category by which we understand beings: hence the ultimate emphasis of Denys' theology is unknowing rather than knowing.

This doctrine Denys inherited from Proclus, and it is present in Plotinus, being in part the outworking of Plato's declaration in *Republic* 509B8, that the supreme Form of the Good is beyond being. It may be puzzling then that the Cambridge Platonists rejected it; but since they received from Erasmus and the humanists not only doubts about the identity of the author of Denys' works, but also an admiration for Origen, there was another major early Christian theological authority to whom they could turn. With this change of theological authority came a change in theological content. If Denys the Areopagite was the great spokesman of apophatic theology, Origen could be read as providing the basis for an altogether more optimistic theological epistemology, turning readily to the Septuagint translation of Exodus 3:14, in which God is identified as not as non-Being but as Being Itself. In *On First Principles* 1.3.6 and his *Commentary on the Gospel of John*, this identification of God with Being is central. Origen combines Exodus 3:14 with Matthew 19:17 as he identifies Being with the concept of the Good: God is both Being and Goodness. Origen in *On First Principles* does say that God is "above" Being, but he also claims that God is rational and self-conscious, and thus the finite mind can attain some rational apprehension of the divine mind. This more sanguine epistemology, one in which the divine mind plays a positive role, was enthusiastically endorsed by the Cambridge Platonists. Meanwhile, Cudworth, when discussing the "Platonick Trinity", identified radical apophaticism of the sort we find in Dionysius, in particular the denial of thought to the first principle, as a "kind of *Mysterious Atheism*".[23]

For Whichcote, as for More, Cudworth and Smith, philosophy and theology belong together, and human reason is grounded in the eternal dictates of divine wisdom. They are all committed to a 'top down' metaphysics in which the higher, i.e., the divine intellect, explains the lower, i.e., the material cosmos. Unsurprisingly, the Platonic ideas play a constitutive explanatory role: these are not abstract objects of thought but they are collectively the plenitude and power of the divine mind as the source of all reality, actual and potential. As Cudworth writes:

> It is all one to affirm that there are eternal rationes, essences of things, and verities necessarily existing, and to say that there is an infinite, omnipotent, and eternal Mind, necessarily existing that always actually comprehendeth himself, the essences of all things, and their verities, or, rather which is the rationes, essences, and verities of all things.[24]

These eternal "essences of things" provide the basis for epistemology, and it is the divine mind that constitutes a vital explanatory principle in their metaphysics. The divine ideas are God's thoughts, and sensible objects are 'ectypes' or images of divine archetypes; man can apprehend the ideas by communing with the divine mind: epistemology implies, literally, theology. And so for the Cambridge Platonists it must be, if they are, as Henry More aimed, to "cut the sinews of the Spinozan and the Hobbesian cause".[25] Hence Cudworth deemed it necessary to construct a metaphysical system, by "joyning Metaphysicks or Theology, together with Physiology, to make up one entire System of Philosophy" (*True Intellectual System*, 175), one in which a thoroughgoing apophaticism is impossible, insofar as the sensible world necessarily presupposes the intelligible world of the divine intellect.

An Antidote to Materialism and Atheism

The Cambridge Platonists were determined to face the challenges their age posed to their cherished view of a hierarchically ordered and ensouled cosmos and to counter atheistic arguments against divine providence. Writing in his *Platonism and Naturalism* (Ithaca, NY: Cornell University Press, 2020), Lloyd Gerson defines Platonism essentially as opposition to five theories: materialism, mechanism, relativism, scepticism and nominalism. The first is the view that only the material world exists. Mechanism is a distinct but related theory: the tenet that an entirely material world can be explained solely in terms of material and efficient causation and the denial of free agency. Relativism repudiates the existence of objective values and places subjective preference in their stead; scepticism denies the possibility of genuine knowledge; nominalism concludes that universals are mere names with no corresponding reality. All these the Cambridge Platonists reject.

Cudworth states the essential 'true' intellectual system of the universe succinctly in opposition to mechanistic naturalism:

> First, for making a Perfect Incorporeal intellect to be the Head of all; and Secondly, for resolving that Nature, as an Instrument of this Intellect, does not merely act according to the Necessity of

Material Motions but for Ends and Purposes, though unknown to it self; Thirdly, for maintaining the Naturality of Morality; and Lastly, for asserting the τὸ ἐφ' ἡμῖν, Autexousie, or Liberty from Necessity.[26]

This is to avow and defend a top-down metaphysics, one in which God is the summit of reality, perfect immaterial Being, with the spirit of nature as the instrument of the divine, and finite freedom in the created world:

> Whereas these three things are (as we conceive) the fundamentals or essentials of true religion. First, that all things in the world do not float without a head and governor; but that there is a God, an omnipotent understanding Being, presiding over all. Secondly, that this God, being essentially good and just, there is φύσει καλὸν καὶ δίκαιον, something in its own nature immutably and eternally just and unjust; and not by arbitrary will, law, and command only. And, lastly, there is something ἐφ' ἡμῖν or, that we are so far forth principles or masters of our own actions, as to be accountable to justice for them, or to make us guilty and blameworthy for what we do amiss, and to deserve punishment accordingly.[27]

In this passage it is evident that the affirmation of God as the first principle, the spirit of nature, and freedom are bound to a commitment that the goodness of God means that values are objective and accessible to the human mind. Nominalism, relativism and scepticism are rejected alongside materialism and the exclusively mechanistic mode of explanation. Accountability rests not upon convention or society but nature itself, the good and the just.

Henry More argues for "a *Sympathy of parts*" in the cosmos that is linked

> into the *Unity* of the *Soul of the Universe*, which is interested in all Plastick powers, and into the *Continuity of the subtile Matter*, which answers to our *Animal Spirits*. And in this sense it is that *Plotinus* sayes, that the World is ὁ μέγας γόης, *the grand* Magus or *Enchanter*.[28]

The plastic power of the spirit of nature is an integral part of a providential order subordinate to a transcendent divine mind. Whilst contemplating divine providence, More happily turns to Plotinian images of the theatre or dance. More writes:

> The *fear* and abhorrency therefore we have *of Death*, and the *sorrow* that accompanies it, is no argument but that we may live after it, and are but due affections for those that are to be spectatours of the great *Tragick-Comedy* of the World; the whole plot thereof being contrived by Infinite Wisdom and Godness, we cannot but surmise that the most sad representations are but a *shew*, but the delight *real* to such as are not wicked and impious; and that what the ignorant call *Evil* in this Universe is but as the shadowy strokes in a fair picture, or the mournful notes in Musick, by which the Beauty of the one is more lively and express, and the Melody of the other more pleasing and melting.[29]

In another beautiful passage More employs the image of a society ball:

> This is a small glance at the Mysteries of Providence, whose fetches are so large, and Circuits so immense, that they may very well seem utterly incomprehensible to the *Incredulous* and *Idiots*, who are exceeding prone to think that all things will ever be as they are, and desire they should be so; though it be as rude and irrational, as if one that comes into a *Ball* and is taken much with the first

Dance he sees, would have none danced but that, or have them move no further one from another then they did when he first came into the room; whereas they are to trace nearer one another, or further off, according to the measures of the musick, and the law of the Dance they are in. And the whole Matter of the Universe, and all the parts thereof, are ever upon Motion, and in such a Dance, as whose traces backwards and forwards take a vast compass, and what seems to have made the longest stand, must again move, according to the modulations and accents of the musick, that is indeed out of the hearing of the acutest ears, but yet perceptible by the purest Minds and the surest Wits.[30]

More's analogy between living and a ball draws upon the deeply Plotinian image of life as a drama and a dance:

In this dance the soul sees the spring of life, the spring of intellect, the principle of being, the cause of good, the root of the soul; these are not poured out from him with the result that they diminish him; for there is no bulk; otherwise the things generated from him would be perishable. But, as it is, they are eternal, because their principle remains the same, not divided up into them but abiding as a whole. So they also abide; just as the light abides if the sun abides. For we are not cut off from him or separate, even if the nature of body has intruded and drawn us to itself, but we breathe and are preserved because that Good has not given its gifts and then gone away but is always bestowing them as long as it is what it is.[31]

This is a typical instance of the direct and thoroughgoing influence of "deep Plotin" upon Henry More. Yet his admiration for Plotinus was never slavish, and indeed More's opinions on many philosophical issues changed through his career, though the main thrust of his Christian Platonic metaphysics remained constant. His approval of contemporary philosophers was often critical. Thus, he praised Descartes as "that sublime and subtill Mechanick" but disagreed with Descartes over the latter's denial of animal souls.[32] Another instance would be More's affirmation of impenetrability and penetrability as the hallmarks of matter and spirit, rather than the Cartesian opposition of extension and thought. It is important to note that there was also disagreement among the Cambridge Platonists: Henry More's distinctive notions of spiritual extension and spissitude are not accepted by Cudworth. But we should not lose sight of the fact that these disagreements occur within a broader context of agreement against atheistic materialist or deterministic philosophies.

The Critique of Theological Voluntarism

God does not, because of his Omnipotency, deal Arbitarily with us; but according to Right, and Reason: and whatever he does, is therefore Accountable; because Reasonable.

Benjamin Whichcote[33]

One of the most widespread ancient and modern critiques of theology, from Xenophanes to Feuerbach and Freud, is the projection theory: the idea that theories of the gods emerge out of all-too-human projections onto the universe. As cultivated humanists, the Cambridge Platonists were particularly hostile to any crude anthropomorphism in theology. Moreover, they objected forcefully to the principle that God's omnipotence or sovereignty alone provides the basis for truth or morality. This is also one of the implications of the doctrine of divine ideas: if the visible transient world is an image of the invisible and eternal world of the divine mind, it cannot be viewed as the product of arbitrary divine will. Indeed, the divine will for the Cambridge Platonists is subordinate to divine wisdom and goodness. Right and wrong, true and false are grounded in eternal verities.[34] Henry More insisted that Platonism is the soul, while Cartesianism is the body, of the true philosophical system.[35] Yet Descartes' theological voluntarism—the doctrine that God's will takes metaphysical priority over his mind, so that he could change the nature of even supposed eternal truths if he so willed, for example making what is evil to be good—is severely criticised by all the major figures in the school. Not even God could make clear and distinct ideas false: "power hath no dominion over understanding, truth, and knowledge". Cudworth defends the theological legitimacy of his position by noting that voluntarism was rare among the "ancient fathers of the Christian church" who "were very abhorrent from the doctrine" and Cudworth notes: "it crept up afterward in the scholastic age" especially in the thought of William of Ockham.[36]

Love, Fear and Supreme Goodness

Removing fear was a central goal for much ancient philosophy. The concept of *ataraxia* is central for Epicureanism and other philosophical traditions like Stoicism. The work of Pierre Hadot, in particular, has witnessed most eloquently to the profound practical dimension of ancient thought and the removal of fear in particular is a central aspect of this.[37] Thomas Hobbes, a brilliant and learned humanist, revived the concern with the problem of fear in an audacious manner. Hobbes' theory of the political state, and his theology too, is grounded upon the emotion. If, indeed, life is to be conceived of not merely as "solitary, poor, nasty, brutish, and short", the war of all against all, then only a powerful sovereign, be it monarch or parliament, can serve to redress the anarchy generated by the relentless selfishness that characterises all human beings, and only the threat of punishment and the efficacy of the law can check these selfish instincts.[38] Yet in this stress on fear, Hobbes seems to steer close to aspects of Calvinism, in particular the terrifying God of the Westminster Confession and the doctrine of double predestination, and Hobbes' theology is shaped by the continual fear and danger of violent death.

Samuel I. Mintz in his work *Hunting for Leviathon: Seventeenth Century Reactions to the Materialism and Moral Philosophy of Thomas Hobbes* (South Bend, IN: St Augustine's Press, 1996) provides a useful protocol of the range of attacks on the philosophy of Hobbes and in particular his prodigious impiety. The Cambridge Platonists were certainly opposed: their theology rested upon the principle of God's goodness rather than fear of his sovereignty. Origen was adamant on this point: God must be envisaged as absolute goodness, and the Cambridge Platonists present the self-communication of the supreme goodness as the justification of creation. John Smith writes that God

> hath copied forth Himself in the creation; and in this outward world we may read the lovely characters of the Divine goodness, power, and wisdom . . . That Divine Wisdom, that contrived and beautified this glorious structure, can best explain her own art, and carry the soul back again in these reflected beams to Him who is the Fountain of them.[39]

The Neoplatonic language of reflection and the fountain is conventional, but Smith's is not the path of the Dionysian *via negativa*, the negative way. The physical world is a glorious mirror of the divine source and good folk will find traces of the transcendent goodness in the world. Only those who are blinded by selfishness and pride will fail to behold God in this world.

God must not be envisaged as an object of terror, and much less as a bargaining partner. God has no reason to create humanity except out of disinterested love: Cudworth writes of the "Love of infinite activity". Smith explicitly attacks the idea that God's creation was "out of a piece of Self-Interest, as if he had had any design to advance himself, or to enlarge his own stock of glory and happiness". He avers that

> he need neither our Happiness nor our Misery to make himself more illustrious by; being full in himself, it was his good pleasure to communicate of his own fullness. The communication of his goodness: God does then most glorifie and exalt himself in the most triumphant way that may be . . . when he most of all communicates himself.[40]

Similarly, Henry More's metaphysical theology is emphatically based upon the conviction of divine plenitude and abundance: his characteristic doctrines of spiritual extension and divine space are grounded in the sense of the boundless and creative goodness of God.

Enthusiasm and Deification

The insistence in Dionysius the Areopagite upon a theophany grounded in an ecclesiastically mediated hierarchy could tend to proscribe any other theophanies, such as the sense of the numinous in nature or individual experiences of the divine presence. Religious experience is a decisive topic for the Cambridge Platonists, and one that they bequeathed in turn to the English Romantics, Emerson and William James. The states of ecstatic union with the divine as described by Plato or Plotinus are linked to the indwelling Christ of St Paul. The potent but perplexing theme of divine inspiration or even madness Plato's dialogues becomes in Neoplatonism a doctrine of ecstasy—that is, a doctrine of union with the divine though a gradual process of assimilation to God, known as deification, and in fleeting moments of mystical union with God. The problem of whether religious madness is divine inspiration or human ailment became particularly pressing in the aftermath of the Civil War because of the emergence of sects claiming special and direct knowledge of God. Henry More, in particular, addressed this question of enthusiasm and its dangers with trenchant arguments. Yet More himself was far removed from a complacent and worldly Restoration divine. Describing himself as "drunk with Divinitie", More's critique of enthusiasm presupposes a true version of the indwelling divine principle, something of which once again Smith wrote eloquently:

> The true Metaphysical and Contemplative man . . . endeavours the nearest union with the Divine Essence that may be, κέντρον κέντρῳ συνάψας, as Plotinus speaks; knitting his owne centre, if he have any, unto the centre of the Divine Being . . . This life is nothing else but God's own breath within him, and an Infant-Christ (if I may use the expression) formed in his Soul, who is in a sense . . . the shining forth of the Father's glory.[41]

This "Metaphysical and Contemplative man" is an image of Plotinus, the "divine philosopher". Cudworth remarked:

> Plotinus aimed at such a kind of Rapturous and Ecstatick Union with the Τὸ ἕν and Τἀγαθόν, the First of the Three Highest Gods, (called The One and The Good) as by himself is described towards the latter end of this Last Book [Ennead VI 9], where he calls it ἐπαφὴν, and παρουσίαν ἐπιστήμης κρείττονα, and τὸ ἑαυτῶν κέντρον τῷ οἷον πάντων κέντρῳ . . . συνάπτειν, a kind of Tactual Union, and a certain Presence better than Knowledge, and the joyning of our own Centre, as it were, with the Centre of the Universe.[42]

This idea of the κέντρον, or centre, of the soul has parallels with the doctrine of the spark or *apex mentis* in the Eckhart school of German mysticism. Tuckney objected to the revival of this medieval Platonic mystical doctrine as a "A kinde of a Moral Divinitie minted; onlie with a little tincture of Christ added: nay, a Platonique faith unites to God!".[43] Yet this Platonic doctrine of the centre of the soul is an aspect of the epistemological optimism of the Cambridge Platonists. It is the divine-in-the-mind that makes knowledge and ethics possible. Yet it is also part of a critique of the prevailing Protestant doctrine of imputed righteousness, according to which the Christian's righteousness before God is nothing inherent in them but accounted to them on the basis of their divine election and their faith in Christ's atoning sacrifice. Salvation, for the Cambridge Platonists, cannot be the result of an external forensic attribution but rather must entail the transformation of the soul into its divine archetype—its deification. Salvation is the renewal of the soul through the indwelling of the eternal Logos in the spirit.[44]

Trinity and Unity

The doctrine of salvation in the Cambridge Platonists brings us to the Christian doctrine of the Trinity as a point at which philosophy and theology coincide. It is perhaps ironic that the doctrine which, if considered in purely numerical terms, seems to present an egregious instance of theological irrationalism (how can multiple divine persons nevertheless amount to one God?), constitutes one of the great stimuli of the development of Christian Platonism, demanding a high degree of philosophical-theological rigour and creativity. Some vision of the unity of the absolute first principle of being and nevertheless its relationality forms the philosophical foundation for the doctrine that the one God is at once the three persons of Father, Son and Holy Spirit. Whilst we cannot explore here the origins of this theme within the philosophical tradition, the significance for the Christian doctrine of the triune identity of the Godhead of the Platonic doctrines of a supreme unity and an indeterminate 'dyad' attributed to Plato's Academy and the Neoplatonic exegesis of Plato's triad of principles in his dialogue Parmenides cannot be doubted. Neither can the Noetic triad, which Marius Victorinus translated from the conception of the divine mind as being, life, and thought, which in the reflections of Augustine and others developed though the Western tradition of Christian philosophical theology. Nor can we explore the reception of the Logos doctrine as a model of the creative dimension of the Godhead, and the story of how the Logos became identified with the ideas as the thoughts of God.[45] In this manner, philosophy and theology were fused.

With much of this background, the Cambridge Platonists, learned in both the Platonic tradition and in patristics, were familiar. What must be stressed here is the ongoing significance for them of the doctrine of the Trinity, in the light of persisting tendencies to view the Cambridge Platonists as Arians, or even Deists.[46] The Cambridge Platonists were Christian theologians, and like Locke, Stillingfleet or Boyle, believed that reason must be supplemented by revelation. By contrast, the Deists denied the need for revelation altogether. The tendency of some Latitudinarians of the Restoration to avoid doctrinal controversy in favour of a stress upon practical faith and virtue should not blind us to the deep interest of the Cambridge Platonists in doctrinal questions. The great Jesuit scholar Petavius (1583–1652) argued that the Council of Nicaea represented a break with Platonism and the pre-Nicaean fathers could not be regarded as properly orthodox; Cudworth, on the contrary, argued that the *homousion* was compatible with a moderate form of subordinationism. Cudworth's forays into the minutiae of recondite patristic scholarship was philosophically motivated, since he, too, was drawing upon the Platonic themes and arguments that had inspired his Alexandrian forebearers.

The philosophical theology of the Cambridge Platonists culminates in the vision of a unity that thinks itself, creates the visible cosmos in its own image, and both calls and impels the return of the world to itself. In this sense, the problem of identity and difference, two of Plato's 'great categories', become models of both the imminent and the economic life of the divine. The orthodoxy of the manner in which they mapped the Christian Trinity according to these Platonic distinctions is for others to judge; yet the seriousness with which they treat the core doctrines of Christianity is indisputable. And, in addition to this, we forget the deep link between early modern definitions of the 'person' and 'consciousness' and the debates around the doctrine of the Trinity in the late seventeenth century.[47]

A True Intellectual System

In their own day, the Cambridge Platonists were often criticised for their rationalism and uninhibited and candid engagement with the critics of Christian theism. To this day they have been accused of facilitating the very atheism they were attacking.[48] This is a view based upon just the kind of historicist or relativist premises that the Platonists would reject. If sustained analysis and critique of the intellectual objections to theism should be the ultimate advantage of the atheistic camp, then Henry More or Ralph Cudworth would in principle concede victory to the atheists.

In his influential work, *The Mind of God and the Works of Man* (Oxford: Clarendon Press, 1997), Edward Craig contrasted two paradigms of philosophy since the seventeenth century. One presents the human mind as a natural object within a physical world and which deploys the methods of the natural sciences—the paradigm employed by Hobbes and Hume. This model constitutes a critique of what Craig calls the 'Similarity Thesis'—Craig's other paradigm, in which human agents are made in the image of God and obliged to imitate God as far as possible:

> When . . . man is compared to God in point of his ability to acquire a certain type of knowledge, the thought very naturally follows that that its acquisition is itself a moral value, something that we have an obligation to pursue. In doing so we ourselves approach more nearly to perfection; for since it is such items of knowledge that, among other things, compose the mind of God, it follows that in acquiring them we approach more nearly the divine state, the summit of all good.[49]

One might be inclined to associate the Cambridge Platonists with an obsolete philosophical prototype. Add to this the verdict of Ernst Cassirer, that the Cambridge Platonists constituted an intellectual dead end, and the renewed interest in the Cambridge Platonists might seem a Sisyphean and fruitless task.

Yet there are four areas where the legacy of these writers is of persisting philosophical relevance: the problem of consciousness, the question of freedom and responsibility, the problem of nature, and the relation between philosophy and religion.

1. The problem of consciousness has been designated the "hard problem".[50] Various attempts to 'dissolve' the problem of consciousness have failed signally. Some philosophers have even proposed that consciousness is an illusion, which is somewhat paradoxical since presumably holding that theory presupposes the possession of consciousness. Behaviourism and functionalism have their respective difficulties: behaviourism just omits the relevant data of the first person perspective, and the frequent gap between behaviour and belief that we find, for example, in the hypocrite or the imposter; functionalism is a more sophisticated theory, but in identifying the mind with functions rather than particular phenomenal qualities or physical properties, it sidesteps the problem.

By shifting the emphasis upon function, the enigma of the mind itself can remain unheeded—a functionalist can be a materialist, dualist or panpsychist, but the ontological question still persists. The emergence of panpsychism is linked to the difficulty of explaining consciousness from a materialistic perspective. Anne Conway's *Principles of the Most Ancient and Modern Philosophy*, which constitutes a monistic rejection of both Henry More and Spinoza, is an indication of the array of positions forged in this seminal phase of early modern philosophy.

2. Freedom. Since the seventeenth century it has been customary for philosophers to claim that since the world of objects is causally determined, and human agents belong to this world, they must be determined. Yet, as many moralists, especially Kant, have insisted, "ought implies can". The question of freedom remains as elusive as the problem of consciousness. We are not, as moral beings, just a 'pack of neurons'. Indeed, moral realism—the view that there are agent independent facts about morality—is hard to reconcile with materialism, whether its Hobbesian form or in a neo-Darwinian guise. And yet moral realism is an increasingly popular view among ethicists, with many contemporary philosophers, such as Michael Smith or John McDowell holding to it.

3. The mechanomorphic model of the universe as a 'machine' has been a useful trope, but it clearly has limitations. The rejection of final causes and the establishment of a domain of efficient and material causes has been the dominant model since the seventeenth century; yet there has always been critique of the over-weaning ambitions of the reductionists, and it is not clear that the case for teleological explanation is redundant. Thomas Nagel has recently criticised the capacity of materialism to account for biological phenomena. For Nagel, the mind-body problem is not merely an isolated issue related to the interstices between mind and brain that is relevant for our appreciation of the entire cosmos and the history thereof. He is committed to the intelligibility of the world we find ourselves in, and argues that teleology means that in addition to physical laws of the familiar kind, there are other laws of nature that "bias towards the marvelous".[51] If one is not convinced by the idea that the systematic features of the world are a collection of brute facts generated by a gigantic coincidence, then behind the marvellous emergence of life from genes to proteins and cells lies some goal-directed activity, *nisus formativus*:

> The view that rational intelligibility is at the root of the natural order makes me, in the broad sense, an idealist—not a subjective idealist, since it doesn't amount to the claim that all reality is ultimately appearance—but an objective idealist in the tradition of Plato and perhaps also of certain post-Kantians, such as Schelling and Hegel, who are usually called absolute idealists.[52]

The Cambridge Platonists, as the most important idealist school of philosophy between the Platonic Renaissance and the revival of Neoplatonism in the late eighteenth century, offer one of the most trenchant critiques of the mechanomorphic paradigm in modern philosophy. Nagel does not mention the Cambridge Platonists, but Henry More and Ralph Cudworth represent precisely the view that "rational intelligibility is at the root of the natural order", and they argue that this is because it reflects the divine mind. The visible world is a transient image of an eternal and immutable archetype.

4. Philosophy and religion. The beginning of the twenty-first century saw a revival of powerful advocates of atheism, from Dawkins, Hitchens and Harris, to philosophers A.C. Grayling, Daniel Dennett and Michael Martin.[53] The Cambridge Platonists are among the most notable early avowed critics of atheism. Moreover, these figures attack atheism as a *philosophical* theory. Whilst critics might object that 'atheism' in the seventeenth century could mean an array of positions despised by any given author, the Cambridge Platonists were consciously targeting a *philosophical* position, and one that had existed in the philosophical landscape at least since the *Laws* of Plato.

It is possible, however, to accept the failure of modern materialism to account for consciousness, moral value and purpose, and yet reject any religious response to these questions. Thomas Nagel is a good example of such an attitude. Yet as Nagel is well aware, the idea of the rational intelligibility of the universe is a powerful motivation for religious belief. Yet theology in the last century has been deeply shaped by anti-intellectualist movements, often buttressed by the notion of belief as an act of will. This current of anti-intellectualism comes down from glittering intellects like Pascal, Kierkegaard and William James. Yet the Cambridge Platonists stand opposed to any such theological anti-intellectualism. Perhaps the most significant early statement of this is Whichote's critique of Tuckney's Calvinist faith, in the course of which Whichcote said stridently "I oppose not rational to spiritual, for spiritual is most rational".[54] For indeed, "Reason is the *Divine* Governor of man's life; it is the very Voice of God".[55]

Conclusion

> In the case of the "Cambridge Platonists," it is eminently true that, with all their faults, philosophy in England never reached a more ideal height—a summit of pure intellectual contemplation—than it did in them.
>
> John Tulloch[56]

The Cambridge Platonists have been often presented as irksome in their antiquated erudition and remote, if not repugnant to, current philosophical and theological concerns. Yet one can, we submit, make a strong case for the real urgency of many of the questions raised by the Cambridge Platonists and their relevance for contemporary thought. They were amongst the first to grapple with those keen issues of abiding significance since the scientific revolution, developments that have raised powerful questions about the human condition, shaken inherited structures in society, and appear to have generated an infinite world apparently devoid of transcendence and bereft of value. Notwithstanding the complex syntax, learned citations, and baroque Carolingian eloquence, these are thinkers toiling with and reflecting upon the metaphysical and theological legacies of Copernicus, Kepler, Descartes and Newton. The crisis of meaning that emerged from the age of genius, and the interrogation of the various attempts to expound and explicate the new relation between mind and world that came to the fore with the 'new science' has been the object of manifold studies and theories of secularisation, with its much vaunted 'disenchantment' of the cosmos. The ramifications for ethics or aesthetics have been just as radical as for religious belief; yet among the Cambridge Platonists we find an intuitive sensibility for the sacred, the championing of the contemplation of goodness, truth and beauty, the advocacy of the indispensability of the spiritual life, and the poignant and consoling awareness of the eternal amidst the debris and tumult of existence.

Notes

1. *The Republic of Plato*, 3.
2. This can be accessed at www.cambridge-platonism.divinity.cam.ac.uk/.
3. For Cudworth's reception of Harvey see *True Intellectual System*, 161.
4. See Brucker's discussion in chapter IV of *Kurtze Fragen aus der Philosophischen Historie*, 353–448.
5. *Eight Letters of Dr. Antony Tuckney, and Dr. Benjamin Whichcote*, 38.
6. *Eight Letters of Dr. Antony Tuckney, and Dr. Benjamin Whichcote*, 97.
7. Hans-George Gadamer, *Gesammelte Werke VII* (Tübingen: Mohr Siebeck, 1991), 409.
8. Aristotle, *Metaphysics* I,6 987a30.
9. J.N. Findlay, *Plato: The Written and Unwritten Doctrines* (Abingdon: Routledge, 1974), 337.

10. Ernst Benz, "Christus und Sokrates in der alten Kirche", *Zeitschrift für die Neutestamentliche Wissenschaft und die Kunde der Älteren Kirche,* 43 (1951): 195–224.
11. Ilaria Ramelli, "Origen the Christian Middle/Neoplatonist: New Arguments for a Possible Identification", *Journal of Early Christian History* 1, no. 1 (2011): 98–130.
12. For a detailed discussion of Parker's objections, see Douglas Hedley, "Samuel Parker's Free and Impartial Censure of the Platonick Philosophie", in *Harmony and Contrast: Plato and Aristotle in the Early Modern Period*, eds. Anna Corrias, and Eva Del Soldato (London: Cambridge University Press, 2022), 122–146.
13. On this philosophical debate see Paul M. Gould (ed.), *Beyond the Control of God?: Six Views on the Problem of God and Abstract Objects* (London: Bloomsbury, 2014).
14. Heinrich Dörre, "Was ist „spätantiker Platonismus"? Überlegungen zur Grenzziehung zwischen Platonismus und Christentum", *Theologische Rundschau* 36, No. 4 (1971): 285–302.
15. Mark Edwards, *Origen against Plato* (Farnham: Ashgate, 2002).
16. For an account of Beierwaltes' scholarship see Douglas Hedley, "Werner Beierwaltes and the Yearning for Transcendence", *International Journal of the Platonic Tradition* 16, no. 2 (2022): 115–133.
17. See More's philosophical poem *Democritus Platonissans, or, An essay upon the infinity of worlds out of Platonick principles* of 1646.
18. Praefatio Generalissima VII–VIII [Opera omnia II/1, p. vi].
19. C.A. Staudenbaur, "Galileo, Ficino, and Henry More's Psychathanasia", *Journal of the History of Ideas* 29, no. 4 (1968): 565–578; see also A. Jacob, "Henry More's Psychodia Platonica and its relationship to Marsilio Ficino's Theologia Platonica", *Journal of the History of Ideas* 46, no. 4 (1985): 503–522.
20. Philosophischen Schriften III, 646.
21. Smith, *Select Discourses*, 430.
22. Eriugena, *Periphuseon* 681A. See Werner Beierwaltes, "Eriugena's Platonism", *Hermathena* no. 149 (1990): 53–72, esp. 59ff.
23. Cudworth, *True Intellectual System*, 585.
24. Cudworth, *Eternal and Immutable Morality*, 128.
25. A. Jacob, *Henry More's Refutation of Spinoza* (Hildesheim: Georg Olms Publishers, 1991).
26. Cudworth, *True Intellectual System*, 55.
27. Cudworth, *True Intellectual System*, Preface.
28. More, *Immortality of the Soul* II,X,7, 137.
29. More, *Immortality of the Soul*, III,XV,9, 278–279.
30. More, *Immortality of the Soul*, III,XIX,7, 307.
31. Plotinus, *Enneads* VI.9.9.1ff.
32. *Democritus Platonnisans*, 403. On the question of animal souls, see further L.D. Cohen's discussion, "Descartes and Henry More on the Beast-Machine", *Annals of Science* 1, no.1 (1936): 48–61.
33. *Moral and Religious Aphorisms*, No.417
34. On the Cambridge Platonists' understanding of the divine ideas see Brunello Lotti, "Universals in English Platonism: More, Cudworth, Norris", in *The Problem of Universals in Early Modern Philosophy*, eds. Stefano Di Bella, and Tad M. Schmaltz (New York: Oxford University Press, 2017), 166–197; and Bogdan-Antoniu Deznan, "The Eternal Truths in Henry More and Ralph Cudworth", *Journal of Early Modern Studies* 11, no.1 (2022): 93–114.
35. More, *Several Philosophical Writings*, xii.
36. Cudworth, *Eternal and Immutable Mortality*, 14.
37. Pierre Hadot, *Philosophy as a Way of Life: From Socrates to Foucault* (Malden, MA: Wiley-Blackwell, 1995), 187.
38. Hobbes, *Leviathan* XIII.
39. Smith, *Select Discourses*, 430.
40. Smith, *Select Discourses*, 142.
41. Smith, *Select Discourses*, 20.
42. Cudworth, *True Intellectual System*, 549.
43. *Eight Letters of Dr. Antony Tuckney, and Dr. Benjamin Whichcote*, 39
44. On this see John Russell Roberts, "Whichcote and the Cambridge Platonists on Human nature: An Interpretation and Defence", in *Oxford Studies in Early Modern Philosophy Volume* VI, eds. Daniel Garber, Donald Rutherford (Oxford: Oxford University Press, 2017), 29–74.
45. On the philosophical dimension of Neoplatonic trinitarian speculation within Christian theology, see the work of Werner Beierwaltes, especially "Unity and Trinity in Dionysius and Eriugena", *Hermathena* no.157

(1994): 1–20; see also David Albertson, *Mathematical Theologies: Nicholas of Cusa and the Legacy of Thierry of Chartres* (Oxford: Oxford University Press, 2014); and Markus Enders and Rolf Kühn (eds), "*Im Anfang war der Logos . . .*": *Studien zur Rezeptionsgeschichte des Johannesprologs von der Antike bis zur Gegenwart* (Freiburg im Breisgau: Verlag Herder, 2011); Douglas Hedley, "Pantheism, Trinitarian Theism and the Idea of Unity: Reflections on the Christian Concept of God", *Religious Studies* 32, no.1 (1996): 61–77 ; and Dale M. Schlitt, *German Idealism's Trinitarian Legacy* (Albany, NY: State University of New York Press, 2016).
46. A tendency found, for example in Nicholas Lash, *The Beginning and the End of Religion* (Cambridge, UK: Cambridge University Press, 1996), 14.
47. On this issue specifically see Udo Thiel, "Cudworth and Seventeenth-Century Theories of Consciousness", in *The Uses of Antiquity. Australasian Studies in History and Philosophy of Science*, Volume 10, ed. S. Gaukroger (Springer, 1991), 79–99; for a general survey see Thomas Dixon, *Nice and Hot Disputes* (London: T&T Clark, 2005).
48. David Leech's monograph, *Hammer of the Cartesians* (Leuven: Peeters, 2013), provides an instance of this.
49. Craig, *The Mind of God and the Work of Man*, 22.
50. David Chalmers, *The Conscious Mind* (New York: Oxford University Press, 1996), 2.
51. Thomas Nagel, *Mind and Cosmos: Why the Materialist Neo-Darwinian Conception of Nature is Almost Certainly False* (New York: Oxford University Press, 2012), 92.
52. Nagel, *Mind and Cosmos*, 17.
53. On this phenomenon see Tina Beattie, *The New Atheists: The Twilight of Reason and the War on Religion* (London: Darton, Longman & Todd, 2007).
54. *Eight Letters of Dr. Antony Tuckney, and Dr. Benjamin Whichcote*, 108.
55. Whichcote, *Moral and Religious Aphorisms*, No.76.
56. John Tulloch, *Rational Theology and Christian Philosophy* vol. I (Edinburgh: William Blackwood and Sons, 1872), viii.

Chapter 2

The Cambridge Platonists
A Very Brief History

Marilyn A. Lewis

The philosophical-theological movement which nineteenth century historians would call 'Cambridge Platonism' began in the second oldest university in England at a time of political, social and theological conflict. During the long reign of Elizabeth I (r.1558–1603), the Crown had been able to hold the 'Elizabethan Settlement' of the Church of England in place, although calls for a more thorough Protestant Reformation had reached a peak in small separatist movements during the 1590s. English soteriology had become increasingly Calvinist, despite the lone voice of the proto-Arminian Peter Baro of Peterhouse and the moderation of Richard Hooker. Puritan hopes rose with the accession of James I (r.1603–1625), but they were frustrated when no official relaxation of liturgy or church polity was allowed. Such hopes increasingly found expression in disobedience to the rubrics of the Book of Common Prayer. The principal points at issue were episcopal church polity and set prayers, alongside the liturgical requirements of the surplice, the sign of the cross in baptism, kneeling for Communion and the ring in marriage. At the same time, an English form of Arminianism which stressed sacramental grace began to develop, and it came to the fore during the reign of Charles I (r.1625–1649). The ecclesiastical reforms of William Laud (bishop of London 1628–1633, archbishop of Canterbury 1633–1646) imposed tighter adherence to episcopal church polity and ceremonial liturgy, while English Arminianism became the preferred soteriology of the royal court and Laud's friends among the ecclesiastical hierarchy. The constant backdrop to this enduring and often fierce friction was a fear of Roman Catholic resurgence, especially because both James' and Charles' queens adhered to Rome and had access to their own chaplains and services at court. These tensions would find violent expression in the Civil War and Interregnum, cause societal discord at the Restoration and come to only partial resolution in the Act of Toleration of 1689 during the first year of William III and Mary II's reign.

Against this complicated scene, in which even illiterate lay people in parishes held strong opinions, Emmanuel College, Cambridge, developed into the preeminent Puritan seat of learning. Founded by the Elizabethan courtier Sir Walter Mildmay in 1584 as an institution for the training of preachers, this was one of two colleges which gave rise to the Cambridge Platonist movement. Benjamin Whichcote (1609–1683) entered the college in 1626, when Charles I was in the first year of his reign, and he was tutored by the Calvinists Anthony Tuckney and Thomas Hill. As a tutor himself from 1633, Whichcote came to reject their harsh doctrine of double predestination and turned towards a more generous soteriology which incorporated a Platonic emphasis on God as absolute goodness and the possibility of human participation in that goodness through a life of deiformity. Although the Cambridge Platonists were sometimes accused of being Arminians and therefore considered heretical by their Calvinist contemporaries, their soteriology was more Platonic than Arminian. Theirs was truly a third, and distinctive, way between the warring theological factions in seventeenth century England. Whichcote's pupils included several leading members of the Cambridge Platonist circle, including Ralph Cudworth (1617–1688), John Smith (1618–1652) and John Worthington (1618–1671). Cudworth, too, was a popular tutor at Emmanuel, before moving on to become master of Clare Hall in 1645 and of Christ's College in 1654. Smith would become a fellow of Queens' College, preaching sermons in the college chapel which were published by Worthington in 1660, after Smith's early death in 1652. Worthington would become the Interregnum master of Jesus College and the husband of Whichcote's niece Mary.

At the other locus of Cambridge Platonism's origin, Christ's College, the young Henry More (1614–1687) suffered an emotional breakdown soon after performing brilliantly in his Bachelor of Arts disputation in 1636, fearing that mere erudition would not enable him to lead a holy life. During this period which he called his 'deep retirement', he sought answers through reading, especially the *German Theology* in Sebastian Castellio's Latin translation and Marsilio Ficino's edition of Plotinus' *Enneads*, and he came to a new consciousness of the importance of inner purgation and holiness. He was elected to a Christ's fellowship in 1641, and his early *Philosophicall Poems* (1642, 1647) reflect his new-found Plotinianism. In one of these poems, *Psychozoia*, in an allegory where birds represent various churchmen and Puritans, Laud appears as 'a gay Pye in his rich attire', suggesting that More was critical of church ritual, although he had moved decisively away from his own Calvinist upbringing. He would have heard Whichcote preach at the Round Church in Cambridge on Sunday afternoons (c.1636–c.1656), and his friendship with Cudworth definitely predated Cudworth's arrival at Christ's as master in 1654.

The early years of More's fellowship coincided with the beginning of the Civil War between the king and Parliament in August 1642. The Long Parliament, which met from November 1640, abolished episcopacy and liturgy according to the *Book of Common Prayer* and confiscated the privileged wealth of the Church of England. From 1643, the predominantly Calvinist Westminster Assembly met to frame a new Presbyterian polity for the national church and reform church services by means of the *Directory for Public Worship*. At Cambridge, the Earl of Manchester was charged by the Long Parliament with a purge based on subscription to the Solemn League and Covenant, a document coming to the Westminster Assembly from the Scottish Kirk which endorsed Presbyterian church polity. Across the University, 217 fellows and nine heads of house were ejected for refusal to subscribe, and there were some arrests. At Christ's College, only the aged and moribund master Thomas Bainbridge and three fellows—Henry More, William Moore and Ralph Widdrington—survived the purge, although More and Widdrington always denied having subscribed. Archbishop Laud was executed by Parliament in January 1645, and King Charles I, Supreme Governor of the Church of England, met the same fate four years later in January 1649. Yet the Long Parliament failed in its attempt to impose Presbyterianism nationally and was itself replaced by the Barebone's Parliament of 1653 and then by the Protectorate of Oliver Cromwell. The Cromwellian religious establishment outlawed both Roman Catholicism and 'prelacy', i.e., the services of the pre-war Church of England, while supporting the preaching ministry of thoroughly vetted Presbyterians, Congregationalists and Baptists. Quakers and other radical sects were still illegal and punished as such. Whichcote, Cudworth and More had taken Anglican orders before the Civil War and Worthington was ordained in 1646, but their liberal principles allowed them to function as ministers within Cambridge colleges during the Interregnum, a fact which was later held against them by their opponents.

Whichcote was appointed provost of King's College by Parliament in 1645. The content of his preaching from the 1640s and 1650s is not recorded, since his posthumously published sermons are generally thought to date from his time as rector of St Lawrence Jewry in the City of London (1668–1683), but a sermon he preached in 1650 when he became vice-chancellor of the University of Cambridge was sufficiently Platonist and anti-Calvinist to evoke a highly critical letter from his former tutor Tuckney. An exchange of letters followed, ceasing only when they agreed to disagree. In 1647, Cudworth preached a famous sermon to the House of Commons urging the Parliamentarians to try to live according to the true moral precepts of Christianity rather than taking refuge in the party strife associated with theological opinions. Two other sermons, *A Discourse concerning the True Notion of the Lord's Supper* (1642) and *The Union of Christ and the Church; in a Shadow* (1647), established his reputation as a Platonist and a Hebraist. He maintained a friendly correspondence with John Thurloe, secretary of state to both Oliver Cromwell and his son Richard, recommending Cambridge men for promotion in the service of the Protectorate. Alongside Whichcote, Cudworth served on Cromwell's Whitehall Conference in 1655 to consider the readmission of the Jews to England, although their contributions to proceedings are not recorded.

More soon began to attract younger men to Christ's to read towards their Master of Arts and Bachelor of Divinity degrees. He was able to establish, with Cudworth's later assistance, a community within which Christian Platonist studies could flourish, despite the persistent opposition of Widdrington, who tried to obstruct the two Platonists for three decades. George Rust (c.1627–1670) was the most thoroughly Platonist of More's protégés, and his two disputations for the degree of Bachelor of Divinity give evidence of the support and encouragement of both Cudworth and More. Rust was a fellow of Christ's from 1649 to 1659. Five of his Cambridge sermons and discourses are extant, and they all demonstrate that he had become a major contributor to the Cambridge Platonist movement by the time he resigned his fellowship. After leaving Christ's, Rust was most likely engaged in writing *A Letter of Resolution concerning Origen* (1661), a controversial work which fully betrayed its author's Origenian sympathies. At Christ's he was tutor to Henry Hallywell (1641–1703), who would hold a fellowship at the college from 1662 to 1667. Hallywell later corresponded with More, proving that they had been friendly during the years before he succeeded his father as a parochial incumbent in a series of Sussex parishes. Hallywell was not only responsible for saving, editing and publishing Rust's Cambridge writings but also wrote eight short books of his own distilling and presenting the basic Cambridge Platonist message for other clergy and literate laity.

Another of More's protégés was John Finch, the elder half-brother of Lady Anne Conway (1631–1679), who would become More's 'heroine pupil' and a life-long friend. As a woman, Anne was unable to attend Cambridge University, but More was persuaded to take her through a course of Cartesian philosophy by correspondence. More was the first English academic to teach the philosophy of Descartes and would correspond with him between 1648 and the French philosopher's death in 1650. When More recommended Rust to his friend Jeremy Taylor for promotion within the Church of Ireland, Rust travelled to Ireland with Lord and Lady Conway, who were journeying there to visit their Irish estates and would extend their ecclesiastical patronage to their new friend. Rust was ordained deacon and priest in Ireland in 1661. He served as dean of Connor and rector of Lisburn before succeeding Taylor as bishop of Dromore in 1667. More would spend many summers at the Conways' country house, Ragley Hall in Warwickshire. There, he met the Kabbalist Francis Mercury Van Helmont, the Quaker George Keith and other thinkers whose conversation over some years would assist Anne to conceive the highly original work found in her room after her death in 1679, which was translated into Latin and published in 1690 as *Principia philosophiae antiquissimae et recentissimae*. An English translation, *The Principles of the most Ancient and Modern Philosophy*, appeared in 1692, but Anne's original English manuscript has been lost. Anne's companion and librarian, Elizabeth Foxcroft, a sister of Benjamin Whichcote, took an active interest in the intellectual life at Ragley.

More's role was less public than those of Whichcote and Cudworth, but he began to write philosophical prose in earnest during the 1650s. A bad-tempered exchange with Thomas Vaughan in 1650–1651 about the true nature of Platonism was republished in 1656 with More's classic *Enthusiasmus Triumphatus*, a short treatise in which he diagnosed 'enthusiasm' as a symptom of the medical condition then known as melancholy. In 1653, More dedicated *An Antidote against Atheisme*, his first attempt to prove the existence of God by means of natural theology, to Lady Conway. He dedicated his 1653 *Conjectura Cabbalistica* to his 'eminently learned and truly religious friend' Cudworth. This was his own conception of what the ancient Jewish Cabbala should consist of, although he later learned a much more accurate version from Van Helmont and Christian Knorr von Rosenroth. More's last work before the Restoration, *The Immortality of the Soul* of 1659, was dedicated to Lord Conway. It explores the journey of the pre-existent soul through terrestrial life to an eventual return to its celestial state. He was also at work on *The Grand Mystery of Godliness*, which would be published in the year of the Restoration. Rust's 1658 Bachelor of Divinity discourse on the Resurrection body at the Cambridge annual Commencement shows that he had already seen both of these works in manuscript and doubtless discussed them with More. This Commencement was chaired by Worthington, vice-chancellor for the year, and also included a Doctor of Divinity disputation by Nathaniel Ingelo of Queens' College on the virtues of Origen's philosophy. It was a high point of Cambridge Platonist public utterance in Cambridge which coincided with the publication of William Spencer's Greek/Latin edition of Origen's *Contra Celsum*. In 1660, Worthington brought out his edition of *Select Discourses* by John Smith with the funeral sermon preached in 1652 by Symon Patrick of Queens'.

Yet another protégé was Joseph Glanvill (1636–1680), an Oxford man who was educated at Exeter College and then held a fellowship at Lincoln College before becoming rector of Bath Abbey. Glanvill was hugely impressed by More's *Enthusiasmus Triumphatus* and *Immortality of the Soul*, and he paid extravagant compliments to More in his own first book, *The Vanity of Dogmatizing* (1661). By the time it was published, Glanvill had made friends with Rust, probably in London before Rust travelled to Ireland with the Conways. After Rust's death, Glanvill brought out an edition of Rust's essay, *What is Truth*, together with his own *The Way of Happiness and Salvation* and a short, almost hagiographical, biography of Rust (1677). In an earlier manuscript version of his 1676 essay *Antifanatick Theology, and Free Philosophy*, Glanvill created an imaginary portrait gallery of divines whom he called 'Cupri-Cosmits' and later historians would call 'Latitudinarians', which included Whichcote, Cudworth, More and Rust. After both Glanvill's and More's deaths, some of their friends extracted the section on More and prepared it for publication as an obituary, but it was never published. Glanvill and More carried on an extensive correspondence, and they supported each other in writing about the pre-existence of the soul and the existence and real malevolence of witches. Glanvill himself is often classified as a Latitudinarian, but some of his writings after the Restoration are strident in their denunciation of dissent from the established church.

At the Restoration of the monarchy in 1660, the episcopal Church of England was also reinstated, with bishops being appointed to English sees by the crown as early as the summer of that year. By the Act of Uniformity of 1662, all college heads and fellows were required to swear allegiance to the crown, conform to the liturgy of the *Book of Common Prayer* and renounce the Solemn League and Covenant. Those who were in holy orders (and most college fellows were required to take orders) were also required to have received episcopal ordination and to subscribe to the 39 Articles of the Church of England, and parish clergy must also have sworn obedience to their diocesan bishop. Nearly 2,000 parish ministers from the Interregnum period and not a few Oxbridge fellows lost their positions when the law went into effect on 24 August, and this marked the beginning of a bitter antagonism between the Church of England and Dissent. The so-called Clarendon Code, passed by the Cavalier Parliament (1661–1679) made it illegal for Dissenters to hold public office or meet for worship separately from their parish churches and for Dissenting ministers to live within five miles of their former cures or any incorporated town. Again, the commitment of our Platonists to toleration and moderation meant that they were capable of accepting the Restoration settlement, although their sincerity was challenged by a cohort of new High Church heads of Cambridge colleges as well as their old enemy at Christ's, Ralph Widdrington.

At the Restoration, the Crown attempted to force a change of course on Cambridge, which had been more Puritan than Oxford and was perceived to be disinclined to implement the Restoration settlement. The heads of eleven Cambridge colleges, including Whichcote and Worthington, were ejected and replaced with High Churchmen, but Cudworth, after a struggle, remained. Although he was a known collaborator with Parliament and the Protectorate, he received valuable support from Gilbert Sheldon, bishop of London and soon to become archbishop of Canterbury. Widdrington, who probably wanted to supplant Cudworth as master of Christ's, embarked on a campaign to discredit both Cudworth and More. In August 1660, he petitioned the king against Cudworth, after which Cudworth managed to eject him from his fellowship, only to have him reinstated by the Privy Council. In June 1665, More wrote to Anne Conway that Widdrington loaded Cudworth 'with whatever his malice could invent or catch at'. He had characterised the college as a 'Seminary of Heretics' and called More and Cudworth 'Latitude-Men'. Widdrington was able to enlist the aid of a group of new heads of house—Joseph Beaumont at Peterhouse, Peter Gunning at Corpus Christi and then St John's, John Pearson at Jesus and then at Trinity and Anthony Sparrow at Queens'—as well as Herbert Thorndike, a restored fellow at Trinity. Following the publication of More's *Grand Mystery of Godliness*, Beaumont privately circulated a manuscript list of accusations of heresy against him. More published it without Beaumont's permission in his *Apology* in 1664, defending himself especially against charges that he was lukewarm in his advocacy of episcopacy and that his understanding of the role of reason in religion, of the divinity of Christ and of the Resurrection body was heretical. More and Cudworth survived this campaign of attacks against them, but at Christ's College they had to battle Widdrington's machinations until at least the middle of the 1670s. In doing so, they were able to build a fellowship of scholars supportive of their leadership, some of whom would become authors of texts strongly inclined to Platonism and Origenism. One of Widdrington's specific targets in the mid-1660s was probably Henry Hallywell, who, as we have seen, was a fellow of Christ's from 1662 to 1667. Hallywell's first two books, published anonymously, were written during his fellowship. *A Private letter of Satisfaction to a Friend*, an Origenian account of a morally dynamic afterlife, was composed in 1665 and published in the final year of his fellowship, while *Deus Justificatus*, an Origenian attack on Calvinist double predestination, followed in 1668.

These were perilous times for Cudworth and More, who stood in real danger of losing their Cambridge positions, yet they were not without supporters, particularly a younger generation of men educated during the Civil War and Interregnum who turned Widdrington's insult—'Latitudinarian'—into a term of approbation. As we saw with Glanvill's Cupri-Cosmits, contemporary writers did not make the sharp distinction between Cambridge Platonists and Latitudinarians which later historians have sometimes imposed. In 1662, 'S. P. of Cambridge'—most likely Symon Patrick of Queens'—set out the basic Latitudinarian programme in *A Brief Account of the New Sect of Latitude-Men*. Patrick had been much influenced by John Smith, whose funeral sermon he had preached, and he had been supplanted as master of Queens' by Anthony Sparrow, although he was elected by the fellows. S. P. wrote of the willingness of 'Latitude-men' to receive episcopal ordination and conform to the *Book of Common Prayer*, as well as accepting the Thirty-nine Articles, the *Book of Homilies* and the historic creeds, including the Athanasian creed. They were Arminians who valued both faith and a holy life, but they rejected all rigid doctrines, relying on the church fathers and guiding reason—'the candle of the Lord', to use a favourite phrase of Whichcote's—in the interpretation of Scripture. They took an active interest in the discoveries of the new experimental natural philosophy but did not abandon their 'old loving Nurse, the *Platonick Philosophy*'. Seven years later, the Scot Gilbert Burnet's *Modest and Free Conference betwixt a Conformist and a Nonconformist* was published anonymously. In his assertion that 'Religion was given of God to transform man into the Divine likeness, and to a real participation of the Divine Nature', Burnet showed that he was already greatly influenced by reading the early works of the Cambridge Platonists. He had met Whichcote, More and Cudworth on a journey to England in 1663, as well as the Latitudinarians John Wilkins, John Tillotson and Edward Stillingfleet, who all acknowledged a strong debt to Cambridge Platonism. When Burnet was bishop of Salisbury in the Reign of William and Mary, he included a laudatory list of 'Latitudinarians' in his *History of his own Time*, including Whichcote, Cudworth, John Wilkins, More and Worthington, with Tillotson, Stillingfleet and Patrick preeminent among their second-generation disciples. In 1670, Edward Fowler of Corpus Christi College, Oxford, anonymously published a full-length book defending Latitudinarianism, republished in 1671 with an expanded title: *The Principles and Practices of certain moderate Divines of the Church of England, abusively called Latitudinarians (greatly mis-understood) truly represented and defended*. Fowler's thinking was so similar to More's that the Calvinist Thomas Barlow, keeper of the Bodleian Library and a fellow of the Queen's College, Oxford, thought it must be his.

At Christ's College, Widdrington continued to try to influence fellowship elections and other college matters until the mid-1670s, requiring More and Cudworth to be ever vigilant against his destructive interference. Their friendship was a great support to both of them, although they quarrelled briefly in January 1665. More was a prolific writer, publishing a collection of his philosophical works in 1662, beginning a lengthy series of publications against Roman Catholicism and concerning the apocalypse and bringing out several major new works during the 1660s. Cudworth worked more slowly, although his massive *True Intellectual System of the Universe* was taking shape during this decade. More and Cudworth had discussed the need for a new book on ethics, and Cudworth thought that More had ceded this project to him, only to discover in January 1665 that More's own *Enchiridion Ethicum* was nearly ready for the press. Worthington and Thomas Standish, who would become the longest serving fellow at Christ's, helped the two friends to resolve this painful quarrel. More's book was published in 1667 and became a popular university textbook. It was translated into English by Edward Southwell in 1690. In 1668, More brought out his deeply Platonic *Divine Dialogues*, followed by his major work against Spinoza, *Enchiridion Metaphysicum* in 1671. In that year, Cudworth's *True Intellectual System* received the *imprimatur*, but opposition to him at court, probably orchestrated by Widdrington, prevented its publication until 1678. Hallywell seems to have temporarily filled the gap by anonymously publishing his short work, *A Discourse of the Excellency of Christianity* in 1671. John Cockhsute, a young admirer of More and a friend of John Finch, died in 1670, leaving More £300 to cover the cost of translating his English philosophical works into Latin and publishing them. The result was the three-volume *Opera Omnia* of 1675–1679.

Despite his willingness to conform to the restored Church of England, Whichcote was ejected from the provostship of King's College in 1660 to make way for a royal nominee. In 1668, when John Wilkins vacated the vicarage of St Lawrence Jewry in the City of London to become bishop of Chester, Whichcote was appointed vicar there. Wilkins had already established a tradition of liberal preaching in the benefice, which Whichcote was able to augment. The parish had endowed lectureships for weekday preaching, mainly filled by John Tillotson and John Sharp, who became archbishops of Canterbury and York, respectively, after the Glorious Revolution. Tillotson was the preeminent Latitudinarian, and Sharp, although he became something of a High Churchman as archbishop, was deeply embedded in the Cambridge Platonist network. A graduate of Christ's and a protégé of More, he had been a domestic chaplain to Sir Heneage Finch, Lady Conway's elder half-brother. As Lord Chancellor, Finch entrusted all his ecclesiastical patronage to Sharp, making him a powerful figure in ecclesiastical employment. Whichcote preached twice a week at St Lawrence Jewry until his death in 1683 at Cudworth's house in Cambridge. Hallywell almost certainly heard Whichcote when he visited Walter Kettilby at the sign of the Bishop's Head in St Paul's churchyard. Kettilby was More's London bookseller and publisher, and he handled most of Hallywell's books, too. The similarity of Whichcote's and Hallywell's sermon cycles on Philippians 4:8, both masterpieces of Christian Platonist theology, is so close as to suggest that Hallywell took inspiration from sermons he had heard at St Lawrence Jewry. Hallywell's book on this text, *The Excellency of Moral Vertue* (1692), was dedicated to Tillotson, who had just presented him to the vicarage of Cowfold in Sussex, and his final book, *A Defence of Revealed Religion* (1694) was dedicated to his old friend Sharp.

Henry More felt a profound affection for Lady Anne Conway, although the final years of her life, when she became a Quaker and her health deteriorated severely, brought about something of a separation between them. Since girlhood, she had suffered from crippling headaches, which became more frequent as the years went by despite the advice she sought from a number of physicians. In 1666, Rust accompanied the Irish 'stroker' Valentine Greatrakes to Ragley Hall to attempt to effect one of his famous cures on her. The attempted cure failed, but the party gathered to witness it gives us a rare glimpse of several of the people we have been discussing gathered in a setting of human affection and compassion. More, Rust and Lord Conway were present, while Cudworth and Whichcote testified to the efficacy of Greatrake's healing on other occasions. Rust wrote to Glanvill describing and commenting on the attempted healing. It may well have been the last time that the assembled party saw Rust alive, since he soon returned to Ireland and died in 1670. At Ragley, More met the famous Flemish physician Francis Mercury van Helmont, who was resident as Lady Conway's person physician during the 1670s. Van Helmont introduced More to the Lurianic Cabbala, so different from More's Cabbalistic imaginings of 1653, and put him in touch with the famous German Cabbalist Christian Knorr von Rosenroth. More and von Rosenroth would collaborate on a book presenting the Cabbala to Christian readers, *Kabbala denudate* (1677). Van Helmont shared Anne's growing interest in Quakerism, and prominent Quakers including George Fox, Robert Barclay, George Keith and William Penn visited Ragley. In 1677–1678, Anne and van Helmont became Quakers, despite the strenuous opposition of Lord Conway and More. More had attempted to become more understanding and sympathetic towards Quakerism because of his deep affection for Anne, but some of his earlier published views on the errors of the sect are reflected in Hallywell's 1673 *Account of Familism*. Shutting herself off even from More's visits, Anne surrounded herself with Quaker servants in the remaining months before her death in 1679, saying how grateful she was for their silence.

Glanvill and More collaborated and supported each other on two issues which brought Cambridge Platonism into controversy: the pre-existence of the soul and the reality of witchcraft. Following More's advocacy of pre-existence in his early poems and in *The Immortality of the Soul* and *The Grand Mystery of Godliness*, and Rust's probable writing on the subject in *A Letter of Resolution concerning Origen*, Glanvill wrote a letter, probably to Rust, asking for further clarification of the doctrine. He then anonymously published *Lux Orientalis* in 1662, strongly supporting pre-existence. He was answered very critically by Samuel Parker in 1666 and Edward Warren in 1667, but More remained silent until 1682, when he wrote ample annotations in a new edition of the book, published together with Rust's *Discourse of Truth*. Hallywell replied to Parker almost immediately, in a short tract published together with his anonymous *Deus Justificatus*, but he took Parker to task for emphasising God's will at the expense of his goodness rather than discussing pre-existence. Glanvill and More shared an interest in the paranormal, believing that it was an essential support to belief in God. When Glanvill's early *Blow at Modern Sadducism* (1668) was attacked by John Webster, our authors began collecting witchcraft stories which they believed to be verified by eyewitness statements. Glanvill died in November 1680 before they had fully prepared a much-expanded edition of his book, but More was able to publish the first edition of *Saducismus Triumphatus* in 1681. This was followed by a supportive contribution from Hallywell, *Melampronoea, or a Discourse of the Polity and Kingdom of Darkness*, also in

1681, and then by a second, even further expanded, edition of *Saducismus Triumphatus* in 1682. For the modern reader who remains unconvinced by the witchcraft stories, perhaps the most interesting thing about these books is the way in which they demonstrate how widespread witchcraft belief was among the Cambridge Platonist circle and how their correspondence sheds light on their friendship networks.

During the 1680s, More continued to write about the apocalypse and to denounce Roman Catholic idolatry, while Cudworth dictated many pages to a series of amanuenses in an attempt to complete the second and third parts of his *True Intellectual System*. In 1731, his *Treatise concerning Eternal and Immutable Morality* would be published for the first time, followed by *A Treatise of Freewill* in 1838. As we have seen, Whichcote died in 1683, having published nothing in his lifetime. Several strands of manuscript tradition and printed collections were combined in an edition of ninety-seven sermons, published anonymously in Aberdeen in 1751. A collection of 1,200 Aphorisms, drawn from Whichcote's own notes, was published by Samuel Salter in 1753, together with his correspondence with Anthony Tuckney.

The 1680s were years of rising political tension as Parliament tried and failed to exclude James, duke of York, from the succession, followed by James's accession in 1685. The Church of England briefly joined forces with prominent Dissenters to resist James' attempts to reintroduce Roman Catholicism as the national religion. When this resistance seemed doomed to fail, Parliament invited James' son-in-law and nephew, William of Orange, who was married to the king's elder daughter, Mary, to take the throne in November 1688. But neither More, who died in September 1687, nor Cudworth, who died in July 1688, lived to see the Glorious Revolution. Of the original group of Cambridge Platonists, only Hallywell lived on into the eighteenth century, affirming in his final book of 1694 that William's reign was beneficial not only to England but to the whole of Europe. When a number of bishops (the Nonjurors) refused to swear loyalty to the new regime, they were deprived of their sees and replaced by a strong group of Latitudinarians, thus bringing the apparently subversive Platonic theology of the Civil War period into the established Church of England and the House of Lords.

Chapter 3

From the Latitude Men to the Cambridge Enlightenment

Changing Nomenclatures

Christian Hengstermann

The first contemporary designations to be attached to the group of 17th century divines and philosophers now commonly known as the "Cambridge Platonists" were coined in the Restoration era. Their purpose was to denigrate the likes of Benjamin Whichcote, John Smith, Ralph Cudworth and Henry More for what members of the higher echelons of the newly restored Anglican Church viewed as their opportunistic turncoat mentality. The so-called "Latitude Man", most notably Cudworth and More who had retained their university posts at the Restoration were now charged with refusing for reasons of self-interest to support either the Calvinism or the Arminianism of the civil war factions in ecclesiastical organization or soteriological dogma. Closely tied to the contemporary invectives against their reservation of judgement in matters of church organization were designations targeted at their philosophical allegiance to highly dubious authors like Plato himself or his most unorthodox Christian follower Origen of Alexandria. While the Cambridge Platonists did not take exception to "Origenian Platonism" as a designation of their variety of an ancient Christian theology of a recognizably idealist stamp, they were reviled by their Restoration foes as "Praeexistentiaries" who subscribed to heterodox teachings like the pre-existence of souls or worse. The original two-part definition of Cambridge Platonism in terms of church politics and of patristic and Platonic philosophy continues to inform the various nomenclatures suggested in both classical and contemporary research in the field.

Cambridge Platonist Nomenclatures

"Cambridge" and "Platonism" may be seen to designate the Cambridge Platonists' place in Revolutionary and Restoration politics and in perennial philosophy respectively. "Cambridge Platonists", the most well-known of these modern group designations, was coined by John Tulloch in his two-volume *Rational Theology* of 1872. The "Cambridge Platonists", to whom the second volume of Tulloch's magisterial and influential work is devoted, carried the torch of an undogmatic and tolerant Christian religion lit by the "Liberal Church Men" of the Great Tew Circle, of whom the first volume provides a comprehensive exposition. In reaction against the stern Puritanism of Emmanuel College where most of them were originally educated and against the Calvinist creeds of the Westminster Conference on the one hand and against the excessive Laudian ritualism on the other, the Cambridge Platonists put ancient pagan and patristic Platonism and early modern Cartesiansim alike at the service of a pioneering first Protestant natural theology. It was designed to eschew the extremes of Calvinism and Arminianism and bring about the longed-for reconciliation of warring Christian parties of the civil war era. In his 1932 classic *The Platonic Renaissance in England (and the School of Cambridge)*,[1] Ernst Cassirer duly acknowledged the seminal importance of Tulloch's view of the eponymous group of early modern thinkers as "the most important representative of 'rational theology' to emerge in 17th century England" (Cassirer, *Platonische Renaissance*, 225). However, the "school of Cambridge" is, above all, defined by its major representatives' staunch resistance to all things distinctly early modern and modern. Theirs, in Cassirer's unfavourable estimate, is a philosophy entirely out of touch with the new age of the natural sciences and the experimental method to which they opposed a quaint humanist *prisca theologia* in wistful longing for the venerable Platonism of old. However, in several more positive remarks which run counter to his overall negative view, Cassirer grudgingly pays respect to the group as a chief foil to British empiricism in general and to John Locke's anti-innatism in particular. In combatting Hobbes's empiricism, the Cambridge Platonists were careful to lay out the inevitable aporiai of an empiricist theory of knowledge and a contractualist theory of moral and political obligation. Their emphasis throughout lay upon the practical and formal religious *a priori* in metaphysics and ethics. Its chief corollary of a universalist rational religion at once looks back to the humanistic visions of Nicolas of Cusa's *On the Peace of Faith*, Marsilio Ficino's *Christian Religion* and Thomas More's *Utopia* and forward to the ethical rationalism of Gottfried W. Leibniz's *Theodicy* and Immanuel Kant's *Religion within the Limits of Reason*. While unique and unsurpassed in sheer erudition and the scope of the exposition of the "school of Cambridge's" place in Enlightenment Europe, Cassirer's landmark study, despite its occasional reluctant praise, did the Cambridge Platonists more harm than good. It effectively relegated the Cambridge Platonists to the outer fringes of intellectual history. In sharp divergence from Cassirer's negative account of their philosophical achievement, two relatively recent sobriquets instead emphasize the Cambridge Platonists' pivotal role in early modern philosophy and beyond. "Cambridge Origenists", the first of these two novel designations, was coined by the two (originally) Münster-based German scholars Alfons Fürst and Christian Hengstermann in a series of German translations of selected Cambridge Platonist writings with introductions and interpretative essays. It highlights the group's profound debt to the heterodox Church Father Origen of Alexandria. The chief rationale for the proposed new nomenclature is the 1661 *Letter of Resolution Concerning Origen and the Chief of His Opinions* written by Henry More's friend and follower George Rust and published anonymously after the Restoration in 1661 (Fürst/Hengstermann, *Cambridge Origenists*). They borrowed from Origen's "Metaphysics of Freedom" (Kobusch, *Christliche Philosophie*; Hengstermann, *Ursprung der Freiheitsmetaphysik*) the key insight into moral freedom and agency as the first principle of all reality, whether divine or human. In defending divine goodness and human free will against the denial of any objective moral value and choice in the determinist systems of Thomas Hobbes and Baruch de Spinoza, the Cambridge Origenists were instrumental in shaping a distinctly early modern view of a world endowed with the creator's life and driven by nothing else but his own and his creatures' autonomous moral agency. "Cambridge Enlightenment", the second new group designation, was suggested by Sarah Hutton whose pioneering research work on the subject, perhaps more than any other, helped rediscover and re-evaluate Cambridge Platonism. While not a school in any strict institutional sense, the Cambridge Enlightenment thinkers shared a common body of doctrines, notably a libertarian theory of action, an ethical realism and an idealist metaphysics upon which they based an emphatically anti-Calvinist and anti-voluntarist rational theology of divine goodness (Hutton, *British Philosophy*, 136–159). Despite their frequent recourse to the philosophical tradition, their philosophy of religion is not an exercise in anachronistic humanism, but a response both to the political upheavals of the Commonwealth and Restoration eras and the philosophical paradigm shift effected by the advent of the natural sciences. Far from insignificant, therefore, the Cambridge Platonists, several of whom held important posts in the Interregnum body politic and were members of the Royal Society at the Restoration, helped shape early modern politics and philosophy. One of the comprehensive expositions of Cambridge Platonism, Henry More's 1679 *Enchiridium metaphysicum*, is perhaps even "the most substantial work of metaphysics to be produced in seventeenth-century Britain" (Hutton, *British Philosophy*, 148). Nor were the Cambridge Platonists, as is frequently alleged, without any lasting influence upon subsequent English and European theology and philosophy. The subsequent Latitudinarian movement in the Church England clearly bore the imprint of their theological libertarianism. In addition, two major varieties of British ethics, rationalism and sentimentalism, can be traced back to the Cambridge Platonists' pioneering work in practical philosophy. The new designation was key to the major three-year AHRC-funded project The Cambridge Platonists at the Origins of the Enlightenment (2016–2019) led by Douglas Hedley, Sarah Hutton and David Leech. It led to a decisive *Revisioning* of *Cambridge Platonism* in terms of its *Sources and Legacy* (Leech/Hedley) and produced an online Sourcebook of Cambridge Enlightenment thought meant to furnish further evidence for its pioneering role in British and Continental philosophy and religion.

Only relatively recently, therefore, have the Cambridge Platonists come to be seen as major early modern British Enlightenment philosophers in their own right whose thought has been unjustly eclipsed by their more well-known rationalist and empiricist contemporaries. In the process, their contributions to numerous principal philosophical disciplines have increasingly been re-evaluated as well. In terms of the differing nomenclatures attached to the members of the group, it is perhaps indicative of the growing interest in their religious as well as in their theoretical and practical philosophy that the Cambridge Platonists have been recognized as seminal thinkers in a great variety of modern disciplines. As a consequence, several various philosophical "isms" have been applied to their thought. Not only did Ralph Cudworth coin the term in his 1671/1678 *True Intellectual System of the Universe*, but he may in fact be regarded as the early modern founder of the "philosophy of religion" who remedied several shortcomings of the Cartesian notion of God (Taliaferro, *Evidence and Faith*, 11–56), In metaphysics, the "Cambridge Enlightenment" has been recognized for its innovative contributions to theories of subjectivity (Thiel, *Early Modern Subject*, 67–71) and to "panentheism" as the major alternative to classical theism. On the Cambridge Platonist view, God is both transcendent and immanent to all things, interacting with them in such a fashion as, possibly, adds to the ever-growing perfection of his own supremely consummate life (Cooper, *Panentheism*, 72–74). In response to the Cartesian bifurcation of nature, all of the Cambridge Enlightenment thinkers either carefully offset traditional Platonist substance dualism by introducing mediating entities, most notably "plastic nature" and the "spirit of nature", or rejected it altogether in favour of a panpsychistic cosmology so as to allow for the Deity's creative and formative omnipresence in all of infinite space and nature (Hengstermann, "God or Space and Nature?"). Their religious philosophy hinged upon an epistemology of God's symbolic self-revelation in nature and history. It has recently been revived and refined in a comprehensive theory of the *Iconic Imagination* and its *Living Forms* which also admits of the tragic in a theodicy revolving around the *Sacrifice Imagined* in terms of a world rehearsing God's own eternal kenotic act in creation (Hedley). Of equal importance are the Cambridge Platonists' contributions to practical philosophy in which they are now recognized as major "British moralists". Among their lasting contributions are a particularly elaborate "libertarianism" in the theory of action (Leisinger, "Cudworth on Freewill") and theories of a moral sense and a rational and universalist internal ought in systems bracketed both sentimentalist and internalist in systematic outlook (Darwall, *British Moralists*, 109–148; Gill, *British Moralists*, 7–74). Cudworth in particular opposed to Hobbes's compatibilism his own highly original account of accountable libertarian agency in a review of the latter's historic controversy with John Bramhall and in a yet largely unpublished series of massive manuscript remains. While there is as of yet no comparable rediscovery of Cudworth's fellow Cambridge Platonist More's system of theoretical and practical philosophy in monographs on metaphysics or ethics yet, two recent more analytic book-length expositions by Jasper Reid (*Philosophy*) and by David Leech (*Hammer of the Cartesians*) have highlighted its merit, clearly encouraging contemporary philosophers of the analytic and continental tradition to engage in fruitful dialogue with the most speculatively profound of the Cambridge Enlightenment philosophers.

Note

1. Strangely enough, the English translation by James P. Pettegrove omits the latter half of the title which expressly affirms the existence of a "School of Cambridge" linked by bonds of friendship and by substantial doctrinal agreement: *Die platonische Renaissance in England* **und die Schule von Cambridge**.

Chapter 4

From Campagnac to Taliaferro and Teply

Cambridge Platonist Anthologies Old and New

Christian Hengstermann

Not surprisingly given the sheer magnitude of the Cambridge Platonists' literary production, there have been important anthologies from the early 20th century to the present day. These four previous anthologies of Cambridge Platonism share the focus upon authors and texts, privileging writings which lend themselves more readily to anthologizing, notably sermons and briefer treatises which can be reproduced in their entirety. All of the previous anthologies contain introductions of varying length which place the Cambridge Platonists in their political and philosophical contexts. In the process, they inevitably reflect the changing fortunes of the Cambridge Platonists in historical and philosophical research. The four anthologies differ signally in the general principles and preferences of selection.

A more narrow focus underlies the texts selected in E.T. Campagnac's pioneering anthology of 1901, and C.A. Patrides's now classical one of 1969. Campagnac's *The Cambridge Platonists*, somewhat surprisingly, reproduces texts by a triad of authors only, namely Benjamin Whichcote, John Smith and Nathaneal Culverwell (the latter of whom is now no longer generally regarded as a member of the group). Cudworth and More receive only occasional mention. In a brief reflection on past and present nomenclatures of the group, Campagnac names these two major Cambridge Platonists alongside several of the "lesser" ones, including "Worthington, Rust, and Norris" who make up "the School of the Cambridge Platonists, or as they were called by some of their contemporaries, the Latitude men" (Campagnac, *The Cambridge Platonists*, xi). It is with great succinctness that the author proceeds to define the "middle course" between Calvin's and Laud's extremes as the core characteristic of the group's emphatically rational religion. Their signature rationalism is shown to have flown from their belief in doctrinal latitude as the sole means by which to put an end to the fierce religious strives of their day:

> "Their efforts were directed towards the discovery of a middle course between the party which was dominated by the ecclesiastical statesmanship of Laud on the one hand, and, on the other, the party which was encumbered by the subtle and formal and all too complete theology of the Puritans. Against the first they urged that conduct and morality were of more moment than Church polity; against the latter they claimed that reason must not be fettered; and against both, that in the conscience of the individual, governed by reason, and illuminated by a revelation which could not be inconsistent with the reason, itself a 'seed of Deiform nature,' lay the ultimate seat of authority in religion"
>
> (Campagnac, *The Cambridge Platonists*, xiii).

The rights of human reason, not weakened or annulled, but strengthened and illuminated by divine revelation, are the chief focus of this first anthology's corpus of texts. Whichcote's original defence of reason in his celebrated sermons and aphorisms is expanded upon from a more Calvinist and a more Platonist perspective by his students John Smith and Nathaneal Culverwell. Given its surprising omission of Ralph Cudworth and Henry More, the two inarguably most prolific and most influential Cambridge Platonists, Campagnac's anthology may well be regarded as documenting a kind of Ur-Cambridge Platonism, a first Christian rational theology which was yet to be developed into a comprehensive system of a Christian philosophy of religion. Whichcote and his Calvinist and Platonist students laid the groundwork of the blend of Cartesian physics and Platonic metaphysics which came to be known as Cambridge Platonism. While also comparatively narrow in the choice of texts, C.A. Patrides's 1969 *The Cambridge Platonists* reproduces excerpts from several principal writings by the now canonical Cambridge Platonist core group of Benjamin Whichcote, Ralph Cudworth, Henry More and John Smith. Each of the texts selected is accompanied by a number of detailed notes on the great variety of classical and contemporary sources of philosophical thought either quoted or alluded to. Patrides's equally erudite introduction is noteworthy for its careful analysis of the Cambridge Platonists' place in the tradition of Christian Platonism. Theirs is a Platonism deeply shaped by "the mighty Origen" (Patrides, *Cambridge Platonists*, 2) whose own distinct metaphysics with its stress on human freedom and the divine image they consistently opposed to the prevalent Augustinianism of the Reformed Christian tradition and its preoccupation with man's sin and fall from God's grace. Above all, however, the Cambridge Platonists, in Patrides's view, compare highly unfavourably to their late antique and early modern humanist forebears. Cambridge Platonism at large is seen as an "even more modest edition" of the living Platonist tradition than that of the Florentine Neoplatonists Marsilio Ficino and Pico della Mirandola. Patrides's special ire is directed against Henry More. In a somewhat forced comparison of the Cambridge Platonists to their ancient and late antique forebears, More is summarily dismissed as the misguided Cambridge Iamblichus to the group's Plato Whichcote and its Porphyry Smith and, above all, to its Plotinus and Proclus Cudworth:

> "Their inspiration came from their Plato, Benjamin Whichcote; their best writing issued from their Porphyry, John Smith; their perversities became most apparent with Iamblichus, Henry More; while Ralph Cudworth as an acute and subtle philosopher was their Plotinus, and as a scholastic systematiser their Proclus"
>
> (Patrides, *Cambridge Platonists*, 2).

Cambridge Platonism is shown to differ from contemporary Puritanism and sectarianism in a *sui generis* rationalism which, while defending with great determination the rights of reason in matters of religion, also admits of the profundity of mystical vision and intimacy with God. Patrides is ahead of his time in placing the school's epistemology at the centre of his introduction and selection. It is the firm conviction of the soul's capacity for comprehensive divine vision that underlies the Cambridge Platonist's ethics of man's assimilation to the Divine and their politics of religious toleration. It is also crucial to their view of nature as suffused by God in "plastic nature". Patrides's *Cambridge Platonists* is the only anthology to reproduce Cudworth's famous *Digression* on the subject, thereby highlighting a particularly important part of their religious philosophy. While Patrides's anthology is rightly held in high regard, its overall negative estimate of the authors and texts in general and of More in particular takes away from the work's quality.

The two other anthologies of Cambridge Platonism opt for a broader approach and include a larger number of authors. Besides the canonical four Cambridge Platonists, Gerald R. Cragg's 1968 *The Cambridge Platonists* comprises substantial excerpts from Nathanael Culverwel and John Norris. Its structure is thematic. Divided into ten parts of unequal length, it contains a large section on the relationship between faith and reason followed by chapters on key areas of Cambridge Platonist thought, including epistemology, ethics and the theory of action as well as, strikingly, the theory of religious toleration and political sovereignty. A particularly noteworthy difference between Cragg's anthology and the earlier and contemporaneous ones of Campagnac and Patrides is the inclusion of More's spirited plea for religious toleration in the last book of the 1661 *Grand Mystery of Godliness* and Cudworth's long critique of Hobbesian and Spinozist contractualism on the final pages of his 1671/1678 *True Intellectual System*. Coupled with several excerpts highlighting the Cambridge Platonists' belief in man's freedom, the two long passages by the group's two prime representatives is clearly designed to further defend it from Cassirer's verdict of pious otherworldliness. In many ways, Cragg's circumspect selection of carefully modernized texts may well provide the most satisfying account of Cambridge Platonism, including its principal proponents' overriding political aim of a "middle way" meant to reconcile the warring sects of their day. Cragg's equally well-argued definition of the two-part sobriquet "Cambridge Platonists" revolves around their emphasis upon their Latitudinarianism to which any stern and unrelenting dogmatism dissevered from a conduct of sincere Christian charity and love was anathema. In civil war Cambridge, they sought to forge a median theology between Laudianism and Calvinism, inevitably incurring the ire of either party in the process. While Platonists well-read in the master's dialogues, especially the *Theatetus* and the *Euthyphro* upon which they based their own theory of *a priori* knowledge and the primacy of divine goodness vis-à-vis power respectively, their Platonism bears the imprint of Plato's late antique diadochi Plotinus and Origen. The body of doctrines to which all of the Cambridge Platonists subscribed hinges upon the inviolability of practical and theoretical reason which exercises its irreducible autonomy in both responsible action and the acquisition of knowledge. While Cudworth's *Digression* on "plastic nature" (alongside any other of the Cambridge Platonist treatises and texts on the school's important philosophy of nature) is missing from Cragg's anthology, its seminal influence on various panpsychistic systems, including Henri Bergson, is duly noted and discussed.

The latest of the anthologies of the Cambridge Platonists, *Cambridge Platonist Spirituality*, edited by Charles Taliaferro and Alison J. Teply, follows Cragg in emphasizing the early modern philosophical school's overriding political agenda. Not coincidentally, the first text included is Ralph Cudworth's *Sermon Preached before the Honorable House of Commons at Westminster, March 31, 1647* which showcases the primarily ethical Christian spirituality advocated by the school in an age of appalling violence perpetrated in the name of religion. Taliaferro and Teply's selection is even broader than Cragg's and includes texts by Nathanael Culverwell and Peter Sterry as well as, importantly, the woman philosopher Anne Conway. The group's Platonism, notably the goodness of the creator and creation and the spirit of joyous enquiry as man's chief source of participation in God, is delineated in great detail. At the same time, the two editors are careful to stress that the "descriptive title *Platonic Christianity* cannot be adopted without some qualification". Instead, the group's Platonism is one deeply steeped in the universalism of Alexandrian Christianity. The Christian Platonists of Alexandria were instrumental in freeing their Platonism from its aristocratic disdain of the *hoi polloi*: "Origen recognizes the sublimity and awesomeness of Plato's view of the Good and the difficulty of finding God, while he counters that such difficulties can be surmounted by God's abundant generosity" (Taliaferro/Teply, *Cambridge Platonist Spirituality*, 6).

From Early Conversion to Mature System—Principles of Selection in the *An Anthology of the Cambridge Platonists*

Despite its numerous debts to them, the *An Anthology of the Cambridge Platonists* parts ways with the previous four in several crucial regards. Most strikingly, unlike the early anthologies, its overall organising principle is not prosopographic, but systematic. While principal texts by all of the major and several of the minor Cambridge Platonists are included, the focus of the *Anthology* is upon their contributions to theoretical and practical philosophy. Framed by an introductory and a commentary section, the texts selected in each of the chapters of *An Anthology of the Cambridge Platonists* are intended to highlight the Cambridge Platonists' contributions to a major discipline of theoretical and practical philosophy. They highlight both the school's principal doctrinal agreements and disagreements, thereby throwing into relief and rendering accessible to a specialist and non-specialist readership alike the body of doctrines defining of Cambridge Platonism as a school of distinctly early modern thought. Throughout the *Anthology*, the approach to Cambridge Platonism is that of constellation research first pioneered by the German philosopher Dieter Henrich in the field of German Idealism studies and introduced into Cambridge Platonist scholarship by Sarah Hutton ("Eine Cambridge-Konstellation?"; "Radical Review"). It was subsequently made extensive use of by Marilyn A. Lewis to detail the original emergence and subsequent flourishing of the Cambridge Origenist network in the Revolutionary and the Restoration period ("'Origenian Platonisme'"; "Expanding the 'Origenist Moment'"; "'Christ's College and the Latitude-Men' Revisited"). Of particular importance is the Cambridge Platonists' critical engagement with several major philosophers of the day against whom they directed several in-depth refutations. A substantial part of the *Anthology* is devoted to this body of polemical writings which highlight their distinctly early modern style of philosophising. Notwithstanding their somewhat dated predilection for humanist-style argument, the Cambridge Platonists are first and foremost early modern thinkers closer in technical philosophical diction and substance to their contemporaries Thomas Hobbes, René Descartes and Baruch de Spinoza than to the humanists of Renaissance Italy or the Netherlands such as Ficino, Pico or Erasmus. In sharp divergence from Cassirer's and Patrides's dismissal of Cambridge Platonism, the present anthology views the Cambridge Platonists as major philosophers of the early modern period. Not only do their critiques of the aforementioned thinkers rank among the Cambridge Platonists' finest and most influential writings, but they also reveal their chief philosophical concerns in their critiques of materialism, dualism and panpsychism.

Of great importance to this principle of text selection is the Cambridge Platonist Henry More unduly dismissed by Cassirer and Patrides as a largely inept writer out of touch with the scientific and philosophical thought of his day. His influential Latin writings, notably his widely-read handbooks on ethics and metaphysics, the 1667 *Enchiridion Ethicum* and the 1671 *Enchiridium Metaphysicum*, as well as his early correspondence with René Descartes and his late refutations of Jacob Böhme und Baruch de Spinoza, reveal More as a major early modern English moralist and metaphysician. Some of the excerpts from More's Latin works are taken from pre-existing English translations, notably Robert Southwell's early modern *Account of Virtue*, a highly spirited English rendering of More's 1664 *Enchiridium Ethicum*, and from the modern English translations by Alexander Jacob. However, given the significance of More's two handbooks and his principal polemical works, a substantial body of notes have been added to Southwell's translation to indicate the numerous differences between the translator's readable, yet overly ornate and frequently misleading, English and the author's own more concise and sober Latin. Though pioneering efforts which helped make accessible to a wider readership several of More's most important works, Jacob's translations are not without mistakes which occasionally distort the author's argument. All of the excerpts from his English renderings of *Henry More's Manual of Metaphysics* and *Refutation of Spinoza* have therefore been carefully checked and revised. The majority of extracts from More's principal polemical Latin writings are reproduced in new English translations made by Christian Hengstermann for the purposes of the present anthology. Our anthology also departs from previous ones in further stressing the contribution of the so-called minor Cambridge Platonists, most notably George Rust and his student and editor Henry Hallywell. Not only did Rust author the *Letter of Resolution*, the most Origenist of the Cambridge Origenists' works, but his sermons rank among the finest of the group's philosophical essays. Despite his own protestations to the contrary and his exuberant praise of More, Rust himself cannot be dismissed as a spirited, yet unoriginal, disciple of his revered Christ's teacher. Instead, he may well be deserving of a re-evaluation as the fifth major Cambridge Platonist besides the canonical four and a major early modern religious philosopher in his own right. Likewise, Henry Hallywell is shown to be another unduly neglected Cambridge Platonist whose work provides some of the most accessible and most tightly argued expositions of the school's religious philosophy.

The bibliography at the end of the *An Anthology of the Cambridge Platonists* contains references to all modern editions of Cambridge Platonist writings as well as a list of introductory and specialist literature on the topics of each of the chapters.

Part II

Historical Context and Philosophical Programme

Introduction

Conversion and Original Insight

More's original insight at "Aeton School" in 1628, when the young student was sent there by his uncle, a staunch Calvinist, revolved around "that hard Doctrine concerning Fate" which he came to reject in a sudden insight. In an autobiographical sketch in the preface to the Latin translation of his philosophical works of 1679 **(5 A–B)**, More confides in his reader the "proper sentiments of his own Mind drawn and derived" as he is careful to point out, neither from his education nor his reading, but solely "from my most intimate Nature", i.e. in the manner of an unprejudiced Cartesian "Meditation". Though probably written with the benefit of theological hindsight, the "Dr.'s little narrative of himself" encapsulates in a piece of vividly written autobiographical theology the unshakable foundation of the Cambridge Platonists' theistic metaphysics. Underlying all their philosophical thought is the firm conviction of God's goodness and justice and man's freewill to reject his universal grace or embrace it in sincere moral endeavour. It was at Cambridge where he begins his studies three years later that More, deeply immersed in the Greek Neoplatonist Plotinus's *Enneads* with Marsilio Ficino's Latin commentaries and, above all, the medieval *Theologia Germanica*, viewed practical virtue, the purgation of self-will in a life of universal love, as the soul's "true Life" in God, whether in heaven, on earth or indeed in hell. Having overcome a tormenting ἀπορία of skepticism—"O Father Jove", he laments in his earliest surviving verses, "'Tis brave, we Mortals live in clouds like thee", his original insight into God's goodness and justice and man's freedom finds its first poetical expression in the Εὐπορία, a moving Neoplatonist hymn on the Soul's procession from and return to God in a life of purgative self-denial and universal love. His heartfelt early poetry **(5 C–D)**, notably two of his lyrical Latin poems, shed further light upon More's motives for his two-stage conversion Calvinism to an emphatically practical Platonism, notably his fervent belief in human free will. Man's insight into the infinity of divine benignity frees him from necessity and its ubiquitous rule in nature.

Ralph Cudworth underwent a similar conversion to More's. In a 1668 fragmentary letter, Cudworth relates why he rejected Calvinism in favour of Christian Platonism. The author's Latin letter to the Dutch Remonstrant Philipp van Limborch with whom he and Henry entertained close amicable ties throughout is important for two reasons. For one thing, it is crucial evidence of a seminal 17th century constellation placing Cambridge Platonism in the larger context of liberal European theology in the vein of Erasmus of Rotterdam and his later Arminian followers which thrived, above all, in the relatively tolerant Netherlands. Not only did Jean LeClerc, van Limborch's Arminian friend and colleague, go on to publish excerpts from Cudworth's *True Intellectual System of the Universe* in a French translation, but Dutch and English liberal theologians subsequently came to join forces in the historic Dutch Bredenburg Disputes about Spinoza and the rationalist materialism and determinism of his *Ethics*. For another, Cudworth's letter, shows the same concern with divine goodness and human freedom to be the driving force of nascent Cambridge Platonism and its staunch opposition to Calvinism. It links the foremost Cambridge Platonist's early conversion from Calvinism to Christian Platonism to a public Commencement disputation held in 1651. The Commencements or *magna comitia* were major public events at the university at which the higher degrees were conferred upon the candidates. A Commencement was a two-day event taking place on the first Tuesday of July called the "Commencement Day" and the preceding evening or "Commencement Eve". At its centre was a public discussion held in the university church Great St. Mary's where the candidate incepting his degree was called upon to defend a thesis as "respondent". The Latin Commencement verses distributed at the event were intended to serve as verse summaries of the thesis under discussion. Not surprisingly, the divinity Commencements were of particular political importance as they were meant either to showcase the university's orthodox faith or to serve as "a gauge of the theological positions found acceptable in the University" (Hall, *Cambridge Act and Tripos Verses*, 17). The latter clearly holds true for the Cambridge Commencement at which Cudworth ventured openly and vocally to champion key tenets of Cambridge Platonist metaphysics in the face of what must have been determined Calvinist opposition. The Commencement took place on 1st July 1651, towards the end of the British civil war. Presided over by Benjamin Whichcote, the then vice chancellor of the university, it saw Ralph Cudworth defend the school's landmark moral and theological realism of a strictly universal and univocal eternal and immutable morality binding upon God and man alike. As can be seen from the verse summary of his Commencement thesis, Cudworth was vocal in his rejection of the Calvinist notion of unlimited divine omnipotence. In what must be seen as a major turning point in the history of the university, Cudworth repudiated prevalent Calvinist orthodoxy as an egregious anthropomorphism, charging its Cambridge proponents with falsely ascribing to a good God the defining characteristic of a fickle and capricious human tyrant. Predating his *opus magnum* by two decades, the vibrant verses of the two Commencement poems, thus, provide a dense, yet remarkably lucid and elegant, first exposition of Cudworth's metaphysics of divine goodness and love. God's every action is shown to be subject to his universal goodness, which renders conceptually impossible the spectre of a Calvinist deity damning human souls at will. Besides their intrinsic historical and philosophical importance as an early public proclamation of the Cambridge Platonists' rational theology, the two poems are also remarkable for their idiosyncratic authorship. In keeping with general Commencement custom, Cudworth had not composed the Latin verses distributed to those attending the event in Great St. Mary's himself. Instead, he had had a gifted younger Cambridge friend, the mathematician and theologian Isaac Barrow, write them on his behalf. Barrow, while not a Cambridge Platonist himself, shared many of the group's theological key convictions. A document written in close temporal proximity to Cudworth's religious crisis in the mid-1630s is his letter to his foster father John Stoughton **(5 G)**. It reveals in emotional language the preoccupation with divine infinity as another early concern of the precocious Cudworth. The preface to his mature 1671/1678 **(7 A–B)** shows the remarkable continuity of his thought. From first to last, Cudworth sought to defend human freedom from theological and philosophical determinism alike.

Political Platonism and Early Sermons on Rational Theology

Benjamin Whichcote, Ralph Cudworth, Henry More, George Rust, Henry Hallywell and Joseph Glanvill were all ordained priests of the Church of England. Whichcote, Cudworth and More had been ordained before the Civil War but continued to minister within Cambridge colleges throughout the Interregnum. They were willing to cooperate with the Protectorate regime which outlawed prelacy and imposed a more reformed Protestant settlement on the national church, but they conformed to the re-established Church of England at the Restoration. John Smith became a fellow of Queens' College following the Earl of Manchester's purge of the university in 1644, so there was no question of his taking Anglican orders, and he died in 1652, well before the Restoration. Our younger authors, Rust, Hallywell and Glanvill took orders between 1660 and 1662. Rust would become a bishop in the Church of Ireland, while Hallywell and Glanvill were parish priests in England. All our authors were regular preachers, and this section attempts to demonstrate something of the distinctive theology of their sermons.

An Augustinian Calvinist theology predominated in Interregnum Cambridge, and the few Arminian voices raised were quickly accused of heresy. Belief in double predestination was deemed an essential component of orthodox Christianity, and Arminianism was associated with the outlawed Laudian ritualism which had been a major Puritan grievance before the Civil War. The Cambridge Platonists are often classified as Arminians or as providing a third way, a compromise position, between the two warring theological factions. Yet, while Arminianism opened the gate of salvation to a much larger proportion of the human race than Calvinism, it still held that human reason was irremediably damaged by the Fall. By distinct contrast, the Cambridge Platonists believed that human reason, while wounded, could be redeemed, and that it formed an essential component of intellectual adherence to the truth of the Gospels. They also advocated a process of becoming deiform, imitating God's moral virtues as exemplified by Jesus Christ, with the eventual goal of attaining fitness for the society of heaven. In these beliefs, they were heavily influenced by Plato, Plotinus and Origen of Alexandria, all authors who compounded their guilt in the eyes of their Calvinist colleagues.

Whichcote's sermons at the Round Church in Cambridge c.1636–c.1656 were very popular, but we know little of their content because he liked to preach extempore from notes and never prepared his sermons for publication. His sermons at St Lawrence Jewry in the City of London 1668–1683 were captured in shorthand notes by several auditors. These notes, combined with some of the preacher's own, were published as sermons after his death, with the most complete edition not appearing until 1751. In 1753, 1000 of his Aphorisms were published, and our selection here is taken from these, which are surely representative of Whichcote's thinking in sermon preparation. Smith's chapel discourses at Queens' College were published by his friend John Worthington in 1660, eight years after Smith's death. In college, he perhaps reached only a small auditory, but his *Select Discourses* are one of the classics of Cambridge Platonist theology. More's sermons represent only a very small proportion of his total writings, but a selection of those he preached in Christ's College chapel and Great St Mary's, the Cambridge University Church, in the 1640s and 1650s were collected and published in 1692 by John Worthington, and a brief passage from Discourse XIII is selected here. Cudworth published only four sermons; our selection, *A Sermon Preached before the House of Commons*, was preached in 1647 and has become one of the most quoted writings within Cambridge Platonist literature. Rust's sermon, *A Discourse of the Use of Reason in Matters of Religion*, was preached in Latin in Great St Mary's in early 1659, translated into English and annotated by Hallywell, dedicated to More and published in 1683. Hallywell did publish two sermon cycles in the 1690s, but our selection is taken from his 1677 *The Sacred Method of Saving Human Souls by Jesus Christ*, his attempt to present a concise Cambridge Platonist soteriology. The passage on the Atonement must have figured regularly in his parochial preaching. Glanvill's essay *The Agreement of Reason and Religion* began life as a clerical visitation sermon in 1670, preached while he was rector of Bath Abbey. He then included it as the fifth essay in his 1675 *Essays on Several Important Subjects in Philosophy and Religion*, dedicated to his patron the marquess of Worcester, a relative of his wife.

The New Sect of Latitude-Men: Religious Toleration and Moderation in Revolution and Restoration England

In an age of theological and ecclesiological party strife, 'Latitudinarian' and 'Latitude-Men' were originally terms of abuse levelled at moderate clergy by both strict Calvinist Presbyterians and Anglican High Churchmen. Latitudinarians were generally Arminians in their soteriology, although our Cambridge Platonists often embraced a more Origenian doctrine of salvation through deiformity. In church polity, they were moderate episcopalians, receiving ordination from bishops but not rejecting other forms of authorisation for ministry outright. Liturgically, they were satisfied with the set prayers of the Book of Common Prayer but eschewed Laudian ritualism. They also rejected contentious doctrines which they considered unscriptural, not only predestination but also Roman Catholic transubstantiation, believing adherence to them to be unnecessary to salvation. They had often cooperated with the Cromwellian religious establishment of the Interregnum but conformed to the restored Church of England when the Act of Uniformity became law in August 1662. Historians have sometimes drawn a sharp distinction between the Cambridge Platonists and a younger generation of their followers who became London parish priests at the Restoration, but contemporaries drew no such distinction, often grouping them together. 'Latitudinarian' is an older term than 'Cambridge Platonist' to describe the entire group. A more nuanced prosopography views them as inhabiting overlapping circles with porous borders. Their principles kept most of them from preferment before the Glorious Revolution, but a number of London Latitudinarians became bishops under the politique William III, thus bringing Latitudinarian principles into the hierarchy of the Church of England.

'S. P. of Cambridge', the author of *A Brief Account of the New Sect of Latitude-Men* (1662) **(6★ A)**, was most likely Symon Patrick (1626–1707) of Queens' College, Cambridge.[1] The 'Mr G. B. at Oxford' to whom he wrote has not been identified and is likely to have been a fictional correspondent. As a student, Patrick was strongly influenced by John Smith, who was a fellow of Queens' but not his tutor. Smith helped him to leave behind the Calvinist predestinarianism of his upbringing, and Patrick would preach his funeral sermon, published with Smith's *Select Discourses* in 1660. G.B.'s letter is dated 15 May 1662. On 29 April, the restored president of Queens', Edward Martin, had died and Patrick had been informed that the majority of the fellows wished to elect him. By 5 May, on his way to Cambridge from London, Patrick learned that the royal nominee, Anthony Sparrow, had already been installed as president. The issue dragged on in the courts, but by 1665 Patrick had dropped his claim. Sparrow was a High Churchman, and Patrick's Latitudinarianism was doubtless held against him as the crown attempted to install its supporters in Restoration Cambridge. Against this backdrop, Patrick was setting out his vision of a restored Church of England without unnecessary doctrinal and liturgical commitments and free to exercise an intellectual appraisal of credenda. During the reigns of Charles II and James II, Patrick was rector of St Paul's Covent Garden, but after the Glorious Revolution, he became bishop first of Chichester and then of Ely.

George Rust (c.1627–1670) was a pupil and protégé of both More and Cudworth at Christ's College and the student who most completely adhered to More's Origenian theology, which he also instilled in his own pupil Henry Hallywell. He went to Ireland in 1661 on More's recommendation to Jeremy Taylor, bishop of Connor and Down and administrator of the diocese of Dromore. Travelling to Ireland with the Conways, who were going to attend to their Irish estates, he developed a deep intellectual friendship with Lady Anne. He succeeded Taylor as bishop of Dromore in 1667 but died in 1670 of a fever and was buried in the same vault as Taylor in Dromore cathedral, a small building rebuilt by Taylor in 1661 after destruction during the Civil War. The funeral sermon selected here **(6★ B)** was preached in 1663 while Rust was still dean of Connor and printed the following year. It commemorates Hugh Earl of Mount Alexander, an Irish royalist nobleman who died suddenly in Dromore at the age of 38. Very soon after his election to the Irish Parliament in May 1661, Earl Hugh had moved a declaration that all Irish subjects should accept episcopal church government and the Book of Common Prayer. He was created Earl of Mount-Alexander by Charles II very soon after that, in recognition of his military efforts on behalf of the exiled king during the Interregnum. The sermon is dedicated to his widow, Katharine, whom he had married as his second wife in 1660. It was preached in Newtown, now known as Newtownards, in County Down, where he was buried on 29 October 1663.

At the Restoration, Ralph Widdrington, a fellow of Christ's College, Cambridge, attempted to have Cudworth and More removed from their respective posts as master and fellow. He allied himself with several new college heads who had been appointed by the crown in an effort to expunge the Puritanism and Latitudinarianism of Interregnum Cambridge. Although Widdrington made life very uncomfortable for the Platonists, they were able to turn his opposition into an advantage by carefully managing fellowship elections for a quarter of a century, thereby building up a community in which the study of Christian Platonism could flourish. An important source for our knowledge of the Widdrington affair is the *Conway Letters* **(6★ C)**, a large deposit of correspondence originally edited by Marjorie Hope Nicolson in 1930 and revised with additional material by Sarah Hutton in 1992. At the time of the writing of the two selected letters—the summer of 1665—Widdrington still represented a real danger but would soon be brought to something approaching a manageable position within the college. In these letters, we find 'Latitude men' and 'latitudinarian' reportedly used as terms of abuse against More and Cudworth.

Gilbert Burnet's (1643–1715) *Modest and Free Conference betwixt a Conformist and a Nonconformist* **(6★ D)** was published anonymously. Burnet was a Scot who lived most of his adult life in England, but he was still resident in Scotland as a young, ordained minister when he wrote the pamphlet, which dealt with 'the present distempers in *Scotland*'. Although it would later be established as a Presbyterian church, the Scottish Church at that time had been restored on the same pattern as the Church of England, governed by bishops and worshipping according to the Book of Common Prayer. Burnet was already greatly influenced by reading the early works of the Cambridge Platonists, and he had met Whichcote, More and Cudworth on a journey to England in 1663. He also met the Latitudinarians John Wilkins, John Tillotson and Edward Stillingfleet at that time. From 1675, he would become close friends with Tillotson and Stillingfleet as well as with William Lloyd, who all acknowledged a strong debt to Cambridge Platonism. William III would appoint Burnet to the bishopric of Salisbury in 1689. He was the author of *A History of his own Time*, first published in 1724, with its well-known list of 'Latitudinarians'.

Edward Fowler's (1632–1714) anonymously published *The Principles and Practices of certain moderate Divines of the Church of England* **(6★ E)** appeared in 1670. A second edition of 1671 inserted the phrase '*abusively called Latitudinarians*' into the title. Fowler became a leading London Latitudinarian and was made bishop of Gloucester in 1691 by William III. At the time of his first book, *Principles and Practices*, Fowler was curate of Northill, Bedfordshire, but he was already a friend of Henry More. A manuscript note opposite the title page in Thomas Barlow's copy of the book in the Bodleian Library reads:

> This discourse is a justification of a Latitudinarian (the word was hatch'd at Cambridge . . . and it looks soe like some discourse of Dr. Hen: Moore of the aforesaid University, that tis probable he may be the Author of it.

Farther down the page, however, this attribution is corrected to 'one Mr. Fowler', the owner of the book having been informed 'by those who should know' at Cambridge. The book is framed as a discourse between 'two Intimate Friends', whose agreement is virtually complete, so the speakers have not been differentiated in the selected passages here.

Joseph Glanvill (1636–1680) invented a fictional portrait gallery of Latitudinarian divines whom he denoted 'Cupri-Cosmits', in a land he called Bensalem, preserved in an unpublished manuscript which formed an early draft of his *Anti-Fanatical Religion and Free Philosophy* (1676) **(6★ F)**. In the published version of this essay, he lauded the moderation of Anglican divines like Jeremy Taylor and Henry Hammond, alongside those whom we would designate Cambridge Platonists and Latitudinarians. Here was a vision of the established church in conformity to the earliest centuries of Christianity before Roman corruption set in, rational in contrast to the fanaticism of the mid-seventeenth-century sects, Platonist but eager to accept the findings of the new experimental philosophy. Glanvill was rector of Bath Abbey when he wrote this essay, which is styled as a continuation of Francis Bacon's *New Atlantis*.

Note

1 Nicholas Fisher, *Symon Patrick (1626–1707) and his Contribution to the Post-1660 Restored Church of England*, Newcastle upon Tyne, 2019, pp. 14–17, disputes the attribution to Patrick, mainly because of the lack of evidence elsewhere for his interest in the 'new philosophy'.

Chapter 5

Conversion and Original Insight

Christian Hengstermann

A Henry More, "The Dr's little narrative of himself" (*Opera omnia*, II/2, v–vi. Translation: Ward, *Life of Henry More*, 59–61)

Concerning which Matter, I am the more assur'd; in that the Sensations of my own Mind are so far from being owing to Education, that they are directly contrary to it: I being bred up, to the almost 14th year of my Age, under Parents and a Master that were great Calvinists (but withal very pious and good ones): At which Time, by the Order of my Parents, persuaded to it by my Uncle, I immediately went to Æton School; not to learn any new Precepts or Institutes of Religion, but for the perfecting of the Greek and Latin Tongue. But neither there, nor yet anywhere else, could I ever swallow down that hard Doctrine concerning Fate. On the contrary I remember, that upon those words of Epictetus, Ἄγε με ὦ Ζεῦ κὶ [καὶ] σὺ ἡ πεπρωμένη, Lead me, O Jupiter, and thou Fate, I did (with my eldest Brother; who then, as it happened, had accompanied my Uncle thither) very stoutly, and earnestly for my Years, dispute against this Fate or Calvinistick Predestination, as it is usually call'd: And that my Uncle, when he came to know it, chid me severely; adding menaces withall of Correction, and a Rod for my immature Forwardness in Philosophizing concerning such Matters: Moreover, that I had such a deep Aversion in my Temper to this Opinion, and so firm and unshaken a Perswasion of the Divine Justice and Goodness; that on a certain Day, in a Ground belonging to Æton College, where the Boys us'd to play, and exercise themselves, musing concerning these Things with my self, and recalling to my Mind this Doctrine of Calvin, I did thus seriously and deliberately conclude within [60] my self, viz., "If I am one of those that are predestinated unto Hell, where all Things are full of nothing but Cursing and Blasphemy, yet will I behave my self there patiently and submissively towards God; and if there be any one Thing more than another, that is acceptable to him, that will I set my self to do with a sincere Heart, and to the utmost of my Power:" Being certainly persuaded, that if I thus demeaned my self, he would hardly keep me long in that Place. Which Meditation of mine, is as firmly fix'd in my Memory, and the very Place where I stood, as if the Thing had been transacted but a Day or two ago.

And as to what concerns the Existence of GOD: Though in that Ground mention'd, walking, as my Manner was, slowly, and with my Head on one Side, and kicking now and then the Stones with my Feet, I was wont sometimes with a sort of Musical or Melancholick Murmur to repeat, or rather humm to my self, those Verses of Claudian:

Saepe mihi dubiam traxit sententia mentem;
Curarent Superi terras; an nullus ineffet
Rector, et incerto fluerent Mortalia casu.

[Oft hath my anxious Mind divided stood;
Whether the Gods did mind this lower World;
Or whether no such Ruler (Wise and Good)
We had; and all things here by Chance were hurl'd.]

Yet that exceeding hail [whole] and entire Sense of GOD, which Nature herself had planted deeply in me, very easily silenced all such slight and Poetical Dubitations as these. Yea, even in my first Childhood, an inward Sense of the [61] Divine Presence was so strong upon my Mind; that I did then believe, there could no Deed, Word, or Thought, be hidden from him; Nor was I by any others that were older than my self to be otherwise persuaded. Which Thing since no distinct Reason, Philosophy, or Instruction taught it me at that Age; but only an internal Sensation urg'd it upon me; I think it very evident, that this was an innate Sense or Notion in me, contrary to some witless and sordid Philosophasters of our present Age. And if these cunning Sophisters shall here reply; that I drew this Sense of mine *ex Traduce*, or by way of Propagation, as being born of Parents exceedingly Pious and Religious, I demand, how it came to pass that I drew not Calvinism also in along with it? For both my Father and Uncle, and so also my Mother, were all earnest Followers of Calvin. But these Things I pass; since Men Atheistically disposed cannot so receive them, as I from an Inward Feeling speak them.

B More, "Little narrative" (*Opera omnia*, II/2, vi–vii. Translation: Ward, *Life of Henry More*, 61–66)

I go on therefore with my little Narrative. I was endued with these Principles, that is to say, a firm and unshaken Belief of the Existence of GOD, as also of his unspotted Righteousness and perfect Goodness, that he is a God infinitely Good, as well as infinitely Great; (and what other would any Person, that is not doltish or superstitious, ever admit of).

At the Command of my Uncle, to whose care my Father had committed me, having spent about three Years at Aeton, I went to Cambridge; recommended to the Care of a Person both [62] learned and pious, and, what I was not a little sollicitous about, not at all a Calvinist; but a Tutour most skilful and vigilant: Who presently after the very first Salutation and Discourse with me, ask'd me, whether I had a Discernment of Things Good and Evil? To which, answering in somewhat a low voice, I said "I hope I have:" When at the same Time, I was Conscious to my self, that I had from my very Soul, a most strong Sense and savoury Discrimination, as to all those Matters. Notwithstanding, the mean while, a mighty and almost immoderate Thirst after Knowledge possess'd me throughout. Especially for that which was Natural; and above all others, that which was said to dive into the deepest Cause of Things, and Aristotle calls the first and highest Philosophy, or Wisdom.

After which when my prudent and pious Tutour observed my Mind to be inflam'd, and carried with so eager and vehement a Career; He ask'd me on a certain Time, "Why I was so above Measure intent upon my Studies"; that is to say, for what End I was so? Suspecting, as I suppose, that there was only at the Bottom a certain Itch, or Hunt after Vain-glory; and to become, by this means, some famous Philosopher among those of my own Standing. But I answered briefly, and that from my very Heart; "That I may know." "But, young Man, What is the Reason," saith he again, "that you so earnestly desire to know Things?" To which I instantly return'd; "I desire, I say, so earnestly to know, That I may know." For even at that Time, the Knowledge of natural and divine [63] Things, seem'd to me the highest Pleasure and Felicity imaginable.

Thus then persuaded, and esteeming it what was highly Fit, I immerse my self over head and ears in the study of Philosophy; promising a most wonderful happiness to my self in it. Aristotle therefore, Cardan, Julius Scaliger, and other philosophers of the greatest Note, I very diligently peruse. In which, the Truth is, though I met here and there with some things wittily and acutely and sometimes also solidly spoken; yet the most seem'd to me either so false and uncertain, or else so obvious and trivial that I looked upon my self as having plainly lost my time in the Reading of such Authors. And to speak all in a Word, Those almost whole Four Years which I spent in Studies of this kind, as to what concern'd those Matters which I chiefly desired to be satisfied about, (for as to the Existence of a God, and the Duties of Mortality, I never had the least Doubt) ended in nothing, in a manner, but mere Scepticism. Which made me that, as my manner was, (for I was wont to set down the present State of my Mind, or any Sense of it that was warmer or deeper than ordinary, in some short Notes, whether in Verse or Prose; and that also in English, Greek, or Latin) it made me, I say, that as a perpetual Record of the Thing, I compos'd that stanza of eight Verses, which is call'd Ἀπορία, and is to be found inserted in the end of my Second Philosophicall Volume, viz. –

[64] Οὐχ ἔγνων etc.
know I:
Nor whence, nor who I am, poor Wretch!
Nor yet, O Madness! Whither I must goe:
But in Grief's crooked Claws fast held I lie;
And live, I think, by force tugg'd to and fro.
Asleep or wake all one. O Father Jove,
'Tis brave, we Mortals live in clouds like thee.
Lies, Night-dreams, empty Toys, Fear, fatal Love,
This is my Life: I nothing else do see.

And these things happen'd to me before that I had taken any Degree in the University.

But after taking my Degree, to pass over and omit abundance of things; I designing not here the Draught of my own Life (though some, and those very Famous Men too, have done that before me;) but only a brief Introduction for the better Understanding the Occasion of writing my First Book; It fell out truly very Happily for me, that I suffer'd so great a Disappointment in my Studies. For it made me seriously at last begin to think with myself; whether the Knowledge of things was really that Supreme Felicity of Man; or something Greater and more Divine was: Or, supposing it to be so, whether it was to be acquir'd by such an Eagerness and Intentness in the reading of Authors and contemplating of Things; or by the Purging of the Mind from all sorts of Vices whatsoever: Especially having begun to read now the Platonick Writers, Marsilius Ficinus, Plotinus himself, Mercurius Trismegistus; and the Mystical Divines; among whom there was frequent mention made of the Purification of the Soul, and of the Purgative [65] Course that is previous to the Illuminative; as if the Person that expected to have his Mind illuminated of God, was to endeavour after the Highest Purity.

But amongst all the Writings of this kind, there was none, to speak the Truth, so pierced and affected me, as that Golden little Book, with which Luther is also said to have been wonderfully taken, viz. *Theologia Germanica*: Though several Symptoms, even at that time, seem'd ever and anon to occur to me, of a certain deep Melancholy; as also no slight Errors in Matters of Philosophy. But that which he doth so mightily inculcate, viz.: That we should thoroughly put off and extinguish our own proper Will; that being thus Dead to our Selves we may live alone unto God, and do all things whatsoever by his Instinct, or plenary Permission; was so Connatural, as it were, and agreeable to my most intimate Reason and Conscience, that I could not of anything whatsoever be more clearly or certainly convinced. Which Sense yet (that no one may here use that dull and idle Expression, *Quales legimus, Tales evadimus*, Such as we read, Such we are) that truly Golden Book did not then first implant in my soul, but struck and rouz'd it, as it were, out of Sleep in me; Which it did verily as in a Moment, or the twinkling of an Eye. But after that the Sense and Consciousness of the great and plainly Divine Duty was thus awaken'd in me; Good God! what Stragglings and Conflicts follow'd presently between this Divine Principle and the Animal [66] Nature! For since I was most firmly perswaded, not only concerning the Existence of God, but also of His Absolute both Goodness and Power, and of His most real Will that we should be Perfect, even as our Father which is in Heaven is perfect; there was no room left for any Tergiversation, but a necessity of immediately entring the Lists, and of using all possible Endeavours, that our own Will, by which we relish our selves, and what belongs to us, in things as well of the Soul as of the Body, might be oppos'd, destroy'd, annihilated; that so the Divine Will alone, with the New Birth, may revive and grow up in us. And, if I may here freely speak my Mind, before this Conflict with the Divine Will, and our own proper Will or Self-Love, there can no certain signs appear to us of this New Birth at all. But this Conflict is the very Punctum saliens, or First Motion of the New Life or Birth begun in us. As to other Performances, whether of Morality or Religion, arising from mere Self-Love, let them be as Specious or Goodly as you please, they are at best but as Preparations, or the more refin'd Exercises of a sort of Theological Hobbianism.

C More, Necessity Vanquished Or Man's will is not necessarily determined to one thing (1638/1639) (Bullough, *Philosophical Poems of Henry More*, 139–140. Translation: Christian Hengstermann, "That Miracle of the Christian World", 301–303)

Oh goddess, thou carriest a spike and a wedge in thy proud hands and pressest down all things in a structure made up of liquid lead. Thou art wont to impose upon them thy fierce law, but doth thy regiment extend so far, oh thou fiercest of all things, that thou bindest unto thee all things alike in dire bond? Thine is the earth and so are the flowers which it brings forth in springtime and whatever it seeds in its dark entrails. Rivers go wherever thou biddst them go, as do salty waters and the celestial bodies which wander the width of the world. The air is under thy dominion, the rushing rainstorms and whatever fearsome thunder reverberates through the hoarse firmament. And if even all of this may appear too small a realm for thee, extend it to the underworldly shadows and the seats of the dead and to Tartarus belching forth horrific fires from its jaws. Add to that all kinds of living brutes and the countless species of beasts and birds. Nature is thy possession, the one sadder and pressed down by the sun below in gloomy darkness, the other warmed by the ethereal Sun and his midday rays. Thou art entitled to give to all of them, to put them in sterns chains and tie them to *one* ineluctable thing with stinging knots. However, the rest is not benumbed by this mindless law.

No, mankind is free. It is like an unmarried virgin not yet promised to the wedding torch of any husband. Many men, rendered eloquent by love and by the desire of the night, woo her with their pleas and their flattering words. We feel that our souls are besieged by shadows, some from the seats below, some from those in the middle and some from those high above. Indeed, Jove himself has descended into our heart in chaste play to inspire in it both virtue and holy love. Hence it is that our mind is free from the laws of eternal fate and the severity of *one* thing. If the iron goddess were to determine the motions of the soul, fixing it of old with iron nails, all of its assents would be fictitious and its freedom nothing but inane fantasy. If someone has made this up, it is necessary that he burn in the chains which he helped forge, and sweat while rolling Chrysippus' cylinder.

D More, *Monocardia or The Single Heart* (1639/1640) (Bullough, *Philosophical Poems*, 150–151. Translation: Hengstermann, "That Miracle", 305–307)

What power is it that stirs my bowels and begins to hit my heart with gentle motion? New furies shake my mind. New loves I feel. I sense how all myself is vanishing into liquid fire. A gentle flame, tender and living, has permeated all my limbs and with its heat calls forth a sense of joy in in all my body and in all my spirit. Let one poet extol his beautiful play, another sing the praise of his fair Carinna, yet I myself am being consumed by Monocardia's gentle fire. She calls me to be her holy poet. O fair Simplicity! Happy maid! Thy splendour outshines the rays of Phoebus and thy beauty surpasses that of all the stars combined. For who could behold thy heart, thy open bosom and the splendour of thy ivory-white treasure? Yea, may the moon herself be somewhat darkened by a raincloud of the warm east wind and every star more black and an image of the night, yet it is white and ivory even amid the darkness of Hyle itself. When, therefore, I see pleasant and lovely spheres and shining fires, those delightful incentives of love, the Sun vanishes at once and the form of the broad day passes away, submerged in the darkness of the noon. Oh thou first of the Charites, thou goddess of goddesses, thou splendour of heaven and one and only pleasure of the human race, thou chain with golden knots who link'st gods and men. The winged youths of Mount Olympus nimbly fly around thee, sustaining thy gentle steps with their hands and strengthen thy tender limbs, oh thou gentle care of the gods and Venus of the heavens! Oh thou source of joy and pious play! Oh thrice fair girl! Gentle maid! Sitting gently in our bowels and filling our minds with heavenly love, thou placest us in the assembly of the gods above.

E Ralph Cudworth, [Fragment of] *Letter to Limborch* (1668) (Hertling, *John Locke und die Schule von Cambridge*, p. 164 n. 2. Translation: Christian Hengstermann)

As for me personally, I admit that I had drunk in different doctrines with my mother's milk and imbibed them thoroughly in the first years of my youth.[1] Nevertheless, the power of truth prevailed and tore down the confines of these prejudices. One of my main motives was that I came to realize that all of the ancient philosophers, not only the Peripatetics, but also the Platonists, whom I enjoyed reading every now and then, kept asserting τὸ ἐφ' ἡμῖν.[2] But when I considered ethics more attentively and saw clearly both that there were wholly immutable natures of moral good and bad and that in reality they did not depend upon God's will, this difference between honest and disgraceful rather being necessarily derived from God's immutable nature, I could not ascribe to God those horrible decrees by which he, as he pleases, condemns innocent people to guilt and sin, inevitably punished by eternal tortures. Moreover, it seemed absolutely certain to me that the proponents of these decrees did away with the very nature of sin itself entirely. Hence, when, fifteen years later, I set about to gain my doctorate, I put all my trust in the truth and decided to defend the following thesis in the public assembly: "There are eternal and immutable reasons of good and bad."

F Cudworth, "There are eternal and immutable reasons of good and bad" (1651) (Allen, *A Treatise of Freewill* By Ralph Cudworth, 90–92. Translation: Christian Hengstermann)

The Honest is the image and the form of the unchanging God, his unborn offspring. It is older than all ages and prior to all principles, recognizing none as its parent and deriving from no origin. Not even God's caring will, the creator of both worlds,[3] brought it forth from its fertile womb. Nay, God himself, not rejecting them with an iniquitous intent, honours the awesome Decrees of the Good, those rights which are older than any word, neither known from his orders nor issued by his will. To the Right he willingly submits heaven's eternal fasces and its world-ruling sceptres. It is divine to assist the Good in quiet allegiance and lack the ability to stray from the Just. But stop! Who is he that dare impose laws upon the heavens and put Jove into chains and the gods into shackles? Who is he that, knowing the heaven's prerogatives, dare claim that the Thunderer himself will bear the yoke around his compliant neck? Who can lay a bridle upon the mouth of him who carries in his hands the rein of all things? Do not be astonished! Not even the giants, therefore, could conquer the heavens.

He reigns and restrains himself. Mount Olympus limits itself, the immeasurable being its measure, the right its rule. God is to himself what he is to others, binding himself within the bounds of unbounded virtue. Infinite power makes the Just its bars. It is not a sea-born outward Venus who has subdued him, but the burning passion of his invincible love for his own Goodness. The gods neither could nor would be dissimilar to themselves, destroy the radiant paradigm of their proper Honesty or leave its prescribed trails. Nor have they ever been led astray in their external dealings by any devious error, following their own north star that guides their every step in safety. Indeed, if theirs were a rule without reason and a liberty indiscriminately to confound right and wrong, sending the bad into Elysium and casting down the innocent into Tartarus with a brute lightning strike, would it not be easy to say: 'What difference does it make if God governs the Earth or natives from here?' It is characteristic of God that he cannot will the bad, and of a tyrant that he can. Those laws are observed by the Idea of the Good, as they are by Beauty's coeternal shadow, Evil, its opposite and foe. These two are the twofold city of Camarina,[4] fixed in the depth and unshaken even by the floods of roaring eternity. They laugh at the Sisters' feeble fingers and powers, at the threads weaved together not with their own distaff, but decreed before the Parcae turned a single strand with their nimble fingers. Nay, from this wool Fate itself spins its threads, and from this metal Vulcan forges his chains. It is not easy for the latter to emerge into the heights, thereafter concealing its humble head in the first waters, as the helper Apollo changed his rays. Unlike him, our Sun, shining in unchanging splendour, cannot extinguish his flames. He is bound by those chains of which no age can be freed and by the edict of the Stygian water. It would tire Jove's fingers to unravel its knots, nor must this fixed North Pole sink into the sea. The good things would refuse to accept mendacious dyes or cast off the supreme grace of their native form, while deformed evil could never exchange its Ethiopian looks for the form of radiant Nobleness. Imagining God yielded to evil, covering up deceit and concealing crime in safe night, it would be sin to speak and do the truth, check the unruly passions, worship the gods with pious incense or our parents in dutiful mind, deserving of the blows of righteous Nemesis. Imagine, then, the gods to die, the dark to dispel the sun, the stones to be sentient and wisdom to be foolish. Snow burns fire with faithful flames. Man would be without reason and the lamb would act the lioness' part, devastating the Libyan woods in burning rage. If God willed, deeds done would be undone. The past would cease to have been, and Clotho would dissolve her threads. One and the same thing would differ from itself, contraries joined in one.

Evidently, divine wisdom protects the Ideas of Right, secure from all danger, in the citadel of her mind.

G Cudworth, "There are incorporeal substances that are by their nature immortal" (Allen, *Treatise of Freewill*, 93–95. Translation: Christian Hengstermann)

"There is a holy kind [i.e. of being] visible to the sanctified mind that is eternal and devoid of body", declares the seer Apollo in unambiguous words, confirming it with his oracle, as his secret power puts the Pythia into a prophetic frenzy with its flames and as her frantic speech makes itself heard from the temple's inner round. How often did the Dodonian doves and horned Father of Libya declare this? How often did this spark of truth shine forth from the deep vaults of Trophonius?[5] Yea, even the sad shadows of dirty Avernus directed their eyes towards it. Whose ear is stirred by the prayers of the Thessalian priestess, and who is moved by her rites? Which power makes the concealed and convulsed water stop[6] and drives away the winds and summons them? What mechanism pulls back the returning streams to their mouths much to the admiration of their banks? Why do the fleeting clouds and shaking mountains listen to the orders of an old woman? Which eyes did the magician from Ephesus foresee the Roman tyrant's fate with?[7] His own? What is it that inspires the seers' hearts, freeing them from their bodies' limitations so that the light of foreknowledge shines into the little blind eye of the Theban old man? Such signs prove an unknown power, the dark revealing the truth. How far could I see with my heavenly eyes with which I can contemplate those other realms of the higher world absorbing a light of limpid clarity for immeasurable distances, if only the space of my mind, utterly freed from the ugly dirt of stinking matter, lay open like the lonely Libyan desert, unfilled by men? Why should the body, from its blind cave, see so much, while the mind perceives nothing of itself? If even the palace of the high heavens lacks any retinue, while a more illustrious crowd throng the Persian tyrant's shining Susa, heavenly ministers will more frequently be sought in vain to fill the higher offices.

Is indeed spiritless ether supposed to roll the gigantic orbs in their constant orbits? Who is to celebrate the solemn festival of Minerva's palm and sign the swan songs?[8] Who is God to shine upon and to whom is he to lay open his august breast, rich in glory? Who is to admit the radiance of the divine light into his heart and reflect it back? Who is to carry man's pious prayers above on trustful wings and bring back the rewards? Who is to protect cities, men and provinces from unjust Fortune's ambushes? What has prevented the world's Origin to this day from founding a lineage so useful and so holy? Could he not do it? It is easier for him to light pure flames similar to their own parent than force foul vapours out of earthly dregs so utterly dissimilar to their beautiful father! Did he not want to do it? Divine Benignity ungrudgingly shares its rays! Vanquished, old Epicurus strolls through his deserted garden, dying at the hands of his own cruel doctrine. Reason, Faith, and the Oracles pronounce as certain that "Angelical forms exist".

Hence, there is a species [i.e. of being] purer than ether, finer than the subtle wind, which rejects the vile chains of poisonous matter, the evil tinder of death.

G Cudworth, Second Letter to Dr Stoughton (1638/39) (Solly, *The Will*, 289–291)

> To the right worshipful, my very much-honoured father, Dr Stoughton,
> at his house in Aldermanbury these.

Dear and loving father,

I am glad to hear of your and my mother's safe return from the country, which I did the last week by Mr Man. And I present you with my thankful remembrances [290] for your invitation of me by Mr Coxe to go with you, but, besides other things, his letter came too late to me according to that time which it afterward informed me of.

It is a noble thing to walk in the beams of divine light, in St John's phrase, ἐν τῷ φωτὶ περιπατεῖν.[9] Our souls, as the substance of them is cloistered up within the thick walls of the body, so their apprehensions are much bounded and imprisoned within the dark dungeon of sense and because all their actions are from sense and through sense like pure sunbeams that receive a material impression of colour if they pass through coloured glass, so they, by percolation through the body, have a gross and earthy tincture and indeed have also lost their own primitive purity. The highest excellency of our nature is in the deep apprehension of God's infinite majesty and glorious transcendent excellency to become nothing in ourselves in the deepest degree of holy annihilation, being swallowed up in him and losing the little drop of our own being in the vast ocean of our eternal God, making him in the Lord Christ, the fountain of all, in humble acknowledgement the centre of all in motion and tendency, moving towards him by faith, for faith in Christ is our προσαγωγή to God, and it is somewhere in the Scriptures defined by a coming to God, and then moving and rolling in him by a circulation of holy love. No such wonder in the world as that God which is all in everything and πλήρωμα πάντων,[10] as the Platonists call the soul, should be lost and by so few fully discerned. What a little thing is heard of him, says divine Elihu when he had reckoned up all his works. Nay, our souls themselves are so narrow and their highest thoughts so unworthy that when they grasped with all their might to reach after him and lift themselves up towards him, they fall down in the midst of a thick darkness. And perhaps, therefore, the Holy of Holies called God's throne in the Revelation was not only negatively dark, because it had not windows, but there was also a cloud there and, moreover, the priest never went in, but he was to make a cloud before him by his incense. In imitation of which the gods in Homer never went anywither but wrapped up in a cloud. But the best is in heaven our souls shall be filled with him and not only as [291] buckets drawn full out of well, but as open vessels swimming in the ocean. We shall be baptized in God. I think the expression may be used, for so both Casaubon and the Greek scholiast expound that in the Acts: βαπτισθήσεσθε ἐν πνεύματι ἁγίῳ[11]: *Domus enim, in qua hoc peractum erat, Spiritu Sancto fuit repleta, ita ut in eam tanquam in Κολυμβήθραν quandam apostoli demersi videantur,*[12] elegantly.

But I trouble you with tediousness. Thus, with my duties to my mother and my brother and sisters best remembrances to you both, I leave you to the protection of the Lord,

Your much-obliged Son,
R. Cudworth

Notes

1 Cudworth refers to his early Calvinist upbringing under his stepfather John Stoughton, a renowned Puritan preacher.
2 Translated literally "what is in our power", the term denotes the freedom of choice in ancient philosophy.
3 I.e., in Platonism, of the intelligible and the empirical worlds.
4 An ancient Sicilian city with access both to see and land. As such, it is used by the poet as a symbol of the two contradictory opposites of eternal and immutable morality, good and evil.
5 A legendary Greek hero and mythical builder of the temple of Delphi.
6 The ambiguous sentence—*celata concussaque* may either qualify *vis* or *freta*—probably refers to the lapping of water by which the Pythia was believed to tell the future.
7 The assassination of Emperor Domitianus, predicted by the legendary pagan would-be messiah Apollonius of Tyana.
8 Celebrated on 19th March, the annual Roman Minerva festival was particularly famous for its fortune-tellers who were usually consulted by women on that occasion.
9 1 Jn. 1:2: "walk in the light".
10 The fullness of all things.
11 Acts 1:5: "Ye shall be baptized with the Holy Ghost."
12 "For the house in which this came to pass, was filled with the Holy Spirit so that the apostles dived into it as into a baptismal font."

Chapter 6

Political Platonism and Early Sermons on Rational Theology

Christian Hengstermann

A Benjamin Whichcote, *Moral and Religious Aphorisms* (1753)

8. God made man Intelligent and Voluntary: and the Law of Nature, and the Reason of his Mind, God intended for the great *Rule* of his Life; to take place in all particulars, where God did not think good, farther to express his Will, and declare his Pleasure.
50. *We* must *be* in our measure, degree, and proportion, in respect of Moral Perfection; of Holiness, Righteousness, Goodness and Truth; what *God* is, in his Highth [sic], Excellency, and Fulness: for in all Moral Perfections, God is imitable by us; We may resemble God: God is communicable to us; We may partake of Him.
71. There is nothing proper and *peculiar* to Man; but the Use of Reason and the Exercise of Virtue.
76. To go against *Reason*, is to go against *God*: it is the self same thing, to do that which the Reason of the Case doth require; and that which God Himself doth appoint: Reason is the *Divine* Governor of Man's Life; it is the very Voice of God.
98. If Reason may not *command*, it will *condemn*.
99. Reason *discovers*, what is Natural; and Reason *receives*, what is Supernatural.
121. In the Use of *Reason*, and the exercise of *Virtue*, we enjoy God.
161. *Habits* of Virtue are Acquired, by a right Use of our selves; and they are spoiled, by Unnatural practice.
162. We are *Good*; by Imitation Participation and Resemblance of God; and in the same way, we are Happy.
214. In Intellectual Nature, a Principle of *Knowledge* is Vital to the Understanding; and an *habitual Disposition* is Vital to the *Will*.
229. The Mind is to be *Informed* with Knowledge and *Refined* by Virtue. By the several Virtues the Mind is purified, and made fit to converse with God, and to receive from Him.
248. We *Worship* God best; when we Resemble Him most.
262. *Holiness*, in Angels and Men, is their *Dei-formity*; likeness to God in Goodness, Righteousness, and Truth. Such *real* Holiness sanctifies the Subject by its Presence: and where That is, the person is made Pure, Good, and Righteous.
277. Give me the man, of whom I may say; This is the person, who, in the true use of *Reason*, (the Perfection of Humane Nature) who, in the Practice and Exercise of *Virtue* (its Accomplishment) hath brought himself into such a *Temper*; as is *Connatural* to those Principles, and Warranted by them.
296. The *Perfection* of the *Happiness* of Humane Nature, consists in the right Use of our Rational Faculties; in the vigorous and intense Exercise of them, about their Proper and proportional Object; which is God.
339. If you would be Religious, be *Rational* in your Religion.

523. Nothing is more *Unnatural* to men, than *Wickedness*; for wickedness is contrary to the *Reason* of the *Mind*, and to the *Reason* of *Things*; contrary to the Reason of the Mind, which is our *Governor*; and contrary to the Reason of Things, which is our *Law*.

544. God will not *Destroy* any thing, that partakes of his own Nature; but will foster and cherish every thing, that is *God-like*.

591. Religion is τὶς ὁμοίωσις Θεοῦ, κατὰ δυνατὸν ἀνθρώπου the being as much like God as Man can be like him.

633. Reason if the *first* Participation from God; and Virtue is the *second*.

644. True *Reason* is so far from being an Enemy to any matter of *Faith*; that a man is disposed and qualified by Reason, for entertaining those matters of Faith that are proposed by God.

708. *Religion*, which is in Substance our Imitation of God, in his Moral Perfections of Goodness, Righteousness, and Truth; is that, wherein our *Happiness* doth consist.

820. The *Effect* of our Religion, is our Agreement with God; in Mind and Temper: and it is the *Use* of our Religion, by it, as a Means, to introduce that Agreement: The *Accomplishment* of our Religion is, by the Exercise of it, to Enjoy God; who is our Ultimate End, and Happiness.

877. Where *Reason* speaks, it is the voice of our Guide; a natural voice, we cannot but hear; it is according to the very make of our nature. It is also true in *Religion*, [*Idem est, sequi Deum & rectam Rationem;*] to follow God and to follow right Reason is all one: a man never gives God an offense; if he doth that, which Reason requires.

1004. We are not Men, so much by bodily Shape; as by Principles of Reason and Understanding: wherefore those, who discharge Reason from having any thing to do in matters of Religion, do no true Service to Religion: do rather pursue the Apostasy of the first *Adam*, and raze the foundations of God. For all the greater Rights, *majora jura*, αἰώνια δίκαια are founded in Reason; are supposed in Christianity, are acknowledged and reinforced.

1183. If any speak, in a Language I *do* understand, concerning things I *should* understand; as having studied and considered them: and what is said is not at all Intelligible to Me; though he pretends to the Spirit, I do not violate Charity to think, the Speaker understands not Himself well: but that he speaketh Words without Sense. For the Parts of men are not so vastly dis-proportionate; and what is most Spiritual is most Rational.

B John Smith, *Of the Existence and Nature of God* (1660), Chapter 2 (*Select Discourses*, 126–128)

First, There is nothing whereby our own Souls are better known to us then by the Properties and Operations of *Reason:* but when we reflect upon our own *Idea* of *Pure* and *Perfect Reason*, we know that our own [127] Souls are not it, but onely partake of it; and that it is of such a Nature that we cannot denominate any other thing of the same rank with our selves by; and yet we know certainly that it is, as finding from an inward sense of it within our selves that both we and other things else beside our selves partake of it, and that we have it κατὰ μέθεξιν and not κατ' οὐσίαν neither doe we or any *Finite* thing contain the source of it within our selves: and because we have a distinct Notion of the *most Perfect Mind* and *Understanding*, we own our deficiency therein. And as that *Idea* of *Understanding* which we have within us points not out to us This or That *Particular*, but something which is neither This nor That, but *Totall, Understanding;* so neither will any elevation of it serve every way to fit and answer that *Idea*. And therefore when we find that we cannot attain to *Science* but by a *Discursive* deduction of one thing from another, that our knowledge is confined, and is not fully adequate and commensurate to the largest Spheare of Being, it not running quite through it nor filling the whole *area* of it; or that our knowledge is *Chronical* and *successive*, and cannot grasp all things at once, but works by intervals, and runs out into *Division* and *Multiplicity;* we know all this is from want of Reason and Understanding, and that *a Pure and Simple Mind and Intellect* is free from all these restraints and imperfections, and therefore can be no less then *Infinite*. As this *Idea* which we have of it in our own Souls will not suffer us to rest in any conception thereof which represents it less then *Infinite:* so neither will it suffer us to conceive of it any otherwise then as *One Simple Being:* and could we multiply Understandings into never so vast a number, yet should we be again collecting and knitting them up together in some Universal one. So that if we rightly reflect upon our own *Minds* and *the Method* of their *Energies*, we shall find them to be so framed, as not to admit of any other then *One Infinite* source of all that *Reason and Understanding* which themselves partake of, in which they live, move and have their Being. And therefore in the old Metaphysical Theology, an Originall and Uncreated μόνας or *Unity* is made the Fountain of all Particularities and Numbers which have their Existence from the Efflux of its Almighty power.

C Henry More, Discourse XIII, 394–395, 415–418. *Discourses on Several Texts of Scripture* (1692)

1 Peter 1:22–23. Seeing ye have purified your souls in obeying the truth through the Spirit, unto unfeigned love of the brethren; see that ye love one another, with a pure heart, fervently: Being born again, not of corruptible seed, but of incorruptible, by the word of God which liveth and abideth for ever.

The Text is an Exhortation to *Christian Love*, The Duty is enforced from a double Argument.

1. From the end of our Sanctification, in those words, Seeing ye have purified your Souls in obeying the Truth through the Spirit, φιλαδελφίαν ἀνυπόκριτον, unto (or for) unfeigned brotherly love. And this ushers in the Precept or Duty, Love one another with a pure heart, fervently.
2. The other Argument follows, of no less force than the former, which is drawn from the condition of our new Birth; *Being born again, not of corruptible seed, but of incorruptible, by the word of God, which liveth and abideth for ever.*

The *Incitements* to this Duty are many: But I will confine my self to the Text, and cull out some three: As,

1. *From the Seed of the New Birth.*

For what is this Seed but the Son of God, by union with whom we also become the Sons of God, petty Deities? But sith that the Deity it self is nothing else but a sufficient and overflowing Goodness, creating all things, and sustaining them from no other principle than the Spirit of Goodness; though we cannot act as this absolute Deity, yet we may will according to that uncreated Will, which is nothing else but pure overspreading Love.

Again, this Seed, (as hath been shewed) which is the Word, is a living Seed. But where Life is, and Understanding or Sense, there must needs be Love, for it is the flower and sweet of all desire. What then can be the desire of the living Word but Love; and how can he want desire, sith he is Life; and what can he so much desire as the good and welfare of Mankind? What therefore should that part of Mankind that partake of this Divine Nature, desire more than the good of one another, and of those also, that as yet have not partaked of that Divine Nature: For God also loves those, or else how could ever any partake of it?

2. *From the Regeneration of the Soul.*

It is the Holy Ghosts own arguing, 1 *John.* 4. 7. *Beloved, let us love one another: for love is of God; and every one that loveth, is born of God, and loveth God.* Ver. 16. *And we have known and believed the love that God hath to us. God is love; and he that dwelleth in love, dwelleth in God, and God in him.* By Righteousness and Unrighteousness, by Love and Hatred, are the Children of God and the Children of the Devil manifested. 1 *John* 3. 10. *In this the children of God are manifest, and the children of the devil: Whosoever doeth not righteousness, is not of God, neither he that loveth not his brother.* Ver. 14. *We know that we have passed from death unto life, because we love the brethren: he that loveth not his brother, abideth in death.* If Water or Earth be turn'd into Fire, we expect it should burn and be hot. How shall then a Son of Satan, or the Earthly man, be turn'd by Regeneration into the Son of God, and not love?

3. *From the end of our Sanctification.*

Love is the very End of it. Shall Envy, shall Hatred, shall Lust, Ambition, Luxury, *&c.* shall all these enormous Desires and Affections be cast out of the Soul by Sanctity and Purity, that she may be but a transparent piece of Ice, or a spotless fleece of Snow? Shall she become so pure, so pellucid, so christalline, so devoid of all stains, that nothing but still shadows and night may possess that inward diaphanous Purity? Thus would she be no better than the nocturnal Air, no happier than a statue of Alabaster; it would be but a more cleanly sepulchre of a dead starved Soul. Nay, certainly all this cleansing and preparing is for something well worth that labour. The *Stoicks* themselves, that were such severe Sentencers of Passion, would retain φιλανθρωπία. Stoicism it self brings in, upon that deadness and privation of other Passions, that divine motion of the Soul, which is Love or Goodwill to all Mankind. And shall Christianity be but a cold grave to the mortified Soul of man? No surely, there is a Resurrection to Life, Love and the Divinity, as well as a Death of the enormous Affections of this Mortal Body. Bitter Zeal, harsh Censure, busie Revenge, etc. are so far from being able to supply the place of Charity, that it's a manifest sign that we are as yet carnal and unsanctified.

D Ralph Cudworth, *A Sermon Preached before the House of Commons* (1647), Preface

The Scope of this *Sermon*, which not long since exercised your Patience (*Worthy Senatours*) was not to contend for *this* or *that Opinion*; but onely to perswade men to the *Life of Christ*, as the Pith and Kernel of all Religion. Without *Which*, I may boldly say, all the severall *Forms* of *Religion* in the World, though we please our selves never so much in them, are but so many severall *Dreams*. And those many *Opinions* about *Religion*, that are every where so eagerly contended for on all sides, where *This* doth not lie at the Bottome, are but so many *Shadows* fighting with one another: so that I may well say, of the true Christian, that is indeed possessed of the Life of Christianity, in opposition to all those that are but lightly tinctured with the Opinions of it, in the language of the Poet, Ὅιος πέπνυται τοὶ δ' ὡς σκιαὶ ἀΐσουτι. Wherefore I could not think any thing else, either more Necessary for Christians in generall, or more Seasonable at this time, then to stirre them up to the reall Establishment of the *Righteousnesse of God* in their hearts, and that *Participation of the Divine Nature*, which the *Apostle* speaketh of. That so they might not content themselves, with mere *Phancies* and *Conceits* of Christ, without the *Spirit of Christ* really dwelling in them, and *Christ* himself inwardly *formed* in their hearts. Nor satisfie themselves, with the mere holding of right and Orthodox Opinions, as they conceive; whilest they are utterly devoid within of that *Divine Life*, which Christ came to kindle in mens Souls; and therefore are so apt to spend all their zeal upon a violent obtruding of their own Opinions and Apprehensions upon others, which cannot give entertainment to them: which, besides its repugnancy to the Doctrine and Example of Christ himself, is like to be the Bellows, that will blow a perpetuall Fire of Discord and Contention, in Christian Commonwealths: whilest in the mean time, these hungry, and starved *Opinions*, devoure all the Life and Substance of Religion, as the *Lean Kine*, in *Pharaohs* Dream, did eat up the *Fat*. Nor lastly, Please themselves, onely in the violent Opposing of other mens *Superstitions*, according to the Genious of the present times; without substituting in the room of them, an inward *Principle* of *Spirit*, and *Life*, in their own Souls: for I fear many of us that pull down *Idols* in Churches, may set them up in our Hearts; and whilest we quarrel with *Painted Glasse*, make no scruple at all, of entertaining many soul *Lusts* in our Souls, and committing continuall Idolatry with them.

E George Rust, *A Discourse of the Use of Reason in Matters of Religion*, translated by Henry Hallywell (1683), 23–25, 40–41

I am not ashamed of the Gospel of Christ, said the Great Apostle who was bred up at the feet of *Gamaliel*, and fully instructed in all the Learning both of the *Jews* and *Greeks*. Wherefore when the Christian Religion was every where oppressed and despised, when it was a scandal to the *Jews*, and foolishness to the *Greeks;* yet then despising the shame, and undervaluing the Afflictions he should meet withal, *I am ready* (says he) *to preach the Gospel to you that are at Rome,* among the famous Philosophers and Orators of that City, renowned as well for Arts as Arms. For although there are not wanting some, the Eyes of whose Minds are covered with gross Ignorance and Darkness, yet glorying mightily in the mean while of their own Wisdom who endeavour to expose and ridicule the Doctrine of the Gospel as the greatest Piece of Folly; nevertheless he that laying aside his Prejudices and Tumultuous Affections, shall weigh the thing it self, in the Balance of a sincere and incorrupted Judgment, will really find the Christian Religion to be *the Power and Wisdom of God*, wholly agreeable to Reason and worthy of all belief.

By Right Reason therefore I understand that innate Faculty of the Soul of Man, by which it discerns the Reasons and Mutual Affections of things, and argues, and concludes one thing from another, And now I say that Christian Religion is not contrary to Reason thus understood.

A Fourth Argument I take from the Nature of Right Reason; from whence arises a clear Demonstration, that no Divine Revelation can be contrary to it. For the Souls of Men are derived from the Divine Mind, and Right Reason is of a Celestial Original, framed after the Image of Uncreated Wisdom and Knowledge. It is a certain Beam or Ray of the Intellectual Sun, bearing the Resemblance of Primigenial light. For Divine Wisdom is nothing else but a steady Comprehension of the Idea's of Things, together with those Reasons, Affections, and Mutual Relations whether of Concord or Discord, which Immediately slow from the Nature of Things themselves, as Relations *posito fundamento & termino*. And the Divine Intellect does intimately penetrate and behold at one view these Affections together with the Idea's of the Things themselves and discerns their Order and Reciprocations. Now what is this but fixed and stable Reason looking upon the Reasons and Connections of all things at once, and as it were with an Unmoved Eye? Whose express and accurate Resemblance is Right Reason engraven on Humane Minds, which though it cannot know and lay open all things, and their respective Reasons, by one single Act, yet it explicates and unfolds them successively and in order. Moreover, we have a clear and distinct Perception of the Consent or Discrepancy of so many of these Idea's and Reasons as we have an Entire and Comprehensive view of, and accordingly undertake either the Probation or Refutation of one from another. Wherefore Humane Reason does truly imitate and express Divine Wisdom, with this only Difference, that what she comprehends at once with one single Act, Reason deduces by many and operose Consequences.

That God should therefore reveal any thing contrary to Right Reason, is alike impious as to suppose him to be a Liar, and to contradict the internal Conceptions of his own Wisdom. For Right Reason and Divine Wisdom give the same Judgment of things, and if Humane Understanding shall at any time determine otherwise, that must not be looked upon as the Fault of Reason, but of Ignorance. Therefore if any thing propounded under the Plausible Name of Divine Revelation shall seem to contradict Reason, I ought to suspect that I do not fully conprehend [sic] the meaning of it, and therefore must insist upon a further search, and resolve that God intended that to be believed, which should be most consonant to the Principles of Nature. Nevertheless I would not have Humane Understanding arrogate too much to it self, nor rashly attempt to condemn presently that which exceeds its Capacity. For if the chiefest Part of those things which are delivered and consigned by Divine Testimony, be worthy of God, and Consonant to our Faculties, as to other things we ought to yield an implicit Faith to Divine Revelations, though they seem otherwise to clash with Reason, yet to give our Assent to them, at least according to the sense of the Spirit of God, although what that is, we cannot yet so fully understand.

F Henry Hallywell, *The Sacred Method of Saving Humane Souls by Jesus Christ* (1677), 15–18

1. In finding out a way, whereby God might demonstrate, both his just and implacable hatred of sin, and his exuberant Love and Goodness in saving Men. Sin is no part of God's Creation, nor any thing of the true Nature of the Soul, but an extraneous and adventitious Being, brought first into the World by the Devil, the great Enemy of Mankind. It is the Destruction and Ruine of the Workmanship of God's own hands, and being so infinitely contrary to his Sacred Life and Nature, it is no wonder, if he bear an irreconcileable hatred against it, and seek by all means, the driving it quite out of the World. But although God, by reason of the Infinite Purity and Holiness of his Nature, could not look with any favourable eye upon sin, yet his Almighty Love pitied his Creatures, and *his bowels yerned over them*, being, as it were, grieved and troubled at the heart, that they should be miserable for ever. Wherefore, God, through his Eternal Wisdom, resolved upon a course, which should both effectually extirpate and eradicate sin and evil out of the World, and yet reduce those strayed souls, which through it, had revolted from his blessed Life and Nature, to a participation of it again. And this he hath done, by sending his own Son into the World, to become an Expiatory Sacrifice for the sins of all Mankind. For should God have cast Men off for ever, and thrown them into Hell, though he had still been Just and Righteous in his Actions, and declared but a high dislike of that, which his Essential Holiness could never patronize or countenance, yet his Goodness and Love had not so conspicuously and gloriously appeared. On the other hand, should God have received the World into grace and favour, forgiving their Iniquities, without any previous satisfaction for sin, though he might have done this, without any breach of the Eternal Purity and Justice of his Nature, yet he had not so sensibly affected the minds of Men, with his just aversation of sin, nor so effectually discovered to them, his Anger and Displeasure against all evil and wickedness. But now in the Death of Jesus Christ, God has reconciled Goodness and Holiness, Justice and Mercy, punishing sin, and yet saving the sinner.

G Joseph Glanvill, *The Agreement of Reason and Religion Essays on Several important Subjects in Philosophy and Religion* (1676), Essay V: 1, 2, 3, 5, 8–9

There is not any thing that I know, which hath done more mischief to *Religion*, than the disparaging of *Reason*, under pretence of respect and favour to it: For hereby the very Foundations of Christian

Faith have been undermin'd, and the World prepared for Atheism. And true *Reason* if Reason must not be heard, the *Being* of a *God*, and the *Authority* of *Scripture*, can neither be proved nor defended; and so our Faith drops to the Ground like an House that hath no Foundation.

[2] So that, in my Judgment, it is the great duty of all sober and reasonable Men, to rise up (as they can) against this Spirit of Folly and Infatuation: And something I shall attempt now, by shewing, That *Reason* is very serviceable to *Religion;* and *Religion* very friendly to *Reason.*

[3] For *Religion* first; It is taken either strictly for the Worship of God; or in a more comprehensive sense, for the *sum* of those *Duties* we owe to Him: And this takes in the other, and agrees with the Notation of the Name, which imports *Binding*, and implies *Duty*. Now all Duty is comprised under these two, *viz. Worship* and *Vertue:* Worship comprehends all Duties that immediately relate to God, as the Object of them; Vertue, all those that respect our Neighbour and our Selves. So that Religion primarily, and mainly consists in *Worship* and *Vertue.*

[5] Reason is sometimes taken for *Reason* in the *Faculty*, which is the *Understanding;* and at other times, for *Reason* in the *Object*, which consists in those *Principles* and *Conclusions*, by which the Understanding is informed. This latter is meant in the Dispute concerning the Agreement or Disagreement of Reason and Religion. And Reason in this sense, is the same with *natural Truth*, which I said is made up of Principles and Conclusions. By the *Principles* of Reason we are not to understand the Grounds of any Man's *Philosophy;* nor the Critical Rules of *Syllogism;* but those imbred *Fundamental Notices*, that God hath implanted in our Souls; such as arise not from external Objects, nor particular Humours or Imaginations, but are immediately lodged in our Minds; independent upon other Principles or Deductions; commanding a sudden assent; and acknowledged by all sober Mankind.

[8] These two great Truths, *The Existence of God*, and *Authority of Scripture*, are the first in our Religion; and they are *Conclusions* of Reason, as well as *Foundations* of Faith. And [9] thus briefly of those Principles of Religion that are *presupposed* unto it; we have seen how Reason serves for the Demonstration of them.

Chapter 7

The New Sect of Latitude Men
Religious Toleration and Moderation in Revolutionary and Restoration England

Marilyn A. Lewis

A S[ymon] P[atrick], A Brief Account of the New Sect of Latitude-Men (1662), 5, 7, 8–9, 10, 11, 24

[5] But you would think I had a mind to shuffle with you, if I should give you onely this general account; for you will not imagine I can be so short-sighted, but that I may be able to see farther into the matter than so; that I may not therefore frustrate your expectation, I will tell you all that I am able to understand or conjecture concerning it; the greatest part of the men that seem to be pointed at under that name, are such, whose fortune it was to be born so late, as to have their education in the University, since the beginning of the unhappy troubles of this Kingdom, where they ascended to their preferments by the regular steps of election, not much troubling themselves to enquire into the Titles of some of their Electours; they are such as are behind none of their neighbours either in Learning or good manners, and were so far from being sowred with the Leaven of the times they lived in, that they were always looked upon with an evil eye by the successive usurping powers, and the general out-cry was, that the whole University was over-run with *Arminianisme,* and was full of men of a Prelatical Spirit, that had apostatized to the Onions and Garlick of *Egypt,* because they were generally ordained by Bishops; and in opposition to that hide-bound, strait-lac'd spirit that did then prevail, they were called *Latitude-men;* for that was the first original of the name, what ever sense hath since been put upon it: this was a certain barr to their preferment, as they were sure to find, if any of them came before the Committee of Tryers, who (as it was reported) had gotten a List of all those that were Ordained by the Bishop of *Norwich;* and truly if they that were turned out of their preferment, were esteemed Martyrs, I know not why these that were debarred thereof upon the same grounds may not be called Confessors.

[7] Our Latitudinarians therefore are by all means for a Liturgy, and do preferre that of our own Church before all others, admiring the Solemnity, gravity and primitive simplicity of it, its freedome from affected phrases, or mixture of vain and doubtfull opinions; in a word they esteem it to be so good, that they would be loth to adventure the mending of it, for fear of marring it. As for the Rites and Ceremonies of Divine worship, they do highly approve that vertuous mediocrity which our Church observes between the meretricious gaudiness of the Church of *Rome,* and the squalid sluttery of Fanatick conventicles.

[8] In like mannner they have a deep veneration of her Government, which they stedfastly beleive to be in it self the best, and the same that was practised in the times of the Apostles. . . . Lastly for the Doctrine of the Church, they do cordially adhere to it, as doth sufficiently appear by their willingness to subscribe to the thirty nine Articles, and all other points of Doctrine contained either in the Liturgy or book of Homilies, [9] and particularly (whatsoever may be privately whispered to the contrary) they do both devoutly adore the blessed Trinity in the Letany, and make solemn profession

of their Orthodox faith, both concerning it and other points, in the three Creeds, not excepting that which is commonly ascribed to *Athanasius,* nor is there any Article of Doctrine held forth by the Church, which they can justly be accused to depart from, unlesse absolute reprobation be one, which they do not think themselves bound to believe.

[10] For Reason is that faculty whereby a man must judge of every thing, nor can a man beleve any thing except he have some reason for it, whether that reason be a deduction from the light of nature, and those principles which are the candle of the Lord, set up in the soul of every man that hath not wilfully extinguished it; or a branch of Divine revelation in the oracles of holy Scripture; or the general interpretation of genuine antiquity, or the proposal of our own Church consentaneous thereto, or lastly the result of some or all of these: for he that will rightly make use of his Reason, must take all that is reasonable into consideration.

[11] I shall always think him most consciencious who leads the most unblameable life, though he be not greatly scrupulous about the externals of Religion; and for their lives I think the *Latitude-men* were never taxed by their greatest enemyes.

[24] True *Philosophy* can never hurt sound *Divinity*. Christian Religion was never bred up in the *Peripatetick school,* but spent her best and healthfullest years in the more Religious *Academy,* amongst the primitive Fathers; but the Schoolmen afterwards ravished her thence, and shut her up in the decayed ruines of *Lyceum,* where she served an hard servitude, and contracted many distempers: why should she not at last be set at liberty, and suffered to breath in a free air? let her alone be Mistress, and choose her Servants where she best likes; let her old loving Nurse the *Platonick Philosophy* be admitted again into her family; nor is there any cause to doubt but the Mechanick also will be faithful to her, no less against the open violence of *Atheisme,* than the secret treachery of *Enthusiasm* and *Superstition,* as the excellent works of a late learned Author have abundantly demonstrated.

B George Rust, A Sermon Preached at New-Town the 29 of Octob. 1663 (1664), 37–38

I can make this sincere profession, that I should sooner choose to be of the Communion of the Church of *England,* than any Church that I know in the Christian world; for though it requires conformity in some things of external worship, yet they are, to speak the least of [38] them, so harmless and innocent, so undetermin'd by any Law of God, and so much in the disposition of lawful Authority, that it is a wonder to me, that wise and sober men should ever raise any controversie about them: But in matters of opinion, where the minde and understanding is concern'd, which is not in a man's power to command, and can be subject to no other dictates, and impositions, but those of infallible revelation, the Church of *England* does here allow so fair a latitude, that a sober and ingenuous spirit can hardly desire a greater, I am sure he will no where else find nere so much.

C Letters from Henry More to Lady Conway, letters 161–162, on pp. 242–243, Conway Letters (1992)

161 [29 June 1665] In that letter I signifyde to your Ladiship that the maine charge was intended against Dr Cudworth, Dr Widdrington loading him with whatever his malice could invent or catch at. But it is the judgement of all men that I hear say any thing, that the things are so frivolous and so common to all, that it can not amount to any danger to him. I am collaterally concerned in this charge but onely as to the point of Discontinuance. But I have this advantage, that my late Discontinuance at Ragley did so divide it self into the last year and this current, that I have not transgressed the statute above 2 or 3 dayes. Some in the town to make sport with it reported at the coffy house,

that R. Widdrington had layd a charge against me that I had discontinued a whole day above the allowance of the statute. The Master gave in answer touching me that besydes that I had been ill of late, that it did not appear that I had discontinued otherwise then was allowable by statute: which R. Widdrington when he replyde to other thinges, declin'd to make any reply to, as finding, I suppose, himself at a losse to do any great hurt in that point. And this is the onely point that concerns me in the whole Charge. For other things the moderation of their Superiours and my own Integrity, I conceive, keepes them of[f]. But Ra. Widdrington had petitioned the Archbishop against the Colledge as a seminary of Heretics.

162 [10 July 1665] Concerning the Colledge affaire I know not what will be the end of it. A long rabble of accusations was fram'd by Dr Widdrington against Dr Cudworth, which the judges or Referees look upon as matters of small weight. But he has interserted one accusation at random, on purpose to seek a pretense to have the Masters accounts reaudited by the Vice-chancellour, whenas they are legally ratifyde by the Colledge. This is to pick quarrels and to finde a pretense of casting the charges of the late sute upon the Master. They push hard at the Latitude men as they call them, some in their pulpitts call them sons of Belial, others make the Devill a latitudinarian, which things are as pleasing to me as the raillery of a jack-pudding at one end of a dancing rope. For I understand not the looseness of their language nor whom they mean, nor what they would have. I believe to all sober men such things cannot but be unsavoury. But the world is the world, which could make no good man afrayd to leave it, and to come into the order of a better scheme.

D [Gilbert Burnet], A Modest and Free Conference betwixt a Conformist and a Nonconformist (1669), 82–83, 89–90

Nonconformist: I See we have no reason to hope for any good from you, who are so fierce against us but God be thanked, an ill-willed Cow hath short horns.

Conformist: If by fiercenesse you mean a desire to see you ruined and destroyed, you mistake me quite; since there is none living, more averse from fierce and violent courses than my self. I love all Christians, who live according to the rules of the Gospel: And I pity such as I judge mistaken, knowing how subject I am to errour my self. I quarrel with no man for his opinion in these matters, which are, as the late incomparable King in his divine work calls them, *But the Skirts and Suburbs of Religion*. And as all the thoughts of that divine Book bewray an augustnesse, which speaks the Author a King indeed; so his moderation in these matters looks like the paternal clemency which becomes the Father of a Countrey; he then adviseth his Son, our Gracious Sovereign, thus, *Beware of exasperating any Factions, by the crossnesse and asperity of some mens passions, humours, or private opinions, imployed by you, grounded only upon the differences in lesser matters, which are but the Skirts and Suburbs of Religion: wherein a charitable connivance and Christian-tolleration often dissipates their strength, whom rougher opposition fortifies; and* [83] *puts the despised and oppressed party into such combinations, as may most enable them to get a full revenge on those they count their persecutors, who are commonly assisted by that Vulgar commiseration which attends all that are said to suffer under the notion of Religion.* And a little after, *Take heed, that outward circumstances and formalities of Religion, devour not all, or the best incouragements of Learning, Industry, and Piety.* Thus that Great and glorious Prince.

Nonconformist: By this it seems you are a Latitudinarian, and I have heard much ill of these new sort of people.

Conformist: Truly I own no name, but that of Jesus Christ, in which I was baptized; and these are invidious Arts, to coyn names of parties, and to affix them on such as disown them; I am, and desire to be a sincere Christian, but of no party nor Sect. But if by latitude, you mean charity, truly I must tell you, I glory in it, which is no newer way, than the *new commandment* which our Saviour gave to his Disciples, *to love one another, as he loved them.*

[89] Nonconformist: I will hear you in these with all my heart; for though you have said many things that do much displease me, yet as uncharitable as you think me, I am full of kindness for you; and I love to hear good spoken by any body: therefore we will dispute no more.

Conformist: Ah, how strangely is the world mistaken in matters of Religion! Some placing it wholly in debates, others in external forms; others in some private devotions, and others in a regulation of the outward man; but true Religion is power and life, and far above all these shadows. *The Kingdom* [90] *of God is not meat and drink, but righteousness and peace, and joy in the holy Ghost*; it doth not levell at externals only, but secretly insinuats it self into the Soul; whereas a divine seed it propagates, diffusing its vertue through the whole man: In a word, Religion was given of God to transform a man into the Divine likeness, and to a real participation of the Divine Nature.

E [Edward Fowler], The Principles and Practices, of certain Moderate Divines of the Church of England (1670), 8–13, 23, 41–42

[8] They are characterized as people, whose onely Religion it is to temporize, & transform themselves into any Shape for their secular interests, and that judge no Doctrine so Saving, as that which obligeth to so complying and condescending a humour, as to become [9] all things to all men, that so by any means they may gain something.

[9] Have you not heard the Cholerick Gentlemen distinguish these persons, by a long nick-name; which they have taught their tongues to pronounce as roundly, as if it were shorter then it is, by four or five syllables? . . . I hear, ever and anon, the word of a foot and a half long sounded out with a great grace; and that not onely at Fires and Tables, but sometimes from *Pulpits* too.

[10] I have heard them give a description of their *Latitudinarian*; and 'tis this short one, *He is a Gentleman of a wide swallow.* . . . Very good! It seems then his *Conscience* is the Seat of his Latitude.

[12] [Latitudinarians say that] the Foundations of all Religion, viz. That Moral good and evil are not only such, because God commands the one and forbids the other; but [13] because the things themselves are so essentially and unalterably. That there is an eternal Reason, why that which is good should be so and required, and why that which is evil should be so and is forbidden; which depends not so much on the divine will as the divine nature.

[23] In short, the grand fault that is found by some in their practice, is their *Conformity* to the present Ecclesiastical Laws; which enjoyn some Rites in the worship of God, which there is no express warrant from the Scriptures for.

[41] In their Discourses generally, they handled those subjects that are of the weightiest and most necessary importance: I mean such as have the greatest influence into the reformation of men's lives, and purification of souls. Nor had I ever so lovely an *idea* of the divine *nature*, which is the most powerful incentive to obedience to the divine *will*, nor so clear a sense of the excellence of the Christian Religion, the Reasonableness of its precepts, the nobleness and generosity of its design, and its admirable fitness for [42] the accomplishment of it; as, through the blessing of God, I have gained by the hearing of these men.

F Joseph Glanvill, Anti-fanatical Religion and Free Philosophy, Essays on Several important Subjects in Philosophy and Religion (1676), Essay VII: 11. . .13

One of the *first* things they *did,* was, to deliver their *own* Minds (and to endeavour the same for *others*) from the *Prepossessions,* and *Prejudices* of *Complexion, Education,* and implicit *Authority;* Asserting the Liberty of Enquiry, and thereby freeing their Reasons from a base and dishonourable Servitude, and vindicating this just Right of Humane Nature. For though they knew, That *Green Youth,* and *Vulgar*

Inquirers, ought not pragmatically to call their Teachers to account for their Doctrines, or to venture upon deep [12] Speculations without assistance; Yet they thought, that *Men* who were bred in the way of Study, had first submisly heard the Opinions of their Instructors, and been well acquainted with their Dictates, who were arriv'd to maturity of Understanding, and a good capacity to seek after Truth; might at length be permitted to *judge for themselves;* that *so* they might *choose,* like *reasonable* Creatures, and not have their Principles *brutishly obtruded* on them. This they saw was a *natural* Right, and that the Tyrannical Custom of over-ruling and suppressing it, had held the greatest part of Mankind in fatal Chains of Ignorance and Error.

Here, I say, They begun, and taught, That all lovers of Truth, whose Judgements were competently matur'd, ought to free their Minds from the Prejudices of Education, and usurping Authorities; that is, so far, as not to conclude any thing certainly true, or false, *meerly* on the account of *those Impressions:* But to *try all things,* as Scripture and Reason require, and incourage us; and to suspend the giving up our *full,* and resolv'd assent to the Doctrines we have been taught, till we have impartially consider'd and examin'd them *our selves.* That in our Researches, we ought to retain a Reverence for *Antiquity,* and *venerable Names;* but not *blindly* to *give up* our Understandings to them, against clear Evidence of the Divine Oracles, or Impartial Reason. That when other Considerations, on both sides, were *equal,* the Inducements of *old Belief,* and *reverend Authorities* ought to determine us to a *probable* assent on *that* side: But when God's Word, or our Faculties stood on the *other,* we ought not to be enclin'd.

Thus they modestly asserted the *Liberty* of *Judgment,* and bounded it with so much Caution, that no Prejudice could arise to Legal Establishments from that freedom: For they allow'd it not to *immature* Youth; or to *illiterate* or *injudicious* Men, who are not to be *trusted* to conclude for themselves in things of *difficult* Theory: But advised *such,* to submit to their Instructors, and so practise the plain things they are taught, without busie intermedling in Speculative Opinions, and things beyond their reach. Such a *Liberty* of *Judgment* as *this* they taught, and *such* was necessary for the Age, in [13] which the Minds of Men were inthrall'd by the Masters of Sects, and the Opinions then stil'd *Orthodox,* from which it was accounted *Heresie* and *Damnation* to recede. So that nothing could be done, to set them at large from those vain Fancies and Ways, till they were perswaded to examine them with *freedom* and *indifference,* and to conclude according to the Report of their Faculties. They knew, That Truth would have the advantage, could it but procure an *impartial* Tryal: That the False Doctrines, and Fanatical Practices of the Times would be detected and sham'd, were it not for the superstitious straightness that supprest all Enquiry; and that those *Old Truths* that were exploded with so much abhorrence, would, in all likelyhood, gain upon the Judgments and Assents of all that were *free,* and *durst* to be *inquisitive.* On such accounts they prest the *Liberty* of *Judgment;* and in a time when it was very *seasonable,* and no hurt could directly arise from it.

Chapter 8

True Theism and the Philosophy of Religion

Christian Hengstermann

A Ralph Cudworth, *The True Intellectual System of the Universe* (1671/1678), Preface to the Reader (pp. 3r–4v)

[3r] THOUGH, *I confess, I have seldom taken any great pleasure, in reading other men's* Apologies, *yet must I at this time make some myself. First therefore, I acknowledge, that when I engag'd the Press, I intended only a Discourse concerning* Liberty *and* Necessity, *or to speak out more plainly,* Against the Fatall Necessity *of all* Actions *and* Events; *which upon whatsoever* Grounds *or* Principles *maintain'd, will (as We conceive)* Serve *the Design of* Atheism, *and* Undermine *Christianity, and all Religion; as taking away all* Guilt *and* Blame, Punishments *and* Rewards, *and plainly rendering a* Day of Judgment *Ridiculous: And it is Evident that some have pursued it of late, in order to that End. But afterwards We consider'd, That this which is indeed a* Controversy, *concerning The* True Intellectual System of the Universe, *does, in the full Extent thereof, take in Other things; the* Necessity *of all* Actions *and* Events *being maintained by* Several Persons, *upon very* Different Grounds, *according to that* Tripartite Fatalism, *mentioned by us in the beginning of the* First Chapter. For First, The Democritick Fate, *is nothing but The* Material Necessity of all things without a God: *in supposing* Senseless Matter, Necessarily Moved, *to be the only Original and Principle of all things: Which therefore is called by* Epicurus, The Physiological; *by us, the* Atheistick Fate. *Besides which, The* Divine Fate *is also* Bipartite; *Some* Theists *supposing* God, *both to* Decree *and* Doe *all things in us,* (Evil *as well as* Good) *or by his* Immediate Influence *to* Determinate *all* Actions, *and so make them alike* Necessary *to us. From whence it follows, That his Will is no way* Regulated *or* Determined, *by any* Essentiall *and* Immutable Goodness, *and* Justice; *or that he hath nothing of* Morality *in his* Nature, *he being only* Arbitrary Will Omnipotent. *As also That all Good and Evil Morall, to us Creatures, are mere* [4v] Theticall *or* Positive *things; νόμῳ and φύσει, by* Law *or* Command *onely, and not by* Nature. *This therefore may be called The* Divine Fate Immorall, *and* Violent. *Again, There being other* Divine Fatalists, *who acknowledge such a Deity, as both* suffers *other things, besides it self, to* Act, *and hath an Essential* Goodness *and* Justice *in its* Nature; *and consequently, That there are things,* Just *and* Unjust *to us Naturally, and not by* Law *and* Arbitrary Constitution *onely; and yet nevertheless take away from men, all such* Liberty, *as might make them capable of* Praise *and* Dispraise, Rewards *and* Punishments, *and Objects of* Distributive Justice: *they conceiving* Necessity *to be* Intrinsicall *to the* Nature *of every thing, in the* Actings *of it; and nothing of* Contingency *to be found any-where; from whence it will follow, That nothing could possibly have been* Otherwise, *in the whole World, than it* Is. *And this may be called The* Divine Fate Morall *(as the other* Immorall) *and* Naturall *(as the other* Violent); *it being a* Concatenation, *or* Implexed Series *of* Causes, *all in themselves* Necessary, *depending upon a* Deity Morall *(if we may so speak); that is, such as is Essentially* Good, *and Naturally* Just, *as the Head thereof; the* First Contriver *and* Orderer *of all. Which kind of* Divine fate *hath not only been formerly asserted by the* Stoicks, *but also of late by divers* Modern Writers. *Wherefore, of the* Three Fatalisms, *or False Hypotheses of the Universe, mentioned in the beginning of this*

Book, One is Absolute Atheism, *Another* Immorall Theism, *or* Religion *without any* Naturall Justice *and* Morality *(all* Just *and* Unjust, *according to this* Hypothesis, *being mere* Theticall *or* Factitious *things, Made by* Arbitrary Will *and* Command *onely); The Third and Last, such a* Theism, *as acknowledges not onely a* God, *or* Omnipotent Understanding Being, *but also* Natural Justice *and* Morality, Founded *in him, and* Derived *from him; nevertheless no* Liberty *from* Necessity *anywhere, and therefore no* Distributive *or* Retributive Justice *in the World.*

B Cudworth, *True Intellectual System*, Preface (pp. 4v–7r)

Whereas these Three Things *are (as we conceive) the* Fundamentals *or* Essentials *of* True Religion. *First, That all things in the World do not Float without a* Head *and* Governour; *but that there is a* God, *an* Omnipotent Understanding Being, Presiding over all. *Secondly, That this* God, *being* Essentially Good *and* Just, *there is* φύσει καλὸν καὶ δῖκαιον, *Something in its own* Nature, Immutably *and* Eternally Just *and* Unjust; *and not by* Arbitrary Will, Law, *and* Command *onely. And, Lastly, that There is Something* ἐφ' ἡμῖν, *or, That we are so far forth* Principals *or* Masters *of our own* Actions, *as to be* Accountable *to* Justice *for them, or to make us* Guilty *and* Blame-worthy *for what we do* Amiss, *and to* Deserve Punishment *accordingly. Which* Three Fundamentals [^{5r}] *of* Religion *are Intimated by the Authour to the Hebrews in these Words*: He that Cometh to God must Believe that He Is, and That He Is a Rewarder of those who seek him out. *For to* Seek out God *here, is nothing else but to* Seek *a* Participation *of his* Image, *or the* Recovery *of that* Nature *and* Life *of his, which we have been* Alienated *from. And these Three Things, namely, That all things do not Float without a* Head *and* Governour; *but there is an* Omnipotent Understanding Being Presiding over all: *That this* God *hath an* Essential Goodness *and* Justice, *and That the Differences of* Good *and* Evil Morall, Honest *and* Dishonest, *are not by meer* Will *and* Law *onely, but by* Nature; *and consequently, That the* Deity *cannot* Act, Influence, *and* Necessitate *men, to such things as are in their* Own Nature, Evil: *and Lastly, That* Necessity *is not* Intrinsicall *to the* Nature *of every thing; But that men have such a* Liberty *or* Power *over their own* Actions, *as may render them* Accountable *for the same, and* Blame-worthy *when they do* Amiss; *and consequently, That there is a* Justice Distributive *of* Rewards *and* Punishments *running through the World; I say, These* Three, *(which are the most* important Things, *that the* Mind *of man can employ it self upon)* taken all together, make up the Wholeness *and* Entireness *of that, which is here called by us,* The True Intellectual System of the Universe; *in such a Sense as* Atheism *may be called, a* False System *thereof: The Word,* Intellectual, *being added, to distinguish it from the other, Vulgarly so called,* Systems of the World, *(that is, the* Visible *and* Corporeal World) *the* Ptolemaick, Tychonick, *and* Copernican; *the Two Former of which, are now commonly accounted* False, *the* Latter True. *And thus our Prospect being now* Enlarged, *into a* Threefold Fatalism, *or* Spurious *and* False Hypothesis *of the Intellectual System, making all things* Necessary *upon several* Grounds; *we accordingly designed the confutation of them all, in three several books. The First,* Against Atheism, *(which is the* Democritick Fate) *wherein all the* Reason *and* Philosophy *thereof is* Refelled, *and the* Existence *of a* God *Demonstrated; and so that* ὑλικὴ ἀνάγκη, *or* Material Necessity *of all things,* Overthrown. *The Second, For such a* God *as is not meer* Arbitrary Will Omnipotent, Decreeing, Doing, *and* Necessitating *all* Actions, Evil *as well as* Good, *but* Essentially Moral, Good, *and* Just; *and For a* Natural Discrimen Honestorum & Turpium; *whereby another Ground of the* Necessity *of all* Human Actions *will be* Removed. *And the* Third *and* Last, *Against* Necessity Intrinsicall *and* Essentiall *to all* Action; *and for such a* Liberty, *or* Sui-Potestas, *in* Rational Creatures, *as may render them* Accountable, *capable of* Rewards *and* Punishments, *and so* Objects *of* Distributive *or* Retributive Justice: [^{6v}] *by which the now onely remaining Ground, of the* Fatal Necessity *of all* Actions *and* Events, *will be* Taken away. *And all these* Three *under that* One General Title, *of* The True Intellectual System of the Universe. *Each Book having besides, its own* Particular Title: *as, Against* Atheism; *For* Natural Justice *and* Morality, *Founded in the* Deity; *for* Liberty *from* Necessity, *and a*

Distributive Justice *of* Rewards *and* Punishments *in the World. And this we conceive may fully satisfy, concerning our* General Title, *all those, who are not extremely* Criticall *or* Captious, *at least as many of them as ever heard of the* Astronomical Systems *of the World: so that they will not think us hereby Obliged, to Treat of the* Hierarchy of Angels, *and of all the Several* Species *of* Animals, Vegetables, *and* Minerals, *&c. that is, to write* De Omni Ente, *of whatsoever is Contained within The* Complexion of the Universe. *Though the Whole* Scale *of* Entity *is here also taken notice of; and the* General Ranks *of* Substantiall Beings, *below the* Deity (*or* Trinity *of* Divine Hypostases) *Consider'd: which yet, according to our* Philosophy, *are but* Two; Souls *of several Degrees,* (Angels *themselves being included within that Number) and* Body, *or* Matter: *as also the* Immortality *of those* Souls *Proved. Which notwithstanding is Suggested by us, onely to Satisfy some mens* Curiosity. *Nevertheless, we confess, that this* General Title, *might well have been here spared by us, and this* Volume *have been Presented to the Reader's View, not as a* Part *or* Piece, *but a* Whole Complete *and* Entire *thing by it self, had it not been for* Two Reasons; *First, Our beginning with those* Three Fatalisms, *or* False Hypotheses *of the* Intellectual System, *and Promising a Confutation of them all, then when we thought to have brought them within the Compass of One Volume; and Secondly, Every other Page's, throughout this whole Volume, accordingly bearing the* Inscription *of* Book the First *upon the Head thereof. This is therefore that, which, in the First place, we here* Apologize *for our Publishing* One Part *or* Book *alone by it self; We being surprised in the Length thereof; Whereas we had otherwise Intended Two more along with it. Notwithstanding which, there is no Reason why this Volume should be therefore thought* Imperfect *and* Incomplete, *because it hath not All the* Three Things *at first Designed by us; it containing All that belongeth to its own* Particular Title *and* Subject, *and being in that respect no* Piece, *but a* Whole. *This indeed must needs beget an Expectation, of the Two following Treatises,* (*especially in such as shall have receiv'd any Satisfaction from this First;*) *concerning those* Two other Fatalisms, *or False Hypotheses mentioned; to make up our Whole* Intellectual System Compleat: *The One to Prove, That* God *is not meer* Arbitrary Will Omnipotent (*without any* Essential Goodness *and* Justice) Decree-[ʳ]-ing *and* Doing *all things in the World, as well* Evil *as* Good; *and thereby making them alike* Necessary *to us; from whence it would follow, that all* Good *and* Evil Moral *are meer* Thetical, Positive, *and* Arbitrary *things; that is, not* Nature, *but* Will; *Which is the* Defence of Natural, Eternal, *and* Immutable Justice *or* Morality: *The Other, that* Necessity *is not* Intrinsical *to the* Nature *of Every thing,* God *and all* Creatures, *or* Essentiall *to all* Action; *but, That there is Something* ἐφ' ἡμῖν, *or, That we have some* Liberty *or* Power *over our own* Actions: *Which is the* Defence *of a* Distributive *or* Retributive Justice, *dispensing* Rewards *and* Punishments *throughout the whole World. Wherefore we think fit here to advertize the Reader concerning these, That though they were, and still are, really intended by us; yet the Complete Finishing and Publication of them, will notwithstanding depend upon many* Contingencies; *not only of our* Life *and* Health, *the Latter of which, as well as the Former, is to us very Uncertain; but also of our* Leisure, *or* Vacancy *from other Necessary Employments.*

Commentary

While relatively brief and written a long time after the events related, More's and Cudworth's few autobiographical notes **(5 A–B. E)** are nevertheless revealing. They show the guiding convictions of Cambridge Platonism, namely its concern with the objective nature of divine goodness which not even omnipotent will can compromise in any way. Instead, God cannot but act in accordance with the highest of his attributes. To the rational belief in divine goodness corresponds closely that in human freedom which More and Cudworth championed equally vocally early on. Their early Latin poetry **(5 C–D. F–G)** in particular contains several arguments for human freedom. More views the first rational insight into God's goodness as proof for man's free will. The vision of God's fullness is of such magnificence that the soul cannot but feel the chasm between the supreme divine ideal and the abject reality which it is both called upon and able to bridge in autonomous charitable action.

Cudworth likewise emphasises the fullness of God's being in which the soul is invited to share in a life of pious action and contemplation **(5 H)**.

The selection from Whichcote's *Aphorisms* that begins the next chapter **(6 A)** presents his main ideas on reason and deiformity succinctly and forcefully, making it clear that human reason is created with the capacity to participate in the divine reason through the continuous choice of virtuous behaviour.

The brief selection from Smith's discourse *Of the Existence and Nature of God* **(6 B)** expands on Whichcote's idea of human reason as an efflux of the perfect divine reason, through which human beings can participate, within creaturely limits, in the divine mind.

More's sermons **(6 C)** deal mainly with deiformity, presenting a rigorous path of self-purgation to an auditory which must have been mainly composed of very young men. They reflect his own emotional breakdown after success in his BA examinations, during which he sought healing by reading the *German Theology* and the *Enneads* of Plotinus, both of which counsel humility and inner purity.

Cudworth's sermons established his credentials as a Platonist well before the publication of his massive *True Intellectual System of the Universe*. In his famous *Sermon before the House of Commons* **(6 D)**, he rebukes the warring theological factions, urging them to follow the life of Christ as "the Pith and Kernel of all Religion".

Rust **(6 E)** echoes Whichcote and Smith on the nature of "right reason". This sermon is aimed at "Atheists and Deists", but his specific targets are sectarians who rely on emotionally based "revelation" rather than reason and Roman Catholics who insist on "implicit faith" in doctrines which defy rational explanation.

Hallywell **(6 F)** briefly addresses one of the weak points in Cambridge Platonist theology: how to explain the sacrifice of the cross, while eschewing penal substitution but also going beyond a mere exemplary doctrine of the Atonement. He adopts the Grotian or governmental theory which states that God could simply forgive the sin of the world but that this would not allow human beings to grow to spiritual maturity. Christ therefore willingly dies on the cross as a representative and expiatory sacrifice to show God's abhorrence of sin, opening floodgates of grace to human beings who believe in him and wish to become deiform.

Glanvill **(6 G)**, like Rust, wishes to correct the misconceptions of the use of reason in religion by both sectarian enthusiasts and Roman Catholics. In this sermon, originally delivered to fellow clergy, he argues that human acceptance of the existence of God and the authority of Scripture is dependent on the correct use of reason.

Symon Patrick **(6★ A)** sets our quite clearly what he means by a "Latitude-Man", who emerges as a moderate Anglican at a time when such a position was suspect. He refers to a list of those ordained by the bishop of Norwich. This was Joseph Hall (1574–1656), who was translated from the see of Exeter to that of Norwich by Charles I in 1641 but was imprisoned by Parliament as he travelled to his new diocese. In 1618, Hall had been an English delegate to the Synod of Dort, which strongly affirmed Calvinist double predestination. He left the synod early on grounds of ill health but was thought to be relieved that he did not have to subscribe to its harsh soteriological articles. A staunch royalist, Hall quietly ordained a number of candidates to the Anglican priesthood, including Patrick, in the late 1640s. Patrick also refers to a recent author who had written about the pernicious conjunction of atheism, enthusiasm and superstition. This was Henry More, whose *Enthusiasmus Triumphatus* had first appeared in 1656 and was republished in his *Collection of Several Philosophical Writings* in expanded form in 1662.

Rust's funeral sermon for the earl of Mount-Alexander **(6★ B)** suggests that he agreed with both Jeremy Taylor and Henry More about the slight credenda necessary for salvation. He found that the Church of England was sufficiently moderate in imposing articles of belief and practice, allowing ample intellectual engagement with theology without doctrinal restrictions. The major part of this sermon deals mainly with the immortality of the soul, continuing Rust's thinking on the Resurrection body from his Bachelor of Divinity discourse at Cambridge in 1658.

Henry More's letter of 29 June 1665 to Lady Conway (6★ C) indicates that Ralph Widdrington was accusing him of contravening the Christ's College statutes by an absence exceeding that which was allowed to fellows. More thinks he is in the clear, especially if a few days on which he was unwell are taken into consideration. More will have tried to maximise his annual summer visit to Lady Conway, and Widdrington has spotted this as a point of vulnerability. In the second letter of 10 July, More claims not to understand the term "Latitude man" but notes the real danger of an external audit of the college's accounts. The auditor was to be the college's visitor, Vice-chancellor Anthony Sparrow, whom we have met as Patrick's opponent at Queens'. There appears to be no extant record of the audit, but Widdrington's machinations went on for another decade.

Gilbert Burnet spends the first five dialogues of his *Conference betwixt a Conformist and a Nonconformist* (6★ D) arguing for episcopacy and the Book of Common Prayer against the Nonconformist whom he considers to be a fanatic. In the final dialogue, the Nonconformist accuses the Conformist of being a Latitudinarian, and Burnet tries to explain the term favourably. A Latitudinarian is a charitable person of good morals, neither an atheist nor a Socinian and certainly not a papist. He believes that a holy life is necessary for salvation, but there is nothing to be gained by owning the contentious term "Arminian". Burnet quotes the irenic advice given by Charles II to his son, the eventual Charles II, in his *Eikon Basilike* (pp. 240-241), published in 1649 very soon after the regicide. Burnet's final assertion that "Religion was given of God to transform a man into the Divine likeness, and to a real participation of the Divine Nature" betrays his agreement with the Cambridge Platonists.

Edward Fowler's *Principles and Practices* (6★ E) begins with a witty account of what both Puritans and High Churchmen say about Latitudinarians, but he makes a number of solid points which indicate his agreement with the Cambridge Platonists. Basic to his whole understanding of the Christian religion is the Platonic question: does God order certain laws because they are good or are they good merely because God has ordered them? Fowler sides with his friend Henry More in presenting the absolute goodness of God as the foundation of all morality. He is well satisfied with the restored Church of England, but he sees virtuous behaviour – by which we can participate in the divine nature – as more important than mere compliance with episcopacy and the Book of Common Prayer.

Under the cover of a description of the Bensalemites, Glanvill (6★ F) sets out the necessity of but also the correct limitations upon free intellectual inquiry in theological questions. Such inquiry is not to be undertaken by the uneducated nor by the very young, but mature men who have been taught how to handle such matters should have the freedom to reject some aspects of authority in the education they have received. Undue reverence for antiquity can be just as harmful as the ill-considered suggestions of enthusiasm. Truth will emerge without damaging the religious establishment if such *"Liberty of Judgment"* is used judiciously. Glanvill was an eager advocate of the new philosophy practised by the Royal Society but also a vigorous apologist for the Church of England, rejecting toleration of the "sects".

Cudworth's preface (7 A–B) provides a précis of Cambridge Platonist philosophy. It is opposed to Calvin's voluntarism, Stoic determinism and, above all, Hobbes's materialism. To the false theisms, Cudworth opposes a three-article rational faith of a benign Deity, a strictly realistic notion of good and evil and a libertarian concept of human freedom. While the moral (and epistemological) realism is introduced as a corollary of the true theism of a good God, free will is the *sine qua non* of his justice. Only if man is free and, thus, accountable for his deeds and misdeed can he be rewarded and punished in the end. Both in intent and diction, the school's tripartite new Platonism is a recognizably early modern philosophy of religion.

Part III

Cambridge Platonism in Early Modern Thought

Christian Hengstermann

Introduction

The Cambridge Platonists engaged critically with all the foundational thinkers of early modern philosophy. In reaction to the spectre of the theological voluntarism which they had imbibed in their childhood and youth, they came to espouse a theology based not upon God's unbounded omnipotence, but upon his universal and disinterested goodness. From More's early poetry collected in the *Platonicall Song of the Soul* to Cudworth's massive prose work *The True Intellectual System* of the Universe, the circle's prodigious literary production is concerned chiefly with a "rational soteriology" (Beiser, *Defence of Reason*, 159–183) that hinges upon the twin pillars of God's supreme goodness and the soul's free will. All of the Cambridge Platonists concur in their vociferous rejection of Calvin's twin doctrines of unrestricted, rather than morally bound divine omnipotence or theological voluntarism and imputed, rather than inherent human righteousness or justification. Not coincidentally, Calvinism or "divine fate immoral" is one of the three false theisms rejected in the preface to the comprehensive exposition of Cambridge Platonism in Cudworth's 1671/78 *True Intellectual System*. It is shown to be opposite to all the three articles of their own rational faith, i.e. a benign Deity, a morality exempt from and binding for his omnipotent decree and human free will. In the 1640s, the revulsion at the doctrine of the predestination of the large majority of humankind for eternal damnation without any demerit on their part fuelled their seminal first philosophical efforts. Both Cudworth and More report in vivid autobiographical narratives their conversion from the arbitrary God of the Calvinism of their childhood and youth to the good God of the Platonism of their early adulthood and maturity. The Cambridge Platonists emerged as vociferous critics of Calvinism in the era of the civil war and the Commonwealth and the Protectorate in the 1640s and the 1650s. In the process, they ushered in a momentous transition from Puritanism to Platonism at their Cambridge colleges. As early as 1647, we find the landmark tenets of the group's anti-Calvinist soteriology put forward with great audacity in the youthful Cudworth's *Sermon Before the House of Commons* **(1A–B)**, a deliberately topical reading of 1 John 2,3–4: "And hereby we do know that we know him, if we keep his Commandments. He that saith, I know him, and keepeth not his Commandments, is a liar, and the truth is not in him." The 30-year-old philosopher's sermon, preached to the divided Parliament at the height of the civil war of the 1640s, is one of the earliest programmatic expositions of Cambridge Platonism. It contains in dense argument and in stirring language the outlines of the Cambridge Platonists' emphatically anti-Calvinist rational soteriology, coupled with an epistemology of religious knowledge whose chief Johannine criterion of truth is not one of theoretical reasoning, but one of practical moral and political conduct. Cudworth is outspoken in his plea for "*a true Reformation*" (*Sermon Before the House of Commons*, 82). At its heart is a religion of humble pious *orthopraxy*, rather than notoriously zealous and unforgiving *orthodoxy* which the Cambridge Platonist preacher impresses upon his audience as the sole means whereby peace can be brought to the warring Christian sects and factions of the day. Throughout his sermon, Cudworth opposes to the narrowness of flat and unprofitable dogmatic religion with its stress on stale creed and formula the enlivening sense of the infinite width of God's love which the soul intuits and embraces in sublime vision and is called upon to translate into corresponding ethical and political action. The sermon is directed against the Westminster Assembly of Divines and the Calvinist creed which they were drafting at the time of its delivery. The spectre of Calvin's elusive Deity and his inscrutable decrees by which he chooses to damn most of humanity and exempt from damnation in an arbitrary exercise of unlimited power only a happy few is rejected as the chief foil to the practical first truth of the universalist rational religion proclaimed in the homily. Calvin's notion of immoral divine omnipotence, which the young Cudworth repeatedly decries as the πρῶτον ψεῦδος of all philosophical religion, is to be replaced with Plato's first principle of God's goodness and his disinterested self-giving in creation and salvation. Cudworth's critique is two-fold. In a more restrained epistemological censure of what he regards as the voluntarist first principle of Calvinism, he rejects any possibility on the part of the human soul to fathom the divine degrees. Instead of overbearingly and sacrilegiously purporting to pry into God's counsels, he follows the apostle and evangelist in laying down obedience to the divine law, i.e. practical moral conduct in a spirit of disinterested and universal love, as the sole criterion by which a Christian soul may tell whether it is among those redeemed or not. In a set of sharper invectives, he lambasts the Calvinists' very idea of an omnipotence unbound by any prior moral standard whatsoever as an act of despicable idolatry. In Calvinist soteriology, man worships none other than himself in the mirror of a thoroughly anthropomorphist deity created in the human image of caprice and fickleness. Like the pre-Socratic Xenophanes' Ethiopians whose God inevitably shares their black colour of skin, the Calvinist hypostasizes his own self-will and lust. In response, Cudworth views God's omnipotence as being identical with the highest of his predicates. It is his disinterested goodness in which the creator cannot but choose to share the fullness of his being with all of creation in unbegrudging self-communication. Through the soul's gradual sanctification, wrought by its own free will, none other than the Father himself exercises his omnipotence, bestowing upon it his very being as consummate goodness and holiness in the Son and the Holy Spirit's work of salvation. There is on the first principles of Cambridge Platonist soteriology no contradiction between theonomy and autonomy with grace designating freedom informed by God's spirit of universal love. Cudworth's universalist vision of divine goodness, juxtaposed with great rhetorical virtuosity with the Calvinists' particularist notion of arbitrary divine omnipotence, is deeply indebted to the Alexandrian Christian Platonist Origen whom all of the Cambridge Latitudinarians preferred over the Latin Church Father Augustine. It is hardly surprising that leading Calvinists objected to the Origenist soteriology of the new Christian party. In another of the foundational documents of Cambridge Platonism, a series of eight letters exchanged with his erstwhile Cambridge tutor in late 1651, the philosopher preacher Benjamin Whichcote, Provost of King's College and Vice-Chancellor of the university at the time, responded to charges of preaching a highly suspect unscriptural Christian rationalism **(C)**. In many ways, Whichcote was the Socrates of the Cambridge Platonist movement, acting as a midwife helping to give birth to the liberal and rational religion espoused by its major representatives. Ordained deacon and priest and appointed Sunday afternoon lecturer at Trinity Church in 1636, he exerted seminal influence upon a young generation of divines. In particular, he was instrumental in transforming Emmanuel College from the stronghold of English Puritanism that it was founded as in 1584 into the cradle of Cambridge Platonism that is became under the influence of his pupils. Among the hearers to imbibe his Cambridge Enlightenment creed of human reason as the "candle of the Lord" (Prov. 20:27) were the young Cudworth, John Worthington and John Smith. In 1644, following the Earl of Manchester's purge of the Cambridge colleges, Whichcote was appointed

Provost of King's College and Regius Professor of Divinity. The charge of a "kinde of Moral Divinitie" far removed from the gospel and "onlie with a little tincture of Christ added" (*Eight Letters*, 39) was levelled at him by the then Master of Emmanual College, Benjamin Tuckney, a celebrated Cambridge preacher and teacher and member of the Westminster Assembly. Tuckney was the mouthpiece of a growing group of more traditionally-minded Puritans who took exception to what they believed to be the popular preacher's overly rationalist message. In addition, the Cambridge divine felt personally offended by his erstwhile student's Commencement Sermon of 7th September 1651 which he believed—and despite Whichcote's subsequent protestations to the contrary continued to believe— to have been directed against an earlier Commencement address of his own. The ensuing exchange of letters between the Cambridge Calvinist and the Socrates of Cambridge Platonism from September to November 1651 revolved around the role of both practical and theoretical reason in matters of religion. Like Socrates, Whichcote was accused by his former university tutor of leading astray the youth entrusted to his spiritual care. Plato and his followers, much to Tuckney's dismay, tended to be quoted more frequently in his homilies than Scripture and were clearly praised over and above the latter's inspired penman and protagonists. In brief, Whichcote's Christian religion was no longer that of the venerable Reformer Calvin and his equally authoritative English successors, several of whom are mentioned by name in the correspondence. Instead, it veered perilously close to Arminianism and Socinianism in the stress which Whichcote placed upon man's own autonomous rationality. Naturally, a chief bone of contention in the two Cambridge divines' exchange of letters was the doctrine of salvation. As well as over-emphasizing human reason as the "candle of the Lord" at the expense of God's revelation in the Holy Writ, Whichcote was charged by Tuckney with prioritizing human will over the free gift of divine grace. In his response, Whichcote, intriguingly, reproduced notes of the sermon in question which he believed to prove unfounded the charge of downplaying the importance of divine grace. In so doing, Whichcote highlighted key concerns of the Cambridge Platonists' rational soteriology, notably God's unchangeable goodness and the soul's assimilation to him as the essence of salvation. His student John Smith's *Discourses* **(C)**, delivered in the early 50s, when the preacher was Dean of Queen's College and Catechist, and edited and published by John Worthington, a friend of his and another member of the group, after his untimely death in 1652, expose as egregiously anthropomorphic the Calvinists' adulation of God's supreme power to the detriment of his superior moral and intellectual perfection. Smith's detailed refutation of the Calvinist theology of unrestrained divine omnipotence comes at the end of a lengthy meditation upon God's goodness defined in the Neoplatonist terms of an ungrudging self-communication in creation and salvation. In careful conceptual reasoning, God's will is shown to be one governed entirely by the two higher principles of his perfect goodness and love and by his supreme intellect. It was under the tutelage of his revered teachers Cudworth and More at Christ's College that the gifted young sizar George Rust contributed significantly to the nascent new movement of rational theology which he helped shape in several of his early treatises. His most influential shorter work is the *Discourse of Truth*, a university sermon delivered as a reading of the Latitudinarian group's Old Testament motto "The spirit of man is the candle of the Lord" (Prov. 20:27) at Christ's College chapel in 1651 and as an exegesis of the New Testament "What is truth" (Jn. 18:38) at Great St. Mary's in 1655 **(E–F)**. Its subsequent publication history bears testimony to the significance which his fellow Platonists attached to his concise treatise. The *Discourse* was published with extensive commentary by his teacher Henry More in the 1682 *Two Choice and Useful Treatises* alongside their common friend Joseph Glanvill's *Lux Orientialis* and republished by his student Henry Hallwell as part of the 1686 posthumous *Remains* of his works. In his *Discourse of Truth*, Rust repudiates Calvinist predestination upon the grounds of divine goodness defined as the "everlasting Proportion and symmetry between fulness and its overflowing and dispreading of it self" in the group's shared Christian rationalism. The author mounts a powerful *reductio* argument against the Calvinists' pernicious theological voluntarism in conjuring up the spectre of a good God revoking all his promises of eventual salvation and instead damning all of humanity at a whim. In support, Rust cites an unidentifiable anonymous Calvinist *"Pamphleteer"* who expressly ascribes to God the ability to break his every prior vow so as to demonstrate his unrestrained power in the end. However, as well as following his revered teachers Cudworth and More in decrying such a deity as a "a worse Devil than is in Hell", Rust furnishes a tightly argued précis of the Cambridge Platonists' early rational soteriology which views God's immutable predicates and man's hope for salvation as grounded in the immutable first principle of divine goodness.

The Cambridge Platonists continued to oppose Calvinism after the 1660 Restoration of the Church and the Crown, critiquing what they perceived to be the Calvinists' improper hypostatization of divine power both from the pulpit and in print. Cudworth's second sermon, delivered to the prestigious Lincoln's Inn in 1664 **(G–H)**, exposed the soteriological inanity of an external satisfaction unaccompanied by any internal participation in God's goodness and intellect. It is particularly noteworthy for the way Cudworth weaves together his rational soteriology and his ontology, notably the distinction between primary and secondary qualities and the spirit of nature as the medium by which God informs and guides the natural world. The soul's activity by which it gives rich and varied life to a cosmos consisting of lifeless atoms only evidences its divine descent. If it duly prepares itself in purification, it may come to resemble the spirit of nature in receiving and distributing the beautiful intelligible principles and forms encompassed in the divine intellect. In addition, there are in-depth critiques of Calvinism in several of the Cambridge Platonists' more popular works published at a time of transition in church and state and clearly meant to disseminate their gospel of the Christ within among wider circles of interested clergy and laity in the newly restored Anglican Church. Of these works, Henry More's anti-Calvinist invective in the third of the five *Divine Dialogues* **(I)** and Hallywell's book-length rebuttal *Deus Justificatus* **(J–L)** are of particular philosophical significance. Both works appeared in 1668. For the most part, More's long-winded third *Dialogue* is designed to reproduce enough ethnological material to lend further metaphysical credence to the subsequent argument for the hypothesis of the pre-existence of souls to which More held on despite the official censure he had incurred prior to the work's publication at the hands of Bishop Samuel Parker. Such is the extent of human depravity in the Old World and the New that egregious trespasses committed in an earlier state must account for it. However, More's expositions of miscellaneous indigenous customs and rituals, taken from then popular New World travelogues, turns into a remarkable exercise in comparative religion. It is on the basis of the Cambridge Platonists' shared ontology of a single perfect archetypal divinity revealed in a plethora of images that More, following the principle of charity, sets out to find hints and traces of the eternal truth in a range of *prima facie* barbarous cultural and religious practices described in graphic detail in the ethnographic sources consulted. The refusal to wear any kind of garment, for instance, is taken as a symbol of original purity and chastity not unlike the Biblical myth of the Garden of Eden and the brutal practice of a host putting to death a virtuous guest at night is at least motivated not by hatred, but by the love of the moral excellencies which the misguided, yet well-meaning, perpetrator believes to acquire in the process. Even the ritual slaughtering of some 20,000 followers of the late "Great *Cham* of the *Tartars*" at the latter's funeral, however appalling, testifies to that uncultivated people's firm belief in "the Immortality of the Soul and personal distinctness of the deceased in the other life" (*Divine Dialogues*, 3,10 [2nd edition, 200]). Even more remarkably, More's review of New World religion and ritual contains a damning critique of European colonialism. For one thing, the violence of several of the appalling rituals described pales in comparison to that perpetrated by "our modern Europeans". On the topic of cannibalism, More berates in no uncertain terms the excesses of wanton violence committed by the Spanish conquistadors: "Besides, whether is it more barbarous out of scorn and hatred to kill Men to feed their Dogs withal, as the *Spaniards* used the poor *Indians*, or for the *Indians* or other *Barbarians*, out of an appetitious liking of Man's flesh, more honourable to bury it in their own bowels?" (*Divine Dialogues*, 3,12 [2nd edition, 203].). For another thing, it is in his critique of European colonialism that More lashes out against the strict "*Superlapsareans*" who insist that God's predestination of the elect and the reprobates precedes Adam's fall **(I)**. Theirs, insists More, is a theology far more unforgiving and cruel even than that of any of the worst devil worshippers in the New Word. Not only is their "Imagination of *Omnipotent Power* and *Will* acting without any regard to *Justice* or *Goodness*" an act of idolatry comparable to the most execrable excesses of primitive satanism, but their strict Calvinism vies with the cruel practice of human sacrifice in the extent of cruelty in having an evil idol of infinite arbitrary power condemn to eternal suffering the vast reprobate majority without any prior trespass on their part. For the most part, the second-generation Cambridge Platonist Henry Hallwell, a student of Rust's at Christ's and the editor of his posthumous *Remains*, acted as a popularizer of the circle's Christian Platonism. His is, therefore, a "pastoral Origenism" meant to translate into more accessible language the major Platonists' systems of rational theology. However, his 1668 principal work *Deus Justificatus* is a densely argued speculative treatise. It is also the only book-length refutation of Calvinist theology from the pen of a Cambridge Platonist. While the author's arguments are largely the group's tried-and-tested ones of the priority of God's goodness and wisdom vis-à-vis his power, Hallywell's chef-d'oeuvre is remarkable for its balanced critical account. It provides long excerpts from the writings of several principal major Calvinists past and present, including Calvin himself and Theodore Beza. In careful critical reading, he argues that there is not "in any Scheme of the Supralapsarian or Sublapsarian Doctrines" any possibility of not making God the author of Adam's original sin for which he then punishes the large majority of reprobate humanity in egregious anthropomorphist vindictiveness entirely unbecoming of his goodness. Hallywell's work is the only one to address in detailed philosophical argument the incompatibility of God's pre- or postlapsarian predestination with man's free will. In a substantial appendix, Hallywell also provides a powerful rejoinder to Samuel Parker's attempt at a reconciliatory middle way between more traditional Calvinism with its emphasis on divine sovereignty and power and more liberal currents of Protestant Christianity, including Arminianism and Cambridge Platonism with their stress on divine goodness. In a concise axiomatic reassertion of the Cambridge Platonist metaphysics of divine goodness, Hallwell rejects Parker's notion of a creator constrained by the pact gone into at creation to ensure to his creatures a state better than utter non-existence, thus enlarging the scope of divine freedom and defending traditional tenets of Christian faith like eternal damnation. It is Cudworth who mounts the most powerful *reductio* argument against Calvinist voluntarism which he believes to undoes all knowledge and, by implication, all religion, philosophy and science **(M)**.

To the opposition to the *theology* of John Calvin corresponds closely in both style and argument the opposition to the *philosophy* of Thomas Hobbes whose voluntarism in ethics and politics with its stress on might, rather than right they found to mirror in crucial regards the French reformer's emphasis upon unbounded divine omnipotence. However, Hobbes's political and theological theory of unlimited royal and divine power, popularized, above all, in the widely-read 1651 *Leviathan*, hinged upon a comprehensive materialist and determinist account of reality laid down in his three-volume *Elements of Philosophy* (1642–1658) and in the celebrated Commonwealth-era literary debate with the Arminian High Churchman and bishop John Bramhall about *Liberty and Necessity* (1654–1656). While they were unwavering in their belief in a God of universal goodness revealing himself to man in infallible intuitive vision, they met Hobbes on his own terms and exposed the fallacies and shortcomings of his argument in careful conceptual analyses of his materialism. Henry More mounted several in-depth attacks upon the Cambridge Platonists' archfoe in his mature prose writings of the

1650s. Both the 1653 *Antidote*, advertised in the preface as a pioneering first English "Draught *of Natural Theology or* Metaphysicks", and the 1659 *Immortality of the Soul*, the most comprehensive account of Cambridge Platonism at the close of the 1650s, contain several of the Cambridge Platonists' most substantive responses to Hobbes's philosophy. More is careful to highlight the Cambridge Platonists' close cooperation in combatting as formidable foe as Hobbes by dedicating the first and third work in his trilogy of principal works—the third being the 1653 allegorical Genesis commentary *Conjectura Cabbalistica*—to Lady and Lord Conway, respectively. The nobleman Edward Conway promoted the latitudinarian and philosophical agenda of More's group and protected him and Cudworth from harm when the pendulum at the university swung in their disfavour at the Restoration. Ragley Hall, the family's estate, served as a frequent meeting place of the Cambridge Platonist network fondly remembered in the preface to the *Immortality of the Soul* for "the solemness of the Place, those shady Walks, those Hills and Woods, wherein often having lost the sight of the rest of the World, and the World of me, I found out in that hidden solitude the choicest Theories in the following Discourse." Conway's wife Anne, whom More had begun tutoring in Descartes's *Principles* and in his own synthesis of Cartesianism and Origenism in the early 1650s, was his extraordinarily gifted "heroine pupil" eulogized in the preface to his *Antidote* as a woman philosopher of "singular Wit and Vertues" and worthy to converse with "that Plato" himself, "if he were alive again". More's writings are firmly rooted in his debates with his fellow Platonists in Cambridge and at Ragley Hall. The first work to emerge from this fruitful discourse, the *Antidote*, is an exercise in a Christian rationalism close to Descartes in both method and substance. As such, it contains no in-depth refutations of Hobbes' materialism. Nevertheless, the latter's materialism and sensualism clearly informs the spectre of a mock theology of a "*Matter*" that "*does necessarily exist of it self.*" More even comes close to mimicking an atheist of unmistakably Hobbesian stamp when he has a *fictus interlocutor* argue with some rhetorical bravado that "*Matter* is palpable and *sensible* unto us, but God is not, and therefore we pronounce confidently that it is, though *God* be not" (*Antidote*, I,8,11–12 [*Collection*, 24]). In response, More insists upon the prerogatives of reason among whose innate ideas is that of a most perfect being inaccessible to sense. On no account, therefore, must the soul impoverish itself by overprivileging sense, while disregarding the higher epistemic power of reason. In contrast to the brief critical notes on the unnamed Hobbes in the 1653 *Antidote*, the 1659 *Immortality of the Soul* contains several chapters wholly dedicated to the refutation of the *Elements*, the *Leviathan* and the *On Liberty and Necessity* of which, significantly, the author first provides remarkably fair and balanced accounts. A major first part of More's critique revolves around the first principles of Hobbes's ontology and epistemology, notably his dismissal of the very notion of incorporeal substance as a contradiction in terms **(2A–C)**. Hobbes's rejection of spirit is shown to beg the question. On the principles of his reductionist mechanist atomism, he takes for granted what he sets out to prove by ruling out the possibility of incorporeal substance in a wholly corporeal universe. Nor is the knowledge about incorporeal substance solely due to appearances of ghosts or the deluded imagination, i.e. "Dreams and *Fears* of Melancholick and Superstitious persons". More himself clearly believed that apparitions, of which he went to great pains to provide accurate reports, furnished valuable evidence for the existence of incorporeal substances. Of greater philosophical significance to his rational theology, however, were the classical subjects of metaphysics, i.e. God, the soul and the world. Each single one of them, More insists, is defined exclusively by or exhibits to various degrees operations and perfections that defy a description in the conceptual apparatus of Hobbes's reductionist atomism and mechanism. Still, while continually maligning Hobbes as an overly "confident exploder of *incorporeal substance*", More readily acknowledges the force of one of the latter's most formidable arguments against the existence of incorporeal substance. In the 1659 *Immortality*, he expresses agreement with Hobbes in rejecting as grossly counter-intuitive, if not downright absurd the classical ancient and medieval account of incorporeal substance or spirit being present as a whole in each and every part of its body. However, whereas Hobbes believed that the absurd notion of a spirit inhabiting its body in its entirety both as a whole and in its every part further supported his rejection of incorporeal substance as a contradiction in terms, More, clearly, chose to hold on to incorporealism. However, he revisited and revised his earlier ontologies of mind in the light of his chief adversary's cogent critique. In his 1671 *Enchiridium Metaphysicum*, a manual intended to supersede similar scholastic and Cartesian ontological handbooks in the university curriculum, he expanded significantly upon what he acknowledged as Hobbes's valid censure of classical incorporealism **(E)**. Strikingly, More enlisted the Cambridge Platonists' chief philosophical adversary as an aide in his struggle against one of what he came to perceive to be the two chief errors in the dualistic substance ontologies of his day (identified, in Latin and Greek neologisms of his own coinage, as Cartesian "nullibism" and as scholastic "holenmerism"). His counter-arguments against the latter error carry to its logical extreme Hobbes's *reductio* refutation of the notion of incorporeal spirit. In the first of these quasi-Hobbesian arguments, More exposes as absurd inevitable implications of a holenmerian concept of incorporeal substance such as a spirit's potential division into an infinity of "wholes" or the reduction of God or any other spiritual substance into an unextended geometric point. In response to the aporiae and the general explanatory weakness of classical holenmerianism, More advocates his own concept of a *sui generis* spiritual extension which at once ensures the mind's indivisibility and eschews the aforementioned absurd corollaries. Another set of objections levelled against Hobbes in More's *Immortality of the Soul* target the latter's determinism **(D)**. In lines of reasoning analogous to those directed against his materialism, More defends the coherence of the concept rejected as contradictory by the philosopher from Malmesbury. Libertarian free will, conceived of as the incorporeal mind's capacity of initiating an action independently of any prior external stimulus, is shown to be possible. While possibly apocryphal and an invention of his biased biographer meant to add to his subject's fame, Hobbes' remark reported in Richard Ward's The *Life of Henry More* that if he did not hold his own philosophy, he would embrace More's is testimony to its level of sophistication: "And even Mr. *Hobbs* himself, as I have been informed, hath been herd to say, *That if his* own Philosophy *was not* True, *he knew of none that he should sooner like* than MORE's *of Cambridge*" (Ward, *Life*, I 5 [ed. Hutton et al., 55]).

Like More, Ralph Cudworth devoted considerable space in his principal writings to the refutation of Hobbes's materialism and determinism. Hobbes's "mechanistic fate" is one of the four possible atheisms rebutted in the *True Intellectual system* and considered the most formidable variety alongside Spinozist "hylozoism" **(F)**. Throughout the anti-Hobbesian parts of the published first part of his *System*, Cudworth's critique revolves around rational self-activity **(G–L)**. Cudworth establishes the existence of an inherently active incorporeal substance on the basis of Hobbes's and his own shared atomistic cosmology. Like his fellow Cambridge Platonists, Cudworth embraced the scientific revolution and its paradigm of matter particles interacting in the void, an account which, he acknowledges, is "unquestionably true". Mechanistic atomism provides an apposite explanatory framework for the interaction of bodily phenomena in the visible world without having to resort to the made-up substantial forms of the Platonist and Aristotelian tradition. Significantly, however, the exhaustive atomist definition of body in terms of its primary qualities, i.e. "magnitude, figure, sight, motion, and rest" renders necessary the assumption of a second substance to account for its secondary qualities, i.e. a body's visual or olfactory qualities. Otherwise, these sensual attributes would have to arise from nothing. In the overall architecture of the published first part of Cudworth's *System*, Hobbes's atomism is shown to be a truncated variety of the ancient theology. It deviates from Moses's own ancient cosmology of matter particles in motion by excising from it the incorporeal second substance and, therefore, falls short of its time-honoured truth. Nor does Hobbes's sensationalist epistemology fare better in Cudworth's review of atheism. Hobbes's attempt to reduce to mere sense impression every higher thought and concept is equally doomed to failure as, clearly, the mind's judgement about the contents of the five organs of sensation cannot itself be sensual in nature. Nor can there be such a thing as truth in a sensationalist epistemology, since this concept lies beyond the confines of the senses which are not yet capable of being either true or false. Hence, Hobbes's attempt at a materialist denial of the existence of God whose idea is inscribed into a rational being's mind cannot but in principle come to naught. Cudworth's critique of Hobbes goes further than More's in laying out in considerable detail the incompatibility of Hobbesian materialism and sensualism with any serious Christian rational theology. Abundant evidence is provided by Hobbes' own theological nominalism. God's sublime predicates are reduced to merely doxological manners of speaking meant to worship his single actual attribute, i.e. his unbounded power as the source of all motion. On the first principles of Hobbes' mechanistic atomism, there is, and cannot be, be any "natural justice" restraining God who is entitled to humanity's worship solely on the grounds of his unlimited power. Hobbes's denial of "natural justice" in favour of authority as the sole source of moral obligation also underlies the aporetic contractualist account of political power in the *De cive* and the *Leviathan* in which the author emerges as the leader and luminary of "our modern atheistic philosophers and politicians." No contract or agreement can possess any binding power whatsoever without an agent's *a priori* obligation to honour it. Towards the end of his posthumously published *Essay Concerning Eternal and Immutable Morality*, Cudworth is outspoken in the overall practical and political purpose underlying the Cambridge Platonists' staunch opposition to Hobbes' *Elements of Philosophy* (**L**). If it were not for the inherent power and activity of man's reason, there could be no foundation for either morality or politics. The Cambridge Platonists' preoccupation with the sources of authority in human conduct reveals the topical nature of their critical engagement with Hobbes's materialism and sensualism which they believed ill-equipped to provide any guidance to a nation torn by religious and civil wars. The belief in the inherent activity of the responsible agent as the source of theoretical as well as moral and political concepts also informs Cudworth's critique of Hobbes' determinism. In the posthumous *Treatise of Freewill* (**M**), he exposes the logical fallacies of his philosophical foe's theory of action. Hobbes is shown to confuse causality with necessity. While an agent possesses the power to perform an action, she may choose to abstain from doing so. Nor does the "necessity of a disjunctive proposition" render obsolete the contingency of free and responsible action. While it is necessary that one of the two events will occur, this does not by itself confer necessity upon either of them. Conway apparently commended More's refutation of atheism in the 1653 *Antidote* dedicated to her. In the 1656 *Mastix His Letter* of which she is the most likely addressee, More contrasts her negative reaction to his anti-enthusiast pamphlets with her positive estimate of his principal anti-atheist treatise: "That you wish they were as effectuall an *Antidote* against *Enthusiasme*, as That other is against *Atheisme*, it does imply that you think they are not; and I thank you for your freedome in declaring your opinion; to which I willingly subscribe" (1 [original edition, 294]). Clearly, she shared with him and the other Cambridge Platonists the defining tenets of a philosophy of religion based upon God's goodness, objective morality and human free will. However, hers is a different critique of the group's chief adversary. Like her teacher, Conway acknowledged that there were aspects common to his misguided modern philosophy and her own. In particular, in contradistinction to her teacher and the other Cambridge Platonists, she embraced a monistic ontology herself. It even makes her fend off the charge of subscribing to a variety of Hobbesian materialism herself. Her monism is not one of dead matter, but one of living spirit guided by the theological conviction that all of reality can and indeed is called upon to become more and more perfect in approximating the infinity of divine perfection itself. It is a key conviction that underlies her assumption that the member of any created species can evolve or devolve into any other created species. At the same time, her ontology of a living dynamic continuum makes her question More's critique of

Hobbes. While he is right in rejecting Hobbesian materialism, his dualism is no less deleterious to the first truth of the universal capacity for perfection than Hobbes's variety of monism.

Among the Cambridge Platonists' works on Cartesian philosophy, More's correspondence with the French philosopher himself takes pride of place. For one thing, it marked the beginning of the Cambridge Platonists' four-decade-long critical engagement with Descartes' philosophy. More's first letter in particular **(3C)**, written at the behest of the Christ's College network and meant to articulate its philosophical agenda in polished humanist Latin, contained a first rich and tightly argued outline of several of the major topics on which the major and the minor members of the group disagreed with the celebrated French philosopher. For another, More's *Four Letters to Descartes*, published in the two major editions of the Cambridge Platonist's complete works in the early 1660s and the late 1670s and continually revised in the process, was to figure prominently in all the subsequent phases of the Cambridge Platonists' engagement with the dualistic ontology and quasi-mechanistic cosmology of the French philosopher's *Principles of Philosophy* and the internalist foundationalism of his *Meditations*. More himself had first adopted tenets of Cartesian cosmology in one of the later didactic epics added to the original *Psychozoia* **(A–B)**. In the preface to the 1646 *Democritus Platonissans* **(A)**, he related how Descartes' *Principles of First Philosophy*, published two years earlier, had convinced him to give up the notion of a world of necessarily finite extension in favour of an infinitist cosmology. The creator's goodness called for an infinite creation to harbour the riches of its generous and ungrudging self-communication. It is likely that More's dense verse exposition of Cartesian cosmology helped establish his reputation as a major connoisseur of Descartes' thought on British soil **(B)**. Among its early readers was, in all likelihood, the celebrated Prussian polymath and pedagogue Samuel Hartlib, who, at that time, was already acquainted with More's Cambridge friends and colleagues Benjamin Whichcote and Ralph Cudworth and close friends John Worthington. In November 1648, Hartlib and Cudworth approached More, persuading him to write a first letter to Descartes on 11th December the same year. In a letter to Hartlib, More recalled with great candour how he had initially felt no little apprehension at the prospect of engaging in an exchange of letters with one of the age's foremost thinkers. Eventually, however, he gave in to "the importunity of friends (amongst whom I must ever reckon yourself)" and dared to write to a philosopher of "great fame": "I must confesse such is my natural rusticity and aversnesse from affecting acquaintances, and correspondencyes with men of great fame and noized partes and worth, that it was a hard task for me to dispense with the obstinacy of my own nature and disposition on this point" (Webster, "Some New Sources", 364). However, in the subsequent vivid exchange, cut short by Descartes' unexpected move to Sweden in 1649 at the invitation of Queen Christina and his subsequent illness and death the following year, More exhibited considerable aplomb in putting forward what amounted to a comprehensive critique of Descartes's dualism of thought and extension. While the first letter begins with an unusually ornate *captatio benevolentiae* in praise of the famous addressee and purports to critique only *paucula* or "minor aspects" of his system, More's five objections in reality amount to no less than a formidable onslaught upon Descartes's fundamental distinction between thought and extension, his notion of divine agency and his denial of animal souls. In answer to the perceived shortcomings of Cartesian metaphysics and physics **(C–F)**, More posited a *sui generis* spiritual extension by which God imparted motion to an extended world of indivisible atoms at will. In his reply on 5th February 1649, Descartes, while rejecting his English critic's own alternative ontology of spiritual and material extensions, duly acknowledged the general astuteness of his objections. Descartes' favourable reaction encouraged More to send him another letter dated 5th March. Building upon his earlier critique, More rejected the concept of a transfer of motion or a mode from one body or substance to another as impossible on logical grounds. Instead, he restated in concise prose the early panpsychist cosmology of his philosophical poetry, attributing to every body a rudimentary form of life and a capacity for self-motion. The French philosopher replied in a letter of 15th April and he may well have started writing a reply to another set of objections in More's third letter of 23rd July in late August before he accepted the invitation of Queen Christina and began preparations for his move to Sweden. Understandably, More was taken aback by the expected interruption of the correspondence caused by Descartes' move to Stockholm. And, not surprisingly, he was devastated by the news of the philosopher's untimely death shortly afterwards which appeared to spell the inevitable end of their exchange.

However, More's *Four Letters to René Descartes* continued to be the major reference text both in his own and in his students' Cartesian writings of the 1650s, which marked the extraordinarily fertile second phase of the Cambridge Platonists' critical engagement with the French philosopher. More himself not only composed a major trilogy of works which bore the unmistakeable imprint of Cartesian rational theology, but he also engaged in fruitful discussions with two of his most gifted students. When her half-brother John Finch, a student and friend of his, left for Europe in 1651, he began tutoring Anne Conway in philosophy, using his own English translation of Descartes's *Principles* produced for that purpose. Conway immediately proved a student with an extraordinary independence of mind who did not shrink from questioning key tenets of her teacher's own philosophy. Among the Cartesian topics **(G–H)** discussed was the ontological proof of God's existence which Conway apparently rejected on the grounds that it inevitable proved any substance qualified by a predicate in the superlative. Her critique was also directed at the critique raised in the first of More's *Four Letters*. Of the five *paucula*, the distinction between the creator's infinity and creation's indefinite extent was of particular concern to More's circle of followers and friends. Conway embraced the fourth and followed More in rejecting Descartes's concept of the *indefinite* which they both concurred in viewing as an undue argumentative evasion from the question of the world's finiteness. However, she sided with the French philosopher against her tutor in rejecting the second *pauculum* of the vacuum. There could, on her deeply held philosophical convictions, be no void in which there was no interaction between the infinitely good and wise creator and his infinitely many creatures destined to share in his fullness. More, on the other hand, was at pains to eschew the infinity of matter which he believed to be a necessary corollary of the denial of empty space. If there were to be no void, infinity and necessity existence would inevitably have to be attributed to a matter which would acquire attributes specific to God alone. Whereas More's original critique of Descartes' philosophy in the *Four Letters* bore chiefly upon the ontology of Descartes's *Principles of Philosophy*, notably his variety of dualism of extended matter and unextended mind, Rust's anti-Calvinist and anti-Cartesian 1651 sermon *Discourse of Truth*, delivered a second time in 1655 and subsequently supplemented by his 1658 *God is Love* homily, was the first Cambridge Platonist treatise to subject the epistemology of the *Meditations* to detailed critique **(I–J)**. Rust exposed the circular nature of Descartes' attempt to overcome the spectre of an "evil demon" and to ground *clare et distincte* knowledge in the proof of the existence of an all-perfect God who as such was unable to deceive the I of the *cogito*. However, the inference of God's veracity from his supreme perfection clearly presupposes the very reliability of the soul's faculties which the argument sets out to establish. Instead of the *cogito*, Rust, in self-consciously foundationalist language, posits divine goodness as the "grand and fundamental truth" upon which to base all knowledge. This superior "fundamental truth" of Christian rationalism is unhampered by any circularity. It rules out as a matter of metaphysical principle the possibility of a human mind created with fundamentally flawed epistemic powers. Instead, the finite created mind is shown to participate in God's infinite uncreated intellect in it its every act of clear and distinct cognition. The absolute divine infinity in which it participates in the process is that of the creator's qualitative goodness by which he is obliged to give life to a creation of the (relative) infinity of all conceptually possible beings which are capable of participating in his fullness without inevitably doing harm to their fellow creatures. Not only did More, in the 1650s, tutor his students, most notably Conway and Rust, in Cartesian philosophy but he also produced two of his most Cartesian works in 1653, when he published his Genesis commentary *Conjectura Cabbalistica* and the *Antidote against Atheism* (to which he went on to add a substantive *Appendix* in 1655) **(K)**. His own version of Descartes' ontological argument of the *Antidote*, which he may well have put forward in reply to Conway's critique of Descartes's *Fifth Meditation*, and the Cartesian vortex cosmology of the *Conjectura Cabbalistica*, upon which More bestowed the honour of Mosaic pedigree, bear impressive testimony to his abiding interest in Cartesian metaphysics and physics. Given his own and his students' uninterrupted work on Cartesian physics and metaphysics, More was not entirely honest when he told Claude Clerselier, the editor of Descartes's letters, who approached him in 1654, that his interest in the French philosopher's thought had waned after the celebrated philosopher's unexpected death in 1650. Clerselier asked him for his copies both of his own objections and Descartes' replies to include them in his edition of the French philosopher's correspondence. More answered only on 13th May 1655. Apologizing profusely for the delay, he related that Clerselier's letter had reached him only on 15th April of that year, when, for health reasons, he had not been in Cambridge, but in the countryside of his hometown of Grantham. He applauded Clerselier's editorial project, even expressing hope that a publication of his own letters in that forthcoming edition might lead Cartesians of the day to respond to his queries left unanswered by the master himself. Above all, Clerselier sent More both the "inventory of Stockholm", a list of Descartes' works left in Chenut's house in Stockholm, where the philosopher had died. Most importantly, he forwarded to More a brief two-page fragment of a third Descartes letter to him of which, he had hoped, More might possess and share with him a complete copy. Surprisingly given his earlier high opinion of his young English correspondent, Descartes's fragmentary letter is overall dismissive of More's thought and scathing in tone. It culminates in an impatient rejection of his speculations on angels and demons and his flirtations with panpsychism as "downright amusing" (Op. omn. II/2, 268). More wrote a response to the fragment **(L)** which he included in a letter to Clerselier, defending his original metaphor of the world as a "shadow" of God's own perfect life with which every body, however minute, shared the fundamental capacity for self-motion. More's answer does not signal a break with Descartes. The philosophical substance of his cosmological sketch is recognizably that of his earlier panpsychist ontology with its occasionalist concept of causality.

Only in 1659, when he published his principal philosophical prose work *The Immortality of the Soul*, did More reject his monism of life in favour of a dualism of living spirit and dead matter. The 1660s marked the third stage in the Cambridge Platonists' critical appropriation of Cartesian thought. In the preface to his 1662 *Collection of Several Philosophical Writings*, More explicitly referenced the "Catalogue of what Writings Cartesius had left behind him". Nor, apparently, had the later philosopher's scorn expressed in the letter fragment taken away from the high esteem in which he continued to hold the French rationalist. Instead, More cited with approval Descartes's early exercise on Prov. 1:7 as yet another piece of evidence for the close elective affinity between him and the French philosopher. Among the *Several Philosophical Writings* included in his *Collection* is an edition of the *Four Letters* which now included Descartes's "Fragment" and More's "Response" as well as the letters exchanged with Clerselier. In addition, this new edition was supplemented by another letter on Cartesianism entitled *Epistola ad V.C.*, advertised in the *Correspondence*'s table of contents as "a defence of Descartes" and "an introduction to the whole of Cartesian philosophy" (Op. omn. II/2, 229). While the inclusion of a letter addressed to a different (anonymous) recipient in an exchange of letters between More and Descartes may at first seem odd, the explanations for Cartesian errors provided in the *Epistola ad V.C.* are evidently intended by the author to be read as a commentary on those exposed in his original *Epistolae Quatuor ad Renatum Des-Cartes*. Descartes's identification of matter and extension may well be attributed to his predilection for mathematics which falsely led him to reduce living nature to operations within a Cartesian coordinate system. Still, Descartes, for all his errors, must be credited with a compelling account of a cosmogony of bodies initially endowed with motion and following mechanistic laws inserted into them by the creator God. Towards the end of the decade, More coined the concept of "nullibism" to denigrate the Cartesian denial of spiritual extension as inevitably equalling atheism **(P)**. Besides a substantially enlarged edition of his original *Four Letters* and the anti-Cartesian chapters of his *Enchiridium Metaphysicum* published and written in the early and the later years of the decade respectively, the 1660s saw a first powerful response to More's list of critical *paucula* detailed in the first of the *Four Letters*. When Cudworth composed his massive *True Intellectual System of the Universe* sometime in the course of that decade, he rejected in detailed argument major aspects of his friend and fellow Platonist's critique of Cartesianism, most notably that of More's signal doctrine of spiritual extension **(Q–U)**. There is no record of how the second major Platonist came to know and appreciate Descartes's thought. However, as is clear from the fact that he followed Hartlib in repeatedly encouraging an initially reluctant More to approach Descartes and engage in an intellectual exchange with him on behalf of the Prussian polymath's and their own shared Cambridge Platonist networks, Cudworth must have begun studying his *Principles* and his *Meditations* at about the same time as More. Nor can there be any doubt that he engaged in discussions with More himself and with their common friends and followers at Christ's College and at Ragley Hall, including Rust. While neither mentioning his fellow Cambridge Platonist by name nor quoting verbatim any of the anti-Cartesian passages in his early and mature writings, Cudworth clearly took exception to More's critique of Descartes in the early *Four Letters*. Despite his attempts at respectful anonymity, the Cartesian passages of Cudworth's *System* document an ongoing controversial exchange between them about a proper Platonist reading of the first principles of Cartesian philosophy. In ontology, Cudworth first pretends to waver between leaving open the question of the (divine and human) mind's extension or defending a holenmerist account of its formative presence in the world and the body from More's charges of nullibist atheism. However, his sympathies clearly lay not with More's idiosyncratic concept of spiritual extension, but with the time-honoured Neoplatonist and scholastic holenmerist one of a spirit being present in its body's every part in its indivisible entirety. Cudworth had More's anti-Cartesian concept of nullibism in mind when he sought to allay his reader's fear "that whatsoever doth not take up *Space*, and is in no *Place*, is *Nothing*." He even invoked the authority of Origen as a particularly able "Asserter of Incorporeal Substance" who rejected all anthropormorphic conceptions along the lines of More's spiritual extension. At the same time, Cudworth was careful to lay out his own philosophical concern which was not so much with the opposition between extension and inextension, but that between activity and inactivity. Spirit is defined not as static being, but as dynamic action. They are "*Substantial Powers, Vigours*, and *Activities*; which though they act upon *Bulk* and *Extension*, yet are themselves *Unbulkie* and devoid of *Quantity* and *Dimensions*". As well as rejecting More's anti-Cartesian incorporealism, Cudworth defended Descartes's concept of the *indefinite*, one of the original *paucula* criticised in the *Four Letters*. Without quoting the critical remarks in the *Four Letters* which he sought to rebut, Cudworth adopted the notion of the indefinite extension of nature. Creation, including time and space, is of indefinite *quantitative* extension. As such, it by definition admits of the "*Addition of Finites*, never making up *Infinite*". Actual infinity is ruled out as a contradiction in terms. Instead, Cudworth closely follows Descartes in replacing it with qualitative perfection. The infinity predicated of the creator refers to the supreme perfection of each of the "*Substantial Powers, Vigours*, and *Activities*" by which the most perfect divine being is defined. However, his infinite or perfect power is such that it is bounded by his supreme moral and intellectual perfection. It is on the basis of the Cambridge Platonists' general animus against voluntarism in religion and philosophy that Cudworth singles out for critique Descartes's doctrine of created eternal truth which the latter had laid out in his correspondence with

Marin Mersenne. If God's will were to be the source of the truths contained in his intellect, his own knowledge would be subject to future arbitrary changes of mind. It would, therefore, lack the conceptual necessity by which knowledge is defined and, hence, inevitably cease to be knowledge at all. As the 1660s drew to a close, More provided both a rich literary account of the Cambridge Platonists' collaborative engagement with Descartes' philosophy and a concise précis of his own two major misgivings about Cartesianism (**M–O**). At the 1668 *Divine Dialogue*'s lavish estate, an obvious stand-in for Ragley Hall, Philotheus lectures his friends, who all bear labelling names denoting their piety or philosophical affiliation, about the extension of spirit and motion as a *vis agitans* inherent to all created finite substance. As in the original correspondence with Descartes, More was adamant that motion was not a reciprocal relationship between bodies which remained extraneous to the mobile and the immobile body alike, but an intrinsic force defining of a substance's being. Its inner power is such that it gradually guides each and every creature towards the end inscribed into its very essence by its supremely benign creator. In the preface to the 1669 second edition of his *Enchiridium Ethicum*, More detailed his two-part rationale for his opposition to the celebrated French philosopher, i.e. the necessary existence of indefinite material extension and the denial of final causation. More opposed to the twin errors of Cartesianism his own doctrine of the infinity of God's spatial extension which encompassed a finite reality endowed with life and guided not solely or even predominantly by efficient, but by final causation. Whereas he had originally been prepared to acknowledge the existence of inanimate beings driven exclusively by efficient causation, he now believed that the principle of parsimony required that in reality none was exempt from the final causation exercised by the spirit of nature at the behest of an infinitely good Deity.

The 1670s marked a final phase of Cambridge Cartesianism, ushered in by Cudworth's *True Intellectual System* which was given its *imprimatur* in 1671 and by More's *Enchiridium Metaphysicum* which was published that same year. Both Cudworth and More continued to engage with Descartes's thought. Cudworth expanded significantly upon More's own and Rust's critique of Descartes's internalist project, viewing the *clare et distincte* as the defining feature of man's epistemic powers which was neither capable nor in need of any grounding in a proof of the necessary existence of a perfectly veracious God. Instead, "clear intelligibility" is the essence of the truths comprised in the eternal divine intellect in which man comes to share in *clare et distincte* knowledge (**V**). While More had expressed his animus against the Cartesianism of his day in the anti-nullibist polemics of the closing chapters of his 1671 *Enchiridium Metaphysicum*, he was nevertheless careful to distinguish between the well-meaning, albeit problematic or aporetic, theism of Descartes and the outright atheism of many of his contemporary followers in England, France and the Netherlands (**Y–Z**). While he viewed Descartes' "nullibism" or the denial of extension and place to spirit as a chief source of a particularly potent variety of contemporary atheism, he exempted Descartes himself from that charge. In the *scholia* on the *Epistola ad V.C.*, he commented on Descartes's fragmentary third letter in which, despite his continual protestations to the contrary, he came close to acknowledging the existence of a created substance by which God imparts motion to creation. In the *scholia* on the *Quatuor Epistolae*, More even attributed to Descartes his own notion of spiritual extension with which he now found himself in astonishing agreement. However, while More restated his original critique in the more polemic parts of the 1671 *Enchiridium* and in a few places of *Scholia* written sometime between 1675 and 1679, it was in his pupil Conway's *Principia* that his original critique was given a full systematic expression in the middle of the final decade of the Cambridge Platonists' engagement with Descartes' *Principles* and *Meditations* (**W–X**). Conway's is a system based upon the qualitative infinity of the creator's goodness by which he is compelled to give life to a strict quantitative infinity of creatures. As well as being infinite in number, the creatures proceeding from the creator's own fullness are all composed of infinitely many creatures themselves. Each of Conway's living beings is endowed with vital self-motion which it exercises in unison with all the others so as to fulfil the supreme end of its nature in acquiring an ever-growing participation in the divine fullness. Despite some shared terminology, hers, clearly, is not a Cartesian system, but a restatement of More's early anti-Cartesian panpsychism with its stress upon self-motion as the defining feature of all living substance. In a nod to her teacher, her treatise ends with an outline of More's occasionalist theory of causation which Descartes had rejected as "downright amusing".

From first to last, the Cambridge Platonists' chief philosophical concern is with a supremely benign Deity who is not removed from, but suffuses all of visible reality, guiding it towards fulfilment in the contemplation of his riches. It is a concern which also informs their reception of another major figure of early modern intellectual history, i.e. the Lusatian philosopher mystic Jacob Böhme. In a seminal 1660 vision in Görlitz, Böhme had come to reject the transcendent Deity of traditional Christian belief, instead embracing one immanent to and coextensive with nature. His is a dynamic view of God who is composed of seven principles or "source spirits", each of which marks a stage of a theogonic process occurring at all places at all times. The Deity is originally an abyss or a chaotic all-oneness longing for vision and comprehension acquired in the interaction of the source spirits of which he is composed. From the Father's contradictory attractive and expulsive powers emerges a violent fiery tension which erupts in the light of the Son in which God acquires self-knowledge and self-love. Their loving union is that of the Holy Spirit in which the angels and, subsequently, nature and man participate. The Cambridge Platonists' reception of the German cobbler visionary's hugely influential theosophical system with its pioneering early modern notion of God as the contradictory power of life is documented, above all, in More's multifaceted literary production on the subject. However, More never leaves any doubt about the seminal influence which his sprawling network of friends, followers and fellow philosophers exerted upon his numerous conflicting accounts of the Teutonic Philosopher. His four-decade engagement with Jacob Böhme, which culminated in a book-length *Critique of the Teutonic Philosophy*, unfolded in an astounding variety of divine dialogues.

A first stage in the late 1640s and early 1650s coincided with the beginnings of Radical Behmenism which flourished from that time onwards. John Sparrow, Böhme's "foremost English translator" (Ariel Hessayon, title), and his associates undertook the Herculean labour of translating all of the German master's voluminous writings into English. They were also vocal in their political commitment to the cobbler mystic's sublime vision of a God immanent in universal nature and in the individual soul alike. The Teutonic philosophy which they helped disseminate in translations and treatises was believed by them to be an instrument of providence by which God sought to reconcile the warring factions of British Christendom. More's first fleeting interest in the Teutonic Philosopher was kindled at a first major Behmenist moment in English theology, when his Cambridge friend Charles Hotham, the foremost Radical Behmenist philosopher of the day, advertised with considerable daring the circle's translation of the Lusatian master's works at a public Tripos event at the University of Cambridge in 1646. He went on to publish his dissertation in its original Latin in 1648 and in an English translation in 1650, asking More to contribute a commendatory poem. While More did oblige his friend's request, his lacklustre Latin dedicatory verse to the 1648 *Manuductio* amounted to little more than a flimsy excuse for his headstrong refusal to take Böhme seriously as a philosopher. His reluctance to engage in a close study of his friend's *Manuductio* is all the more perplexing given its significance both as a pioneering work of British Behmenism and as a major metaphysical treatise in its own right. Hotham subscribes to a traducianist view of a child's soul coming into existence in biological procreation. His rational psychology hinges upon a panpsychist philosophy of nature deeply steeped in Böhme's cosmic theogony. It envisages a world "full of radiant life, and as throughly furnisht with possibilities of propagation into thousands of thousands in its own kinde, as that childe of the drossie Earth, the Brutall spirit, is fruitful in his kinde" (*Manuductio*, 8–9 = *Introduction*, 15). In technical vocabulary clearly indebted to More's early Cartesian writings, most notably his holenmist concept of divine infinity and ubiquity, Hotham views the animate world as "an infinite immeasurable space, in every imaginable point whereof dwelt the whole Deity" (ibid., 20–21 = ibid., *Introduction*, 33). While More continued to ignore Charles Hotham's treatise, he apparently read with great care and interest the younger Hotham brother Durand's 1656 *Life of Jacob Boehme*. Alongside Böhme's youthful chef-d'oeuvre *Aurora*, published in John Sparrow's English translation in the same year, Durand Hotham's biography was instrumental in piquing his serious interest in the saintlike cobbler philosopher. Hotham's *Life* depicts Jacob Böhme as the embodiment of an "equal, humane, sociable principle" (Hotham, *Life* [7])" above reason by which God, in Böhme's English follower's own day, seeks to redeem fallen humankind and war-riven British Christendom. Intrigued by Hotham's biographical account, More began studying Böhme in the mid-1650s, which mark a second phase of Cambridge Behmenism. The first literary account of Behmenism to emerge from More's critical engagement with the German mystic and his English followers is a brief refutation of alchemistic pantheism in his 1656 anti-sectarian handbook *Enthusiasmus Triumphatus* **(4A)**. While it is overly terse and even fails to mention the Teutonic Philosopher by name, More's doxographic account of a pantheism of divine feeling is not without philosophical interest. It betokens a first fascination with Böhme whose *Aurora*, translated by Sparrow in the same year, More apparently chose to read on learning about the mystic's saintlike life from Hotham's biography. The most important work to hail from this second period of More's engagement with Böhme is *Mastix His Letter* **(B)** appended to the *Enthusiasmus Triumphatus* in the same year. It contains two chapters solely devoted to the Teutonic Philosopher. In a remarkable partial retraction of the earlier critique levelled against his enthusiasm and alchemistic pantheism, More is now prepared to set him apart from all other major enthusiasts of his day. It is with sincere admiration that he acknowledges the "sanctity of the Man", noting with special approval his unwavering loyalty to the Protestant church even amidst persecution at the hands of the higher Görlitz clergy. Even more importantly, given the extraordinary sanctity which Böhme exhibited in his saintlike life, More no longer rejects his metaphysics of a cosmic Deity *tout court*, but finds words of guarded praised for the "vigour of his Phansie: Which", for all the shortcomings of the vision of God to which it inevitably gave rise, "being so well qualified with holinesse and sanctity, proved not unsuccsessfull." The seeds of a more positive reading of the Teutonic philosophy of which there is ample evidence in the two chapters devoted to its author in the 1656 *Mastix His Letter* came to fruition in two lengthy treatises on the subject composed a decade later.

In the second half of the 1660s, which mark the third phase of his engagement with the Teutonic Philosopher, More exchanged several long letters on Böhme with John Worthington and Anne Conway, two of his closest associates and friends. His *Divine Dialogues* about the flourishing of radical religion of the Behmenist stamp in Restoration England provide a literary account of More's Behmenist discussions. The centre of the most fertile quinquennium of More's engagement with Böhme was Ragley Hall, the estate of the politically influential noble Conway family in Warwickshire. Lord Conway's wife Anne was the addressee of the "Epistle about Ja. Beh." originally written at her entreaty in 1667/1668 and published in the second volume of the 1679 *Opera omnia* in a substantially enlarged Latin translation entitled *Critique of the Teutonic Philosophy. A Private Letter to a Friend*. Worthington reports that More had his "ears full of Behmenism" at Ragley Hall at that time (*Diary and Correspondence*, II/2, 287). As we learn from the same letter, he had by then acquired a complete edition of the English works of the Teutonic Philosopher which undoubtedly provided the foundation for the extended debates at Ragley Hall: "I sent several times to enquire of your return, but could not hear of it, till I received yours. I believe, you had your ears full of Behmenism at Ragley; for when I was at London, I met with one, who was to buy all Jacob Behmen's works, to send thither" (Worthington, ibid., II/2, 287). More's deeply Platonist *Divine Dialogues* of 1666 and

1668 pay tribute to "*Ragley*, and its Woods" eulogized in heartfelt literary *locus amoenus* tropes as a "little Arbour stored with such choice Guests" or "free Spirits" as Anne Conway and her half-brother John Finch as well as other fellow Platonists like Cudworth, Rust and Glanvill with whom More enjoyed "the liberty of Philosophizing without any breach of Friendship" over a cup of wine (*Divine Dialogues*, 1,2 [Second edition, 5–6]). Strikingly, in the preface, More does not hesitate to list the Behmenists alongside the Platonists and Cartesians as three major contemporary sects of Christian philosophers whom he is about to subject to critique in the subsequent work **(C)**. In the fifth *Divine Dialogue*, which, alongside the fourth, was published in 1666 prior to the first three, More provides a vivid literary account of the debates about Böhme at Ragley Hall **(D)**. His interlocutors concur in their critique of the Teutonic Philosopher's melancholy enthusiasm. Drawing upon his earlier enquiry into the causes of religious delusion in his *Enthusiasmus Triumphatus*, More continues to view Böhme as "a very serious and well-minded Man, but of a nature extremely melancholick". At the same time, however, Böhme's metaphysical acumen is now duly acknowledged. Even more importantly, More is prepared to follow the contemporary Radical Behmenists in according Böhme a pivotal providential role. His religion of an interior Christ saving the soul from within and transforming it into his likeness through its own autonomous moral agency is praised by the Ragley Behmenists as God's providential means by which he seeks to rid the war-riven British Isles from the yoke of a religion of merely external liturgical pomp in the present painful "trials of Mens spirits": "For at present, by a kind of oblique stroke, God does notable execution upon the dead Formality and Carnality of Christendom by these zealous Evangelists of an *internal* Saviour". More's substantive epistolary treatise, originally entitled "Epistle about Ja. Beh." (Worthington, *Diary and Correspondence*, II/2 294) and privately circulated among friends, grew from his committed Ragley group's extended discussions about Böhme and about Revolutionary and Restoration enthusiasm and his correspondence with Worthington and Conway on that subject. Probably sometime in 1665 or early 1666, when her life-long sickness finally granted her some brief respite, Conway approached her friend and mentor and posed to him the five "questions" which he went on to answer in the original English "Letter about Ja. Beh." of 1666/7. The first three of the five questions answered in More's principal work on Böhme's life and work are epistemological in nature and deal with the distinction between true and false religious knowledge **(E)**. Whereas true knowledge is derived from the soul's boniform vision, false knowledge originates in its enthusiastic imagination. Böhme's practical philosophy of the soul's new birth in humility is shown to be derived from boniform vision and, hence, infallibly true. By contrast, his theoretical metaphysics is largely marred by his vigorous imagination which time and again led him astray. As a consequence, he projected his own spiritual anguish prior to and his exuberant joy upon his 1660 vision of God onto a Trinity undergoing change from the Father or as yet desolate matter to the Son or spirit capable of feeling and thought. On a more charitable reading, however, Böhme emerges as a panpsychist, rather than a materialist. The lengthy fourth "question" is devoted to the distinction between Behmenist and Platonist ontology. It is unique in More's substantial corpus of anti-enthusiastic writings in that Böhme's is the only materialism of the enthusiast variety which he did not simply reject out of hand. Instead, following Conway's entreaty, he goes to considerable lengths to provide a translation of Böhme's vision of a cosmic Deity into his own time-honoured ancient theology **(F–H)**. Böhme's theogonic account of an abyss acquiring feeling and thought in the interaction of atoms given life and form by the spirit of nature may be read as a theistic cosmology of unmistakably panpsychist stamp. To this end, More adds to his own Platonist system the novel hypostasis of a "world soul". It designates a material world gradually gaining more complex mental characteristics and even serving God as his "register" duly recording his dealings with man. The deletion of the central Christological source spirit from Böhme's seven-principle theogonic scheme enables his Platonist interpreter to translate the cosmic vision of a natural deity into an account of a God who is at once transcendent and immanent to all of reality. As "Trinity of pure divinity", God is beyond the created cosmos, defined as the "supreme good" which encompasses in itself the fullness of forms as "eternal intellect" and which chooses to share it with creation as "Divine Soul". Conversely, as "trinity of universal nature", the "abyss of physical monads" is endowed with living forms by "the spirit of nature", thereby gradually becoming a "world soul". Combined they make up the one God. It is impressive testimony to the grudging admiration which he had come to feel for the Teutonic Philosopher that More, when preparing his magisterial three-volume *Opera Omnia* (1675–1679) for print, chose to translate his originally private "Epistle about Ja. Böh." to Conway into Latin, the academic vernacular of the European republic of letters.

The final phase of More's Behmenism extended from the mid- to the late 1670s, when the nobleman John Cockshute acted as his Maecenas, funding the major enterprise of a Latin translation of More's principal writings. Retitled *Philosophiae Teutonicae Censura*, More's principal work on Böhme was first published in the *Opera omnia*. As we learn from the later additions to the work and the correspondence with Worthington, Conway and several other close associates and friends, More translated his private letter on the subject in answer to the growing success of the Quakers and other sects in his day. It was at the time of the work's translation that More noted with increasing concern both Conway's growing sympathies for the Society of Friends, to which she eventually converted, and the real threat of Quaker rebellion against the Church and the Crown. In the process, somewhat paradoxically, More's admiration for the shoemaker philosopher from Görlitz reached its apogee. Not only was Böhme a precursor of his own political and ecclesiastical latitudinarianism, but he even matched the most celebrated of early modern philosophers in the depth of his speculative vision of divine nature. Besides translating his *Private Letter to A Friend* into Latin, More added to the original work a biographical *Praefatio ad lectores* **(I)** and a political *Conclusio* **(J–K)** in which he credited him with boniform insight into God and with a political latitudinarianism conspicuously close to that of the Cambridge Platonists in its blend of millenarianism and Origenian universalism. In addition, he discussed the intent and purpose of the original work in the *praefatio generalissima* and added several *scholia* **(J)** which are of considerable historical and philosophical interest. More implicitly acknowledges the extent to which he had fallen under the spell of Böhme, retracting several crucial aspects of his earlier Platonist reading of Böhme, notably the identification of God with the trinity of divinity and nature. His chief argument for a stricter distinction between the creator and creation is one dealt with in great detail in his critique of Baruch de Spinoza, i.e. the "holiness of the divine majesty", which must on no account be compromised by implicating God in the woes and evils of the visible world. Far from viewing Böhme as an amateurish alchemist philosopher led astray by the vigour of a rampant imagination, as he had originally assumed in the late 1640s and the 1650s, More now confers upon him the honorary epithet of a Christian Neoplatonist. He even enlists his aid against that new formidable enthusiast-atheist threat to Christian religion, i.e. the Dutch rationalist Baruch de Spinoza. The holiness of God, defined in terms of his supreme moral perfection exercised in his disinterested self-communication in creation and salvation, is the major theme of More's trilogy of writings directed against the Spinoza.

Ralph Cudworth was the first of the Cambridge Platonists to respond in print to Baruch de Spinoza's monistic system clearly presupposed in the critique of biblical hermeneutics and politics in the *Tractatus Theologicus-Politicus* published anonymously in 1670. Henry More followed suit and, while praising Cudworth's pioneering effort, expanded significantly upon the critical notes on Spinoza's denial of miracles and his panpsychistic variety of atheism in his friend's *True Intellectual System of the Universe*. There are only a handful of references to Spinoza in Cudworth's massive work, published in 1678, but finished in 1671, when it was given its *imprimatur*. In a brief remark, Cudworth alludes to the title of the Dutch rationalist's *Theological-Political Treatise* of 1670, dismissing as slight and insubstantial the critique which "that late Theological Politician" had levelled at the notion of miraculous divine intervention in that work **(5A)**. Of more philosophical significance are Cudworth's detailed refutations of the so-called "hylozoist" variety of atheism in his principal work **(B–D)**. "Hylozoism", one of several philosophical neologisms of Cudworth's own coinage, designates one of only four conceptually possible varieties of atheism in total. The two materialist atheisms of Democritic or "atomist" and the Anaximandrian or "hylopathian" stamp trace all life back to matter and its qualities respectively. By contrast, the two panpsychistic varieties, i.e. Strato's hylozoism and the Stoics' cosmo-plasticism, posit life as a defining feature either of each part or of the whole of matter, thereby rendering obsolete the theistic notion of a superior "mind senior to the world" (*True Intellectual System*, 736). Cudworth ascribes this erroneous doctrine to a major representative of ancient thought. Strato of Lampsacus, successor to Theophrastus as head of Aristotle's Lyceaum in the first half of the 3rd century AD and a "natural philosopher" (*physicus*) of considerable renown, was the first to subscribe to the erroneous doctrine of living matter. However, as is clear from the author's own ominous remark that "*Strato's Ghost* had begun *to walk* of late" (Cudworth, *True Intellectual System*, 145), his critique of panpsychism was directed against contemporary systems of philosophy, notably the 1672 *Tractatus de natura substantiae energetica, sive de vita naturae* of the English physician philosopher Francis Glisson and the 1670 *Tractatus* (and, probably, if Cudworth had access to the unpublished manuscript or added passages for the eventual 1678 publication, the 1677 *Ethica*) of the Dutch rationalist Baruch de Spinoza. His critical expositions of hylozoism are placed in different parts of his *opus magnum*. Both his brief critical remark of Spinoza's *Tractatus* **(A)** and his pioneering first formulation of the combination problem are to be found in the unpolished draft-like fifth chapter **(B)**. The main body of his critique of Spinoza and Glisson **(C–D)** is part of his carefully structured survey of the four principal varieties of atheism. It is testimony to Cudworth's acute awareness of how formidable a threat Spinoza's panpsychism posed to his cause of a Christian philosophy of religion that he viewed it as the most well-argued atheism besides Hobbes's materialism. Cudworth's estimate was shared by his fellow Cambridge Platonist Henry More.

More's first acquaintance with Spinoza is likely to go back to 1671, when he first mentioned him in his correspondence. In a letter to Robert Doyle, possibly dating from 4th December 1671, More relates how a friend, probably the Dutch Remonstrant Philippus van Limborch, who was instrumental in introducing the work of the Dutch rationalist in England, told him "that *Spinoza*, a *Jew* first, after a *Cartesian*, and now an atheist, is supposed the author of *Theologico-Politicus*" (*Conway Letters*, 519). In the same year, van Limborch also warned Oliver Doiley, another Cambridge divine, of Spinoza's controversial critique of revealed religion. It is probable that in a letter to van Limborch of 1675, Henry Jenkes, a Fellow of Gonville and Caius College and a friend of More's, had the Cambridge Platonists (or perhaps even More in particular) in mind when mentioning "Pious Readers and True Christians" opposed to Spinoza's execrable teachings (Colie, *Light and Enlightenment*, 96). The Dutchman van Limborch and the Cambridge men Doiley and Jenkes may have been the "highly gifted men" mentioned in the introductory chapter of More's *Ad V.C. epistola altera* who had for some time been "persistently" entreating him to write a refutation of the *Tractatus* (epist. alt. 1 [*Opera omnia* II/1,565]). Only in 1677, however, did More finally decide to give in to his European and English friends' earnest entreaties and write the first major book-length refutation of Spinoza in the English tongue. At that time, the Flemish polymath Francis Mercury van Helmont (1614–1698), a common friend of More's and his heroine pupil Anne Conway, gave him a copy of *The Secrets of Atheism Revealed* by the Dutch Collegiant Frans Kuyper, a refutation of Spinoza's *Theological-Political Treatise*. While having the collection of loose sheets bound by the bookbinder, More chose to read Spinoza's original work. Realizing how menacing an atheist onslaught upon rational Christian religion it contained, he proceeded to provide an in-depth refutation of both Spinoza's original rationalist work and Kuyper's fideist rebuttal. There can be no doubt that the common "friend in Holland" (*Conway Letter*, 429) was indeed the Dutch Remonstrant Philipp van Limborch mentioned in a letter and that van Helmont himself was the anonymous V.C. or *vir clarissimus* to whom More's refutation of Spinoza was originally addressed.

From the outset, therefore, the Cambridge Platonists' engagement with Spinoza's hylozoism unfolded against the backdrop of a European network which included major Flemish, Dutch and English thinkers. More in particular wrote his trilogy of anti-Spinozist works in response to two closely linked controversies in early modern European intellectual history. The first of these debates centred around the reception of Jacob Böhme and the Cabbalah. More's anti-Spinozist writings are tied closely to his discussions with Francis Mercury van Helmont Not only did van Helmont acquaint him with Spinoza in the first place, but he was also at the centre of a network at the Conways' estate at Ragley where More engaged in debates about rational and radical religion of which he furnished vivid accounts in his correspondence and in his *Divine Dialogues*. The three late anti-Spinozist writings both postdate and build upon his earlier critiques of Jacob Böhme's theosophy and Isaac Luria's Cabbala in his *Censura Philosophiae Teutonicae* and a series of Kabbalistic commentaries which he contributed to Christian Knorr von Rosenroth's magisterial textbook *Kabbala Denudata* (1677–1684). Of even greater significance to that late body of polemical writings is a second major European controversy. The Englishman More's Latin *Epistola altera*, as is clear from his critique of the volatile Dutch Remonstrant turned Socinian turned Collegiant Frans Kuyper (1629–1691), was written against the backdrop of the Dutch Bredenburg Controversy raging over Spinoza's *Theological-Political Treatise* at that time. While a book of scandal raising an outcry in all of European Christendom right after its anonymous publication in 1670, the debate in the Netherlands was particularly vitriolic. Published in 1676, the *Secreta Atheismi Revelata* by Kuyper, against which More originally reacts in his first anti-Spinozist work, was directed as much against Johannes Bredenburg's *Enervatio Tractatus Theologico-Politici* of 1675 as it was against Spinoza's original work. The Amsterdam wine merchant Jan or Johannes Bredenburg (1643–1691), after whom the increasingly acerbic Disputes were named, was an important member of the Dutch Collegiant movement. The Collegiants were a group of Christians who, prizing the inner light and the spirit of free and amicable enquiry over dogma, were originally renowned for their religious toleration. Spinoza himself had entertained close ties to the Collegiant movement and his friends Jarig Jelles and Pieter Balling, in the 1650s, were figureheads of a radically rationalist group in its midst. It was Bredenburg's anti-Spinozist work *Enervatio Tractatus Theologico-Politici* of 1675 that ignited the bitter conflict within the liberal Christian group of which he and Kuyper were the major representatives. In that work, Bredenburg provided an exposition of Spinoza's system which he believed to underlie the critique of revealed religion in the *Tractatus*. Despite his best of efforts, however, the author soon proved a "Rotterdam Collegiant under the Spell of Spinoza" (van Bunge, *Johannes Bredenburg*, title) as he had to admit to having failed to expose any *non sequitur* that could undermine Spinoza's naturalist and determinist philosophy of *Deus sive natura*. Not surprisingly, Bredenburg's *de facto* concession that Spinoza's philosophy was irrefutable made him the subject of scathing critique by his chief foe within the Collegiant community, Frans Kuyper whose intensely polemical pamphlet *Den Philosoperenden Boer* of 1676, co-written with a like-minded friend, was the first of many works to accuse him of being a Spinozist and atheist himself. Kuyper's own solution envisaged a fideism that denied reason any role in religious matters apart from a purely philological enquiry into the Holy Writ along Socinian lines. Bredenburg's own radical solution hinged on a theory of double truth, one philosophical, one religious, which, in turn, was to evoke the ire of van Limborch in the mid-1680s of which their celebrated exchange of letters, published in Rotterdam in 1686, provided ample evidence. Considering the European significance attaching to the Dutch Bredenburg debates, it is not surprising that van Helmont, given his and More's joint work on Böhme and the Cabbala at Christ's College and at Ragley Hall, should have taken a keen interest in his friend's view about Kuyper and Spinoza. Likewise, there was an extended correspondence between Cudworth and the Remonstrants around van Limborch and Jean LeClerc with whom the two most influential Cambridge Platonists felt a close elective affinity in their deepest-held philosophical and political convictions. It was a natural choice for the English and Dutch liberal theologian to join forces in combatting both in the atheist Spinoza's naturalism and his misguided Dutch opponents' fideism.

Like Cudworth and van Limborch, More's attitude towards the philosopher Spinoza with whom he shared a number of signature doctrines, most notably the notion of infinite divine extension, was one of grudging respect. While he apparently first believed the Dutch rationalist to be yet another atheist whom he could rebut with ease, wielding his tried and tested arsenal of anti-atheist arguments once again, he was soon proven wrong by the first of his two principal works. Notwithstanding Spinoza's execrable impiety, against which he continually inveighed in his at times acrimonious polemics, More, on his own admission, "found in the author of this *Treatise* a mind a little more complex and astute than" the most well-known atheists of the early modern period, including Thomas Hobbes (epist. alt., [praef.] (Opera omnia, II/1,565). The tripartite structure of the *Ad V.C. Epistola altera* mirrors the two-part structure of the *Theological-Political Treatise*'s and the work's overall context of the Anglo-Dutch debates in rebutting Spinoza's immanentist theology (1–36 [Op. omn. II/1, 565–587]) and contractualist political philosophy (37–46 [II/1,587–595]) as well as Kuyper's misguided fideist response in *The Secrets of Atheism* (47–50 [II/1,595–601]). It ends with a brief creed-like summary of the key tenets of More's own mature rational theology (51 [II/1, 601]. In response to Spinoza's rational theology of the *Deus sive natura*, More restates with great argumentative vigour the Cambridge Platonists' cherished notion of God as a supreme moral agent committed to univocal goodness as the first and most noble of his attributes. As goodness in person, God cannot be identified with nature, but must be transcendent to it. In his rebuttal of the two principal objections levelled against classical theism in Spinoza's *Treatise*, i.e. God's supernatural revelation and intervention in natural and human affairs, More first sets out to defend his concept of an intuitive insight into God. The chief power by which the prophets acquired the most sublime of truths about God, the soul and the world was their "boniform faculty" or, as he chose to term it in his *Ad V.C. Epistola altera*, a "natural sagacity" or an "internal sense" (20; II/1, 574). The God intuited in prophetic vision is one who both preserves the natural order of things and at times intervenes in its course, temporarily suspending the laws laid down at creation in occasional miraculous intervention **(E–F)**. More builds on Cudworth's defence of miracles in the *True Intellectual System* of which he provides a philosophical account in terms of the Cambridge Platonists' cosmology of the spirit of nature. On the one hand, "the spirit of nature which embraces the common laws of nature in a living fashion" (epist. alt., 18 [II/1,573]) is the principle whereby God displays his *universal* care and providence in law-governed organic processes in nature. On the other hand, he is at liberty to act contrary to its laws and exercise his libertarian agency "as he sees fit" to grant to humanity *special* pledges of his love. More's interest in Spinoza did not wane after he had completed his refutation of Spinoza's *Tractatus*. On the contrary, he soon immersed himself in Spinoza's complete works and took issue with several of the key tenets of his hyolozoism in two more polemical writings. It was with a view to confirming the authorship of the anonymous 1670 *Tractatus* that More chose to study his *Principles of Descartes' Philosophy*, including the *Appendix Containing Metaphysical Thoughts*, and purchase Spinoza's *Opera Posthuma* shortly after their publication in 1677. In a second set of notes on the first *scholia* on his original *Ad V.C. Epistola altera*, More recalls in vivid detail how he chanced upon an edition of Spinoza's collected works at a London bookseller and felt obliged to buy it to make sure that he had not judged the first of his two principal works too severely. More's *Scholia In Epist. Ad V.C.* is more than two series of notes on the original *Epistola altera*. Instead, it is a second work in his anti-Spinozist trilogy of works that expands significantly upon his earlier critique of the Dutch rationalist's naturalist account of divine agency and adds to it a first sustained critique of his adversary's strict determinism. In addition, it includes a long refutation of Glisson's *Tractatus de Natura Substantiae Energetica seu de vita naturae eiusque tribus primis facultatibus* **(G)**. More's interest in "that most famous physician Francis Glisson", whom he identified as a panpsychist in the Spinozist vein, appears to have been aroused by Cudworth's 1678 *True Intellectual System* which he apparently studied at the same time as *Glisson's* Natura Substantiae Energetica and Spinoza's *Opera Posthuma*. In the process, he endorsed his friend and fellow Platonist's landmark general division of philosophical atheism into a materialist and a panpsychist variety. More's warm praise of "learned author of the *True Intellectual System of the Universe*", whose newly coined concept he uses alongside his own of "biousian", is a remarkable piece of evidence for their joint effort in combatting a particularly perilous variety of contemporary atheism. More's critique of the Cambridge physician and metaphysician Glisson's audacious draft of "hylozoism" or "biusianism" is a watershed work in his own and the Cambridge Platonists' reception of two major strands of early modern panpsychism. More rejects the novel bottom-up-causality of living matter and reasserts the top-down-causality of a spirit of nature and supreme mind. If it were not for a higher divine intelligence both beyond and immanent to matter, atom lives could hardly be believed to coalesce so as to form higher organisms endowed with sensation and perception, let alone intellection. At the same time, however, More is prepared to adopt a panpsychism close to that first laid down in his early poetry and correspondence with Descartes. All reality, proceeding from God, resembles him in possessing life. However, only if there is an immutable divine intellect guiding these atoms of life to increasingly higher forms of conscious unity does panpsychism have explanatory power. Not surprisingly, More, on reading with care Spinoza's *Opera Posthuma*, chose to devote an entire work to the refutation of Spinoza's principal works, the *Ethics* **(G–M)** Inarguably the most significant of his anti-Spinozist writings, his *Confutation* views Spinoza's atheism as resting on the titular two *Chief Columns* of the singularity and necessary existence of substance qua substance. If there is but one substance, matter qua substance must be viewed as existing of necessity, thereby either replacing the perfect mind as the sole Deity or compromising his defining supreme perfection. God must not be viewed as an infinitely extended matter adopting infinitely many forms in a never-ending process of chaotic motion and rest, but as a mind of infinite benignity and spiritual extension who gives life to a plurality of self-moving spiritual and material substances individuated and separated from him and from one another not by attribute or mode, but by "real" or spatial "distinction". More exhibits a remarkable awareness of the considerable common ground between his own rationalism and Spinoza's as he credits his adversary with "prophetic" insight into extension as an attribute of the divine first substance. In their day, both More and Spinoza were unorthodox Cartesians who deviated from Descartes in subscribing to a deity of supreme cogitation *and* extension. At the same time, it was Spinoza's chief fault that he failed to acknowledge two distinct extensions, the one divisible and imperfect, the other indivisible and perfect. The *Confutatio* thus contains both an account of the core doctrines of Cambridge Platonism at large and More's own idiosyncratic trialism of three distinct extensions. While it is impossible to date the *scholia* with exact precision, it is clear that they hail from the same period as the latest of his Latin works. Alongside several major new works, including his anti-Spinozist trilogy, More's *Opera omnia* of 1675–1679 included Latin translations of several earlier published and unpublished English writings such as the *Immortality of the Soul* and the *Philosophiae Teutonicae Censura* alongside a substantial number of occasional substantive *scholia* on his earlier publications. Among the *scholia* on More's *Correspondence with Descartes* in the late 1640s are several in which he restates his earlier critique of the French philosopher in the light of Spinoza's metaphysics **(N)**. It is clear from the explicit mention of Spinoza's *Opera Posthuma* that these *scholia* postdate the *Ad V.C. Epistola altera* and the *Scholia* in which More relates how he purchased them in London. In all likelihood, these Scholia were, therefore, written after the completion of the anti-Spinozist trilogy. When More revisited his correspondence with Descartes in the light of his detailed critique of what he now believed to be the French philosopher's most formidable follower, he deliberately rephrased the charge of nullibism in Spinozist wording. In particular, More took exception to Descartes's notion of the extension attributed to spirit which, as the French philosopher had insisted in the original exchange of letters, was "one of power only, not of substance". It was with the benefit of Spinozist hindsight that More now viewed nullibism as denying spirit as a mere epiphenomenal mode of matter. Paradoxically, Spinozist hylozoism had in part turned out to be the logical upshot of Cartesian nullibism.

Chapter 9

The Critique of John Calvin
Divine Fate Immoral

A Ralph Cudworth, *A Sermon Before the House of Commons* (1647) (pp. 8–11)

Hereby we know that we know him, if we keep his Commandments. He that saith, I know him, and keepeth not his Commandments, is a liar, and the truth is not in him. (1 John: 2,3–4)

I Come now unto these words themselves, which are so pregnant, that I shall not need to force out any thing at all from them: I shall therefore onely take notice of some few observations, which drop from them of their own accord, and then conclude with some Application of them to our selves.

First then, If this be the right way and methode of discovering our *knowledge of Christ,* by our *keeping of his Commandments;* Then *we may safely draw conclusions concerning our state and condition, from the conformity of our lives to the will of Christ.* Would we know whether we know Christ aright, let us consider whether the life of Christ be in us. *Qui non habet vitam Chri*[8]*sti, Christum non habet;* He that hath not the life of Christ in him, he hath nothing but the name, nothing but a phansie of Christ, he hath not the substance of him. He that builds his house upon this foundation; not an airy notion of Christ swimming in his brain, but Christ really dwelling and living in his heart; as our Saviour himself witnesseth, he *buildeth his house upon a Rock*; and when the flouds come, and the winds blow, and the rain descends, and beats upon it, it shall stand impregnably. But he that builds all his comfort upon an ungrounded perswasion, that God from all eternity hath loved him, and absolutely decreed him to life and happinesse, and seeketh not for God really dwelling in his soul; he builds his house upon a Quicksand, and it shall suddenly sink and be swallowed up: *his hope shall be cut off, & his trust shall be a spiders web; he shall lean upon his house, but it shall not stand, he shall hold it fast but it shall not endure.* We are no where commanded to pry into these secrets, but the wholesome counsell and advise given us, is this; to *make our calling and election sure.* We have no warrant in Scripture, to peep into these hidden [9] Rolls and Volumes of Eternity, and to make it our first thing that we do when we come to Christ, to spell out our names in the starres, and to perswade our selves that we are certainly elected to everlasting happinesse: before we see the *image of God,* in righteousnesse and true holinesse, shaped in our hearts. Gods everlasting decree, is too dazeling and bright an object for us at first to set our eye upon: it is far easier and safer for us to look upon the raies of his goodnesse and holinesse as they are reflected in our own hearts; and there to read the mild and gentle Characters of Gods love to us, in our love to him, and our hearty compliance with his heavenly will: as it is safer for us if we would see the Sunne, to look upon it here below in a pale of water; then to cast up our daring eyes upon the body of the Sun it self, which is too radiant and scorching for us. The best assurance that any one can have of his interest in God, is doubtlesse the conformity of his soul to him. Those divine purposes, whatsoever they be are altogether unsearchable and unknowable by us, they lie wrapt up in everlasting darknesse, and co[10]vered in a deep Abysse; who is able to fathom the bottome of them? Let us not therefore make this out first attempt towards God and Religion, to perswade our selves strongly of these everlasting Decrees: for if at our first flight we aime so high, we shall happily but scorch our wings, and be struck back with lightning, as those *Giants* of old were, that would needs attempt to invade and assault heaven. And it is indeed a most *Giganticall* Essay, to thruft our selves so boldly into the lap of heaven; it is the pranck of a *Nimrod*, of a *mighty Hunter* thus rudely to deal with God, and to force heaven and happinesse before his face whether he will or no. The way to obtain a good assurance indeed of our title to heaven, is not to clamber up to it, by a ladder of our own ungrounded perswasions; but to dig as low as hell by humility and self-denyall in our own hearts: and though this may seem to be the furthest way about; yet it is indeed the neerest, and safest way to it. We must ἀναβαίνειν κάτω and καταβαίνειν ἄνω, as the Greek Epigramme speaks, *ascend downward*, & *descend upward*; if we would indeed come to hea[11]ven, or get any true perswasion of our title to it.

B Cudworth, *Sermon Before the House of Commons* (1647) (pp. 34–39)

And God forbid, that *Gods own Life* and *Nature* here in the World, should be forlorn, forsaken, and abandoned of God himself. Certainly, where-ever it is, though never so little, like a sweet, young, tender *Babe*, once born in any heart; when it crieth unto God the *father* of it, with pitifull and bemoning looks imploring his compassion; it cannot chuse but move his *fatherly bowels*, and make them *yerne*, and turn towards it, and by strong sympathy, draw his compassionate arm to help and relieve it. Never was any tender Infant, so dear to those Bowels that begat it, as an *Infant new-born Christ, formed in the heart* of any true believer, to God the *father* of it. Shall the *children of this World*, the *sonnes of darknesse*, be moved with such tender affection, and compassion, towards the fruit of their bodies, their own Naturall offspring; and shall God who is the *Father of lights*, the fountain of all goodnesse, be moved with no compassion towards his true Spirituall Offspring, and have no regard [35] to those sweet *Babes of Light*, ingendered by his own beams in mens hearts, that in their lovely countenances, bear the resemblance of his own face, and call him their *father*? Shall he see them lie fainting, and gasping, and dying here in the World, for want of nothing to preserve and keep them, but an *Influence* from him, who first gave them life and breath? No; hear the language of Gods heart, heare *the sounding of his bowels* towards them: *Is it Ephraim my dear sonne? Is it that pleasant child? since I spake of him I do earnestly remember him, my bowels, my bowels are troubled for him; I will surely have mercy upon him, saith the Lord*. If those expressions of goodnesse and tender affection here amongst creatures, be but drops of that full Ocean that is in God; how can we then imagine, that this *Father* of our *spirits*, should have so little regard to his own dear Ofspring, I do not say our souls, but that which is the very Life and Soul of our souls, the *Life of God* in us; which is nothing else but Gods own Self communicated to us, his own Sonne born in our hearts; as that he should suffer it to be cruelly murdered in its *Infancy* by our Sinnes, [36] and like young *Hercules* in its very *cradle*, to be strangled by those filthy *vipers*; that he should see him to be crucified by wicked *Lusts*, nailed fast to the crosse by invincible *Corruptions*; pierced and gored on every side with the poisoned spears of the Devils *temptations*, and at last to give up the Ghost; and yet his tender heart not at all relent, nor be all this while impassionated with so sad a spectacle? Surely, we cannot think he hath such an *adamantine* breast, such a *flinty* nature as this is. What then? must we say that though indeed he be willing, yet he is not able, to rescue his crucified and tormented *Sonne*, now bleeding upon the crosse; to *take him down* from thence *and save him*? Then must Sinne be more powerfull then God: that weak, crasie, and sickly thing, more strong then the *Rock of ages*: and the Devil the Prince of Darknesse, more mighty, then the God of Light. No surely, there is a weaknesse and impotency in all Evil, a masculine strength and vigour in all Goodnesse: and therefore doubtlesse the *Highest Good*, the πρῶτον ἀγαθὸν as the Philosophers call it, is the strongest thing in the World. [37] *Nil potentius Summo Bono.* Gods *Power* displaied in the World, is nothing but his *Goodnesse* strongly reaching all things, from heighth to depth, from the highest Heaven, to the lowest Hell: and irresistibly imparting it self to every thing, according to those severall degrees in which it is capable of it. Have the Fiends of Darknesse then, those poore forlorn spirits, that are fettered and locked up in the Chaines of their own wickednesse, any strength to withstand the force of infinite *Goodnesse*, which is infinite *Power*? or do they not rather skulk in holes of darknesse, and flie like Bats and Owls, before the approching beams of this Sun of Righteousnesse? Is God powerfull to kill and to destroy, to damne and to torment, and is he not powerfull to save? Nay, it is the sweetest Flower in all the Garland of his Attributes, it is the richest Diamond in his Crown of Glory, that he is *Mighty to save*: and this is farre more magnificent for him, then to be stiled *Mighty to destroy*. For that, except it be in the way of Justice; speaks no Power at all, but mere Impotency, for the Root of all Power, is Goodnesse. Or must we say lastly, that God [38] indeed is able to rescue us out of the Power of sinne & Satan, when we sigh & grone towards him, but yet sometimes to exercise his absolute Authority, his uncontrollable Dominion, he delights rather in plunging wretched souls down into infernall Night, & everlasting Darknesse? What shall we then make the God of the whole World? Nothing but a cruell and dreadfull *Erynnis*, with *curled fiery Snakes* about his head, and *Firebrands* in his hands, thus governing the World? Surely this will make us either secretly to think, that there is no God at all in the World, if he must needs be such, or else to wish heartily, there were none. But doubtlesse, God will at last, confute all these our *Misapprehensions* of him, he will unmask our *Hypocriticall pretences*, and clearly cast the shame of all our sinfull Deficiencies, upon our selves, and vindicate his own Glory from receiving the least stain or blemish by them. In the mean time, let us know, that the Gospel now requireth, far more of us, then ever the Law did; for it requireth a *New Creature*, a *Divine Nature*, *Christ formed in us*: but yet withall, it bestoweth a *quickening Spirit*, an [39] *enlivening Power*, to inable us, to express that, which is required of us. Whosoever therefore truly *knows Christ*, the same also *keepeth Christs Commandments*. But, he *that saith, I know him, and keepeth not his Commandments, he is a liar, and the truth is not in him.*

C Benjamin Whichcote, *Eight Letters of Dr. Antony Tuckney and Dr. Benjamin Whichcote* (1650), First Letter in Answer (ed. Salter, 13–16)

For the point of Reconciliation—I shall write you out a copy of my notes, in that point: whereby you will easily understand, how you wrong both my wordes and meaning.

> Christ doth not save us; by onely doing for us, *without* us: yea, we come at that, which Christ hath done for us, with God; by what he doth for us, *within* us. For, in order of execution, it is, as the wordes are placed in the text; Repentance, before Forgiveness of sins; Christ is to be acknowledged, as a principle of grace *in* us; as well as an advocate *for* us. For the scripture holdes-forth Christ to us, under a double notion; [14] 1. To be felt in us, as the new man; in contradiction to the old man: as a divine nature; in contra-distinction to the degenerate and apostate nature: and as a principle of heavenly life; contrary to the life of sin, and spirit of the world: 2. To be beleeved-on by us, as a sacrifice for the expiation and atonement of sin; as an advocate and meanes of reconciliation between God and Man. And Christ doth not dividedly performe these offices; one and not the other. For reconciliation between God and Us, is not wrought, as sometimes it is said and pretended to be in the world, between parties mutually incensed and exasperated one against another:

when the urgency of a case makes them to forbear hostility, and acting one against the other; their inward antipathie and enmitie in the mean while rather increated, inflamed: because they take not up the difference fairely; nor come to agree in the cause; but *causa continens odii* still continues: so that, though an amnestie be consented-to, yet are they not friendes; but in heart enemies. Wherefore our saviour, to distinguish, saith; If ye from your hearts forgive not, etc. But with God there can not be reconciliation; without Our becoming God-like; for God's acts are not false, overly, imperfect; God cannot make a vaine shew; God, being perfectly under the power of goodnesse, [15] can not denie himself: because, if he shou'd, he wou'd depart from goodnesse; which is impossible to God. Therefore *We* must yeelde, be subdued to the rules of goodnesse, receeve stamps and impressions from God; and God can not be farther pleased, than goodnesse takes place. They therefore deceive and flatter themselves extremely; who thinke of reconciliation with God, by meanes of a Saviour, acting upon God in their behalf; and not also working in or upon them, to make them God-like. Nothing is more impossible than this; as being against the nature of God: which is in perfect agreement with goodnesse, and hath an absolute antipathie against iniquity, unrighteousnesse and sin. And we cannot imagine, that God by his Will and Pleasure can go against his Nature and Being.

(The phrase, "Divinity *minted* or *taught* in Hell;" I finde not in my notes: but it was suddainly spoken; upon this abuse of God and cheat of our-selves.)

To put this upon a Saviour to doe; and impotently to flatter our-selves in the conceit of such a thing, which *a parte Dei ponit repugnantiam*; were, instead of reconciling Heaven and Earth, to divide God against Himselfe. And this is a demonstration in Divinity; beyond which no demonstration in Astronomie is more certain. If we wou'd be true to our-selves, let our faith have no contradiction from within us; let not our sense give our conceits the lye, let us taste and see, etc.

[16] Now, whether there be anie thing in all this, contrary to "free grace, freely justifying the ungodly;" as you seeme to inferr: I leave to your self upon second thoughts to judge. Or whether this whole discourse be not, as was by me intended, wholly pointed against those, that "turn the grace of God into wantonnesse;" and pretend to be reconciled to God, through *Justification*; whereas they continue enemies to God, through want of *Sanctification*; and the renewing of the spirit by Christ.

Sir, You wrong me very much; in misquoting, *oritur e nobis*; and attributing it to the ground of our acceptance with God. I finde in my notes these words, "*Salvatio nascitur e nobis, suscipitur a nobis;*" in the gloss I had upon the wordes, *viz.* "*the true notion of salvation*: a saviour to give repentance and forgiveness. Some look at salvation, as at a thing at distance from them; the benefit of some convenient place to be in; exemtion from punishment; freedom from enemies abroad: but it is the mending of our natures, and the safety or our persons, our health and strength within our selves," (Nothing in this is intended to leave-out the authour of our salvation; or *a quo salvatio oritur*) "and our good state and condition with God; the work of grace and favour towards us and upon us; our being restored to righteousnesse, goodnesse and truth; and our being reconciled to God, so as we may truly finde the kingdom of God with us."

D John Smith, *Select Discourses* (1650), 5,8,5 (ed. Williams, 156–158)

The former deduction leads me to another akin to it, which shall be my last; and it is that which Cicero intimates in his *De Legibus*, viz. *That seeing there is such an intercourse and society, as it were, between god and men, therefore there is also some law between them, which is the bond of all communion.* God Himself, from whom all law takes its rise and emanation, is not *exlex*, and without all law, nor, in a sober sense, above it. Neither are the primitive rules of His economy in this world the sole results of an absolute will, but the sacred decrees of reason and goodness. I cannot think God to be so unbounded in His legislative Power, that He can make every thing law, both for His own dispensations and our observance, that we may sometime imagine. We cannot say, indeed, that God was absolutely determined from some law within Himself to makes us; but I think we may safely say, when He had once determined to make us, He could neither make us sinful, seeing He had no idea nor shadow [157] of evil within Himself; nor wrap up those dreadful fates within our natures, or set them over us, that might, *arcana inspiratione*, (as some are pleased to phrase it) secretly work our ruin, and silently carry us on, making use of our own natural infirmity, to eternal misery. Neither could He design to make His creatures miserable, that so He might show Himself just. These are rather the byways of cruel and ambitious men, that seek their own advantage in the mischief of other men, and contrive their own rise by their ruin: this is not Divine Justice, but the cruelty of degenerated men.

But, as the Divinity could propound nothing to itself in the making of the world, but the communication of its own love and goodness; so it can never swerve from the same scope and end in the dispensation of itself to it. Neither did God so boundlessly enlarge the appetite of souls after some all-sufficient good, that so they might the more unspeakably tortured in the missing of it; but that they might more certainly return to the Original of their beings. And such busy-working essences as the souls of men are, could neither be made as dull and senseless of true happiness as stocks and stones are; neither could they contain the whole sum and perfection of it within themselves: therefore they must also be informed with such principles as may conduct them back again to Him from whom they first came. God does not makes creatures, for the mere sport of His Almighty arm, to raise and ruin, and toss up and down, at mere pleasure. No: that εὐδοκία, or good pleasure of that will that made them is the same still: it changes not, though we may change, and make ourselves incapable of partaking the blissful fruits and effects of it.

And so we come to consider that law embosomed in the souls of men which ties them again to their Creator, and this is called *the law of nature*; which, indeed, is [158] nothing else but a paraphrase or comment upon the nature of God, as it copies forth itself in the soul of man.

E George Rust, *Discourse of Truth* (1651/1655/1682), Section 3 (*Two Choice and Useful Treatises*, 167–168)

Sect. III.

An Instance or two of gross and horrid Absurdities, consequent to the denying the mutual respects and relations of things to be eternal and indispensable.

Can the infinite Wisdom it self make the damning of all the Innocent and the unspotted Angels in Heaven a proportionate means to declare and manifest the unmeasureableness of his Grace and Love, and goodness towards them? Can Lying, Swearing, Envy, Malice, nay Hatred of God and Goodness it self, be the most acceptable Service of God, and the readiest [168] way to a mans Happiness? And yet all these must be true, and infinitely more such contradictions than we can possibly imagin, if the mutual respects and relations of things be not eternal and indispensable: which that they are, I shall endeavour to prove.

F Rust, *Discourse of Truth*, Sections 6–7 (*Treatises*, 173–175)

Sect. VII.

An hideous, but genuine Inference of a Pamphleteer from this principle, that absolute and Sovereign Will is the Spring and Fountain of all Gods actions.

And therefore from this principle, that absolute and Soveraign Will is the Spring and Fountain of all God's Actions, it was rightly inferr'd by a later *Pamphleteer*, that God will one day damn all Mankind, Good and Bad, Believers and Unbelievers, notwithstanding all his Promises, Pretensions or Engagements to the contrary; because this damning all mankind in despight of his Faithfulness, Justice, Mercy and Goodness will be the greatest advancement of his Soveraignty, Will and Prerogative imaginable. His words are, *God hath stored up Destruction both for the perfect and the wicked, and this does wonderfully set forth his Soveraignty; his exercising whereof is so perfect, that when he hath tied himself up fast as may be, by never so many promises, yet it should still have its scope, and be able to do what it will, when it will, as it:* Here you have this principle improved to the height. And however you may look upon this Author as some new Light, or *Ignis fatuus* of [174] the times, yet I assure you in some pieces by him set forth, he is very sober and rational.

Sect. VIII.

That the Denial of the mutual Respects and Relations of Things unto one another to be eternal and unchangeable, despoils God of that universal Rectitude of his Nature.

In the next place, to deny the mutual respects and *rationes rerum* to be immutable and indispensible, will spoil God of that *universal rectitude* which is the greatest Perfection of his Nature: For then Justic, Faithfulness, Mercy, Goodness *etc.* will be but contingent and arbitrarious Issues of the Divine Will. This is a clear and undeniable Consequence. For if you say these be indispensible perfections in God, for instance, if *Justice* be so, then there is an eternal relation of Right and Equity betwixt very Being and the giving of it that which is its propriety; if *Faithfulness*, then there is an indispensible agreement betwixt a promise and the performance of it; if *Mercy*, then there is an immutable and unalterable suitableness and harmony between an indigent Creature, and pity and commiseration; if *Goodness*, then there is an everlasting Pro[175]portion and symmetry between fulness and its overflowing and dispreading of it self, which yet is the thing denied: For to say they are indispensibly so, because God understands them so, seems to me extream incogitancy; for that is against the nature of all understanding, which is but the Idea and Representation of things, and is then a true and perfect Image, when it is exactly conformed to its Object: And therefore, if things have not mutual respects and relations eternal and indispensible, then all those perfections do solely and purely depend upon absolute and independent Will, as *Will*; And consequently, it was and is indifferent in it self that the contrary to these, as, *Injustice, Unfaithfulness, Cruelty, Malice, Hatred, Spite, Revenge, Fury*; and whatever goes to the constitution of Hell it self, should have been made the top and highest perfections of the Divine Nature: which is such Blasphemy as cannot well be named without horror and trembling. For instead of being a God, such a nature as this is, joined with Omnipotency, would be a worse Devil than any is in Hell. And yet this is a necessary and infallible consequence from the denial of these mutual respects and relations of things unto one another, to be eternal and unchangeable.

G Cudworth, *A Sermon preached to the Honourable Society of Lincolnes-Inne* (1664) (pp. 18–23)

Wherefore it was so farre from being the Ultimate End of Christ's undertaking to die for Sin, that men might securely live in it, that on the contrary the Death of Christ was particularly intended as an Engine to batter down the Kingdom of Sin & Satan, and to bring men effectually unto God and Righteousness, as the Scripture plainly witnesseth, 1 *Pet.* 2. 24. *His own self bare our Sins in his Body on the Tree, that we being dead to Sin, might live to Righteousness.* The Death of Christ conducing to this great End not onely as it was Exemplary, and Hierogly[19]phically instructed us, that we ought to *take up our Cross* likewise, and *follow our crucified Lord and Saviour, suffering in the Flesh and ceasing from Sin*: but also as it doth most lively demonstrate to us God's high Displeasure against Sin, and the malignant Nature of it, that could not otherwise be expiated then by the Bloud of that innocent and immaculate Lamb, the onely-begotten Son of God: and lastly, as the Hope of Pardon and free Remission of Sin in the Bloud of Christ for the truly Penitent might invite and animate men to chearful & vigorous endeavours against Sin.

Others there are that tell us there is indeed something farther aimed at in the Gospel besides the bare *Remission of Sins*, but that it is nothing else but the *Imputation of an External Righteousness* or *another's Inherent Holiness*, which is so completely made ours thereby to all intents and purposes, as if we our selves had been really and perfectly righteous; and this upon no other Condition or Qualification at all required in us, but onely of mere Faith scrupulously prescinded from all Holiness and Sanctification, or the laying hold and apprehending onely (as they use to phrase it) of this External and Imputed Righteousness, [20] that is, the merely believing and imagining it to be ours: Which kind of Faith therefore is but the Imagination of an Imagination, or of that which really is not, and, as *Pindar* calls Man, Σκίας ὄναρ, *the very Dream of a Shadow*.

For though this be pretended by some to be spoken onely of *Justification* as contradistinct from *Sanctification*, the latter of which they conceive must by no means have any Conditional Influence upon the former; yet it is plain, that it will unavoidably extend to the taking away of the Necessity of *Inherent* Righteousness and Holiness, and all Obligation to it: upon which very account it is so highly acceptable, because under a specious shew of Modesty and Humility it doth exceedingly gratify mens Hypocrisie and Carnality. For he that is thus completely Justified by the Imputation of a mere External Righteousness, must needs have *ipso facto* a Right and Title thereby to Heaven and Happiness without Holiness; for *Rom.* 8. 30. *Whom he justifieth, them he also glorifieth.* Neither can any thing be required inherently in them, where all *Inherency* is perfectly supplied by *Imputation*. And though it be pretended that *Sanctification* will spontaneously follow after by way of *Gratitude*; yet this is [21] like to prove but a very slippery hold, where it is believed that *Gratitude* it self, as well as all other Graces, is already in them by Imputation. Neither can it be reasonably thought that true Holiness should spring by way of *Gratitude* or *Ingenuity* from such a Principle of Carnality as makes men so well contented with a mere Imaginary Righteousness.

But this Opinion as it makes God in Justifying to pronounce a false Sentence, and to conceive of things otherwise then they are, and to doe that which himself hath declared to be abominable, *to Justifie the wicked* (in a forensick sense,) and as it is irreconcileable to those many Scriptures that assure us *God will render to every man according to his Works*; so it also takes away the Necessity of Christ's Meritorious and Propitiatory Sacrifice for the Remission of Sins: for where a complete Righteousness is imputed, there is no Sin at all to be pardoned. And lastly, it vainly supposes *Righteousness* and *Holiness* to be mere Phantastical and Imaginary things; for otherwise it were no more possible that a Wicked man should be made Righteous by another's Righteousness imputed, then that a Sick man should be made Whole by another's imputed [22] Health. *If a Brother or Sister be naked and destitute of daily food, and one of you say unto them, Depart in peace, be you warmed, and be you filled; notwithstanding you give them not those things which are needful for the body; what doth it profit?* James 2. 15, 16. *Even so, what doth it profit, my Brethren, if a man say he hath Faith* (or Imputed Righteousness) *and have not Works?* (that is, Real and Inherent Righteousness, or Inward Regeneration) *can such a Faith* (that is, Imagination, or Imputation) *save him?* Certainly no more then mere words can clothe a naked mans Back, or feed a hungry mans Belly, or warm and thaw him whose Bloud is frozen and congealed in his veins. Nay it is no more possible for a man to be made *Holy*, then to be made *Happy*, by mere Imputation, which latter few men would be contented withall; and, were it not for their Hypocrisie, they would be as little contented with the former; and it would as little please them to be *Opinione tantùm Justi*, as *Opinione tantùm Beati*, to use *Tully's* expressions against the *Epicureans*. Nay, since it is most certain that the greatest part of our *Happiness* consisteth in *Righteousness and Holiness*, it will unavoidably follow, that if we have no other then an *Imputative Righteousness*, we can have [23] no other then an *Imputative Happiness*, and a mere Imaginary Heaven, which will little please us when we feel our selves to be in a true and real Hell.

H Cudworth, *Sermon Before Lincolnes-Inne* (pp. 38–41)

Doubtless God hath no other Design upon us in Religion and the Gospel of his Son then what is for our good, and to restore us to the Rectitude and Perfection of our own Beings: Wherefore he seeks to redeem and call off our Affections from the perishing Vanities of this [39] World, which being so infinitely below us do debase and pollute our Spirits; wherefore he would not have us to addict ourselves wholly to the Gratifications of our *lower Faculties*, which are but the *Brute* in us, but he would have the Best in us to be uppermost, *the Man* to rule the *Brute*, and the τὸ Θεῖον, that that is of God in us, to rule our Manly and Rational Faculties. He would not have us, *Narcissus*-like, to be alwaies courting our own Shadow in the Stream; for, according to the ancient *Democritical* Philosophy, this whole visible World is nothing else but mere extended Bulk, and hath nothing Real in it but *Atomes* or *Particles* of a different Magnitude, diversely placed and agitated in a continual Whirlpool. But all the Colour, Beauty and Varnish, all that which charms and bewitches us in these Objects without us, is nothing but the Vital Sensations and Relishes of our own Souls. This gives all the Paint and Lustre to those Beauties which we court and fall in love withall without us, which are otherwise as devoid of Reality and as Phantastical as the Colours of the Rainbow. So that this *Outward World* is not unfitly compared to *an inchanted Palace*, which seems indeed mighty pleasing and ra[40]vishing to our deluded Sense, whereas all is but imaginary and a mere prestigious Shew. Those things which we are enamoured with, thinking them to be without us, being nothing but the Vital Energies of our own Spirits. In a word, God would have Man to be a Living Temple for himself to dwell in, and his Faculties Instruments to be used and employed by him; which need not be thought impossible, if that be true that Philosophy tells us, that there is *Cognatio quaedam* a certain near *Kindred* and *Alliance* between the Soul and God.

Lastly, we must observe, though this inward Victory over Sin be no otherwise to be effected then by the Spirit of Christ through Faith, and by a Divine Operation in us, so that in a certain sense we may be said to be *Passive* thereunto; yet notwithstanding we must not dream any such thing, as if our *Active* Cooperation and Concurrence were not also necessarily required thereunto. For as there is a Spirit of God in Nature which produceth Vegetables and Minerals, which humane Art and Industry could never be able to effect, namely that *Spiritus intus alens* which the Poet speaks of, which yet notwithstand [41] ing doth not work *Absolutely*, *Unconditionately* and *Omnipotently*, but requireth certain Preparations, Conditions and Dispositions in the Matter which it works upon; (For unless the Husbandman plow the Ground and sow the Seed, the Spirit of God in Nature will not give any increase:) In like manner the Scripture tells us that the Divine Spirit of Grace doth not work *Absolutely*, *Unconditionately* and *Irresistibly* in the Souls of men, but requireth certain Preparations, Conditions and Cooperations in us; forasmuch as it may both be *quenched*, and *stirred up* or *excited* in us. And indeed unless we *plow up the Fallow-ground of our hearts and sow to our selves in Righteousness* (as the Prophet speaks) by our earnest endeavours; we cannot expect that the Divine Spirit of Grace will showr down that Heavenly increase upon us. Wherefore if we would attain to a *Victory over Sin* by the Spirit of Christ, we must endeavour to *fight a good Fight and run a good Race*, and to *enter in at the streight gate*, that so overcoming we may receive the Crown of Life.

And thus much shall suffice to have spoken at this time concerning the First Particular, *The Victory over Sin*.

I Henry More, *Divine Dialogues* (1668), 3,15–16 (Second edition, 209–211)

Euist.   Can there be any thing possibly parallel to this, *Cuphophron*, amongst our Civilized *Europaeans*?

Cuph.   I think nothing, unless it be the Religion of the *Superlapsarians*, the Object whereof is *Infinite Power* unmodified by either *Justice* or *Goodness*: which is that very Idol of *Typhon* or *Arimanius* I spoke of. For this Imagination of *Omnipotent Power* and *Will* acting without any regard to *Justice* or *Goodness*, is but an Idol, no real thing. If it were, it were more horrible then the *Indian Deumo*, or any Devil that is. But it could not be God: For God is Love, and every thing acts according to what it is.

Sophr.   Very well argued, *Cuphophron*.

Philop.   In many things *Cuphophron* seems to be on a more then ordinary good pin today.

Euist.   But I believe he must stretch his wit to an higher pin then he has done hitherto, to pretend to make any tolerable answer to what follows.

[210] *Cuph.*   Why, what strange thing is that which follows, *Euistor*?

Euist.   The Sacrificing of men to the Devil. Those of *Peru* frequently sacrifice their Children for the success of the affairs of their *Ingua*, for Health, Victory, or the like. The Son was also frequently sacrificed for the health of the Father. They of *Mexico* had a Custome of sacrificing of their Captives. Whence their Kings were often stirred up by their Priests to make war upon their neighbours, to get Captives to sacrifice to the Devil, they telling them their Gods died for hunger, and that they should remember them. The Devil also himself is said to appear in *Florida*, and to complain that he is thirsty, that humane blood may be presently shed to quench his thirst. The solemnity of sacrificing Captives to *Vitziiputzly* in *Mexico* within the Palisado of dead mens Sculls is most horrid and direfull: where the high Priest cut open their Breasts with a sharp Flint, and pulled out their reeking Hearts, which he first shew'd to the Sun, to whom he offered it, but then suddenly turning to the Idol, cast it at his face; and with a kick of his foot tumbled the Body from the Tarrass he stood upon down the Stairs of the Temple, which were all embrew'd and defiled with blood. These Sacrifices also they ate, and clothed themselves with the Skins of the slain.

Cuph.   Now certainly this Custome of the *Americans* is very horrible and abominable, thus bloodily to sacrifice men to that Enemie of Mankind, the Devil. And therefore it were very happy if we had nothing in these Civilized parts of the World that bore the least shadow of similitude with it.

Euist.	Why? have we any thing, *Cuphophron?*
Cuph.	Why? what is the greatest horrour that surprises you in this Custome, *Euistor?*
[211] *Euist.*	To say the truth, *Cuphophron*, I do not find my self so subtile and distinct a Philosopher as explicitly to tell you what, but I think it is, first, That mankind should worship so ugly and execrable an object as the Devil; and then in the second place, That they should sacrifice so worthy and noble a thing as an *humane Body*, which is in capacity of becoming the Temple of the Holy Ghost, to so *detestable* an Idol.
Cuph.	You have, I think, answered very right and understandingly, *Euistor*, if you rightly conceive what makes the Devil so detestable.
Euist.	Surely his *Pride, Cruelty* and Malignity of nature, and in that all *Love* and *Goodness* is extinct in him, which if he could recover, he would presently become an Angel of Light.
Bath.	*Euistor* has answered excellently well, and like a Mysticall Theologer.
Euist.	To tell you the truth, I had it out of them.
Cuph.	But if he has answered right, *Bathynous*, it is a sad consideration, that we have in the Civilized parts of the World those that profess a more odious Religion then the *Mexicans* that sacrifice men to the Devil, I mean, the *Superlapsarians*. For the Object of their Worship is a God-Idol of their own framing, that acts merely according to *Will* and *Power* sequestred from all respect to either *Justice* or *Goodness*, as I noted before, which is the genuine *Idea* of a *Devil*. To which Idol they do not, as the *Mexicans*, sacrifice the *mere Bodies* of men, but their very *Souls* also; not kicking them down a Tarrass, but arbitrariously tumbling them down into the pit of Hell, there to be eternally and unexpressibly tormented, for no other reason but because this their dreadfull Idol will have it so. Can any Religion be more horrid or blasphemous then this?

J Henry Hallywell, *Deus Justificatus* (1668), 3 (pp. 104–108)

I have now finished this Argument from the consideration of the Divine Nature, and have deduced such genuine and legitimate Conclusions, that if rightly estimated and weighed, cannot but implant for the future in every unprejudic'd mind more generous and serene Apprehensions of the Dei[105]ty, then are offered in any *Scheme* of the *Supralapsarian* or *Sublapsarian* Doctrins; both which concurr in that which appears most deformed to every pure and defecate eye, *viz*. The Eternal Reprobation and Confusion of the greatest part of Mankind, the one upon pretence of Gods sole Will and Pleasure, and the other under the mantle and cover of *Adam*'s transgression, in whose loins the whole race of Mankind was included, when he fell and lost his Paradise. Both which opinions, though never so fairly guilded over, do really make God put on the mask of cruelty and rigour, that he might appear just in his Oeconomy and Administration of the affairs of the World: and that which is most barbarous and infamous in the eye of reason is made to speak the glory of the Deity. And that God might bring about this dismal and black design of Damning his Creatures, he must compass it by injurious artifices, and tyrannical contrivances; not unlike that inhumane fraud *Tiberius* used to *Brutus* and *Nero* the sons of *Germanicus*, *Variâ fraude induxit ut concitarentur ad convitia, &concitati perderentur*. How deep a stain doth this cast upon the lovely rayes and efflorences of the Divine Goodness and Mercy, making him [106] to become the Executioner to his own off-spring, and rend that dear life in pieces, which his own hands gave Being to? And although the *Sublapsarian Dogma* be entertained of some, on purpose to mollifie that harsh decree of the *Supralapsarian Reprobation;* yet if we divest it of those terms and artifices of words wherewith it is mantled over to appear more specious to the World, we shall find it cast as great a blot upon the Divine Nature as the other. For, whether is it better to say,

That God by his Eternal Prerogative of Absolute Dominion over all his Creatures, has adjudged the greatest part of Mankind to inevitable misery, for no other reason but upon the impulse of his own Will, and to shew the glory of his Power: Or to say, That God for the sin of one Man (whom he made the Representative of the succeeding Generations of Men to the end of the World) committed some thousands of years ago, and imputed only to his Posterity, who were no more able to help it, than to hinder their being born into the World, should take the advantage of his lapse, and decree the greatest number of Mankind to Everlasting destruction. And if we impartially view this latter, it will appear no less precarious and absurd than [107] the former. For though it be true, that we are really and formally guilty of Original Sin; yet to say, that God did physically predetermine *Adam*'s fall: or in the mildest sense, That he looked upon man as fallen (for the *Reprobationists* are not consistent with themselves) and so took the opportunity which he foresaw would offer it self by his lapse to bring about his design of ruining the greatest number of Mankind, is to bring Almighty God the Father of compassions upon the stage of the World, speaking unto the calamitous Off-spring of *Adam*, like the Wolfe when he intended to devour a Lamb:

Ante hos sex menses, ait, maledixisti mihi;
Respondit agnus: Equidem natus non eram.
Pater hercule tuus, inquit, maledixit mihi:
Atque ita correptum lacerat injustâ nece.

Should God take the souls of men being yet innocent, so soon as he set them upon acting in the World according to those Principles and Powers he bestowed upon them at their first production, and cast them into everlasting burnings, they would have this comfort left to them, that they suffered innocently, and never in the least measure violated any of the sacred Laws of Heaven: [108] But when they shall hear that their Creator and Father (who upon that very account could not inflict a greater evil than the good he bestowed on them) hath contrived their death, and drawn them into sin, that he might with the fairer shew of equity, punish them with infinite tortures both in body and soul, this injustice must needs appear unspeakably grievous. For although some would seem to excuse this Oeconomy from all harshness, iniquity and rigor by substituting the softer termes of Preterition or negative Reprobation; yet if they will unmask their apprehensions and speak plain sense, the difference will appear only in words, not in the thing it self, and is all one as if a man should seek to alleviate the calamity of a condemned Malefactor, by telling him he should not die by Common but Noble hands; For the event declares Gods intention: and the denial of his help to extricate them from misery, is equivalent to a positive Reprobation.

K Hallywell, *Deus Justificatus*, (pp. 182–185)

3. But he that makes good use of Gods gifts, and behaves himself as a good Souldier [183] of the Lord Christ, and conquers and subdues his rebellious lusts by the power of his Spirit, descendihg into the grave with the holy Jesus by a profound humility and mortification, and becoming perfectly ἀναυταίθητος, dead to all the self-feeling and the luscious relishes of the corporeal life, he is arrived to the highest dispensation of Christianity, which is to be under the νόμος τοῦ πνεύματος τῆς ζωῆς, *Law of the Spirit of life in Christ Jesus*. Such a man is wholly alive unto God, and though he be encumbred with many hardships, afflictions and outward calamities which threaten approaching ruine to his body of earth, yet his life is holy, harmless and innocent, like the life of Christ upon Earth, and his soul is so affected as his was, having but one only will in the World, which is to annihilate himself that God may be all in him. And whoever is arrived to this high pitch of Divine perfection hath attained

an enlarged and boundless freedom, his life being melted into the Divine life, and his will fitted and adapted to the comprehension of the Divine Will. For the true liberty of our wills consists not in an uncertain indifferency and dubious fluctuation between two different objects presented to our choice (For this arises out of [184] the darkness and imperfection of our understandings) but when our wills are conformable to reason, and spontaneously elect that which the Intellect propounds to them as best, and in it self most eligible. Having thus declared the amplitude and extent of the liberty of mans Will in all it's respective capacities, I shall now manifest and shew how it's taken away by asserting and maintaining of *Inconditionate Decrees;* which will be no hard matter to evince, if we consider that both the Predestination of the Good to life, and of the Reprobates to destruction, necessarily pervades and casts a fatal influence upon their whole lives, I mean that that eternal decree invincibly orders and disposes the actions of men to their respective ends, so that he who is preordained to happiness shall certainly and necessarily be good, and the other who is destin'd to perdition shall inevitably be wicked and vitious. A cast of which Doctrine we have delivered to us by *Zanchy* in these words, *Non dubitamus itaque confiteri ex immutabili Reprobatione necessitatem peccandi, & quidem sine resipiscentia ad mortem usque peccandi, eóque &aeternas poenas dandi, reprobis incumbere:* that is, *We doubt not to profess* [185] *that from the immutable Decree of Reprobation there lies upon Reprobates a necessity of sinning, and that without Repentance even unto death, and consequently of suffering eternal punishments.*

L Hallywell, *Deus Justificatus* (pp. 275–277)

[275] Let us see now how he confutes the *Platonists*, with whom he is very angry for asserting, *That God being Infinite Goodness, will necessarily do that which is best, page* 27. His first Argument to prove the [1] falsity of this Position he sets down *page 29, 30. etc.* the sum of which in brief is this, *That the necessity of Infinite Wisdom doing that which is best, takes away the liberty and freedom of the Divine Will.* To which I answer, That the liberty of the Divine Will consists not in an Arbitrary Indifferency of acting or not acting; but in acting always sutably and conformablely to his own Infinite Rectitude and Perfection: As the true Excellency and Freedom of our wills consists not in an indifferency or dubious suspension between Good and Evil (for this is a debility and imperfection in us) but in a constant Election of that which Right Reason and Intellect propound to them as Best: So that when once that Eternal Providence which sent us down upon Earth, shall reinstate us in the Possession of our Native Glory, our Wills which shall then obtain their freedom in it's greatest latitude and dimensions, yet shall not be left to a bare Indifferency: but will as certainly adhere to that which is Good, as a wise and [276] prudent man will always give the same judgment of the same thing in the same circumstances. Wherefore to answer in short, I say, that Gods actions are not so fatal and necessary as the motions of an *Automaton* or *Engine*, because he is endued with an Energetical Power of Reason and Intellect; but are free and unconstrained by any external Principle: but because his Nature is infinitely Good, it will always do that which is Best, because Goodness is the chief and first active Principle in it. The proof of this lies in *Axiome* II. III. IV.

[2] His second Argument is this, *That if the Divine Goodness or Beneficence be necessary, it would then destroy it's own Nature, because 'tis absolutely necessary to the Nature of Beneficence, that it proceed from a free and elective Principle, page* 33. I suppose this Argument is only cast in as a surplusage, and not with any intent to convince any of his Readers, unless Mr. *P.* imagine them so unwary and credulous as to be imposed upon by fallacies and sophisms; For if by Gods Bounty and Beneficence, he mean his gracious Donations and Benefits above [277] what may render his Creatures happy in their several states and capacities; then, I say, it is most free, because when any Beings have forfeited their Felicity, God is not obliged to reinstate them in all the circumstances of it again: But if we take Bounty or Goodness for the Eternal Perfection of Gods Blessed Nature, whereby he communicates himself to

all capable receptacles, this is as necessary as his Being: and against this Mr. *P.* ought properly to have levell'd his Argument. Nor does this make the Divine Goodness ever a whit the less Moral, because then none of Gods actions would be capable of Being Morally Good; for this impossible and blasphemous to assert, That the Divine Will is indifferent either to Good or Evill. God doth necessarily Love himself as the highest and most Absolute Good, and cannot but embrace every thing that is like himself; nor is the Divine Will Indifferent either to Love or Hate it's own Image and Similitude. And if the Communications of the Divine Goodness to such Beings as bear his Impresses upon them, and never defiled themselves with the least contagion of sin and vice be not necessary, then he is left free to destroy them, and consequently he can destroy something of his own Life and Nature, which no sober Person will affirm. And if this Hypothesis of his be true, I know no ground Mankind can have (setting aside those Declarations God hath made of himself in Holy Scripture) to believe and trust in him, and depend upon him for the advancement of their happiness after Death. But we find the sober and wise Heathens, who believed the soul of man to be τοῦ θεοῦ, and ἀθανάτοις ὁμώνυμον, as *Hermes* and *Plato* speak, constantly relying upon the Almighty Goodness of God, which they confidently believed did always that which was Best, and thence became assured and raised a strong foundation for their hopes, that it should go well with them in the other World, and that that Eternal Providence would take their better parts into it's tutelage and care, when they laid down their bodies in their beds of Earth.

M Ralph Cudworth, *Eternal and Immutable Morality* (1831), Book I, Chapter 1, Section 5

5. But whatsoever was the true meaning of these Philosophers, that affirm Justice and Injustice to be only by Law and not by Nature (of which I shall discourse afterwards,) certain it is, that divers Modern Theologers do not only seriously, but zealously contend in like Manner, *That there is nothing Absolutely, Intrinsecally and Naturally Good and Evil, Just and Unjust, antecedently to any positive Command or Prohibition of God; but that the Arbitrary Will and Pleasure of God,* (that is, an Omnipotent Being devoid of all Essential and Natural Justice) *by its Commands and Prohibitions, is the first and only Rule and Measure thereof.* Whence it follows unavoidably, that nothing can be imagined so grossly wicked, or so foully unjust or dishonest, but if it were supposed to be commanded by this Omnipotent Deity, must needs upon that Hypothesis forthwith become Holy, Just and Righteous. For though the Ancient Fathers of the Christian Church were very abhorrent from this Doctrine, (as *shall be shewed* hereafter) yet it crept up afterward in the Scholastick Age, *Ockham* being among the first that maintained *That there is no Act Evil but as it is prohibited by God, and which cannot be made good if it be commanded by God. And so on the other hand as to Good.* And herein *Petrus Alliacus* and *Andreas de Novo Castro*, with others, quickly followed him.

But this Doctrine hath been since chiefly promoted and advanced by such as think nothing so essential to the Deity as *Uncontroulable Power* and *Arbitrary Will*, and therefore that God could not be God if there should be any Thing Evil in its own Nature which he could not do; and who impute such dark Counsels and dismal Actions unto God, as cannot be justified otherwise than by say[11]ing, that whatsoever God can be supposed to do or will, will be *for that Reason* Good or Just, because he wills it.

Now the necessary and unavoidable Consequences of this Opinion are such as these, *That to love God is by Nature an indifferent thing, and is morally Good only, because it is commanded by God; That to prohibit the Love of God, or command the Hatred of God, is not inconsistent with the Nature of God, but only with his Free Will; That it is not Inconsistent with the Natural Equity of God to command Blasphemy, Perjury, Lying, etc. That God may command what is contrary, as to all the Precepts of the Decalogue, so especially to the*

First, Second, Third; *That Holiness is not a Conformity with the Nature of God*; [12] *That God may oblige Man to what is impossible*; *That God hath no Natural Inclination to the Good of the Creatures*; *That God can justly doom an innocent Creature to Eternal Torment*. All which Propositions, with others of like Kind are Word for Word asserted by some late Authors. Though I think not fit to mention the Names of any of them in this Place, excepting only one, *Joannes Szydlovius*, who in a Book published at *Franeker*, hath professedly avowed and maintained the grossest of them. And yet neither he, nor the rest, are to be thought any more Blame-worthy herein, than many others, that holding the same Premises have either dissembled, or disowned those Conclusions which unavoidably follow there-from: But rather to be commended for their Openness, Simplicity and Ingenuity, in representing their Opinion nakedly to the World, such as indeed it is, without any Veil or Mask.

Wherefore since there are so many, both Philosophers and Theologers, that seemingly and verbally acknowledge such things as *Moral Good and Evil, Just and Unjust*, that contend notwithstanding that these are [13] not by *Nature*, but *Institution*, and that there is nothing *Naturally* or *Immutably Just* or *Unjust*; I shall from hence fetch the Rise of this Ethical Discourse or Inquiry *concerning things Good and Evil, Just and Unjust, Laudable and Shameful*: (For so I find these Words frequently used as synonymous in *Plato*, and other Ancient Authors,) demonstrating in the first Place, that if there be anything at all *Good* or *Evil, Just* or *Unjust*, there must of Necessity be *something Naturally and Immutably Good and Just*. And from thence I shall proceed afterward to shew what this *Natural, Immutable, and Eternal Justice is*, with the Branches and Species of it.

Chapter 10

The Critique of Thomas Hobbes
Mechanistic Fate

A Henry More, *The Immortality of the Soul* (1659), Book 1, Chapter X, Sections 1–3 (*Collection of Several Philosophical Writings*, 36–37 = ed. Jacob, 53–55)

Chap. X.

1. *An Answer to the first Excerption.* 2. *To the second.* 3. *An Answer to the third.* 4. *To the fourth Excerption.* 5. *An Answer to the fifth.* 6. *To the sixth.* 7. *To the seventh.* 8. *An Answer to the eighth and last.* 9. *A brief Recapitulation of what has been said hitherto.*

    1. WE have set down the chiefest passages in the Writings of Mr. *Hobbs*, that confident Exploder of *Immaterial Substances* out of the world. It remains now that we examine them, and see whether the force of his Arguments bears any proportion to the firmness of his belief, or rather mis-belief, concerning these things. To strip therefore the first Excerption of that long *Ambages* of words, and to reduce it to a more plain and compendious forme of reasoning, the force of his Argument lies thus: *That seeing every thing in the Universe is* Body (*the Universe being nothing else but an Aggregate of Bodies*) Body *and* Substance *are but names of one and the same thing; it being called* Body *as it fills a place, and* Substance *as it is the Subject of several Alterations and Accidents. Wherefore* Body *and* Substance *being all one,* Incorporeal Substance *is no better sense then an* Incorporeal Body, *which is a contradiction in the very termes.* But it is plain to all the world that this is not to prove, but to suppose what is to be proved, That the Universe is nothing else but an Aggregate of Bodies: When he has proved that, we will acknowledge the sequel; till then, he has proved nothing, and therefore this first argumentation must pass for nought.

    2. Let us examine the strength of the second, which certainly must be this, if any at all; *That which has its originall merely from Dreams, Fears and Superstitious Fancies, has no real existence in the world: But Incorporeal Substances have no other Original.* The Proposition is a Truth indubitable, but the Assumption is as weak as the other is strong; whether you understand it of the real Original of these Substances, or of the Principles of our knowledge That they are. And be their Original what it will, it is nothing to us, but so far forth as it is cognoscible to us, by Axiome first. And therefore when he says, they have no other Original then that of our own Phansy, he must be understood to affirme that there is no other Principle of the knowledge of their Existence then that we vainly imagine them to be; which is grossly false.

    For it is not the *Dreams* and *Fears* of Melancholick and Superstitious persons, from which Philosophers and Christians have argued the Existence of *Spirits* and *Immaterial Substances*; but from the evidence of Externall Objects of Sense, that is, the ordinary *Phaenomena* of Nature, in which there is discoverable so profound Wisdome and Counsell, that they could not but conclude that the Order of things in the world was from a higher Principle then the blind motions and jumblings of *Matter* and *mere Corporeal* Beings.

To which you may adde what usually they call *Apparitions*, which are so far from being merely the *Dreams* and *Fancies* of the Supersti[37]tious, that they are acknowledged by such as cannot but be deemed by most men over-Atheistical, I mean *Pomponatius* and *Cardan*, nay by *Vaninus* himself, though so devoted to Atheisme, that out of a perfect mad zeale to that despicable cause he died for it. I omit to name the *Operations of the Soul*, which ever appeared to the wisest of all Ages of such a transcendent condition, that they could not judge them to spring from so contemptible a Principle as *bare Body* or *Matter*. Wherefore to decline all these, and to make representation onely of *Dreams* and *Fancies* to be the occasions of the world's concluding that there are *Incorporeal Substances*, is to fancy his Reader a mere fool, and publickly to profess that he has a mind to impose upon him.

3. The third argumentation is this: *That which appears to us as well sleeping as waking, is nothing without us: But Ghosts, that is Immaterial Substances, appear to us as well sleeping as waking*. This is the weakest Argument that has been yet produced: for both the Proposition and Assumption are false. For if the Proposition were true, the Sun, Moon, Stars, Clouds, Rivers, Meadows, Men, Women, and other living creatures were nothing without us: For all these appear to us as well when we are *sleeping* as *waking*. But *Incorporeal Substances* do not appear to us as well *sleeping* as *waking*. For the Notion of an *Incorporeal Substance* is so subtile and refined, that it leaving little or no impression on the *Phansy*, its representation is merely supported by the free power of *Reason*, which seldome exercises it self in *sleep*, unless upon easy imaginable Phantasmes.

B More, *Immortality*, I,10,4. 7–8 (*Collection*, 37. 38–39 = ed. Jacob, 55. 57–58)

4. The force of the fourth Argument is briefly this: *Every Substance has dimensions; but a Spirit has no dimensions*. Here I confidently deny the Assumption. For it is not the Characteristicall of *a Body* to have *dimensions*, but to be *Impenetrable*. All Substance has *Dimensions*, that is, Length, Breadth, and Depth: but all has not *Impenetrability*. See my Letters to Monsieur *Des-Cartes*, besides what I have here writ in this present Treatise.

[. . .]

7. In this seventh Excerption is contained the same Argument that was found in the first; but to deal fairly and candidly, I must confess it is better back'd then before. For there he supposes, but does not prove, the chief ground of his Argument; but here he offers at a proof of it, couched, as I conceive, in these words [*and hath the dimensions of Magnitude, namely Length, Breadth and Depth*] for hence he would infer that the whole Universe is *Corporeal*, that is to say, every thing in the Universe, because there is nothing but has *Length, Breadth* and *Depth*. This therefore is the very last ground his Argument is to be resolved into. But how weak it is I have already intimated, it being not *Trinal Dimension*, but *Impenetrability*, that constitutes a *Body*.

[39] 8. This last Excerption seems more considerable then any of the former, or all of them put together: but when the force of the Arguments therein contained is duly weighed, they will be found of as little efficacy to make good the Conclusion as the rest. The first Argument runs thus; *Whatsoever is real, must have some place: But Spirits can have no place*. But this is very easily answered. For if nothing else be understood by *Place*, but *Imaginary Space*, Spirits and Bodies may be in the same *Imaginary Space*, and so the Assumption is false. But if by *Place* be meant the *Concave Superficies of one Body immediately environing another Body*, so that it be conceived to be of the very Formality of a *Place*, immediately to environ the *corporeal* Superficies of that Substance which is said to be placed; then it is impossible that a *Spirit* should be properly said to be in a *Place*, and so the Proposition will be false.

Wherefore there being these [43] two acceptions of *Place*, that Distinction of being there *Circumscriptivè* and *Definitivè* is an allowable Distinction, and the terms may not signify one and the same thing. But if we will with Mr. *Hobbs* (and I know no great hurt if we should doe so) confine the Notion of *Place* to *Imaginary Space*, this distinction of the Schools will be needless here, and we may, without any more adoe, assert, That *Spirits* are as truly in Place as *Bodies*.

His second Argument is drawn from that Scholastick Riddle, which I must confess seems to verge too near to profound Non-sense, That the Soul of man is *tota in toto* and tota in qualibet parte corporis. This mad Jingle it seems has so frighted Mr *Hobbs* sometime or other, that he never since could endure to come near the Notion of a *Spirit* again, not so much as to consider whether it were a mere Bug-bear, or some real Being. But if Passion had not surprised his better Faculties, he might have found a true settled meaning thereof, and yet secluded these wilde intricacies that the heedless Schools seem to have charged it with: For the *Immediate Properties* of a *Spirit* are very well intelligible without these Ænigmatical flourishes, viz. That it is *a Substance Penetrable and Indiscerpible*, as I have already shewn at large.

Nor is that Scholastick Aenigme necessary to be believed by all those that would believe the Existence of an *Incorporeal* Soul; nor do I believe Mr *Hobbs* his interpretation of this Riddle to be so necessary. And it had been but fair play to have been assured that the Schools held such a perfect contradiction, before he pronounced the belief thereof necessary to all those that would hold the Soul of Man *an Immaterial Substance, separable from the Body*. I suppose they may mean nothing by it, but what *Plato* did by his making the Soul to consist ἐκ μεριστῆς καὶ ἀμερίστου οὐσίας nor *Plato* any thing more by that *divisible* and *indivisible Substance*, then an Essence that is intellectually divisible, but really indiscerpible.

C More, *Immortality* II,3,1. 5–7 (*Collection*, 68–70 = ed. Jacob 94–97)

1. HIS first Argument runs thus (I will repeat it in his own words, as also the rest of them as they are to be found in his Treatise of *Liberty and Necessity*;) *I conceive,* (saith he) *that nothing taketh beginning from it self, but from the action of some other immediate agent without it self; and that therefore, when first a man hath an appetite or Will to something to which immediatly before he had no appetite nor Will, the cause of his Will is not the Will it self, but something else not in his own disposing: So that whereas it is out of controversy, that of voluntary actions the Will is the necessary cause, and by this which is said the Will is also caused* [69] *by other things, whereof it disposeth not, it followeth, that voluntary actions have all of them necessary causes, and therefore are necessitated.*

[. . .]

5. The Entrance into his first Argument is something obscure and ambiguous, *Nothing taketh beginning from it self:* But I shall be as candid and faithfull an Interpreter as I may. If he mean by *beginning,* beginning of *Existence,* it is undoubtedly true, That no Substance, nor Modification of Substance, taketh beginning from it self; but this will not infer the Conclusion he drives at. But if he mean, that *Nothing taketh beginning from it self, of being otherwise affected or modified then before*; he must either understand by *nothing,* no Essence, neither *Spirit* nor *Body,* or no *Modification* of Essence. He cannot mean *Spirit,* as admitting no such thing in the whole comprehension of Nature. If *Body,* it will not infer what he aims at, unless there be nothing but *Body* in the Universe; which is a mere precarious Principle of his, which he beseeches his credulous followers to admit, but he proves it no where, as I have already noted. If by *Modification* he mean the *Modification of Matter* or *Body*; that runs still upon the former Principle, That there is nothing but *Body* in the world, and therefore he proves nothing but upon a begg'd Hypothesis, and that a false one; as I have elsewhere demonstrated. Wherefore the most favourable Interpretation I can make is, That he means by *no thing*, no Essence, nor Modification

of Essence, being willing to hide that dearly-hug'd Hypothesis of his (*That there is nothing but Body in the World*) under so general and uncertain termes.

6. The words therefore in the other senses having no pretence to conclude any thing, let us see how far they will prevail in this, taking [70] *no thing*, for *no Essence*, or *no Modification of Essence*, or what will come nearer to the matter in hand, *no Faculty of an Essence*. And from this two-fold meaning, let us examine two Propositions that will result from thence, viz. *That no Faculty of any Essence can vary its Operation from what it is, but from the action of some other immediate Agent without it self*; or, *That no Essence can vary its Modification or Operation by it self, but by the action of some other immediate Agent without it*. Of which two Propositions the latter seems the better sense by far, and most natural. For it is very harsh, and, if truly looked into, as false, to say, *That the Mode or Faculty of any Essence changes it self*; for it is the Essence it self that exerts it self into these variations of Modes, if no externall Agent is the cause of these changes. And Mr *Hobbs* opposing an *External Agent* to *this Thing* that he saies does not change it self, does naturally imply, That they are both not *Faculties* but *Substances* he speaks of.

7. Wherefore there remains onely the latter Proposition to be examined, *That no Essence of it self can vary its Modification*. That some Essence must have had a power of moving is plain, in that there is *Motion* in the world, which must be the Effect of some Substance or other. But that *Motion* in a large sense, taking it for mutation or change, may proceed from that very Essence in which it is found, seems to me plain by Experience: For there is an Essence in us, whatever we will call it, which we find endued with this property; as appears from hence, that it has variety of perceptions, *Mathematical*, *Logical*, and I may adde also *Moral*, that are not any impresses nor footsteps of Corporeal Motion, as I have already demonstrated: and any man may observe in himself, and discover in the writings of others, how the Mind has passed from one of these perceptions to another, in very long deductions of Demonstration; as also what stilness from bodily Motion is required in the excogitation of such series of Reasons, where the Spirits are to run into no other posture nor motion then what they are guided into by the Mind it self, where these immaterial and intellectual Notions have the leading and [73] rule. Besides in grosser Phantasmes, which are supposed to be somewhere impressed in the Brain, the composition of them, and disclusion and various disposal of them, is plainly an arbitrarious act, and implies an Essence that can, as it lists, excite in it self the variety of such Phantasmes as have been first exhibited to her from External Objects, and change them and transpose them at her own will. But what need I reason against this ground of Mr *Hobbs* so sollicitously? it being sufficient to discover, that he onely saies, that *No Essence can change the Modifications of it self*, but does not prove it; and therefore whatever he would infer hereupon is merely upon a begg'd Principle.

D More, *Immortality* II,3,8–10 (Collection, 70–71 = ed. Jacob, pp. 97–98)

8. But however, from this precarious ground he will infer, that *whenever we have a Will to a thing, the cause of this Will is not the Will it self, but something else not in our own disposing*; the meaning whereof must be, *That whenever we Will, some corporeal impress, which we cannot avoid, forces us thereto*. But the Illation is as weak as bold; it being built upon no foundation, as I have already shown. I shall onely take notice how Mr. *Hobbs*, though he has rescued himself from the authority of the Schools, and would fain set up for himself, yet he has not freed himself from their fooleries in talking of *Faculties* and *Operations* (and the absurditie is alike in both) as separate and distinct from the *Essence* they belong to, which causes a great deal of distraction and obscurity in the speculation of things. I speak this in reference to those expressions of his, of the *Will being the cause of willing*, and of its being the *necessary* cause of voluntary actions, and of things not being in its disposing. Whenas, if a man would speak properly, and desired to be understood, he would say, *That the Subject in which is this power or act of*

willing, (call it Man or the Soul of Man) is the cause of this or that voluntary action. But this would discover his Sophistry, wherewith haply he has entrapt himself, which is this, *Something out of the power of the Will necessarily causes the Will; the Will once caused is the necessary cause of voluntary actions; and therefore all voluntary actions are necessitated.*

9. Besides that the first part of this Argumentation is groundless (as I have already intimated) the second is Sophisticall, that sayes *That the Will is the necessary cause of voluntary actions:* For by *necessary* may be understood either *necessitated*, forced and made to act, whether it will or no; or else it may signify that the Will is a *requisite* cause of voluntary actions, so that there can be no voluntary actions without it. The latter whereof may be in some sense true, but the former is utterly false. So the Conclusion being inferred from assertions whereof the one is groundless, the other Sophisticall, the Illation cannot but be ridiculously weak and despicable. But if he had spoke in the *Concrete* in stead of the *Abstract*, the Sophistry had been more grossly discoverable, or rather the train of his reasoning languid and contemptible. Omitting therefore to speak of the *Will* separately, which of it self is but a blind Power or Operation, let us speak of that *Essence* which is endued with *Will, Sense, Reason*, and other Faculties, and see what face this Argumentation of his will bear, which will then run thus;

F Enchiridium Metaphysicum (1671), chapter 27, sections 1. 13 (Opera omnia, II/1, 307. 314. Translation: Jacob, Henry More's Manual of Metaphysics, I, 98. 110–111)

1. *A representation of the opinions of the Nullibists and the Holenmerians.*

[...]

The second is of those who very willingly concede spirit to be somewhere, indeed add, besides, that they are not only entire in their own Ubi or place, but are entire even in individual points or parts of their Ubi at the same time; they describe the nature of spirit in such a way as if it were whole in the whole and whole in any part of it. Which the Greeks therefore aptly and concisely call οὐσίαν ὁλενμέρη and this very property (τῶν ἀσωμάτων οὐσιῶν τὴν ὁλενμέρειαν) the Holenmerism of incorporeal things. Whence even these other philosophers, diametrically opposed to the first, can be called by the most significant and sufficiently compendious term Holenmerian.

13. A Refutation of the First Reason of the Holenmerians

Now indeed, as for the reasons on account of which the Holenmerians adhere to such absurd opinions, these are certainly such as in no way can compensate those enormous difficulties and contradictions under which the opinion itself labours. For, the first, which so solicitously provides for the indivisibility of spirits, seems to me to undertake a superfluous or ineffectual trouble. Superfluous, indeed, if extension can be without all divisibility, as we have demonstrated clearly above it can be in the infinite immoveable extension distinct from moveable matter; ineffectual, indeed, if all extension is divisible and the essential presence of a spirit which pervades and is extended through the whole body CDE can for that very reason be divided. For thus the entire essence which occupies the whole body CDE is divided into parts. By no means, you may say, since it is wholly in the individual parts of the body. Therefore it would be divided into so many totalities, if I may say so. But what logical ears can bear such an absurd saying, and so removed from all reason, as that the whole is not divided into parts but into wholes? Indeed, you may say, let us at least understand this, that it is acknowledged that an essential presence can be divided according to so many totalities distinct in site which occupy the whole body CDE at the same time. Certainly, it would be so granted when you would have demonstrated a spirit not greater than a physical monad to be able to occupy in the same τῷ νῦν all the parts of the body CDE, but on this condition that you further acknowledge that not many totalities, but one entire essence, although most minute, occupies that entire space and, where necessary, is able to occupy in a moment an infinite one. Which it is necessary for the Holenmerians to hold of the divine essence, since, according to their option accepted in the second sense (by which they confine the entire essence of a spirit, in turn, in a minute point), even the divine essence is not greater than any physical monad. Whence it is clearly established that all those three objections which we brought in initially recur again here, and bury deep this first reason of the Holenmerians, so that the remedy applied by them is more intolerable than the illness itself.

G Ralph Cudworth, *The True Intellectual of the Universe* (1671/1678), Preface to the Reader (pp. 10r–10v)

And whereas we conceive this Atomick Physiology, *as to the Essentials thereof, to be Unquestionably True,* viz. *That the onely* Principles of Bodies, *are* Magnitude, Figure, Site, Motion, *and* Rest; *and* [¹⁰ᵛ] *that the* Qualities *and* Forms *of* Inanimate Bodies, *are Really nothing, but several* Combinations *of these, Causing several* Phancies *in us: (Which excellent Discovery therefore, so long agoe made, is a Notable Instance of the Wit and Sagacity of the* Ancients:) *So do we in the Next place, make it manifest, that this* Atomick Physiology *rightly understood, is so far from being either the* Mother *or* Nurse *of* Atheism, *or any ways Favourable thereunto, (as is* Vulgarly *supposed;) that it is indeed, the most directly* Opposite *to it of any, and the greatest* Defence *against the same. For, First, we have Discovered, That the* Principle, *upon which this* Atomology *is Founded, and from whence it Sprung, was no other than this*, Nothing out of Nothing, *in the True Sense thereof; or,* That Nothing can be Caused by Nothing: *from whence it was concluded, that in* Natural Generations, *there was no new* Real Entity *produced, which was not before: the Genuine Consequence whereof was Two-fold; That the* Qualities *and* Forms *of* Inanimate Bodies *are no* Entities Really distinct from the Magnitude, Figure, Site *and* Motion of Parts; *and, That* Souls *are Substances* Incorporeal, *not* Generated *out of* Matter. *Where we have shewed, That the* Pythagorick Doctrine, *of the* Prae-Existence *of* Souls, *was founded upon the very same* Principle *with the* Atomick physiology. *And it is from this very Principle, rightly understood, that Ourselves afterwards undertake to Demonstrate the Absolute Impossibility of all Atheism. Moreover, we have made it undeniably Evident, That the* Intrinsick Constitution *of this* Atomic Physiology *also is such, as that whosoever admits it, and rightly understands it, must needs acknowledge* Incorporeal Substance; *which is the Absolute Overthrow of* Atheism. *And from hence alone it is certain to us, without any* Testimonies *from* Antiquity, *that* Democritus *and* Leucippus, *could not possibly be the* First Inventors *of this* Philosophy, *they either not rightly Understanding it, or else wilfully Depraving the same: and the* Atomick Atheism, *being Really nothing else, but a* Rape *committed upon the* Atomick Physiology. *For which Reason, we do by no means here Applaud* Plato, *nor* Aristotle, *in their Rejecting this most* Ancient Atomick Physiology, *and Introducing again, that* Unintelligible First Matter, *and those* Exploded Qualities *and* Forms, *into* Philosophy. *For though this were probably done by* Plato, *out of a Disgust and Prejudice against the* Atomick Atheists, *which made him not so well Consider nor Understand that* physiology; *yet was he much disappointed of his Expectation herein; That* Atomology, *which he Exploded, (rightly understood,) being really the* Greatest *Bulwark against* Atheism; *and on the contrary, Those* Forms *and* Qualities *which he Espoused, the* Natural seed *thereof; they, besides their* Unintelligible Darkness, *bringing* Something out of Nothing, *in the* Impossible Sense; *which we shew to be, the* Inlet of all Atheism. *And thus in this* First Chapter, *have we not onely quite* Disarmed Atheism *of* Atomicism, *or shewed that the* Latter, *(rightly understood,) affordeth no manner of* Shelter *or* Protection *to the* Former; *But also made it manifest, that it is the greatest* Bulwark and Defence *against the same. Which is a thing afterwards further insisted on.*

H Cudworth, *True Intellectual System*, Chapter 5 (pp. 634–635)

We begin with the First. That we can have no *Idea, Conception,* or *Thought* of any thing, not *Subject to* Sense; nor the least *Evidence* of the *Existence* of any thing, but from the same. Thus a Modern *Atheistick* Writer[1]; *Whatsoever* [. . .] *we [can] conceive, hath been Perceived first by Sense, either at once or in parts; and a man can have no Thought representing any thing not Subject to Sense.* From whence it follows, that whatsoever is not *Sensible* and *Imaginable*, is utterly *unconceivable* and to us *Nothing*. Moreover the same Writer adds, *That the only Evidence which we have of the Existence of any thing, is from Sense*[2]; the Consequence whereof is this, That there being no *Corporeal Sense* of a *Deity,* there can be no *Evidence* at all of his *Existence.* Wherefore according to the Tenour of the *Atheistick Philosophy,* all is Resolved into *Sense;* as the only Criterion of Truth, accordingly as *Protagoras* in *Plato's Theaetetus*[3] concludes, *Knowledge to be Sense;* and a late Writer of our own[4] determins, *Sense to be Original Knowledge.* Here have we a wide Ocean before us, but we must contract our Sayls,[5] Were *Sense, Knowledge* and *Understanding;* then he that sees *Lights* and *Colours,* and feels *Heat* and *Cold,* would understand *Light* and *Colours, Heat* and *Cold,* and the like of all other Sensible Things: neither would there be any *Philosophy* at all concerning them. Whereas the Mind of man remaineth altogether unsatisfied, concerning the Nature [635] of these Corporeal Things, even after the Strongest Sensations of them, and is but thereby awakened, to a further *Philosophick Enquiry* and Search about them, what this Light and Colours, this Heat and Cold, etc. really should be; and whether they be indeed *Qualities* in the *Objects* without us, or only Phantasms and Sensations in our selves. Now it is certain, that there could be no Suspicion of any such thing as this, were *Sense* the Highest Faculty in us; neither can *Sense* it self ever decide this Controversie; since one Sense cannot judge of another, or correct the Error in it; all Sense as such, (that is, as *Phancy* and *Apparition*) being alike True. And had not these Atheists been Notorious Dunces in that *Atomick Philosophy* which they so much pretend to, they would clearly have learne'd from thence, That *Sense* is not *Knowledge* and *Understanding,* nor the *Criterion* of Truth as to *Sensible* things themselves; it reaching not to the *Essence* or *Absolute Nature* of them, but only taking notice of their *Outside,* and perceiving its own *Passions* from them, rather than the Things themselves: and That there is a Higher Faculty in the Soul, of *Reason* and *Understanding,* which judges of Sense, detects the *Phantastry* and *Imposture* of it; discovers to us that there is nothing in the Objects themselves like to those forementioned *Sensible Ideas;* and resolves all Sensible Things into *Intelligible Principles;* the Ideas whereof are not *Foraign* and *Adventitious,* and meer *Passive Impressions* upon the Soul from without, but *Native* and *Domestick* to it, or *Actively Exerted* from the Soul it self: no Passion being able to make a Judgment either of it self, or other things. This is a thing so Evident, that *Democritus* himself could not but take notice of it, and acknowledge it, though he made not a right use thereof; he in all Probability, continuing notwithstanding a *Confounded* and *Besotted Atheist.*

I Cudworth, *True Intellectual System*, 5 (pp. 636–637)

But to prove that there are *Cogitations* not subject to *Corporeal Sense,* we need go no further than this very *Idea* or *Description* of God; *A Substance Absolutely Perfect, Infinitely Good, Wise, and Powerful, Necessarily Self-existent, and the Cause of all other things.* Where there is not One Word unintelligible to him, that hath any Understanding in him, and yet no Considerative and Ingenuous Person can pretend, that he hath a *Genuine Phantasm,* or *Sensible Idea,* answering to any one of those words; either to *Substance,* or to *Absolutely Perfect,* or to *Infinitely,* or to *Good,* or to *Wise,* or to *Powerful,* or to *Necessity,* or to *Self-existence,* or to *Cause;* or indeed to *All,* or *Other,* or *Things.* Wherefore it is nothing but want of *Meditation,* together with a *Fond* and *Sottish Dotage* upon *Corporeal Sense,* which hath so far imposed upon some, as to make them believe, that they have not the least *Cogitation* of any thing not subject to *Corporeal Sense,* or that there is nothing in *Humane Understanding* or *Conception,* which was not First in *Bodily Sense*; a Doctrine highly favourable to Atheism. But since it is certain on the contrary, that we have many Thoughts not Subject to Sense, it is manifest, that whatsoever falls not under External Sense, is not therefore *Unconceivable*, and *Nothing*. Which whosoever asserts, must needs affirm *Life* and *Cogitation* it self, *Knowledge* or *Understanding*, *Reason* and *Memory*, *Volition* and *Appetite*, things of the greatest Moment and Reality, to be Nothing but mere Words without any *Signification*. Nay *Phancy* and *Sense* it self, upon this *Hypothesis*, could hardly escape from becoming *Non-Entities* too, forasmuch as neither *Phancy* nor *Sense* falls under *Sense*, but only the Objects of them; we neither *seeing Vision*, nor *feeling Action*, nor *hearing Audition*, much [637] less *hearing Sight*, or *seeing Taste*, or the like. Wherefore though God should be never so much Corporeal, as some Theists have conceived him to be; yet since the *Chief of his Essence*, and as it were his *Inside*, must by these be acknowledged to consist in *Mind*, *Wisdom* and *Understanding*, he could not possibly, as to this, fall under *Corporeal Sense* (Sight or Touch) any more than *Thought* can. But that there is *Substance Incorporeal* also, and therefore in it self altogether *Insensible*, and that the Deity is such, is demonstrated elsewhere.

J Cudworth, *True Intellectual System*, 5 (pp. 650–651)

But in the next place we add, that though it be true, that the Nature of things, admits of nothing *Contradictious*, and that whatsoever plainly Implies a *Contradiction*, must therefore of necessity be a *Non-Entity*, yet is this *Rule* notwithstanding, obnoxious to be much abused, when whatsoever mens Shallow and Gross Understandings cannot Reach to, they will therefore presently conclude to be *Contradictious*, and *Impossible*. As for example, the *Atheists* and *Materialists* cannot Conceive of any other *Substance* besides *Body*, and therefore do they determine presently, that *Incorporeal Substance* is a *Contradiction* in the very Terms; it being as much as to say *Incorporeal Body*; wherefore when God is said by Theologers, to be an *Incorporeal Substance*, this is to them an *Absolute Impossibility*. Thus a Modern Writer[6]; *The Universe, that is, the whole Mass of all things, is Corporeal; that is to say, Body. Now every Part of Body is Body, and Consequently every Part of the Universe is Body; and that which is not Body is no part thereof. And because the Universe is All, that which is no part of it, is nothing. Therefore when Spirits are called Incorporeal, this is only a name of Honour, and it may with more Piety be attributed to God himself, in whom we consider, not what Attribute best expresseth his Nature which is Incomprehensible; But what best expresseth our Desire to Honour him.* Where, *Incorporeal*, is said to be, an *Attribute of Honour*, that is, such an *Attribute*, as expresseth only the *Veneration* of mens Minds, but signifieth nothing in Nature, nor hath any *Philosophick Truth* and *Reality* under it: a *Substance Incorporeal* being as *Contradictious*, as *Something* and *Nothing*. Notwithstanding which, this *Contradiction* is only in the Weakness and Childishness of these mens Understandings, and not the thing it self; it being *Demonstrable*, that there is some other *Substance* besides *Body*, according to the *True* and *Genuine Notion* of it. But because, this mistake is not proper to Atheists only, there being some Theists also, who labour under this same Infirmity of Mind, not to be able to Conceive any other *Substance* besides *Body*, and who therefore assert a *Corporeal Deity*: we shall in the next place show, from a passage of a *Modern Writer*, what kind of *Contradictions* they are, which these Atheists impute to all Theology; namely such as these, that it supposes God, *to Perceive things Sensible, without any Organs of Sense; and to Understand and be Wise without any Brains.* Pious men (saith he)[7] *attribute to God Almighty for Honours sake, whatsoever they see Honourable in the world, as Seeing, Hearing, Willing, Knowing, Justice, Wisdom, etc., But they deny him such poor things, as Eyes, Ears and Brains, and other Organs, without which we Worms, neither have, nor can conceive, such Faculties to Be; and so far they do well. But when they dispute of God's Actions Philosophically, then do they Consider them again, as if He had indeed such Faculties. This is not well, and thence is it, that they fall into so many Difficulties. We ought not to dispute of God's Nature. He is no fit Subject of our Philosophy.* [651] *True Religion consisteth in Obedience to Christ's Lieutenants, and in giving God such Honour, both in Attributes and Actions, as they in their several Lieutenancies shall ordain.* Where the plain and *Undisguised* meaning of the Author seems to be this; That God is no Subject of Philosophy, as all Real things are: (accordingly as he declareth elsewhere,⁸ that *Religio non est Philosophia sed Lex, Religion is not a Matter of Philosophy, but only of Law and Arbitrary Constitution*) He having no *Real Nature* of his own, nor being any *True Inhabitant of the World or Heaven,* but (as all other *Ghosts* and *Spirits*) an *Inhabitant of mens Brains* only, that is, a *Figment of their Fear and Phancy,* or a meer *Political Scare-Crow.* And therefore such Attributes are to be given to him, without any Scrupulosity, as the Civil Law of every Country shall appoint, and no other. The Wise and Nasute,⁹ very well understanding, that all this Business of Religion, is nothing but meer *Pageantry,* and that the *Attributes* of the *Deity,* indeed signifie neither *True* nor *False* nor any thing in *Nature,* but only mens *Reverence* and *Devotion* towards the Object of their *Fear*: the manner of expressing which, is determined by Civil Law.

K Cudworth, *True Intellectual System*, 5 (pp. 662–663)

Accordingly a late Pretender to Politicks,¹⁰ who in this manner, discards all *Natural Justice* and *Charity,* determines concerning God, *Regnandi & Puniendi eos qui Leges suas violant, Jus Deo esse*¹¹ *à Solâ Potentiâ Irresistibli, That he has no other Right of Reigning over men, and of Punishing those who transgress his Laws, but only from his Irresistible Power.* Which indeed is all one as to say, *That God has no Right at all of Ruling over mankind, and imposing Commands upon them,* but what he doth in this kind, he doth it only by *Force* and *Power; Right,* and *Might,* (or *Power*) being very different things from one another, and there being no *Jus* or *Right* without *Natural Justice*; so that the word *Right* is here only Abused. And Consentaneously hereunto the same Writer further adds,¹² *Si Jus Regnandi habeat Deus ab Omnipotentia sua, manifestum est Obligationem ad praestandum ipsi Obedientiam incumbere Hominibus propter Imbicillitatem, That if God's Right of Commanding, be derived only from his Omnipotence,* [663] *then is it manifest, that mens Obligation to obey him, lies upon them only from their Imbecillity.* Or as it is further explained by him,¹³ *Homines ideò Deo subjectos esse, quia Omnipotentes non sunt, aut quia ad Resistendum satis Virium non habent, That men are therefore only Subject to God, because they are not Omnipotent, or have not sufficient Power to Resist him.* Thus do we see plainly, how the Atheists by reason of their *Vice* and and *Ill Nature,* (which makes them deny all *Natural Justice and Honesty, all Natural Charity and Benevolence*) transform the Deity into a monstrous shape; such an *Omnipotent Being,* as if he were, could have nothing neither of *Justice,* in him, nor of *Benevolence* towards his *Creatures;* and whose only *Right* and *Authority* of Commanding them, would be his *Irresistible Power;* whom his Creatures could not place any *Hope, Trust* and *Confidence* in, nor have any other *Obligation* to obey, than that of *Fear* and *Necessity,* proceeding from their *Imbecillity,* or *Inability to resist him.* And such a Deity as this, is indeed a *Mormo* or *Bug-bear,* a most *Formidable* and *Affrightful thing.*

L Cudworth, *True Intellectual System*, 5 (pp. 893–895)

But let us in the next place see, how our Modern *Atheistick Philosophers* and *Politicians,* will mannage and carry on this *Hypothesis,* so as to *Consociate* men by *Art,* into a *Body Politick,* that are *Naturally Dissociated* from one another, as also *Make Justice,* and *Obligation Artificial,* when there is none in *Nature.* First of all therefore these *Artificial Justice-Makers, City-Makers,* and *Authority-Makers,* tell us, that though men have an *Infinite Right* by *Nature,* yet may they *Alienate* this *Right* or part thereof, from themselves, and either *Simply Renounce* it, or *Transfer* the same upon some other Person; by means whereof it will become Unlawful for themselves, afterwards, to make use thereof. Thus late Writer,¹⁴ Men *my by Signs Declare, Velle se non Licitum sibi amplius fore, certum aliquid facere quòd Jure anteà fecisse poterant. That it is their Will, it shall no longer be Lawful for them, to do something which before they had a*

Right to do; and this is called by him, a *Simple Renunciation* of *Right*; and further saith he, they *may declare again, Velle se non Licitum sibi amplius fore aliui Resistere, etc, That it is their Will, it shall be no longer Lawful for them, to Resist this or that particular Person, whom before they might Lawfully have resisted*; and this is called a *Translation of Right*. But if there be Nothing in its own *Nature Unlawful*, then cannot this be *Unlawful*[15] for a man afterwards, to make use of such Liberty as he had before in *Words Renounced* or *Abandoned*. Nor can any man by his meer *Will*, make any thing *Unlawful* to him, which was not so in it self; but only Suspend the Exercise of so much of his *Liberty*, as he thought good. But however, could a man by his *Will, Oblige* himself, or make any thing *Unlawful* to him, there would be Nothing got by this, because then might he by his *Will, Disoblige* himself again, and make the same *Lawful* as before. For what is *Made* meerly by *Will*, may be *Destroyed* by *Will*. Wherefore these *Politicians* will yet urge the business further, and tell us, That no *man can be Obliged but by his own Act*, and that the *Essence of Injustice*, is Nothing else, but *Dati Repetitio*, The *taking away of that, which one had before given*. To which we again Reply, that were a man *Naturally Unobliged* to any thing, then could he no way be *Obliged*, to stand to his own *Act*, so that it should be Really *Unjust* and Unlawful for him, at any time upon Second thoughts, *Voluntarily to undo*, what he had before *voluntarily done*. But the Atheists here plainly Render *Injustice*, a meer *Ludicrous thing*; when they tell us, that it is Nothing but such an *Absurdity in Life*, as it is in *Disputation*, when a man Denies a *Proposition that he had before Granted*. Which is no Real Evil [894] in him as a *Man*, but only a thing Called an *Absurdity*, as a *Disputant*, That is, *Injustice* is no *Absolute Evil* of the *Man*; but only a *Relative Incongruity* in him, as a *Citizen*. As when a man speaking Latine, observes not the *Laws* of *Grammar*, this is a kind of *Injustice* in him, as a Latinist or *Grammarian*; so when one who lives in *Civil Society*, observes not the *Laws* and *Conditions* thereof, this is, as it were. The *False Latine* of a *Citizen*, and nothing else. According to which *Notion* of *Injustice*, there is no such Real *Evil* or *Hurt* in it, as can any way withstand, the *Force* of *Appetite* and *Private Utility*, and *Oblige* men to *Civil Obedience*, when it is Contrary to the same. But these *Political Juglers* and *Enchanters*, will here cast yet a further *Mist* before mens Eyes with their *Pacts* and *Covenants*. For men by their *Covenants*, say they, may Unquestionably *Oblige* themselves, and make things *Unjust* and *Unlawful* to them, that were not so before. Wherefore *Injustice* is again Defined by them, and that with more Speciousness, to be the *Breach* of *Covenants*. But though it be true, that if there be *Natural Justice; Covenants* will *Oblige*; yet upon the Contrary *Supposition*, that there is *Nothing Naturally Unjust*; this cannot be *Unjust*, neither to *Break Covenants. Covenants* without *Natural Justice*, are nothing but meer *Words* and *Breath*; (as indeed these *Atheistick Politicians* themselves, agreeably to their own *Hypothesis*, call them) and therefore can they have no *Force to Oblige*. Wherefore these *Justice-Makers*, are themselves at last necessitated, to fly to *Laws* of *Nature*, and to Pretend, this to be a *Law* of *Nature*, That men should *Stand to their Pacts and Covenants*. Which is plainly to Contradict their main *Fundamental Principle*, that by *Nature* nothing is *Unjust* or *Unlawul*[16]; for if it be so, then can there be no *Laws* of *Nature*; and if there be *Laws* of *Nature*, then must there be something Naturally Unjust and Unlawful. So that this is not to *Make Justice*, but clearly to *Unmake* their *own Hypothesis*, and to suppose *Justice* to have been already Made by *Nature*, or to be in *Nature*; which is a *Gross Absurdity* in *Disputation*; to *Affirm* what one had before *Denied*. But these their *Laws of Nature* are indeed nothing but *Jugling Equivocation*, and a meer *Mockery*; themselves again acknowledging them to be no *Laws*, because *Law is* nothing but the *Word of him, who hath Command over others*; but only *Conclusions or Theorems concerning what conduces* to the *Conservation* and Defence of themselves; upon the Principle of *Fear*; that is, indeed the *Laws* of their own *Timorous*, and *Cowardly Complexion:* for they who have Courage and Generosity in them, according to this *Hypothesis*, would never Submit to such sneaking Terms of *Equality*, and *Subjection*, but venture for *Dominion*; and resolve either to *Win the Saddle*, or *Loose the Horse*. Here therefore do our *Atheistick Politicians* plainly daunce round in a *Circle*; they first deriving the *Obligation* of *Civil Laws*, from that of *Covenants*, and then that of *Covenants* from the *Laws of Nature*; and Lastly, the *Obligation* both of these *Laws of Nature*, and of *Covenants* themselves, again, from the *Law, Command*, and *Sanction* of the Civil *Sovereign*; without which neither of them would at all Oblige. And thus is it manifest, how vain the *Attempts* of these *Politicians* are, to Make *Justice Artificially*, when there is no such thing *Naturally*; (which is indeed no less than, to make *Something* out of *Nothing*) and [895] *by Art to Consociate into Bodies Politick*, those whom *Nature* had *Dissociated* from one another: a thing as impossible as to Ty *Knots* in the *Wind* or *Water*, or to build up a Stately *Palace* or *Castle* out of Sand. Indeed the *Ligaments*, by which these *Politicians* would tie the Members of their huge *Leviathan*, or *Artificial Man* together, are not so good as *Cobwebs*; they being really nothing, but meer *Will* and *Words*. For if Authority and Sovereignty be made only by *Will* and *Words*, then is it plain, that by *Will* and *Words*, they may be *Unmade* again at pleasure.

M Cudworth, *A Treatise Concerning Eternal and Immutable Morality* (1731), Book IV Chapter 6, Sections 4–7

4. But I have not taken all this Pains only to Confute Scepticism or Phantasticism, or meerly to defend and corroborate our Argument for the Immutable Natures of Just and Unjust; but also for some other Weighty Purposes that are very much conducing to the Business that we have in hand. And first of all, that the Soul is [287] not a meer *Rasa Tabula*, a Naked and Passive Thing, which has no innate Furniture or Activity of its own, nor any thing at all in it, but what was impressed upon it without; for if it were so, then there could not possibly be any such Thing as Moral Good and Evil, Just and Unjust; Forasmuch as these Differences do not arise meerly from the outward Objects, or from the Impresses which they make upon us by Sense, there being no such Thing in them; in which Sense it is truly affirmed by the Author of the *Leviathan*, Page 24. *That there is no common Rule of Good and Evil to be taken from the Nature of the Objects themselves*, that is, either considered absolutely in themselves, or Relatively to external Sense only, but according to some other interior Analogy which Things have to a certain inward Determination in the Soul it self, from whence the Foundation of all this Difference must needs arise, as I shall shew afterwards; Not that the Anticipations of Morality spring meerly from intellectual Forms and notional Idea's of the Mind, or from certain Rules or Propositions, arbitrarily printed upon the Soul as upon a Book, but from some [288] other more inward, and vital Principle, in intellectual Beings, as such, whereby they have a natural Determination in them to do some Things, and to avoid others, which could not be, if they were meer naked Passive Things. Wherefore since the Nature of Morality cannot be understood, without some Knowledge of the Nature of the Soul, I thought it seasonable and requisite here to take this Occasion offered, and to prepare the Way to our following Discourse, by shewing in general, that the Soul is not a meer Passive and Receptive Thing, which hath no innate active Principle of its own, Because upon this Hypothesis there could be no such Thing as Morality.

5. Again, I have the rather insisted upon this Argument also, because that which makes Men so inclinable to think that Justice, Honesty and Morality are but thin, airy and phantastical Things, that have little or no Entity or Reality in them besides Sensuality, is a certain Opinion in Philosophy which doth usually accompany it, that Matter and Body are the first Original and Source of all Things; that there is no Incorporeal Substance superior to Matter and independent upon it: And therefore that sensible Things are the only real and substantial Things in Nature; but Souls and Minds springing secondarily out of Body, that Intellectuality and Morality belong unto them, are but thin and evanid Shadows of sensible and corporeal Things, and not natural, but artificial and factitious Things that do as it were border upon the Confines of Non-Entity.

6. This is a Thing excellently well observed by *Plato*, and therefore I shall set down his Words at large concerning it. "These Men making this Distribution of Things, that all Things that are, are

either by Nature, or Art, or Chance, they imagine that the greatest and most excellent Things that are in the World, are to be attributed to Nature and Chance; which working upon those greater Things which are made by Nature, does form and fabricate certain smaller Things afterward, which we commonly call artificial Things. To speak more plainly, Fire, Water, Air, and Earth, they attribute wholly to Nature and Chance, but not to any Art or Wisdom; in like manner those Bodies or the Earth, the Sun, Moon and Stars, they will have to be made out of them fortuitously agitated; and so by Chance causing both divers Systems and Compages of Things: thus they would have the whole Heavens made, and all the Earth and Animals, and all the Seasons of the Year, not by any Mind Intellect, or God, not by any Art or Wis[291]dom, but all by blind Nature and Chance. But Art and Mind afterwards springing up out of these, to have begotten certain ludicrous Things, which have little Truth and Reality in them, but are like Images in a Glass, such as Picture and Musick produces. Wherefore these Men attribute all Ethicks, Politicks, Morality and Laws, not to Nature, but to Art, whose Productions are not real and substantial."

7. Now this Philosopher, that he may evince that Ethicks, Politicks and Morality are as real and substantial Things, and as truly natural as those Things which belong to Matter, he endeavours to shew that Souls and Minds do not spring secondarily out of Matter and Body, but that they are real Things in Nature, superior and antecedent to Body and Matter. His Words are these: "These Men are all ignorant concerning the Nature of Mind and Soul, as in other Regards, so especially in respect of its Original, as it is in order of Nature before Matter and Body, and does not result out of it; but does command it, govern it, and rule it." And I have in like manner in this antecedent Discourse, endeavoured to shew that Wisdom, Knowledge, Mind and Intellect, are no thin Shadows or Images of corporeal and sensible Things, nor do result secondarily out of Matter and Body, and from the Activity and Impressions thereof; but have an independent and self-subsistent Being, which in order of Nature, is before Body; all particular created Minds being but derivative Participations of one Infinite Eternal Mind, which is antecedent to all corporeal Things.

N Cudworth, *Treatise of Freewill*, Chapter 22

Another argument for the natural necessity of all actions much used by the Stoics was this, that οὐδέν ἀναίτιον nothing can be without a cause, and whatsoever has a cause must of necessity come to pass. Mr Hobbes thinks to improve this argument into a demonstration after this manner. Nothing can come to pass without a sufficient cause, and a sufficient cause is that to which nothing is needful to produce the effect, wherefore every sufficient cause must needs be a necessary cause, or produce the effect necessarily.

To which childish argumentation the reply is easy, that a thing may have sufficient power, or want nothing of power necessary to enable it to produce an effect, which yet may have power also or freedom not to produce it. Nothing is produced without an efficient cause, and such an efficient cause as had a sufficiency of power to enable it to produce it. But yet that person, who had sufficient power to produce an effect might notwithstanding will not to produce it. So that there are two kinds of sufficient causes. One is such as acteth necessarily and can neither suspend nor determine its own action. Another is such as acteth contingently or arbitrarily, and hath a power over its own action, either to suspend it or determine it as it pleaseth.

I shall subjoin to this another argument, which Mr Hobbes glories of, as being the sole inventor of. From the necessity of a disjunctive proposition nothing can be so contingent but that it was necessarily true of it beforehand that it will either come to pass or not come to pass. Therefore, says he, if there be a necessity in the disjunction, there must be a necessity in one or other of the two parts thereof alone by itself. If there be no necessity that it shall come to pass, then must it be necessary that it shall not come to pass, as if there could not be no necessity in the disjunction though both members of it were contingent, and neither of them necessary. This is a most shameful ignorance in logic, especially for one who pretends so much to geometrical demonstration.

And yet this childish and ridiculous nonsense and sophistry of his was stolen from the Stoics too, who played the fools in logic after the same manner. Every proposition, said they, concerning a supposed future contingent, that it will come to pass, was either true or false beforehand and from eternity. If it were true then it must of necessity come to pass, if false, then was it necessary it should not come to pass. And yet this ridiculous sophistry puzzled not only Cicero but also Aristotle himself so much as to make them hold that propositions concerning future contingents were to be neither true nor false.

O Anne Conway, *Principles of the Most Ancient and the Most Modern Philosophy* (1690), Chapter 9, Sections 3–4 (van Helmont, *Opuscula Philosophica*, 136–137)

[§.3. Nor the Philosophy of Hobbs and Spinosa, (falsely so feigned,) but diametrically opposite to them.]

§.3. BUT, Secondly, as to what pertains to Hobbs's Opinion, this is yet more contrary to this our Philosophy, than that of Cartes; for Cartes acknowledged God to be plainly Immaterial, and an Incorporeal Spirit. Hobbs affirms God himself to be Material and Corporeal; yea, nothing else but Matter and Body, and so confounds God and the Creatures in their Essences, and denies that there is any Essential Distinction between them. These and many more the worst of Consequences are the Dictates of Hobbs's Philosophy; to which may be added that of Spinosa; for this Spinosa also confounds God and the Creatures together, and makes but one Being of both; all which are diametrically opposite to the Philosophy here delivered by us.

[§.4. That they who have attempted to refute Hobbs and Spinosa, have given them too much advantage.]

§.4. BUT the false and feeble Principles of some who have undertaken to refute the Philosophy of Hobbs and Spinosa, so called, have given them a greater advantage against themselves; so that they have not only in effect, not refuted them, but more exposed themselves to Contempt and Laughter.

But if it be Objected, That this our Philosophy seems, at least, very like that of *Hobbs*, because he taught that all Creatures were originally one Substance, from the lowest and most ignoble, to the highest and noblest; from the smallest Worm, Insect, or Fly, unto the most Glorious Angel; yea, from the least Dust or Sand, unto the most excellent of all Creatures; and then this, that every Creature is Material and Corporeal; yea, Matter and Body it self; and by consequence the most Noble Actions thereof, are either Material and Corporeal, or after a certain Corporeal manner. Now I Answer to the First, I grant that all Creatures are originally one Substance, from the lowest to the highest, and consequently convertible or changeable, from one of their Natures into another; and although *Hobbs* saith the same, yet that is no prejudice to the Truth of it, as neither are other parts of that Philosophy where *Hobbs* affirms something that is true, therefore an *Hobbism*, or an Opinion of *Hobbs* alone.

P Conway, *Principles*, 9,6 (van Helmont, *Opuscula Philosophica*, 139–139)

§.6. SECONDLY, If it be said, by way of Objection, that according to this Philosophy, every Creature is Material and Corporeal; yea, Body and Matter it self, as *Hobbs* teacheth. Now I Answer, That by Material and Corporeal, as also by Matter and Body, here the thing is far otherwise understood, than

Hobbs understood it, and which was never discovered to *Hobbs* or *Cartes*, otherwise than in a Dream: For what do they understand by Matter and Body? Or, What Attributes do they ascribe to them? None, certainly, but these following as are Extension and Impenetrability, which nevertheless are but one Attribute; to which also may be referred Figurability and Mobility. But, suppose, those are distinct Attributes, certainly this profits nothing, nor will ever help us to understand what that excellent Substance is, which they call Body and Matter; for they have never proceeded beyond the Husk or Shell, nor ever reached the Kernel, they only touch the Superficies, never discerning the Centre, they were plainly ignorant of the noblest and most excellent Attributes of that Substance which they call Body and Matter, and understood nothing of them. But if it be demanded, what are those more excellent Attributes? I Answer, these following, Spirit, or Life, and Light, under which I comprehend a capacity of all kind of Feeling, Sense, and Knowledge, Love, Joy, and Fruition, and all kind of Power and Virtue, which the noblest Creatures have or can have; so that even the vilest and most contemptible Creature; yea, Dust and Sand, may be capable of all those Perfections, *sc.* through various and succedaneous Transmutations from the one into the other; which according to the Natural Order of Things, require long Periods of Time for their Consummation, although the Absolute Power of God (if it had pleased him) could have accelerated or hastened all Things, and effected it in one moment: But this Wisdom of God saw it to be more expedient, that all Things should proceed in their Natural Order and Course; so that after this manner, that Fertility or Fruitfulness, which he hath endued every Being with, may appear, and the Creatures have Time by Working still to promote themselves to a greater Perfection, as the Instruments of Divine Wisdom, Goodness and Power, which operates in, and with them; for therein the Creature hath the greater Joy, when it possesseth what it hath, as the Fruit of its own labour.

But this capacity of the afore-mentioned Perfections is quite a distinct Attribute from Life, and Understanding, or Knowledge, quite distinct from the former, *viz*. Extension and Figure; and so also a Vital Action is plainly distinct from Local, or Mechanical Motion, although it is not nor cannot be separated from it, but still useth the same at least, as its Instrument, in all its concourse with the Creatures.

Notes

1 Thomas Hobbes, *Leviathan I* 3 (ed. N. Malcolm), 17 ("can" is an addition by Cudworth).
2 This is a gloss and not a *verbatim* quotation from the section just quoted above.
3 Plato, *Theaetetus* 152a1–4 = Protagoras, fr. B1 (eds. H. Diels-W. Kranz).
4 See Thomas Hobbes, *Leviathan I* 7 (ed. N. Malcolm), 40: "as for knowledge of fact, it is originally sense, and ever after, memory".
5 See n. 1.
6 Thomas Hobbes, *Leviathan III* 46 (ed. N. Malcolm), 440–441.
7 Thomas Hobbes, "Questions Concerning Liberty, Necessity & Change" (1654/6), in W. Molesworth (ed.), *The English Works of Thomas Hobbes* V, 435–436.
8 Thomas Hobbes, *De Homine* (1642), in W. Molesworth (ed.), *Thomae Hobbes Opera Philosophica quae Latine scripsit omnia II*, London: J. Bohn, 1839, 119. Hobbes words are as follows: *religio itaque philosophia non est, sed in omni civitate lex.*
9 *nasute* : *fault-finding.*
10 Thomas Hobbes, *De cive* XV 5 (Howard Warrender (ed.), The Clarendon Edition of the Works of Thomas Hobbes 2: De Cive: The Latin Version, XV 5, 221).
11 *esse* 1 : *est* ed. Molesworth.
12 Thomas Hobbes, *De cive* XV 7 (Howard Warrender [ed.], The Clarendon Edition of the Works of Thomas Hobbes 2: De Cive: The Latin Version, XV 7, 222).
13 Thomas Hobbes, *De cive* XV 7 (Howard Warrender (ed.), The Clarendon Edition of the Works of Thomas Hobbes 2: De Cive: The Latin Version, XV 7, 223). This is Hobbes' footnote to *propter imbecillitatem.*
14 Thomas Hobbes, *De Cive* II 4, 100 (ed. Howard Warrender).
15 *Unlawful* corr. : *Unlwful* 1.
16 *Unlawful* corr. : *Ulawful* 1.

Chapter 11

The Critique of René Descartes
Infinity and Nullibism

A Henry More, *Democritus Platonissans*, To the Reader (Second edition, 189–190 = ed. Jacob, 403f.)

Nay and that sublime and subtill Mechanick too, Des-Chartes, though he seem to mince it must hold infinitude of worlds, or which is as harsh, one infinite one. For what is his mundus indefinitè extensus, *but* extensus infinitè? *Else it sounds onely* infinitus quoad nos, *but* simpliciter finitus.[1] *But if any space be lest out unstuffd with Atoms, it will hazard the dissipation of the whole frame of Nature into disjoynted dust; as may be proved by the Principles of his own Philosophie. And that there is space whereever God is, or any actuall and self-subsistent Being, seems to me no plainer then one of their* κοιναὶ ἔννοιαι.[2]

For mine own part, I must confesse these apprehensions do plainly oppose what heretofore I have conceived; but I have sworn more faithfull friendship with Truth then with my self. And therefore without all remorse lay battery against mine own edifice: not sparing to shew how weak [190] *that is, that my self now deems not impregnably strong. I have at the latter end of the last Canto of Psychathanasia, not without triumph concluded, that the world hath not continued ab* aeterno *from this ground:—Extension That's infinite implies a contradiction. And this is in answer to an objection against my last argument of the souls Immortalitie, viz. divine goodnesse. Which I there make the measure of his providence. That ground limits the Essence of the world as well as its duration, and satisfies the curiositie of the Opposer, by shewing the incompossibilitie in the Creature, not want of goodnesse in the Creatour to have staid the framing of the Universe. But now roused up by a new Philosophick furie, I answer that difficultie by taking away the Hypothesis of either the world or time being finite: defending the infinitude of both. Which though I had done with a great deal of vigour and life, and semblance of assent, it would have agreed well enough with the free heat of Poesie, and might have passed for a pleasant flourish: but the severity of my own judgement and sad Genius, hath cast in many correctives and coolers into the Canto it self; so that it cannot amount to more then a discussion. And discussion is no prejudice but an honour to the truth: for then and never but then is she victorious. And what a glorious Trophee shall the finite world erect when it hath vanquished the Infinite; a Pygmee a Giant!*

H. M.

B More, *Democritus Platonissans*, Cantos 8–14. 45 (Second edition, 193–194. 202 = ed. Jacob, 407–409. 418)

8

All in just bignesse and right colours dight.
But totall presence without all defect
'Longs onely to that Trinity by right,
Ahad, Aeon, Psyche with all graces deckt,
Whose nature well this riddle will detect;
A circle whose circumference no where
Is circumscrib'd, whose Centre's each where set,

But the low Cusp's a figure circular,
Whose compasse is ybound, but centre's every where.

9

Wherefore who'il judge the limits of the world
By what appears unto our failing sight
Appeals to sense, reason down headlong hurld
Out of her throne by giddie vulgar might.
But here base senses dictates they will dight
With specious title of Philosophie,
And stiffly will contend their cause is right
From rotten rolls of school antiquity,
Who constantly denie corporall Infinitie.

10

But who can prove their corporalitie
Since matter which thereto's essentiall
If rightly sifted's but a phantasie.
And quantitie who's deem'd Originall
Is matter, must with matter likewise fall.
What ever is, is Life and Energie
From God, who is th' Originall of all;
Who being everywhere doth multiplie
His own broad shade that endlesse throughout all doth lie.
[194]

11

He from the last projection of light
Ycleep'd *Shamajim*, which is liquid fire
(It *Aether* eke and centrall *Tasis* hight)
Hath made each shining globe and clumperd mire
Of dimmer Orbs. For Nature doth inspire
Spermatick life, but of a different kind.
Hence those congenit splendour doth attire
And lively heat, these darknesse dead doth bind,
And without borrowed rayes they be both cold and blind.

12

All these be knots of th' universall stole
Of sacred *Psyche*; which at first was fine,
Pure, thin, and pervious till hid powers did pull
Together in severall points and did encline
The nearer parts in one clod to combine.
Those centrall spirits that the parts did draw

The measure of each globe did then define,
Made things impenetrable here below,
Gave colour, figure, motion, and each usuall law.

13

And what is done in this Terrestriall starre
The same is done in every Orb beside.
Each flaming Circle that we see from farre
Is but a knot in *Psyches* garment tide.
From that lax shadow cast throughout the wide
And endlesse world, that low'st projection
Of universall life each thing's deriv'd
What er'e appeareth in corporeall fashion;
For body's but this spirit, fixt, grosse by conspissation.

14

And that which doth conspissate active is;
Wherefore not matter but some living sprite
Of nimble nature which this lower mist
And immense field of Atoms doth excite,
And wake into such life as best doth fit
With his own self. As we change phantafies
The essence of our soul not chang'd a whit
So do these Atomes change their energies
Themselves unchanged into new Centreities.
[. . .]
[202] 45

Wherefore this wide and wast Vacuity,
Which endlesse is out stretched thorough all.
And lies even equall with the Deity,
Nor is a thing meerly imaginall,
(For it doth farre mens phantasies forestall
Nothing beholden to our devicefull thought)
This inf'nite voidnesse as much our mind doth gall,
And has as great perplexities ybrought
As if this empty space with bodies were yfraught.

C More, *Four Letters of Henry More to René Descartes*, First Letter (11th December 1648) (*Opera omnia*, II/2, 234–236 = Adam/Tannery, V, 283–242. Translation: Christian Hengstermann)

Firstly, the definition which you give of matter or body is far broader than is warranted. For God also seems to be an extended substance, as do angels and indeed every thing subsisting through itself. Hence, extension is apparently coterminous with the absolute essence of things, although the latter may differ according to the differences between the essences themselves. I view God as being extended in his own way on account of his omnipresence, occupying as he does the whole fabric of the world and each of its particles in an intimate fashion. How else could he impress motion upon matter, which, as you yourself concede, he did at some point and which he does to this day, unless he touches, or had at least at some point touched, the matter of the universe from close up? He could not have done so at any time had he not been present everywhere and occupied every single place. Hence, God is extended and expanded in his own way, and therefore is an extended substance.

Nor does it follow from this that he is a body or matter which your mind, that ingenious artist, has so skilfully formed into little orbs and grooved particles. For this reason, "extended substance" is broader than "body".

[. . .]

Your argument to support this definition of yours is so misguided and downright sophistical that I am further encouraged to disagree with you in this matter. A body, you argue, would be a body even if it were deprived of its softness and hardness as well as its heaviness or lightness. Thus, it would continue to be a body if all those together with all the other qualities perceived in a material body were to be removed from it. It is as though you were to say that a waxen pair of scales could be such without having a round, cubic or pyramidal shape, or that it could remain a complete waxen pair of scales without any shape at all, which is impossible. For even though neither this nor that figure is tied to the wax so closely that it could not cast off one or the other of them, it is nevertheless an absolute and inescapable necessity that wax should always have a shape. Thus, even though matter is not necessarily soft or hard and hot or cold, it is absolutely necessary that it is *sensible* or, if you will, *tangible* according to that most apposite definition of Lucretius:

> For nothing, if it be not body, can touch and be touched.[3]

Certainly, this notion need not at all be at odds with your views, since your philosophy most clearly follows those ancient philosophers mentioned in Theophrastus' *Περὶ αἰσθήσεως* in making all sensation consist in touch, which I most willingly accept as perfectly true. However, should you take exception to body being defined by its relationship to our senses, I allow for this tangibility to be broader and more general, signifying the mutual contact between bodies and their power of touching one another, whether they are animate or inanimate. Let it be defined then as the surfaces of two or more bodies being situated immediately adjacent to each other. And this reveals another property of matter or body which we could call "impenetrability": one body cannot penetrate or be penetrated by another body. From that the difference between the divine and the corporeal nature becomes quite clear: the former is able to penetrate the latter, while the latter cannot penetrate itself. Hence, Virgil, following his Platonists, seems to argue altogether more felicitously than Descartes himself, singing the following song in accordance with their views:

> The spirit within nourishes, and mind instilled throughout the living parts activates the whole mass, and mingles with this vast body.[4]

I omit other more remarkable properties of the divine extension because it is not necessary to expound them here. These few should suffice to demonstrate that it is much safer to define matter as a tangible or, as I have explained above, an impenetrable substance than as an extended thing. For the tangibility or impenetrability mentioned can be attributed to body universally. Your definition, by contrast, infringes the law of *καθόλου πρῶτον*, as it is not reciprocal with the thing defined.[5]

[. . .]

Secondly, you imply that it is not possible even by divine power that there could exist a vacuum in the proper sense of the word. Thus, for example, if every body were to be removed from a vessel, its sides would necessarily meet. However, this seems to me to be both wrong and at odds with what you have said before. For if God impresses motion upon matter, as you have shown earlier, can he not press against it, preventing the sides of the vessel from meeting? However, it is a contradiction to say [, you argue,] that the sides of a vessel are distant from one another without there being anything between them. Moreover, the learned ancients Epicurus, Democritus, Lucretius and others also took a different view. However, let us not dwell on that slight kind of argument any further. I contend that the divine extension lies between them, that your supposition that only matter is extended is ill-founded, and that, as I have said before, the sides will approach each other not by logical, but by natural necessity, and God alone can prevent them from meeting again. For since the particles, notably those of the first and second elements, are impelled forward in such violent motion, it is necessary that they rush to the vacated place, forcing those adjacent to them with them.

[. . .]

Fourthly, I do not understand your notion of the indefinite extension of the world. For that indefinite extension is either infinite in itself or in relation to us. If you conceive extension to be infinite [sc. in itself], why do you obscure your view with such overly restrained and moderate words? If you believe it infinite in relation to us only, extension will in reality be finite, for our mind is neither the measure of truth nor reality. And therefore, since there is another expansion that is infinite itself, namely that of the divine essence, the matter of your vortices will move away from its centres and the whole fabric of the world will dissipate into wandering particles and atoms.

Indeed, I find your modesty and restraint in not subscribing to the infinity of matter all the more surprising seeing that you yourself acknowledge the particles to be both infinite and divided in actuality in Articles 34 and 35. But even if you had not done this, you can still be shown to be committed to matter's infinity in the following fashion. If a quantity is infinitely divisible, it must actually have infinite parts. Therefore, just as it is completely ἀμέχανον or impossible to take a small knife or some other instrument and mechanically cut a body into visible parts which are not actual parts, so it is likewise completely ἄλογον and contrary to reason, even notionally, to divide a quantity into parts which are not actual real parts of this whole.

Moreover, you may add to this the fact that the hypothesis that the world is simply and truly infinite can explain and prove the modes of rarefaction and condensation propounded in Articles 6 and 7 above, as well as your principle "that only body is extended and an extension cannot be of nothing". Thus, what is established by the necessity of logic or contradiction in the one case is established with utmost certainty by the necessity of physics and mechanics in the other.

D More, *Four Letters to Descartes*, Second Letter (5th March 1649) (II/2, 245–246 = AT, V, 305–308)

III

"And therefore you assume that God has parts external to each other and is divisible, attributing to him the whole essence of a corporeal thing."

I do not attribute to him any such essence. For I deny that extension belongs to a body, insofar as it is a body, but rather insofar as it is a being or at least a substance. Besides, God, insofar as the human mind comprehends God, is everywhere in his entirety. He is present in all places and all spaces as well as in each point of space in his whole essence. However, it does not follow that he has parts external to each other or that, by implication, he is divisible, even though he occupies all places very closely and tightly without leaving any gaps in between. Hence, I acknowledge the divine presence or amplitude, as you call it, to be measurable, but I deny that he is divisible in any way.

However, absolutely everybody—fools as well as philosophers—agree, and I too perceive and assent in my mind to the truth that God occupies every single point of the world. Now the divine essence is the same both inside and outside the world. Thus, if we envisage the visible starry sky as the boundary of the world, the centre of the divine essence and its total presence replicates itself outside the world in the same way as we clearly conceive it to replicate and reiterate itself inside it. However, it is appropriate that this reproduction of the divine centre which occupies the world continues beyond it, expanding with itself the infinite spaces outside the visible heavens. And if it is not accompanied by your indefinite matter, your vortices will be lost. In order to make this more acceptable, let us test our conclusions with regard to God's successive duration.

God is eternal, i.e. the divine life comprehends at once all ages as they pass and all the things past, future and present as they unfold. Still, this eternal life is present to every single point of time and, as it were, astride every single moment, so that we can rightly and truly say that God rests in his eternity for so many days, months or hours. If, for instance, we assume that the world was created 100 years ago, has not the one whole and all-embracing eternity of God then lasted for so many hours, days, months and years up to this very day, i.e. 100 years? And yet, God's existence after the world's creation does not differ from that before the world's creation.

Hence, it is obvious that God not only possesses infinite eternity, but also a temporal succession of infinite duration. If we admit this, why should we not likewise attribute to him an extension that also fills infinite spaces as well as a temporal succession of infinite duration?

Indeed, when (as I do often) I think about these things more deeply and more diligently by myself, I take the view that we may attribute both extensions, that of space and that of time, to non-beings and beings alike. And I suspect that both views might have equally well arisen from prejudice. Since all things we perceive by sense and touch are solid and corporeal and, therefore, always extended, conversely we jump to the conclusion that all corporeal things must be extended; and similarly some prejudice originating in the senses could in principle lead us to believe that incorporeal things are likewise extended.

However, what has led me to assume that non-being also possesses extension is the fact that being "extended" means only that there exist parts external to each other. However, "part" and "whole", "subject" and "predicate", "cause and effect", "contraries" and "relatives", "contradictories" and "privatives" and other such universals are logical notions which we apply to non-beings as well as beings. From this it does not follow that whatever we conceive as having parts external to each other must be conceived as a real being.

But how often does the human mind here struggle with its own shadow, or rather, like a foolish dog, play with its own tail? For it is our own mind that makes us engage in such playful struggle, while it reflects upon those logical notions and modes according to which it considers external things, not merely as its own modes of thought, but as though they were something in the things themselves distinct from it [i.e. the mind itself]. Reaching for them as for its tail, it is teased to exhaustion and ensnared in deep misery. But I have imprudently babbled more than I had originally intended to. I therefore hasten to move on.

[. . .]

V.

"Nevertheless, I believe there is a crucial difference between the amplitude of that corporeal extension", etc.

I, too, am equally convinced that there is a major difference between the divine and corporeal amplitudes. Firstly, the former is not an object of sense, whereas the latter is. Secondly, the former is uncreated and independent, the former dependent and created. The former, moreover, is penetrable and pervades all things, while the latter is solid and impenetrable. Finally, the former proceeds from the ubiquitous reiteration of its complete and total essence, the latter from the external position of its parts lying immediately adjacent to each other, so that nobody, if he is not completely dumb and utterly stupid, could suspect that

> We are entering on impious elements of reason,
> and embarking on a course of crime,

as the poet puts it. There are, after all, theologians, and ones for that matter who are perhaps sufficiently cautious in other fields, who, for all that, acknowledge that God, had he wanted to, could have created the world from all eternity. And yet, it seems equally absurd to attribute to the world either an infinite duration or an infinite size.

E More, *Four Letters to Descartes*, Second Letter (II/2, 247–247 = AT, V, 312–314. Translation: Hengstermann)

3. Regarding Part 2, art. 20: If body AB moves away from body CD, I wonder why it should be so clear that this motion is reciprocal. Assuming that CD is a tower and AB the western wind going past the sides of the tower, the tower CD either rests or at least does not move away from wind AB. If it moves away, or, as you put it, is transferred in its motion, it must be moving westwards. However, it does not move westwards, since both the earth and the wind head eastwards. It therefore seems to be at rest in relation to the wind, since it receives no motion from it. And still you say that the transfer of the tower itself and the wind, a transfer which surely is motion, is reciprocal. They would, therefore, simultaneously be in motion and at rest in relation to the same wind, which strikes me as quite a contradiction.[6] Let us assume someone walks away from me, say by a thousand feet, while I am sitting. While he will be red with sweat, there will be neither redness nor sweat on my face because all along I have been sitting. This shows that he alone has been in motion, while I have been at rest the whole the time. It is therefore only in my mind that I experience a change of distance between him and myself in his movement, rather than a real and physical motion.

[. . .]

6. Regarding Part 4, art. 189: "The soul or mind is intimately linked to the brain." Here I should very much like to hear your opinion about the soul's union with the body. Is it joined to the whole body or to the brain alone? Or is it in fact confined to the pineal gland as though to some very little prison cell? For I follow you in believing that it is the seat of the common sense and the ἀκρόπολις[7] of the soul. However, I suspect that the soul might in fact pervade the whole body. Furthermore, I ask you how the soul can join so closely with the body, lacking as it does particles shaped like hooks or branches. And I should also like to know whether there might not be some power[8] in nature which cannot be explained mechanistically in any way. How does the αὐτεξούσιον,[9] of which we are conscious in ourselves, come to be? And how can our souls command the animal spirits and send them into this or that part of the body? How can the spirits of witches, commonly called familiars, form and compress matter for their purposes so ably that they can assume visible and palpable shapes for those execrable old hags? Not only old hags, but quite a few young witches have told me freely and without compulsion that this is true.

Further, is it this very power that we ourselves experience in our souls in some way when we set our animal spirits in motion or make them stop, send them somewhere and call them back at our own discretion[10]? I wonder, therefore, whether a philosopher should not acknowledge that there is in the whole fabric of things some incorporeal substance which can nevertheless, as bodies do on one another, impress on some body all or at least most corporeal properties such as motion, shape and the structure of its parts. Nay more, since this clearly holds true of motion and rest, may this incorporeal substance not also add to a body whatever is consequent upon motion? May it not divide and join, disperse and bind together, give shape to particles and then arrange them, make them rotate or move in any other way and stop them again, as well as all other such things as necessarily give rise to light, colour and other sense impressions of that kind, as your excellent philosophy has shown?

Moreover, nothing either corporeal or incorporeal can act on any other thing in any other way than by applying its essence to it. I also deem it necessary, therefore, that, whether it is an angel, a demon, a soul or God who acts on matter in the modes mentioned above, their essence is, as it were, riding on either those parts of matter upon which they act or some others acting upon them through the transfer of motion. Consequently, they must at some point be present to the whole of the matter which they control and modify. This can be seen in genii both good and evil who have appeared to the eyes of men. For how else should they have compressed matter and kept it in their respective shapes?

Finally, an incorporeal substance possesses such an extraordinary power that it can contract, dilate, divide and simultaneously projecting and retaining matter simply by applying itself to it, without ropes or hooks, nets or wedges. Does it not seem probable then that it can also contract itself into itself, since there is no impenetrability to hinder it, and then expand itself again and many more such things?

F More, *Four Letters to Descartes*, Third Letter (23rd July 1649) (II/2, 254–256 = AT, V, 379–383. Translation: Hengstermann)

Finally, then, I am utterly surprised that you fail to see that the human mind or an angel are extended in just this fashion as though this implied a contradiction. By contrast, I personally am more inclined to think that it implies a contradiction that the power of the mind is extended, while the mind itself is not in any way. For, since the power of the mind is an intrinsic mode of the mind, it obviously cannot be outside the mind itself. And the same argument applies to God. Hence, I am equally surprised that in your answer to the penultimate instances you admit that he is everywhere in respect of his power, but not in respect of his essence. How could the divine power, which is a mode of God, be outside God, even though every real mode always inheres most intimately in the thing of which it is a mode? Hence, it is necessary that God is everywhere if his power is everywhere.

And I cannot but suspect that by the power of God you want to understand an effect transferred into matter. However, if you understand it this way, I cannot see how that should not equally come to naught. For there is no other way for this effect to be transferred than by the divine power touching matter and matter receiving it; in other words, by some real mode united to the matter and, therefore, extended. Nor can it all the while be separated from the divine essence itself. There seems to be an obvious contradiction here, as I have said. However, I do not want to dwell on this any longer.

[. . .]

As to the third, I have gained the following useful things from your example of the boat: 1. in motion there is a mutual resistance between the bodies that are said to be moving. 2. Rest is action, namely some resistance or opposition. 3. For two bodies to move means that they separate immediately. 4. That immediate separation is precisely that motion or transfer.

Indeed, when two bodies separate themselves from each other, this motion, unless you add to this notion of translation or motion some separating or parting power in the one or the other, will be nothing more than a wholly extrinsic relationship at best. Being separated either means that the surfaces of bodies which beforehand touched each other, distance themselves from each other (the distance between the bodies, however, being a wholly extrinsic relation) or it means that bodies no longer touch each other which did so previously. However, this is merely a privation or negation. I am obviously not yet sufficiently certain about your view on this matter.

Personally, however, I would, if I may, deem motion to be that power or action by which those bodies which, you say, are in motion separate themselves from each other. Their immediate separation is the effect of the said motion, even though it is either merely a bare relation or a privation. However, you yourself seem to have argued differently in your explanation of the definition of motion given in Part II, art 25, where, to tell you the truth, I do not yet fully understand your view.

[. . .]

Indeed, I have been thinking upon these first principles so rigorously that I am faced with another difficulty regarding the nature of motion. If the motion of a body is a mode like shape, the structure of its parts, etc., how is it any more possible for it to move from one body to another than for any other corporeal mode? And in general I cannot imagine how it is possible that anything that cannot exist outside a subject (which applies to all modes) might pass to another subject. Moreover, I have another question: when a body hits a smaller one that is at rest, pulling it with it, does the rest of the body that is at rest pass to the one in motion just as the motion of the one moving passes its motion to the one resting? For rest seems to be something so idle and indolent that it is loath to move. And yet, it is as real as motion and, therefore, reason forces us to suppose that it, too, is passed on.

Finally, I am completely baffled when I consider that a thing as tiny and as vile as motion, which is also capable of being separated from its subject and passing to another, and which is of so frail and so transient a nature that it would cease to be at once if it were not for a subject sustaining it, should nevertheless stir its subject up so potently and impel it here and there so forcefully. I, for one, am more inclined to assume that there is no transfer of motion whatsoever. Rather, on account of the impulse of one body, another body is, as it were, awakened into motion, just as the soul is awakened into thought on this or that occasion. Instead of receiving motion, a body stirs itself into motion on being alerted by another body. And, as I have said before, motion is to body what thought is to mind, that is to say, neither of them is received from without, but both proceed from within the subject in which they are to be found. And in fact every so-called body is also alive in a mindless and befuddled way, since in my view it is the last und lowest shadow and image of the divine essence which, I hold, is most perfect life. However, it is devoid of all sense and animadversion.

G Henry More to Anne Finch, C.C.C. Septemb. 9 [1650] (*Conway Letters*, 484)

Madame!

YOUR letters came not to my hands till Saturday last when they very acceptably bad me welcome out of Bedfordshire where I had been with Dr. More my uncle. I am glad I have now the opportunity of making my promise good to you. And will forth with endeavour to answer your objections so well as I can. The Idea of God or what is the same of a fully perfect Being, conteining in it necessary existency, demonstrates to us that God dos exist, this in brief is Cartesius his reasoning. Now your objection against it, if I rightly understand you, is this. That then the idea of a fully imperfect Being should emply the existence of a

Being fully imperfect. But it is quite contrary. For that idea, if we may call it so, of what is fully imperfect (for we cannot call it a Being) emplyes a necessary non-existence. And the idea of this fully imperfect, tells us that it is impossible for it to exist or be any thing, as the idea of the fully perfect tells us that it dos necessarily exist. But in your further progresse in this objection when you conceive you have sufficiently proved, that some ideas do emply no necessarie existence of things of wch they are the ideas, you then inferre that therefore the idea of God will not emply his necessary existence. But there is not like reason in both. For no idea but that of God, conteines in it necessary existence, but only possible or els impossible, is that idea of what is fully imperfect.

H Henry More to Anne Finch, C.C.C. May. 5. [1651] (*Conway Letters*, 486–489)

Madam!

NOT to spend much time in professions how welcome your letter is to me, (though I can professe no more then is true in that point, it being a messenger to me of that wch I am heartily glad of, viz. of your recovery of your health, wch I pray God continue to you, and of your persistency in your noble designe upon Philosophy, wch I begin to think you are likely to continue in.) I will forthwith fall upon the matters your Ladiship has propounded to me, by way of objections. The first whereof is upon the 18 Paragr. Of the 2 Part of Des Cartes his Principles, where he contendes than an empty space emplyes a contradiction. And here you sett Des Cartes and myself together by the eares to make your Ladiship merry. But we shall prove good friends and agree well in the end. For his so superstitiously excluding all possibility of an empty space, is but to get an indefinite or indeed and infinite body to frame out his vortices in. For indeed his supposition of the impossibility of a vacuum dos ipso facto make the matter infinite. My contending for a true infinite distance in space, in my Infinity of Worlds, is onely to facilitate the possibility of that Infinity. But your Ladiship in courtesy seemes to take the strangers part and lean towards his opinion that there can not be an empty space or any distance but by the interposition of body or matter. But to win you over to my syde, I shall propound these arguments following. And your Ladiship in your next shall tell me your judgement wch of them is ye weakest. For I will not professe them all unconfutable.

[487] 1. The first argument therefore that an empty space emplyes no contradiction, is that almost all men, hold the world finite, nay hold it a contradiction that it should be infinite, and then beyond the world there will be an empty space and besides, those that held the world infinite or an infinity of worlds, held a vacuum, as the Epicureans, but it is much that the generality of men, not forced by superstition, or aw of education, should of their own accords hold that true that emplyes no contradiction. Therefore there is no contradiction emplyde in this notion of empty space.

2ly. That affection that will accrew to a body nothing at all being done to that body to wch it doth accrew, is no reall or physical affection, and therefore may be also there where no body or reall being is, but distance will accrew to a body nothing at all done to that body to wch it doth accrew. As so if B be removed from A already distant 7 foot 7 foot more, this 7 foot more distance dos accrew to A without any thing done to A at all. Therefore distance may be conceived in Non-entityes as well as in Entityes.

3ly. Distance or extension, in its very nature emplyes nothing more then this, to have partem extra partem, yt is, to have explicated partes. But pars and Totum as subject and adjunct and the rest of logicall notions, are applicable as Non-entityes as well as to Entityes, therefore, extension or distance in an empty space emplyes no contradiction.

[. . .]

[488] 1. That extension can not be of nothing. This is answered by my 2d, 3d and 4th argument.

2ly. That space is impenetrable as well as matter, therefore it emplyes something reall or is matter itself. And it is impenetrable, because 20 foot space can not be in 10 foot space, no more than 20 foot of matter in 10 foot. This very handsome and witty. But I answer, if it were possible to remove ten foot space to another ten foot they would not exclude one another, but ly very quietly in one. But space is immovable, and impassible. All the porters in London will not be able to carry one foot square of it from Cheepsyde to Charing Crosse. But that wch you ayme at is done already. For ten foot of timber dos ly in ten foot of space, so that there is twenty in ten, according to our hearts desire. And this proves space to have no impenetrability. So that space would ly in space if it were possible to bring one to the other.

3ly. That there is no reason why bodyes touch, but because there is no body betwixt. Yet the reason is because there is no space betwixt, for the mere distance of space keeps them from touching, as is plaine from my sixt argument.

And hitherto concerning space upon the 18th Paragraph. Now we come to Paragraph 20. To divide a thing in our thoughts is to perceive clearly and distinctly that the thing in its own nature is divisible. But you do not thus divide the soul in your thoughtes. Now Madam! I suppose you plainely understand the meaning of the place.

[489] Paragr. 21. For infinite and indefinite in Des Cartes sense, truly Madam, I can not easily absteine from being of your Ladiships opinion in that, that they come much to one. But it is no more essentiall to a body to have a superficies, or to a line, to have terminating pointes, then to Platos world-animal to have eares, nose and eyes. These belong to a particular animal, and those to a particular body, or this or that part of the matter, not to the whole. And if you can once phansy an infinite body you will easily phansy a body without any superficies, and line unterminated by any pointes. But to say the truth we do not so much phansy these things as reach them by reason, nor comprehend them as apprehend them, as we may also hold, though not so fast, what we are not able to graspe with our hand. Thus Madam, have I endeavoured to satisfy all your objections, but if any scruple is stille behind concerning any of them it is my duty to add what is wanting, and your ingenious proposals are no small pleasure and encouragement therein to

Yr Ladiships humbly devoted servant
H. More

I George Rust, *Discourse of Truth* (1651/1655/1682), Section 9 (*Two Choice and Useful Treatises*, 178–179)

[*That the Denial of the unchangeableness of the said mutual Respects and Relations of things to one another, takes away all* Knowledge of God *and of our* own Happiness*, and lays a Foundation of the most incurable Scepticism imaginable*]

. . . But suppose we should come to know that there is a God, which, as I have demonstrated, denying the necessary and immutable truth of common Notions, and the indispensible and eternal relations of things, is altogether impossible: However, let it be supposed; yet how shall we know that these common Notions, and principles of natural instinct, which are the foundation of all Discourse and Argumentation, are infallible Truths; and that our *Senses*, (which with these former Principles, we suppose this Divine to have given us to converse with this outward world) were not on purpose bestowed upon us, to befool, delude and cheat us; if we be not first assured of the *Veracity* of God? And how can we be assured of that, if we know [179] not that Veracity is a perfection? And how shall we know it is so, unless there be an intrinsical relation betwixt Veracity and Perfection? For if it be an arbitrarious respect depending upon the Will of God, there is no way possible left whereby we should come to know that it is in God at all; And therefore we have fully as much reason to believe that all our common Notions and Principles of natural instinct, whereupon we ground all our reasonings and discourse, are meer Chimaera's to delude and abuse our faculties; and all those Idea's, Phantasms and Apprehensions of our external senses, we imagine are occasioned in us by the presence of outward objects, are meer Spectrums and Gulleries, wherewith poor mortals are befooled and cheated; as that they are given us by the first Good and Truth to lead us into the Knowledge of himself and Nature.

This is a clear and evident consequence, and cannot be denied by any that doth not complain of darkness in the brightest and most Meridian Light. And here you have the foundations laid of the highest Scepticism; for who can say he knows any thing, when he hath no basis on which he can raise any true conclusions?

J Rust, *God is Love* (1658) (*Remains*, 14. 17–18)

Thus have you some imperfect Account of that grand and fundamental Truth, That God is Love; and you see I have not been curious in ranking my Arguments, or methodizing my Discourse, nor did I think it needfull; for I do not know that I have spoken any thing which, as to me, is not as clear and evident as common Notions, and of whose Truth I make no more doubt than I do of my own Existence which the so much admired Monsieur hath made the first Principle of his Philosophy.

I could now from this single Principle of Divine Goodness, that we have hitherto been speaking of, by mathematical and demonstrative Evidence deduce the noblest Conclusions that the Mind of Man can entertain it self withal: But this is too large and spacious a Field, and I must draw my Thoughts into a narrower compass.

[. . .]

And we are first chiefly to consider, that such is the infinite Goodness and infinite Wisedom of God, as he knows how to bring good out of evil, and is acquainted with all the Circumstances of Beings, and clearly sees how to bestow his Goodness with the greatest Advantages: But it is very hard, and too presumptuous to determine, that this or that particular Line of divine Providence is not agreeable to infinite Goodness. But if this look too like an evasion, I farther add, that there are infinite degrees of Beings within the Sphere of Omnipotency, and it is suitable to Divine Goodness in its productions to reach the utmost limits of Possibility. Now among other possible *Ided's* we find one of a Being, as to its inward Essence spiritual and immaterial, yet having so near and vital Union with matter, that it shall be in a kind of Indifferency to the Divine and Animal Life, and this we call Man; nor must we require, that he should be created in a state of Impeccability; for then he had not been what he is, but some other higher order of Being, which, according to the former Principles, is to be supposed already produced. But this being once made, it is agreeable to the Wisedom of God to suffer it to act according to those Faculties and Powers, he hath indued it with, and [18] consequently by its free choice and election to bring sin into the World. Nor must we easily expect,

God should be at the expence of a Miracle in treating with his Creatures; but that he should deal with them in a way suitable to their Natures. Wherefore the Objection can onely be made against the production of such a lapsible Being as this is; and for that, besides what hath been said already, I have farther to add several Considerations. First, It is very suitable to the Wisedom of the Creatour, that seeing he made such a visible World, as this is wherein we live, and furnished it with variety of Creatures, which are suited to various Functions, that he should make such a Creature as Man is, to be Governour and Master over them; and consequently, that he should be thus vitally united to a Terrestrial Body, which *ipso facto* puts him into a State of Peccability. I might say farther, that hereby was place given us to demonstrate the reality and sincerity of our Affections to the Divine Life; which God would the rather have accepted, because of our being so addicted another way; and had we stuck close to the dictates of the Divine Life, notwithstanding all suggestions to the contrary; it would have been a matter of very great Triumph, and the avoiding of so hazardous a Temptation. And it is not to be doubted, but that there were far beyond the number of those that fell many Myriads of Rational Beings, our Kindred and Allies, that maintain'd their Innocency, and are ingrafted into the Will of God, beyond all possibility of Apostasie. Besides God hath the greater advantage to magnifie his love in our Recovery, and Man will have the transcendent Pleasure, to have escaped out of so great Dangers and Miseries; and lastly, hereby is an occasion given us of exercising those Perfections, which otherwise there could not have been opportunity for, as Patience, Self denial as to the most delightfull Pleasures, Pity, Compassion, Fortitude and Magnanimity of Spirit, Dependance upon God, and Faith in him: Therefore ought it not to be [19] expected that the Wisedom of God should step beside the course of Nature to prevent these Objects and Occasions, which these Divine Excellencies are to be conversant about. These things I have briefly touched on; more might be said, if I believed it requisite and suitable. I now hasten to a Conclusion, and have but two words to detain you with.

K More, *Antidote Against Atheism* (1653), Book 1, Chapter VIII, Sections 1–4 (*Collection of Several Philosophical Writings*, 21–23)

[1. *That the very* Idea *of God implies his necessary Existence*]

1. And now verily casting my eyes upon the true *Idea* of God which we have found out I seem to my self to have struck further into this businesse then I was aware of. For if this *Idea* or *Notion* of God be true, as I have undenyably proved, it is also undeniably true that he doth [22] exist; For this *Idea* of God being no arbitrarious Figment taken up at pleasure, but the necessary and naturall Emanation of the mind of Man, if it signifies to us that the Notion and Nature of God implyes in it *necessary Existence* as we have shown it does, unlesse we will wink against our own naturall light, wee are without any further Scruple to acknowledge *that God does exist*.

[2. *That his Existence is not* hypothetically *necessary, but* absolutely, *with the occasion noted of that slippery Evasion*]

2. Nor is it sufficient grounds to diffide to the strength of this Argument, because our fancy can shuffle in this Abater, viz. That indeed this *Idea* of God, supposing God did exist, shews us that his Existence is necessary, but it does not shew us that he doth necessarily exist. For he that answers thus, does not observe out of what prejudice he is inabled to make this Answer, which is this: He being accustomed to fancy the Nature or Notion of every thing else without Existence, and so ever easily separating Essence and Existence in them, here unawares hee takes the same liberty, and divides

Existence from that Es|sence to which Existence it self is essentiall. And that's the witty fallacy his unwarinesse has intangled him in.

[3. *That to acknowledge God a Being* necessarily Existent *according to the true Notion of him, and yet to say he may not Exist, is a plain Contradiction*]

3. Again when as we contend that the true *Idea* of God represents him as a *Being necessarily Existent*, and therefore that he does exist; and you to avoid the edge of the Argument reply, If he did at all exist; by this answer you involve your self in a manifest contradiction. For first you say with us, that the nature of God is such, that in its very Notion it implyes its *Necessary Existence*, and then again you unsay it by intimating that notwithstanding this true *Idea* and *Notion* God may not exist, and so acknowledge that what is absolutely necessary according to the free Emanation of our Facultyes, yet may be otherwise: Which is a palpable Contradiction as much as respects us and our Facultyes, and we have nothing more inward and immediate then these to steer our selves by.

[4. *That* Necessity *is a Logical term, and implies an indissoluble connexion betwixt Subject and Predicate, whence again this Axiome is necessarily and eternally true,* God doth Exist.]

4. And to make this yet plainer at least if not stronger when wee say that the *Existence* of God is *Necessary*, wee are to take notice that *Necessity* is a *Logicall Terme*, and signifies so firme a Connexion betwixt the *Subject* and *Praedicate* (as they call them) that it is impossible that they should bee dissevered, or should not hold together, and therefore if they bee affirm'd one of the other, that they make *Axioma Necessarium*, an Axiome that is necessary, or eternally true. Wherefore there being a *Necessary Connexion* betwixt *God* and *Existence;* this Axiome, *God does Exist, is* an Axiome Necessarily and Eternally true. Which we shall yet more clearly understand, if we compare *Necessity* and *Contingency* together; For as *Contingency* signifies not onely the *Manner of Existence* in that which is contingent according to its *Idea*, but does intimate also a *Possibility* of *Actual Existence*, (so to make up the true and easy Analogy) *Necessity* does not only signify the *Manner of Existence* in that which is *Necessary*, but also that it does *actually Exist*, and *could never possibly do otherwise*. For ἀναγκαῖον εἶναι and ἀδύνατον μὴ εἶναι, Necessity of Being and Impossibility of Not-being, are all one with *Aristotle*, and the rest of the [23] *Logicians*. But the *Atheist* and the *Enthusiast*, are usually such profess'd Enemyes against *Logick;* the one meerly out of Dotage upon outward grosse sense, the other in a dear regard to his stiffe and untamed fancy, that shop of Mysteryes and fine things.

5. Thirdly, wee may further add, that whereas wee must needs attribute to the *Idea* of God either *Contingency, Impossibility, or Necessity* of *Actuall Existence*, (some one of these belonging to every *Idea* imaginable) and that *Contingency* is incompetible to an *Idea of a Being absolutely perfect*, much more *Impossibility*, the *Idea* of God being compiled of no Notions but such as are *possible* according to the light of Nature, to which wee now appeal: It remains therefore that *Necessity of Actuall Existence* bee unavoidably cast upon the *Idea* of God, and that therefore God does *actually Exist*.

L More, *Four Letters to Descartes, Answer to Descartes' Fragment in the Letter of Henry More to Claude Clerselier* (July/August 1656) (Opera omnia, II/2, 270–271 = AT, V, 644–646. Translation: Hengstermann)

5. A transfer does seem to have less being than shape, because the latter is a more absolute predicate of the body in which it is than the former, which is only a relation to another body. As regards the

motive force, he may have placed it either in God and the divine mind or, agreeing with the Platonists, in the world soul. Either way, however, it is extraordinary that such an excellent philosopher has not attributed this power to matter itself, but to some other subject which, therefore, cannot but be immaterial or incorporeal. Thus, undoubtedly, this most farsighted man had realized that unless we were to usurp the freedom of affirming and denying things arbitrarily and at will, it was necessary to acknowledge that the whole of matter was by its very nature homogeneous in accordance with its idea observed in our minds, especially since we could not invent any reason for any diversity in it. Hence, it follows that the whole of worldly matter either is in motion or at rest by its very nature. However, if, as a whole, it were moved through itself, there would not, even for one single moment, be any permanent structure in anything. Instead, the particles would at once drift apart by themselves, or rather they would never coalesce into any unity at all, as I have proved in abundant detail in my letter to Descartes.

[. . .]

8. I am inclined to believe that if those "amusing" things of mine, as he likes to call them, and the sterner ones of his were mixed, it would yield the best possible blend. Meanwhile, I personally bow most willingly to the beautiful rigour of Descartes' genius, although there is one thing that I have observed quite frequently: those who seek mathematical certainty in all things with such tenacity vacillate in some of the same in the most infelicitous fashion possible. For once a line of arguing that purports to be a demonstration has been shown to be illegitimate, it cannot rightly be judged to be an argument of any worth.

Besides, there cannot be any deceit hidden in the use of metaphors and similitudes as long as we keep in mind that things are not designated by their proper names, but by figurative ones. Hence, in saying that matter or the universal body of the world was, as it were, the shadow of the divine essence, I did not mean to say they were a shadow in reality. For the meaning of this metaphor is not that it is a shadow in actual fact, but that it depends upon God as does the shadow upon the body. Further, just as a shadow reflects some image of the body, albeit a very obscure and base one, there are in body or matter some blind and faint traces of the divine essence. However, since the latter, as I have said, is most perfect life, the analogy itself requires that matter is not wholly deprived of the image of life. It counterfeits some semblance of life in the meeting of two bodies, as their motion is adjusted in such a way that both, notifying one another of the acceleration and deceleration of motion respectively, eventually agree in the continued course of their motion. And the same holds true of the other laws of transfer. For not even Descartes dares to affirm that the motion which is in one body passes to another.

Moreover, I appreciate what he proceeds to add, namely, that there is some external power, be it from God or from another incorporeal substance created by God, by which matter is stirred into motion, because it is undoubtedly very true in general. If, however, he understands it in such a way that the divine power immediately impels each single body that is in motion, a major difficulty will arise, as the mutual impulses of bodies will be in vain. However, it is clear from experience that one body impels another, as we can see from stones cast by men's hands or iron balls fired from instruments of war. If, then, this power immediately rouses some parts, while not[11] rousing others, those parts stirred by God will by their own impulse stir the others into motion. Since, in reality, no motion passes from one body to another, it is manifest that one awakens the other from sleep, as it were, and that the bodies awakened this way transfer themselves from one place to another by their own power. And I, for one, call this property of body a shadow or image of life, as it were. Hence, it finally becomes clear that we are not reaching for hollow shadows here at all. Instead, they are quite useful and a very good illustration of a truth which can also be proved by a much stricter mode of argumentation.

M More, *Divine Dialogues* (1668), Book II, Chapter 25 (Second edition, 49–52)

XXV. That there is an Extension intrinsecal to Motion

Philoth. Well then, give me leave, *Hylobares*, to attaque you some other way. Did you not say even now, that what-ever has no Extension or Amplitude is nothing?

Hyl. I did, and do not repent me of so saying. For I doubt not but that it is true.

Philoth. Wherefore *Extension* or *Amplitude* is an intrinsecall or essential Property of *Ens quatenus Ens*,[12] as the Metaphysicians phrase it.

[50] *Hyl.* It is so.

Philoth. And what is an intrinsecall or essential Attribute of a thing, is in the thing it self.

Hyl. Where should it be else?

Philoth. Therefore there is Extension in every *thing* or *Entity*.

Hyl. It cannot be deny'd.

Philoth. And it can as little be deny'd but that Motion is an *Entity*, I mean a *Physicall Entity*.

Hyl. It cannot.

Philoth. Therefore Extension is an intrinsecall property of Motion.

Hyl. It must be acknowledged; what then?

Philoth. What then? Do you not yet see, *Hylobares*, how weak an Assertion that of *Des-Cartes* is, That Extension and Matter are reciprocall? for you plainly see that Extension is intrinsecall to Motion, and yet Motion is not Matter.

Hyl. Motion is not *Ens*, but *Modus Entis*.

Philoth. Nay, by your favour, *Hylobares*, Motion is *Ens*, though in some sense it may be said to be *Modus corporis*.

Hyl. Methinks I am, I know not how, *Philotheus*, illaqueated, but not truly captivated into an assent to your Conclusion.

Philoth. That is because you are already held captive in that inured Conceit of *Des-Cartes*, that makes you suspect solid Reason for a Sophism.

Hyl. If Motion were a thing that was loose or *exemptitious* from Matter, then I could not but be convinced that it had Extension of its own; but being it is a mere Mode of Matter, that cannot pass from it into another Subject, it has no other Extension then that of the Matter it self it is in.

Philoth. But if it have another Essence from the Matter it self, by your own concession it must however have another Extension. Besides, you seem mistaken in what I mean by Motion. For I mean not simply the *Translation*, but the *vis agitans* that pervades the whole body that is moved. [51] Which both *Regius* and *Des-Cartes* acknowledge *exemptitious* and loose, so that it may pass from one part of Matter to another.

Hyl. But what is that to me, if I do not?

Philoth. It is at least thus much to you, that you may take notice how rashly and groundlesly both *Des-Cartes* and *Regius* assert Extension and Matter to be reciprocall, while in the mean time they affirm that which according to your own judgement does plainly and convincingly inferr that Extension is more general then Matter.

[52] *Hyl.* It is, I must confess, a sign that the apprehensions of men are very humoursome and lubricous.

Philoth. And therefore we must take heed, *Hylobares*, how we let our mindes cleave to the Opinion of any man out of admiration of his Person.

Hyl. That is good advice, and of great consequence (if it be given betimes) for the keeping out of Errour and Falshood. But when a Phancy is once engrafted in the Minde, how shall one get it out?

Philoth. I must confess I marvell much, *Hylobares*, that you being so fully convinced that every real and Physicall *Entity* has an intrinsecall Extension of its own, and that Motion is a Physicall Entity different from Matter, you should not be presently convinced that Motion has also an intrinsecall Extension of its own. To which you might adde, that the manner of the Extension of Matter is different from the nature of the Extension in Motion: the former being one single Extension, not to be lessened nor increased without the lessening and increase of the Matter it self; but the other a gradual Extension, to be lessened or augmented without any lessening or augmenting the Matter. Whence again it is a sign that it has an Extension of its own, *reduplicative* into it self, or reducible to thinner or weaker degrees; while the Extension of the Matter remains still single and the same.

Hyl. I must confess, *Philotheus*, that I am brought to these streights, that I must either renounce that Principle, That every Physicall Entity has an intrinsecall Extension of its own, as much as it has an intrinsecall Essence of its own, (which I know not how to doe;) or else I must acknowledge that something besides Matter is extended. But I must take time to consider of it. I am something staggered in my judgement.

N More, Preface to the Reader about the 2nd edition [of the *Enchiridion Ethicum*] (1669) (*Opera omnia*, II/1, 4–5. Translation: Christian Hengstermann)

In fact, it is mainly two conclusions in that philosophy which pose a major threat to piety. The first one is "that the matter itself of which the world consists cannot not exist, being extended indefinitely in every direction." For that indefinite extension which we cannot in any way expel from our minds as inexistent must, according to Descartes' view, necessarily be corporeal. Whilst we have only critically touched on this view in this present work, we have given a comprehensive and sound refutation in our first and second letters to Descartes.

5. And there is certainly one single argument in particular, one which we have already put forward,[13] namely that from the motion of the earth, which makes it perfectly clear to everyone not either mentally retarded or obsessed by great prejudices that this necessary existence does not belong to the extended matter of the world, but to some other immaterial extension. In fact, there is in all philosophy, including even mathematics, no other speculation of which I am as capable due both to my character and my knowledge as the one which I am about to expound now. All the philosophers of a better stamp agree that the body of this earth in its annual orbit describes an elliptical orbit, its distance from the sun being everywhere that of certain semi-diameters. However, every form must be described within some extension and it cannot be described in some worldly matter that is external to it like, say, the vortex in which the earth moves, since it does not move through the parts of the vortex, but is carried around with the vortex itself at a certain distance from the sun. Hence, it clearly follows that there is some more inward extension within which that whole vortex in which this elliptical orbit is described by the body of the earth is situated. Moreover, this more inward extension is immobile and the whole vortex moves within it. And that extension, finally, is the one to which alone that necessary existence belongs, since it is something that neither our mind nor our imagination can in any way eliminate or remove from the totality of all things. Rather, we hit on it, even against our will, wherever we direct our mind.

6. Moreover, it follows that, if we want to listen to Descartes who never grows tired of inculcating on us the principle that "there is no property of nothing", that this immobile and necessary extension is also some essence or substance. It cannot be corporeal, since it everywhere penetrates body or matter. Hence, it only remains that it is incorporeal or spirit or, if you prefer, the amplitude of some immense spirit. ★ However, necessary existence can belong to no other thing but to God. Therefore, this immense amplitude whose necessary existence we grasp can be no other than the divine extension itself in which we live, move and subsist.

7. If this is so, we shall by a certain right and absolutely incontestable method, reach both Aristotle's "first unmoved mover" which the latter calls τὸ πρῶτον κινοῦν ἀκίνητον[14] and Anaxagoras' νοῦς ἀμιγής, i.e. "unmixed mind".[15] For it is obviously clear from this that the first origin of all physical motions is immobile, and that the divine numen is unmixed with matter, not only insofar as it is mind, but also insofar as it is a certain power moving the whole of worldly matter. For that immense unmoved extension is not pulled around with the countless vortices of matter, as it moves in circles, and therefore God does not (★ as it happens in particular animals) coalesce with the body of the world in such a way that he is pulled away with its motion, but he is only close to it, imprinting with a kind of higher and more sublime magic the requisite motions and forms upon the particles of matter.

O More, Preface to 2nd edition (II/1, 6–7. Translation: Hengstermann)

14. The second opinion which smacks of some impiety is the following: *all phenomena of the world, including even plants and animal bodies and organisms, can arise from purely mechanical principles, namely from locomotion and matter alone. Moreover, the necessary causes and reasons of all of them can be deduced from these sources.* I have certainly repeatedly criticized this ill-conceived view in several places in this letter itself. However, there is only single instance, namely that on the formation and motion of grooved particles, in which I undertook to give a more thorough refutation here. Nor must you be surprised that I am content with one single argument in a matter of such importance, even though there are so many others. After all, I had in my other writings dealt with the matter in so clear and limpid demonstrations that I deemed it superfluous to devote too much labour to this same subject once again. The demonstrations to which I refer are those given in my books *Against the Atheists* and *On the Immortality of the Soul*. Among them is that taken from that celebrated experiment of a large weight attached to the sucker of an air-pump and being carried upwards by it, ascending, as if spontaneously, once the air is removed.[16] Another is that of the descent of heavy objects.[17] And you may finally add the ascent of a wooden plate from the bottom of a vessel filled with water and suspended in almost complete balance.[18] All these phenomena might be extremely simple ones. Still, not only do they defy every attempt at a purely mechanical explanation, but they are indeed in most obvious contradiction to the common laws of mechanics. We have provided most compelling proof regarding the former two in the aforementioned treatises and regarding the latter one in other places.

15. Thus, the mechanical philosophy, so much-belaboured in our times, is subject to egregious hallucinations about phenomena that are neither complex nor sophisticated in any way, but easily comprehensible and perfectly clear to our mind. Could there, then, be a hope more ill-conceived or a promise more insane, I pray you, than that somebody can find the purely mechanical causes of all phenomena of the world, even those contrived by the greatest and most intricate art and craft? This strikes me as not dissimilar to the impudence and temerity of that man who, even though he had destroyed a two-bench boat in the harbour, boasted that he could steer the ship of the Argonauts in the Black Sea, as Lucius Crassus, according to Cicero, argues wisely and soundly in his own case.

16. Indeed, as far as I am concerned, I hold the view that not only those most intricate phenomena cannot be explained on purely mechanical principles, but that, in fact, none can. It is true that an excessive love and zeal for Descartes made me concede to him in that letter that there were a few golden chains held together by a purely mechanical link. Now, however, moved not by a changeable and inconstant mind, but by compelling arguments, I have changed my view and revoked my gift. I do not doubt that everyone who has a mind free of all prejudice would rather prefer to acknowledge one single and uniform principle everywhere than one diverse and different in kind in one place and another in the next. And therefore, since I was certain that some phenomena had their origin in a more divine principle than one pure mechanical, I brought myself to believe that all the others likewise proceeded from the same source. Furthermore, the σύμφυσις or coalescence of physical monads into particles clearly appears to be a thing entirely inexplicable in any mechanical fashion. Lastly, even if the first rudiments of the world should have come into existence through such swirling and smoothing as Descartes imagines it, there would in fact be such a mass of the most subtle element ★ that it would flood back even above the orbit of Saturn. And I think it suffices briefly to have mentioned these arguments in this way here. It is, after all, not the place here to dwell upon them any longer, but only to note them in passing.

17. Moreover, since I am not prepared to admit any purely mechanical phenomenon anywhere in the word, it follows necessarily that I very gladly subscribe to the view that the enquiry into final causes should also be introduced into natural philosophy. Indeed, I thought that so fitting for a philosopher that I should much rather attribute the fact that Descartes removed them from this philosophy to some honest cunning of his than to his ignorance of so sound a truth. If I have erred in this matter, this should certainly rather be attributed to my kindness than some despicable penchant for servile dishonesty. However, I, for one, certainly deem the careful enquiry into final causes to be the most enjoyable part of natural philosophy. It is also, I should like to add, the most useful one both for other things and, above all, true piety and religion. No other gift given to humanity by the immortal God is more excellent, more agreeable and more pleasant or, finally, more perfect.

18. Let us assume, therefore, that somebody, moved either by some blind fate or by his own arrogance, were to boast that he could deduce all phenomena in the world from purely mechanical causes, i.e., that he could—in one fell swoop, as it were—take away from the nature of things all those most excellent and sound arguments for the existence of God (even though in reality it is impossible that anyone should give purely mechanical explanations for even the most simple phenomenon). Would that person not make himself a risible spectacle for all others? Would he not yield himself up to the ridicule or even the utter contempt of gods and men? This, surely, is that man who creates worlds in a mechanical fashion, but cannot even explain the descent of a stone on purely mechanical grounds. This is that man who destroys a two-bench boat in the harbour, but nevertheless imagines being able to steer the Argo. This is that astonishing smatterer who rather chooses to arrogate to himself the knowledge about the creation of worlds than allow anyone to gain sound knowledge about God from the phenomena of the created world.

P More, *Enchiridium Metaphysicum* (1671), Chapter 27
(*Opera omnia*, II/1, 307. 309. Translation: Jacob, *Henry More's Manual of Metaphysics*, I, 98. 101)

1. A representation of the opinions of the Nullibists and the Holenmerians.

The first is of those who, although they not unwillingly acknowledge that incorporeal things exist in nature, they very sharply contend that they are nowhere in the entire universe. Which opinion indeed, although it is seen even at first sight to be sufficiently ridiculous, is, however, held fast to by the maintainers of it, not without contempt and superciliousness, or at least with secret contempt of other philosophers who feel otherwise, as being less intellectual and too indulgent of their imagination. These people, therefore, since they so boldly affirm spirit to be nowhere, have deservedly obtained the title of Nullibists.

[...]

5. A clear demonstration that all things are in some way extended from the corollary of the third principle of the Nullibists.

As regards the second axiom or principle, namely, Whatever is extended is material, there is no lack of any new argument for proving its falsity, since it has been so clearly and firmly refuted by me above, from the fact that I have demonstrated by so many such irrefutable arguments in Chaps. 6, 7 and 8 that there exists some immobile extension distinct from moveable matter in the universe. Although it may suffice to refer the reader to these, we shall however demonstrate here further from the corollary of the third principle, and clearly prove by the same effort, that all spirits are somewhere (against the ridiculous and insane opinion of the Nullibists).

The third principle of which, and from which they conclude precisely and immediately that spirits are nowhere, is What is inextended is nowhere. Which I certainly grant most willingly, but on this condition that they in turn concede (I do not doubt but that it is freely to be conceded) that Whatever is somewhere is also extended. From which, as I have said, I shall prove the consectary with plainly mathematical certainty, that God and our soul and, therefore, all other immaterial things are in some way extended. For, even the Nullibists acknowledge and affirm that the operations with which the soul acts in the body are in the body, and that divine power by which God acts in matter and moves it is present in the individual parts of matter. Whence it is easy to infer that the operation of the soul and the motive power of God are somewhere, namely in the body and in matter. And, indeed, the operation of the soul by which it acts in the body and the soul itself, and the divine power by which God moves matter and God himself, are together, nor can they be mutually separated from one another, not even in thought, the operation indeed from the soul, and the power from God. Therefore, if the operation of the soul is somewhere, the soul is somewhere, namely, there where the operation is: if the power of God is somewhere, God is somewhere, there, namely, where the divine power is, the latter in the individual parts of matter, the soul in the human body. Whoever, indeed, can deny this would by the same reason deny that that common mathematical notion that Those individual things which are equal to a third are equal between themselves.

Q Ralph Cudworth, *The True Intellectual System of the Universe* (1671/1678), Preface to the Reader (pp. 17v–17r)

Again, we shall here Advertise the Reader, (though we have Caution'd concerning it, in the Book it self) That in our Defence of Incorporeal Substance *against the* Atheists, *However we thought our selves concerned, to say the utmost that possibly we could, in way of Vindication of the* Ancients, *who generally maintained it to be* Unextended, *(which to some seems an Absolute* Impossibility;*) yet we would not be supposed Ourselves,* Dogmatically *to Assert any more in this Point, than what all* Incorporealists *agree in, That there is a Substance Specifically distinct from* Body; *namely such, as* Consisteth *Not of Parts Separable from one another; and which can* Penetrate Body; *and Lastly, is* Self-Active, *and hath an* Internal Energy, *distinct from that of* Locall Motion. *(And thus much is undeniably Evinced, by the Arguments before proposed.) But whether this* Substance, *be altogether* Unextended, *or* Extended *otherwise than* Body; *we shall leave every man to make his own Judgment concerning it.*

Furthermore, We think fit here to Suggest, That whereas throughout this Chapter *and* Whole Book, *we constantly Oppose the* Generation of Souls, *that is, the* Production *of* Life, Cogitation, *and* Understanding, *out of* Dead *and* Senseless Matter; *and assert all* Souls *to be as* Substantiall *as* Matter [17r] *it self; This is not done by us, out of any fond* Addictedness *to* Pythagorick Whimseys, *nor indeed out of a meer* Partiall Regard *to that Cause of* Theism *neither, which we are engaged in, (though we had great reason to be tender of that too;) but because we were enforced thereunto, by* Dry Mathematicall Reason; *it being as certain to us, as any thing in all* Geometry, *That* Cogitation *and* Understanding *can never possibly* Result *out of* Magnitudes, Figures, Sites, *and* Locall Motions, *(which is all that ourselves can allow to Body) however Compounded together. Nor indeed in that other way of* Qualities, *is it better Conceivable, how they should emerge out of* Hot *and* Cold, Moist *and* Dry, Thick *and* Thin; *according to the* Anaximandrian Atheism. *And they who can persuade themselves of the Contrary, may Believe, That any thing may be Caused by any thing; upon which Supposition, we confess, it Impossible to us, to prove the* Existence of a God, *from the* Phaenomena.

R Cudworth, *True Intellectual System*, Chapter 5 (pp. 643–644)

Nay, we will yet go further in compliance with them and acknowledge likewise, That as for those *Infinities*, of *Number*, of *Corporeal Magnitude*, and of *Time* or *Successive Duration*, we have not only no *Phantasm*, nor *Full Intellectual Comprehension* of them, but also no manner of *Intelligible Idea, Notion* or *Conception*. For though it be true, that Number be somewhere said by *Aristotle*[19] to be *Infinite*, yet was his meaning there only in such a negative Sence as this, that we can never possibly come to an End thereof by Addition, but may in our minds still add Number to Number *Infinitely*; which is all one as if he should indeed have affirmed, that there can be no *Number* Actually and Positively *Infinite*, according to *Aristotle*'s own Definition of Infinite elsewhere given,[20] namely, *That to which nothing can be added:* no Number being ever so Great, but that One or More may still be added to it. And as there can be no *Infinite Number*, so neither can there be any *Infinity of Corporeal Magnitude*; not only because if there were, the parts thereof must needs be Infinite in Number; but also because, as no Number can be so great, but that More may be added to it; so neither can any *Body* or *Magnitude* be ever so Vast, but that more *Body* or *Magnitude* may be supposed still further and further; this *Addition* of *Finites*, never making up *Infinite*. Indeed *Infinite Space*, beyond the *Finite World*, is a thing which hath been much talked of; and it is by some supposed to be *Infinite Body*, but by others to be an *Incorporeal Infinite*; through whose Actual Distance notwithstanding (Mensurable by Poles and Miles) [644] this *Finite World* might rowl and tumble *Infinitely*. But as we conceive, all that can be demonstrated here, is no more than this, That how vast soever the Finite World should be, yet is there a *Possibility* of more and more *Magnitude* and *Body*, still to be added to it, further and further, by *Divine Power, Infinitely*; or that the World could never be made so Great, no not by God himself, as that his own Omnipotence could not make it yet Greater. Which *Potential Infinity* or *Indefinite Encreasableness* of *Corporeal Magnitude*, seems to have been mistaken for an *Actual Infinity* of *Space*.[21] Whereas for this very Reason, because more could be added to the Magnitude of the Corporeal World *Infinitely*, or without *End*; therefore is it *Impossible* that it should ever be *Positively* and *Actually Infinite*; That is, such as to which nothing more can Possibly be added. Wherefore we conclude concerning *Corporeal Magnitude*, as we did before of *Number*, that there can be no *Absolute* and *Actual Infinity* thereof; and that how much Vaster soever, the World may be, than according to the Supposition of Vulgar Astronomers, who make the *Starry Sphere* the *Utmost Wall* thereof, yet is it not *Absolutely Infinite*, such as Really hath *No Bounds* or *Limits* at all; nor to which Nothing more could by *Divine Power* be added. Lastly, we affirm likewise concerning *Time* or *Successive Duration*, that there can be no *Infinity* of that neither, no *Temporal Eternity* without *Beginning:* and that not only because there would then be an *Actual Infinity* and more than an Infinity of Number; but also because upon this Supposition, there would always have been an Infinity of *Time Past*, and consequently an Infinity of *Time Past*, which was never *Present*. Whereas all the Moments of *Past Time*, must needs have been once *Present*; and if so, then all of them, at least save One, Future too; from whence it will follow, that there was a *First Moment* or *Beginning* of *Time*. And thus does Reason conclude, neither the *World* nor *Time* it self, to have been *Infinite* in their *Past Duration*, or *Eternal* without *Beginning*.

S Cudworth, *True Intellectual System*, 5 (pp. 646–648)

First therefore it is here observable, that this *Omnipotence* or *Infinite Power* asserted by *Theists*, has been commonly either ignorantly mistaken, or wilfully misrepresented by these *Atheists*, out of design to make it seem *Impossible* and *Ridiculous*; as if by it were meant, a Power of Producing and Doing any thing whatsoever without Exception, though never so *Contradictious*. As a late *Atheistick Person*, seeming to assert this *Divine Omnipotence* and *Infinite Power*, really and designedly notwithstanding abused the same, with this *Scoptick Irony, That God by his Omnipotence, or Infinite Power, could turn this Tree into a Syllogism*. Children indeed have sometimes such childish apprehensions of the *Divine Omnipotence*; and *Ren. Cartesius*, (though otherwise an Acute Philosopher) was here no less *Childish*, in affirming, that all things whatsoever, even the Natures of *Good and Evil*, and all *Truth* and *Falshood*, do so depend upon the *Arbitrary Will* and *Power of God*, as that if he had pleased, *Twice Two should not have been Four*, nor the *Three Angles of a Plain Triangle, Equal to Two Right ones*, and the like: he only adding, that all these things notwithstanding, when they were once settled by the Divine Decree, became *Immutable*; that is, I suppose, not in themselves or to God, but unto us. Than which, no Paradox of any old Philosopher, was ever more *Absurd* and *Irrational*: and certainly if any one did desire, to perswade the World, that *Cartesius*, notwithstanding all his pretences to Demonstrate a Deity, was indeed but an *Hypocritical Theist*, or *Personated* and *Disguised Atheist*, he could not have a fairer pretence for it out of all his Writings, than from hence. This being plainly to destroy the Deity, by making one *Attribute* thereof, to *Devour* and *Swallow* up another; *Infinite Will and Power, Infinite Understanding and Wisdom*. For to suppose God to *Understand* and to be *Wise* only by his *Will*, is all one as to suppose [647] him, to have Really no *Understanding* at all. Wherefore we do not affirm, God to be so *Omnipotent* or *Infinitely Powerful*, as that he is able to Destroy or Change the *Intelligible Natures* of things at Pleasure; this being all one, as to say, that God is so *Omnipotent* and *Infinitely Powerful* that he is able to Destroy, or to *Baffle* and *Befool* his own *Wisdom* and *Understanding*; which is the very *Rule* and *Measure* of his *Power*. We say not therefore, that God by his *Omnipotence* or *Infinite Power*, could make *Twice Two* not to be *Four*, or turn a *Tree* into a *Syllogism*; but we say, that *Omnipotence* or *Infinite Power*, is that which can *Produce* and *Do*, all whatsoever is *Possible*, that is, whatsoever is *Conceivable*, and Implies no manner of *Contradiction*: the very *Essence* of *Possibility* being no other than *Conceptibility*.[22] And thus has the Point been stated all along, not only by Christian Theists, but even the Ancient *Pagan Theologers* themselves; that *Omnipotence* or *Infinite Power*, is that which can do all things, that do not imply a *Contradiction*; or which are not *Unconceivable*. This appearing from that of *Agatho*, cited before out of *Aristotle, That nothing is exempted from the Divine Power, but only to make* πεπραγμένα ἀγένητα, *what hath been done, to be Undone*; or the like hereunto.[23] Now *Infinite Power*, being nothing else, but a *Power* of Doing whatsoever is *Conceivable*, it is plainly Absurd to say; That a *Power* of doing nothing but what is *Conceivable*, is *Unconceivable*.

But because the Atheists look upon *Infinity*, as such a *Desperate* and *Affrightful* thing; we shall here render it something more easie, and take off that Frightful Vizard from it, which makes it seem such a *Mormo* or Bugbear to them; by declaring in the next place, that *Infinity*, is Really nothing else but *Perfection*.[24] For *Infinite Understanding* and *Knowledge*, is nothing else but *Perfect Knowledge*, that which hath no Defect or Mixture of Ignorance with it; or the Knowledge of whatsoever is *Knowable*. So in like manner, *Infinite Power* is nothing else but *Perfect Power*, that which hath no *Defect* or Mixture of *Impotency* in it; a *Power* of *Producing* and *Doing* all whatsoever is *Possible*; that is, whatsoever is *Conceivable*. Infinite Power can Do, whatsoever *Infinite Understanding* can *Conceive*, and nothing else: Conception being the Measure of *Power* and its *Extent*, and whatsoever is in it self *Unconceivable*, being therefore *Impossible*. Lastly *Infinity of Duration* or *Eternity*, is Really nothing else, but *Perfection*, as including Necessary Existence and Immutability in it. So that it is not only Contradictious to such a Being, to Cease to Be, or Exist; but also to have had a *Newness* or *Beginning* of Being; or to have any Flux or Change therein, by *Dying* to the *Present*, and acquiring something New to it self which was not before. Notwithstanding which, this Being comprehends the differences of *Past, Present*, and *Future*, or the *Successive Priority* and *Posteriority* of all *Temporary Things*. And because *Infinity* is *Perfection*, therefore can nothing which includeth any thing of *Imperfection*, in the very *Idea* and *Essence* of it, be ever Truly and Properly *Infinite*; as Number, Corporeal Magnitude, and Successive Duration. All which can only, *Mentiri Infinitatem, Counterfeit and Imitate Infinity*,[25] in their having more and more added to them *Infinitely*, whereby [648] notwithstanding they never reach it or overtake it. There is nothing *truly Infinite*, neither in *Knowledge*, nor in *Power*, nor in *Duration*, but only One *Absolutely Perfect Being* or *The Holy Trinity*.

T Cudworth, *True Intellectual System*, 5 (pp. 776–778)

And as for Christian Writers, besides *Origen*, who was so famous an Asserter of *Incorporeal Substance*, that (as *Socrates* recordeth)[26] the Egyptian Monks and Anthropomorphites, threatned death to *Theophilus* the *Alexandrian* Bishop, unless he would at once execrate and renounce the Writings of *Origen*, and profess the Belief of a *Corporeal God, of Humane Form*; and who also maintained *Incorporeal Substance* to be *Unextended*, as might be proved from Sundry Passages, both of his Book against *Celsus*, and that *Peri Archon*; we say (besides *Origen and others of the Greeks*) St. *Austine* amongst the Latins, clearly asserted the same, he maintaining in his Book, *De Quantitate Animae*,[27] and else where, concerning the *Humane Soul*, that being *Incorporeal*, it hath no Dimensions of *Length, Breadth* and *Profundity*, and is *Illocabilis, No where* as in a *Place*. We shall conclude, with the Testimony of *Boetius*, who was both a Philosopher and a Christian,[28] *Quaedam sunt* (saith he) *Communes Animi Conceptiones, per se notae, apud Sapientes tantum; Ut Incorporalia non esse In Loco; There are certain Common Conceptions, or Notions of the Mind, which are known by themselves amongst wise men only; as this for example, That Incorporeals are in No Place*. From whence it is manifest, that the generality of reputed Wise men, were not formerly of this opinion, *Quod Nusquam est nihil est, That what is No where, or in no certain Place, is Nothing*; and that this was not look'd upon by them as a *Common Notion*, but only as a *Vulgar Errour*.

By this time we have made it unquestionably Evident, that this Opinion of *Incorporeal Substance* being *Unextended, Indistant*, and *Devoid of Magnitude*, is no Novel or Recent thing, nor first started in the *Scholastick Age*, but that it was the general Perswasion, of the most ancient and learned Asserters of *Incorporeal Substance*; especially, that the *Deity* was not Part of it *Here*, and Part of it *There*, nor the *Substance* thereof *Mensurable* by Yards and Poles, as if there were so much of it contained in one Room, and so much and no more in another, according to their several Dimensions; but that the whole *Undivided Deity*, was at once in Every *Part* of the world, and consequently No where *Locally* after the manner of *Bodies*. But because this opinion, seems so *Strange* and *Paradoxical*, and lies under so great [777] *Prejudices*, we shall in the next place show, how these ancient *Incorporealists*, endeavoured to acquit themselves in repelling the several *Efforts* and *Plausibilities* made against it. The First whereof is this, That to suppose *Incorporeal Substances, Unextended* and *Indivisible*, is to make them *Absolute Parvitudes*, and by means of that, to render them all, (even the *Deity* it self) contemptible; since they must of necessity, be either Physical *Minimums*, that cannot *Actually* be *Divided* further by reason of their *Littleness*, (if there be any such thing) or else meer *Mathematical Points*, which are not so much as *Mentally Divisible:* so that *Thousands* of these *Incorporeal Substances*, or *Spirits*, might *Dance together at once upon a Needles Point.*²⁹ To which it was long since thus Replied by *Plotinus*,³⁰ οὐχ οὕτω δὲ ἀμερές ὡς μικρόν· οὕτω γὰρ οὐδὲν ἧττον καὶ μεριστὸν ἔσται· καὶ οὐ παντὶ αὐτῷ ἐφαρμόσει οὐδ' αὖ αὐξομένῳ τὸ αὐτὸ συνέσται· ἀλλ' οὐδ' οὕτως ὡς σημεῖον, οὐ γὰρ ἓν σημεῖον ὁ ὄγκος, ἀλλ' ἄπειρα ἐν αὐτῷ, [. . .] οὐδ' ὡς ἐφαρμόσει, *God and all other Incorporeal Substances, are not so Indivisible, as if they were Parvitudes, or Little things, as Physical points; for so would they still be Mathematically Divisible; nor yet, as if they were Mathematical Points neither, which indeed are no Bodies nor Substances, but only The Termini of a Line. And neither of these wayes, could the Deity Congruere, with the world; nor Souls with their respective Bodies, so as to be all present with the whole of them.* Again he writeth particularly concerning the Deity thus,³¹ οὔτε οὕτως ἀμερές, ὡς τὸ μικρότατον· μέγιστον γὰρ ἁπάντων οὐ μεγέθει, ἀλλὰ δυνάμει· [. . .]ληπτέον δὲ καὶ ἄπειρον αὐτὸν οὐ τῷ ἀδιεξιτήτῳ ἢ τοῦ μεγέθους ἢ τοῦ ἀριθμοῦ, ἀλλὰ τῷ ἀπεριλήπτῳ τῆς δυνάμεως. *God is not so Indivisible as if he were the Smallest or Least of things, for he is the Greatest of all, not in respect of Magnitude, but of Power. Moreover as he is Indivisible, so is he also to be acknowledged Infinite, not as if he were either a Magnitude or a Number, which could never be past thorough; but because his Power is Incomprehensible.* Moreover the same Philosopher,³² condemneth this for a *Vulgar Errour*, proceeding from *Sense* and *Imagination*, that whatsoever is *Unextended* and *Indistant*, must therefore needs be *Little*, he affirming on the contrary the Vulgar to be much mistaken, as to *True Greatness* and *Littleness*, μέγα νομίζοντες τὸ αἰσθητὸν ἀποροῦμεν, πῶς ἐν μεγάλῳ καὶ τοσούτῳ ἐκείνη ἡ φύσις ἐκτείνεται. Τὸ δέ ἐστι· τοῦτο τὸ λεγόμενον μέγα μικρόν· ὃ δὲ νομίζεται μικρόν, ἐκεῖνο μέγα, εἴ γε ὅλον ἐπὶ πᾶν τούτου μέρος φθάνει, μᾶλλον δὲ τοῦτο πανταχόθεν τοῖς αὐτοῦ μέρεσιν ἐπ' ἐκεῖνο ἰὸν εὑρίσκει αὐτὸ πανταχοῦ πᾶν καὶ μεῖζον ἑαυτοῦ, *We commonly looking upon this Sensible world as Great, wonder how that* (Indivisible and Unextended) *Nature of the Deity, can every where comply and be present with it. Whereas that which is Vulgarly called Great, is indeed Little, and that which is thus Imagined to be Little, is indeed Great. For as much as the whole of This diffuseth it self through every part of the other; or rather this whole Corporeal Universe, in every one of its parts, findeth that Whole and Entire; and therefore Greater than it self.* To the same purpose also *Porphyrius*,³³ Τὸ ὄντως ὂν οὔτε μέγα οὔτε μικρόν ἐστι· (τὸ γὰρ μέγα καὶ μικρὸν κυρίως ὄγκου ἴδια) ἐκβεβηκὸς δὲ τὸ μέγα καὶ μικρὸν καὶ ὑπὲρ τὸ μέγα ὂν καὶ ὑπὲρ τὸ μικρὸν καὶ ὑπὸ τοῦ μεγίστου καὶ ὑπὸ τοῦ ἐλαχίστου ταὐτὸ καὶ ἓν ἀριθμῷ ὄν, εὑρίσκεται καὶ ἅμα ὑπὸ παντὸς μεγίστου τοῦτο καὶ ὑπὸ παντὸς ἐλαχίστου· μήτε γὰρ ὡς μέγιστον αὐτὸ ὑπονοήσῃς· εἰ δὲ μή, ἀπορήσεις πῶς μέγιστον ὂν τοῖς ἐλαχίστοις ὄγκοις [778] πάρεστι, μὴ μερισθὲν ἢ μειωθὲν ἢ συσταλέν· μήτε ὡς ἐλάχιστον, εἰ δὲ μή, ἀπορήσειςπῶς ἐλάχιστον ὂν τοῖς μεγίστοις ὄγκοις πάρεστι, μὴ πολλαπλασιασθέν, ἢ αὐξηθέν, *The Deity, which is the only true Being, is neither Great nor Little,* (*For as much as Great and Little properly belong to Corporeal Bulk or Magnitude*) *but it exceedeth both the Greatness of every thing that is Great, and the Littleness of whatsoever is Little (it being more Indivisible and more One with it self, than any thing that is Little, and more Powerful than any thing that is Great) So that it is above both the Greatest, and the Least; it being found, all one and the same, by every Greatest and every Smallest thing, participating thereof. Wherefore you must neither look upon God, as the Greatest thing,* (*that is in a way of Quantity*) *for then you may well doubt, how being the Greatest, He can be all of him present with every Least thing, neither diminished nor contracted: nor yet must you Look upon him, as the Least thing neither; for if you do so, then will you be at a loss again, how being the Least thing, he can be present, with all the Greatest Bulks, neither Multiplied nor Augmented.* In a word, the Sum of their Answer amounts to this, that an *Incorporeal Unextended Deity* is neither a *Physical Point*, because this hath *Distance* in it, and is Mentally *Divisible*; nor yet a *Mathematical One*; because This though having neither *Magnitude* nor *Substance* in it, hath notwithstanding *Site* and *Position*, a Point being according to *Aristotle*,³⁴ *a Monad having Site and Position. It is not to be conceived as a Parvitude or very Little thing*, because then it could not *Congruere*,³⁵ with all the Greatest things; nor yet as a *Great thing*, in a way of Quantity and Extension, because then it could not be All of it Present, to every *Least thing*. Nor does *True Greatness* consist, in a way of *Bulk* or *Magnitude*, all *Magnitude* being but *Little*, since there can be no *Infinite Magnitude*, and no *Finite Magnitude* can have *Infinite Power*, as *Aristotle* before urged. And to conclude, though some who are far from Atheists, may make themselves merry, with that *Conceit*, of *Thousands of Spirits, dancing at once upon a Needles Point*, and though the *Atheists*, may endeavour, to *Rogue* and *Ridicule*, all *Incorporeal Substance* in that manner; yet does this run upon a clear Mistake of the Hypothesis, and make nothing at all against it; for as much as an *Unextended* Substance, is neither any *Parvitude*, as is here supposed (because it hath no *Magnitude* at all) nor hath it any *Place*, or *Site*, or *Local Motion*, properly belonging to it; and therefore can neither Dance upon a Needles Point, nor any where else.

U Cudworth, *True Intellectual System*, 5 (pp. 778–780)

But in the next place, it is further *Objected*; That What is neither *Great* nor *Little*, what possesses no *Space*, and hath no *Place* nor *Site* amongst Bodies, must therefore needs be an *Absolute Non-Entity*, for as much as *Magnitude* or *Extension*, are the very *Essence* of *Being* or *Entity*, as such; so that there can be neither *Substance* nor *Accident* Unextended. Now since whatsoever is *Extended*, is *Bodily*, there can therefore be no other *Substance* besides *Body*, nor any thing *Incorporeal*, otherwise then as that word may be taken, for a *Thin and Subtile Body*, in which Sense Fire was by some in *Aristotle*,[36] said to be, μάλιστα τῶν στοιχείων ἀσώματον, and ἀσωματώτατον; *The most Incorporeal of all the Elements*; and *Aristotle* himself useth the word in the same manner, [779] when he affirmeth, that all *Philosophers* did define the *Soul*, by Three things, *Motion, Sense*, and *Incorporiety*; several of those there mentioned by him, understanding the Soul to be no otherwise *Incorporeal*, than as σῶμα λεπτομερὲς, *A Thin and Subtle Body*. In answer to which Objection; we may remember that *Plato* in the passage before cited, declareth this to be but a *Vulgar Errour*, that whatsoever doth not take up *Space*, and is in no *Place*, is *Nothing*. He Intimateing the Original hereof, to have sprung, from men's adhering too much to those *Lower Faculties*, of *Sense* and *Imagination*, which are able to conceive Nothing, but what is *Corporeal*. And accordingly *Plotinus*[37]; ἡ μὲν γὰρ αἴσθησις, ᾗ προςέχοντες ἀπιστοῦμεν τοῖς λεγομένοις, λέγει ὅτι ὧδε καὶ ὧδε, ὁ δὲ λόγος τὸ ὧδε καὶ ὧδέ φησιν οὐκ ἐκταθεῖσαν ὧδε καὶ ὧδε γεγονέναι, ἀλλὰ τὸ ἐκταθὲν πᾶν αὐτοῦ μετειληφέναι ὄντος ἀδιαστάτου αὐτοῦ. *Sense indeed, which we attending to, disbelieve these things, tells us of Here and There; but Reason dictates, that Here and There, is so to be understood of the Deity, not as if it were Extendedly Here and There, but because every Extended thing, and the several Parts of the World, partake every where of that, being Indistant and Unextended*. To the same purpose *Porphyrius*,[38] δεῖ τοίνυν ἐν ταῖς σκέψεσι κατακρατοῦντας τῆς ἑκατέρου ἰδιότητος μὴ ἐπαλλάττειν τὰς φύσεις· μᾶλλον δὲ τὰ προσόντα τοῖς σώμασιν ἢ τοιαῦτα μὴ φαντάζεσθαι καὶ δοξάζειν περὶ τὸ ἀσώματον· οὐ γὰρ ἂν τὰ ἴδιά τις τοῦ καθαρῶς ἀσωμάτου προσγράψειε τοῖς σώμασι. τῶν μὲν γὰρ σωμάτων, ἐν συνηθείᾳ πᾶς· ἐκείνων δὲ μόλις ἐν γνώσει γίνεται. ἀοριστῶν περὶ αὐτά, [. . .] ἕως ἂν ὑπὸ φαντασίας κρατῆται, *We ought therefore, in our Disquisitions concerning Corporeal and Incorporeal Beings, to conserve the Property of each, and not to confound their Natures. But especially to take heed, that our Phancy and Imagination, do not so far impose upon our judgments, as to make us attribute to Incorporeals, what properly belongeth to Bodies only. For we are all accustomed to Bodies, but as for Incorporeals, scarcely any one reaches to the knowledge of them; men alwaies fluctuating about them and diffiding them, so long as they are held under the Power of their Imagination*. Where afterwards he propoundeth a Form for this, How we should think of *Incorporeals*, so as not to *Confound* their *Natures* with *Corporeals*[39]; ἐν ἀπείροις μέρεσιν [. . .] τοῦ διαστατοῦ παρὸν ὅλον τὸ ἀδιάστατον, οὔτε μερισθὲν πάρεστι, τῷ μέρει διδὸν μέρος, οὔτε πληθυνθὲν τῷ πλήθει παρέχον ἑαυτὸ πολλὰ πλασιασθέν· ἀλλ' ὅλον πᾶσί τε τοῖς μέρεσι τοῦ ὀγκωμένου, ἑνί τε ἑκάστῳ τοῦ πλήθους, [. . .] ἀμερῶς καὶ ἀπληθύντως καὶ ὡς ἐν ἀριθμῷ· τὸ δὲ μερικῶς καὶ διῃρημένως ἀπολαύειν αὐτοῦ. *That the Indistant and Unextended Deity, is the Whole of it present in Infinite Parts of the Distant World, neither Divided, as applying part to part; nor yet Multiplied into many Wholes, according to the multiplicity of those things that partake thereof. But the whole of it (One and the same in Number) is present to all the Parts of the Bulkie World, and to every one of those many things in it, Undividedly and Unmultipliedly; that in the mean time partaking thereof Dividedly.* It was granted therefore by these *Ancients*, that this *Unextended and Indistant Nature, of Incorporeals, is* ἀφάνταστον, *a thing altogether Unimaginable*; and this was concluded by them, to be the only Reason, why so many have pronounced it to be *Impossible*, because they attended only to *Sense* and *Imagination*, and made them the only *Measure of Things* and *Truth*; it having been accordingly maintained by divers of them, (as *Porphyrius* tells us)[40] that *Imagination* and *Intellection*, are [780] but Two different Names, for one and the same thing; ὀνόματος διαφορᾶς προστεθείσης τῇ τοῦ νοῦ ὑποστάσει καὶ τῆς φαντασίας· ἡ γὰρ ἐν λογικῷ ζώῳ φαντασία δέδοκτο αὐτοῖς νόησις, *There is a difference of Names only and no more, betwixt Mind and Phancy. Phancy and Imagination in Rational Animals, seeming to be the same thing with Intellection.* But there are many things, which no man can have any *Phantasm* or *Imagination* of, and yet are they notwithstanding by all Unquestionably acknowledged for *Entities* or *Realities*; from whence it is plain, that we must have some other *Faculties* in us, which Extend beyond *Phansie* and *Imagination.* Reason indeed dictates, that whatsoever can either *Do or Suffer* any thing, must therefore be undoubtedly *Something:* but that whatsoever is *Unextended*, and hath no *Distant Parts*, one without another, must therefore needs be *Nothing*, is no *Common Notion*, but the *Spurious Suggestion of Imagination* only, and a *Vulgar Errour.* There need to be no fear at all, Lest a Being *Infinitely Wise* and *Powerful*, which Acts upon the whole world; and all the Parts thereof, in Framing and Governing the same, should prove a *Non-Entity*, meerly for want of *Bulk* and *Extension*, or because it *Swells* not out into *Space* and *Distance* as Bodies do, therefore Vanish into *Nothing*. Nor does *Active Force* and *Power*, as such, depend upon *Bulk* and *Extension*, because then, whatsoever had the greater *Bulk*, would have the greater *Activity.* There are therefore, *Two kinds* of *Substances* in the Universe, the *First Corporeal*, which are Nothing but ὄγκοι, *Bulks*, or *Tumours*, devoid of all *Self-Active Power;* the *Second Incorporeal*, which are ἄογκοι, *Substantial Powers, Vigours*, and *Activities;* which though they act upon *Bulk* and *Extension*, yet are themselves *Unbulkie* and devoid of *Quantity* and *Dimensions;* however they have a certain βάθος in them in another *sense*, an *Essential Profundity*, according to this of *Simplicius*,[41] Μεριστὴ μὲν ἁπλῶς ἡ σωματικὴ οὐσία πᾶσα, ἄλλων ἀλλαχοῦ τῶν μορίων κειμένων· ἀμέριστος δὲ εἰλικρινῶς ἡ νοερά, πολὺ δὲ βάθος ἔχουσα, *All Corporeal Substance, is simply Divisible, some Parts of it being here and some there, but Intellectual Substance, is Indivisible, and without Dimensions, though it hath much of Depth ond Profundity in it in another Sense.*

V Cudworth, *A Treatise Concerning Eternal and Immutable Morality* (1731), Book IV, Chapter 5, Sections 5–6

5. But probably it may be here demanded, how a man shall know when his conceptions are conformed to the absolute and immutable natures of essences of things and their unchangeable relations to one another? Since the immediate objects of intellection exist in the mind itself, we must not go about to look for the criterion of truth without ourselves, by consulting individual sensibles, as the exemplars of our ideas, and measuring our conceptions by them. And how is it possible to know by measuring of sensible squares, that the diameter of every square is incommensurable with the sides? Nay, as was observed before, the necessary truth of no geometrical theorem can ever be examined, proved, or determined by sensible things mechanically. And though the eternal divine intellect be the archetypal rule of truth, we cannot consult that neither to see whether our conceptions be commensurate with it. I answer therefore, that the criterion of true knowledge is not to be looked for

any where abroad without our own minds, neither in the height above, nor in the depth beneath, but only in our knowledge and conceptions themselves. For the entity of all theoretical truth is nothing else but clear intelligibility, and whatever is clearly conceived is an entity and a truth. But that which is false, divine power itself cannot make it to be clearly and distinctly understood because falsehood is a nonentity, and clear conception is an entity. And omnipotence itself cannot make a non-entity to be an entity.

Wherefore no man ever was or can be deceived in taking that for an epistemonical truth which he clearly and distinctly apprehends, but only in assenting to things not clearly apprehended by him, which is the only true original of error.

6. But there is another opinion that seems to have gained the countenance of some very learned philosophers, which differs but a little from the Protagorean doctrine. Though for my part I conceive it not to be an opinion, but only a certain scheme of modesty and humility, which they thought decorous to take upon themselves that they might not seem to arrogate too much either to themselves, or to their excellent performances, by not so much as portending to demonstrate any thing to be absolutely true, but only hypothetically, or upon supposition that our faculties are rightly made.

For if we cannot otherwise possibly be certain of the truth of any thing, but only *ex hypothesi* that our faculties are rightly made, of which none can have any certain assurance but only he that made them, then all created minds whatsoever must of necessity be condemned to an eternal *scepsis*. Neither ought they ever to assent to any thing as certainly true, since all their truth and knowledge as such is but relative to their faculties arbitrarily made, that may possibly be false, and their clearest apprehensions nothing but perpetual delusions.

Wherefore according to this doctrine, we having no absolute certainty of the first principles of all our knowledge, as that *quod cogitat, est, Aequalia addita aequalibus efficiunt aequalia, Omnis numerus est vel par vel impar.* We can neither be sure of any mathematic or metaphysical truth, nor of the existence of God, nor of ourselves.

For whereas some would endeavour to prove the truth of their intellectual faculties from hence, because there is a God, whose nature also is such as that he cannot deceive, it is plain that this is nothing but a circle, and makes no progress at all, forasmuch as all the certainty which they have of the existence of God, and of his nature, depends wholly upon the arbitrary make of their faculties, which for aught they know may be false. Nay, according to this doctrine, no man can certainly know that there is any absolute truth in the world at all, because it is nothing but his faculties which makes him think there is, which possibly may be false. Wherefore upon this supposition, all created knowledge as such is a mere fantastical thing.

Now this is very strange to assert, that God cannot make a creature which shall be able certainly to know either the existence of God, or of himself, or whether there be any absolute truth or no.

W Anne Conway, *Principles of the Most Ancient and Most Modern Philosophy* (1690), Chapter 3, Sections 4–7 (van Helmont, *Opuscula Philosophica*, 72–75)

§.4. THESE Attributes duly considered, it follows, that Creatures were created in Infinite Numbers, or that there is an Infinity of Worlds or Creatures made of God: For seeing God is infinitely powerful, there can be no Number of Creatures so great, that he cannot always make more: And because, as is already proved, he doth whatsoever he can do; certainly his Will, Goodness, and Bounty, is as large and extensive as his Power; whence it manifestly follows, that Creatures are Infinite, and created in Infinite Manners; so that they cannot be limited or bounded with any Number or Measure: For Example; Let us suppose the whole Universality of Creatures to be a Circle, whose Semi-diameter shall contain so many Diameters of the Earth, as there are Grains of Dust, or Sand, in the whole Globe of the Earth; and if the same should be divided into Atomes, so small that 100000 of them could be contained in one grain of Poppy-seed: Now who can deny, but the Infinite Power of God, could have made this Number greater, and yet still greater, even to an Infinite Multiplication? Seeing it is more easie to this Infinite Power, to multiply the real Beings of Creatures, than for a skilful Arithmetician to make any Number greater and greater, which can never be so great, but that it may be (by Addition or Multiplication) encreased *ad infinitum*: And farther, seeing it is already demonstrated, that God is a necessary Agent, and doth whatsoever he can do: It must needs be, that he doth multiply, and yet still continues to multiply and augment the Essences of Creatures, *ad infinitum*: Concerning Infinity see *Philosoph. Kabbal. Dissert.* 1. *Cap.* 6. *Dissert.* 3. *C.* 1. in *Kabbal. denud.* Tom. 1. Part. 3. Whence Creatures are rather termed Indefinite than Infinite.

§.5. ALSO by the like Reason is proved, that not only the whole Body or System of Creatures considered together, is Infinite, or contains in it self a kind of Infinity; but also that every Creature, even the least that we can discern with our Eyes, or conceive in our Minds, hath therein such an Infinity of Parts, or rather entire Creatures, that they cannot be numbred; even as it cannot be denied, that God can place one Creature within another, so he can place two as well as one, and four as well as two, so also eight as well as four, so that he could multiply them without end, always placing the less within the greater. And seeing no Creature can be so small, that there cannot be always a less; so no Creature is so great that there cannot be always a greater: Now it follows that in the least Creature there may exist, or be comprehended Infinite Creatures, which may be all of them Bodies, and after a sort, in regard of themselves, impenetrable one of another. As to those Creatures which are Spirits, and can penetrate each other, in every created Spirit, there may be some Infinity of Spirits, all which Spirits may be of equal extension, as well with the aforesaid Spirit, as they are one with another; for in this case those Spirits are more Subtile and Æthereal, which penetrate the Gross and more Corporeal, whence here can be no want of Room, that one must be constrained to give place to another. Of the Nature of Bodies and Spirits, more shall be said in its proper place, this being sufficient to demonstrate, that in every Creature, whether the same be a Spirit or a Body, there is an Infinity of Creatures, each whereof contains an Infinity, and again each of these, and so *ad infinitum*.

§.6. ALL these do greatly extol and set forth the great Power and Goodness of God, for that his Eternity is clearly seen by the Works of his Hands; yea in every Creature that he hath made: Nor can it be objected, we make Creatures equal with God; for as one Infinite may be greater than another, so God is still Infinitely greater than all his Creatures, and that without any comparison. And thus indeed the Invisible Things of God are clearly seen, as they are understood by, or in those things, which are made; for by how much the greater and more Magnificent the Works are, by so much the more is the Greatness of the Workman seen: Therefore those who teach, that the whole Number of Creatures is Finite, and consists of so many Individuals as may be numbred; and that the whole Body of the Universe takes up just so many Acres or Miles, or Diameters of the Earth, according to Longitude, Latitude, and Profundity, consider so great Majesty with too low and unbeseeming a Conception; and so that God which they fansie to themselves, is not the true God, but an Idol of their own Imagination, whom they confine to so narrow an Habitation, as a few little Bees shut up within the limits of an Hive, containing the measure of a few Inches: for what else is that World, which they suppose, in respect of that truly great and Universal World above described?

§.7. BUT if they say, they do not shut up God within this Finite Universe, but do imagine him to exist in Infinite Imaginary Spaces, as well without as within it. To this may be answered, If those Spaces are merely imaginary; certainly then they are nothing but Foolish Fictions of the Brain; but if they are real Beings, what can they be but Creatures of God? Besides, either God Works in those Spaces, or he doth not: if he doth not, then God is not there; for wheresoever he is, there he worketh;

seeing this is his Nature, that he must so act, as it is the Nature of Fire to burn, or of the Sun to shine: For so God perpetually worketh; and his Work is to Create, or give Being to Creatures, according to that Eternal *Idea* or Wisdom which is in him. According to the *Hebrews*, God is Infinite, whom they call *Ænsoph;* for that he is said to exist without the Space of the World, because the Creature could not contain the Immensity of his Light. See what is said in Annotations on the First Chapter. Neither is he said to exist in imaginary Spaces, because no place plainly agrees with God; but he may be said to operate there by his simple activity: But whatsoever is wrought in, and by the way of the Creatures, is done by the *Messias*, who is not so Immense as *Ænsoph* himself.

X Conway, *Principles*, 9,2. 9 (*Opuscula Philosophica*, 135–136.)

§.2. AND none can Object, That all this Philosophy is no other than that of *des Cartes*, or *Hobbs* under a new Mask. For, First, as touching the *Cartesian* Philosophy, this saith that every Body is a mere dead Mass, not only void of all kind of Life and Sense, but utterly uncapable thereof to all Eternity; this grand Errour also is to be imputed to all those who affirm Body and Spirit to be contrary Things, and inconvertible one into another, so as to deny a Body all Life and Sense; which is quite contrary to the grounds of this our Philosophy. Wherefore it is so far from being a *Cartesian* Principle, under a new Mask, that it may be truly said it is *Anti-Cartesian*, in regard of their Fundamental Principles; although it cannot be denied that *Cartes* taught many excellent and ingenious Things concerning the Mechanical part of Natural Operations, and how all Natural Motions proceed according to Rules and Laws Mechanical, even as indeed Nature her self, *i.e.* the Creature, hath an excellent Mechanical Skill and Wisdom in it self, (given it from God, who is the Fountain of all Wisdom,) by which it operates: But yet in Nature, and her Operations, they are far more than merely Mechanical; and the same is not a mere Organical Body, like a Clock, wherein there is not a vital Principle of Motion; but a living Body, having Life and Sense, which Body is far more sublime than a mere Mechanism, or Mechanical Motion.

But it is a matter of great debate how motion can be transmitted from one body to another since it is certainly neither a substance nor a body. If it is only a mode of the body, how can this motion pass properly from one body to another since the essence or being of a mode consists in this, namely, that it inheres or exists in its own body? The answer to this objection which seems to me best is [70] this: that motion is not communicated from one body to another by local motion, because motion itself is not moved but instead moves the body in which it exists. And if motion were communicated by local motion, this motion would be communicated by another, and this again by yet another, and so on to infinity, which is absurd. Therefore, the way motion is communicated is through real production or creation, so to speak. Just as God and Christ alone can create the substance of any thing, since no creature can create or give being to any substance, not even as an instrument, likewise a creature gives existence to motion or vital action, not from itself, but only in subordination to God as his instrument. In the same way motion in one creature can produce motion in another. And this is all that a creature can do to move itself or its fellow creature, namely as an instrument of God. Through these motions a new substance is not created, but only new kinds of things, so that creatures are multiplied in their own kind, while one acts upon or moves another. And this is the entire work of the creature or creation as an instrument of God. But if it moves against his will, whose instrument it is, then it sins and is punished for it. But God is not the cause of sin, as stated above, because when a creature sins, it abuses that power which God granted it. Thus, the creature is culpable and God is entirely free from every spot or stain.

If therefore we apply what has already been said about the attributes of the body, namely that it not only has quantity and shape but also life; and that it can be moved not only mechanically and locally but also vitally, and that it can transmit its vital actions wherever it wishes, provided it has a suitable medium; and that if it lacks this, it can extend itself through the subtle emanation of its parts, which then become the most fitting and appropriate medium for receiving and transmitting its vital action; then by these means it is easy to respond to all the arguments by which some people wish to prove that the body is altogether incapable of sense or perception. And it can be easily shown how the body gradually attains that perfection, so that it is not only capable of such perception and knowledge as brutes have, but of whatever perfection can befall any human being or angel. Thus, without taking refuge in some forced metaphor, we can understand the words of Christ, that "God can raise up children to Abraham from stones" (Mt. 3:9). And if anyone should deny the omnipotence of God and his power to raise up the sons of Abraham from external stones, this surely would be the greatest presumption.

§.9. LIKEWISE, Local and Mechanical Motion (*i.e.*) the carrying of Body from place to place, is a Manner or Operation distinct from Action or Vital Operation, altho' they are inseparable, so that a Vital Action can in no wise be without all Local Motion, because this is the Instrument thereof. So the Eye cannot see, unless Light enter it, which is a Motion, and stirs up a Vital Action in the Eye, which is Seeing; and so in all other Vital Operations in the whole Body. But an Action of Life is a far Nobler and Diviner manner of Operation than Local Motion; and yet both agree to one Substance, and consist well together; for as the Eye receives the Light into it self, from the Object which it seeth from without; so also it sends the same Light to the Object, and in this Spirit and Life is a Vital Action, uniting the Object and Sight together.

Wherefore *Hobbs*, and all others who side with him, grievously erre, whilst they teach that Sense and Knowledge is no other than a reaction of Corporeal Particles one upon another, where, by reaction, he means no other than Local and Mechanical Motion. But indeed Sense and Knowledge is a Thing far more Noble and Divine, than any Local or Mechanical Motion of any Particles whatsoever; for it is the Motion or Action of Life, which uses the other as its Instrument, whose Service consists herein; that is, to stir up a Vital Action in the Subject or Percipient; and can like Local Motion be transmitted through divers Bodies, although very far distant asunder, which therefore are united, and that without any new Transition of Body or Matter, *ex. gr.* a Beam of Wood of an exceeding great length, is moved by one Extream from the North to the South, the other Extream will necessarily be moved also; and the Action is transmitted through the whole Beam, without any Particles of Matter sent hither to promote Motion, from one Extream to the other; because the Beam it self is sufficient to transmit the said Motion: After the same manner also, a Vital Action can proceed together with Local Motion from one thing to another, and that too at a great distance, where there is an apt and fit *Medium* to transmit it, and here we may observe a kind of Divine Spirituality or Subtilty in every Motion, and so in every Action of Life, which no created Body or Substance is capable of, *viz.* by Intrinsecal Presence, which (as before is proved) agrees to no created Substance; and yet agrees to every Motion or Action whatsoever: For Motion or Action is not a certain Matter or Substance, but only a manner of its Being; and therefore is intrinsically present in the Subject, whereof there is a *Modus*, or Manner, and can pass from Body to Body, at a great distance, if it finds a fit *Medium* to transmit it; and by how much the stronger the Motion is, so much the farther it reacheth; so when a Stone is cast into standing Waters, it causes a Motion every way from the Centre to the Circumference, forming Circles still greater and greater at a great distance, by how much longer the time is, till at length it vanishes from our sight; and then without doubt, it makes yet more invisible Circles for a longer space of Time, which our dull Senses cannot apprehend, and this Motion is transmitted from the Centre to the Circumference, not conveighed thither by any Body or Substance, carrying this Motion with it from the Stone. And as the External Light also, seeing it is an Action or Motion stirred up by some illuminate Body, may be transmitted through Glass, Chrystal, or any other transparent

Body, without any Substance, Body, or Matter, conveighed from that illuminate Body from whence the said Action proceeded, not that I would deny that abundance of subtile Matter continually flows from all illuminate Bodies, so that the whole Substance of a burning Candle is spent in such Emanations: And this hath in it that Motion or Action, which we call Light; but this Motion or Action may be increased, *v. g.* by Chrystal, where those subtile Emanations of Bodies may be restrained, that they cannot pass out at least in such abundance, as may be sufficient to communicate the whole Light: But seeing Chrystal (which doth so easily transmit the Light) is so hard and solid, How can it receive so many Bodies, and transmit them so easily through it, when other Bodies, neither so hard nor solid, do let or resist it? for Wood is neither so hard nor solid as Chrystal, and yet Chrystal is transparent, but Wood not; and certainly Wood is more Porous than Chrystal, because it is less solid, and consequently the Light doth not enter by the Pores of the Chrystal, but through the very Substance of it; and yet so as not to adhere to it, or make any turgescency or increase of Quantity, but by a certain intrinseck presence, because it is not a Body or Substance, but a mere Action or Motion. Now Chrystal is a fitter *Medium* to receive this Motion, which we call Light, than Wood is; and hence it is, that it pervades or passeth through that and not this; and as there is a great diversity of the Motion and Operation of Bodies, so every Motion requires its proper *Medium* to transmit the same. Therefore 'tis manifest, that Motion may be transmitted through diverse Bodies, by another kind of penetration, than any Body or Matter (how subtile soever it be) is able to make; to wit, by intrinseck Presence. And if mere Local or Mechanical Motion can do that, then certainly a Vital Action (which is a nobler kind of Motion) can do the same; and if it can penetrate those Bodies, it passeth through by intrinseck Presence, then it may in one moment be transmitted from one Body to another, or rather require no time at all, I mean Motion or Action it self requires not the least time for its transmission, although 'tis impossible but that the Body, wherein the Motion is carried from place to place, ought to have some time, either greater or lesser, according to the quality of Body and vehemency of Motion which carries it.

And therefore we see how every Motion and Action, considered in the Abstract, hath a wonderful subtility or spirituality in it, beyond all created Substances whatsoever, so that neither Time nor Place can limit the same; and yet they are nothing else but Modes or Manners of created Substances, *viz.* their Strength, Power and Virtue, whereby they are extendible into great Substances, beyond what the Substance it self can make. And so we may distinguish Extension into Material and Virtual, which two-fold Extension every Creature hath; Material Extension is that which Matter, Body, or Substance hath, as considered without all Motion or Action; and this Extension (to speak properly) is neither greater or lesser, because it would still remain the same. A Virtual Extension is a Motion or Action which a Creature hath, whether immediately given from God, or immediately received from its Fellow Creature. That which is immediately given of God (from whom also it hath its Being,) and which is the natural and proper effect of its Essence, is in a more proper way of speaking, a proper Motion of the Creature, proceeding from the innermost parts thereof; and therefore may be called Internal Motion, as distinguished from External, which is only from another; and therefore in respect thereof may be called Foreign; and when the said External motion endeavours to carry a Body, or any Thing, to a place whereunto it hath properly no natural inclination, then it is preternatural and violent; as when a Stone is thrown up into the Air, which Motion being preternatural and violent, is plainly Local and Mechanical, and no way vital, because it doth not proceed from the Life of the Thing so moved: But every Motion, proceeding from the proper Life and Will of the Creature, is vital; and this I call a Motion of Life, which is not plainly Local and Mechanical as the other, but hath in it a Life, and Vital Virtue, and this is the Virtual Extension of a Creature, which is either greater or lesser, according to that kind or degree of Life wherewith the Creature is endued, for when a Creature arrives at a Nobler Kind and Degree of Life, then doth it receive the greater Power and Virtue to move it self, and transmit its vital Motions to the greatest distance.

But how Motion or Action may be transmitted from one Body to another, is with many a matter of great debate; because it is not a Body or Substance; and if it be only Motion of Body, how Motion can pass properly with its own subject into another, because the very being of *Modus*, or Manner, consist herein, *viz.* to exist or be inherent in its own Body: The Answer to this Objection, which seemeth to me best, is this, That Motion is not propagated from one Body to another by Local Motion, because Motion it self is not moved, but only moves the Body in which it is; for if Motion could be propagated by Local Motion, this Motion would be propagated of another, and this again of another, and so *ad infinitum*, which is absurd. Therefore the manner of the said propagation is (as it were) by real Production or Creation; so that as God and Christ can only create the Substance of a Thing, when as no Creature can Create or give Being to any Substance, no not as an Instrument; so a Creature, not of it self, but in subordination to God, as his Instrument may give existence to Motion and vital Action, and so the Motion in one Creature may produce Motion in another: And this is all a Creature can do towards the moving it self or its Fellow Creatures, as being the Instrument of God, by which Motions a new Substance is not created, but only new *Species* of Things, so that Creatures may be multiplied in their Kinds, whilst one acts upon, and moves another; and this is the whole Work of the Creature, or Creation, as the Instrument of God; but if it moves against his Will, whose Instrument it is, then it Sins, and is punished for it: But God (as before was said) is not the cause of Sin; for when a Creature Sins, he abuseth the Power God hath granted him; and so the Creature is culpable, and God intirely free from every spot or blemish hereof. If therefore we apply those things which have been already spoken, concerning the Attributes of a Body, *viz.* that it hath not only Quantity and Figure, but Life also; and is not only locally and mechanically but vitally moveable, and can transmit its vital Action whithersoever it pleaseth, provided it hath a *Medium* aptly disposed, and if it hath none it can extend it self by the subtile Emanation of its parts, which is the fittest and most proper *Medium* of it, to receive and transmit its vital Action. Hereby it will be easie to Answer to all the Arguments; whereby some endeavour to prove that a Body is altogether uncapable of Sense and Knowledge; and it may be easily demonstrated, after what manner some certain Body may gradually advance to that Perfection, as not only to be capable of such Sense and Knowledge as Brutes have, but of any kind of Perfection whatsoever may happen in any Man or Angel; and so we may be able to understand the Words of Christ, *that of Stones God is able to raise up Children to* Abraham, without flying to some strained Metaphor; and if any one should deny this Omnipotence of God, *viz.* that *God is able of Stones to raise up Children to* Abraham; that certainly would be the greatest Presumption.

Y More, Scholia on Letter to V.C. (1679) (Opera omnia, II/1, 124–125. Translation: Christian Hengstermann)

Sect. 9: "One can find quite a few truly golden little chains", etc. If "truly golden" is supposed to mean purely mechanical, I have come to believe now that one cannot even find "a few", but rather none at all. On this question see what I have written in the second preface to the *Enchiridion Ethicum*, sects. 16 and 22.

"Whether you rather want to call it soul with Descartes", etc. I should very much like to adduce a passage from "Descartes' fragment", which Claude Clerselier sent me (sect. 5). There he states: "However, the moving power may well be that of God himself preserving the same amount of transfer in matter which he put into it at the first moment of creation. Alternatively, it could be that of a created substance like our mind or some other thing to which he has given the power of moving a body. And that power in a created substance is certainly its own mode and not in God. Since everybody finds this difficult to understand, I chose not to deal with this question in my writings. I was afraid that I might seem to endorse the view of those who consider God the world soul united with matter." Descartes, I must confess, is indeed quite abstruse and unforthcoming in these matters and rather reluctant to state and explain his view. However, from what I, for one, can gather from these words, he apparently wants to state roughly the following: for one thing, he is inclined to assume that there may be some created substance which receives its modes from a power like the one by which it moves worldly matter. It might, therefore, have to be considered something like the world soul. For another, however, he chose to conceal his view for fear that he might seem to lean towards the opinion of those who acknowledge no other God than this soul. Hence, suppressing this created principle, which he nevertheless silently admits for himself, he attributes the task of moving matter to God alone. However, we provide abundant evidence in the *Enchriridium Metaphysicum* that matter is moved by a created principle, which we call the "hylarchic principle", and which is devoid of mind and reasoning. Therefore, it is not God, but the plastic spirit of the world created by God, to whose existence it witnesses with the greatest clarity. Descartes' reference to "a created substance like our mind or some other thing to which he has given the power of moving a body" might very well be taken to denote this principle, as it points to a spirit devoid of mind, but not life.

Z More, *Scholia on [Descartes's] Response to Letter 1* (1679) (*Opera omnia*, II/2, 241–242. Translation: Christian Hengstermann)

First difficulty: "If someone should say that God, because he is everywhere, is extended in a certain way, I do not mind at all. And yet, I do deny . . . a real extension, such as is generally conceived by everybody", etc. It is evident in this place that Descartes only denies that extension to God which everybody conceives to be in a body, i.e., corporeal extension. He does not by any means deny to him the metaphysical extension as described in our *Enchiridium*. We may observe here how far the Cartesian nullibists diverge from Descartes, their founder, who acknowledges that God is everywhere and extended in some way, whereas they contend that he is neither extended nor anywhere.
[. . .]
Second difficulty: "Should rather want to say that the divine extension fills the space in which there is no body", etc. However, I am perfectly correct in stating that wherever we picture that there is imaginary space, in reality it is the divine amplitude. In the *Enchiridium Metaphysicum*, we have with more than mathematical evidence—if this is possible!—proved that there is an immobile extended thing distinct from mobile matter.

"And there should still remain in it an extension which I do not conceive differently from the way I previously conceived the body contained in it", etc. But, for all that, it is absolutely clear from what I have shown in the said *Enchiridium* that this conception is false. In this work, I demonstrate that there is an extended immobile thing distinct from mobile matter which possesses attributes opposite to the attributes of matter. See Ench. Met., chs. 6–8.

Fourth Difficulty: "For I understand God alone to be positively infinite", etc. Assuming Descartes is serious here, we perfectly agree about this matter. And it certainly seems to me that I have given sufficiently sound evidence in the said *Enchiridium* that the world, however indefinite, cannot be infinite, so that the pure divinity extends beyond the limits of the world (like Aaron's body whose head, hands and feet extended beyond the priestly garment. See Ench. Met., ch. 10. sect. 8–9, etc.

"I say that it extends further than everything that can be conceived by man", etc. And a little latter he calls the amplitude of the divine essence "absolutely infinite", the corporeal extension "indefinite". If that indefinite extension of the corporeal world is to be understood in the sense that the human imagination cannot exhaust or comprehend it, it accords well with reason. However, right reason dictates to us by necessity that the divine amplitude exceeds it to an infinite degree, lying around it like a crown, as it were. This is why it is called Kether among the Cabbalists.

Notes

1 "An indefinitely extended world but an infinitely extended world"; "infinite in respect of us, but simply [i.e. absolutely] infinite".
2 (Innate) "common conceptions".
3 Lucretius, *On the Nature of Things*, I, 304.
4 Virgil, *Aeneid*, VI 726–727.
5 Both *adaequate*, which means that a definition applies to all things supposed to fall under it, and καθόλου πρῶτον, as defined by the following *reciproca*, which stipulates that the predicates given in a definition be true of all and only of all the members of a class, are examples of More's use of the technical vocabulary of the logic of definition, as prescribed by scholastic manuals steeped in Aristotelian vocabulary (see e.g. Isaac Watts, *Logick or the Right Use of Reason*, London ¹²1763, p. 105). If correct, More argues, a definition can be substituted for the thing defined in all sentences. The French translation does not reproduce More's technical vocabulary at all, rather giving a loose paraphrase of this difficult passage that captures only part of his formal anti-Cartesian argument: "au lieu que votre définition pèche contre les règles, et ne convient point au seul defini." The Italian translator misunderstands the first technical term altogether, rendering it as a mere figure of speech: "invece, la vostra, *per dire in breve*, viola anzitutto la regola, ed infatti non è reciproca col definito."
6 The text in the *Collection* reads *maxime*, that in the *Opera omnia proxime* which alone makes sense here.
7 Fortress.
8 *Aliquid exerit se in natura*, literally "that something exerts itself in nature", rather points to a "power" than "effets" and "efectos" in the French and Latin translations. In fact, More's expression suggests a non-mechanistic "cause". As such, it points both to his notion of a "spirit of nature" as well as to free will mentioned in the following sentence. The Italian translation even construes it to be a strictly non-mechanistic power of self-creation: "in natura si produca qualcosa di cui non si possa dare alcuna ragione meccanica."
9 The stoic technical term for "free will".
10 The *arbitrium* or "judgement" is part of the Latin phrase *liberum arbitrium* which corresponds to the Greek αὐτεξούσιον mentioned a few lines earlier.
11 The *non* is only in the text of Descartes' *Correspondence*, not in that of More's *Collection*. While the former text has been chosen as the basis of this translation, the latter makes sense too: "If, then, this power rouses some parts, and some of them directly, those parts stirred by God will by their own impulse stir the others into motion."
12 Being as being.
13 It is not entirely clear what *quod jam occurrit* is supposed to refer to. More probably wants to state that the argument is not new within the context of his preface.
14 Famously, Aristotle defines God as "the first unmoved mover" in metaphy.1074a37.
15 More invokes famous description of the transcendent creative intellect given by the Presocratic philosopher in DK 59 B 12: "The other things have a share of everything, but the intellect is unlimited and self-ruling and has been mixed with no thing, but is alone itself by itself. For if it were not by itself, but had been mixed with anything else, then it would partake of all things, if it had been mixed with anything (for there is a share of everything in everything just as I have said before); and the things mixed together with it would thwart it, so that it would control none of the things in the way that it in fact does, being alone by itself. For it is the finest of all things and the purest, and indeed it maintains all discernment about everything and has the greatest strength."
16 More refers to *Antidote*, Book II, Chapter 1, Section 9 (*Collection of Several Philosophical Writings*, 44–45): "According to which that notable *phaenomenon*, which now at last I come to, cannot be brought to pass, namely, That the Sucker of the Aire-pump, the Cylinder being emptied of Aire, should draw up above an hundred pound weight, moving up as it were of its own accord."
17 See Immortality III 13,1 (AIHI 122, 258): "And a farther confirmation that I am not mistaken therein, is what we daily here experience upon Earth, which is the descending of heavy Bodies, as well them. Concerning motion whereof I agree with *Des-Cartes* in the assignation of the immediate corporeal cause, to wit, the *Aethereal* matter, which is so plentifully in the Air over it is in grosser Bodies; but withall do vehemently surmise, that there must be some *Immaterial* cause, such as we call *The Spirit of Nature* or *Inferiour Soul of the World*, that must direct the motions of the Aethereal particles to act upon these grosser Bodies to drive them towards the Earth.
18 Chapter XII of More's late *Enchiridium metaphysicum* provides a thorough philosophical reading of this experiment.

19 Aristotle, *Metaphysics* XI 11.
20 Pseudo-Aristotle, *On Marvellous Things Heard* III 9.
21 See also John Locke, *Essay* II 17 (ed. P.H. Nidditch), 209–223.
22 Here, we find Descartes' conceivability argument applied to God.
23 See Aristotle, *Nicomachean Ethics* 1139b9–11: διὸ ὀρθῶς Ἀγάθων, "μόνου γὰρ αὐτοῦ καὶ θεὸς στερίσκεται, ἀγένητα ποιεῖν ἅσσ' ἂν ᾖ πεπραγμένα".
24 Cudworth in connecting infinity and perfection follows Descartes: "God, on the other hand, I take to be infinite, so that nothing can be added to his perfection" (AT VII 47).
25 Cf. Joannes Maxentius (c. 520), *Against the Nestorians* I 11 (PG, 86a, 1446b): *Deum mentiri, propter infinitatem* (τὸν θεὸν ψεῦσασθαι, διὰ τὸ ἀπερίγραπτον).
26 Socrates, *Ecclesiastical History* VI 7.
27 Cf. *De quantitate animae* 1.2. 5.9.
28 Boethius, *De Hebdomadibus* (PL, 64, 1311).
29 We find this image of angels or spirits dancing on a needle's point in Henry More's *The Immortality of the Soul* (1659): "the Schools . . . rashly take away all extension from spirits, whether souls or angels, and then dispute how many of them booted and spur'd may dance on a needle's point at once" (341–342). See also William Chillingworth's *Religion of the Protestants* (1638)—"whether a million angels may not sit upon a needle's point (§ 19)"—, and in the early 14th-century German mystical treatise '*Sister Catherine' Treatise*: "the Masters say, a thousand souls in heaven sit on the point of a pin" (trans. in Bernard McGinn [ed.], *Meister Eckhart, Teacher and Preacher*, New York, 1986, 382).
30 P. 656 [P. Perna (ed.), *Plotini Opera Omnia, cum latina Marsilii Ficini interpretatione et commentatione*, 656 = Plotinus, *Ennead* VI 4.13.19–24].
31 P. 764 [P. Perna (ed.), *Plotini Opera Omnia, cum latina Marsilii Ficini interpretatione et commentatione*, 764 = Plotinus, *Ennead* VI 9.6.6–11].
32 P. 645 [P. Perna (ed.), *Plotini Opera Omnia, cum latina Marsilii Ficini interpretatione et commentatione*, 645 = Plotinus, *Ennead* VI 4.2.28–34].
33 *Sent.* p. 243 [L. Holstenius (ed.), *Porphyrii philosophi pythagorici . . . Sententiae ad intelligibilia ducentes . . .* , 243 = Porphyry, *Sententia* 34.1–11 (ed. Lamberz, 1975)].
34 *De anima* II 6.
35 *congruere* : *congruous, be in agreement with* or *conform to.*
36 Aristotle, *De anima* 405a6–7.
37 P. 656 [P. Perna (ed.), *Plotini Opera Omnia, cum latina Marsilii Ficini interpretatione et commentatione*, 656 = Plotinus, *Ennead* VI 4.13.2–6].
38 ἈΦ. p. 242 [L. Holstenius (ed.), *Porphyrii philosophi pythagorici . . . Sententiae ad intelligibilia ducentes . . .* , 242 = Porphyry, *Sententia* 33.42–49 (ed. Lamberz, 1975)].
39 Porphyry, *Sententia* 33.22–27 (ed. Lamberz, 1975).
40 P. 224. ἈΦ. [L. Holstenius (ed.), *Porphyrii philosophi pythagorici . . . Sententiae ad intelligibilia ducentes . . .* , 224 = Porphyry, *Sententia* 43.36–38 (ed. Lamberz, 1975)].
41 *In Ar. Phys.* p. 3 [<Simplicius>, *In Aristotelis libros de anima commentaria*, 11.26–27 (ed. Hayduck)].

Chapter 12

The Critique of Jacob Böhme
The Critiques of Enthusiasm and Alchemistic Pantheism

A Henry More, *Enthusiasmus Triumphatus* (1656), Section 44 (*Collection of Several Philosophical Writings*, 30–31)

That all is God's self.

That a man's self is God, if he live holily.

That God is nothing but an hearty Living, friendly Seeing, good Smelling, well Tasting, kindly Feeling, amorous Kissing, etc. Nor the Spirit, say I, that inspires this mystery any thing but *Melancholy* and *Sanguine*.

That God the Father is of himself a dale of darkness, were it not for the light of his Son.

That God could not quell *Lucifer*'s rebellion, because the battle was not betwixt God and a Beast, or God and a man, but betwixt God and God, *Lucifer* being so great a share of his own Essence.

That Nature is the Body of God, nay, God the Father, who is also the World, and whatsoever is any way sensible or perceptible.

That the Star-powers are Nature, and the Star-circle the mother of all things, from which all is, subsists, and moves.

That the Waters of this world are mad, which makes them rave, and run up and down so as they do in the channels of the Earth.

[31] That the blue Orb is the waters above the Firmament.

That there be two kinds of Fires, the one cold and the other hot, and that Death is a cold fire.

That Adam was an Hermaphrodite.

That the fire would not burn, nor there have been any darkness, but for Adam's fall.

That it is a very suspicious matter that Saturn before the fall was where Mercury, and Mercury where Saturn is.

That there are three Souls in a Man, Animal, Angelical, and Divine; and that after Death the Animal Soul is in the grave, the Angelical in Abraham's Bosome, and the Divine Soul in Paradise.

That God has Eyes, Ears, Nose, and other corporeal Parts.

That every thing has Sense, Imagination, and a fiducial Knowledge of God in it, Metals, Meteors and Plants not excluded.

B More, *Mastix His Letter* (1656), 2–3 (pp. 294–295)

2. Methinks he is something bold with some Authours that considerable men set no small price upon. But let him look to that; You know the man and the manner of his disposition, how free and exert he is, and what a sincere zeal he has to the Truth. What he writes concerning David George and that other so near akin to him, I must confesse I dare not blame his boldnesse therein, they seeming to

me (so farre as I can possibly fathome them) at the best but Enthusiastick Sadduces. But as for Jacob Behmen I do not see but that he holds firm the Fundamentalls of the Christian Religion, and that his minde was devoutly united to the head of the Church, the crucified Iesus, to whom he breathed out this short ejaculation with much Fervency of spirit upon his deathbed, *Thou crucified Lord Iesus, have mercy on me, and take me into thy kingdome.* But though I be very well assured of the sanctity of the Man, and look upon him as one that is as much beyond the other two, as his boastings of his own person are lesse then theirs who either equalized themselves with, or set themselves above our Saviour, who is God blessed for ever; yet it is to me no argument at all, that whatsoever he writes is from an infallible spirit; But the case seems to me to stand thus.

3. There being two main wayes whereby our mind is wonne off to assent to things. viz. The guidance of Reason, or The Strength and vigour of Fancy; and according to the complexion or constitution of the body we being led by this Faculty rather then by that, suppose, by the strength or fulnesse of [295] Fancy rather then the closenesse of reason (neither of which Faculties are so sure guides that we never miscarry under their conduct; in so much that all men, even the very best of them that light upon truth, are to be deemed rather fortunate then wise) Jacob Behmen, I conceive, is to be reckoned in the number of those whose Imaginative facultie has the preheminence above the Rationall; and though he was an holy and good man, his naturall complexion notwithstanding was not destroyed, but retained its property still; and therefore his imagination being very busie about divine things, he could not without a miracle fail of becoming an Enthusiast, and of receiving divine truths upon the account of the strength and vigour of his Phansie: Which being so well quallified with holinesse and sanctity, proved not unsuccesfull in sundry apprehensions, but in others it fared with him after the manner of men, the sagacity of his imagination failing him, as well as the anxietie of reason does others of like integrity with himself.

C More, *Divine Dialogues* (1666/1668), "The Publisher to the Reader" (Second edition, xxvi–xxvii)

Nor can I divine what Particulars may any ways disgust any one that is Christianly affected, unless the *Behmenists*, *Cartesians*, and *Platonists* may fansie themselves not so civilly dealt withal. The first, because their great Author, Jacob Behmen, though acknowledged a poius and well-meaning Writer, and not unuseful for the exciting of the Sentiments of sincere Piety in others, is not allowed to be such an inspired Man, as that all that he dictates should go for infallible Oracles. But it being so discernible to the Intelligent that he is an *Enthusiast*, there is no faithful Mi[xxvii]nister of the Kingdom of God will ever stick to declare it, for fear of that great Dis-interest that would be done to Religion, if those that are the most zealous Well-willers thereto should not discover themselves to be of so sound a Mind, as not to be imposed upon by the highest Heats and strongest Surmises or Confidences of any Man's Melancholy, whenas the Prophaner Wits are so prone to suspect that there is no Religion but is such.

D More, *Divine Dialogues*, Book 5, Chapter 18 (Second edition, 467–470)

XVIII. Bathynous his judgment touching J. Behmen, with some Cautions how to avoid the being ensnared by Enthusiasts.

Bath.   To declare my conjecture of him freely and impartially, Euistor, I will in the first place allow him to be a very serious and well-minded Man, but of a nature extremely melancholick. And in the second place, I conjecture that he had been a Reader of H.N. and Paracelsus his Writings Both which being Enthusiastick elevations of Spirit, and produced a Philosophy in which we all-over discover the Foot-steps of Paracelsianism and Familism, Love and Wrath, [468] Sulphur and Sal-niter, Chymistry and Astrology being scattered through all.

I do not deny, Euistor, but that H.N. and J. Behmen were inspired; but I averr withal that their Inspiration was not purely Spiritual. Intellectual and Divine, but mainly Complexional, Natural, and Daemonical: Ἡ γὰρ φύσις δαιμονία, οὐ θεία, as Aristotle speaks[1]; which is best understood by that of Plotinus, Θεὸς μὲν οὖν τὸ πᾶν καὶ χωριστῆς ψυχῆς συναριθμουμένης τὸ δὲ λοιπὸν δαίμων μέγας τὰ δὲ πάθη ἐν αὐτῷ δαιμόνια (*Ennead* 2. *Lib.* 3. *cap.* 10).[2] This therefore was an Inspiration too far removed from the first pure Fountain to come clear Complexional Love, the noblest Motion impress'd upon us by the Spirit of Nature, first oppress'd in the Constriction, Compunction and Anguish of a down bearing Melancholy, and after burning and flaming out into a joyful liberty, and carrying captive with it those severer Particles, that would have smothered it, into a glorious Triumph of Light and cheerful Splendour of the Spirits, which makes the Soul overflow with all kindness and sweetness, this, I conceive, is all the peculiar Inspiration or Illumination these Theosophists had at bottom. Which yet is not so contemptible, but that they justly magnify it above the grim ferocities and superstitious Factions in the imbittered Churches of the World, who have not so good an Inspiration as this, but their *Tongues* and Hearts are *set on fire of Hell* (Jas. 3:6). This Light of Nature, I say is abundantly well appointed, both for Right and Skill, to chastise and reproach the gross and grievous Immoralities of Hypocritical Religions, and to be subservient to that Truth and Life that is really Divine.

Euist. But they writ professedly as from the Spirit of God. And J. Behmen seems to have had the assistance of a good Angel, by that Story of an Old Man, who, upon pretence of buying a pair of shoes of him, read him his destiny, and gave him holy and pious Instructions.

[469] *Bath.* Who knows but that it was really a Man? For he carried the Shoes away with him which he bought, nor did he vanish in his sight. And suppose he was a good Angel, not a Devil, does it follow straight that he was infallible? The Inhabitants of the other World are good Physiognomists, and know very well who are most for their turn in this.

Cuph. As an Hose-courser knows and Horse by his Marks.

Bath. And lastly, that Jacob declares what he writes is from God, that is but that which is necessary for all Enthusiasts to do. For if they did not think themselves inspired, they were not Enthusiasts. But there is a very powerful Magick in this then heightened Confidence for the captivating others to them.

Hyl. How shall a Man do then, Bathynous, to keep himself from being ensnared by their Writings, and from being hurried away with their Enthusiasms?

Bath. For him that reads them there is only this one short Remedy and safe, To observe the moral and pious Precepts they tumble out with such extraordinary Zeal and Fervour, and to endeavour to be as really good as they declare themselves and all Men ought to be, and to make that your first and chief care, without any design of engrasping great Mysteries. This is the only way of being assuredly able to judge them and of coming to that state which David blesses God for; *I have more understanding than my Teachers, because I keep thy Commandments* (Ps. 119:99).

Philoth. That is very good advice, Hylobares, and the most certain way of keeping out of the snares of Enthusiasts, and one of the greatest good effects that God intends by the

	permission of them, to inveigle certain Complexions in the ways of Holiness, and to exercise the gift of discerning of Spirits in others to whom he has gi[470]ven it, for the safety of his Church and the magnifying the Ministry of the Gospel of his Son Jesus in the true and Apostolick Promoters thereof.
Sophr.	In this way were taken, my fears and jealousies, O Philotheus, were all hush'd, nor could I doubt but the pure Apostolic Religion would carry all before it.
Philoth.	And verily as touching those two Sects, I must farther confirm to you, O Sophron, that there is not any such great danger in them, no not in that more suspected one, (for as for the Behmenists, I am of Bathynous his Mind, that they are unjustly suspected). For at present, by a kind of oblique stroke, God does notable execution upon the dead Formality and Carnality of Christendom by these zealous Evangelists of an internal Saviour: and if any of them out of mistake and errour should in a manner antiquate that part of Religion that respects the eternal, which I hope are not many, nor will be, yet (and mark what I say), if they continue sincere, I do not doubt but they will be fetched in again at the long run, as being to be found in that third part of the Cities that are to *fall by the Sword of him that sitteth on the white Horse* at the time of the effusion of the last Vial (Apoc. 6:2).

E More, *Philosophiae Teutonicae Censura* (1667/1668: unpublished English original/1679: Latin translation), quaest. I, 11–13 (*Opera omnia* II/1,538. Translation: Christian Hengstermann)

11. However, his inspiration also led him astray in more important matters such as the nature of God whom, as is clear from his *Aurora*, he frequently makes discerpible and corporeal (assuming we can understand a man's mind from his own words). "The heaven", he says, "the earth and everything above the heavens, taken together, are the total God" (ch. 2, v. 61). And in ch. 4: "Light, heat, cold, soft, gentle, sweet, bitter, sour, acid and tone, they all are in God the Father, though in a mild, pleasant and placid mode" (3,16). And this is what he calls "divine salitter". And v. 58: "God created the angels not out of any external matter, but out of himself" (4,58). And ch. 7: "The holy angels were created out of himself, being, as it were, little gods and corresponding to the total God in their qualities" (7,24). And ch. 8: "In the Father are light and darkness, air and water, heat and cold, hard and soft, thick and thin, sound and tone, sweet and sour, bitter and astringent" (8,7). However, all of that was uncorrupted in him before the fall of Lucifer. And in v. 16 the water in him is "likened to the sap or juice in an apple, but very bright and lightsome, like heaven" (8,16). And in ch. 13, v. 65, he likewise says: "The innermost pith or kernel of the total Deity has a very tart and terrible sharpness, a horrible, dark and cold attraction not unlike winter with its cold frost." In this same chapter he also says that "an angel is a part or piece of the total Deity, not the total God himself" (13,45). He says so again in v. 145: "God himself is all things, and all things whatsoever are formed or framed out of him, be it in love or in wrath" (13,145).

12. And with regard to the fact that God did not defeat Lucifer in battle at once, he replies in ch. 14: "O dear blind man, it was not a man or a beast rising against God, but God against God" (14,96), i.e. one huge piece of God against the rest of God. And in ch. 21,12, he says that "no new thing has ever been created that is distinct from God himself." And v. 69: "The whole or universal God is that one body of which all things consist and which is all things" (21,69). And ch. 23: "God is the total or universal essence of things, not excluding water and earth" (23,3). And v. 6: "Now if thou art of any other matter than God himself, how then canst thou be his child?" (23,6). And v. 7: "If the Deity is another substance or thing than his body, then there must be two deities" (23,7). And let us briefly go back to ch. 22, v. 37 where he says that "if God is not in beasts, worms, leaves, herbs and grass, nor in heaven and earth, and if all of this is not God himself, he will commit his book

to flames." Could anyone describe God as more discerpible and corporeal than the author of these passages? And there are many more to this effect. Hence, it is obvious that there was no infallible inspiration directing his pen every time he took it up.

13. However, after that, this erroneous mystery is carried even further for the sake of a more precise and accurate explanation of the eternal generation of the Deity, the Father, the Son and Holy Spirit, from the seven source spirits of God. You can easily see how corporeal the latter are according to his general description once you have heard their names: "Sour, sweet, bitter, heat, light, tone and body" or, as he calls them in his other treatises, "sour, bitter, pain, heat, etc." And just as he confounds God and nature, he also calls them the "seven spirits of *nature*". And he states explicitly that "nature is the whole body of God" (ch. 2, v. 17). And ch. 3,13: "When we consider the whole of nature and its properties", he says, "then we contemplate the Father." And yet, in his view, the Father is identical specifically with the first four of the source spirits or forms of eternal nature before we come into the light. And therefore, he says in v. 55: "If the Son did not shine in the Father, the Father would have been a dark valley" (3,55). And he says so in other places in his writings as well. And ch. 7, v. 42: "The Father is the power and the kingdom, the Son the light and splendour in the Father and the Holy Spirit the motion of the powers of the Father and the Son forming all things."

F More, *Censura*, quaest. IV, 1–6 (II/1, 546–547. Translation: Hengstermann)

We are now coming to the fourth question which is both more difficult to answer and stranger than all the others. I do not consider it my duty to enquire as to which truth his soul might have aspired in every single one of his aforementioned errors, but only in those which seem to me to be the most significant ones and in which we are more likely to succeed. Before dealing with the matter itself, I think it may be worthwhile to present to you that chart or diagram of the "seven spirits" appended to his *Key*. In brief, it looks like this:

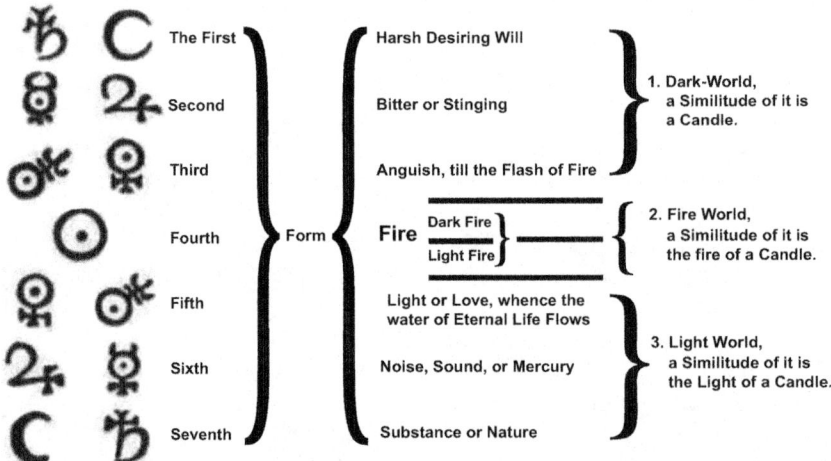

2. This is the chart of the "universal forms" in the complete comprehension of all things. He makes them seven because of his predilection for that number. However, it is superfluous to distinguish the fire world from the light and dark worlds. * And therefore, we shall cross out ☉, the sun. And since ☾ is not a fitting symbol of the divine body or the substance of the light world, we shall

do away with this rather vile planet and put the Sun, ☉, which is a very bad emblem of the dark world, in its place. In this way, ☉, the sun, and ♄, Saturn, will correspond to one another in complete opposition. Thus, in his *Aurora*, he, too, calls ♄ or Saturn an "astringent, frigid and austere sun" as well as the heart of "all corporeality and palpability" (26, 1–2).

3. Now it is also worth mentioning what J.B. himself says about this chart. "Above all", he says, "it is to be observed that the seventh and the first properties are always considered to be one, as are the second and the sixth and, likewise, the third and the fifth, and that the fourth is only a boundary" or limit that sets things apart. Hence, the syzygies ☽ and ♄, ☿ and ♃ and ♂ and ♀ are all meant to show the analogy that obtains between those of one world and those of another, i.e. those of dark fire and light fire or those of love and wrath. "And so", he says, "the effluence of divine manifestation, in terms of the three properties, is *natural* in the first principle, *before* the light, but *spiritual* in the second principle, *in* the light." And hence, I say, let us cross out ☽ and replace it with ☉ in these couplings. And then ♄ will correspond to ☉, the sun, in the light world, and ☉ to ♄, Saturn, in the dark world.

4. And in this way there will be a close affinity and similarity to the old cabbalistic diagram of the six universal forms in the complete comprehension of all things of which I shall provide a structured overview in the following chart:

♄	☉		1 Supreme Good	
☿	♃		2 Eternal Intellect	Trinity of Pure Divinity
♂	♀		3 Divine Soul	
♀	♂	Form	4 World Soul	
♃	☿		5 Spirit of Nature	Trinity of Universal Nature
☉	♄		6 Abyss of Physical Monads	

Here the hypostases of the two trinities correspond to one another in a clear ἀντιστοιχία,[3] ☉ (the sun) to ♄ (Saturn), ♃ (Jupiter) to ☿ (Mercury), and ♀ (Venus) to ♀ (Mars). The trinity of universal nature is like a shadowy projection of the Trinity of pure divinity through the divine soul. It resembles a tree standing above the bank of a river which projects its shadows into the water with the highest of its branches being the lowest in the projection, while the latter correspond to the former and bear a necessary similarity to them. Likewise, the ♃ or abyss of physical monads reflects the image of ☉, the sun, or the supreme good, which the Platonists call τἀγαθόν.[4]

5. Hence, just as the supreme good is divine tactility or intellectual sweetness, so is the abyss of physical monads the source of natural tactility or palpability. And as τἀγαθόν is the uniform lucidity and clarity of divinity, so the abyss of monads is uniform darkness, albeit one that can be ignited into universal splendour and light, thereby creating the "one element" mentioned by J.B. And it is the true Lucifer with his divine salitter who corresponds to ☉, the sun or the supreme good, that "Father of lights" (Jas. 1:17) and inaccessible Phosphor who is most properly called the "heart of God", since he is the first centre of life and light in the Trinity of pure divinity. And on this hypothesis, therefore, the "Lucifer of nature" corresponds to the "heart of God", not the Son, as he is not the heart of the godhead, but its mind and intellect, i.e. ♃.

6. To this mind or intellect, i.e. ♃, otherwise named Zeus or Jupiter (as the mythologers call the eternal intellect, the Son of the divine ♄, Saturn, or Κρόνος, which, in Proclus, means the same as Ἀκρόνος, i.e. τἀγαθόν, to which corresponds τὸ ἀγαθοειδές[5] in human souls), which is also called ὁ θεῖος λόγος,[6] corresponds in exact analogy ☿, Ἑρμῆς, i.e. the λόγος προφορικός,[7] the interpreter, the word spoken, or the λόγος σπερματικός,[8] namely the spirit of nature in the projected shadow. Indeed, Jupiter or ♃ is *perceptive* intellectual omniformity, whereas Mercury or ☿ is *imperceptive and plastic* omniformity. And conversely note that J.B. calls ♃, this Mercury, sound and tone as well, to which, in *Aurora*, he ascribes the forming of all things.

Nor must we omit here that as ♄, Saturn, once ignited into light, becomes the Lucifer of nature, so ☿, because of a natural Nemesis incorporated into it, becomes the Michael of nature, and ♃ the Michael of divinity who brandishes the sword of eternal reason against all transgressors who have sinned against the supreme good, and pleads the cause of the latter in all rational creatures.

G More, *Censura*, quaest. IV, 7–9 (II/1,548. Translation: Hengstermann)

7. And to ♀, Venus, finally, ἡ θεία ψυχή or the divine soul (which Plotinus calls ἡ οὐράνια ἀφροδίτη), κατ᾽ ἀντιστοιχίαν, very appositely corresponds ♂ (Mars), since the one is the fire of love, the other the fire of anguish. Venus, ♀, as it is the true Uriel in the fire of divine love in pure divinity, plunges itself wholly into the enjoyment of divine wisdom and goodness, into the free and shining majesty of the divine. ♂, Mars or the world soul, on the other hand, as it is the Uriel of nature, has its own longing and imagining which is directed towards and determined by nothing but particularities and selfities,[9] and, being wholly bereft of divine influx, it is the origin of fiery desire and strife.

The divine soul is impregnated by the eternal mind or intellect and, on account of its union with the supreme good, instilled with ineffable lust. The world soul is the source only of sensation, imagination and the association of phantasmata[10] and it is exclusively occupied with sensing and grasping the variety of corporeal nature. It rudely seduces us into false reasonings caused by self-love, which blocks out the illumination of pure divinity.

8. This is a brief description of the two general spheres of all things, the one of pure divinity, and the other of universal nature. And if the latter could be severed from the former, notably the world soul from the divine soul, it would certainly, as Plotinus says, change into a δαίμων μέγας[11] or, as I should rather like to put it, a μέγας δράκων.[12] If, by contrast, it were so fully exposed to the sphere of pure divinity, it would all but completely change into one enormous paradise of God. And taken together and viewed as one immense six-fold sphere, whose forms penetrate one another throughout, all the six forms—this Whole, or Universe—is called Θεός by that same philosopher, ★ i.e. the whole or complete Deity or universal origin from which all particular things proceed.

9. And this, surely, could help us in our attempt to conjecture what it is that J.B. probably strives for in his errors. For, even where the target is not hit, the proximate reach reveals the original target of those who shot the arrow. And certainly we cannot but surmise that ★ in reality Jacob Böhme, absorbed as he was with his "seven forms" or "source spirits", aimed for no more than these six. And therefore, in terms of numbers, he was not far off the target.

H More, *Censura*, quaest. IV, 27–29. 32 (II/1,551–552. Translation: Hengstermann)

27. His view about hell or the world of fire and darkness which he believes to be everywhere is true only about its *potentiality*. The total sphere of universal nature could certainly change into a world of fire and darkness. And then Mars would be its great devil or universal Beelzebub. And the infernal Mercury would fill the universe with monstrous and horrendous forms by means of his corrupted and contaminated divine salitter (section 19).

However, no such thing as a world of fire and darkness, viewed as one universal form of nature, exists yet in reality. For the Lucifer of universal nature proves to be everywhere beneficent as well as pure and paradisiac except for places where darkness or another tendency towards it have taken hold and adjacent regions which have let in these forces of darkness. Compared to the other spheres of universal nature, however, their number is less than is one grain of sand in comparison to the whole globe of the earth. Divine providence is so triumphant throughout the immense sphere of nature that it almost constitutes a universally flourishing paradise of nature.

Indeed, the seeds of this paradise insert themselves into the elemental world and the regions of darkness so that its power is felt by the pure and more perfectly regenerated souls. There is very little of hell anywhere except in the devil and in vicious men who make a hell for themselves in this elemental world.

That Adam did not see the sun before the fall and that good angels cannot perceive darkness nor the light of evil unless we want to attribute sensation to naked spirits without a body seems to me to have been said without any reason whatsoever, nor can I conjecture what he might want to say here unless he wanted speak by way of moral allegory.

However, the notion that the soul is propagated in the same way as a small shoot or a young twig is from a tree, is true only in that it is by virtue of the tree that a shoot, rooting itself in the ground, subsequently becomes a cause and principle by which it grows by itself, bearing fruit and blossoms. However, this principle is not a substance taken from the tree, but the spirit of nature operating in it. The tree certainly provided the occasion for the spirit of nature to pursue its work in the shoot and carry it on till the tree was complete. In this way, the foetus in the uterus furnishes an individual soul with the occasion to exercise its life and operation upon this body, directing it, actuating it and governing it for a certain period of time. However, unlike the foetus which is made from their bodies it is not a part of the parents. And somewhere J.B. writes as if he had held the pre-existence of the soul (section 21).

29. However, as to the eternal successive struggle of the seven spirits before the creation of the angels, I believe that he wanted this successive struggle to be of such infinite duration that, counting from our time backwards, we cannot exhaust it with any number as though the eternity of pure and shining divinity were not beyond that. However, J.B. did not reach further in his *Afterglow*, but lost his way in the sphere of ♂, Mars, as I have already said above (section 22).

[. . .]

32. . . . And as regards the shapes and shadows of all things and words which, as J.B. insists time and again—though he fails to explain in what they actually consist—will endure beyond the play of this world without either a spirit or a substance, it certainly cannot be understood in the sense that they will be floating around in the universe without any subject. Instead, they will be inscribed ★ in the memory of the world soul which serves as God's immense register, as it were. Alternatively, all of this was meant solely as a fiction or as nothing but a simple insanity of his.

I More, Censura, Praefatio ad lectorem, 20 (II/1, 534–535. Translation: Hengstermann)

20. The circumstances of J.B.'s death prove with some certainty that he was loved by the heavenly powers. Thus, a few hours before his death, he heard remarkable musical harmonies. After he had predicted the hour in which he was to die, he bade farewell to his family and gave them his blessing. He asked his son to turn him to the other side in his bed and said: "Now, I am going from here to paradise." And so at once he breathed out his soul. I, for my part, confess that I believe that he was not wrong in his prediction at all. For I do not share the opinion of the Mohammedans (who, to that end, leave a curl on their heads so that Mohammed can grab them by that) that man is pulled upwards into paradise by his head, but rather by his heart, in which the root of our regeneration lies and which is the source from which those most divine and delicate sensations of which the human soul is capable spring forth.

21. It was, I believe, primarily because of the perfection of this part that J.B. was so dear to the invisible powers. And notwithstanding his shortcomings in other fields, he was accompanied by such strokes of providence as made him famous all over the world and, as it were, a miracle amongst many good and intelligent men. Furthermore, although he was, for the most part, devoid of it, the repute of his philosophical inspiration nevertheless was like a bait that drew many others towards a sincere reformation of their character and the endeavour to attain that of which no-one need be devoid unless he wants to be. *This is the spirit of Life in the new birth* which, even if it were without any philosophical science, would rightly continue to be the object of man's highest striving and such a precious pearl that it is to be cherished above all other things in the universe.

22. Hence, my dear reader, as regards the productions of his brain, which are mere speculations, we certainly cannot praise J.B. for an infallible spirit residing in him. However, from the few little hints which I have given (and you may find fuller and more satisfactory information by reading his *Life* written by that learned man D.H.) it is clear, I think, that he was not so contemptible an author that anyone sober and interested in things of some importance needs to feel ashamed of undertaking the labour of studying his writings. And this is the aim that I have been pursuing. Farewell.

J More, *Censura, Conclusio,* 1–3 (II/1,558. Translation: Hengstermann)

1. Even though we cannot by any means admit that he was infallibly inspired, we cannot but confess that it is an extraordinary event and quite admirable that such an uneducated man should so manifestly stumble upon the main outlines of the ancient wisdom which was really inspired. We have every reason to believe that his education, insofar as it was Christian, acquainted him with the doctrine of the Trinity. But what could have made him choose the Pythagorean system of the world over the Aristotelian one had it not been for his great mind or something superior to it that gave him aid and guidance? And the fact that he attributes an angelical body to Adam before his fall, if we interpret it cabbalistically, clearly implies the pre-existence of the souls, that excellent third dogma in the *Mosaic Cabbala*.

2. Even though he expressly opposes this doctrine in saying that it is propagated like a shoot from a tree, he nevertheless says in his book on *The Threefold Life of Man*, as if being driven by a kind of ecstatic paroxysm, that "the mind is generated from the eternal quiet peace and existed before the time of this world in the wisdom God and was fertile rain in its eternal quiet mother where it had not yet been created a spirit." Here it is clear from ★ the expression "it had not yet been created a spirit" that it must be conceived as still being in a state in which, perhaps, it did not yet actuate or form a body or, at least, no terrestrial one.

And his expression "was fertile rain" accords extremely well with the Mosaic Cabbala which views souls which descend εἰς γένεσιν[13] into these elemental bodies, as "higher waters". Likewise, Synesius calls his soul a λιβὰς οὐράνια, i.e. "a drop of heavenly rain".

3. And the fact that he calls the soul "mind" rather than "soul" here may well be interpreted as referring to a state of the soul in which it might conceivably have been before the Lucifer of universal nature and the paradise, ★ when the Mars and Mercury of universal nature were in absolute silence and Saturn, if he did exist at all, was still only a monadic abyss. For then the pure mind rested in its mother, in Venus, i.e. the sphere of pure divinity, namely the divine soul, while its plastic part, in terms of its corporeal operations, was entirely silent. Its intellect, by contrast, was wholly actuated by the eternal omniform Intellect and its boniform faculty was firmly focused on the Supreme Good.

However, he seems to intimate that the human minds, even though they were once fixed in divine tranquillity, nevertheless subsequently rained down from the sphere of pure deity into paradise. After their fall there, they sank even further, some even into this elemental world.

This is thoroughly Platonic, even reaching to the sublime level of Plotinus. Apart from that, it would require * a more thorough inquiry whether or to what degree it is right. However, it cannot in any way be disputed that he holds the *pre-existence of the soul*.

K More, *Censura, Conclusio*, 14–18 (II/1,560. Translation: Hengstermann)

14. And his prediction about these times is so far beyond and above his usual ways (in one respect, at least) that his mind may rightly seem to have been in another state of ecstasy when writing down this prophecy. Though a most formidable slanderer and assailant of reason, he can nevertheless write the following about these times: "The lily will not be found in strife and warfare, but in a friendly, humble and benign spirit, coupled with good and sound reason. This will dissipate and dispel the smoke of the devil and flourish in due time."

What character could suit the Philadelphian church better than "a friendly, humble and benign spirit"? Or what could be a better prefiguration of that clarity and comprehensibility by which those times will be graced than "good and sound reason"? That, for sure, will dispel the mist and dust raised so far either by the devil or by wrathful superstition.

15. And speaking about the Jews, the Turks and the other Gentiles, he says: "It is not necessary at all that you expect any other time. No other time is imminent but the time of the lily, and the sign of that time is the sign of Elijah."

This is said as though it referred to the seven successive ages of the churches. In that sense, no other time is imminent than that of the lily, i.e. that of Philadelphia which stirs the expectation of the Jews, the Turks or all other nations. For it is in these times that the whole of Israel will be saved and that all the nations will walk in the light of the New Jerusalem. This name, "Church of the Lily" (that pure, sincere, immaculate, meek, friendly and benevolent church), is the one that the Philadelphian church bears.

16. And he says that the sign of the approach of these times will be the arrival of Elijah in the spirit. As he has pointed out concerning "good and sound reason" above, the latter will be the great restorer of a wisdom and theosophy so holy, so heavenly, so sound and so coherent that no power and reason of the human mind will ever find any stain or weakness in it or seek to refute it in any way.

17. And accompanying this light will be a fire and, with it, a fiery spirit that shall go forth to smoulder and burn all improbity and hypocrisy. The light of that wisdom will seek to correct our life and strengthen our faith and redeem our souls from the vain desires and pleasures of this region of decay and death, leading us to the perpetual thirst for true justice and perfect holiness and to an incessant yearning for those pleasures and glories which are above in the sight of God and his holy angels.

18. The heat of this heavenly fire will devour all the terrestrial fervour of wrath, lust, distrust, pride, contention, persecution and whatever else opposes our love of God and our neighbour. This is the promised spirit of Elijah which will convert the hearts of fathers to their sons and the hearts of sons to their fathers. This is the spirit which will infuse princes with paternal love for their subjects and the subjects with filial reverence for and sincere obedience to their princes. And this, finally, is that dispensation of life and power which will fill all the countries of the globe with sound, true and sanctifying knowledge, with justice, prosperity and peace.

L More, *Censura, Scholia in Qu. IV* (II/1,555. Translation: Hengstermann)

Sect. 2. "And therefore, we shall cross out ☉, the sun": And rightly so, for the sun or fire or rather the fiery world is, as it were, a genus which comprises the dark world and the light world. For the dark world is fiery too, and so is the light world, as ♂ clearly indicates. And therefore, I suspect that by "boundary or limit that sets things apart" he understood the common boundary or terminus in which both worlds concur and coincide, as do two opposing species that concur in their genus. However, owing to his ignorance of logic, he said "limit" (i.e. "boundary") instead of "genus".

Sect. 3. "i.e. the whole or complete deity or universal origin, etc." It is true that Plotinus conceived of the world or the universe as God. However, if one pays sufficient regard to the holiness of the divine majesty, one will both in word and matter make a most religious distinction between the sphere of pure divinity and the sphere of universal nature.

Sect. 9. "In reality Jacob Böhme aimed for no more than these six, etc." This is clear from what we have said in Sect. 2, where we have proved that the fire world is only a genus which comprises the dark world and the light world. As each of them has only three forms, it is necessary that there are six in total.

. . .

Sect. 32. "in the memory of the world soul which serves as God's immense register, as it were, etc." To my mind, it is absolutely certain that the world soul possesses neither reason nor free will. And without reason, it also lacks recollection, but (if it has any at all) it may have some passive memory at least, one that is almost mindless and, if it has any remembrance in it, it must be elicited by someone else. However, these things are covered in immense and impenetrable obscurity and darkness.

Notes

1. *On Divination in Sleep*, 2: "Nature is demonic, not divine."
2. *Enneads*, II,3,9: "The Universe is a God when the divine soul is counted in with it; rest, we read, is 'a mighty demon' and its ways are demonic."
3. Opposition.
4. The good.
5. Boniform
6. The divine word.
7. The word uttered.
8. The spermatic word.
9. The neologism *ipsitates*, literally translated as "selfities", designates the egocentric striving of the lower hypostasis.
10. I.e. mental images.
11. A great demon.
12. A great dragon.
13. Into coming-to-be.

Chapter 13

The Critique of Baruch de Spinoza
Atheism and Hylozoism

A Ralph Cudworth, *The True Intellectual System of the Universe* (1671/1678), Chapter 5 (pp. 706–707)

Wherefore it seems, that there are Two Sorts of *Miracles* or *Effects Supernatural*. First, such as though they could not be done by any *Ordinary* and *Natural* Causes here amongst us, and in that respect may be called *Supernatural*, yet might notwithstanding be done, God Permitting only, by the *Ordinary and Natural Power* of other *Invisible Created Spirits, Angels* or *Demons*. As for example, If a Stone or other Heavy body, should first ascend upwards, and then hang in the Air, without any Visible either Mover or Supporter, this would be to us a *Miracle* or *Effect Supernatural*; and yet according to Vulgar Opinion, might this be done, by the *Natural Power* of [707] *Created Invisible Beings, Angels or Demons*; God only permitting, without whose special Providence it is conceived, they cannot, thus intermeddle, with our humane affairs. Again, If a perfectly Illitterate Person, should readily speak *Greek*, or *Latine*, this also would be to us a *Miracle* or Effect *Supernatural*, for so is the Apostles speaking with Tounges accounted; and yet in *Demoniacks*, is this sometimes done, by *Evil Demons*, God only Permitting. Such also amongst the *Pagans*, was that *Miraculum Cotis*, (as *Apuleius* calls it) that *Miracle of the Whetstone*, done by *Accius Navius*, when at his command, it was divided into Two, with a *Razor*.[1] But Secondly there is another sort of *Miracles*, or Effects *Supernatural*, such as are above the *Power* of all *Second Causes*, or any *Natural Created Being* whatsoever, and so can be attributed to none, but *God Almighty* himself, the *Author of Nature*; who therefore can Controul it at pleasure.

As for that late *Theological Politician*, who writing against *Miracles*, denies as well those of the Former, as of this Latter Kind, contending that a Miracle is nothing but a Name, which the Ignorant Vulgar gives, to *Opus Naturae Insolitum, any Unwonted work of Nature, or to what themselves can assign no Cause off*; as also that if there were any such thing done, Contrary to *Nature* or *Above* it, it would rather Weaken than Confirm, Our Belief of the Divine Existence; We find his Discourse every way so Weak, Groundless, and Inconsiderable; that we could not think it here to deserve a Confutation.

But of the *Former Sort* of those *Miracles*, is that to be understood, *Deuter*. the 13. *If there arise among you a Prophet or dreamer of Dreams, and giveth thee a Sign or a Wonder, and the Sign or Wonder come to pass, whereof he spake unto thee saying; Let us go after other Gods, and serve them; thou shalt not hearken to the words of that Prophet or Dreamer of Dreams, for the Lord your God Proveth you, to know whether you love the Lord your God with all your heart, and with all your Soul.* For it cannot be Supposed, that God Almighty would himself, purposely Inspire any man to exhort others to Idolatry, and immediately assist such a one, with his own *Supernatural Power*, of doing Miracles, in Confirmation of such Doctrine. But the meaning is, that by the suggestion of Evil Spirits, some False Prophets might be raised up, to tempt the Jews to Idolatry; or at least, that by Assistance of them, such *Miracles* might be wrought, in Confirmation thereof, as those sometimes done by the Egyptian *Sorcerers* or *Magicians*, God himself not interposing in this case, to hinder them, for this reason, that he might hereby, *Prove* and *Try* their Faithfulness towards him. For as much as both by the Pure Light of *Nature*, and God's Revealed Will, before confirmed by Miracles, *Idolatry*, or the Religious Worship of any but God Almighty, had been sufficiently condemned. From whence it is evident, that *Miracles* alone, (at least such *Miracles* as these,) are no sufficient Confirmation of a *True Prophet*, without consideration had of the *Doctrine* taught by him. For though a man should have done never so many true and real Miracles, amongst the Jews, and yet should perswade to Idolatry, he was by them confidently to be condemned to death, for a false Prophet.

B Cudworth, *True Intellectual System*, Chapter 3, Sections 1–2 (pp. 104–106)

> [1. That the Grounds of the Hylozoick Atheism could not be insisted on in the former Chapter, together with those of the Atomick, they being directly contrary each to other; with a further Accompt of this *Hylozoick Atheism*.]

1. We have now represented the Grand *Mysteries* of *Atheism*, which may be also called the *Mysteries of the Kingdom of Darkness*; though indeed some of them are but briefly hinted here, they being again more fully to be insisted on afterward, where we are to give an account of the Atheists Endeavours to Salve the *Phaenomenon* of Cogitation. We have represented the chief Grounds of Atheisms in General, as also that most Notorious Form of Atheism in particular, that is called *Atomical*: but whereas there hath been already [105] mentioned, another form of Atheism, called by us *Hylozoical*; the Principles hereof could not possibly be insisted on in this place, where we were to make the most Plausible Plea for Atheism; they being directly contrary to those of the Atomical, so that they would have mutually destroyed each other. For, whereas the *Atomick Atheism* supposes, the Notion or Idea of Body to be nothing but *Extended Resisting Bulk*, and consequently to include no manner of *Life* and *Cogitation* in it; *Hylozoism* on the contrary makes all Body, as such, and therefore every smallest Atom of it, to have *Life* Essentially belonging to it (Natural Perception, and Appetite) though without any *Animal Sense* or *Reflexive Knowledge*, as if *Life*, and *Matter* or *Extended Bulk*, were but too Incomplete and Inadequate Conceptions, of one and the same Substance, called Body. By reason of which Life (not *Animal*, but only *Plastical*) all parts of Matter being supposed able, to form themselves *Artificially* and *Methodically* (though without any Deliberation or Attentive Consideration) to the greatest advantage of their present respective Capabilities, and therefore also sometimes, by Organization to improve themselves further, into *Sense* and *Self-enjoyment* in all Animals, as also to *Universal Reason* and *Reflexive Knowledge* in Men; it is plain that there is no Necessity at all left, either of any *Incorporeal Soul* in Men to make them Rational, or of any *Deity* in the whole Universe to salve the *Regularity* thereof. One main difference betwixt these two Forms of Atheism is this, that the *Atomical* supposes all *Life* whatsoever to be *Accidental*, *Generable* and *Corruptible*: But the *Hylozoick* admits of a certain *Natural* or *Plastick Life*, *Essential* and *Substantial*, *Ingenerable* and *Incorruptible*, though attributing the same only to Matter, as supposing no other Substance in the World besides it.

> [2. A Suggestion, by way of Caution, for the preventing of all mistakes, That every Hylozoist must not therefore be condemned for an Atheist, or a mere Counterfeit Histrionical Theist.]

2. Now to prevent all Mistakes, we think fit here by way of Caution to suggest; That as every *Atomist* is not therefore necessarily an *Atheist*, so neither must every *Hylozoist* needs be accounted such. For whoever so holds the *Life* of *Matter*, as notwithstanding to assert another kind of Substance also, that is Immaterial and Incorporeal, is no ways obnoxious to that foul Imputation. However we

ought not to dissemble, but that there is a great Difference here betwixt these two, *Atomism* and *Hylozoism*, in this regard; That the former of them, namely Atomism (as hath been already declared) hath in it self a Natural Cognation and Conjunction with *Incorporeism*, though violently cut off from it by the *Democritick Atheists*; whereas the latter of them, *Hylozoism*, seems to have altogether as close and intimate a Correspondence with *Corporealism*; Because, as hath been already signified, if all Matter, as such, have not only such a *Life*, *Perception*, and *Self-active* Power in it, as whereby it can Form it self to the best advantage, making this a Sun, and that an Earth or Planet, and fabricating the Bodies of Animals most Artificially; but also can improve it self into Sense and Self-enjoyment; it may as well be thought able to advance it self higher, into all the Acts of *Reason* and *Understanding* in Men: so that there will be no need either of an Incorporeal Immortal Soul in Men, or a Deity in the Universe. Nor indeed is it easily conceivable, how any should be induced to admit [106] such a Monstrous Paradox as this is, That every Atom of Dust or other Senseless Matter, is Wiser than the greatest Politician and the most acute Philosopher that ever was; as having an Infallible Omniscience of all its own *Capabilities* and *Congruities*; were it not by reason of some strong Prepossession, against Incorporeal Substance and a Deity, there being nothing so Extravagant and Outrageously Wild, which a Mind once infected with Atheistical Sottishness and Disbelief, will not rather greedily swallow down, than admit a Deity, which to such is the highest of all Paradoxes imaginable, and the most affrightful Bug-ber. Notwithstanding all which, it may not be denied, but that it is possible for one, who really entertains the belief of a Deity and a Rational Soul Immortal, to be perswaded, first, that the Sensitive Soul, in men as well as Brutes, is merely Corporeal; and then that there is a *Material Plastick Life* in the Seeds of all Plants and Animals, whereby they do Artificially form themselves; and from thence afterward to descend also further, to Hylozoism, that all matter, as such, hath a kind of *Natural*, though not *Animal Life* in it; in consideration whereof, we ought not to Censure every *Hylozoist*, professing to hold a Deity and a Rational Soul Immortal, for a mere Disguised Atheist, or a Counterfeit Histrionical Theist.

C Cudworth, *True Intellectual System*, 3,3 (pp. 106–107)

[3. That, nevertheless, such Hylozoists as are also Corporealists, can by no means be excused from the Imputation of Atheism, for Two Reasons.]

3. But though every *Hylozoist* be not therefore necessarily an *Atheist*, yet whosoever is an *Hylozoist* and *Corporealist* both together, he that both holds the *Life* of *Matter* in the Sence before declared, and also that there is no other Substance in the World besides Body and Matter, cannot be excused from the Imputation of Atheism, for Two Reasons. First, because though he derive the Original of all Things, not from what is perfectly Dead and Stupid as the *Atomick Atheist* doth, but from that which hath a kind of Life or Perception in it, nay an *Infallible Omniscience*, of whatsoever it self can Do or Suffer, or of all its own Capabilities and Congruities, which seems to bear some Semblance of a Deity; yet all this being only in the way of *Natural* and not *Animal Perception*, is indeed nothing but a Dull and Drowsy, *Plastick* and *Spermatick Life*, devoid of all *Consciousness* and *Self-enjoyment*. The *Hylozoists Nature*, is a piece of very Mysterious Non-sence, a thing perfectly Wise, without any Knowledge or Consciousness of it self; Whereas a Deity, according to the true Notion of it, is such a Perfect Understanding Being, as with fall Consciousness and Self-enjoyment, is completely Happy. Secondly, because the *Hylozoick Corporealist*, supposing all Matter, as such, to have Life in it, must needs make Infinite of those Lives, (forasmuch as every Atom of Matter has a Life of its own) Coordinate and Independent on one another, and consequently, as many Independent first Principles, no one Common Life or Mind ruling over the Whole. Whereas, to assert a God, is to derive all things

ἀφ' ἑνός τινος, *from some one Principle*,[2] or to suppose one Perfect Living and Understanding Being to be the Original of all things, and the Architect of the whole Universe.

Thus we see that the Hylozoick Corporealist is really an Atheist, though carrying more the Semblance and Disguise of a Theist, than [107] other Atheists, in that he attributes a kind of Life to Matter. For indeed every Atheist must of necessity cast some of the Incommunicable Properties of the Deity, more or less, upon that which is not God, namely Matter: and they who do not attribute Life to it, yet must needs bestow upon it Necessary Self-existence, and make it the First *Principle* of all things, which are the Peculiarities of the Deity. The *Numen* which the Hylozoick Corporealist pays all his Devotions to, is a certain blind *Shee-god* or *Goddess*, called *Nature* or the *Life of Matter*; which is a very great Mystery, a thing that is Perfectly Wise, and Infallibly Omniscient, without any Knowledge or Consciousness at all. Something like to that τῶν παίδων αἰνίγματι (in Plato)[3] τῷ περὶ τοῦ εὐνούχου τῆς βολῆς πέρι τῆς νυκτερίδος, that vulgar Enigm or Riddle of Boys, concerning an Eunuch striking a Bat; *A Man and not a Man, Seeing and not Seeing, did Strike and not Strike, with a Stone and not a Stone, a Bird and not a Bird*, &c. The Difference being only this; that this was a thing Intelligible, but humoursomly expressed, whereas the other seems to be perfect Non-sence, being nothing but a misunderstanding of the Plastick Power, as shall be showed afterwards.

D Cudworth, *True Intellectual System*, 3,34 (pp. 142–144)

[34. That of these Four Forms of Atheism, the *Atomick* or *Democritical*, and the *Hylozoick* or *Stratonical* are the chief; and that these Two being once confuted, all Atheism will be confuted.]

34. This *Quadripartite Atheism* which we have now represented, is the *Kingdom of Darkness Divided*, or Labouring with an *Intestine Seditious War* in its own Bowels, and thereby destroying it self. Insomuch that we might well save ourselves the labour of any further Confutation of Atheism, merely by committing these several *Forms of Atheism* together, and dashing them one against another, they opposing and contradicting each other, no less than they do Theism it self. For first, those two *Pairs of Atheisms*, on the one hand the *Anaximandrian* and *Democritick*, on the other the *Stoical* and *Stratonical*, do absolutely destroy each other; the Former of them supposing the First Principle of all things to be *Stupid Matter* devoid of all manner of Life, and contending, that all *Life* as well as other Qualities is *Generable* and *Corruptible*, or a mere Accidental thing, and looking upon the *Plastick Life* of Nature as a Figment or Phantastick Capritio, a thing almost as formidable and altogether as impossible as a Deity; the other on the contrary, founding all upon this Principle, that there is a *Life* and *Natural Perception* Essential to *Matter, Ingenerable* and *Incorruptible*, and contending it to be utterly impossible to give any accompt of the *Phaenomena* of the World, the *Original of Motion*, the *Orderly Frame and Disposition of things*, and the *Nature of Animals*, without this *Fundamental Life of Nature*.

Again, the Single Atheisms belonging to each of these several Pairs, quarrel as much also between themselves. For the *Democritick Atheism* explodes the *Anaximandrian Qualities* and *Forms*, demonstrating that the Natural Production of such *Entities out of Nothing*, and the *Corruption* of them again into *Nothing*, is of the two, rather more impossible, than a Divine *Creation* and *Annihilation*. And on the other side, the *Anaximandrian Atheist* plainly discovers, that when the Democriticks and Atomicks have spent all their Fury against these *Qualities* and *Forms*, and done what they can to salve the *Phaenomena* of Nature, without them another way, themselves do notwithstanding [143] like drunken men reel and stagger back into them, and are unavoidably necessitated at last, to take up their Sanctuary in them.

In like manner the *Stoical* and *Stratonical* Atheists, may as effectually undo and confute each other; the Former of them urging against the Latter, That besides that Prodigious Absurdity, of making every Atom of Senseless Matter *Infallibly Wise* or *Omniscient*, without any *Consciousness*, there can be no reason at all given by the *Hylozoists*, why the Matter of the whole Universe, might not as well *Conspire and Confederate* together into *One*, as all the single Atoms that compound the Body of any Animal or Man, or why one Conscious Life might not as well result from the *Tótum* of the former, as of the latter; by which means the *whole World* would become an *Animal* or *God*. Again, the Latter contending, that the *Stoical* or *Cosmo-plastick Atheist* can pretend no reason, why the whole World might not have one *Sentient* and *Rational*, as well as one *Plastick Soul* in it, that is, as well be an *Animal as a Plant*. Moreover, that the Sensitive Souls of Brute Animals, and the Rational Souls of Men, could never possibly emerge out of one *Single, Plastick* and *Vegetative Soul* in the whole Universe. And lastly, that it is altogether as impossible, that the whole World should have *Life* in it, and yet none of its Parts have any *Life* of their own, as that the whole World should be White or Black, and yet no part of it have any Whiteness or Blackness at all in it. And therefore that the *Stoical Atheists*, as well as the *Stoical Theists*, do both alike deny *Incorporeal Substance* but in words only, whilst they really admit the thing it self; because *One* and the same *Life*, ruling over all the distant parts of the Corporeal Universe, must needs be an *Incorporeal Substance*, it being all in the Whole, and all acting upon every part, and yet none of it in any part by it self; for then it would be many and not one. From all which it may be concluded, that Atheism is a certain strange kind of *Monster*, with *Four Heads*, that are all of them perpetually biting, tearing, and devouring one another.

Now though these several Forms of Atheism do mutually destroy each other, and none of them be really Considerable and Formidable in it self, as to any strength of Reason which it hath; yet as they are compared together among themselves; so some of them may be more considerable than the rest. For first, as the *Qualities* and *Forms* of the *Anaximandrian Atheist*, supposed to be really distinct from the Substances, are things unintelligible in themselves; so he cannot, with any colour or pretence of Reason, maintain the Natural Production of them out of *Nothing*, and the *Reduction of them again into Nothing*, and yet withstand a *Divine Creation* and *Annihilation*, as an Impossibility. Moreover the *Anaximandrian Atheism*, is as it were swallowed up into the *Democritick*, and further improved in it, this latter carrying on the same Design, with more seeming Artifice, greater Plausibility of Wit, and a more pompous Show of Something where indeed there is Nothing. Upon which accompt, it hath for many Ages past beaten the *Anaximan[144]drian Atheism* in a manner quite off the Stage, and reigned there alone. So that the *Democritick* or *Atomick Atheism*, seems to be much more considerable of the Two, than the *Anaximandrian* or *Hylopathian*.

Again; as for the two other Forms of Atheism, if there were any *Life* at all in Matter, as the First and Immediate Recipient of it, then in reason this must needs be supposed to be after the same manner in it, that all other Corporeal Qualities are in Bodies, so as to be *Divisible* together with it, and some of it be in every part of the Matter; which is according to the *Hypothesis* of the *Hylozoists*: Whereas on the contrary the *Stoical Atheists* supposing one *Life* only in the whole Mass of Matter, after such a manner, as that none of the parts of it by themselves should have any Life of their own, do thereby, no less than the *Stoical Theists*, make this *Life* of theirs to be no *Corporeal Quality* or *Form*, but an *Incorporeal Substance*; which is to contradict their own *Hypothesis*. From whence we may conclude, that the *Cosmo-plastick* or *Stoical Atheism* is, of the two, less considerable than the *Hylozoic* or *Stratonical*.

E Henry More, Ad V.C. Epistola altera (1677), 18–19 (Opera omnia, II/2, 571–573. Translation: Christian Hengstermann)

18. The sixth chapter is wholly about miracles where he first makes fun of two opinions chiefly held, as he has it, by the common people. The first is that that "they imagine two powers numerically distinct from one another, i.e. the power of God and the power of natural things which is determined by God in a certain way or (as most of them" he says "rather tend to see it nowadays) created." The

second is that "God's power and providence are most clearly evident when they see something happen contrary to the usual course of things" and "imagine the power of nature to be subdued by God, as it were" (*Tractatus*, 6,1). However, since he taunts these opinions as "opinions of the common people", he obviously believes them to be errors, even though they are highly reasonable and true doctrines, not at all unworthy of the wisest of philosophers. For it is manifest from the very idea of God, at which Spinoza grumbles so often here, that nature was created by God. Otherwise, he would not be an absolutely perfect being. God and creation, however, are numerically distinct from one another and, consequently, their powers are numerically distinct from one another as well unless you wanted to imagine creation and, hence, the whole of nature to be created without any other power involved, which would be an insane delusion. Hence, it is evident that the power of God and the power of nature are two powers numerically distinct from one another. And therefore, since the divine power is greater than that of nature and one that can give orders to nature, as it sees fit, there can be real miracles. And the other opinion which he calls an "opinion of the common people" is likewise true, i.e., as regards divine providence, it is most clearly evident that the divine nature is really distinct from matter and the spirit of nature which embraces the common laws of nature in a living fashion. And Spinoza did very badly, trying so much and so hard to destroy this opinion about miracles from men's minds.

19. He then tries to achieve the latter in the following four ways. Firstly, he proves that "nothing happens contrary to nature, but the latter maintains its eternal, fixed and immutable order" (*Tractatus*, 6,2). Secondly, "we cannot know either of God's essence and existence or, hence, his providence from miracles" (ibid.). Thirdly, he shows from several examples of Scripture "that Scripture itself understands by God's decrees and volitions and, hence, by providence nothing other than the order of nature itself, which necessarily follows from his eternal laws" (ibid.). And fourthly and lastly, he adds "a few remarks on how to interpret the miracles in Scripture" (ibid.), etc. He pretends that the first can be proven in the following way: if something happened in nature that really contradicted its universal laws, it would necessarily contradict the divine decree, intellect and nature as well, i.e.: "If God were to do something against the laws of nature, he would also necessarily act against his own nature, because the universal laws of nature are God's decrees which follow from the necessity and perfection of the divine nature. For nothing is true", he says, "except by the necessary divine decree alone. However, everything that is true is such only by divine decree, because in God understanding and will are the same thing, God's understanding not being distinct from God's will" (*Tractatus*, 6,3). However, this last principle to which the whole proof boils down is utterly false, as I have proven above, for God *understands* the evil order of things, but he does not *will* it. He understands all the possible varieties of universes that he could create, even though only a single kind exists in actuality. According to this principle, however, all of them would exist, since—assuming he understood nothing without also willing it—he would will all of them to exist, which is an obvious contradiction. Rather, since he has inserted into matter or the spirit of nature certain universal laws of nature, *understanding* that real miracles are contrary to these laws, he, therefore, *wills* real miracles and, hence, they occur occasionally. Behold the impious sophist caught in his own ties! As God and nature are two distinct things, the one created by the other, and as matter is moved by the created spirit of nature according to certain universal laws inserted into it, it is manifest (unless someone deliberately seeks to blind others) that God, who is infinitely more powerful than nature, can suspend or alter the operations of these laws as he sees fit. However, I suspect that Spinoza has secretly cherished in himself this monstrous error all along that there is no God but nature. In fact, he states it most bluntly in another scrap of an argument in the following words. He says: "The same thing could also easily be shown from the fact that the power of nature is the divine power and virtue itself and the divine power is the very essence of God, but this I am happy to leave aside for the time being" (ibid.). I leave it to

everyone who still has a little wit left to judge whether he prays to anything other than motion and matter and what they produce, especially since a little later he attributes to nature an infinite power: nothing can be imagined that is superior to or more divine than it. And yet, to conceal this impiety and adapt his argument to the common people, he says it would be unworthy for "God to have created a nature so impotent and with laws and rules so feeble that he must continually give it a helping hand if he wants to preserve it so that things keep going according to his wishes, etc." (*Tractatus*, 6,4). To this I reply that nature has deliberately been created by God in such a way that it obeys its creator and his pleasure as well as the free ministers of his providence in departing from its accustomed order, as these ministers see fit, for the existence of God, the angels and divine providence to be made all the more evident by the fact that not everything depends upon nature alone. However, nature, as it is, is sufficiently perfect in its kind, and God need not "give nature a helping hand for its preservation", but for the salvation of those who have fallen, nearly all of them understanding God's existence and providence better from miracles than if nothing were to happen above the powers of nature. Spinoza, however, takes a different view, claiming in the second place that "from miracle we cannot know either of God's essence and existence or, hence, his providence" (*Tractatus*, 6,2).

F More, *Ad V.C. Epistola altera*, 43 (II/2, 593–594. Translation: Hengstermann)

7. Does not the third argument look good! Yet, on closer inspection, it reeks of the very same kind of atheism. For he intimates that God cannot will and decree anything that does not "involve eternal truth and necessity". Thus, he neither wills nor decrees anything, as he says quite frequently, but what transpires in reality and with necessity and what, if we consult his fourth chapter to which he refers us, he does solely by the necessity of his nature and perfection. For in Spinoza God's will and his understanding are the same thing, as are the power of God and that of nature. Hence, by these eternal decrees he seems to me to mean necessary motions and events, as they occur according to the mechanical laws of nature. If it is not like this, why should not God, if he exists and if he is a being distinct from worldly matter, be able to inscribe laws in the minds of men, doing it in such a way, however, that it is up to them to obey them or not and after their disobedience try in new ways to lead them to good fruits, as he is said to have done on Mount Sinai in giving the Laws to Moses? But if there is nothing but worldly matter and its intrinsic power and motion as well as, by implication, the latter's necessary results, i.e. all kinds of sense, appetite and intellect, then there will certainly no longer be a God who can do anything of his own free will, but only according to the necessary chain and sequence of mechanical motions. Then the only lawgivers will be the supreme powers who as princes will enact laws that the people will sometimes obey and sometimes disobey. This is the horrible and monstrous belief that I suspect Spinoza secretly favours, as no other hypothesis seems to accord as well with his arguments and doctrines as he expresses them throughout. See my notes on chapter four. 8. This is the fourth and final argument in which he seeks to prove from experience that "God has no kingdom over men except through those who hold power", even though experience clearly testifies the opposite, as in the pagan Roman Empire. For the first Christians cultivated piety and charity most diligently even in defiance of those who wielded the supreme power. And where the unjust rule, the countless complaints about injustice show that there is a sense of justice ruling in the hearts of the oppressed and that with this sense God rules in them. He does so by virtue of his laws written into their minds or the motions of the Holy Spirit who can illuminate men in a supernatural fashion, strengthening them against the flood of the vices of this world. Thus, you can see how little force these four arguments of his have in confirming his first conclusion that "religion has the power of law only by decree of those who exercise the right of government".

G More, *Scholia in Epist. ad V.C.* (1679), Sect. 51 (II/2, 608–609. Translation: Hengstermann)

It is sufficient that we have shown that the most learned Glisson has not put forth any compelling argument either *a priori* or *a posteriori* by which an energetic nature of matter, i.e. its primordial life consisting in perception, appetite and motion, might be proved. Instead, those samples of life which can be seen to emerge in matter may also be the effects of some immaterial principle which transforms sufficiently compliant and malleable matter into various modes. Nor can those samples prove any life in matter other than one that is merely passive and incapable of perception, being, as it were, a shadow and imitation of the true principle of life, which is certainly immaterial and which precedes every single motion.

Indeed, this applies to all natural motions. And it is completely useless to invent perception and appetite in violent motions such as those of projectiles. For the lead released from a ballista is carried on neither by perception nor by appetite. And it is ridiculous to imagine that, assuming it has lost all its appetite and perception, it should also lose its capability of being shot and fired. And yet it must be admitted that lead, once roused to motion in a determinate fashion, continues by its own powers. However, it does so in a vital fashion, albeit without any appetite or perception. Hence, it is manifest that there may be a life without perception or appetite and without any original αὐτοκινησία. A life modifiable by an immaterial principle in various ways is the one and only life that I am prepared to admit as being deeply rooted in matter. In fact, I am all the more willing to concede that lest the ultimate emanation from the first source of life seem entirely devoid of life.

Meanwhile, it is clear from what we have said that Kuyper's modern atheists who, having rejected mechanical causes of the world's creation, have sought refuge in a primordial life of matter, can in no way hold on to their cause unless they find stronger reasons than Glisson's. Nor can they continue to claim that there is nothing in the world that is more divine than matter. And it is certainly not easy to decide whether it betrays more ἀπαιδευσία[4] to contend that the world was made by mechanical necessity and without any aim or providence or to attribute to worldly matter alone both perception and the providence for the creation of all things. The mechanical philosophers, for sure, do at least affect some ingenuity in offering distinct mechanical reasons by which matter is arranged so that it assumes a certain form and consistency and adopts such an order. However, the biusians (who are termed "hylozoists" by the learned author of the *True Intellectual System of the Universe*) only state in general that matter is αὐτόζωος and is capable of perception, appetite and motion from itself, thus everywhere arranging itself into all the different kinds of things as it sees fit. Not only may this way of philosophizing be rightly deemed all too terse, simple and easy as well as precarious and gratuitous, lacking as it does any solid foundation, but it also involves insuperable difficulties. How, for example, should matter, which is the least unitary of all substances, consisting only of countless physical monads and natural atoms, fulfil those tasks which require unity in the most absolute sense imaginable? For such must be that substance which foresaw and understood the most beautiful order and the mutual relationships of all the ideas of all these things at once, always contemplating in itself the ideas of all things with one single stabile and immutable glance. It must be a kind of eternal perfect mind which preconceives in itself the ideas of all future created things and which pours them forth into its vicarious power, the spirit of nature, and over all matter in a vital, not in an intellectual fashion. Indeed, if there were a kind of primordial life of matter, it would only be generic. As regards its *specific modifications*, it would be spread and disseminated across vast distances. It is no more helpful to assume this kind of life to account for the order and beauty of the world than it is to assume none at all. If there is not something preconceiving and foreseeing the whole fabric of the world and the mutual relationships between its single parts at once, its creation will indeed occur as blindly and fortuitously as if it were created by mere mechanical motion. Of so little worth is the notion of that primordial life that is supposed to split up into various physical forms afterwards.

Moreover, let us assume that the life of matter is such that it perceives the aim and objective of things and that, moved by its striving for that, the single parts set themselves in motion. Let me ask then how credible it is that, say, a stone or a piece of lead, endowed with a sluggish and stupid sense of its own modal subsistence, should retain an idea of the aim of the descent of solid bodies. Does this idea, moreover, include knowledge about the fabric of all the bodies of breathing animals and the utility of pure air for them? And do those more solid bodies also know that if, floating in the air, they are inhaled by these animals, they obstruct their lungs and suffocate them? "It is said", says the most learned Glisson in ch. 34, sect. 26, "that aquatic birds extract with their beak some thick matter from the glands near the uropygium, with which they besmear their wings. Thereby they strengthen them so that, even though they frequently dive into the water, as they are wont to do, on emerging again they can easily shake off the fluid which hardly sticks to them." However, let me ask this learned man once again: is it with this prior aim that the parts of this thick matter both form themselves into this fatty subsistence and move forth to the uropygium so that, say, a duck, a goose, a swan or any other aquatic bird can, as the need arises, extract it from there to besmear its wings with it? That is to say, do those parts possess an idea of said birds extracting this paste or oil from their uropygia with their beaks to besmear their wings with it? The same applies to the spurs of cocks. Did those single parts of matter or those natural atoms possess knowledge about the aim of its eventual hard and hornlike consistency, shape and place in order to adopt this very form and place as an adequate means for fighting? However, all of that would have certainly been impossible without the idea of some scene of a warlike battle between two cocks for the sake of which the parts of the matter of their spurs grew together in such consistency, shape and place. Oh, what express ideas and imaginings must they hence possess, notably of their bladelike spurs with which to gouge out or tear apart their rivals' brains in a consciously dealt out blow!

H More, *Demonstrationis Duarum Propositionum . . . Confutatio* (1679), 44 (*Opera omnia*, II/2, 616. Translation: Alexander Jacob, *Henry More's Refutation of Spinoza*, 58–60)

That quite a different judgement can be passed about this sixth proposition[5] is established by the determinate mark of either universal or particular affirmation, that is, it is said *that no substance can be produced by another*, or *that some substance can be produced by another substance*. If the proposition is understood in the first sense, I say that it is completely false. For it implies no contradiction that a substance exists as infinitely perfect as possible. Nor, indeed, is it contradictory that a substance exists which did not exist before. Therefore, an infinitely perfect substance can easily effect it, and, indeed, anyone who acquired logic in earliest childhood has learnt that it does not imply a contradiction for a substance to exist which did not exist earlier, though it implies existence and non-existence simultaneously. That, however, a perfect substance exists so absolutely and infinitely perfect that no perfection is wanting to it that is not entirely contradictory to what is contained in it is manifest from the common principle which is agreed upon by: *From the essence, certainly, or from the definition of a thing, its existence can be concluded*. Therefore, that the existence of an absolutely perfect Being can be deduced from the true essence of its idea is evident from what has been said above. Since, therefore, a sufficient cause exists by which a substance can be produced, it is manifestly false that no substance can be produced by another. And, certainly, if the absolutely perfect being, or infinitely perfect substance, of whose perfections one is omnipotence (i.e. the power of creating), by virtue of the perfection of its nature is, as it were, the cause of itself, that is, of a being infinitely perfect, is it surprising that it can be the cause of things inferior to it by infinite degrees, namely worldly matter, the spirit of nature and the spirits of men and angels? As regards the particular affirmation of the sixth proposition, that *a substance cannot be produced by another substance*, I concede that it is true, but it is true of no substance except of the absolutely and consummately perfect substance, of which kind there is only one, i.e. the true God or that infinite, omniscient and omnipotent spirit described above. Hence, the proposition so understood does not contribute anything to Spinoza's aim. From this it does not in the least follow that material substance indeed cannot be produced by another substance, which he wishes so much.

However, this geometric method of his does not desist from demonstrating that no substance can be produced from any other substance. The demonstration is as follows: *In nature there cannot be two substances of the same attributes*: (by Prop. 5) that is (by Prop. 2) *which have something in common so that* (by Prop. 3) *one cannot be the cause of the other or be produced by the other.* Q.E.D. I see the mimomathematic order of things, and quite long for the demonstration. From falsehoods indeed nothing can be demonstrated. We shall therefore bring forward those fifth, second and third propositions. The fifth is: *In nature there cannot be two or more substances of the same nature or attributes.* The second is: *Two substances having different attributes have nothing in common.* The third, finally, is: *Of those things which have nothing in common, one cannot be the cause of the other.* The force of the demonstration, stripped of its geometric mask, is briefly this: There cannot be two substances of the same attributes or having something in common, and indeed, if they have nothing in common, they cannot be the cause of the other. So, let us then examine the truth of the individual propositions.

The fifth proposition is indeed manifestly false. There cannot indeed be two or more substances in nature with the same attributes, that, is, on Spinoza's own interpretation, having something in common, which seems to suggest that there can be things of different attributes. Indeed, on the contrary, I say, if you suppose that two or more substances exist which you believe to have dissimilar or diverse attributes, they necessarily have this in common between them, that they are substances. This assertion especially contradicts common sense and experience, since six hundred myriad examples occur in stones, metals, plants and animals, of which it can be demonstrated that many substances of the same nature, or having something in common, exist in nature. One could also mention souls, spirits of angels, and the infinite particles of the universal matter, water, air, ether, which are individual substances having something in common and yet really distinct from one another.

I More, *Confutatio* (II/1,617. Translation: Jacob, *Refutation*, 62–63)

And indeed, that most subtle philosopher, not obstructed by these innumerable examples, has proved his fifth proposition that there cannot be in nature many distinct substances of the same nature or attributes, in the following manner: *If there are many distinct things, they should be distinguished from one another either by the diversity of attributes or by the diversity of modifications*, by Prop. 4: *If of attributes, then not unless there is but one substance of the same attribute. And if from the diversity of modifications, since substance is by nature prior to its modifications,* by Prop. 1, *the substance considered in itself, apart from those modifications posited in it, cannot be conceived of as distinguished from another,* that is, by Prop. 4, *there cannot be many but rather one.* Q.E.D. This is the manner in which he seems to have settled the matter for himself. However, I deny that fourth proposition on which especially rests the force of demonstration, namely, *that two or more distinct things are distinguished from one another either by the diversity of the attributes of substances or by the diversity of their modes.* There is still a third distinction, which we may call "real distinction". We find it wherever a plurality of attributes possess the same attributes and modes. This is the distinction between all individual substances, by which substance A is not substance B, nor B A, etc. This modified matter which is called a bear is not that modified matter which is called a lion, and yet they have the attribute of extension in common. And if the aforementioned matter is deprived of its modifications so that they differ neither by mode nor by attribute, they are still distinguished by that real distinction by which they are different from one another. This is well in keeping with his first axiom: *All things that are, are either in themselves or in other things.* Indeed all those things which are in themselves either exist or can exist outside. This is their real distinction, which plainly differs from the modes or attributes which constitute or rather indicate their essence. That the innermost and bare essence of nothing can be perceived except those essential attributes or essential qualities I have reckoned, in the *Enchiridion Ethicum*, among the fundamentals of the true wisdom that is to be acquired.

J More, *Confutatio* (1679), 44 (II/1,619–620. Translation: Jacob, *Refutation*, 69–72)

After we have demolished and destroyed that column of atheism which states that existence pertains to substance as substance, let us now approach the other which was to be joined to the mind-destroying danger which would, in other times, threaten the heads of atheists. Now, from that first principle which ascribes necessary existence to substance as substance, by which matter would be proved to be self-existent and have nothing to do with God the Creator, the inconvenience of continually flowing things, if there could be several substances in the universe, will be immediately seen. However, from this it can be demonstrated that an immense and eternal spiritual substance, that is, the true God properly called, can exist just as that corporeal substance which the vulgar call a matter. Against this, therefore, Spinoza invidiously places a barrier. According to the second principle, he adds in Epistle 29 the other necessary pivot, as it were, of atheism: *Substance cannot exist in nature as a multiple entity, but only as a single* entity, just as Proposition 14 of Part I of the *Ethics* expressly asserts that *there is but one substance in nature*. In that same fourteenth Proposition, he calls it God in his humorous manner. In his writings, clearly, matter, nature and God mean the same thing. The same proposition pronounces thus: *Besides God no substance can be or can be conceived.* Behold pure and putid Behmenism! O surprising conspiracy and consensus of two opposing intelligences, one of a mathematician demonstrating everything by geometric method, and the other of a consummate enthusiast! Jacob Böhme, who indeed was a simple and sincere man, not an apostate from Moses or from Christ or a promoter and patron of any principles which countenance bad conduct, finally rose to the knowledge of those clearer things, and recognized the *fixed, tranquil and bright Eternity* as being wholly distinct from nature. By contrast, this one, immersed in the filth of atheism, to my knowledge, perished impenitent in it. It is true that this sordid and vile atheist seems to breathe nothing but God in that fourteenth proposition: *Besides God no substance can be or can be conceived.* However, this proposition necessarily implies the crassest atheism.

From this clearly it follows that matter is God, since that substance both is and can be easily conceived by us, and no other substance apart from God can be conceived according to this proposition God. Consequently, stones, dirt, lead and dung would be God, since they are matter. Spinoza himself acknowledges this in the Corollary of Proposition 25: *Individual things are nothing but modes of the attributes of God, expressing those attributes in a certain and determinate manner.* And in Proposition 28, he expressly affirms: *Besides substance and modes there is nothing.* I deny that this is by any means true, especially if that Definition of Spinoza's is admitted: *By attribute*, he says, *I understand that which the intellect perceives of substance as constituting its essence* (Definition 4). He establishes that there are two attributes of this kind in God, i.e. thought and extension (*Ethics*, Part II, Propositions 1 and 2). Since, therefore, stones, lead, dung, an ass, a toad, a louse and all things of that sort are individual things, it is necessary that they be modes of the attributes of God, expressing them in a certain and determinate manner. And since besides substances and modes there is nothing and since modes cannot be without substance, it is clear that the substance of God is the substance of stones, lead, dung, an ass, a toad, and a louse, and those extended things modes of divine extension and those thoughts modes of divine thought. Consequently, the God of Spinoza thinks in an ass as an ass, in a toad as a toad, in a louse as a louse, and indeed in a stone, lead and dung as a stone, as lead and as dung. Hence, it would be necessary for him to have asinine and leaden thoughts, not to mention the rest, provided that lead thinks, which it is necessary that it do if thought is an attribute of God and not a mode, of which kind it certainly is, and modifies certain parts of God, unless all individual things think as well. What I have noted incidentally in the *Enchiridion Metaphysicum*, Ch 4, Sect. 4, from Descartes himself is quite true, that mode is the same as attribute and quality unless we call what we commonly consider to be a substance varied by attribute and quality mode, as what modifies and constitutes a subject in what it is also makes it differ, etc. If, therefore, properly speaking, Spinoza makes thought an attribute of God, it is necessary to ascribe thought to God universally, that is, to the individual parts of God so that lead and stones think. And this can also be noted from that place. Just as a restricted attribute is a mode, so mode, not taken in a restrictive sense, can be said to be an attribute. In this sense It is probable that Spinoza has taken it where he says: *Besides substance and mode there is nothing*, but if not that, he seems to have confused attribute with essence or substance. In whichever way he does it, our argument is sufficiently sound that in that fourteenth Proposition he understands by God matter. Since an ass and lead with all the rest above mentioned are doubtless material things, he affirms matter to be indeed the same everywhere in the *Ethics*, Part I, Prop. 15, page 15.

K More, *Confutatio* (II/1,623. Translation: Jacob, *Refutation*, 81–82)

In reply to the second[6] I say that man, on considering the finest of all particular things in his mind, is right in judging God to be, as it were, similar to himself and to view him as an eternal, infinite, most perfect and omniscient mind who watches over all things. Is this not indeed infinitely preferable to that blind and tumultuous matter? I cannot fail to note how unworthily the fool accuses others here who fashion God in the image of their own minds, insofar as they are free agents pursuing ends of their own given that he, too, fashions him in the image of the matter of his own mathematical mind, if you please. In mathematics one can find long sequences of deductions without respect to any ends, connected and linked with one another by necessary bonds. Likewise, truths emerge and follow from one another inevitably. Spinoza hardly differently views the parts of matter as they are of necessity transformed by one another into these modes, thus forming an eternal sequence, as it were. They do so without any design, but through a blind and mechanical impetus. However, the parts of matter or physical monads, as I have demonstrated in the *Enchiridium Metaphysicum*, do not cohere more closely among themselves than mud without chalk. Whether indeed it is more appropriate to posit a God, an eternal, infinite, omniscient and entirely provident mind or a blind, senseless, geometric matter, unconsciously but necessarily producing the most beautiful order of things from loose grains of those monads, let anybody of sound mind judge.

L More, *Confutatio* (II/1,623–624. Translation: Jacob, *Refutation*, 83–87)

In Epistle 64, however, he apparently wishes to give an account of his definition of God, for which purpose he adds that among others, namely, that all the properties of a subject can be deduced. He argues in the following matter: *But in order that I may know from which idea of a thing, out of many, all the properties of the object may be deduced, I observe one thing only, that the idea or definition of the thing should express its efficient cause. For example, in order to investigate the properties of a circle, I ask whether from this idea of a circle, namely, that it is composed of innumerable right angles, I can deduce all its properties: I inquire, I say, whether this idea involves the efficient cause of a circle. Since this is not so, I seek another, namely that a circle is the space which is described by a line of which one point is fixed and the other moveable. Since this definition expresses the efficient cause, I know that I can deduce from it all the properties of a circle, etc. So also, when I define God as the supremely perfect Being, since this definition does not express the efficient cause (for I conceive that an efficient cause can be internal as well as external) I shall not be able to discover all the properties of God from it. However, when I define God as a being absolutely infinite, etc.* (in which way he is defined in the sixth Definition). From this indeed he suggests that all the properties of God may be deduced.

I shall deliberately pass over unexamined the initial proposition of the comparison, since it applies merely to the illustration. I shall only observe how ignorantly and indolently he argues in the subsequent proposition, how obscurely and falsely. Obscurely indeed, since he says the definition of God does not express the efficient cause. It is uncertain whether he understands it as of itself or of other things. However, he seems to suggest in the added parenthesis that it does not express an efficient cause, neither of itself nor of any other thing. However, it clearly implies both. A being absolutely and supremely perfect is indeed the cause of itself (since its essence involves existence according to Spinoza's first definition), as I have copiously and soundly demonstrated in the *Appendix to the Antidote against Atheism*. Since it involves omnipotence, it is clear that it is the cause of all other things and all the divine properties may be deduced from the Cartesian definition of God. Indeed, by contrast, from Spinoza's definition, unless by a being absolutely infinite, one understands a being supremely and absolutely perfect, not, however, a being of infinity in general, containing thought and extension, neither will it be the cause of itself nor the cause of all other things. Who indeed unless a man of rash and precipitate judgement would declare extension or infinity that is mobile but only endowed with slight and little thought to be the cause of itself any more than if not endowed with thought at all? Who thinks of the cause of himself to be endowed with no thought unless he is someone stupid or of a disturbed mind? The essential idea of this entity does not necessarily involve existence at all. For, to substance, insofar as it is substance, existence does not pertain, as I have shown. From that general attribute of thought, to deduce reason and human intellect is the same as if you were to argue from genus to species, which is not logical, and an argument indeed to be laughed at by boys. Since, therefore, the sixteenth proposition is based on such a false and weak foundation, it is clear that it itself is weak and false. To say that *infinite things of infinite modes must by necessity follow*, not from counsel, but the necessity of divine nature is to seek subterfuges and to hide oneself in clouds and confusions, as the ink-fish blackens the water and is not caught. If from the necessity of infinite matter (so indeed that divine nature is understood), agitated by infinite mechanical modes infinite worldly phenomena arise, how is it that the descent of a stone to the earth is not found among those infinite things? I have by mathematical proof plainly demonstrated in the *Enchiridium Metaphysicum* that that phenomenon is not produced by mechanical causes. And how is it that σφάλματα[7] occur so rarely in the organization of animals? It is clear therefore that the third argument does not have any force against final causes.

Let us approach the fourth, which denies that God acts from free will. This is the Corollary to Proposition 32. There Spinoza further asserts that, although from a given will or intellect infinite things follow, God cannot, for that reason, be said more to act from free will than those things which follow from motion and rest (indeed infinite things follow from these) can be said to act from freedom of motion and rest. He thereby clearly insinuates that the will of God is moved and driven by things existing externally, as all bodies are moved, which we can both deny and affirm. Indeed, he supposes an infinite succession of motions, which I have demonstrated in the *Enchiridium Metaphysicum* to be impossible. For Spinoza here speaks of God in the same way as of some infinite matter, whose parts are pushed and pulled by one another from eternity. But if not so, then motion begins in matter from within at some time unless God, as he is indeed, distinct from matter who not from sportiveness, doubt or hesitating will and counsel, but from a mind that is never incapable of foresight and counsel (since that mind is eternal and infinite which, as it were, in a flash of the eye can see what is best in each things) according to his eternal ideas which include the cause and the end of all things has produced the entire creation as soon as he was capable of creating it.

M More, *Confutatio* (1679), 44 (II/1,628–629. Translation: Jacob, *Refutation*, 98–99)

The first principle on which that demonstration is based is the definition of God by whom, he says, we understand *a being absolutely infinite, that is, a substance consisting of infinite attributes each one of which expresses eternity and infinity*. The definition is rather obscure, but let us hear the explanation of it: *I say*, he declares, *absolutely infinite but not infinite in its own kind, for of whatever is infinite only in its own kind we can deny infinite attributes; but to the essence of that which is absolutely infinite pertains whatever expresses essence and involves no negation, that is, whatever is positive*. From this explanation certainly anyone who is sufficiently discerning can easily trace what he wishes, indeed that the substance of all things is single and infinite, and that God is nothing but the universality of things (which consist in the various modifications of the said substance). This is necessarily to be understood from the words: *What, however, is absolutely infinite, to its essence pertains that which expresses essence*. He thereby affirms that there is a single essence or substance in the universality of things. Those infinite diverse things, however, which are separated are infinite attributes or modes of this single substance. Everyone of sound mind will at once deny that this is the definition of the true God. And so he has constructed his demonstration on a plainly precarious foundation, which he supposes and does not prove, unless that is to be taken for an argument *that that which is absolutely infinite must be God, not, however, that which is infinite only in its own kind*. However, this is an assertion which I reject as no infinity but one that expresses perfection must be attributed to the divine nature. Hence, infinite corporeity, if it could exist, would have to be denied to God.

Hence, absolute infinity in God must not be understood in such a fashion as if it were not an infinity of his own kind and an infinity corresponding to his most absolute perfection. For there is a certain essential sanctity and purity of the divine majesty by which he is different and distant from all the rest of things by his very kind, as it were. No infinity, therefore, is denied to God which expresses perfection, but that alone which involves imperfection. And whatever is perfect in the essence of creatures, as long as it pleases God, must be referred to him as the source and principle which. While not encompassing them *formally*, he encompasses the essences and perfections of all created things *eminently* and *causally*. Since this blind and demented philosophaster cannot comprehend this truth, this definition of God by which he impresses his readers has been shown to be false.

N Henry More, *Epistolae Quatuor ad Renatum Descartes*, Scholia In Respons. Ad Epist. 1 (*Opera omnia*, II/2,242. Translation: Christian Hengstermann)

"No incorporeal substances are extended in the proper sense of the word. Instead, I conceive them as powers or forces which, while attaching themselves to extended things, are not therefore extended themselves—just as fire, while being in white-hot iron, is not therefore iron itself." And yet the fire is extended throughout the iron, which I find sufficient. I must admit openly, though, that I find this place a bit obscure, nor is it clear to me what the philosopher wants to insinuate when he says: "Instead, I conceive them as powers or forces", since the fire is not only extended throughout the iron, but it is also a modification of it. For I do hope that this is not meant to imply what Descartes' pupil Spinoza states so bluntly in his *Posthumous Works*, namely that angels, human minds and all so-called "incorporeal substances" are nothing other than powers and forces of worldly matter, the latter being the only substance in the universe.

Instance 2: "The extension attributed to incorporeal things is one of power only, not of substance. Since this power is only a mode in the thing to which it is applied, it cannot be understood as extended once the extension with which it coexists is removed." Indeed, here he says more expressly what he has already said a little earlier, promoting openly the cause of nullibism, perhaps even that of the nullity of incorporeal things. After all, he implies that the power which we assume to be in spirits is a mode of extended matter, as Spinoza holds. See our notes in the scholia on his answer to the first letter, Difficulty 1.

Commentary

The opposition to Calvin's theology revolves around his voluntarist notion of God, the doctrine of double predestination and the forensic concept of salvation defined in terms of an imputed, rather than internal righteousness. All the Cambridge Platonists inveigh strongly against the notion of a Deity who damns a substantial portion of humankind prior to any trespass or demerit on their part. Regardless of whether he does so prior to or in response to Adam's fall in the supralapsarian and sublapsarian varieties of Calvinism, a God who exercises his omnipotent power not to reform humanity in disinterested goodness, but to reveal his unlimited sovereignty in omnipotent will (perhaps even to the point of revoking all his biblical promises and damning all of humanity) is no better than "a cruel and dreadful Erinys" of Greek mythos or indeed the devil of the Christian tradition **(B, F, I)**. Instead, God must be conceived of as pure goodness which, as such, cannot but overflow and share with a creation of free agents the riches of his being. For the most part, the major Platonists repudiate any voluntarist account of Calvinist stamp in emotionally charged *reductio* arguments in which the biblical and philosophical notion of divine benignity is contrasted with the Calvinist God's outrageous condemnation of countless innocent souls. Divine goodness emerges as the first article of the Cambridge Platonists' rational Christian faith which they time and again inculcate upon their hearers and readers **(A–C, F, I, L)**. It is the first principle of the divine nature superior even to his intellect or wisdom and, above all, to his will. Goodness is defined as "an everlasting Proportion and symmetry between fulness and its overflowing and dispreading of it self". God cannot act contrary to his own nature, which is ruled out both as religious sacrilege and conceptual contradiction. Calvinist voluntarism inevitably robs God of all his ethical and intellectual perfections alike. Like their first principle, the former such as "*Faithfulness*" and "*Mercy*" are defined in terms of necessary relationships between the creator and creation which, given the possibility of change on the part of God's sovereign will and pleasure, cannot but become merely contingent and accidental. The latter, on the principle of the classical theory of truth as correspondence, presuppose an intelligible subject and its predicates of which mind acquires a "true and perfect image". Once again, truth and, by implication, the supreme perfection of the divine mind become moot once a changeable volition is placed above them. Instead, it is God's eternal and immutable goodness which ensures the truth of the ideas encompassed in his intellect or wisdom and which unfailingly guides his omnipotent will. It is in accordance with the first principle of his nature that God cannot but will to give existence and life to creation, allowing it to participate in his moral and intellectual perfection in autonomous practical virtue and theoretical contemplation. It is strictly impossible for him to act contrary to his revealed intents so as to demonstrate a power unrestrained even by the binding force of his own promises. To the notion of God's goodness, conceived of as his fullness of being shared with creation in disinterested self-communication, corresponds closely an ontological concept of redemption as participation (**A, C, H**). In both print and preaching, the Cambridge Platonists time and again oppose the Christian Platonist notion of the soul's participation in and assimilation to an all-benign Deity to Calvin's concept of a forensic justification of imputed righteousness. Cudworth's detailed two-part argument against the notion of imputed righteousness hinges upon the Cambridge circle's shared Platonist ontology. For one thing, Calvin's soteriology is based on a contradiction in terms. It is impossible for one agent, i.e. the sinner's soul, to acquire the virtue and moral perfection of another, namely Christi, without the requisite change of character. For another, a mere imputation of Christ's righteousness in Calvin's judicial sense of the word is soteriologically inane. It cannot but by definition remain extraneous to a sinner's soul, thus leaving him entirely unreformed and in the hell of his vicious former character. Instead, man is able and called upon to participate in God's goodness by actively following his example in creation and salvation in Christ both before and after his incarnation in exercising virtue in his dealings with his fellow creatures. Rather than aspiring to knowledge about God's eternal decrees in irreligious hybris, we should actively strive for "righteousness and true holiness shaped in our hearts", which is the sole criterion of salvation. Given that a soul's virtuous conduct is nothing less than God or goodness in person becoming incarnate in its heart, the Father cannot but come to it as another son of his. The notion of redemption as participation in God's supreme goodness generally underlies the Cambridge Platonists' Christian latitudinarianism with its stress upon universal charity transcending denominational and even religious boundaries. It is intended to unite British Christendom in the civil war and Restoration eras. In response to the critique levelled at their rational soteriology of divine self-communication and human assimilation to God by Restoration divines like Samuel Parker, Hallywell gives an account of the doctrine of freedom underlying it. Parker's charge that the necessity of God's self-communication in creation and salvation undercuts his freedom and, by implication, his benignity of which free will is the *sine qua non* is shown to be ill-founded. It attributes to God an imperfect anthropomorphist freedom incompatible with his supreme perfection conceived of as an unwavering commitment to the principle of his own nature, i.e. consummate goodness, which does not admit of moral error or evil. Cambridge Platonist soteriology offers a strictly realist account of the nature of God and salvation deeply steeped in the tradition of Alexandrian Platonism in late antiquity and opposed to the nominalist and voluntarist tradition represented by William of Ockham in the Middle Ages and by the major Reformers in the Early Modern Period. The strict opposition to a voluntarist and nominalist account of the Christian tradition underlies the Cambridge Platonists' critique of key tenets of Thomas Hobbes's theoretical and political philosophy.

In their reply to Hobbesian materialism and sensualism as well as his determinism, the Cambridge Platonists lay bare several major argumentative flaws and fallacies in their opponent's reductionist account of the human mind (**A–C, G, I**). Hobbes is shown to commit a classic *petitio principii* in defining the universe as "nothing else but an Aggregate of Bodies" to go on to argue that there can be no incorporeal substance. His subsequent dismissal of "incorporeal Body" as a *contradictio in adiecto* is based upon his ill-argued prior identification of substance with body. Nowhere, therefore, does Hobbes, contrary to his stated aim, come close to proving the impossibility of spirit whose notion, as has been admitted even by the majority of atheists, is not contradictory at all. As his shown by More's adoption of a key element of Hobbes' critique of incorporealism, however, the Cambridge Platonists' stance towards the latter's philosophy is not one of complete rejection. Despite its overall untenability, Hobbes's repudiation of the "Scholastick Riddle" of a spirit being present in the body as a whole in its every part is valid. More ascribes to spirit dimensions and a spatial presence located not in the scholastics' imaginary space—a non-existent stand-in for the point of contact between two actual bodies—but in the same real place occupied by other incorporeal and corporeal substances. He even builds significantly on Hobbes' *reductio* argument when laying out in detail his concept of extended spirit in his 1671 *Enchiridium Metaphysicum* **(E)**. With Latinising and Graecising neologisms of his own coinage, More views the scholastics' "holenmerian" account of the spirit's whole presence in a body's each and every part as the second grave error of incorporealism besides the Cartesians' "nullibism". It is rejected as both "superfluous" and "ineffectual", as it is inferior to the univocal extension espoused by More in Hobbes-inspired argument and admits of the patently absurd possibility of a spirit's division into an infinity of identical wholes. It is by virtue of a conspicuously Hobbes-inspired line of reasoning that More, significantly, further fends off his adversary's charge of the concept of spirit's intrinsic incoherence. As well as failing to prove the contradictory nature of incorporeal nature, Hobbes is mistaken in his equally reductionist concomitant sensualist epistemology. In reply to Hobbes' critique, More resorts to the philosophical tradition, emphasizing that the belief in the existence of incorporeal substance, clearly, does not originate solely in daytime hallucinations or dreams about supernatural apparitions. Instead, More follows Plato and his successors from antiquity to the Early Modern Period in invoking God, nature and the soul to establish the necessity of an invisible incorporeal substance. God is "a higher principle" imposing order upon the "blind motions and jumblings of *Matter* and *mere Corporeal* Beings" which, left to its own devices, could not possibly bring about a cosmos of supreme harmony and beauty. The order of nature, therefore, reveals a principle beyond and superior to matter upon which it exercises its defining formative power. Of the greatest importance to the Cambridge Platonists' response to Hobbesian naturalism are "the *Operations of the Soul*, which ever appeared to the wisest of all Ages of such a transcendent condition, that they could not judge them to spring from so contemptible a Principle as *bare Body* or *Matter*". Among the "*Operations of the Soul*", sensation and intellection as well as action establish beyond doubt the existence of a spirit superior to body. While the Cambridge Platonists are outspoken in their attempt to revive an ancient theology of Platonic or even Mosaic pedigree, they do so by making reference to landmark tenets of early modern ontology and epistemology, most notably the distinction between primary and secondary qualities which Cudworth invokes repeatedly in his rebuttal of "Democritic fate". Hobbes's "Democritic" or reductionist materialist variety of atomism is an unduly reduced version of the ancient cosmology of the interaction of atoms in the void or indeed, as the learned author puts it in deliberately repulsive wording, "*a* Rape *committed upon the* Atomick Physiology". The altercation between Hobbes and Cudworth enacted in the *True Intellectual System*'s erudite exposition of the whole corpus of the extant pre-Socratic and Platonist source materials revolves around the corollaries of the new science in general metaphysics and the philosophies of mind and action. In contradistinction to the *Democritus redivivus* Hobbes, Cudworth shows the new atomist physics to confirm the old Platonist metaphysics of a "mind senior to the world" (*True Intellectual System*, 736). The two premises of what Cudworth considers the single most compelling argument against any attempt at a reductionist account of God, nature and the soul are the analytic or *a priori* principle of "Nothing out of Nothing" or "*That* Nothing can be Caused by Nothing" and the empirical or *a posteriori* atomist description of reality in terms of passive extension defined solely and exclusively by size, form, place and locomotion. If, as has been established as a irrefutable scientific fact by the atomists of the ancient and the early modern period alike, the reality of scientific experience and experiment consists of the aforementioned primary qualities alone, secondary ones like colour or heat cannot originate in passive body, but must arise from active spirit which cannot but by definition be distinct from it. It possesses none of its definings traits of "Magnitude, Figure, Site, Motion, *and* Rest" and is defined by its own spontaneity and activity in producing the secondary qualities of the rich and varied contents of perception and sensation. In turn, the sensations prove Hobbes wrong in his radical sensationalism **(H)**. Clearly, the sensation of heat and cold is not identical with knowledge about the respective feelings into which the soul may indeed be motivated to enquire in closer philosophical investigation when subject to them. There is a performative dimension to Cudworth's refutation of sensationalism. Once the soul engages in an enquiry about any of those impressions, it cannot make use of sense itself which cannot arbitrate between conflicting sensations or establish the truth of one and the falsity of another. Sensation is altogether incapable of truth which is a category specific to the rational mind, as it actively "resolves all Sensible Things into *Intelligible Principles*; the *Ideas* whereof are not *Foraign* and *Adventitious*, and meer *Passive Impressions* upon the Soul from without, but *Native* and *Domestick* to it, or *Actively Exerted* from the Soul it self: no Passion being able to make a Judgment either of it self, or other things." Sense impressions like heat and cold or the colour spectrum are not "*Qualities* in the *Objects* without us", but "only Phantasms and Sensations in our selves", which once again highlights the mind's irreducible activity.

The soul's "free power of *Reason*" is the chief argument in More and Cudworth's rejection of Hobbes' determinism as well **(C, M)**. More is careful to connect his foe's determinism to his materialism which is presupposed in his altogether fallacious claim "*that nothing taketh beginning from it self, but from the action of some other immediate agent without it self*". Hobbes's denial of the landmark Platonist notion of a soul's self-motion, in other words, is based upon "a begg'd Hypothesis". While the principle holds true for matter and its various states, it does not for spirit which is capable of effecting changes without the involvement of an external cause. Spontaneity is the defining characteristic of the "variety of perceptions, *Mathematical*, *Logical*, and I may adde also *Moral*, that are not any impresses nor footsteps of Corporeal Motion." It is the soul's prerogative to make use of its ideas within to guide its actions without. Hobbes commits another fallacy when he views the external cause of an agent's will as a sufficient cause which necessitates the latter's action and thereby makes free will another contradiction in terms. His argument is a *non sequitur* based on the equivocal use of necessity. While it is true that an agent must necessarily will a certain course of action in order for it to occur, this necessity is one signally different from the necessity which Hobbes sets out to prove. Clearly, a manner of speaking in the philosophical analysis of human action which involves that modal category does not translate into a determinism of the necessity of all human deliberation and volition. Besides the μετάβασις fallacy, Hobbes makes use of a faculty psychology not unlike that of his opponent John Bramhall which he purports to combat in their controversy.

The determined defence of innate ideas which are the source of the soul's sovereign freedom to instigate practical reasoning and action also underlies Cudworth's rejection of Hobbes' political theology and theory which he shows to be closely intertwined in an altogether faulty account of the one and the other. If there were no concepts inscribed into man's mind, there could not be any eternal and immutable morality. Classical divine attributes such as "*Seeing, Hearing, Willing, Knowing, Justice, Wisdom, etc.*" are reduced to merely doxological figures of speech meant to extol the Deity's unlimited power which is the sole characteristic left in Hobbesian theology. Hobbes's "*Omnipotent Being*", deprived of any "*Justice*, in him" as well as of "*Benevolence* towards his Creatures", is conspicuously close to Calvin's. His theology of supreme divine power is a theology but in name, as it is deliberately stripped by the foremost contemporary Democritic atheist of all reference to objective reality and substance and of all philosophical method and meaning. Worse, it underlies an equally misguided political philosophy in which citizens are obliged to engage "*in Obedience to Christ's Lieutenants, and in giving God such Honour, both in Attributes and Actions, as they in their several Lieutenancies shall ordain*". At the heart of Hobbes' contractualism with its characteristic stress upon political might as the source of legal right is an equivocation of the latter, as "the word *Right* is here only Abused". Besides rendering inane the very concept of right, Hobbes' contractualism signally fails to furnish with consistent philosophical meaning its chief notion of a contract entered into by the people so as to endow a sovereign with the power to protect them from harm. If there is no "*Natural Justice*", Hobbes and other unnamed early modern "*Artificial Justice-Makers, City-Makers,* and *Authority-Makers*" cannot but fail at their task. While the people, threatened by the prospect of a violent death in the state of nature, may indeed choose to forgo "their *Infinite Right* by *Nature*", they may revoke and reclaim their freedom whenever they please. There is no binding force to a political contract: "*Covenants* without *Natural Justice*, are nothing but meer *Words* and *Breath*; (as indeed these *Atheistick Politicians* themselves, agreeably to their own *Hypothesis*, call them) and therefore can they have no *Force to Oblige*." Hobbes' materialism which denies to the soul any autonomous self-activity of its own in knowledge and in action is shown to be the chief error which deprives all political co-existence of a rational foundation.

Anne Conway rejects Hobbes on the grounds of his erroneous concept of matter which falls short of the essential characteristic of all reality, namely dynamic life and development, as it strives to embrace the fullness and perfection of its divine archetype to which it aspires in the "vital action" of constant self-improvement **(M–O)**. While Conway rejects Hobbes's material monism, she is equally critical of her fellow Platonists whose dualisms of mind and matter, activity and passivity or first and secondary qualities reduce to irredeemable active one half of reality. Wary of being identified as a follower of Hobbes on account of her own monism, Conway espouses a concept of being different from his and the other Platonists'.

The Cambridge Platonists are heavily indebted to Descartes both for their overall method and for several key concepts of their metaphysics. In their epistemology, they follow him in subscribing to a foundationalism of the internalist variety. Like Descartes, they posit as certain truth any cognition that qualifies as clear and distinct. And like the French philosopher, they believe an all-perfect God to ensure the reliability of the *clare et distincte* criterion. At the same time, however, the role which they assign to God in their foundationalist epistemology differs crucially from Descartes' account in the *Fifth Meditation* upon which they chiefly draw **(G, J, K, V)**. There is considerable disagreement between More and Conway about the validity of the ontological argument. The teacher and his student rehearse the old Anselm and Gaunilo debate about the necessary existence of any conceptual contents expressed with a superlative form. Conway takes Gaunilo's part, arguing that "a fully imperfect Being" is as entitled to necessary existence as "a fully perfect being". More enacts the role of a Cantabrigian Anselm. While the former must of necessity exist, the latter cannot, as the superlatives of perfection and imperfection in being correspond to necessary and contradictory or impossible existence. As well as engaging in dispute about the ontological argument, the Cambridge Platonists are among the first early modern critics of Descartes to expose as circular his attempt to ground the *clare et distincte* of certain knowledge about mind and matter in the veracity of an all-perfect Deity. Once, as is made clear by Rust and Cudworth, the very possibility of a general unreliability of the supreme powers of the human mind is entertained, neither the existence of a perfect God nor his veracity can be established. In the upshot, dogmatic Cartesian foundationalism is shown to lead to a general scepticism. To the *cogito* and the truthfulness of an all-perfect being the Cambridge Platonists oppose divine goodness as the indubitable first criterion of clear and distinct knowledge. Not only does infinite goodness, intuited by an epistemic power superior to discursive reason, ban the Cartesian twin spectres of the "evil demon" and the unbounded divine volition of created eternal truths, but it also renders moot the notion of a creature's fundamentally flawed intellect. Descartes's "clear intelligibility" is reinterpreted as the defining characteristic of Plato's archetypal forms all of which are encompassed in God's intellect. The eternity and immutability of the intelligible objects, viewed as the *sine qua non* of knowledge both divine and human, is rooted in the superiority within the Platonic Trinity of the first divine attribute of infinite goodness vis-à-vis the second and the third of infinite wisdom and infinite power to each of which it gives both limit and form. In contradistinction to Descartes' God, who originally creates even necessary metaphysical and mathematical truth by an omnipotent *fiat*, the divine intellect is entirely exempt from any possible change wrought by an act of arbitrary omnipotence. In clear and distinct cognition, the mind comes to participate in the divine intellect, acquiring certain knowledge about an object both as proceeding from God's goodness and contributing to it in the order of things and sharing in the "clear intelligibility" of his eternal intellect.

Of the major tenets of Cartesian ontology which the Cambridge Platonists chose to adopt to various extents, none proved more contentious than that of infinity (**A–D, H, J, R–S, W**). The conflicting interpretations which they give of the Cartesian concept can be seen to underlie several divergent systems of rational theism. While they all recognizably take inspiration from Descartes's thought to express Plato's first truth of God's supreme creative benignity, the Cambridge Platonists diverge significantly in the eventual ontology espoused. More is the first to adopt the notion of the infinity of both creator and creation, initially viewing the *quantitative* infinity of the latter to be a corollary of the *qualitative* infinity of the former. Only a creation of infinite extension may express to an adequate degree the creator's infinite goodness and generosity. Both in the preface to the *Democritus Platonissans* and the list of critical *paucula* in his first letter to Descartes, he rejects Descartes's *indefinite* as an inane term. There being no third apart from infinity and finiteness, there can be no intelligible ontological meaning to indefiniteness. However, as is clear both from an early Cartesian *Conway Letter* in the early 50s and the preface to the second edition to the *Enchiridion Ethicum* in the late 60s in which the possibility of ascribing necessary existence to matter is viewed as one of two major censures levelled at Cartesianism, More felt that the notion of an indefinite or infinite creation might perilously blur the boundaries between imperfect creation and perfect creator. Given the impossibility of disimagining an infinite space encompassing all mind and matter, it could well be taken as an argument for an atheism in which an infinite matter endowed with necessary existence supplants the supreme divine mind as first principle. More, therefore, chose to reaffirm the finiteness of creation, reserving qualitative and quantitative infinity alike to God. God is at once a spirit of infinite goodness, wisdom and power and an infinite spatial extension in which all created substances come into being and flourish in participating in the divine riches shared with them in creation and redemption. Cudworth rejects More's account of spatial infinity, whether divine or cosmic, as contradictory. Instead, he defends Descartes's notion of the indefinite which by definition admits of an addition. There is no such thing as actual infinity, but solely a qualitative infinity specific to the Deity alone each of whose defining three powers of goodness, wisdom and power, limited only by the hierarchy obtaining among them, marks a logical maximum. Rust likewise diverges from More in not subscribing to spiritual extension, whether finite or infinite. While he applies the concept of infinity to the creator and creation alike, its meaning clearly differs. Its strict theological meaning is that of the logical maximum of God's creative goodness by which he is compelled to give life to a world outside him in ungrudging generosity. Applied to creation, "infinite" is used to denote the supreme, yet inevitably finite, variety of creatures proceeding from God's goodness and fullness. Not only is the "infinite" scale of beings proceeding from God's infinite goodness limited by logic, i.e. conceptual possibility or non-contradiction, but also by the ethical requirement that no being by its nature inflict violence upon another. Of the Cambridge Platonists, only Conway embraces both strict qualitative and quantitative infinity. From early on, she agrees with More on the *pauculum* of the semantic untenability of Descartes's *indefinite* which she consistently replaces with the two closely correspondent notions of the creator's infinite benignity and creation's infinity diversity. Not only are there infinitely many creatures, but each of them is itself composed of infinitely many creatures or monads itself. At the same time, there is clearly an aspect of the Cartesian *indefinite* to the latter *infinitum* as God is believed by Conway to give life to ever more species and individuals.

Another major bone of contention among the Cambridge Platonists is the interaction between the creator and creation within the infinite or indefinite vastness of nature (**C, E, L–P, Q, T, X**). Again, while all the Cambridge Platonists concur in rejecting Descartes's lifeless extension in favour of a living world informed by the creative and salvific omnipresence of the divine mind, they all express God's supremely beneficent agency by the different conceptual means of their respective ontological frameworks. In response to what he views as a fundamental weakness of the admired Frenchman's ontology and philosophy of nature, More suggests that God must be viewed as "extended in his own way". His novel ontology posits extension as "coterminous with the absolute essence of things". Its theistic rationale is God's creative agency in imparting motion to matter viewed as entirely immobile in and of itself in Cartesian physics. If and only if God is, or was at least once, present in all places, can he "touch", or have touched at least once, the atoms constituting the reality of visible extension. In contradistinction to corporeal extension which is defined by its inability to penetrate or be penetrated by other bodies, spiritual extension penetrates and is penetrated by other spiritual and corporeal extensions alike. Spiritual extension, in turn, is either infinite or finite. Whereas finite spiritual extensions such as the human or the angelic soul may expand or contract, occupying larger or smaller places in matter or mind, God's is, by definition, infinite, hence admitting of neither. Nor does divine extension entail the divisibility of his substance. Instead, God's infinite extension is such that he occupies every single place "in his entirety". More originally conceives of the key tenet of his trialist ontology of extension in what he himself, with a neologism of his own coinage, calls holenmerist terms. It is by virtue of the "ubiquitous reiteration of its complete and total essence" that the infinite spirit may choose to act upon creation, "touching" it and thereby imparting motion to it at will. Another corollary of More's early anti-Cartesian ontology is the possibility of a strict vacuum. If body and extension, on his anti-Cartesian ontological scheme, are no longer identical, there may be a void which God may choose to occupy—or rather exercise his creative and salvific agency in—whenever he pleases. If, therefore, the extension between two sides of one vessel is removed, its collapse is no longer inevitable on conceptual grounds. Instead, God is at liberty to step in and prevent the vessel's two sides from meeting by a special divine intervention. However, while following the logic of his early trialism of extension in disagreeing with Descartes and assuming the *possibility* of a vacuum, More is nevertheless careful to deny its *reality* on theological grounds. He closely links God's spatial ubiquity and nature's universal animation, viewing God's creative agency, exercised in every single place of his infinite extension, as a benign communication of life and motion. Instead of leaving places devoid of its beneficent self-communication, "the divine fecundity", More states as a theological first principle of his Christian Platonism, "is not idle anywhere. It has produced matter in all places without leaving even the minutest of gaps" (Letter 2 [II/2,246]). The ubiquity of divine extension is shown by More to be the ontological *sine qua non* of all empirical causality of which Cartesian cosmology is ill-equipped to provide a satisfactory account. Libertarian human agency in particular is grounded in God's ubiquitous agency. Man's αὐτεξούσιον or free will could not but remain an unsolvable conundrum on the first principles of Descartes's mechanistic physics which admits of no other physical interaction between bodies than that of one pushing another. However, causality in general must be understood along the lines of a finite substance's inner self-activity. "Motion" of which God is the first source poses another major problem to which Cartesian physics and metaphysics alike fail to provide any viable solution. Descartes' concept of motion as a merely relative change of place of two adjacent bodies signally fails to express the power by which one body moves itself or another, its *vis agitans* which constitutes the essence of motion. The concomitant view of the reciprocity of all motion inevitably leads to several absurd consequences. On Descartes' principles, a tower must be said to undergo motion whenever the west wind passes by it. And one person sitting still as another runs away from them, breaking out in sweat as a consequence, must be viewed as moving at the same speed. In metaphysics, the very concept proves elusive as motion as an insubstantial mode should neither be able to act upon a substance nor pass from one to another without inevitably vanishing in the process. More's own solution to the aporia of Cartesian causality hinges upon a sketch of panpsychist cosmology that is closely linked to his panentheism of a spatially-extended infinite Deity. There is, in reality, no transfer of motion whatsoever. Instead, body and motion must be conceived of in analogy to mind and thought with one body exercising its own inherent power in setting itself in motion when occasioned to do so by another hitting it. The body's inherent power or "life" is not yet sensation, but rather a rudimentary kind of self-presence or proto-mentality which, as is required by its role in More's theory of natural causality, enables it to engage in a certain degree of self-motion. Material extension is the "last and lowest shadow and image of the divine essence" from whose infinite extension it derives its own motion at creation. The two primary gripes with Descartes detailed in the 1669 preface show his overriding concerns with the spectre of materialism and atheism and a world devoid of God's creative agency.

More's close friends Cudworth and Conway both take exception to all of or major parts of More's anti-Cartesian argument. Cudworth is staunchly Cartesian in his rejection of More's doctrine of spiritual extension as a figment of his fellow Platonist's imagination. A spiritual substance's activity and causality is strictly *sui generis*. On Cudworth's equally Platonist and Cartesian account, its active causal force by which the mind moves the body appears to be part of the original innate idea of the substance which must defy in principle any attempt at further elucidation. On no account, however, must either its being or its agency be conflated with matter which is opposite to it in both regards. It is with great consistency that Conway adopts and expands upon More's early position, viewing every monad as a centre of agency entirely its own and God's who has the interaction of all the infinitely many monads unfold with Christ or "middle nature" in a never-ending process of perfection and restitution.

The first of More's critiques of the Teutonic Philosophy is a concise heresiological overview in the 1656 *Enthusiasmus Trimphatus* **(4A)**. It nevertheless indicates a certain budding interest in Böhme's grand theogony provided in his newly translated *Aurora* in which all of reality is explained in terms of the successive interactions of the seven source spirits. More advances no sustained argument to rebut the erroneous metaphysical views which, to all intents and purposes, he believes to be so absurd as to warrant no detailed refutation. However, the objections implied in the doxographical notes are clearly epistemological and ontological in character. For one thing, More raises the question of Böhme's claim to inspiration which he views as originating not in the Holy Spirit, but in "*Melancholy* and *Sanguine*". It is a state at once psychological and physiological in nature in which an enthusiastic soul's depression leads to a heating of the bodily fluids. In turn, his animal spirits further exacerbate the enthusiast's psychic condition. For another, it is implied that all of Böhme's errors flow from an erroneous initial identification of "all" things or nature with "God's self" or substance. Man, proceeding from God or nature, is or may become identical with him if he leads a life of holiness. God, erroneously identified with nature, shares with it a dire existence devoid of any centre of unitary consciousness. Instead, he is reduced to an indisposed rubble of conflicting sense perceptions and sensations which rise to the level of understanding and bliss only at the later theogonic stage of the birth of the Son. Nor is this higher state of blissful intellection permanent as God, being identical with nature as a whole, of necessity participates in any clash or conflict waged by any of its parts, including Lucifer's rebellion in the beginning. As a consequence, God or divine nature is inevitably plunged into the original chaos.

More revisited and partially revoked his early critique of the Teutonic philosophy shortly after the publication of his original anti-enthusiastic treatise. In *Mastix His Letter* **(B)**, More goes to some lengths to acquit Böhme of several of the charges levelled at him in the original work. Whereas the original work contains only a brief doxography, More now devotes a substantial section of the later work to Böhme whom he now also mentions by name. Instead of rejecting his thought wholesale, More's critique is more balanced. He continues to leave no doubt that Böhme's theosophical vision does indeed meet all the criteria of an enthusiast's misguided inspiration. There is still no denying the fact that Böhme's philosophy springs not from the sobriety of reason, but from the excesses of fancy. However, he now resolutely disassociates Böhme from his fellow enthusiasts, notably the anabaptist David Joris and the Familist Heinrich Niclaes. Whereas the latter two blasphemously extolled themselves as Christs incarnate, Böhme is praised as a man of great personal sanctity and humility who never wilfully strayed from accepted church teaching. Still, while the chief source of his revelations was indeed his excessive imagination, his personal piety and probity were such that his flights of fancies, almost despite themselves, could not but become "so well qualified with holiness and sanctity" that the "divine truths" which he believed to have been imparted to him by God himself "proved not unsuccessful in sundry apprehensions". While More is reticent about the exact nature of the "sundry apprehensions" and "divine truths" with which he is now prepared to credit Böhme, it is clear that he views the Teutonic philosophy as not entirely without metaphysical merit.

The more substantial sketch of Böhme's philosophy in the early fifth book of the *Divine Dialogues* (**D**) explores in some detail the nature of his enthusiast inspiration which was "not purely *Spiritual, Intellectual* and *Divine*, but mainly *Complexional, Natural,* and *Daemonial*", never quite reaching the heights of the intuitive knowledge exclusive to the vision of God as pure transcendent goodness. More's juxtaposition of true and false inspiration reveals his ongoing principal concern with the epistemology of enthusiasm. It is remarkable for the revised and refined exposition of its subject. More, unsurprisingly, cites two chief authorities of his own ancient theology, i.e. Aristotle and Plotinus, in support of nature as a literally "demoniac" source of misguided enthusiastic knowledge about the Divine. *Prima facie*, therefore, nature appears to be dismissed as a viable source of knowledge. However, More goes to some lengths to expand significantly upon the two Greek philosophers' graphic wording. The two triads of attributes chart two distinct three-stage paths of progress in the knowledge about the Divine. In superior supernatural inspiration, the soul gains insight into God's universal formative presence, his supreme intellect and his disinterested goodness. In inferior natural inspiration, the soul advances from the two lower spheres of "demoniac" matter and "natural" spirit to a sphere defined in terms of "*Complexional* Love". Enthusiastic inspiration, while not wrought by the intellect above, but by the spirit of nature below, is nevertheless capable of producing in the more advanced sectarian's soul a sense of universal charity "which makes the Soul overflow with all kindness and sweetness, this, I conceive is all the peculiar Inspiration or Illumination these *Theosophists* had at the bottom". More's novel scheme of enthusiastic epistemology incorporates the salient aspects of his earlier critique, including its concern with "down bearing Melancholy". It views the "*Spirit of Nature*" as the agent of enthusiastic inspiration which shapes the motions of the animal spirits in the enthusiast's body and the notions arising from their interaction. However, instead of positing a strict *absolute* distinction between true and false enthusiasm, the tripartite scheme of More's *Divine Dialogues* revolves around a more nuanced and dynamic *relative* one which admits of an ascent from the two lower stages of base perception and imagination to a higher third stage defined as a sublime sensation of universal benevolence. Böhme is clearly viewed as an enthusiast of this more commendable variety. More's more charitable account is closely linked to his political concern. Behmenism came to be seen by him as a foil to more radical incarnations of sectarianism, notably Quakerism. To this end, More contrasts Böhme's superior enthusiasm with "the grim ferocities of the superstitious Factions in the imbittered Churches of the World, who have not so good an Inspiration as this, but their *Tongues* and Hearts *are set on fire of Hell*". Indeed, the lesser "Light of Nature" in which Böhme is now credited with having participated is viewed as a means to a "Divine Life" which More championed so vociferously as the chief end of all true religion.

Both in the philosophical concerns and the technical concepts used, More's refutation builds upon his early critical engagement with Hobbes and Descartes. In the epistemological "queries", he draws on the tried-and-tested arguments of his earlier anti-enthusiastic writings to reveal Böhme's ontology of a corporeal and "discerpible" Deity to have arisen from an agitated religious mind eager to experience God **(E)**. On More's critical reading of Böhme's theogony in the *Aurora* and beyond, there is a profound experiential dimension to his materialism and its corollary of a God who is not a simple intelligible substance, but a material composite of infinitely many atoms gradually acquiring consciousness and even sensation and intellection. A God composed of matter cannot but share with that substance its defining attribute of divisibility or, as More puts it in the technical vocabulary of his own substance dualism, "discerpibility". The chaos of its parts hitting one another in uncontrolled motion is a translation of a sick soul's afflicted state of mind into equally disturbing materialist metaphysics. To the restlessness of the animal spirits set in heated motion by Böhme's melancholy religious imagination correspond the eternity and infinity of the erratic motions of the paternal source spirits. As an inevitable consequence, the Father's life, consisting as it does in an infinity of disjointed motions of material parts, is a sombre one devoid of self-understanding or self-enjoyment. None of the parts of the allegedly infinite and eternal divine whole can comprehend any single one, let alone all of the others in a unified vision. Böhme's theogony of the Father achieving subjectivity in the Son is thereby shown to be an anthropomorphism modelled upon an enthusiast's religious experience. More's attempt at a Neoplatonic reformulation of Böhme's pantheism of a corporeal Deity hinges upon a dynamic dualism of a superior "Trinity of Pure Divinity" and an inferior "Trinity of universal nature" **(F)**. More opposes to Böhme's theogonic materialism his own exemplarist idealism of an absolute divine mind both transcendent and immanent to all things in its universal creative goodness. Whereas the first three entities are incorporeal in essence and identical to the Trinitarian God, the last three constitute the visible world of atoms suffused by the spirit of nature. Each of the higher levels of beings is reflected in the corresponding lower one with the latter or the image striving for the archetypal fullness of the former. The abyss of physical monads or atoms of which all things visible are composed is a yet unformed and chaotic, albeit living and evolving, image of the disinterested generosity of the metaphysical One whose "Supreme Goodness" it reflects in its own oneness. Likewise, the "Eternal Intellect" is the timeless archetype of all the transcendent forms which the spirit of nature, in turn, imparts to the infinite diversity of visible creation. It fleshes forth in the varied living works of nature all of what is hidden in the divinity of the "Eternal Intellect" which the creator, as "Supreme Goodness", chooses to share with creation in overflowing generosity and kindness. It may perhaps be seen as evidence for the decisive influence that Böhme's theogonic hylozoism came to exert upon the Cambridge Platonist's religious imagination that More identifies God not with the Trinity of Pure Divinity *tout court*, but with the entirety of the six remaining hypostases. He even invokes Plotinus in support of an audaciously novel interpretation of participation as a relationship of mutuality in which creation participates in the creator and, startlingly, vice versa. While different from Böhme's seven-spirit account, the resultant scheme of "one immense six-fold sphere" envisages God and the world as inhering in one another and jointly giving life and soul to all the transcendent forms encompassed by the divine intellect. There being no creator without creation, the concept of God itself is predicated of the dynamic process of the interpenetration of archetypal being and ectypal becoming: "And taken together and viewed as one immense six-fold sphere, whose forms penetrate one another throughout, all the six forms—this Whole, or Universe—is called Θεός by that same philosopher, i.e. the whole or complete Deity or universal origin from which all particular things proceed." The interpenetration of perfect archetype and imperfect archetype is expressed in terms of the interaction between the "divine soul" and the "world soul" **(G–H)**. The former or the Holy Spirit communicates to the latter the principles and forms which it is given by the Supreme Good or the Father and the Eternal Intellect or the Son. In turn, it enables the "world soul" to shape the "abyss of physical monads", communicating to each single one of them one of the forms encompassed in the "spirit of nature". Intriguingly, in so doing, it gradually acquires a kind of consciousness itself. Its memory in particular serves the providential purpose of acting as "God's immense register" and recording the sensations of a world emerging from the divine soul's ubiquitous creative and formative action. The causality of the "spirit of nature" of which it avails itself in the process is expounded in terms close to the occasionalist theory in the *Four Letters to René Descartes*. It bestows higher shapes and forms upon the abyss of matter whenever any of the monads of which it is composed acquires the capacity of being informed by it. More's examples are those of arboreal and human procreation in which the spirit of nature, while "occasioned" by material processes, exercises its creative agency in a strictly autonomous fashion **(H)**. All the "physical monads" are endowed by the spirit of nature with living forms by which their life is directed from its birth in creation to its eventual biological end and future incarnations. More's chief interest is in the development from potentiality to actuality effected by the spirit of nature in concert with creation which is subject to the laws embodied by it. The capacity for universal salvation and perdition inherent to a cosmos emerging from the fullness of a Deity of supreme goodness is a recurring subject in More's Platonist translation of the Teutonic philosophy undertaken in the work's fourth query. More finds in Böhme his own Origenist concern with free will as the prime motor of all reality. Such is reality in its extraordinary potential for good and evil that it may in principle become either a heaven or hell. There is no limit to the extent of good and evil of which a creation composed of living beings and free agents is capable. It is in this Origenist vein that More reinterprets Böhme's dark world as a representation of an imaginary world altogether cut off from the formative power of the Divine **(H)**. If it were not for God's beneficence, the world in its entirety would indeed be altogether dark and comfortless. While not without egregious errors, Böhme's metaphysics is not simply derived from enthusiastic imagination, but owes several of its deeper insights to the German mystic's boniform vision. More's later biographical sketch of Böhme, closely modelled on Durand Hotham's *Life* and added to the original letter for publication, stresses the heart or practical love and reason as a principle of Behmenist speculation **(I)**. It even made him attain on occasion to "the sublime level of Plotinus", as when he laid down the doctrine of the soul's pre-existence and fall **(J)**. In the *scholia* **(L)** More furnishes another argument for his chief correction of Böhme's cosmology of the seven source spirits, i.e. the excision of the sun which he now views as a genus binding together the dark and light worlds. As archetype and image, the two worlds share the characteristic of self-moving animate intelligibility communicated to the "abyss of physical monads" by the "Supreme Good". The number of "source spirits", reduced from Böhme's enthusiast seven to a rationalist six, is thereby proven to be necessary on the metaphysical grounds of a universal correspondence between the two principal realms of reality. However, while immanent to each and every "physical monad", God dwells beyond the "abyss" in supreme transcendence. In another pair of related *scholia*, More points out with great clarity the rationale for his strict adherence to divine transcendence. Whereas Böhme is prepared to admit of evil and darkness in his abyssal God, even viewing it as his primordial first reality, More's own chief metaphysical concern is with the paternal first principle as a "supreme good" or the "holiness of the divine majesty". It is God's supreme moral perfection which calls for a sufficiently robust notion of divine transcendence. Otherwise, he cannot but be implicated in or even seen as the cause of the woe and evil afflicting his creatures, which More rejects as being incompatible with the first divine attribute of pure goodness. In a remarkable retraction of a major passage of his original *Censura*, More revokes his quasi-Behmenist reading of the creator and creation as being "God". Strikingly, he is even prepared to charge Plotinus himself with coming, on occasion, perilously close to Behmenist pantheism himself. After originally crediting Böhme with reaching "the sublime level of Plotinus", he now criticizes the Neoplatonist philosopher himself remarkably sharply for his Behmenist conflation of God and world. More's animus against certain tenets of Plotinus's ontology is no doubt motivated by the spectre of pantheism of which Spinoza is the most formidable representative in his day.

The Cambridge Platonists' critique of Spinoza chiefly revolves around his concept of God's substance and agency judged to be wanting at best and thinly-veiled atheism at worst. Not surprisingly, a major topic is the question of divine intervention in natural and human affairs which Spinoza rejects on epistemological and ontological grounds in the critique of classical theism in the *Tractatus*. In his brief critique of "that late Theological Politician" **(A)**, Cudworth quotes a memorable expression from a specific passage of that work in which the anonymous author rejects miracles as a superstition of the uneducated "common people". Cudworth restricts his critique to Spinoza's dismissive treatment of miracles as inexplicable occurrences brought about by a good Deity for the benefit of his believers. While the Dutch rationalist is indeed scathing in his critique of the religious *hoi polloi* and their belief in a God arbitrarily intervening in the affairs of nature and man for their benefit, it is only a prelude to his philosophical onslaught upon miracles which he believes both to render impossible any knowledge of God on the part of man and be incompatible with the single agency of God and nature. Cudworth signally fails to oppose to Spinoza's critique any viable concept of divine agency. Tellingly, God's role in his defence of so-called "miracles" is exclusively passive, as he merely allows angelic and demoniac beings or impostors to engage in extraordinary, albeit hardly "miraculous", actions for the sake of a greater providential good. Indeed, Cudworth's own concept of a "plastic nature" effecting God's salvific designs at his behest comes conspicuously close to Spinoza's general rejection of supernatural intervention of which, in fact, neither the Dutch rationalist's naturalism of a single substance nor the English Platonist's dualism of mind and matter appears to admit. The briefness of Cudworth's critique of the rejection of miracles in Spinoza's *Tractatus*, which he simply purports to have found too "Weak, Groundless, and Inconsiderable" to warrant any detailed refutation, may well be meant distract from their shared deeper convictions. Of more philosophical merit is Cudworth's four-part division of atheism **(B–D)**. For one thing, Cudworth establishes that the "*Quadripartite Atheism*" exhausts the possibilities of atheism. Given its defining prioritization of matter over mind, it may either take the form of materialism or panpsychism, as mind either inexplicably emerges from or is somehow an integral part of matter. Each of the two materialist and panpsychist options comes in a superior and an inferior variety showcasing its strengths and weaknesses juxtaposed by Cudworth in great detail so as to highlight the fierce strife within the atheistic enemy camp. On the principles of atheist materialism, either atoms in motion may account for all phenomena in an erroneous, yet economical, account of reality (Democritic atomism) or the atheist takes refuge in elusive qualities of matter (Anaximandrian hylopathianism). Likewise, on the principles of panpsychism, either every particle of matter possesses life as part of its ontological makeup (Stratonic hylozoism) or there is, implausibly, one organism encompassing and imparting life to all living monads (Stoic cosmoplasticism). Besides exploiting the internal disagreement in the two pansychist camps, Cudworth marshals compelling arguments against the superior hylozoist variety. His repeated reference to the alleged "infallibility" of each living atom presupposes the combination problem of which Cudworth's *True Intellectual System* contains the historic first formulation. In order for a large number of living atoms to combine and coalesce, they would have to possess knowledge about the eventual whole of which each of them is meant to be part.

More shares with Cudworth the outrage at what he views as a brazen rejection of divine miracles on the part of "that late theological Politician" **(A)**. He references with approval the *True Intellectual System* and cites its systematic definition of atheism in the *scholia* on his first anti-Spinozist work. Above all, he significantly builds upon his fellow Platonist's critical note on Spinoza's *Tractatus* by providing a sustained philosophical defence of a benign God who reveals himself both by upholding the regular course of law-governed nature and suspending it in occasional interventions. It is one of the principal aims of the *Ad V.C. Epistola altera* to expose the naturalist *Deus sive natura* as the πρῶτον ψεῦδος underlying Spinoza's argument against any kind of divine miraculous intervention in the affairs of nature and man: "However, I suspect that Spinoza has secretly cherished in himself this monstrous error all along that there is no God but nature" **(E)**. In response to Spinoza's "monstrous error", More rejects as unbecoming of God's supreme goodness the naturalist identification of divine intellection and volition with the infinite power of nature. Whereas Spinoza's simple substance or nature both understands and wills the infinity of all possible worlds flowing from its infinite power by necessity, More's creator God is an agent of univocal goodness and libertarian freedom. He *understands* evil when setting out to create a world with which to share his goodness and wisdom in creative power, but he does not *will* it. He is bound both by conceptual and ethical necessity to act in accordance with his infinite goodness and share with a finite reality the fullness of his own being. However, he is free to choose any single one of the many possible worlds envisaged in the beginning. The identity of divine and natural agency must therefore be rejected on strictly conceptual grounds. Of the infinite number of possible worlds, God chooses to create only one, presumably the best of all possible ones, while not actualizing all the others. More grants to Spinoza that nature may be viewed as God's "general providence". The spirit of nature serves God as the *natural* means to his chief *moral* end of universal soul-making. It executes God's beneficent creative intention of disinterested universal self-communication by preparing matter in such a fashion that it becomes capable of bodying forth the forms of all things contained in his perfect archetypal intellect. Originally proceeding from God not by the necessity of his essence, but by the benignity of his will, it thereby gradually effects the "good of the universe" at God's behest. However, at the same time, God's "general providence" or nature and its laws must be complemented by a "special providence" or supernatural agency unrestricted by the laws of nature. God may elect to act contrary to the laws contained in the spirit of nature whenever the "good of the universe", which is the latter's original raison d'être, calls for a demonstration of the enduring benevolence and beneficence of his creative wisdom and power. To the spirit of nature's lesser degree of reality, therefore, corresponds a higher degree of contingency. Nature, by its very design, allows for a space of open contingency in which a great variety of free agents exercise their various kinds of moral agency, including libertarian choice. Among these free beings are God himself, whom More calls "that free uncreated agent" in his *Epistola altera*, and his heavenly host. The role of the spirit of nature in More's refutation of Spinoza's naturalism is, therefore, a somewaht paradoxical one. It accounts both for the regularity of natural processes by which beings capable of participating in God's fullness gradually come into existence and ascend the chain of being and for the contingency of a world open to occasional interventions by supernatural agency, whether divine, angelic or demonic. God's benignity which guides his every action in nature and history is such that it not only admits of, but actively encourages moral agency to flourish. He is a lawgiver who inscribes his own law of universal and distinterested love into the souls at their creation and devises means to redeem them once they have fallen away from him. The world is not primarily governed by "worldly matter and its intrinsic power and motion" whose interaction, on Spinoza's necessaritarian ontology, brings about "necessary results", but by God's "own free will" as he enacts laws which the souls, created in his image and likeness, are free either to obey or disobey": "If it is not like this, why should not God, if he exists and if he is a being distinct from worldly matter, be able to inscribe laws in the minds of men, doing it in such a way, however, that it is up to them to obey them or not and after their disobedience try in new ways to lead them to good fruits, as he is said to have done on Mount Sinai in giving the Laws to Moses?" **(F)**. As well as refuting both the theology and the political philosophy of "that late theological politician Spinoza", More follows Cudworth in viewing their fellow Cambridge metaphysician as a Spinozist or proponent of "Stratonic hylozoism" **(G)**. More's rationale for a Spinozist reading of Glisson's seminal 1672 *Tractatus de natura substantiae energetica, sive de vita naturae* is the author's belief in the necessity of life in matter which he likens to the necessity of the existence of substance in Spinoza. More's refutation of

Glisson's *Treatise* is remarkable on two grounds. First, More, despite his critique, endorses a variety of "hylozoism" on theological grounds. All of reality, proceeding as it does from the Deity's supreme life, is seen as the latter's "ultimate emanation" and as such may possess some rudimentary living "self-motion". Secondly, More holds that panpsychism, while being consonant with, and perhaps even a logical corollary of, the soul's innate notion of a benign deity as all-diffusive life, cannot by itself account for the unity characteristic of the animate cosmos as an ordered whole and its living parts. More's refutation of Glisson's Spinozist panpsychism hinges upon the combination problem which deprives panpsychism of its alleged explanatory power. The complexity of an animal organism militates strongly against the truth of modern Glissonian panpsychism. It is inherently unlikely that the single parts of the generic life of matter, "spread and disseminated across vast distances", should consciously and purposely collude in producing the "specific modifications" required for a well-functioning living organism. In his *Confutation* of Spinoza's *Ethics* (**H–M**) More shows his philosophical foe's hylozoic atheism to hinge upon the "twin columns" of the necessary existence of substance qua substance and its oneness (title). Since there is no denying the substantiality of matter, it must, on Spinoza's atheistic twin principles, be believed to be the sole substance of necessary existence. More vacillates in his critical reading of Spinoza's monism which either identifies material extension with God, reducing all of reality to the interplay of atoms moving and resting in a lifeless void, or endows it with a rudimentary cogitation spread throughout all animate and inanimate objects. Either way, Spinoza's substance, despite occasional insights, falls woefully short of the infinitely perfect being of the ancient theology which gives life to creation so as to enable it to participate in its own fullness of its own free volition. More demolishes both columns of Spinoza's atheism. While More concurs with Spinoza in recognizing the force of the ontological argument, it applies only to God whose essence as "absolutely perfect being" is such that it implies his existence. However, God's necessary existence does not rule out the contingent existence of a great many substances distinct from him. On the contrary, since it does not involve a contradiction for a substance to transition from non-being to being, it is possible for an absolutely perfect being to bring about other substances. Indeed, God's omnipotence, defined by More as the capacity for the creation of substances distinct from him in being and power, is part of his essence which reveals both that he cannot not exist and that he can give existence to others. In response to Spinoza's strict monism, More, therefore, reasserts his Platonist pluralism of a supremely benign first principle from which proceeds a chain of being composed of "worldly matter, the spirit of nature and the spirits of men and angels" (**H**). Nor is Spinoza right in arguing that one substance, for want of an attribute common to both of them, cannot produce another since even the substances at the top and at the bottom of reality, i.e. God and matter, have substantiality in common. The plurality of substances are individuated and distinct from one another neither by "the diversity of attributes" nor by "the diversity of modifications", but by the "real distinction" of occupying different places with God's own infinite spatial extension (**I**). In a rejoinder to the charge of anthropomorphism levelled at the cherished Platonist notions of divine goodness and freedom in the Appendix to the first book of the *Ethics*, More furnishes a detailed defence of supremely beneficent divine agency (**I**). For one thing, More makes use of *Tu quoque* arguments in exposing Spinoza's hypostatization of mathematical as every bit as anthropomorphic as his attribution of moral goodness to the first principle. For another, and more importantly, every perfection must be ascribed to a God who is defined as the epitome of all possible perfections. Among them is the highest of human perfections, i.e. moral agency. God's infinity is not quantitative indefiniteness, but the qualitative one of his goodness or "the essential sanctity and purity of the divine majesty by which he is different and distant from all the rest of things by his very kind, as it were (*toto quasi genere*)" (**M**). It was against the backdrop of his critique of Spinoza that More revisited his earlier Cartesian writings in which he came to see the seeds of his most formidable foe's hylozoist atheism.

As is clear from his *scholia* which he added to his correspondence **(N)**, he now took Descartes' denial of a spirit's spatial presence to be close to an epiphenomalist explanation of all mental operations. Intellection and volition and spirit in general are degraded into "powers of worldly matter" and "a mode of extended matter". However, the fire heating the iron to which Descartes likens a soul acting upon a body clearly suffuses the metal heated, thus strengthening More's case for spiritual extension.

Notes

1 Apuleius, *De Deo Socratis*, VI 4 (ed. J. Beaujeu).
2 Proclus, *Commentary on Plato's Parmenides* I, 108.23 (ed. C. Steel) = 123.23 (eds. C. Luna-A.-Ph. Segonds) = 709.23 (ed. V. Cousin).
3 *De Rep.* l. 5 [*Republic* V 479c1–2].
4 "stupidity".
5 *Ethics*, I, P6: One substance cannot be produced by another substance.
6 I.e. "that, since the human mind estimates the divine nature from its own intelligence and since the latter acts for ends, it thinks that God acts so also" (II/1,623. Translation: Jacob, *Refutation*, 79–80).
7 Blunders.

Part IV

Ontology and Metaphysics

Douglas Hedley

Introduction

John Yolton in his seminal work, *Thinking Matter: Materialism in Eighteenth Century Britain* (Minneapolis, MN: University of Minnesota Press, 1983), pursues the suggestion made by Locke in his *Essay Concerning Human Understanding*, that God might well be able to add to matter the capacity to think. This notion was associated by the religious orthodoxy of the seventeenth century with such bogeymen as Thomas Hobbes and Baruch Spinoza. Yet Yolton begins his discussion of the career of materialism in the eighteenth century with neither of these thinkers, but rather with Ralph Cudworth and in particular his critique of the "Atomickal Physiology", according to which matter is inactive and lacking sense, and the only causation within it mechanical. Cudworth's emphatic attempt to sever the link between thought and matter provided the basis of his critique of atheism, and his alternative—for him the "true intellectual system"—was the affirmation of a metaphysics of mind senior to the material world. Whilst the atheist-materialist banishes intentionality and purpose, mental and divine causality from the universe, Cudworth developed a vision of the cosmos in which teleology and the guidance and direction of mind plays a central role, one without which, according to him, we cannot understand nature.

Cudworth thus endeavoured to combine a Platonic metaphysics with the new corpuscularian science, a goal he shared with his friend and colleague at Christ's College, Henry More. More in many ways represents the radical edge of the Cambridge Platonist critique of materialism, and yet More's particular metaphysical system contains elements which themselves look rather close to materialism: it is perhaps interesting to note that Thomas Hobbes was rumoured to have remarked that, were his own philosophy to be false, there was no other that he preferred to that of his great critic Henry More.[1] More's revision of Platonic principles could be startling, not least in his conception of 'extended spirit', and it is perhaps not surprising that his pupil, Lady Anne Conway, in time came to reject them. But in place of More's Platonic-Cartesian dualism, Conway raised a vision of God, mind and world that in many ways more radical than any of More's doctrines, crafting an intriguing system of gradual monism.

It should be clear from these cursory remarks that metaphysics belonged to the very heart of the intellectual endeavour of the Cambridge Platonists. Their work in this area remained informed by new developments in science and philosophy whilst also displaying the influence of a great variety of ancient and medieval thinkers. The various Cambridge Platonists were not always of one mind in their metaphysics, but it is quite impossible to understand both the philosophical and the theological agenda of this group without grasping the distinctive concepts of God, space, nature, mind and matter that they honed and developed.

Chapter 14

The Character of Metaphysics

A Alexander Jacob, *Henry More's Manual of Metaphysics*, 1–5

1. *The definition of metaphysics and reason of its name.*

Metaphysics is the art of correctly contemplating incorporeal substances insofar as they are revealed in our faculties by the light of nature. Thus, metaphysics is, as it were, natural theology.

As regards the name metaphysics, it is indeed most significant; it is in fact taken from the title prefixed wrongly and ineptly to a certain Aristotelean tract: for, it is entitled τὰ μετὰ τὰ φυσικὰ, when, however, there occur quite rarely there things that are really metaphysical, but, for the most part, either logical or something of some other art or science. However, this art which we treat of here and may be taught after physics is said to be metaphysical since it is the most noble fruit of natural philosophy and most genuine. For, from the more accurate knowledge of nature or the world we emerge into a sufficiently clear knowledge of God and of the other incorporeal substances.

2. *Some maxims and titles with which Aristotle distinguishes metaphysics.*

Most aptly therefore is this discipline said to be metaphysical, although it be adorned with other titles and maxims in Aristotle which, even in that sense in which we treat it, are not in fact inept. For, everywhere it is said to be either σοφία or φιλοσοφία, wisdom, or philosophy, or first philosophy: as only a philosopher or at least one that has acquired the first philosophy, possesses wisdom. Since he truly philosophizes who investigates and discovers the most primal causes of things, which Aristotle contends to be the object of wisdom.

Indeed the most primal causes are doubtless to be found among incorporeal substance, of which God is the most excellent. Ὁ γὰρ Θεός, says he, δοκεῖ το αἴτιον πᾶσιν εἶναι καὶ ἀρχή τις.[2] God is indeed seen to be the cause and principle of all things, not to mention anything of the other universal incorporeal causes. All of which, having the most noble and most simple power of acting, indeed this metaphysics of ours is justly to be distinguished and honored by those expressions which Aristotle has so freely heaped on his first philosophy—αἰτιώτατε, ἁπλουστάτη, ἀρχοειδεστάτη, ἐπιστημονικωτάτη, and let me add even καθολικωτάτη. The influence of those first causes is indeed most universal and noble, although their nature and essence is restricted and circumscribed to a certain kind, namely, to the incorporeal.

3. *Natural philosophy is the most noble end of the knowledge of metaphysical substances.*

See, therefore, where the lawful study of natural philosophy leads, indeed, that it directs us as by a path to knowledge of that sort of principles which are both elevated and divine, as is plainly apprehended to be posited above all corporeal nature, and to exceed its powers. When, in the mean while, however, it is seen to be either the ingenuity or misfortune of the present age that all are engaged in the contemplation of corporeal things, fix eternity, too, there, and disturb and vex matter with well-nigh infinite experiments, not that truth might be acknowledged but that it might be utterly falsified and silenced, And so indeed they seem to me to dig holes in the earth's entrails like moles, not, as it were, dig it like men who throw up the foundations of some magnificent dwelling which may raise its head in the luminous air and be filled with the rays of the sun through its open and pellucid windows. But I return to the definition.

4. *In what sense metaphysics is said to be an art; in which sense knowledge and wisdom.*

Metaphysics is said here to be an art, not in that sense in which Aristotle accepts art, especially as "a rational quality concerned with fabrication", but in that common sense in which well-nigh everybody accepts it, namely insofar as it signifies a doctrinal or methodical comprehension of homogeneous precepts whose end is εὐπραξία, and does not refer to either "speculative" or "fabricative". Here indeed it is speculative, and is the habit of rightly contemplating incorporeal substances. Which habit may, not inappropriately, be said to be knowledge or wisdom. Knowledge, since it most of all makes for πρὸς τὴν στάσιν καὶ ἠρέμησιν διανοίας, from which the reason of the name ἐπιστήμη is traced in Aristotle. Wisdom, indeed, since it is the investigator and discoverer of the most primal and abstruse causes.

5. *What is understood by incorporeal substances and the right contemplation of them.*

By incorporeal substances I understand spirits properly expressed, or substances in themselves entirely immaterial, and their affections or properties. The right contemplation of them is forming true and intelligible notions of them, and disposing of these formed notions in that order whereby one sheds light on the other, so that not only individual things are clearly and distinctly conceived, but all theorems, either of the existence of those things or of their nature, are understood to be sufficiently sound and true.

6. *That metaphysics is restricted to the light of nature, as it is distinguished from supernatural theology.*

Finally, I add, "insofar as are revealed to our faculties by the light nature" so that metaphysics (which Aristotle also calls θεολογικήν) may be distinguished from that supernatural theology which is manifest to men by a certain divine revelation. But not so much that those things which occur in that theology by divine inspiration of which the reason can be perceived by our faculties may not be transferred to the former. Such are things regarding God and of the Trinity of the divine numen, of the human soul and angelic, and other things of this sort. Those things which are revealed to our faculties, or are discovered by them originally, or are transmitted by divine influence, but are known by them only insofar as they are consonant with human reason, can all indeed be the objects of that metaphysics (if we wish to elaborate and not be constrained to the limits of a manual) which we here treat, and nonetheless this metaphysics of ours may be rightly called a certain natural theology.

Notes

1 See Richard Ward, *The Life of the learned and pious Dr. Henry More*, 80.
2 Aristot. Met. 1.983a 9–10.

Chapter 15

The Existence and Nature of God

A John Smith, *Of the Existence and Nature of God* (1660), Chapter 1 (*Select Discourses*, 123–126)

[123] WE shall now come to the other *Cardinal Principle* of all Religion, & treat something *concerning God*. Where we shall not so much demonstrate *That he is*, as *What he is*.

Both which we may best learn from *a Reflexion upon our own Souls*, as *Plotinus* hath well taught us, εἰς ἑαυτὸν ἐπιστρέφων, εἰς ἀρχὴν ἐπιστρέφει,[1] *He which reflects upon himself, reflects upon his own Originall*, and finds the clearest Impression of some Eternall Nature and Perfect Being stamp'd upon his own Soul. And therefore *Plato* seems sometimes to reprove the ruder sort of men in his times for their contrivance of Pictures and Images to put themselves in mind of the θεοὶ or Angelicall Beings, and exhorts them to look into their own Souls, which are the fairest Images not onely of [124] the Lower divine Natures, but of the Deity it self; God having so copied forth himself into the whole life and energy of man's Soul, as that the lovely Characters of Divinity may be most easily seen and read of all men within themselves: as they say *Phidias* the famous Statuary, after he had made the Statue of *Minerva* with the greatest exquisiteness of Art to be set up in the *Acropolis* at *Athens*, afterwards impress'd his own Image so deeply in her buckler, *ut nemo delere possit aut divellere, qui totam statuam non imminueret*. And if we would know what the *Impresse* of Souls is, it is nothing but God himself, who could not write his own name so as that it might be read but onely in Rationall Natures. Neither could he make such without imparting such an Imitation of his own Eternall Understanding to them as might be a perpetual Memorial of himself within them. And whenever we look upon our own Soul in a right manner, we shall find an *Urim* and *Thummim* there, by which we may ask counsel of God himself, who will have this alway born upon its breast-plate. [. . .]

[125] For though God hath copied forth his own Perfections in this conspicable & sensible World, according as it is capable of entertaining them; yet the most clear and distinct copy of himself could be imparted to none else but to intelligible and inconspicable natures: and though the whole fabrick of this visible Universe be whispering out the notions of a Deity, and alway inculcates this lesson to the contemplators of it, ὡς ἐμὲ πεποίηκε ὁ θεός,[2] as *Plotinus* expresseth it; yet we cannot understand it without some interpreter within. The [126] Heavens indeed *declare the glory of God, and the Firmament shews his handy-work*, and the τὸ γνωστὸν τοῦ θεοῦ, *that which may be known of God, even his eternal power and Godhead*, as S. *Paul* tells us, is to be seen in these *externall* appearances: yet it must be *something within* that must instruct us in all these Mysteries, and we shall then best understand them, when we compare that copie which we find of them *within* our selves, with that which we see *without* us. The Schoolmen have well compared *Sensible* and *Intelligible* Beings in reference to the Deity, when they tell us that the one doe onely represent *Vestigia Dei*, the other *Faciem Dei*. We shall

therefore here enquire what that Knowledge of a Deity is which a due converse with our own naked Understandings will lead us into.

B John Smith, *Of the Existence and Nature of God* (1660), Chapter 2 (*Select Discourses*, 128–129)

[128] And that is the next thing which our own Understandings will instruct us in concerning God, viz. *His Eternall Power*. For as we find *a Will* and *Power* within our selves to execute the Results of our own *Reason* and *Judgment*, so far as we are not hindred by some more potent Cause: so indeed we know it must be a mighty inward strength and force that must enable our Understandings to their proper functions, and that Life, Energy and Activity can never be separated from a Power of Understanding. The more *unbodied* any thing is, the more *unbounded* also is it in its *Effective* power: *Body* and *Matter* being the most sluggish, inert and unwieldy thing that may be, having no power from it self nor over it self: and therefore the *Purest Mind* must also needs be the most *Almighty Life and Spirit*; and as it comprehends all things and sums them up together in its Infinite knowledge, so it must also comprehend them all in its own life and power. Besides, when we review our own Immortal Souls and their dependency upon some Almighty Mind, we know that we neither did nor could produce our selves; and withall know that all that *Power* which lies within the compass of our selves, will serve for no other purpose then to apply severall præexistent things one to another, [129] from whence all *Generations* and *Mutations* arise, which are nothing else but the *Events* of different applications and complications of Bodies that were existent before: and therefore that which produced that Substantiall Life and Mind by which we know our selves, must be something *much more Mighty* then we are, and can be no less indeed then *Omnipotent*, and must also be the First architect and δημιουργὸς of all other Beings, and the perpetuall Supporter of them.

C John Smith, *Of the Existence and Nature of God* (1660), Chapter 3 (*Select Discourses*, 135–139)

[135] WE shall once more take a view of our own Souls, and observe how the Motions thereof lead us into the knowledge of a Deity. We alwaies find a *restless appetite* within our selves which craves for some *Supreme and Chief good*, and will not be satisfied with any thing less then *Infinity* it self; as if our own *Penury* and *Indigency* were commensurate to the Divine *fulness*: and therefore no Question has been more canvas'd by all Philosophy then this, *De summo hominis bono*, and all the Sects thereof were antiently distinguish'd by those Opinions that they entertain'd *De finibus Boni & Mali*, as *Tully* phraseth it. But of how weak and dilute a Nature soever some of them may have conceived that *Summum Bonum*, yet they could not so satisfie their own inflamed thirst after it. We find by Experience that our Souls cannot live upon that thin and spare diet which they are entertain'd with at their own home; neither can they be satiated with those jejune and insipid morsels which this Outward world furnisheth their Table with. I cannot think the most voluptuous *Epicurean* could ever satisfie the cravings of his Soul with Corporeal pleasure, though he might endeavour to perswade himself there was no better: nor the most Quintessential *Stoicks* find an αὐτάρκεια and ἀταραξία a Self-sufficiency and Tranquil[136]lity within their own Souls, arising out of the pregnancy of their own Mind and Reason; though their sullen thoughts would not suffer them to be beholden to an Higher Being for their Happiness. The more we endeavour to extract an *Autarchy* out of our own Souls, the more we torment them, and force them to feel and sensate their own pinching poverty. Ever since our Minds became so dim-sighted as not to pierce into that Original and Primitive Blessedness which is above, our Wills are too big for our Understandings, and will believe their beloved prey is to be found where

Reason discovers it not: they will pursue it through all the vast Wilderness of this World, and force our Understandings to follow the chase with them: nor may we think to tame this violent appetite or allay the heat of it, except we can look upward to some Eternal and Almighty goodness which is alone able to master it. [. . .]

[137] God is not better defin'd to us by our *Understandings* then by our *Wills and Affections*: He is not onely *the Eternal Reason*, that *Almighty Mind and Wisdome* which our *Understandings* converse with; but he is also that *unstained Beauty* and *Supreme Good* which our *Wills* are perpetually catching after: and wheresoever we find *true Beauty, Love and Goodness*, we may say, Here or there is *God*. And as we cannot understand any thing [138] of an Intelligible nature, but by some primitive *Idea* we have of God, whereby we are able to guess at the elevation of its Being and the pitch of its Perfection; so neither doe our Wills embrace any thing without some *latent sense* of Him, whereby they can tast and discern how near any thing comes to that Self-sufficient good they seek after: and indeed without such an internal sensating Faculty as this is we should never know when our Souls are in conjunction with the Deity, or be able to relish the ineffable sweetness of true Happiness. Though here below we know but little what this is, because we are little acquainted with fruition and enjoyment; we know well what belongs to longings and languishment, but we know not so well what belongs to plenty and fulness; we are well acquainted with the griefs and sicknesses of this in-bred love, but we know not what its health and complacencies are.

To conclude this particular, μεγάλας ἔχει κινήσεις ἡ ψυχη, the Soul hath strong and weighty motions, and nothing else can bear it up but something permanent and immutable. Nothing can beget a constant serenity and composedness within, but something Supreme to its own Essence; as if having once departed from the primitive Fountain of its life, it were deprived of it self, perpetually contesting within it self and divided against it self: and all this evidently proves to our inward sense and feeling, That there is some Higher Good then our selves, something that is much more amiable and desirable, and therefore must be loved and preferred before our selves, as *Plotinus* hath excellently observ'd, τῶν ὄντων ἕκαστον ἐφιέμενον τοῦ ἀγαθοῦ, βούλεται ἐκεῖνο μᾶλλον ἢ ὅ ἐστιν εἶναι,[3] &c. *Every thing that desires the enjoyment of the First good, would rather be* [139] *That then what it is, because indeed the nature of that is much more desirable then its own*. And therefore the *Platonists*, when they contemplate the Deity under these three notions of τὸ ἕν, τὸ ὄν and τὸ ἀγαθόν, and question which to place first in order of understanding, resolve the preeminence to be due to the τὸ ἀγαθόν, as *Simplicius* tells us, because That is first known to us as the Architect of the world, and, we may adde, as that which begets in us this ἐρωτικὸν πάθος, these strong passionate desires whereby all sorts of men (even those that are rude and illiterate) are first known to themselves, and by that knowledge may know what diminutive, poor and helpless, things themselves are, who can never satiate themselves from themselves, and what an Excellent and Soveraign goodness there is above them which they ought to serve, and cannot but serve it, or some filthy idol in stead of it; though this mental Idolatry be like that gross and external in this also, that howsoever we attend it not (and so are never the more blameless) yet our worship of these images and pictures of Goodness rests not there, it being some all-sufficient Good that (as we observed before) calls forth and commands our adorations.

D Ralph Cudworth, *The True Intellectual System of the Universe* (1671/1678), Chapter 4 (pp. 206–707)

[206] And now we have proposed the three principal attributes of the Deity. The first whereof is infinite goodness with fecundity; the second infinite knowledge and wisdom; and the last infinite, active, and perceptive power. From which divine attributes the Pythagoreans and Platonists seemed to have framed their trinity of archical hypostases, such as have the nature of principles in the

universe, and which though they apprehended as several distinct substances, gradually subordinate to one another, yet they many times extend the τὸ Θεῖον so far as to comprehend them all within it. Which Pythagoric trinity seems to be intimated by *Aristotle* in these words: Καθάπερ γάρ φασι καὶ οἱ Πυθαγόρειοι τὸ πᾶν καὶ τὰ πάντα τοῖς τρίσι διώρισται,[4] *As the Pythagoreans also say, the universe, and all things are determined and contained by three principles.* Of which Pythagoric trinity more after wards. But now we may enlarge and fill up that compendious idea of God premised, of a being absolutely perfect, by adding thereunto (to make it more parti[207]cular) *such as infinitely good, wise, and powerful, necessarily existing, and not only the framer of the world, but also the cause of all things.* Which idea of the Deity is sufficient, in order to our present undertaking.

Nevertheless, if we would not only attend to what is barely necessary for a dispute with Atheists, but also consider the satisfaction of other free and devout minds, that are hearty and sincere lovers of this most admirable and most glorious being, we might venture for their gratification, to propose yet a more full, free, and copious description of the Deity, after this manner. *God is a being absolutely perfect, unmade or self-originated, and necessarily existing; that hath an infinite fecundity in him, and virtually contains all things; as also an infinite benignity or overflowing love, uninvidiously displaying and communicating itself; together with an impartial rectitude or nature of justice: who fully comprehends himself, and the extent of his own fecundity, and therefore, all the possibilities of things, their several natures and respects, and the best frame or system of the whole: who hath also infinite active and perceptive power: the fountain of all things, who made all that could be made and was fit to be made, producing them according to his own nature, (his essential goodness and wisdom) and therefore according to the best pattern, and in the best manner possible, for the good of the whole; and reconciling all the variety and contrariety of things in the universe into one most admirable and lovely harmony. Lastly, who contains and upholds all things, and governs them after the best manner also, and that without any force or violence, they being all naturally subject to his authority, and readily obeying his law.* And now we see that God is such a being, as that if he could be supposed not to be, there is nothing whose existence a good man could possibly more wish or desire.

E Ralph Cudworth, *The True Intellectual System of the Universe* (1671/1678), Chapter 5 (pp. 727–730)

[727] This I say is the *Hypothesis* of *Theists*, that there is *One Absolutely Perfect Being*, Existing of *It self* from all Eternity, from whence all other lesser *Perfections*, or *Imperfect Beings* did gradually *Descend*, till at last they end in *Sensless Matter* or *Inanimate Body*. But the *Atheistick Hypothesis* on the contrary, makes *Sensless Matter* the most *Imperfect* thing, to be the *First Principle* or the only *Self-Existent* Being, and the *Cause* of all other things, and Consequently all *Higher Degrees* of *Perfections*, that are in the world, to have *Clombe* up, or *Emerged* by way of *Ascent* from thence; as *Life, Sense, Understanding,* and *Reason*, from that which is altogether *Dead* and *Sensless*. [. . .]

[728] But to speak more particularly, it is certain, notwithstanding all the vain pretences of *Lucretius* and other *Atheists*, or *Semi-Atheists*, to the contrary; that *Life and Sense* could never possibly spring, out of *Dead and Sensless Matter*, as its only Original, either in the way of *Atoms*, (no Composition of *Magnitudes, Figures, Sites and Motions*, being ever able to produce *Cogitation*) or in the way of *Qualities*, since *Life and Perception* can no more result from any Mixture of *Elements*, or *Combinations* of *Qualities* of Heat and Cold, Moist and Dry, *&c.* than from Unqualified Atoms. This being undeniably Demonstrable, from that very Principle of Reason, which the *Atheists* are so fond of, but, misunderstanding abuse, (as shall be manifested afterward) that *Nothing can come from Nothing*. Much less could *Understanding* and *Reason* in men, ever have Emerged out of *Stupid Matter*, devoid of all manner of *Life*. Wherefore we must needs here freely declare, against the *Darknss* of that *Philosophy*, which hath

been Sometimes unwarily entertained by such as were no Atheists, That *Sense may* Rise from a certain *Modification, Mixture,* or *Organization,* of Dead and Sensless Matter; as also that *Understanding and Reason,* may result from *Sense:* the plain consequence of both which is, that *Sensless Matter* may prove the *Original* of all things, and the only *Numen.* Which Doctrine therefore is doubtless, a main piece of the *Philosophy* of the Kingdom of *Darkness.* But this *Darkness* hath been of late in great measure dispelled, by the Light of the *Atomick Philosophy* restored, as it was in its first Genuine and Virgin State, Undeflowred as yet by Atheists, this clearly Showing how far *Body* and *Mechanism* can go, and that Life and Cogitation can never Emerge out from thence; it being built upon that *Fundamental Principle,* as we have made it evident in the first Chapter, that *Nothing can come from Nothing.* And *Strato* [729] and the Hylozoick Atheists, were so well aware and so sensible of this, that all Life and *Understanding* could not possibly be *Generated* or *Made,* but that there must be some *Fundamental* and *Substantial* or *Eternal Unmade Life* and *Knowledge*; that they therefore have thought necessary, to attribute *Life,* and *Perception,* (or *Understanding,*) with Appetite, and Self-moving Power, to all Matter as such, that so it might be thereby fitly Qualified to be the Original of all things. Than which Opinion as nothing can be more Monstrous; so shall we else where Evince the *Impossibility thereof.* In the mean time, we doubt not to averr, that the *Argument* proposed, is a *Sufficient Demonstration* of the *Impossibility of Atheism*; which will be further manifested in our Answer to the Second *Atheistick Objection* against a *Divine Creation,* because *Nothing can come from Nothing.*

But this *Controversie* betwixt Theists and Atheists, may be yet more Particularly Stated, from the *Idea* of God, as including *Mind* or *Understanding* in it *Essentially, Viz.* Whether *Mind* be *Eternal* and *Unmade,* as being the *Maker* of all; or else Whether all *Mind* were it self *Made* or *Generated,* and that out of Sensless Matter? For according to the Doctrine of the Pagan *Theists,* Mind was προγενέστατος, καὶ Κύριος κατὰ φύσιν, *The Oldest of all things, Senior to the World and Elements; and by Nature hath a Princely and Lordly Dominion over all.* But according to those *Atheists,* who make *Matter* or *Body* devoid of all *Life* and *Understanding,* to be the First *Principle,* Mind must be ὑστερογενὴς, *A Post-Nate thing,* Younger than the world; a Weak, Umbratil, and Evanid Image, and next to Nothing.

And the *Controversie* as thus Stated, may be also Clearly and Satisfactorily decided. *For First,* we say, That as it is certainly True, That If there had been once Nothing at all, there could never have been Any thing; So is it true likewise, that If once there had been no *Life,* in the whole Universe, but all had been *Dead,* then could there never have been any *Life* or *Motion* in it; and If once there had been no *Mind, Understanding* or *Knowledge,* then could there never have been any *Mind* or *Understanding* produced. Because, to suppose *Life* and *Understanding,* to rise and spring up, out of that which is altogether *Dead & Sensless,* as its only Original, is plainly to Suppose, *Something* to come *out of Nothing.* It cannot be said so of other things, as of Corporeal World and Matter, that *If* once they had not been, they could never Possibly have been; because though there had been no World nor Matter, yet might these have been produced, from a *Perfect Omnipotent Incorporeal Being,* which in it self *Eminently* containeth all things. *Dead* and *Sensless Matter* could never have *Created* or *Generated Mind* and Understanding, but a *Perfect Omnipotent Mind,* could *Create Matter.* Wherefore because there is *Mind,* we are certain, that there was some *Mind* or other from *Eternity* without Beginning; though not because there is *Body,* that therefore there was *Body* or *Matter* from *Eternity Unmade.* Now these Imperfect Minds of ours, were by no means Themselves Eternal or without Beginning, but from an *Antecedent Non-Existence* brought forth into Being; but since no Mind could spring out of *Dead* and *Sensless Matter,* and all *Minds* [730] could not Possibly be *Made,* nor one produced from another Infinitely; there must of necessity be an *Eternal Unmade Mind,* from whence those *Imperfect Minds* of ours were derived. Which *Perfect Omnipotent Mind,* was as well the *Cause* of all other things, as of humane *Souls.*

F Ralph Cudworth, *The True Intellectual System of the Universe* (1671/1678), Chapter 5 (pp. 639–640)

[639] It is true indeed, that the Deity is more *Incomprehensible* to us than any thing else whatsoever, which proceeds from the Fulness of its Being and Perfection, and from the Transcendency of its Brightness, but for the very same reason may it be said also, in some sence, that it is more Knowable and Conceivable than any thing. As the Sun, though by reason of its Excessive Splendour, it dazle our weak sight, yet it is notwithstanding far more Visible also, than any of the *Nebulosae Stellae, the Small Misty Stars.* Where there is more of Light, there is more of Visibility, so where there is more of Entity, Reality, and Perfection, there is there more of *Conceptibility* and *Cognoscibility*; such an Object Filling up the Mind more, and Acting more strongly upon it. Nevertheless because our Weak and Imperfect Minds are lost in the Vast Immensity and Redundancy of the Deity, and overcome with its transcendent Light and dazeling Brightness, therefore hath it to us an Appearance of *Darkness* and *Incomprehensibility*. [640] As the unbounded Expansion of Light, in the clear transparent *Ether*, hath to us the *Apparition* of an *Azure Obscurity*; which yet is not an Absolute thing in it self, but only *Relative* to our *Sense*, and a mere *Phancy* in us.

The *Incomprehensibility of the Deity*, is so far from being an Argument against the *Reality* of its *Existence*, as that is most certain, on the contrary, that were there nothing *Incomprehensible* to us, who are but contemptible Pieces, and small Atoms of the Universe; were there no other Being in the world, but what our *Finite* and *Imperfect Understandings* could span or fathom, and encompass round about, look through and through, have a commanding view of, and perfectly Conquer and Subdue under them; then could there be nothing *Absolutely and Infinitely Perfect*, that is, no *God*. For though that of *Empedocles* be not true in a Literal Sence, as it seems to have been taken by *Aristotle*, γαίῃ μὲν γὰρ γαῖαν, &c.[5] *That by Earth we see Earth, by Water Water, and by Fire Fire; and understand every thing by something of the same within our selves*; yet is it certain, that every thing is apprehended by some *Internal Congruity* in that which apprehends; which perhaps was the sence intended by that Noble Philosophick Poet. Wherefore it cannot possibly otherwise be, but that the *Finiteness, Scantness,* and *Imperfection*, of our narrow Understandings must make them *Asymmetral* or *Incommensurate*, to that which is *Absolutely* and *Infinitely Perfect*.

G Ralph Cudworth, *The True Intellectual System of the Universe* (1671/1678), Chapter 5 (pp. 652–653)

[652] It is certain, that no *Simple Idea*, as that of a *Triangle* or a *Square*, of a *Cube* or *Sphere*, can possibly be *Contradictious* to it self; and therefore much less can the *Idea* of a *Perfect Being* (which is the *Compendious Idea of God*) it being more Simple, than any of the other. Indeed this Simple Idea of a *Perfect Being*, is *Pregnant* of many *Attributes*, and therefore the Idea of God, more fully declared by them all, may seem to be in this respect a *Compounded Idea*, or One Idea and Conception, Consisting or made up of Many; which if they were really Contradictious, would render the whole, a *Non-Entity*. As for Example, This, *A Plain Triangle, whose Three Angles are Greater than Two Right ones*; it being Contradictious and Unconceivable, is therefore no *True Idea*, but a *Non-Entitie*. But all the *Genuine Attributes* of the *Deity*, of which its Entire Idea is made up, are Things as *Demonstrable* of a *Perfect Being*, as the *Properties* of a *Triangle* or a *Square* are of those Ideas respectively, and therefore cannot they Possibly be *Contradictious*, neither to it, nor to one another; because those things which agree in one Third, must needs agree together amongst themselves.

Nay the *Genuine Attributes of the Deity*, namely, such as are *Demonstrable* of an *Absolutely Perfect Being*, are not only not *Contradictious*; but also *necessarily Connected together*, and *Inseparable from one another*. For there could not possibly be, One Thing *Infinite in Wisdom Only*, Another Thing *Infinite Only in Power*, and Another thing *Only Infinite in Duration* or *Eternal*. But the very same thing which is *Infinite in Wisdom*, must needs be also *Infinite in Power*, and *Infinite in Duration*, and so *vice versâ*. That which is *Infinite* in any one Perfection, must of necessity, have all Perfections in it. Thus are all the *Genuine Attributes* of the *Deity*, not only not *Contradictious*, but also *Inseparably Concatenate*; and the *Idea of God* no Congeries either of Disagreeing things; or else of such as are unnecessarily Connected with one another.

In very truth, all the several *Attributes of the Deity*, are nothing else but so many *Partial and Inadequate Conceptions*, of *One and the Same, Simple Perfect Being*, taken in as it were by piecemeal: by reason of the Imperfection of our Humane Understandings, which could not fully Conceive it all together at once: And therefore are they Really all but *One thing*, though they have the Appearance of *Multiplicity* to us. As the *One Simple Light* of the Sun, diversly *Refracted* and *Reflected* from a Rorid Cloud, hath to us the *Appearance*, of the variegated Colours of the *Rainbow*.

Wherefore the *Attributes* of God, are no *Bundle of Unconceivables*, and *Impossibles*, huddled up together; nor Attributes of Honour and Complement only, and nothing but the *Religious Nonsence* of Astonish'd Minds, expressing their Devotion towards what they Fear; but all of them *Attributes of Nature*, and of *most severe Philosophick Truth*. Neither is the *Idea of God*, an *Arbitrarious Compilement*, of things *Unnecessarily Connected*, and *Separable* from one [653] another: it is no *Factitious* nor *Fictitious* thing, made up by any *Feigning Power* of the Soul, but it is a *Natural* and most *Simple Uncompounded Idea*; such as to which nothing can be Arbitrariously added, nor nothing detracted from. Notwithstanding which, by reason of the Imperfection of humane Minds there may be, and are, different Apprehensions concerning it For as every one that hath a *Conception* of a Plain Triangle in general, doth not therefore know, that it includes this *Property* in it, to have *Three Angles Equal to Two Right ones*; nor doth every one, who hath an Idea of a *Rectangular Triangle*, presently understand, that the *Square of the Subtense*, is Equal to the *Squares of both the Sides*; so neither doth every one, who hath a Conception of a *Perfect Being*, therefore presently know all that is included in that *Idea*.

H Ralph Cudworth, *The True Intellectual System of the Universe* (1671/1678), Chapter 5 (pp. 692–694)

[692] But that *Theism*, or *Religion*, is no *Gullery* or *Imposture*, will be yet further made unquestionably Evident. That the generality of Mankind have agreed in the acknowledgment of one *Supreme Deity*, as a Being *Eternal* and *Necessarily Existent, Absolutely Perfect*, and *Omnipotent*, and the *Maker of the whole World*, hath been already largely proved in the foregoing Discourse. To which purpose is this of *Sextus* the Philosopher,[6] κοινὴν γὰρ πάλιν πρόληψιν ἔχουσι πάντες ἄνθρωποι περὶ θεοῦ, καθ' ἣν μακάριόν τί ἐστι ζῷον καὶ ἄφθαρτον καὶ τέλειον ἐν εὐδαιμονίᾳ καὶ παντὸς κακοῦ ἀνεπίδεκτον· *All men have this common* Prolepsis, *concerning God, that he is a Living Being Incorruptible, Perfectly Happy, and Uncapable of all manner of Evil*. And the Notion of that God, which *Epicurus* opposed, was no other than this, *An Understanding Being, having all Happiness, with Incorruptibility, that Framed the whole World*. Now, I say, that if there be no such thing [693] as this Existing, and this *Idea of God*, be a meer *Fictitious Thing*, then was it altogether *Arbitrarious*. But it is unconceivable, how the Generality of Mankind, (a few Atheists only excepted) should universally agree, in one and the same *Arbitrarious Figment*. This Argumentation hath been formerly used, by some Theists, as appeareth from the forementioned *Sextus*,[7] τελέως δέ ἐστιν ἄλογον τὸ κατὰ τύχην πάντας τοῖς αὐτοῖς ἐπιβάλλειν ἰδιώμασιν, ἀλλὰ μὴ φυσικῶς οὕτως ἐκκινεῖσθαι· *It is altogether Irrational to think, that all men should by Chance, light upon the same Properties (in the Idea of God) without being Naturally mov'd thereunto*. Neither is that any sufficient account which the Atheists would here give, that *Statesmen* and *Politicians*, every where thus possessed

the Minds of men with One and the same *Idea*; the Difficulty still remaining, how Civil Soveraigns and Law-makers, in all the distant parts of the world, and such as had no Communication nor Entercourse with one another; should universally Jump, in one and the same *Fictitious* and *Arbitrarious Idea*.

Moreover, were there no God, it is Not Conceivable, how that forementioned *Idea* should ever have Entred into the Minds of men, or how it could have been Formed in them. And here the Atheists again, think it enough, to say that this *Notion* or *Idea* was *Put* into the Minds of the Generality of mankind, by *Law-makers* and *Politicians*, *Telling them*, of such a Being, and perswading them to believe his Existence; or that it was from the first *Feigner* or *Inventor* of it, propagated all along and conveyed down, by *Oral Tradition*. But this argues their great Ignorance in Philosophy to think that any *Notion* or *Idea*, is put into mens Minds from without, meerly by *Telling*, or by *Words*; we being Passive to nothing else from words, but their Sounds and the Phantasms thereof; they only occasioning the Soul to excite such Notions, as it had before within it self (whether *Innate* or *Adventitious*) which those words by the Compact and Agreement of men were made to be Signs of; or else to reflect also further, upon those *Ideas* of their own, Consider them more Distinctly, and Compare them with one another. And though all Learning be not the *Remembrance* of what the *Soul* once before actually understood, in a *Pre-existent State*, as *Plato* somewhere would have it, according to that of *Boetius*,[8]

Quod si *Platonis* Musa personat Verum,
Quod quisque Discit, Immenior Recordatur;

Yet *is all Humane Teaching*, but *Maieutical*, or *Obstetricious*; and not the *filling of* the Soul as a *Vessel*, meerly by *Pouring* into it from *Without*, but the *Kindling* of it from Within; or helping it so to excite and awaken, compare, and compound its own *Notions*, as whereby to arrive at the Knowledge, of that which it was before Ignorant of; as the thing was better expressed by the forementioned Philosophick Poet, in these words,[9]

Haeret profecto Semen introrsum Veri,
Quod excitatur Ventilante Doctrina.

[694] Wherefore the meer *Telling* of men, There is a *God*, could not infuse any *Idea* of him into their Minds; nor yet the further giving this Definition of him, that he is a *Being Absolutely Perfect, Eternal and Self-Existent*, make them understand any thing of his Nature, were they not able to Excite *Notions* or *Ideas* from within themselves, correspondent to those several words.

I Ralph Cudworth, *The True Intellectual System of the Universe* (1671/1678), Chapter 5 (pp. 724–725)

[724] Wherefore we shall endeavour, to make out an *Argument, or Demonstration*, for the *Existence of a God*, from his *Idea*, as including *Necessary Existence* in it, some other ways. And First, we shall make an Offer towards it in this manner. Though it will not follow from hence, because we can *Frame an Idea* of any thing in our minds, that therefore such a thing Really Existeth; yet nevertheless, whatsoever we can *Frame an Idea* of, *Implying* no manner of *Contradiction* in its Conception, we may certainly conclude thus much of it, that such a thing was not *Impossible to be*; there being nothing to us *Impossible*, but what is *Contradictious* and *Repugnant* to Conception. Now the Idea *of God* or a *Perfect Being*, can Imply no manner of *Contradiction* in it, because it is only the *Idea* of such a thing as hath all *Possible* and *Conceivable* Perfections in it; that is, all *Perfections* which are neither *Contradictious* in themselves, nor to one another. And they who will not allow of this Consequence, from the *Idea of a*

Perfect Being, including *Necessity of Existence* in it, that it doth therefore *Actually Exist*, yet cannot deny, but that this at least will follow, from its implying no manner of *Contradiction* in it, that is therefore a thing *Possible*, or not *Impossible* to be. For thus much being true of all other *Contingent things*, whose Idea implieth no *Contradiction*, that they are therefore *Possible*; it must needs be granted of that, whose very *Idea* and *Essence* containeth a *Necessity of Existence* in it, as the *Essence* of nothing else but a *Perfect Being* doth. And this is the First Step, that we now make in way of Argumentation, from the *Idea of God* or a *Perfect Being*, having nothing *Contradictious* in it, That therefore *God* is at least *Possible*, or no way *Impossible* to have been. In the next place as this particular *Idea* of that which is *Possible*, includeth *Necessity of Existence* in it; from these *Two things* put together at least, the *Possibility* of such a Being, and its *Necessary Ex*[725]*istence* (if not from the Latter alone) will it according to Reason follow, that *He Actually Is*. If *God* or a *Perfect Being*, in whose *Essence* is contained *Necessary Existence*, be *Possible*, or no way *Impossible* to have been; then *He is*; because upon supposition of his *Non-Existence*, it would be *Absolutely Impossible*, that he should ever have been. It does not thus follow, concerning *Imperfect Beings*, that are *Contingently Possible*, that if they *be Not*, it was therefore *Impossible* for them ever to have been; for that which is *Contingent*, though it be Not, yet might it for all that, *Possibly Have been*. But a *Perfect Necessarily Existent Being*, upon the bare supposition of its *Non-Existence*, could no more *Possibly Have been*, than it could Possibly *Hereafter* be: because if it might Have been, though it be not, then would it not be a *Necessary Existent Being*. The sum of all is this, A *Necessary Existent Being*, if it be *Possible*, it *Is*; because upon supposition of its *Non-Existence*, it would be *Impossible* for it ever to have been. Wherefore *God* is either *Impossible* to have been, or else *He Is*. For if God were *Possible*, and yet be *Not*, then is he not a *Necessary*, but *Contingent Being*, which is contrary to the *Hypothesis*.

Notes

1 Plotinus, *Enneads* VI.9.2.36–37.
2 Plotinus, *Enneads* III.2.3.21.
3 Plotinus, *Enneads* VI.8.13.13–14.
4 De Coel. L.1 c.1.
5 Empedocles, fr. B109 (eds. H. Diels-W. Kranz) = Aristotle, *On the Soul* I 2.404b13–15.
6 *Adv. Math.* 314 [Sextus Empiricus, *Adversus Mathematicos* IX 33.5–8].
7 *Adv. Math.* 314 [Sextus Empiricus, *Adversus Mathematicos* IX 33.8–10].
8 Boethius, *De consolatione philosophiae* III 11.15–16: "Deep down in your heart? If Plato's muse rings true,/ what each man learns, forgetful he recalls" (H. F. Stewart, E. K. Rand, S. J. Tester (trans.), *Boethius, Theological Tractates. The Consolation of Philosophy*, Cambridge, MA: Harvard University Press, 1973, 297).
9 Boethius, *De consolatione philosophiae* III 11.11–12: "Assuredly there sticks within some seed of truth/Which is stirred to life by learning's breeze" (H. F. Stewart, E. K. Rand, S. J. Tester (trans.), *Boethius, Theological Tractates. The Consolation of Philosophy*, Cambridge, MA: Harvard University Press, 1973, 297).

Chapter 16

Space

A Jacob, More's *Manual of Metaphysics*, 54–58

1. *Those who consider immobile extension to be nothing but mere void imitate the rude common folk who imagine the heavens to be free of winds and clouds and only an empty concave; indeed, the Pythagoreans and Democritus, and Epicurus have numbered internal place among real beings.*

Nothing therefore prevents this smaller immobile extension which we have revealed from being something real, although it be not body or any material thing, nor can be it by greater right be judged to be a mere vacuum than the near vault of heaven free of wind and clouds be considered by illiterate people to be a certain empty concave. Who certainly seem to me to exactly imitate the common philosophers who would consider this immobile extension which we have demonstrated to be everywhere to be, as it were, a perfectly void interval, when, however, it is not any more a vacuum than the capacity of a cup devoid of wine, which is filled in the meanwhile with invisible air. And, indeed, although not only air, but also ether and any absolutely subtle matter be moved as well as the most gross, there remains, however, a certain subtle substance, indeed the most subtle of all, which, although it can evade the external senses, can be easily apprehended by the internal eyes of the soul, if only the spectator be sufficiently knowing and shrewd, as is apparent in the Pythagoreans who are presented in Aristotle as having another judgement of space (which is said to be a void) than the common one of philosophers.

For, in this way, they describe "that spirit is from infinity, and permeates the entire universe, so that the world is said to breathe in this space". That this void doubtless suggests spirit or immaterial substance. Of which kind the ancient atomic philosophy, in Diogenes Laertius, likewise, declares space to be, Democritus, indeed, among these, acknowledging no other true and real principle of things than atoms and the void, all the rest to be not things but only appearances excited in our senses, and again Epicurus, with the apt words κενὸν καὶ χώραν, calling void and place, τὴν ἀναφῆ φύσιν, intangible nature, i.e. incorporeal.

2. *The first demonstration that internal place is something real, from the fact that, according to Descartes, extension cannot be of nothing.*

Lest we be seen to be supported only by authorities in such a serious matter, we shall finally confirm our cause with one and another argument taken from the nature of substance. Of which the first will be that in which Descartes himself, as well as all the Cartesians, as far as I know, judge with me, namely, that "No extension can be of nothing". Indeed, we have proved above with clear and perspicacious demonstrations that there is some immobile extension distinct from mobile matter pervading everything. How, therefore, is it that anyone would linger or stay behind and not directly conclude that there is therefore some real being distinct from matter which would pervade everything and occupy all space with its presence although no matter were to exist anywhere?

7. *The second demonstration of the real extension of void or internal place—that, in it, is found an attribute which elsewhere is plainly real.*

The other argument is that something that is the real attribute of some real subject can be found nowhere else except where in the same place there is some real subject under it. And, indeed, extension is the real attribute of a real subject (namely matter), which however is found elsewhere and that independently of our imagination. Indeed, we cannot not conceive a certain immobile extension pervading everything to have existed from eternity, and which will exist to eternity (whether we think of it or not) and really distinct, finally, from mobile matter. Therefore, it is necessary that some real subject be under this extension, since it is a real attribute. This argument is so solid that nothing can be more solid. For, if it be shaky, we can indeed conclude the existence of absolutely no real subject in the universe. For, real attributes can be present and yet no real subject or substance be under them.

8. *An enumeration of more or less twenty titles which metaphysicians attribute to God congruous with immobile extension or internal place.*

For this infinite and immobile extension will be seen to be not something merely real (which we have noted in the last place) but something divine after we shall have enumerated those divine names or titles which suit it exactly, and with the greatest certainty make it not possible to be nothing, seeing that so many and such excellent attributes fit it. Of which kind are those which follow, which metaphysicians specifically attribute to First Being. Such as one, simple, immobile, eternal, complete, independent, existing from itself, subsisting by itself, incorruptible, necessary, immense, uncreated, uncircumscribed, incomprehensible, omnipresent, incorporeal, permeating and encompassing everything, Being by essence, Being by act, pure Act. There are not less than twenty titles by which the divine numen should be designated, which most aptly suit this infinite internal place which we have demonstrated to be in the universe; if we may omit that the same divine numen is called among Cabbalists מוקם, that is, place. It would be an absolutely amazing thing, more than can be expressed, and a wonder, as it were, if all this could merely define nothing.

B Norris-More Correspondence (1684) (John Norris, *Theory and Regulation of Love* [1688], 151–158)

John Norris, The First Letter to the Most Famous Mr Henry More

Excellent Sir,

Since I can see from the genius of your writings that your kindness is on a par with your learning and, moreover, hearing you declare publicly at the beginning of your book that "you labour not for yourself only, but for all them that seek learning" (Sir 33:17), I have so far overcome my inborn anxiety that I am now writing to you (even though we have not met personally yet), asking you questions as my oracle about certain difficulties.

There are then two things (to put it briefly when approaching a man who has extremely little time) that keep my mind in a state of perplexity. In your *Enchiridion Metaphysicum*, you seek to prove that there is a certain immobile extension distinct from mobile matter. Not only am I ready to accept that on the strength of your proofs, but I also believe it most strongly. The only thing that I have difficulty with is that you extend this incorporeal dimension, which we usually designate by the name of space, into infinity, making it immense in every direction. I, for one, must admit that I have as yet been unable to bring my faculties to concede that. For, as that space is an enduring quantity of which all the parts, however many there are or can be, exist at the same time, it seems incongruous to me to maintain that it is extended infinitely, it being contradictory for something to be infinite and nevertheless to exist in act in all its parts. Existing in act in all parts means to be enclosed within certain bounds as, equally, any number, however big, is included in a certain species of number and must therefore be concluded to be finite. I admit that it is different in successive quantity whose parts each exist one after the other and which, since it is capable of further enlargement after each addition, however large, may be deemed infinite in its own way. However, that in which all its parts coexist—and space is of that kind—seems to be finite by necessity, since its parts, as is also indicated by that inclusive term "all", fall under a certain species of number.

The other difficulty that I had when reading this same *Enchiridion* of yours concerned the penetrability of spirit. You say that spirits, notwithstanding their extension, can mutually penetrate each other, i.e. occupy the same "where". However, you explain it with reference to their contraction, illustrating it with the example of wax being compressed into less space. This seems to imply that by the penetration of spirits you understand nothing other than the fact that two spirits, pressed together into a tighter shape by a change in place, can occupy that same place which one of them might perhaps have filled without that change in place. Is that correct? However, this is not the penetration that the schools so harp upon, namely the coexistence of different dimensions in the same "where", but only the fact of being positioned side by side in the same shared place of which bodies are no less capable than spirits.

Perhaps I have not stated this with sufficient clarity, but you will be an able interpreter both of your own mind and mine. Do not decline then, I pray you, to light a torch for me in this darkness (provided it is not due to some weightier matter). My role is not that of one criticizing, but of one asking, nor am I writing to you to charge you with a lack of knowledge, but to seek a cure for my own ignorance. I have diligently read through your complete works published in Latin in three volumes and, because of their enormous learning, have arranged for them to be given a place in our library. If only you could have completed the *Metaphysics* that you have begun! I very much long to know what your plans are in this matter. It would be deeply regrettable indeed if so admirable a work were always to remain fragmentary and incomplete! It would have to be like this unless it were completed by you as author, for who could be that second Apelles daring to give this half-completed work the finishing touch?[1] Do not then fail the eager researchers in those high hopes of theirs for all eternity! All that is left for me to do is to pray to God from all my heart that he may long preserve you, the brightest star in the literary firmament, from setting and, after you have set, include you in his choir and finally quench your immense thirst for knowledge from the source of wisdom itself. That is the sincere wish of

Your and your works' most devout admirer John Norris.

Written in Exeter College, Oxford, on 8th January 1684.

Dr More's Answer

Sir,

I Have received your very civil and elegant Latin Letter, but answer you according to my constant use to our own Countrey men, in English. You have therein such significations of your kindness and esteem for me and my writings, that you have thereby obliged me to a professed readiness to serve you in any thing that lies in my power. And therefore without any further Ceremony I shall endeavour, as touching those two difficulties you propound, to give you the best satisfaction I can. The first difficulty, if I understand you aright, is this: How that *Immobile Extensum* distinct from matter which in my *Enchiridium Metaphysicum* I demonstrate to exist, can truely be said to be infinite, when as it has all its parts that are or can be *coexistent at once*. Because to exist according to *all* its parts at *once* is to be *included* within certain limits, as any number how big soever is conteined under some certain species of Number, and therewithal conceived finite as the [*All*] also implyes. And therefore *successive Quantity* seems more capable of being infinite then *permanent Quantity*, because there may be still more parts coming on; whenas in Permanent Quantity all the parts are at once, and that term [*All*] includes an actual bounding of the whole. This I conceive is the full scope of the first difficult propounded.

To which I breifly answer first, That that *Immobile Extensum* distinct from matter, being really a substance Incorporeal, I do not conceive that the Term [Parts] in a Physical sense does properly belong thereto, every Incorporeal substance or spirit, according to my notion of things, being *Ens unum per se & non per aliud*, and therefore utterly indiscerpible into parts, it implying a contradiction, that this of the substance or Essence should divided from that, the entire substance being *Ens unum pers & non per aliud*. But understanding by parts onely Notional or Logical parts, which will consist with this Indiscerpibility, wee'll admit the phrase in this sense for more easy and distinct discourse sake, and also of *Totum* and *Omne* and whatever is kin to them. And the same caution I premise touching the word [Quantity] that we take it not in that crass Physical sense, such as belongs to matter and bodyes, but meerly in that notional and Logical sense, which is so general that it clashes not at all with the *sacrosanctity*, as I may so speak, of incorporeal substances. [. . .]

Now as for the second difficulty, it seems such to you from your missing my meaning in my bringing in that Instance of Wax drawn out an Ell long. And after reduced into the form of a Globe, suppose no bigger than of an ordinary Nutmeg: An heedless or Idiotick Spectator of this change may haply imagine the dimension of Longitude quite lost thereby, whenas there is not one Atom of the quantity thereof lost by this change of Site, no more than there is of the *substance* of the wax. But what seems lost in Longitude, it is compensated in Latitude and profundity. So say I of the contraction of a created Spirit, suppose from a spherical form, (for we must take some figure or other) of half a yard diameter, to a sphear of a quarter by the Retraction of it self into so much less an *Ubi* (eight times less than before) for as much as nothing of its substance is annihilated thereby, nothing of its dimensions is, but what seems to be lost in Longitude, Latitude, and profundity, is gained or compensated in *Essential Spissitude*, which is that fourth dimension I stand for, that it is in *Rerum Natura*. Which tho it is more particularly belonging to the contraction of one and the same spirit into it self, yet it is also truely found, when any two substances whatever adequately occupy the same *Ubi*.

C John Smith, *Of the Existence and Nature of God* (1660), Chapter 2 (*Select Discourses*, 132)

[132] Now thus as we conceive of God's *Eternity*, we may in a correspondent manner apprehend his *Omnipresence*; not so much by an Infinite Expanse or Extension of Essence, as by an unlimited power, as *Plotinus* hath fitly express'd it, ληπτέον δὲ καὶ ἄπειρον αὐτὸν οὐ τῷ ἀδιεξιτήτῳ ἢ τοῦ μεγέθους ἢ τοῦ ἀριθμοῦ, ἀλλὰ τῷ ἀπεριλήπτῳ τῆς δηνάμεως.[2] For as nothing can ever stray out of the bounds or get out of the reach of an Almighty Mind and Power; so when we barely think of *Mind* or *Power*, or any thing else most peculiar to the Divine Essence, we cannot find any of the Properties of *Quantity* mixing themselves with it: and as we cannot confine it in regard thereof to any one point of the Universe, so neither can we well conceive it extended through the whole, or excluded from any part of it. It is alwaies some *Material* Being that contends for *Space*: Bodily parts will not lodge together, and the more bulky they are, the more they justle for room one with another; as *Plotinus* tells us, τὰ μὲν ἐνταῦθα μεγάλα ἐν ὄγκῳ, τὰ δὲ ἐκεῖ ἐν δηνάμει,[3] Bodily Beings are great onely in bulk, but Divine Essences in virtue and power.

D Ralph Cudworth, *The True Intellectual System of the Universe* (1671/1678), Chapter 5 (pp. 778–780)

[778] But in the next place, it is further *Objected*; That What is neither *Great* nor *Little*, what possesses no *Space*, and hath no *Place* nor *Site* amongst Bodies, must therefore needs be an *Absolute Non-Entity*, for as much as *Magnitude* or *Extension*, are the very *Essence* of *Being* or *Entity*, as such; so that there can be neither *Substance* nor *Accident* Unextended. Now since whatsoever is *Extended*, is *Bodily*, there can therefore be no other *Substance* besides *Body*, nor any thing *Incorporeal*, otherwise then as that word may be taken, for a *Thin and Subtile Body*, in which Sense Fire was by some in *Aristotle*,[4] said to be, μάλιστα τῶν στοιχείων ἀσώματον, and ἀσωματώτατον; *The most Incorporeal of all the Elements*; and *Aristotle* himself useth the word in the same manner, [779] when he affirmeth, that all *Philosophers* did define the *Soul*, by Three things, *Motion*, *Sense*, and *Incorporiety*; several of those there mentioned by him, understanding the Soul to be no otherwise *Incorporeal*, than as σῶμα λεποτμερές, *A Thin and Subtle Body*. In answer to which Objection; we may remember that *Plato* in the passage before cited, declareth this to be but a *Vulgar Errour*, that whatsoever doth not take up *Space*, and is in no *Place*, is *Nothing*. He Intimateing the Original hereof, to have sprung, from men's adhering too much to those *Lower Faculties*, of *Sense* and *Imagination*, which are able to conceive Nothing, but what is *Corporeal*. And accordingly *Plotinus*[5]; ἡ μὲν γὰρ αἴσθησις, ᾗ προσέχοντες ἀπιστοῦμεν τοῖς λεγομένοις, λέγει ὅτι ὧδε καὶ ὧδε, ὁ δὲ λόγος τὸ ὧδε καὶ ὧδέ φησιν οὐκ ἐκταθεῖσαν ὧδε καὶ ὧδε γεγονέναι, ἀλλὰ τὸ ἐκταθὲν πᾶν αὐτοῦ μετειληφέναι ὄντος ἀδιαστάτου αὐτοῦ. *Sense indeed, which we attending to, disbelieve these things, tells us of Here and There; but Reason dictates, that Here and There, is so to be understood of the Deity, not as if it were Extendedly Here and There, but because every Extended thing, and the several Parts of the World, partake every where of that, being Indistant and Unextended.* To the same purpose *Porphyrius*,[6] δεῖ τοίνυν ἐν ταῖς σκέψεσι κατακρατοῦντας τῆς ἑκατέρου ἰδιότητος μὴ ἐπαλλάττειν τὰς φύσεις· μᾶλλον δὲ τὰ προσόντα τοῖς σώμασιν ἢ τοιαῦτα μὴ φαντάζεσθαι καὶ δοξάζειν περὶ τὸ ἀσώματον· οὐ γὰρ ἄν τὰ ἴδιά τις τοῦ καθαρῶς ἀσωμάτου προσγράψειε τοῖς σώμασι. τῶν μὲν γὰρ σωμάτων, ἐν συνηθείᾳ πᾶς· ἐκείνων δὲ μόλις ἐν γνώσει γίνεται. ἀορίστων περὶ αὐτά, [. . .] ἕως ἂν ὑπὸ φαντασίας κρατῆται, *We ought therefore, in our Disquisitions concerning Corporeal and Incorporeal Beings, to conserve the Property of each, and not to confound their Natures. But especially to take heed, that our Phancy and Imagination, do not so far impose upon our judgments, as to make us attribute to Incorporeals, what properly belongeth to Bodies only. For we are all accustomed to Bodies, but as for Incorporeals, scarcely any one reaches to*

the knowledge of them; men alwaies fluctuating about them and diffiding them, so long as they are held under the Power of their Imagination. Where afterwards he propoundeth a Form for this, How we should think of *Incorporeals*, so as not to *Confound* their *Natures* with *Corporeals*[7]; ἐν ἀπείροις μέρεσιν [. . .] τοῦ διαστατοῦ παρὸν ὅλον τὸ ἀδιάστατον, οὔτε μερισθὲν πάρεστι, τῷ μέρει διδὸν μέρος, οὔτε πληθυνθέν τῷ πλήθει παρέχον ἑαυτὸ πολλα πλασιασθέν· ἀλλ' ὅλον πᾶσί τε τοῖς μέρεσι τοῦ ὀγκωμένου, ἑνί τε ἑκάστῳ τοῦ πλήθους, [. . .] ἀμερῶς καὶ ἀπληθύντως καὶ ὡς ἓν ἀριθμῷ· τὸ δὲ μερικῶς καὶ διῃρημένως ἀπολαύειν αὐτοῦ. *That the Indistant and Unextended Deity, is the Whole of it present in Infinite Parts of the Distant World, neither Divided, as applying part to part; nor yet Multiplied into many Wholes, according to the multiplicity of those things that partake thereof. But the whole of it (One and the same in Number) is present to all the Parts of the Bulkie World, and to every one of those many things in it, Undividedly and Unmultipliedly; that in the mean time partaking thereof Dividedly.* It was granted therefore by these *Ancients*, that this *Unextended and Indistant Nature, of Incorporeals, is* ἀφάνταστον, *a thing altogether Unimaginable*; and this was concluded by them, to be the only Reason, why so many have pronounced it to be *Impossible,* because they attended only to *Sense* and *Imagination*, and made them the only *Measure* of *Things* and *Truth*; it having been accordingly maintained by divers of them, (as *Porphyrius* tells us)[8] that *Imagination* and *Intellection*, are [780] but Two different Names, for one and the same thing; ὀνόματος διαφορᾶς προστεθείσης τῇ τοῦ νοῦ ὑποστάσει καὶ τῆς φαντασίας· ἡ γὰρ ἐν λογικῷ ζῴῳ φαντασία δέδοκτο αὐτοῖς νόησις, *There is a difference of Names only and no more, betwixt Mind and Phancy. Phancy and Imagination in Rational Animals, seeming to be the same thing with Intellection.* But there are many things, which no man can have any *Phantasm* or *Imagination* of, and yet are they notwithstanding by all Unquestionably acknowledged for *Entities* or *Realities*; from whence it is plain, that we must have some other *Faculties* in us, which Extend beyond *Phansie* and *Imagination*. Reason indeed dictates, that whatsoever can either *Do or Suffer* any thing, must therefore be undoubtedly *Something:* but that whatsoever is *Unextended*, and hath no *Distant Parts*, one without another, must therefore needs be *Nothing*, is no *Common Notion*, but the *Spurious Suggestion* of *Imagination* only, and a *Vulgar Errour*. There need to be no fear at all, Lest a Being *Infinitely Wise* and *Powerful*, which Acts upon the whole world; and all the Parts thereof, in Framing and Governing the same, should prove a *Non-Entity,* meerly for want of *Bulk* and *Extension*, or because it *Swells* not out into *Space* and *Distance* as Bodies do, therefore Vanish into *Nothing.* Nor does *Active Force* and *Power*, as such, depend upon *Bulk* and *Extension*, because then, whatsoever had the greater *Bulk*, would have the greater *Activity.* There are therefore, *Two kinds* of *Substances* in the Universe, the *First Corporeal*, which are Nothing but ὄγκοι, *Bulks,* or *Tumours*, devoid of all *Self-Active Power;* the *Second Incorporeal*, which are ἄογκοι, *Substantial Powers, Vigours,* and *Activities*; which though they act upon *Bulk* and *Extension*, yet are themselves *Unbulkie* and devoid of *Quantity* and *Dimensions*; however they have a certain βάθος in them in another *sense*, an *Essential Profundity*, according to this of *Simplicius*,[9] Μεριστὴ μὲν ἁπλῶς ἡ σωματικὴ οὐσία πᾶσα, ἄλλων ἀλλαχοῦ τῶν μορίων κειμένων· ἀμέριστος δὲ εἰλικρινῶς ἡ νοερά, πολὺ δὲ βάθος ἔχουσα, *All Corporeal Substance, is simply Divisible, some Parts of it being here and some there, but Intellectual Substance, is Indivisible, and without Dimensions, though it hath much of Depth ond Profundity in it in another Sense.* But that there is some thing ἀφαντάστον *Unimaginable* even in Body it self, is evident, whether you will suppose it to be *Infinitely Divisible* or Not, as you must of necessity suppose, one or other of these. And that we ought not always to pronounce of *Corporeal Things* themselves, according to *Imagination*, is manifest from hence; because though *Astronomical Reasons*, assure us, that the Sun is really more than a *Hundred Times* bigger than the whole Earth, yet can we not possibly for all that, *Imagine* the *Sun* of such a Bigness, nor indeed the *Earth* it self; half so big as we know it to be. The reason whereof is, partly because we never had a Sense or Sight of any such Vast Bigness at once, as that of either of them, and partly because our Sense always representing the Sun to us, but ὡς πεδιαῖον, *as of a Foot Diameter*, and we being accustomed always to *Imagine* the same according to the Appearance of Sense, are not able to frame any *Imagination* of it, as very much Bigger. Wherefore if *Imagination* be not to be *Trusted*, nor made the *Criterion* or *Measure* of *Truth*, as to *Sensible* things themselves, much less ought it to be, as to *Things Insensible*.

E Ralph Cudworth, *The True Intellectual System of the Universe* (1671/1678), Chapter 5 (pp. 769–770)

[769] But in the Management of this *Cause*, there hath been some Disagreement amongst the *Atheists* themselves. For First, the *Democriticks* and *Epicureans*, though consenting with all the other *Atheists* in this, That whatsoever was *Unextended*, and *devoid of Magnitude*, was therefore *Nothing*; (so that there could neither be, any *Substance*, nor *Accident* or *Mode* of any *Substance, Unextended*) did notwithstanding distinguish concerning a *Double Nature*. First, That which is so *Extended*, as to be *Impenetrable*, and *Tangible*, or *Resist the Touch*, which is *Body*. And Secondly, That which is Extended also, but *Penetrably* and *Intangibly*, which is *Space* or *Vacuum:* a *Nature*, according to them, really distinct from *Body*, and the only *Incorporeal Thing* that is. Now since this *Space* which is the only *Incorporeal*, can neither *Do nor Suffer* any thing, but only give *Place* or *Room* to Bodies to Subsist in, or Pass thorough, therefore can there not be any *Active, Understanding, Incorporeal* Deity. This is the *Argumentation* of the *Democritick Atheists*.

To which we Reply; That if *Space* be indeed a *Nature* distinct from *Body*, and a Thing *Really Incorporeal*, as they pretend, then will it undeniably follow from this very Principle of theirs, that there must be *Incorporeal Substance*; and (this *Space* being supposed by them also to be *Infinite*) an *Infinite Incorporeal Deity*. Because if Space be not the *Extension* of *Body*, nor an *Affection* thereof; then must it of necessity be, either an *Accident Existing* alone by it self, without a *Substance*, which is Impossible; or else the *Extension* or *Affection*, of some other *Incorporeal Substance*, that is *Infinite*. But here will *Gassendus* step in,[10] to help out his good Friends, the *Democriticks* and *Epicureans*, at a dead Lift; and undertake to maintain, that though *Space* be indeed an *Incorporeal Thing*, yet it would neither follow of necessity from thence, that it is an *Incorporeal Substance* or *Affection* thereof, nor yet that it is an *Accident*, Existing alone by it self without a *Substance*; because this *Space* is really, neither *Accident*, nor *Substance*, but a certain *Middle Nature or Essence* betwixt both. To which Subterfuge of his, that we may not quarrel about Words, we shall make this Reply; That unquestionably, Whatsoever *Is*, or hath any kind of *Entity*, doth either Subsist by it self, or else is an *Attribute, Affection*, or *Mode*, of something that doth Subsist by it self. For It is Certain, That there can be no *Mode, Accident*, or *Affection*, of Nothing; and consequently, that Nothing cannot be *Extended*, nor *Mensurable*. But if Space be neither the *Extension* of *Body*, nor yet of *Substance Incorporeal*, then must it of necessity be, the *Extension of Nothing*, and the *Affection of Nothing*; and Nothing must be *Mensurable* by *Yards* and *Poles*. We conclude therefore, That from this very *Hypothesis* of the *Democritick* and *Epicurean Atheists*, that *Space* is a *Nature* distinct from *Body* and *Positively Infinite*, it follows undeniably, that there must be [770] some *Incorporeal Substance*, whose *Affection* its *Extension* is; and because there can be nothing *Infinite*, but only the *Deity*, that it is the *Infinite Extension* of an *Incorporeal Deity*; just as some *Learned Theists* and *Incorporealists* have asserted. And thus is the *Argument* of these *Democritick* and *Epicurean Atheists*, against an *Incorporeal Deity*, abundantly confuted; we having made it manifest, that from that very *Principle* of their own, by which they would disprove the same, it is against themselves *Demonstrable*.

Notes

1 A legendary Greek painter living in the 4th century BC. His skill was reputed to be so extraordinary that no one dared complete his unfinished painting of Aphrodite of Kos after his death. See Pliny the Elder, *Natural History* 35.36.79–97.

2 Plotinus, *Enneads* VI.9.6.11–13.
3 Plotinus, *Enneads* II.9.17.11–12.
4 Aristotle, *De anima* 405a6–7.
5 P. 656 [P. Perna (ed.), *Plotini Opera Omnia, cum latina Marsilii Ficini interpretatione et commentatione*, 656 = Plotinus, *Ennead* VI 4.13.2–6].
6 ἈΦ. p. 242 [L. Holstenius (ed.), *Porphyrii philosophi pythagorici . . . Sententiae ad intelligibilia ducentes . . .* , 242 = Porphyry, *Sententia* 33.42–49 (ed. Lamberz, 1975)].
7 Porphyry, *Sententia* 33.22–27 (ed. Lamberz, 1975).
8 P. 224. ἈΦ. [L. Holstenius (ed.), *Porphyrii philosophi pythagorici . . . Sententiae ad intelligibilia ducentes . . .* , 224 = Porphyry, *Sententia* 43.36–38 (ed. Lamberz, 1975)].
9 *In Ar. Phys.* p. 3 [<Simplicius>, *In Aristotelis libros de anima commentaria*, 11.26–27 (ed. Hayduck)].
10 On Gassendi's conception of space as *neither* corporeal, *nor* spiritual, see Gassendi, *Syntagma philosophiae Epicuri*, Lyon: Guillaume Barbier, 1649, sect. I. book II, chap. 1.

Chapter 17

Nature

A Ralph Cudworth, *The True Intellectual System of the Universe,* Chapter 5 (pp. 857–863)

It is true indeed, that the Νοητὸν, or Thing Understood, is in order of Nature before the Intellection and Conception of it, and from hence was it, that the Pythagoreans and Platonists concluded, that Νοῦς, Mind or Intellect, was not the very First and Highest Thing in the Scale of the Universe, but that there was another Divine Hypostasis, in order of Nature before it, called by them Ἕν and Τ'ἀγατὸν, One and The Good, as the Νοητὸν or Intelligible thereof. But as those Three Archical Hypostases of the Platonists and Pythagoreans, are all of them Really but One Θεῖον or Divinity: And the First of those Three, (Superiour to that which is properly called by them, Mind or Intellect) is not supposed therefore to be Ignorant of it self: So is the First Mind or Understanding, no other, than that of a Perfect Being, Infinitely Good, Fecund, and Powerful, and vertually Containing all things; comprehending it self and the Extent of its own Goodness, Fecundity, Vertue, and Power; that is, all Possibilities of things, their Relations to one another, and Verities; a Mind before Sense, and Sensible Things. An Omnipotent Understanding Being, which is it self its own Intelligible, is the First Original of all things. Again, that there must of necessity be some other Substance besides Body or Matter, and which in the Scale of Nature is Superiour to it, is evident from hence, because otherwise, there could be no Motion at all therein, no Body being ever able to move it self. There must be something Self-Active and Hylarchical, something that can Act both from it self, and upon Matter, as having a Natural Imperium, or Command over it. Cogitation is in order of Nature, before Local Motion. Life and Understanding, Soul and Mind, are no Syllables or Complexions of things, Secundary and Derivative, which might therefore be made out of things devoid of Life and Understanding; but Simple, Primitive, and Uncompounded Natures: they are no Qualities or Accidental Modifications of Matter, but Substantial Things. For which Cause Souls or Minds can no more be Generated out of Matter, than Matter it Self, can be Generated out of Something else: and therefore are they both alike (in some sense) Principles, Naturally Ingenerable and Incorruptible; though both Matter, and all Imperfect Souls and Minds, were at first Created by one Perfect Omnipotent Understanding Being. Moreover Nothing can be more Evident than this, that Mind and Understanding hath a Higher Degree of Entity or Perfection in it, and is a Greater Reality in Nature, than meer Sensless Matter or Bulkie Extension. And Consequently the things which belong to Souls and Minds, to Rational and Intellectual Beings as such, must not have Less, but More Reality in them, than the things which belong to Inanimate Bodies. Wherefore the Differences of Just and Unjust, Honest and Dishonest, are greater Realities in Nature, than the Differences of Hard and Soft, Hot and Cold, Moist and Dry. He that does not perceive any Higher Degree of Perfection, in a Man, than in an Oyster, nay than in a Clod of Earth or Lump of Ice, in a Piece of Past, or Pye-Crust, hath not the Reason or Understanding of a Man in him. There is unquestionably, a Scale or Ladder of Nature, and Degrees of Perfection and Entity, one above another, as of Life, Sense, and Cogitation, above Dead, Sensless and Unthinking Matter; of Reason and Understanding above Sense, &c. And if the Sun be Nothing but a Mass of Fire, or Inanimate Subtle Matter Agitated, then hath the most Contemptible Animal, that can see the Sun, and hath Consciousness and Self enjoyment, a Higher Degree of Entity and Perfection in it, than that whole Fiery Globe; as also than the Materials, (Stone, Timber, Brick and Morter) of the most Stately Structure, or City. Notwithstanding which, the Sun in other regards, and as its vastly Extended Light and Heat, hath so great an Influence, upon the Good of the whole World, Plants and Animals; may be said to be a far more Noble and Useful thing in the Universe, than any one Particular Animal whatsoever. Wherefore there being plainly a Scale or Ladder of Entity; the Order of Things was unquestionably, in way of Descent, from Higher Perfection, Downward to Lower; it being as Impossible, for a Greater Perfection to be produced from a Lesser, as for Something to be Caused by Nothing. Neither are the Steps or Degrees of this Ladder, (either upward or downward) Infinite; but as the Foot, Bottom, or Lowest Round thereof, is Stupid and Sensless Matter, devoid of all Life and Understanding; so is the Head, Top, and Summity of it, a Perfect Omnipotent Being, Comprehending it self, and all Possibilities of things. A Perfect Understanding Being, is the Beginning and Head of the Scale of Entity; from whence things Gradually Descend downward; lower and lower, till they end in Sensless Matter. Νοῦς πάντων προγενέστατος,[1] Mind is the Oldest of all things, Senior to the Elements, and the whole Corporeal World; and likewise according to the same Ancient Theists, it is Κύριος κατὰ φύσιν,[2] by Nature Lord over all, or hath a Natural Imperium and Dominion over all; it being the most Hegemonical thing. And thus was it also affirmed by Anaxagoras, Νοῦς βασιλεὺς οὐρανοῦ τε καὶ γῆς, that Mind is the Soveraign King of Heaven and Earth.

B Ralph Cudworth, *The True Intellectual System of the Universe* Chapter 3, "Digression on Plastic Nature" (pp. 147–149)

2. For unless there be such a thing admitted as a Plastick Nature, that acts ἕνεκά του, *for the sake of something*, and *in order to Ends*, Regularly, Artificially and Methodically, it seems that one or other of these Two Things must be concluded, That Either in the Efformation and Organization of the Bodies of Animals, as well as the other Phenomena, every thing comes to pass *Fortuitously*, and happens to be as it is, without the Guidance and Direction of any *Mind* or *Understanding*; Or else, that God himself doth all *Immediately*, and as it were with his own Hands, Form the Body of every Gnat and Fly, Insect and Mite, as of other Animals in Generations, all whose Members have so much of Contrivance in them, that *Galen* professed he could never enough admire that Artifice which was in the Leg of a Fly, (and yet he would have admired the Wisdom of Nature more, had he been but acquainted with the Use of Microscopes.) I say, upon supposition of no *Plastick Nature*, one or other of these Two things must be concluded; because it is not conceived by any, that the things of Nature are all thus administred, with such exact Regularity and Constancy every where, merely by the Wisdom, Providence and Efficiency, of those Inferior Spirits, *Dæmons* or Angels. As also, though it be true that the Works of Nature are dispensed by a *Divine Law* and *Command*, yet this is not to be understood in a *Vulgar Sence*, as if they were all effected by the mere Force of a *Verbal Law* or *Outward Command*, because Inanimate things are not *Commandable* nor *Governable* by such a *Law*; and therefore besides the Divine Will and Pleasure, there must needs be some other Immediate *Agent* and *Executioner* provided, for the producing of every Effect; since not so much as a Stone or other Heavy Body, could at any time fall downward, merely by the Force of a *Verbal Law*, without any other *Efficient Cause*; but either God himself must immediately impel it, or else there must be some other subordinate Cause in Nature for that Motion. Wherefore the *Divine Law* and *Command*, by which the things of Nature are

administred, must be conceived to be the Real Appointment of some *Energetick*, *Effectual* and *Operative Cause* for the Production of every Effect.

3. Now to assert the Former of these Two things, that all the Effects of Nature come to pass by *Material* and *Mechanical Necessity*, or the mere *Fortuitous Motion of Matter*, without any Guidance or Direction, is a thing no less Irrational than it is Impious and Atheistical. Not only because it is utterly Unconceivable and Impossible, that such Infinite Regularity and Artificialness, as is every where throughout the whole World, should constantly result out of the *Fortuitous Motion of Matter*, but also because there are many such Particular *Phænomena* in Nature, as do plainly transcend the *Powers of Mechanism*, of which therefore no Sufficient Mechanical Reasons can be devised, as the *Motion of Respiration* in Animals; as there are also other *Phænomena* that are perfectly Cross to the *Laws of Mechanism*; as for Example, that of the *Distant Poles* of the *Æquator* and *Ecliptick*, which we shall insist upon afterward. Of both which kinds, there have been other Instances proposed, by my Learned Friend Dr. *More* in his *Enchiridion Metaphysicum*,[3] and very ingeniously improved by him to this very purpose, namely to Evince that there is something in Nature besides Mechanism, and consequently Substance Incorporeal.

Moreover those Theists, who Philosophize after this manner, by resolving all the Corporeal *Phænomena* into *Fortuitous Mechanism*, or the *Necessary and Unguided Motion of Matter*, make God to be nothing else in the World, but an *Idle Spectator* of the Various Results of the *Fortuitous* and *Necessary Motions* of Bodies; and render his Wisdom altogether Useless and Insignificant, as being a thing wholly Inclosed and shut up within his own breast, and not at all acting abroad upon any thing without him.

Furthermore all such *Mechanists* as these, whether *Theists* or *Atheists*, do, according to that Judicious Censure passed by *Aristotle* long since upon *Democritus*, but substitute as it were χεῖρα ξυλίνην τέκτονος, *a Carpenters or Artificers Wooden Hand, moved by Strings and Wires, in stead of a Living Hand.*[4] They make a kind of Dead and Wooden World, as it were a Carved Statue, that hath nothing neither *Vital* nor *Magical* at all in it. Whereas to those who are Considerative, it will plainly appear, that there is a *Mixture* of *Life* or *Plastick Nature* together with *Mechanism*, which runs through the whole Corporeal Universe.

And whereas it is pretended, not only that all *Corporeal Phænomena* may be sufficiently salved *Mechanically*, without any *Final*, *Intending* and *Directive Causality*, but also that all other Reasons of things in Nature, besides the *Material* and *Mechanical*, are altogether *Unphilosophical*, the same *Aristotle* ingeniously exposes the Ridiculousness of this Pretence after this manner; telling us, That it is just as if a Carpenter, Joyner or Carver should give this accompt, as the only Satisfactory, of any Artificial Fabrick or Piece of Carved Imagery, ὅτι ἐμπεσόντος τοῦ ὀργάνου τὸ μὲν κοῖλον ἐγίνετο, τό δὲ ἐπίπεδον,[5] *that because the Instruments, Axes and Hatchets, Plains and Chissels, happened to fall so and so upon the Timber, cutting it here and there, that therefore it was hollow in one place, and plain in another, and the like, and by that means the whole came to be of such a Form.*[6] For is it not altogether as Absurd and Ridiculous, for men to undertake to give an accompt of the Formation and Organization of the Bodies of Animals, by mere Fortuitous Mechanism, without any *Final* or *Intending Causality*, as why there was an Heart here and Brains there, and why the Heart had so many and such different Valves in the Entrance and Outlet of its Ventricles, and why all the other Organick Parts, Veins and Arteries, Nerves and Muscles, Bones and Cartilages, with the Joints and Members, were of such a Form? Because forsooth, the Fluid Matter of the Seed happened to move so and so, in several places, and thereby to cause all those Differences, which are also divers in different Animals; all being the Necessary Result of a certain Quantity of Motion at first indifferently impressed, upon the small Particles of the Matter of this Universe turned round in a *Vortex*. But as the same *Aristotle* adds, no Carpenter or Artificer is so simple, as to give such an Accompt as this, and think it satisfactory, but he will rather declare, that himself directed the Motion of the Instruments, after such a manner, and in order to such Ends[7]: βέλτιον ὁ τέκτων, οὐ γὰρ ἱκανὸν ἔσται αὐτῷ, τὸ τοσοῦτον εἰπεῖν, ὅτι ἐμπεσόντος τοῦ ὀργάνου, &c. ἀλλὰ διότι τὴν πληγὴν ἐποιήσατο τοιαύτην, καὶ τίνος ἕνεκα, ἐρεῖ τὴν αἰτίαν, ὅπως τοιόνδε ἢ τοιονδήποτε τὴν μορφήν γένηται. *A Carpenter would give a better account than so, for he would not think it sufficient to say, that the Fabrick came to be of such a form, because the Instruments happened to fall so and so, but he will tell you that it was because himself made such strokes, and that he directed the Instruments and determined their motion after such a manner, to this End that he might make the Whole a Fabrick fit and useful for such purposes.* And this is to assign the *Final Cause*. And certainly there is scarcely any man in his Wits, that will not acknowledge the Reason of the different *Valves* in the Heart, from the apparent Usefulness of them, according to those particular Structures of theirs, to be more Satisfactory, than any which can be brought from mere Fortuitous Mechanism, or the Unguided Motion of the Seminal Matter.

C *Opera omnia*, II/1,9–11. Translation: Christian Hengstermann

Sect. 7: "As it happens in particular animals". I do not want this to be understood in such a way as though God and the world, taken together, were some large animal, although, besides some Platonists and Marcus Aurelius, Aristotle himself, in his *Metaphysics*, likewise makes God a kind of animal: φαμὲν δὴ τὸν θεὸν εἶναι ζῷον ἀΐδιον ἄριστον, ὥστε ζωὴ καὶ αἰὼν συνεχὴς καὶ ἀΐδιος ὑπάρχει τῷ θεῷ· τοῦτο γὰρ ὁ θεός.[8] It is even a bit more absurd, however, to make up an animal without a soul and a body. We must look, therefore, whether he does not make the heaven itself God's body in the following words from his *On the Heavens*: Ἕκαστόν ἐστιν, ὧν ἐστιν ἔργον, ἕνεκα τοῦ ἔργου. Θεοῦ δ᾽ ἐνέργεια ἀθανασία· τοῦτο δ᾽ ἐστὶ ζωὴ ἀΐδιος. ὥστ᾽ ἀνάγκη τῷ θεῷ κίνησιν ἀΐδιον ὑπάρχειν. Ἐπεὶ δ᾽ ὁ οὐρανὸς τοιοῦτος (σῶμα γάρ τι θεῖον), διὰ τοῦτο ἔχει τὸ ἐγκύκλιον σῶμα, ὃ φύσει κινεῖται κύκλῳ ἀεί.[9] However, in his *On the World*, we learn about the highest heaven that God's power reaches to the lower spheres and even the earth itself, while God himself ἐπὶ τῆς ἀνωτάτω χώρας ἱδρῦσθαι.[10] I, for one, think we should neither make God an animal nor place him in the highest heaven so that he sits there καθαρὸς ἐν καθαρῷ χώρῳ.[11] Instead, I believe that the holiness and sublimity rather consist in the fact that he does not move worldly matter without intermediate and secondary causes, but by means of the so-called spirit of nature, as I have proved in great detail in the *Enchiridium metaphysicum*.

"With some higher and more sublime magic", etc. By "magic" I understand a certain power of life or vital motion, insofar as it is opposed to mechanical and corporeal motion in which one body is sometimes pushed and driven forward by another. However, of such a kind is the vital or magical motion proceeding from the spirit of nature to worldly matter. Hence, it is not surprising at all that it is called ὁ μέγας γόης by Plotinus.[12] However, that magic by which the spirit of nature both is acted on and itself acts on the matter is rather crass and vast, even though it does not unite itself to matter in such a fashion when moving it that it could not at the same time free itself of it. In this regard, it comes closer to Anaxagoras' νοῦς ἀμιγής,[13] being a transcription of the latter, as it were, that contains the laws of the world *vitally*, albeit not *intellectually*. Thus, unmixed with matter and not subject to locomotion itself, it moves matter from one place to another by vital motion, both uniting itself with and freeing itself from matter, as it is required. οὕτω γὰρ μόνως κινοίη ἀκίνητος ὢν καὶ κρατοίη ἀμιγὴς ὤν, says Anaxagoras about the divine mind of which the spirit of nature is nothing but the ectype and shadow, insofar as it contains the laws of the universe in a certain *vital* or *plastic* fashion.[14] However, a magic more sublime and more exalted, however, attaches to pure divinity, whose flower and highest point is called τ᾽ἀγαθόν among the Platonists. The latter is the metaphysical τὸ πρῶτον κινοῦν ἀκίνητον, just as the spirit of nature is the physical one. Aristotle himself, too, seems to point to this in his *Metaphysics*: Ἔστι τι ὃ οὐ κινούμενον κινεῖ, ἀΐδιον καὶ οὐσία καὶ ἐνέργεια οὖσα.[15] And a little later: *Ἀρχὴ γὰρ ἡ νόησις. Νοῦς γὰρ ὑπὸ τοῦ νοητοῦ κινεῖται. Νοητὸν γὰρ ἡ ἑτέρα συστοιχία καθ' αὑτήν· καὶ ταύτης ἡ οὐσία πρώτη, καὶ ταύτης ἡ ἁπλῶς καὶ κατ' ἐνέργειαν. Ἔστι γὰρ τὸ ἓν καὶ τὸ ἁπλοῦν οὐ τὸ αὐτό· τὸ μὲν γὰρ ἓν μέτρον σημαίνει, τὸ δὲ ἁπλοῦν πῶς ἔχον αὐτό. Ἀλλὰ μὴν καὶ τὸ καλὸν καὶ τὸ δι' αὑτὸ αἱρετόν, ἐν τῇ αὐτῇ συστοιχίᾳ, καὶ ἔστιν ἄριστον ἀεὶ ἢ ἀνάλογον, τὸ πρῶτον.*[16] What else should this be but a somewhat obscure hint at what the Platonists are wont to call *τὸ ἕν* and *τ'ἀγαθόν*, the supreme goodness of the divine numen? He calls the latter the *στρατηγός* or highest army leader in ch. 10,[17] where he also introduces Anaxagoras who posits as the first mover: *Ἀναξαγόρας δὲ ὡς κινοῦν τὸ ἀγαθὸν ἀρχήν· ὁ γὰρ νοῦς κινεῖ. ἀλλὰ κινεῖ ἕνεκά τινος, ὥστε ἕτερον.*[18] According to Aristotle, therefore, the *τ'ἀγαθόν* or *τὸ ἕν* is the first mover in an absolute sense or the principal *τὸ πρῶτον κινοῦν ἀκίνητον*, since it moves the divine intellect as the highest army leader. Not only is it the *τὸ ἁπλοῦν*, even though it is such indeed, being the most simple thing in itself, but also *τὸ ἕν*, because it is the *τὸ μέτρον*, the measure which gives measure to all things and according to which all things are ordered. *Πρὸς γὰρ ἓν ἅπαντα συντέτακται.*[19] These are the very words of Aristotle himself who has revealed himself as a splendid pupil of Plato in these places. Meanwhile, it is sufficiently clear from what has been said how sublime and exalted this divine magic is.

Sect. 13: "Rational ideas of all things proceed from such a benign and wise principle and must, therefore, be derived from their 'ends' in respect of which they are also called 'good'", etc. No-one can express this more clearly than Aristotle himself does rather succinctly in *The Generation of Animals* I 1: *ὅ τε γὰρ λόγος καὶ τὸ οὗ ἕνεκα ὡς τέλος, ταὐτόν*[20] and more fully in II 1: *Βελτίων γὰρ καὶ θεοτέρα τὴν φύσιν ἐστὶν ἡ αἰτία ἡ κινοῦσα πρῶτον, ᾗ ὁ λόγος ὑπάρχει καὶ τὸ εἶδος τῆς ὕλης.*[21] However, that which first moves is the aim and end of the whole *ἀποτέλεσμα*,[22] as it is conceived in a certain intellectual principle, that is to say, God's intellect, as can be seen very well from what he says earlier in the same chapter: *Ὡς γὰρ διὰ τὸ βέλτιον καὶ τὴν αἰτίαν τὴν ἕνεκά τινος ἄνωθεν ἀπὸ τοῦ παντὸς ἔχει τὴν ἀρχήν.*[23] And a little later: *τὸ γὰρ καλὸν καὶ τὸ θεῖον, αἴτιον ἀεὶ κατὰ τὴν αὑτοῦ φύσιν, τοῦ βελτίονος ἐν τοῖς ἐνδεχομένοις.*[24] This accords nicely with what he says towards the end of the chapter: *Ἡ γὰρ τέχνη, ἀρχὴ καὶ τὸ εἶδος τοῦ γινομένου, ἀλλ' ἐν ἑτέρῳ, ἡ γὰρ τῆς φύσεως κίνησις ἐν αὐτῷ, ἀφ' ἑτέρας οὖσα φύσεως τῆς ἐχούσης τὸ εἶδος ἐνεργείᾳ.*[25] This should be best referred to the divine nature which possesses the ideas of all natural things in intellectual actuality. By contrast, the spirit of nature possesses them only in vital potentiality, although the latter is awakened as matter is prepared accordingly. This is that Platonic and Aristotelian philosophy of the generation of natural things. In comparison to it, the modern phantasies of the mechanical philosophers, reeking of nothing but stupid and putrid atheism, strike me as completely vile.

Notes

1 Aristotle, *De anima* I 5, 410b14.
2 Plato, *Philebus*, 28c7–8.
3 Henry More, *Enchiridion Metaphysicum, sive de Rebus incorporeis Succincta & luculenta Dissertatio*, London: E. Flesher, 1671, caps. VI–VII, 42–64. See also the translation by Alexander Jacob of the second edition (1679) of the *Enchiridion Metaphysicum*, *Henry More's Manual of Metaphysics. A Translation of the Enchiridum Metaphysicum (1679)*, Zürich/New York: Georg Olms, 1995.
4 *De part. An.* l. 1. cap. 1 [Cudworth's Greek is χεῖρα ξυλίνην τέκτονος. But Aristotle's sentence (*Parts of Animals* I 1.640b35–641a1) is very different from the translation given here (trans. A. L. Peck):"Ἔτι δ' ἀδύνατον εἶναι **χεῖρα** ὁπωσοῦν διακειμένην, οἷον χαλκῆν ἢ **ξυλίνην**, πλὴν ὁμωνύμως, ὥσπερ τὸν γεγραμμένον ἰατρόν ("so also no hand of bronze or wood or constituted in any but the appropriate way can possibly be a hand in more than name")].
5 Cudworth gives the Greek only for the first part of the passage ("that because ... here and there"). Here is the rest: ἀλλὰ διότι τὴν πληγὴν ἐποιήσατο τοιαύτην, καὶ τίνος ἕνεκα, ἐρεῖ τὴν αἰτίαν, ὅπως τοιόνδε ἢ τοιόνδε ποτὲ τὴν μορφὴν γένηται.
6 Aristotle, *Parts of Animals* I 1.641a11–12.

7 *De Part. An.* l. 1. c. 1 [*Parts of Animals* I 1.641a11–12].
8 *Metaph.* XII, 1072b28–30: "We say therefore that God is an animal eternal, most good, so that life and duration continuous and eternal belong to God; for this *is* God." Translation: II p. 1695 Ross (modified). The Greek word ζῷον, which Ross translates as "a living being", also means "animal", a meaning which is crucial to More's argument.
9 *Cael.* 286a8–12: "Everything that has a function exists for its function. The activity of God is immortality, i.e. eternal life. Therefore, the movement of God must be eternal. But such is the heaven, viz. a divine body, and for that reason to it is given the circular body whose nature it is to move always in a circle." Translation: I p. 472 STOCKS.
10 The quotation from Pseudo-Aristotle, mun. 398b7, is part of a lengthy comparison between God and the Persian king Xerxes. If the latter governs his empire without being visible, it *a fortiori* holds true for God that "it is more worthy of his dignity and more befitting that he should be enthroned in the highest region, and that his power, extending through the whole universe, should move the sun and moon and make the whole heaven revolve and be the cause of permanence to all that in on this earth." Translation: I p. 636 FORSTER.
11 According to the cosmology outlined *ibid.* 400a6, God, "himself pure", dwells not in the world, but in "a pure region" above. Translation: *ibid.* I p. 638.
12 In Ennead IV 4,40, Plotinus calls the animated universe "the primary wizard and enchanter" *(ὁ γόης ὁ πρῶτος καὶ φαρμακεὺς)*. Translation: ARMSTRONG, LCL 443, 261–263.
13 See n. 2 above.
14 According to Aristotle, phys. VII, 256a24–26, "Anaxagoras is right when he says that intellect is impassive and unmixed, since he makes it the principle of motion; for it could cause motion in this way only by being itself unmoved, and have control only be being unmixed." Translation: I. p. 429 HARDIE/GAYE (slightly modified). In a complex hermeneutical process, More cites the fragments of Anaxagoras preserved by Aristotle whom, following Ralph Cudworth, he views as a Neoplatonist in support of his own Platonist *prisca theologia*.
15 *Metaph.* XLL, 1072a25: "There is a mover which moves without being moved, being eternal, substance and actuality." Translation: II p. 1694 Ross.
16 More provides a densely metaphysical Latin rendering of the first part of the passage *ibid.*, 1072a30—b1, which poses severe textual and philosophical difficulties, in his *Scholia on the Letter to V.C.* (Op. Omn. II/1, 126): "For intellection is the beginning, but the intellect is moved by an intelligible object. However, one of the two orders is that which is intelligible by itself, and of such a kind is the first substance and it is such simply and actually." See also the substantive philosophical comments on this passage *ibid*. The second part of the excerpt quoted reads in Ross's (slightly-modified) translation (II p. 1694): "The one and the simple are not the same; for 'one' means measure, but 'simple' means that the thing itself has a certain nature. But the good, also, and that which is itself desirable are on this same side of the order; and the first in any order is always best, or analogous to the best."
17 The military comparison to which More refers here is to be found *ibid*. 1075a 11–15: "We must consider also in which of two ways the nature of the universe contains the good or the highest good, whether as something separate and by itself, or as the order of the parts. Probably in both ways, as an army does. For the good is found both in the order and in the leader, and more in the latter; for he does not depend on the order, but it depends on him." Translation: *ibid.* II 1699.
18 *Ibid.* 1075b8–9: "Anaxagoras makes the good a motive principle; for thought moves things, but moves them for the sake of something, which must be something other than it." Translation: *ibid.*, II p. 1700.
19 *Ibid.* 1075a18–19: "All things are ordered towards one thing". Our translation.
20 *Gen. animal.* 715a8–9: "For the definition and the 'for the sake of which' or end are identical." Our translation.
21 *Ibid.* 732a3–5: "The first moving cause, to which belong the definition and the form of matter, is better and more divine in its nature." Translation: I p. 1136 PLATT (modified).
22 The ἀποτέλεσμα is the being in the state of perfection reached at the end of its natural development.
23 *Gen. animal.* 731b22–24: "For the fact that they exist because of something better and of an end has something higher as its principle." Our translation.
24 *Ibid.* 731b25–26: "For that which is beautiful and divine is always, by virtue of its nature, the cause of the better in contingent beings." Our translation.
25 *Ibid.* 735a2–4: "For the art is the principle and form of that which is made, albeit in something else, whereas the movement of nature exists in it itself, issuing from another nature which possesses the form in actuality." Translation: I p. 1140 PLATT (modified).

Chapter 18

Body and Spirit

A Joseph Glanvill, "Against Confidence in Philosophy and Matters of Speculation" (*Essays on Several Important Subjects in Philosophy and Religion*, Essay I, 10–14)

II. *BODIES:* I begin with our *Own;* which though we *see,* and *feel,* and have them *nearest* to us, yet their inward Constitution and Frame, is hitherto an undiscovered Region: And the saying of the Kingly Prophet, that *we are wonderfully made,* may well be understood of that *admiration,* that is the Daughter of Ignorance.

For, 1. There hath no good account been yet given, how our *Bodies* are *formed:* That there is *Art* in the contrivance of them, cannot be denied, even by those that are least beholden to Nature: and so elegant is their composure, that this very Consideration saved *Galen* from being an *Atheist:* And I cannot think that the branded *Epicurus, Lucretius* and their Fellows were in earnest, when they resolv'd this Composition into a *fortuitous range of Atoms:* 'Twere much less absurd to suppose, or say, that a Watch, or other curious *Automaton,* did perform divers *exact* and *regular* Motions, by *chance;* than 'tis to affirm, or think, that this admirable *Engine,* an *Humane Body,* which hath so many Parts, and Motions, that *orderly* cooperate for the good of the whole, was framed without the Art of some knowing Agent: But who the skilful, particular *Archeus* should be; and by *what* Instruments, and *Art* this Fabrick is erected, is still unknown. That God hath *made us,* and *fashion'd* our Bodies in *the nethermost parts of the Earth,* is undoubted; But he is the *first* and *universal* Cause, who transacts things in Nature by *secondary* Agents, and not by his own *immediate hand:* (The supposal of *this* would destroy *all Philosophy,* and enquiry after Causes) So that *He* is still *supposed;* but the Query is of the *next,* and *particular Agent,* that forms the Body in so exquisite a manner; a Question that hath not yet been answered. Indeed by some 'tis thought enough to say, That it is done by the *Plastick Faculty;* and by others 'tis believ'd that the *Soul* is that that forms it. For the *Plastick Faculty,* 'tis a *big word,* but it conveys nothing to the Mind: For it signifies but *this,* that the Body is *formed* by a *formative Power;* that is, 'tis *done,* by a *power of doing it.* But the doubt remains still, what the *Agent* is that hath *this power?* The other Opinion of the *Platonists,* hath two Branches: some will have it to be the particular Soul, that fashions its own Body; others suppose it to be the general Soul of the World: If the former be true, By what *knowledg* doth it do it? and *how?* The *means,* and *manner* are still *occult,* though that were granted. And for the *other* way, by a *general Soul;* That is an *obscure* Principle, of which we can know but little; and how that acts (if we allow such a being) whether *by knowledg,* or *without,* the Assertors of it may find difficulty to determine. The former makes it little less than *God* himself; and the *latter* brings us back to *Chance,* or a *Plastick Faculty.* There remains now but one account more, and that is the *Mechanical; viz.* That it is done by *meer Matter* moved after *such,* or *such* a manner. Be that so: It will yet be said, that *Matter* cannot move *it self;* the question is still of the *Mover;* The Motions are *orderly,* and *regular;* Query, *Who guides? Blind Matter* may produce an elegant effect for once, by a great Chance; as the Painter accidentally gave the Grace to his Picture, by throwing his Pencil in rage, and disorder upon it; But then *constant* Uniformities, and Determinations to a *kind,* can be *no Results* of *unguided Motions.* There is indeed a *Mechanical Hypothesis* to this purpose; That the Bodies of *Animals* and *Vegitables* are formed out of *such* particles of Matter, as by reason of their Figures will not lie together, but in the order that is necessary to make *such* a Body; and in *that* they naturally concur, and rest; which seems to be confirm'd by the *artificial Resurrection* of *Plants,* of which *Chymists* speak, and by the regular Figures of Salts, and *Minerals;* the *hexagonal* of *Chrystal,* the *Hemi-spherical* of the *Fairy-Stone,* and divers such like. And there is an experiment mentioned by approved Authors, that looks the same way; It is, That after a decoction of Herbs in a frosty Night, the shape of the Plants will appear under the Ice in the Morning: which Images are supposed to be made by the congregated *Effluvia* of the Plants themselves, which loosly wandring up and down in the Water, at last settle in their natural place and order, and so make up an appearance of the Herbs from whence they were emitted. This account I confess hath something ingenious in it; But it is no solution of the Doubt. For how those *heterogenous* Atoms should hit into their proper places, in the midst of such various and tumultuary Motions, will still remain a question: Let the *aptness* of their *Figures* be granted, we shall be yet to seek for something to *guide* their *Motions:* And let their *natural Motion* be what it will, *gravity* or *levity, direct* or *oblique,* we cannot conceive how *that* should carry them into every particular place where they are to lie; especially considering they must needs be sometimes diverted from their course by the occursion of many other Particles. And as for the *Regular Figures* of many *inaminate* Bodies, that consideration doth but *multiply* the doubt.

B Jacob, More's *Manual of Metaphysics,* 117–119. 123–124

2. The definition of a body in general and such a clear explanation of it that even those who complain of the obscurity of a spirt cannot but confess that they understand it perfectly.

For the rest who despair so much of all knowledge of the true nature of a spirit I would urge that they exert their mind in recognizing and understanding more deeply the nature of body in general, and that they tell me frankly whether they cannot acknowledge this to be the perspicuous and clear definition of it, namely, that body is a material substance devoid in itself of all perception and life, and indeed all motion, or thus, that body is a material substance coalescing into one thing by an alien life, and participating in life and motion from it. I do not doubt but that they will promptly reply that they sufficiently clearly and perfectly understand this as regards those terms themselves, and will not doubt of the truth, unless we deprive body of all motion by itself and equally union and life and perception. That indeed it is a substance, that is, a being subsisting by itself, not a mode of any thing, they cannot not admit willingly. That, further, it is a material substance, that is, composed of physical monads, or at least the most minute particles of matter into which it is divisible, and on account of their ἀντιτυπίαν impenetrable by any other body, so that the essential and positive differentia of body is that it is ἀντίτυπον, or impenetrable, and physically divisible into parts. The fact that it is extended, however, immediately belongs to it insofar as it is a being. There is certainly no reason why they should doubt of the remaining differentia since we have so solidly proved above that matter is endowed with no perception, no life, and no motion from its own nature or from itself. And besides, it is necessary to remember that we are not dealing here with the existence of things but with their intelligible notion and essence.

3. The perfect definition of a spirit and a full explanation of its nature through all its grades.

Which, if it is so easily understood in the corporeal nature or in body, I do not see but that an equal ease of comprehension would be found in the species immediately opposite to body, namely spirit. Let us try, therefore, and define spirit, from the law of opposites, as An immaterial substance intrinsically endowed with life and the faculty of moving. This light and brief and noiselessly flowing definition includes the entire nature of spirit in general. Which, lest what is being said, on account of its lightness and brevity, escape the understanding, just as a spirit may escape sight, I shall add to it a little more copious explanation, that finally it may appear to all that this definition of spirit is not inferiour in clarity and perspicuity to the definition of body and that, by this method, as I have noted above Ch.2, a full and perfect conception and understanding of the nature of spirit is to be derived.

Come, therefore, let us discern through all the grades of the defined thing what precise and immediate properties each of them contains, whence finally the most distinct and perfect knowledge of the entire defined thing may emerge. We shall begin therefore from the very top, and first acknowledge that spirit is a being, and, from the fact that it is a being, is one, true, good, at some time, in some place, and extended. For that there are the affections of being as being I have sufficiently demonstrated above, and it is not necessary to repeat it here. However, being is either a substance or a mode or accident of a substance. That spirit indeed is not a mode or accident of a substance almost all declare with one voice, and we have sufficiently clearly demonstrated above that the matter is thus.

The second essential grade of spirit, therefore, is that it is a substance. From which is understood subsisting by itself, nor does it need any other thing in which it may inhere as in a subject, or whose mode or accident it is, in order to subsist or exist.

The third, indeed, and last, essential grade is that it is immaterial: According to which it immediately agrees with it that it be not only a single being, but single by itself, and not by any other thing, that is, although it, as being, extended, that, however, it be absolutely indivisible or indiscerpible into physical and real parts, and that, besides, it may penetrate matter and (what matter cannot do) pervade things of its own kind, that is spiritual substances. In which two essential attributes, (as is necessary in every perfect and legitimate distribution of a genus) it is fully and accurately contrary to its opposite species, namely, of body. As also in those immediate properties by which it is understood to have life intrinsically in itself and the faculty of moving. Which is true, at least in some sense, of all spirits altogether, since life is either vegetative, or sensitive, or intellectual, one of which, at least, every spiritual substance enjoys, as also the faculty of moving, so that every spirit either moves itself or matter, or both, or at least matter, mediately or immediately or, finally, in both ways. For, in this way all moveable things are moved by God.

4. That from the fact that the definition of a body is clear the definition of a spirit too is necessarily clear.

Therefore I dare to call here the judgement and conscience of any man who is not absolutely illiterate or of a very dull and obtuse mind, whether this notion or definition of a spirit in general be not equally as intelligible and clear, not equally clear and every way distinct as the idea or notion of a body or of any other thing which the human mind can contemplate in the entire universe. And if he cannot equally easily, or rather with the same effort, apprehend the nature of body and spirit, since both agree exactly in proximate genus. The differentia indeed illustrate each other mutually through mutual opposition, so that that it is impossible that some one understand what material substance is without understanding by that very fact what immaterial substance is, or what it is not to have life or motion from itself without readily perceiving what it is to have both in itself or to be able to communicate it to others.

9. *That extension as such does not include divisibility or impenetrability, or indivisibility or penetrability, but is indifferent to either two.*

And from hence is it that, from the fact that a thing is extended, it is immediately imagined that it has parts outside parts, and that a thing is not one by itself, but composed of the juxtaposition of parts. When the idea of extension considered precisely in itself includes no such thing, but only a triple διάστασιν or solid amplitude, that is, not only linear or superficial (if it be permissible to use those terms which properly refer to magnitude) but running out everywhere or towards any direction. This amplitude certainly, but nothing else, includes a bare and simple extension, not penetrability nor impenetrability, not divisibility nor certainly indivisibility, but is, considered in itself, altogether indifferent to either affections or properties, or, if you prefer, essential differentia, namely, divisibility and indivisibility, or penetrability and indivisibility, and can be designated to either two of them.

Wherefore, since we acknowledge some extension, namely material, to be so strongly and invincibly endowed with ἀντιτυπία that it necessarily and by an insuperable resistance repels and excludes every other matter approaching and attempting to penetrate it, nor does it permit it to enter at all, although this wonderful power is not at all contained in the idea of simple extension, but is altogether omitted, as not at all pertaining to it by itself and immediately, why can we not equally easily conceive that another extension, namely, immaterial, although extension in itself include no such thing, is so constituted that it cannot be divided by any other thing, either material or immaterial, into parts, but with an indissoluble, necessary and plainly essential link is so united to and coheres with itself everywhere that, although it may penetrate everything and be in turn penetrated by everything, nothing however can so insinuate itself into it that it disjoin some of its essence anywhere or perforate it or dig or scratches a hole in it? That is, that I may say it in one word, what is there that prevents that it may be some being one by itself and not by any other thing, although every being as being be extended, since extension does not include physical division in its precise notion but the mind itself infected with corporeal imagination falsely and unskillfully supposes it to be there.

C Henry More, *An Antidote against Atheism*, Book 3, Chapter 8, Sections 2–5 *(Collection of Several Philosophical Writings, 111–113)*

[111] 2. A certain Shoemaker in one of the chief Towns of *Silesia*, in the year 1591, *Septemb. 20*. On a Friday betimes in the morning, in the further parts of his house, where there was adjoining a little Garden, cut his own throat with his Shoemakers knife. The Family, to cover the foulness of the fact, and that no disgrace might come upon his widow, gave out that he died of an Apoplexie, declined all visits of friends and neighbours, in the mean time got him washed and laid linens so handsomely about him, that even they that saw him afterwards, as the Parson and some others, had not the least suspicion but that he did dye of that disease; and so he had honeft Burial, with a funeral Sermon and other circumstances becoming one of his rank and reputation. Six weeks had not past but so strong a rumour broke out that he died not of any disease, but had laid violent hands upon himself, that the Magistracy of the place could not but bring all those that had seen the corps to a strict examination. They shuffled off the matter as well as they could at first, with many fair Apologies in the behalf of the deceased, to remove all suspicion of so hainous an act: but it being pressed more home to their Conscience, at last they confessed he died a violent death, but desired their favor and clemency to his widow and children, who were in no fault; adding also, that it was Uncertain but that he might be slain by some external mishap, [112] or if by himself, in some irresistible fit of phrensie or madness.

Hereupon the Councel deliberate what is to be done. Which the Widow hearing, and fearing they might be determining something that would be harsh, and to the discredit of her Husband and her self, being also animated thereto by some busie-bodies, makes a great complaint against those that raised these reports of her Husband, and resolved to follow the Law upon them, earnestly contending that there was no reason upon mere rumours and idle defamations of malevolent people, that her Husband's body should be digged up or dealt with as it he had been either *Magician* or *Self-murtherer*. Which boldness and pertinacity of the woman, though after the confession of the fact, did in some measure work upon the Councel, and put them to a stand.

3. But while these things are in agitation, to the astonishment of the Inhabitants of the place, there appears a *Spectrum* in the exact shape and habit of the deceased, and that not onely in the night, but at mid-day. Those that were asleep it terrified with horrible visions; those that were waking it would strike, pull, or press, lying heavy upon them like an *Ephialtes*: so that there were perpetuall complaints every morning of their last nights rest through the whole Town. But the more freaks this *Spectrum* play'd, the more diligent were the friends of the deceased to suppress the rumours of them, or at least to hinder the effects of those rumours; and therefore made their addresses to the President, complaining how unjust a thing it was, that so much should be given to idle reports and blind suspicions, and therefore beseech'd him that he would hinder the Councel from digging up the corps of the deceased, and from all ignominious usage of him: adding also, that they intended to appeal to the Emperour's Court, that their Wisdoms might rather decide the Controversie, then that the cause should be here determined from the light conjectures of malicious men.

But while by this means the business was still protracted, there were such stirs and tumults all over the Town that they are hardly to be described. For no sooner did the Sun hide his head but this *Spectrum* would be sure to appear, so that every body was fain to look about him and stand upon his guard, which was a fore trouble to those whom the labours of the day made more sensible of the want of rest in the night. For this terrible *Apparition* would sometimes stand by their bed-sides, sometimes cast it self upon the midst of their beds, would lie close to them, would miserably suffocate them, and would so strike them and pinch them, that not onely blew marks, but plain impressions of his fingers would be upon sundry parts of their bodies in the morning. Nay, such was the violence and impetuousness of this Ghost, that when men forsook their beds and kept their dining-rooms, with Candles lighted, and many of them, in company together, the better to secure themselves from fear and disturbance; yet he would then appear to them, and have a bout with some of them notwithstanding all this provision against it. In brief, he was so troublesome, that the people were ready to forsake their houses and seek other dwellings, and the Magistrate so awakened at the perpetual Complaints of them, that at last they resolved, the President agreeing thereto, to dig up the Body.

[113] 4. He had lain in the ground near eight moneths, *viz.* from *Sep.* 22. 1591 to *April* 18. 1592. When he was digged up, which was in the presence of the Magistracy of the Town, his body was found entire, not at all putrid, no ill smell about him, saving the mustiness of the grave Clothes, his joynts limber and flexible, as in those that are alive, his skin only flaccid, but a more fresh grown in the room of it, the wound of his throat gapping, but no gear nor corruption in it; there was also observed a Magical mark in the great toe of his right foot, *viz.* an Excrescency in the form of a Rose. His body was kept out of earth from April 18. to the 24. at what time many both of the same Town and others came daily to view him. These unquiet stirs did not cease for all this, which they after attempted to appease by burying the corps under the Gallows, but in vain; for they were as much as ever, if not more, he now not sparing his own Family; insomuch that his Widow at last went her self to the Magistrate, and told them that she should be no longer against it, if they thought fit to fall upon some course of more strict proceedings touching her Husband.

5. Wherefore the seventh of May he was again digged up, and it was observable that he was grown more senibly fleshly since his last interment. To be short, they cut off the Head, Arms and Legs of

the corps, and opening his Back took out his Heart, which was as fresh and intire as in a Calf new kill'd. These, together with his Body, they put on a pile of wood, and burnt them to Ashes, which they carefully sweeping together and putting into Sack (that none might get them for wicked uses) poured them into the River, after which the *Spectrum* was never seen more.

D Henry More, *The Immortality of the Soul*, Book 3, Chapter 1 (Collection of Several Philosophical Writings, 145–147 = ed. Jacob, 191–198)

1. WE have, I hope, with undeniable evidence demonstrated *the Immortality of the Soul* to such as neither by their slowness of parts, nor any prejudice of Immorality, are made incompetent Judges of the truth of Demonstrations of this kind: so that I have already perfected my main Design. But my own curiosity, and the desire of gratifying others who love to entertain themselves with Speculations of this nature, do call me out something further; if the very Dignity of the present Matter I am upon doth not justly require me, as will be best seen after the finishing thereof: which is *concerning the State of the Soul after Death*. Wherein though I may not haply be able to fix my foot so firmly as in the foregoing part of this Treatise, yet I will assert nothing but what shall be reasonable, though not demonstrable, and far preponderating to whatever shall be alledged to the contrary, and in such clear order and [146] Method, that if what I write be not worthy to convince, it shall not be able to deceive or entangle by perplexedness and obscurity; and therefore I shall offer to view at once the main Principles upon which I shall build the residue of my Discourse.

Axiome XXVII.

The Soul *separate from this* Terrestrial *Body is not released from all* Vital Union *with Matter.*

2. THis is the general Opinion of the *Platonists*. *Plotinus* indeed dissents, especially concerning the most divine Souls, as if they at last were perfectly unbared of all Matter, and had no union with any thing but God himself: which I look upon as a fancy proceeding from the same inequality of temper, that made him surmise that the most degenerate Souls did at last sleep in the bodies of Trees, and grew up merely into *Plantal life*. Such fictions as these of fancyfull men have much depraved the ancient *Cabbala* and sacred Doctrine which the *Platonists* themselves do profess to be δεοπαράδοτον, a holy *Tradition* received from the mouth of God or Angels. But however *Plotinus* himself does not deny but till the Soul arrive to such an exceeding height of purification, that she acts in either an *Aiery* or *Celestial* Body.

But that she is never released so perfectly from all Matter, how pure soever and tenuious, her condition of operating here in this life is a greater presumption then can be fetcht from any thing else, that she ever is. For we find plainly that her most subtile and most Intellectual operations depend upon the *fitness of temper* in the *Spirits*; and that it is the *fineness* and *purity* of them that invites her and enables her to love and look after *Divine* and *Intellectual* Objects: Which kind of Motions if she could exert immediately by her own proper power and essence, what should hinder her but that, having a will, she should bring it to effect? which yet we find she cannot if the *Spirits* be *indisposed*. But, as I said, the Soul cannot be hindred by the undue temper of the Spirits in these Acts, if they be of that nature that they belong to the bare essence of the Soul quite prescinded from all Union with *Matter*. For then as to these Acts it is all one where the Soul is, that is, in *what Matter* she is (and she must be in some, because the Universe is every where thick-set with *Matter*) whether she be raised into the purest regions of the Aire, or plunged down into the foulest Receptacles of Earth or Water; for her *Intellectual* actings would be alike in both; this Conjunction in all likelihood engaging onely the *Plastick* and *Sensitive* powers of the Soul even when she is vitally united with *Matter.* What then is there imaginable in the *Body* that can hinder her in her nobler Operations?

Wherefore it is plain that the nature of the Soul is such, as that she cannot act but in dependence on *Matter,* and that her Operations are some way or other alwaies modified thereby. And therefore if the Soul act at all after death, (which we have demonstrated she does) it is evident that she is not released from all *vital union* with all kind of *Matter* [147] whatsoever: Which is not onely the Opinion of the *Platonists,* but of *Aristotle* also, as may be easily gathered out of what we have above cited out of him.

3. Besides, it seems a very wilde leap in nature, that the Soul of Man, from being so deeply and muddily immersed into Matter as to keep company with Beasts, by vitall union with gross flesh and bones, should so on a suddain be changed, that she should not adhere to any Matter whatsoever, but ascend into an ἀϋλότης competible haply to none but God himself; unless there be such Creatures as the *Platonists* call Νόες or *pure Intellects.* This must seem to any indifferent man very harsh and incongruous, especially if we consider what noble Beings there are on this side the Νόοι or Νόες, that all the Philosophers that ever treated of them acknowledge to be vitally united with either *Aërial* or *Æthereal* Vehicles. For of this condition are all the *Genii* or Angels.

It is sufficient therefore that the Soul never exceed the immateriality of those Orders of Beings; the lower sort whereof that they are vitally united to Vehicles of *Aire,* their ignorance in Nature seems manifestly to bewray. For it had been an easy thing, and more for their credit, to have informed their followers better in the Mysteries of Nature; but that themselves were ignorant of these things, which they could not but know, if they were not thus bound to their *Aiery* bodies. For then they were not engaged to move with the whole course of the *Aire,* but keeping themselves steddy, as being disunited from all Matter, they might in a moment have perceived both the *diurnal* and *annual motion* of the *Earth,* and so have saved the Credit of their followers, by communicating this Theory to them; the want of the knowledge whereof spoils their repute with them that understand the Systeme of the world better then themselves, for all they boast of their Philosophy, so as if it were the Dictate of the highest Angels.

Axiome XXVIII.

There is a Triple Vital Congruity *in the Soul, namely* Æthereall, Aëreal, *and* Terrestrial.

4. THat this is the common Opinion of the *Platonists,* I have above intimated. That this Opinion is also true in it self, appears from the foregoing Axiome. Of the *Terrestrial Congruity* there can be no doubt; and as little can there be but that at least one of the other two is to be granted, else the Soul would be released from all *vital union with Matter* after Death. Wherefore she has a *Vital aptitude* at least to unite with *Aire:* But *Aire* is a common Receptacle of bad and good Spirits, (as the *Earth* is of all sorts of men and beasts) nay indeed rather of those that are in some sort or other bad, then of good, as it is upon Earth. But the Soul of Man is capable of very high refinements, even to a condition *purely Angelical.* Whence Reason will judge it fit, and all Antiquity has voted it, That the Souls of men arrived to such a due pitch of purification must at last obtain *Celestial* Vehicles.

E Anne Conway, *The Principles of the Most Ancient and Modern Philosophy*, Chap. VII, Sec. 3; Chap. VIII, Sec 1

§.3. MY Third Reason is drawn from the great Love and Desire that the Spirits or Souls have towards Bodies, and especially towards those with which they are united, and in which they have their Habitation: But now the Foundation of all Love or Desire, whereby one Thing is carried unto another, stands in this, That either they are of the same Nature and Substance with them, or like unto them, or both; or that one hath its Being from the other, whereof we have an Example in all living Creatures which bring forth their young; and in like manner also in Men, how they love that which is born of them: For so also even Wicked Men and Women (if they are not extremely perverse, and void of Parental Love) do Love their Children, and cherish them with a Natural Affection, the cause whereof certainly is this, That their Children are of the same Nature and Substance, *viz.* as though they were Parts of them; and if they are like them, either in Body, Spirit, or Manners, hereby their Love is the more increased: So also we observe that Animals of one *Species* love one another more than those that are of a different *Species;* whence also Cattle of one Kind feed together; Birds of a Kind flock together; and Fishes of a Kind swim together; and so Men rather converse with Men, than with any other Creatures: But besides this particular Love, there remains yet something of Universal Love in all Creatures, one towards another, setting aside that great confusion which hath fallen out since, by reason of Transgression; which certainly must proceed from the same Foundation, *viz.* in regard of their First Substance and Essence, they were all one and the same Thing, and as it were Parts and Members of one Body. Moreover, in every *Species* of Animals, we see how the Male and Female Love one another, and in all their Propagations (which are not Monstrous, and contrary to Nature) they respect each other; and that proceeds not only from the unity of Nature, but also by reason of a certain eminent similitude or likeness between them. And both these Foundations of Love between a Man and a Woman, are expresly mentioned in *Genesis;* but that which *Adam* spoke concerning his Wife, *This is Bone of my Bone, and Flesh of my Flesh,* &c. pertains unto the Unity of Nature; for she was taken out of him, and was a part of him, and therefore he loved her. Moreover also, concerning Similitude, it is said, there was no Help found for him, or before his Face, as it is in the *Hebrew* (*i.e.*) among all Creatures he saw not his like, with whom he would converse, until *Eve* was made for him. But there is yet another cause of Love, when Beings, that love each other, are not one Substance, but one gave Being to the other, and is the proper and real cause thereof. And so it is in the case between God and Creatures; for he gave to all, Being, Life, and Motion; and therefore he loves all Creatures; neither can he not love them; yea, at the same time when he seems to hate and be angry with them, this his Anger, and what proceeds therefrom, *viz.* Punishments and Judgments, turns to their Good, because he perceiveth they have need of them. So, on the contrary, the Creatures which have not wholly degenerated, and lost all sense of God, do love him; and this is a certain Divine Law, and Instinct, which he put in all rational Creatures, that they might love him, which is the fulfilling of the whole Law: But those Creatures which draw most near unto God in similitude or likeness, do love him the more, and are the more loved of him. But if it be thought there is another principal cause of Love, to wit, Goodness, which is the most vehement or powerful *Magnet* thereof, whence also God is above all the most to be loved; because he is the best; which Goodness is in some measure in Creatures, either really or apparently; wherefore such are loved of their Fellow-Creatures: I Answer: It must be granted indeed, that Goodness is a great, yea the greatest Cause of Love, and the proper Object of it; but this Goodness is not a distinct Cause from those before laid down, but is comprehended in them. Wherefore do we call a Thing Good? But because it either really or apparently pleases us, for the unity it hath with us, or which we have with it: Hence it comes to pass, that Good Men love Good Men, and not otherwise; for Good Men cannot love Evil, nor Evil Men Good Men as such; for there is no greater similitude than between Good and Good: For the reason why we call or esteem a Thing Good, is this, that it benefits us, and that we are made Partakers of its Goodness, and so here the First Cause of Similitude is still Militant: So likewise, when one Thing gives being to another, as when God and Christ give Being to Creatures (as from whom have every true Essence proceeded,) here is in like manner a certain Similitude; for it is impossible that the Creatures should not in some Things be like their Creator, and agree with him in some Attributes or Perfections.

This being supposed a Touch-stone, we shall now return to our subject matter, (*i.e.*) to examine, whether Spirits and Bodies are of one Nature and Substance, and so convertible one into another? Therefore, I demand, What is the reason, That the Spirit or Soul so loveth the Body wherewith it is united, and so unwillingly departs out of it, that it has been manifestly notorious, the Souls of some have attended on, and been subject to their Bodies, after the Body was dead, until it was corrupted, and dissolved into dust. That the Spirit or Soul gave a distinct Being to the Body, or the Body to the Spirit, cannot be the reason of this Love; for that were Creation in a strict sence; but this (*viz.*) to give Being unto Things agrees only to God and Christ; therefore that necessarily comes to pass by reason of that similitude they have one with another, or some Affinity in their Natures: Or, if it be said, there is a certain Goodness in the Body, which moves the Spirit to love it, certainly this Goodness must necessarily answer to something in the Soul which is like it, otherwise it could not be carried unto it; yea, let them inform us what that Goodness in the Body is, for which the Soul doth so fervently love it? or in what Attributes or Perfections a Body is like a Spirit; if a Body is nothing but a dead Trunk, and a certain Mass which is altogether uncapable of any degree of Life, and Perfection? if they say a Body agrees with a Spirit *Ratione entis*, or in respect of Being; that is to say; as this hath Being so that hath the same; this is already refuted in the former Argument; for if this Being hath no Attributes or Perfections wherein it may agree with the Being of a Spirit, then it is only a mere Fiction; for God created no Naked *Ens*, or Being, which should be a mere Being, and have no Attributes that may be predicated of it; besides also, *Ens* is only a Logical Notion or Term, which Logicians do call *Genus generalissimum*, or the most General Kind, which in the naked and abstracted Notion of it, is not in the Things themselves, but only in the Conception or Humane Intellect. And therefore every true Being is a certain single Nature, whereof may be affirmed such and such Attributes: Now what are those Attributes of Body, wherein it resembles a Spirit? Let us examine the principal Attributes of Body, as distinct from a Spirit, according to their Opinion, who so much dispute, that Body and Spirit are so infinitely distant in Nature, that one can never become the other: The Attributes are these, That a Body is impenetrable of all other Bodies, so that the parts thereof cannot penetrate each other; but there is another Attribute of Body, *viz.* to be discerpible or divisible into parts: But the Attributes of Spirit (as they define it) are penetrability and indiscerpibility, so that one Spirit can penetrate another; also, that a thousand Spirits can stand together one within another, and yet possess no more Space than one Spirit. Moreover, that a Spirit is so simple, and one in it self, that it cannot be rent asunder, or actually divided into separate parts. If now the Attributes of Body and Spirit are compared together, they are so far from being like one another, or having any Analogy of Nature (in which nevertheless the true Foundation of Love and Unity doth consist, as before was said,) that they are plainly contrary; yea, nothing in the whole World can be conceived so contrary to any Thing, as Body and Spirit, in the opinion of these Men. For here is a pure and absolute contrariety in all their Attributes; because Penetrability and Impenetrability are more contrary one to another than black and white, or hot and cold: For that which is black may become white, and that which is hot may become cold: But (as they say) that which is impenetrable cannot be made penetrable; yea, God and Creatures do not so infinitely differ in Essence one from another; as these Doctors make Body to differ from Spirit: For there are many Attributes, in which God and the Creatures agree together; but we can find none, wherein a Body can any way agree with a Spirit, and by consequence, nor with God, who is the chiefest and purest of Spirits; wherefore it can be no Creature, but a mere Non-entity or Fiction: But as Body and Spirit are contrary in the Attributes of Penetrability and Impenetrability; so are they no less contrary in Discerpibility and Indiscerpibility: But if they alledge, that Body and Spirit do agree in some Attributes, as Extension, Mobility, and Figurability; so that Spirit hath Extension, and can reach from one place to another, and also can move it self from place to place, and form it self into whatsoever Figure it pleaseth, in which cases it agrees with a Body, and a Body with it: To this I Answer: Supposing the first, that a Spirit can be extended (which yet many of them deny, yea most, who teach that Body and Spirit are essentially distinct) yet the Extension of Body and Spirit, as they understand it, do wonderfully differ; for the Extension of Body is always impenetrable; yea, to be extended, and impenetrable, as pertaining to Body, is only one real Attribute proposed in two Mental and Logical Notions, or ways of speaking; for what is Extension, unless the Body (wheresoever it is) be impenetrable of its own proper parts? But remove this Attribute of Impenetrability from a Body, and it cannot be conceived any longer, as extended. Moreover also, the Extension of Body and Spirit, according to their Notion, infinitely differ; for whatsoever Extension a Body hath, the same is so necessary and essential to it, that it is impossible for it to be more or less extended; when nevertheless a Spirit may be more or less extended; as they affirm; and seeing to be moveable and figurable, are only consequential Attributes of Extension, (for that a Spirit is far otherwise moveable and figurable than a Body, because a Spirit can move and form it self as a Body cannot:) The same Reason which is good against the one is good against the other also.

Chap. 8.

§.1. TO prove that Spirit and Body differ not essentially, but gradually, I shall deduce my Fourth Argument from the intimate Band or Union, which intercedes between Bodies and Spirits, by means whereof the Spirits have Dominion over the Bodies with which they are united, that they move them from one place to another, and use them as Instruments in their various Operations. For if Spirit and Body are so contrary one to another, so that a Spirit is only Life, or a living and sensible Substance, but a Body a certain Mass merely dead; a Spirit penetrable and indiscerpible, but a Body impenetrable and discerpible, which are all contrary Attributes: What (I pray you) is that which doth so join or unite them together? Or, what are those Links or Chains, whereby they have so firm a connexion, and that for so long a space of Time? Moreover also, when the Spirit or Soul is separated from the Body, so that it hath no longer Dominion or Power over it to move it as it had before, What is the cause of this separation? If it be said, that the vital agreement, the Soul hath to the Body, is the cause of the said Union, and that the Body being corrupted that vital Agreement ceaseth. I Answer, We must first enquire, in what this vital Agreement doth consist; for if they cannot tell us wherein it doth consist, they only trifle with empty Words, which give a sound but want a signification: For certainly in that sence which they take Body and Spirit in, there is no Agreement at all between them; for a Body is always a dead Thing, void of Life and sense, no less when the Spirit is in it, than when it is gone out of it: Hence there is no Agreement at all between them; and if there is any Agreement, that certainly will remain the same, both when the Body is sound, and when it is corrupted. If they deny this, because a Spirit requires an organized Body, by means whereof it performs its vital Acts of the external Senses; moves and transports the Body from place to place; which Organical Action ceases when the Body is corrupted. Certainly by this the difficulty is never the better solved. For why doth the Spirit require such an organized Body? *ex. gr.* Why doth it require a Corporeal Eye so wonderfully formed and organized, that I can see by it? Why doth it need a Corporeal Light, to see Corporeal Objects? Or, why is it requisite, that the Image of the Object should be sent to it, through the Eye, that it may see it? If the same were entirely nothing but a Spirit, and no way Corporeal, Why doth it need so many several Corporeal Organs, so far different from the Nature of it? Furthermore, how can a Spirit move its Body, or any of its Members, if a Spirit (as they affirm) is of such a Nature, that no part of its Body can in the least resist it, even as one Body is wont to resist another, when 'tis moved by it, by reason of its Impenetrability? For if a Spirit could so easily penetrate all Bodies, Wherefore doth it not leave the Body behind it, when it is moved from place to place, seeing it can so easily pass out without the least resistance? For certainly this is the cause of all Motions which we see in the World, where one Thing moves another, *viz.* because both are impenetrable in the sence aforesaid: For were it not for this Impenetrability one Creature could not move another, because this would not oppose that; nor at all resist it; an Example whereof we have in the Sails of a Ship, by which the Wind drives the Ship, and that so much the more vehemently, by how much the fewer holes, vents and passages, the same finds in the Sails against which it drives: When on the contrary, if instead of Sails Nets were expanded, through which the Wind would have a freer passage; certainly by these the Ship would be but little moved, although it blew with great violence: Hence we see how this Impenetrability causes resistance, and this makes Motion. But if there were no Impenetrability, as in the case of Body and Spirit, then there could be no resistance, and by consequence the Spirit could make no motion in the Body.

Commentary

More's *Enchiridion Metaphysicum* **(13 A)** is a late text, but it is a good place to start when considering the Cambridge Platonists' ontology and metaphysics. It shows that, while they were familiar with Aristotle and his definition of metaphysics, they viewed the enterprise as special metaphysics, i.e., as theology. Metaphysics is, for More, *natural* theology, 'the art of correctly contemplating incorporeal substances'—above all, God—'insofar as they are revealed in our faculties by the light of nature', and as such it is to be distinguished from *revealed* theology, i.e., meditation upon scripture. The poet in More is evident when he observes that the materialists 'dig holes in the earth's entrails like moles' rather than 'like men who throw up the foundations of some magnificent dwelling which may raise its head in the luminous air and be filled with the rays of the sun through its open and pellucid windows'. His conviction here is that empirical investigation and the new science can and should stimulate and strengthen metaphysics and ultimately theology reveals the character of More's rationalism; and it is not so far from the view of Newton, who wrote in the *General Scholium* to the 1713 edition of the *Principia* that discourse of God 'from the appearances of things, does certainly belong to Natural Philosophy.'

While More is careful to indicate his points of difference from Aristotle in defining metaphysics, his positive reception of the Stagirite should not be overlooked. Within the Neoplatonic tradition Aristotle is generally regarded favourably as a Platonist,[1] and his theory of contemplation in the *Nichomachean Ethics* X and the *Metaphysics* XII was an important constitutive element in this appropriation. Contemplation of divine truth is a major theme in the Cambridge Platonists, not least More himself, for whom it was the summit of human intellectual endeavour. In 1772, Dr Johnson is reported to have told Boswell that 'the happiness of an unembodied spirit will consist in a consciousness of the favour of GOD, in the contemplation of truth and in the possession of felicitating ideas', and that Dr Henry More had carried the task of proving this 'as far as philosophy can'.[2]

John Smith is perhaps the most eloquent of the Cambridge Platonists. In the first extract from his discourse *On the Existence and Nature of God* **(14 A)** he endorses the classic Platonic path of interiority and the 'erotic' ascent of the mind to God, a path first laid down by Plato in the *Symposium* and the *Phaedrus*, and developed by the Neoplatonists and the Christian church fathers, notably Augustine.[3] It is no surprise that Smith's conception of the self here similarly echoes the Neoplatonic conception according to which the self is constituted by and fulfilled in its reversion towards its transcendent divine source.[4] It is this relationship between the soul and God that grounds knowledge for the Cambridge Platonists. The finite mind is conceived as a lesser reflection of the infinite divine mind, and through the Cambridge Platonists' influence on Locke the language of reflection would become important in British philosophy, albeit often shorn of its Neoplatonic associations.

The second extract from Smith's discourse **(14 B)** outlines his understanding of divine omnipotence. Smith begins by explaining that matter is inert and incapable of any autonomous activity: its motion must then be derived from a higher, immaterial agency. Our immaterial souls have the power to govern the matter of our bodies in rational agency; but our power over our bodies, let alone the material world, is limited, and certainly we did not bring ourselves into existence. It seems to Smith that matter is an encumbrance, and he asserts the principle that the "more *unbodied* any thing is, the more *unbounded* also is it in its *Effective* power". This principle is one shared by the Platonic tradition and discussed at length by Plotinus in *Ennead* VI.8, which argues that the One is total power and perfect freedom, the corollary of its absolute metaphysical priority being its absolute transcendence of conditioning by any being whatsoever, least of all by matter.[5] Smith's reasoning is that, if the activity of the material world is intelligible as our actions are intelligible, there must be such a divine agency behind it, one wholly immaterial and vastly superior to us in wisdom and power: a divine creator who functions—again, as is typical in the Platonic tradition—as the archetype of which our own souls, and all other things too, are mere images.

In the third extract **(14 C)**, Smith argues develops an argument for God and the absolute goodness of God from the insatiability of human desire as that for which our souls long. Discovering themselves incapable of satisfaction through worldly things, Smith urges his audience to recognise that peace lies in acknowledging and turning to that divine source which is the transcendent source of these lesser goods. Smith's arguments are finely wrought intellectual endeavours, and here especially we should observe that this Cambridge Platonist is not a dry rationalist: in fact for Smith, despite the emphasis on reason, "God is not better defin'd to us by our *Understandings* then by our *Wills and Affections*". The intellect properly longs not for abstract truths but "that *unstained Beauty* and *Supreme Good* which our *Wills* are perpetually catching after".

The selections from Smith each focus on one member of the triad of divine goodness, wisdom, and power: he focuses on the need for the mind's participation in God as the interpreter within, without which we could not understand nature; he acknowledges the supreme power of God evinced by all created things; and he dwells upon the latent sense of divine goodness as the ultimate inspiration of the will in its affections. An interest in the same qualities can be found in the other Cambridge Platonists, including in our first extract from Cudworth's unfinished opus maximum, the sprawling (and boldly titled) *True Intellectual System of the Universe* **(14 D)**. This triad of goodness, wisdom and power is, according to Cudworth, the "Pythagorean Trinity", part of a supposed 'ancient theology' shared by pagans, Hebrews and Christians. Pythagoras is a pivotal figure for Cudworth, since in the wake of Reuchlin, Pythagoras was perceived to a beneficiary of Mosaic wisdom and therefore a link between Hebrew revelation—the Jewish Cabbala—and Greek reason—Platonism as it emerges with Plato himself. However unlikely genealogy may be, the influence of Pythagoras on Plato is undeniable.[6]

In the next extract, **(14 E)** Cudworth develops an argument for the existence of God by turning the atheist proposition of *ex nihilo nihil fit* on its head. The atheist is correct to claim that nothing can come out of nothing, but false in the conclusion they draw—that there was no creation and thus no creator bur merely the brute fact of "*Dead* and *Sensless Matter*". For empirically (or at least phenomenologically) we are not faced with dead and senseless matter but also mind. Given Cudworth's Platonic premise that effects must pre-exist in their cause and only the metaphysically higher can produce the lower, he presents the existence of mentality as an irresolvable problem for the materialist, and reasons that the existence of finite mentality must be taken to imply the existence of mind at a higher and supreme causal level, i.e., of *divine* mind.

Cudworth's argument in the next extract **(14 F)** deals with divine incomprehensibility. The philosopher relies on the ancient principle that only like understands like. The reality of divinity is what makes the world intelligible as our minds reflect the divine mind. Yet the reflection is finite and imperfect and the reflected infinite and perfect: it is not surprising then that, however our knowledge of the world may advance, we do not come to a level of understanding commensurate with God's own, and certainly we do not fully comprehend God himself. Thus for Cudworth God is both known and unknown to us, and there are strong parallels here to Plato's discussion of the Form of the Good and his Allegory of the Cave in books VI and VII of the *Republic*. God is not understood in himself in his entirety, but he is that by which we understand and without which we could not understand. The principle of intelligibility is dazzling through its very power.

Such is the infinite perfection of God. But as Cudworth discusses in the next extract, **(14 G)** God has all perfect attributes simply, i.e., they are all one in him: "all the *Genuine Attributes* of the *Deity*, not only not *Contradictious*, but also *Inseparably Concatenate*; and the *Idea of God* no Congeries either of Disagreeing things; or else of such as are unnecessarily Connected with one another". This doctrine of 'inseparable concatenation' is better known as divine simplicity. If God is the one absolute, prior to all that is physically or metaphysically, he cannot in any sense be composite, because composition implies component parts which would themselves take metaphysical priority, thus undermining God's absolute divine status. God then is one and simple, and parts cannot be distinguished in him: even his essence cannot be distinct from his existence, for fear of the implication that he received that existence from some other thing. The doctrine of divine simplicity is a commonplace of late platonic and patristic and medieval Christian thought and was held by the majority of philosophical theists into the nineteenth century, though more recently it has come under attack in analytic philosophy of religion on the basis of supposed implantable implications and a feeling that it is hard to combine with the personal conception of deity which many take to be more biblical.[7]

In the penultimate extract of the chapter **(14 H)**, Cudworth deploys a variant of the classic *consensus gentium* argument, according to which the God's existence should be more plausible to us when we reflect that monotheism has been held by most peoples across cultures that are diverse historically and geographically. That monotheism has been so widespread is of course contentious, and while this argument has an ancient pedigree, it was widely debated in the early modern period, not least because of the European exploration of the 'New World' of the Americas and other regions, and the great interest that this fostered in the in the religious beliefs of non-Christian cultures.[8]

Finally, we have Cudworth's own variant on the ontological argument **(14 I)**. Broadly speaking, Cudworth is loath to put as much weight upon the deeply controversial ontological argument as Descartes and is much more inclined to argue for a teleological foundation for natural theology on the basis that God's nature as creative act is the reason for the intelligible structure and harmony of the world. However, it is worth noting that, unlike Aquinas, he does not dismiss the ontological argument totally, but believes it has some cogency.

Henry More's view of space as substantial and as an attribute of the divine, developed in the *Enchiridion Metaphysicum* **(15 A)** has enjoyed a momentous, though much debated, afterlife.[9] The position that he adopts in the *Enchiridion* had precedents in his earlier writings:

> Wherefore this wide and wast Vacuity,
> Which endlesse is out stretched thorough all.
> And lies even equall with the Deity,
> Nor is a thing merely imaginal[10]

The divinity of space is a radical theory grounded upon More's disdain for 'nullibism'—his name for the more typical position that God, the soul and immaterial spirits lack any spatial location—on the grounds that to have no place in existence is to have no existence at all. Thus *to be* for More is *to be in space*, while space itself, which More takes to be infinite, is divine. In the *Enchiridion* we find

More defending his view of space as divine as by way of a lengthy list of attributes philosophers and theologians traditionally apply of God but which More believes are equally applicable to space: God, like space, is said to be "one, simple, immobile, eternal, complete, independent, existing from itself, subsisting by itself, incorruptible, necessary, immense, uncreated, uncircumscribed, incomprehensible, omnipresent, incorporeal, permeating and encompassing everything, Being by essence, Being by act, pure Act." Henry More's mature theory of space as an attribute of God is connected to his affirmation of the substantial and not merely virtual divine presence.

More's theory of space was highly novel and was a point of disagreement with other philosophers and theologians, including amongst the Cambridge Platonists. In our second extract **(15 B)**, the Oxford thinker (sometimes regarded as an 'Oxford Platonist') John Norris and More exchange letters as the former attempts to clarify the latter's position. This correspondence is an illuminating instance of this intra-Platonic debate. In the exchange More speaks of "*Essential Spissitude*, which is that fourth dimension": spissitude, meaning, perhaps, thickness, is a technical term used by More for the extension of spirit as it contracts or expands. The reply to Norris suggests, as More does in the *Enchiridion*, that spirit should not be seen in its three-dimensional length, breadth, and depth, but as belonging to an extra dimension. Quite what he means has been subject to much debate.[11]

In the next two extracts we find Smith **(15 C)** and Cudworth **(15 D)** objecting to More's position, emphasising instead what was undoubtedly the majority view of Platonists historically, that God transcends space and that space itself neither contains all that is, nor is it divine. Cudworth characteristically quotes a number of ancient authorities on the point, while Smith takes up Plotinus' view that God's presence in the world is by virtue of his power, which is active in all things, rather than a result of the divinity of space. Cudworth is keen to point up a possible source of More's erroneous view as he sees it, namely a confusion between imagination and intellection, the former being a capacity of the mind that relies upon mental images of corporeal things, the latter being the higher ability to grasp truth in its pure, incorporeal (and indeed non-spatial) form. As Cudworth argues, imagination and intellection are not identical (there are truths we can know for which we can compose no adequate mental image), and so it is an error to imagine the presence of God as one might the presence of an embodied human being, taking up a certain space.

While from his perspective then More is undoubtedly a maverick on this issue, it should be noted that, in our final extract **(15 E)**, in the face of atheistic arguments that claim space exists distinct from bodies entirely, the judicious mind of Dr Cudworth is willing to concede the point to More: "if *Space* be indeed a *Nature* distinct from *Body*, and a Thing *Really Incorporeal* . . . there must be *Incorporeal Substance*; and (this *Space* being supposed by them also to be *Infinite*) an *Infinite Incorporeal Deity*." In our first extract on the Cambridge Platonist's view of nature **(16 A)**, Cudworth begins with this reference to the Pythagorean-Platonic trinity of the One or the Good in relation to the noetic realm of mind/intellect and soul, which Cudworth presents as three aspects of one deity and which by implication is an image of the Christian doctrine of the Trinity. Lying behind this model is the principle that the natural world should not be understood in materialistic and mechanistic terms but rather through a self-active and hylarchical principle which constitutes the formative power of nature.[12] Linked to this conception of nature as permeated by intelligence is the view that there is a scale or ladder of being, that is to say degrees of reality, so that, while life and intelligence belongs to a level superior to unthinking matter, nature can be seen as pointing to higher perfection.

Cudworth's theme in the following extract **(16 B)** is his doctrine of 'plastic nature', another idea of the Cambridge Platonists that enjoyed an influential afterlife. The term 'plastic' may appear rebarbative, but it is important to bear in mind Greek etymology and the derivation of 'plastic' from the Greek πλάττειν, *plattein*, meaning 'to shape' or 'to form'. The central idea of plastic nature consists in the assertion that nature contains guiding principles that mold or determine matter in an intelligible manner. This vision is reliant upon the central anti-Gnostic treatise of Plotinus, *Ennead* III.8, in which Plotinus presents a picture of nature as slumbering spirit. This Neoplatonic paradigm provided a model for Cudworth with which to repudiate a materialistic and mechanistic conception of nature as determined by the collision of atoms, and to present the natural realm as an image, albeit an indirect image, of the divine mind. That is to say, the divine presence in nature is indirect, insofar as God is neither a remote *Deus ex machina* but nor is he to be identified with the natural realm in the pantheistic or Spinozistic manner.

In the passage of More featured in this chapter **(16 C)** we find More's answer to Cudworth's plastic nature, namely his 'spirit of nature.' We also find an exploration of the Neoplatonic and Stoic image of sympathy, albeit in the somewhat startling form of "some higher and more sublime magic". More makes it perfectly clear that by the term 'magic' he is referring to a strictly philosophical issue, that of explaining the relations between objects in the world which like Cudworth he holds cannot be reduced to mechanical interactions in which as he says a body is "pushed and driven forward by another". Again, More stresses the intellectual lineage by referring not only to Plotinus but to Anaxagoras and to Aristotle here. It is important to bear in mind that the Cambridge Platonists are inclined to regard the real Aristotle, as opposed to the Aristotle of the Scholastics, as "a splendid pupil of Plato", and indeed with some justification. We have in More a contrast to the divine nature which possesses the ideas of all things naturally, and the spirit of nature that does so only potentially, so that nature is conceived of as striving towards the divine. Clearly, on this question of mechanism, More and Cudworth are closely aligned.

A close confederate of Henry More, Joseph Glanvill is an apt starting point for our chapter on body and spirit. In some ways Glanvill's text **(17 A)** is a Platonic precursor of William Paley's natural theology in his avowal of a riposte to neo-Epicurean materialism. Glanvill exhibits an ontological optimism, and he is animated by the question of how the body can develop in so exquisite a manner, whilst questioning, as the Cambridge Platonists all did, whether mechanism can account for its structure and orderliness. Displaying the enthusiasm of both a scientist and a theologian, Glanvill shows nothing of the much-vaunted hostility to the body which is typically said to be 'Platonic'.

Our second text of this chapter **(17 B)** returns us to More. It should be clear from the passage that More is a substance dualist, that is to say that, for him, mind and matter are distinguished as resolutely as in Descartes. However, on examination, the nature of his substance dualism is somewhat more porous than the radical contrast one finds in Descartes: whereas Descartes contrasted mind as a thinking thing, the *res cogitans*, and matter as merely an extended thing, the *res extensa*, we have already seen that for More extension can, indeed must, also be a property of immaterial beings. More's contrast between mind and body is really between discerpability and indiscerpability, penetrability and impenetrability. It is interesting to note that some have argued that More's substance dualism in fact exhibits a propensity towards a crypto-materialism (Henry, "A Cambridge Platonist's Materialism").

In the last major anthology of the Cambridge Platonists, C.A. Patrides included the first two books of Henry More's *An Antidote Against Atheism*, but omitted the third. Readers of our rather ghoulish third extract **(17 C)**, which comes from that part of More's work, will understand why. But though More's 'ghost stories' may strike us as out of place if not distasteful in philosophical works, evidence of supernatural activity, including hauntings, possessions and witchcraft, were of great interest to both More (as also to Glanvill), and they form an important part of his argumentative strategy alongside more purely philosophical reasoning in defence of the reality of the soul.

In our fourth extract **(17 D)** we encounter some of the detail of More's theory of the soul. The doctrine of the vehicle of the soul was a development of later Neoplatonism and there is little or no evidence of such a theory in Plotinus.[13] The attraction of such a theory to a Christian thinker should be evident, since the appeal to a spiritual vehicle of an aerial or an aethereal kind is a means of combining the Platonic theory of the immortality of the soul with the Christian doctrine of a post-mortem heavenly existence and the doctrine of the resurrection of the body.[14] More's elaborate theorising on the soul-vehicle or subtle body is also linked to his interest in apparitions and the ghosts of the departed remaining in this world.

Our passages from More showed that, although he remained a substance dualist, he in some was began breeching the radical contrast between soul and body that one finds in Descrates. In his 'heroine pupil' Lady Ann Conway, we find a radicalisation of More's propensity to blur the division of spirit and body. Indeed, Lady Conway, produces a monistic system in which the difference between body and spirit consists not in kind but merely in degree, and our final extract of this chapter **(17 E–F)** presents some of her arguments.

The key problem for any substance dualist is that of interaction, i.e., how can we properly conceive of an interaction between two radically distinct substances, namely mind and matter. More's answer to this problem is vital congruity, an active kinship between mind and matter, between the soul and its vehicle. Conway plausibly claims that More's purported solution to the problem merely amounts to a restatement of it, because by More's very own account there cannot be congruity between passive dead matter and active spirit. More, according to Conway, has proposed a merely verbal solution without resolving the problem: he has simply stipulated that there is a congruity but in no way explained how the gulf between spirit and matter can be bridged. Conway, for her part, can be seen employing the idea of a ladder of being and the Platonic intuition that all finite things are reflections of the divine that share in its life to argue that mind and matter, body and spirit cannot be held so separate as the more dualistic Platonists have supposed.[15]

Notes

1 For a contemporary exposition of this stance, see Lloyd Gerson, *Aristotle and Other Platonists* (Ithaca, NY: Cornell University Press, 2005).
2 28th March 1772 (471).
3 On this motif see Catherine Osborne, *Eros Unveiled: Plato and the God of Love* (Oxford: Clarendon Press, 1994).
4 See further Gerhard O'Daley, *Plotinus' Philosophy of the Self* (New York: Barnes & Noble, 1973); D.M. Hutchinson, *Plotinus on Consciousness* (Cambridge, UK: Cambridge University Press, 2018); Phillip Cary, *Augustine's Invention of the Inner Self: Legacy of a Christian Platonist* (Oxford: Oxford University Press, 2003); and Charles Taylor, *Sources of the Self* (Cambridge, UK: Cambridge University Press, 1989).
5 Kevin Corrigan, *Ennead VI.8: On the Voluntary and on the Free Will of the One* (Las Vegas, NV: Parmenides Publishing, 2018).
6 On the legacy of Pythagoras see Christiane L. Joost-Gaugier, *Measuring Heaven: Pythagoras and His Influence on Thought and Art in Antiquity and the Middle Ages* (Ithaca, NY: Cornell University Press, 2007).
7 For a survey and exposition of the doctrine see James E. Dolezal, *God without Parts* (Eugene, OR: Wipf and Stock, 2011).
8 See Douglas Hedley, "Gods and giants: Cudworth's platonic metaphysics and his ancient theology", *British Journal for the History of Philosophy*, 25, no.5 (2017): 932–953.
9 See E.A. Burtt's discussion in *The Metaphysical Foundations of Modern Science* (London: Kegan Paul, 1925), 135–150.
10 More, *Democritus Platonissans* 45.
11 On the knotty problem of spissitude, and More's doctrine of space generally, see Jasper Reid's discussion in *The Metaphysics of Henry More* (Springer, 2012), 200ff. For a recent defence of the doctrine, see Jonathan Lyonhart, *Space God: Rejudging a Debate Between More, Newton, and Einstein* (Cascade Books, 2023).
12 See further Lutz Bergmann, *Ralph Cudworth—System aus Transformation Zur Naturphilosophie der Cambridge Platonists und ihrer Methode* (Berlin: De Gruyter, 2012); and Douglas Hedley, "Real Atheism And Cambridge Platonism: Men Of Latitude, Polemics, And The Great Dead Philosophers", in *Platonisms: Ancient, Modern, and Postmodern*, eds. Kevin Corrigan and John Turner (Leiden: Brill, 2007), 155–173.

13 The locus classicus is E.R. Dodds' "The Astral Body in Neoplatonism", appended to his translation of Proclus' *Elements of Theology* (Oxford: Oxford University Press, 1963), 313–322. See also John Finamore, *Iamblichus and the Theory of the Vehicle of the Soul* (Chico, CA: Scholars' Press, 1985).
14 On this topic consult John Thompson's *The Metaphysics of Resurrection in Seventeenth Century Philosophy* (Springer, 2022).
15 For a full discussion of Conway's ingenious system, see Sarah Hutton, *Anne Conway: A Woman Philosopher* (Cambridge, UK: Cambridge University Press, 2009); Jonathan Head, *The Philosophy of Anne Conway: God, Creation and the Nature of Time* (London: Bloomsbury, 2020).

Part V

Epistemology and Ethics

Christian Hengstermann

Introduction

It is one of the chief ironies of Cambridge Platonist literature that the two major works which either in substantial parts or as a whole are devoted to epistemology bear titles that rather mark them as treatises on ethics. There is very little ethical thought in Cudworth's *Treatise Concerning Eternal and Immutable Morality* which is the principal text of Cambridge Platonist epistemology. There is good reason to label the first of these works *Enchiridion Ethicum*. More's *Enchiridion Ethicum*, first published in 1666 and subsequently republished in several new editions, is the first of the two major works of Cambridge Platonist epistemology and ethics. Modelled upon Descartes' *On the Passions of the Soul*, of which it provides a detailed philosophical critique in its outline of an alternative moral psychology, More's hugely successful ethical handbook draws upon a plethora of ancient sources which the author quotes at length both in the original Greek tongue and his own Latin translation, providing in-depth comments. Among the chief texts of reference are Aristotle's *Nicomachean* and *Eudemian Ethics* and his late antique commentators, notably Andronicus of Rhodes, as well as a range of well-known and more elusive Hellenistic Stoic and Neo-Pythagorean sources, notably Marcus Aurelius' *Meditations* and Epictetus' *Handbook* as well as pseudo-epigraphic writings by Neopythagoreans of the early imperial age. While deeply indebted to Platonism or Pythagorism and Stoicism throughout, More's is a deeply original Platonist vision of the soul's happiness or good life and its moral duties. Despite its humanist outlook, the ethical system delineated in the *Handbook* is a distinctly early modern account of the first principles of autonomous and universalist moral agency and a set of values and obligations established in rationalist axiomatic reasoning. It hinges upon what More calls the soul's intuitive "boniform faculty" which, in turn, serves as the basis of discursive "right reason". Besides More's several attempts at a definition of the soul's highest epistemic power, i.e. its boniform faculty, his principal ethical work provides an in-depth account of the Cambridge Platonists' strict realism.

As well as providing a first English translation of More's preface to the second edition of his *Enchiridion Ethicum* and the scholia appended to it in the second tome of the three-volume Opera Omnia of 1675–1679, the following selection of excerpts is meant to highlight the principal tenets of Morean and Cambridge Platonist ethics, including the epistemology of an intuitive vision of divine goodness, the system of objective and universal obligation and the theory of libertarian agency. To this end, the passages selected include all of More's major expositions of the "boniform faculty" and of "right reason", including his long treatise on natural law, as well as his long definition and defence of libertarian freedom. The final chapter reproduced is the eschatological vision put forward at the end of the *Handbook*. Throughout, the English text transcribed is that of the early modern translation by the later politician and diplomat Edward Southwell published in 1690 and republished with several minor corrections in 1701. While it may be an exaggeration to say, as did Anthony Wood, that "it is done so well and the style is so masculine and noble, that I know not as yet any book written in better English" (Lamprecht, "Bibliographical Note"), Southwell's translation entitled *An Account of Virtue or Dr. Henry More's Abridgment of Morals* is an extraordinary literary attainment. It is even more impressing considering that its author was a mere 19 years old at the time of its composition. Southwell's is a vivid and vibrant early modern English prose which frequently lives up to or even surpasses More's equally passionate Latin eulogy of divine goodness and perfectible human freedom. However, Southwell's translation throughout fails to do justice to More's technical vocabulary, which proves particularly detrimental in the case of the author's carefully-written expositions of the core concepts of Cambridge Platonist ethics and epistemology. Worse, Southwell can be seen to have tampered with More's text on numerous occasions, deliberately deleting the author's reference to the Origenist notion of the pre-existence of souls or rephrasing his theological intellectualism in the voluntarist terms loathed by the Cambridge Platonists. The text reproduced in the following selection is that of Southwell's early modern translation. However, it has throughout been compared to More's original Latin. Major divergences and omissions have been noted and commented on in the notes added to the text transcribed. Thus, while making available a major early modern translation of one of the most successful and influential works of the Cambridge Platonists, the following selection is meant to provide the reader with a reliable account of More's own ethical system. At the heart of Cambridge Platonism is the vision of God's all-encompassing goodness. It discloses to the soul is capacity for autonomous moral choice as it must choose either to embrace this vision or act contrary to it. It also informs its every act of cognition as it translates into the Phaedrean plain which serves as the universal frame of all particular knowledge. The ethics of the boniform vision is that of universal virtue exercised both in personal moral and in political action.

Chapter 19

Intuitive Vision and the First Principle of Divine Goodness

A Ralph Cudworth, *A Sermon Preached Before the Honourable House of Commons* (1647) (pp. 76–79)

Love is at once a Freedome from all Law, a State of purest Liberty, and yet a Law too, of the most constraining and indispensable Necessity. The worst *Law* in the World, is *the Law of Sinne, which is in our members*; which keeps us in a condition of most absolute Slavery, when we are wholly under the Tyrannicall commands of our lusts: this is a cruell *Pharaoh* indeed, that sets his hard task-masters over us, and maketh us wretchedly drudge in Mire and Clay. The *Law of the Letter* without us, sets us in a condition of a little more Liberty, by restraining of us from many outward Acts of Sinne; but yet it doth not disenthrall us, from the power of sinne in our hearts. But the *Law of the Spirit of life*, the *Gospel-Law of* [77] *Love*, it puts us into a condition of most pure and perfect Liberty; and whosoever really entertaines this Law, he hath *thrust out Hagar* quite, he hath *cast out the Bondwoman and her Children*; from henceforth, *Sarah the Free woman*, shall live forever with him, and she shall be to him, a Mother of many children; her seed shall be *as the sand of the seashoar for number*, and *as the starres of heaven*. Here is Evangelicall liberty, here is Gospel-freedome, when *the Law of the Spirit of life in Christ Jesus, hath made us free, from the Law of sinne and death*: when we have a liberty from sinne, and not a liberty to sinne: for our dear Lord and Master hath told us, that *Whosoever committeth sinne, he is the servant of it*. He that lies under the power, and vassallage of his base lusts, and yet talks of Gospel-freedome; he is but like a poore condemned Prisoner, that in his sleep dreams of being set at liberty, and of walking up and down wheresoever he pleaseth; whilst his Legs are all the while lock't fast in fetters and Irons. To please our selves with a Notion of Gospel-liberty, whilest we have not a Gospel-principle of Holinesse within [78] us, to free us from the power of sinne, it is nothing else, but to gild over our Bonds and Fetters, and to phancy our selves to be in a Golden Cage. There is a Straitnesse, Slavery, and Narrownesse in all Sinne: Sinne crowds and crumples up our souls, which if they were freely spread abroad, would be as wide, and as large as the whole Universe. No man is truly free, but he that hath his *will* enlarged to the extent of Gods own will, by loving whatsoever God loves, and nothing else. Such a one, doth not fondly hug this and that particular created good thing, and envassal himself unto it, but he loveth every thing that is lovely, beginning at God, and descending down to all his Creatures, according to the severall degrees of perfection in them. He injoyes a boundlesse Liberty, and a boundlesse Sweetnesse, according to his boundlesse Love. He inclaspeth the whole World within his outstretched arms, his Soul is as wide as the whole Universe, as big as *yesterday, to day, and forever*. Whosoever is once acquainted with this Disposition of Spirit, he never desires any thing else: and he loves the *Life* [79] *of God* in himself, dearer then his own Life. To conclude this therefore; If we love Christ, and *keep his commandments, his commandments will not be grievous to us: His yoke will be easie, and his burden light*: it will not put us into a State of Bondage, but of perfect Liberty.

For it is most true of Evangelicall Obedience, what the wise man speaketh of Wisdome; *Her wayes, are wayes of pleasantnesse, and all her paths are peace; She is a tree of Life to those that lay hold upon her, and happy are all they that retain her.*

B Henry More, *Second Lash of Alazonomastix* (1651), 43–44

But I say that a free divine universalized spirit is worth all. How lovely, how magnificent a state is the soul of man in, when the life of God inactuating her, shoots her along with himself through Heaven and Earth, makes her unite with, and after a sort feel herself animate the whole world, as if she had become God and all things. This is the precious clothing and rich ornament of the mind, farre above reason or any other experiment. And in this attire though canst not but dance to that Musick of the Sibylle.

Εἰμὶ δ᾽ ἐγὼ ὁ ἐὼν (σὺ δ᾽ ἐνὶ φρεσὶ σῇσι νόησον) ·
Οὐρανὸν ἐνδέδυμαι , περιβέέλημαι δὲ θάλασσαν,
Γαῖα δέ μοι στήριγμα ποδῶν , περὶ σῶμα κέχυται,
Ἀὴρ ἠδ᾽ ἄστρων με χορὸς περιδέδρομε πάντῃ

I am Jehova, (well my words perpend)
Clad with the frory sea, all mantled over
With the blue Heavens, shoed with the Earth I wend,
The stars about me dance, th' Air doth me cover.

This is to become Deiform, to be thus suspended (not by imagination, but by union of life, Κέντρον κέντρῳ συνάψαντα, joyning centres with God) and by a sensible touch to be held up from the clotty dark Personality of this compacted body. Here is love, here is freedome, here is justice and equity in the superessentiall causes of them. He that is here, looks upon all things as one, and on himself, if he can then mind himself, as a part of the whole. And so hath no self-interest, no unjust malicious plot, no more then the hand hath against the foot, or the ear against the eye. This is to be godded with God, and Christed with Christ, if you be in love with such affected language.

B More, *The Preface general*, 6 (*Collection of Several Philosophical Writings*, vii–viii)

[6. Divine Sagacity a Principle antecedaneous to successful Reason in Contemplation of the highest concernment.]

But in the third and last place, (and which, though it has some considerable influence every where, yet is more peculiarly requisite in perusing writings upon such Subjects as these I treat of) I should commend to them that would successfully philosophize, the belief and endeavour after a certain Principle more noble and inward than Reason it self, and without which Reason will faulter, or at least reach but to mean and frivolous things. I have a sense of something in me while I thus speak, which I must confess, is of so retruse a nature, that I want a name for it, unless I should [viii] adventure to term it *Divine Sagacity*, which is the first Rise of successful Reason, especially in matters of great comprehension and moment, and without which a man is as it were in a thick wood, and may make infinite promising attempts, but can find no open Champain, where one may freely look about him every way, (the πέδιον τῆς ἀληθείας) without the safe conduct of his *Genius*.

C Henry More, Preface to 2nd edition, 22 (Translation: Christian Hengstermann)

22. . . . And I beseech all those who intend to philosophize in earnest: cast off all admiration for persons and all party zeal! Instead, spare no effort in striving for that moral prudence of which we have given such an accurate description in this *Enchiridion*. We shall then have a pure und untainted mind, one freed of all prejudice and gathered and taken back into the divine mind, united with it in closest union and most perfect subjection. Embraced by it, as it were, we shall always be guided by it through the influx of its powers. For all human reason that God does not inform and govern by his divine breath is paralyzed, as it were, and displaced. And something holier and more divine than reason must assist it and carry the torch before it unless we want reason perpetually to lead us into those narrow lanes and mazes from which we are either compelled to escape in shame or exhaust our strength in eternal errors.

D More, *Enchiridion Ethicum*, I 5,1–7

Chap. V.

To shew which are the Faculties whereby we do find and understand what is simply, and its own nature good.

I. IT is now manifest,[1] there is something which is simply and absolutely good, which in all human Actions is to be sought for. That it's Nature, Essence, and Truth are to be judged of by *Right Reason*; But that the relish and delectation thereof, is to be taken in by[2] the *Boniform Faculty*. Also that all Moral Good, properly so called, is *Intellectual* and *Divine*: *Intellectual*, as the Truth and Essence of it is defined and comprehended by the Intellect: and *Divine*, as the Savour and Complacency thereof, is most effectually tasted through that high Faculty, by which we are lifted up and cleave unto God, (that Almighty One, who is the most pure and absolute Good, and who never wills any thing but what is transcendently the Best.)[3] So that for a man thus to know, and thus to ascend,[4] is not only the highest Wisdom, but the highest Felicity. And it is by this Gradation toward things divine, or by this Flower and Perfection of the Soul, that we attain to a sort of Coalition what is perfectly the Best.[5] So it was said of old;

Objectum quoddam est quod mentis flore prehendas.

II. NOW as to those men who shall either rashly or advisedly[6] reject the Truth of our *Noema's*, 'tis easie to guess by this disrelish, what are the Faculties they consult. Nay, it is plain they set up for the *animal Appetite*; and openly declare, that what pleases them most, is only the best. But tho we may here venture to call this a poor brutal delusion,[7] yet these things are most properly referred unto, in the Chapter of *Temperance*.

III. IN the mean time, for what relates even to *Justice*, the Sentiments of those Gentlemen are nothing better. They will not allow for the chiefest Good that which is absolutely and in its own nature just; but that which to *themselves* looks well, without any regard to their Neighbors.[8] And if you enquire into the state of this *Good* they so indulge, and so pursue,[9] they make it no secret to tell you plainly, it is what affords best entertainment to their *Senses*. Alas, how deplorable is it, that man should ever value himself upon such an affinity with the Beast! Nay, in human shape to become the very Beast![10] Whereas he has Title to think higher of himself, and to be one and the same with what is most eminent within him; or what in Dignity stands next thereto: which is doubtless his *Intellect* and *Right Reason*.[11]

IV. FOR as in Numeration the Sum Total is accounted from the last Unite,[12] so is it in other matters; the last and most perfect essential difference makes a Thing to be what it is, and doth distinguish it from all Things else. Wherefore, if any man shall make his *sole good* to be that, which to himself is grateful, as insisting wholly on the delectation of his *animal Appetite*, he plainly publishes himself for a Brute. But if he means and intends such grateful thing, as to the Intellect, or Right Reason, or to the *Boniform Faculty*, is suitable: This indeed (as Plotinus saith) is the Object of a *perfect Man*, I mean of an *intellectual Man*, and for such may pronounce him.[13]

V. FOR this is the plain Character of the intellectual Life, that as in the search of Truth, it is not inquired what may seem true to any one Body of Men, tho ever[14] so numerous, much less to any man in particular, but what is simply and absolutely the Truth: so neither doth it set up that for good,[15] which to any one man, or to any number of men, appears for such; but that which really and absolutely is so; and which, in like Circumstances every intellectual Creature is bound to elect,[16] be the animal Nature never so averse. Now as it happens in *specious Arithmetick*,[17] that every signal Operation stands afterwards for a Theorem or Conclusion: so in Morals let such preference and election, as we have mentioned, stand for an eternal President, to guide our actions in all like cases, when circumstances are the same. And let us acquiesce therein, and acknowledge the Truth thereof, tho it prove never so ungrateful to our Appetites, and seem quite contrary to our external sense.[18]

VI. WHEREFORE as it is an Error in the Intellect, to resign it self so far to the Imagination, or to the Sense, as but to waver in the pursuit of *Truth*: So doubtless is it an error in the Will, to be so captivated, as to resign it self to the animal Appetite, and to forsake what is absolutely good.[19] For if the Will may want at some seasons that relish of good which it ought to have; this is merely the Will's neglect, in not exciting that divine Faculty, by which we not only know what is best, but are elevated, and even ravished when we enjoy it. For it is plain, that when we open our Eyes, such are the Charms of this Joy, that a man would rather venture a thousand deaths, than by any base prevarication to hazard his portion in a state of which, which is so desirable and so divine.[20]

VII. WHEREFORE as it is now plain, that something there is, which of its own nature, and incontestably is *true*: so is there somewhat which of its own nature is simply *good*. Also that as the former is comprehended by the Intellect, so the sweetness and delight of the latter is relished by the Boniform Faculty. Wherefore as to those who pronounce every thing good, so far as at any it can be grateful, and so establish it for the standard of human Actions; this is Madness it self, inasmuch as hereby they rank the Wise, the Fools, and the Mad-men, all in the same state. Nay, perhaps they herein prefer the Fools and Mad men before the Wise; since these are the most likely to persist against all Sense and Reason, and to stick by that which is *grateful*, let it be never so destructive, vile or ridiculous.[21]

E More, *Enchiridion Ethicum*, II,9,13–18

Chap. IX.

Of that Mediocrity, in which Vertue does consist: And of the true measure of such Mediocrity.

XIII. THERE is now but one thing more, to clear before us all the Difficulty that remains. For whereas it may sound as if we give up our prudent Man to Inspirations and to Enthusiasm; while we contend he cannot in any other respect be wise, than as his Mind is reform'd and purg'd: and that it must also needs hence ensure, that whatsoever a Man so purg'd, shall afterwards imagine, must therefore be according to Right Reason, or Right Reason it self, merely because he thinks so: And that, in short, there must be no other Measure, or Principle; but that his Imagination[22] shall be as the standard of Congruity and of Right.

Therefore it is necessary (as *Andronicus Rhodius* speaks) first to inquire and find out, *What is the Mode and Standard of this Right Reason? And what that Principle in human Affairs that is just and congruous?* For surely that alone is Right Reason, which to such Standard, Mode, and Principle, can be apply'd; and this must be some Primitive Good, which is not only most simple, but most excellent, and a true *Basis*, *Norma* and *Standard*,[23] for all the rest.

XIV. NOW while I am in this high pursuit, I call to witness all that is holy, that in my sense (L. 1. c. 2. § 5 etc.)., there cannot, in the whole compass of Nature, be found a greater Good than is that *Love*, which (to free it from all other Imputations) we call *Intellectual*. For what can more fill, elevate, and irradiate the Soul than this intellectual Love (L. 3. c. 8. § 8)? Surely nothing is more exalted or Divine, nothing more ravishing, and complacent, nothing more sharp in distinguishing what in every Case is decorous and right, or more quick in executing whatsoever is laudable and just.

Since therefore this is the most high and most simple good; it ought in preference, to be the Rule and Standard[24] of all the rest; and nothing should pass, or be accounted, for Right Reason, which from this Divine Source and Fountain did not take its Birth.

XV. AND what is all this *Intellectual Love*, we so describe, but an inward Life and Sense, that moves in the *Boniform Faculty of the Soul*[25] (*vid. Margin. supra.*)? 'Tis by this the Soul relisheth what is simply the best; thither it tends, and in that alone it has its Joy and Triumph Hence we are instructed how to set God before our Eyes; to love him above all; to adhere to him[26] as the supremest Good; to consider him as the Perfection of all Reason, of all Beauty, of all Love; how all was made by his Power, and that all is upheld by his Providence. Hence also is the Soul taught how to affect and admire the Creation, and all the Parcels of it; as they share in that Divine Perfection and Beneficence,[27] which is dispersed through the whole Mass: So that if any of these Parcels appear defective or discompos'd, the Soul compassionates and brings help, strenuously endeavouring, as it is able, to restore every thing to that state of Felicity, which God and nature intended for it. In short, it turns all its Faculties to make good Men happy; and all its Care and Discipline is to make bad Men good.

XVI. THEREFORE I say, this most simple and Divine Sense and Feeling in the *Boniform Faculty of the Soul* (*V. Marg. supr.*) is that Rule or Boundary, whereby Reason is examin'd and approves her self. For if she offers or affirms any thing that is contrary to the Sense and Feeling, 'tis spurious and dishonest; if congruous to it, 'tis Orthodox, fit, and just.[28] So that we need not invent any other *external* Idea of Good; or follow those, who vainly dream of remoter Objects; when as this inward Life and Sense points singly at that Idea, which is fram'd not from exterior things, but from the Relish and intrinsick Feeling of the *Boniform Faculty* within. And altho this Idea be but single and alone, yet from thence arise all the Shapes and Modes of Virtue and of Well-doing: and 'tis into this again, that all of them may, by a due and unerring Analysis, be resolv'd. For as all Numbers arise from Unity, and by Unites are all measur'd: so we affirm, that by this *Intellectual Love*, as from a Principle the most pure and most abstracted of all others, all the Modes and Kinds of *Justice*, *Fortitude*, and even or *Temperance* it self, are to be measur'd: for nothing is so detrimental to less and extinguish this Love as it the Exercise and Infection of sensual Delights.

XVII. NOW, in the last place, if any shall object that we have done amiss; and that all this splendid Fabrick of the Virtues is by us laid on a weak and tottering Foundation: As, namely in Passion, such as they may suppose this our Love to be. Let them for their better Information, know, that this *Love* is not more a Passion than is Intellection it self, which surely they cannot but believe to be very valuable, and very Divine.[29] 'Tis true we may as to this point (with *Des Cartes*) allow, that all Intellection has so much of Passion, as it is the Perception of something imprinted from without. However, as this Perception, which is made by Intellection, is not from the Body, but rather from the Soul, exerting and exciting her self into such Action: So neither is this Love form the Body; but either from the Soul it self, or else from God above, who calls and quickens the Soul to such a Divine *Effort*.[30] And tho this Perception may, if they please, be termed a sort of Passion, yet 'twill derogate no more from the Dignity[31] and Excellency of it, than from Intellection it self: Which, because 'tis an Act of Perception, may on that account be also termed a Passion.

XVIII. YET when all is said, perhaps this Love, which we insist upon, may not so truly be termed a Passion, as acknowledg'd to be the Peace and Tranquillity of the Mind: nay a state of such Serenity, as hath no other Motions than those of Benignity and Beneficence. So that this Love may rather be thought a firm and unshaken Benignity, or Bounty of the Soul; such as has nothing more perfect, or more approaching to the immortal Gods. I mean hereby that State of the Blessed Spirits, unto which we ought all to aspire: and surely without this Love, those very Spirits would not be as Gods, but as a Race of Devils. And therefore we may conclude this Love, to be the most perfect, and the most Angelick Think of all others; far excelling even Intellection it self. And, in truth, more aptly deserving those lofty Words, which *Aristotle* bestows upon the Speculative Intellect; where he says, *That according to some Doctors we are not to converse with human things, altho we are Men, nor with things transitory, altho we were Mortals; but, as much as is possible, we should affect to live as do the immortal Gods: And this, by performing every thing in such sort, as conforms to that Principle, which is the most excellent thing within us* (Ethic. Nicom. l. 10. c. 7.). Now *Andronicus* (his Paraphrast) declares, *This most excellent thing within us, to be the Intellect* (L. 10. c. 9). But I beg leave to call it rather by the Name of *Intellectual Love*.

Thus I end a Point, on which some may think I have insisted too long: But the whole will shew our Sense of Virtue; and of its kinds; and how it may be said to consist in a *Mediocrity*; and what also is the *Norma* or Measure of such *Mediocrity*. The next Step will be touching Good that is *external*.

Notes

1 The Latin says: "It is manifest from this", which implies that the subsequent remarks are considered by More to be conclusions from his catalogue of *noemata*.
2 In More's Latin, the "relish and sweetness are perceived in the boniform faculty of the soul".
3 Southwell takes quite a few liberties in the rendering of this crucial description of the soul's foremost moral faculty: "Divine inasmuch as its sweetness is tasted with the greatest joy and passion in that divine faculty by which we cleave to God, that most simple and most absolute good who always wills that which is absolutely and simply good."
4 Even though it is clearly implied by the context, the translator has omitted the object of the soul's boniform knowledge: "Hence, it is man greatest wisdom and greatest happiness to taste this Divine."
5 Again, Southwell introduces the vocabulary of ascent which, though Morean, is not to be found in the original. Moreover, Southwell seeks to relativize More's moral mysticism by qualifying the union with the Divine as "a sort of coalition", providing a Latin translation of the Greek quotation from the *Chaldaic Oracles*: "For it is by virtue of the apex and flower of our soul that we are conjoined with that which is absolutely the best, as that ancient oracle has it: 'There is something intelligible which you must understand by virtue of the flower of the mind'." The *prehendas* is Southwell's distinctly Morean rendering of the Greek χρή σε νοεῖν. The soul's knowledge of the Divine is not "intellection", but "comprehension" in its original meaning of "touching".
6 "Advisedly" may be slightly misleading here. The contrast between "rashly" (*temere*) and "deliberately" (*ex composito*) is probably that between a hedonistic lifestyle and a philosophical hedonism.
7 Southwell seems to have been carried away by the drift of More's anti-hedonistic argument, changing the syntax and adding a pun on "brutal" by which he denigrates the hedonists as "brutes". In the Latin, the reader is called on to "ask them which faculty they consult when putting forward such absurd responses. For you will see that such a person always consults his animal appetite and defines as the best thing whatever he finds to be most pleasant to himself. Clearly, this is the voice of a beast, not that of a man!" The Latin in this passage is generally odd. Not only is there a typological error (*definere* instead of *definire*), but More also uses the indicative instead of the subjunctive (*consulunt* instead of the mandatory *consulant*) and switches from the plural to the singular in his invective against the hedonist.

8 More, for the purpose of additional emphasis, assumes the role of the hedonist himself, providing a précis of the latter's ill-founded position. It is important to give a literal translation of the *intelligo*, which the author deliberately uses twice. Key to the hedonist argument is the alleged unintelligibility of the concept of an absolute good: "I do not understand at all what an 'absolute and simple good' is supposed to be (nor the meaning of 'something that is just by its nature'). The only good I can understand is the one that is good *for myself*, without any regard for my neighbour."
9 Southwell again expands greatly upon More's rather sober "Ask them further then".
10 While more vivid, Southwell's translation once again is a paraphrase of More's Latin which reads: "without realizing all the while how treacherously he denies his human nature and takes on that of a beast instead. Nay, he openly declares himself a beast, rather than a man!"
11 The translation is rather free and adds the concept of man's "dignity": "Whereas we are much more entitled to identify with what is the best in us or what at least is in our midst. However, this is intellect or right reason."
12 The mathematical analogy, which is important to More's rationalist methodology, has been rendered with rather insufficient clarity: "For just as in numbers the final unit determines the kind", i.e. that of the exact number, whether it is below or above ten, one hundred, etc.
13 More's own wording is more careful and precise here. It bears testimony to his systematic endeavour to distinguish right reason, which is intellectual in character, from the boniform faculty to which the good is said to be "pleasant". Moreover, Southwell may have misunderstood Plotinus's concept of the "true man" which designates the intellect as the archetypal essence of humanity: "If, instead, he points to what intellect and right reason approves of and is pleasing to the boniform faculty, this is certainly pleasing to and approved of by 'the true man', as Plotinus calls him, i.e. the one whom one may rightly call the intellectual man."
14 There appears to be a typological error in the text. It should say "never" instead.
15 In the original, More once again clarifies the distinct operation of practical reason, whether boniform or intellectual, which "neither seeks nor embraces" a particular good approved of by one or many, but absolute goodness necessarily applauded by all rational beings.
16 "Bound" retains its original meaning here. Hence, it does not designate necessity, but moral obligation which is categorical in nature: "that which is always to be chosen by every rational creature".
17 "Special arithmetic".
18 Southwell once again mistranslates a mathematical comparison. He also changes More's deeply Platonist terminology of the good choice as an "unchanging and eternal form" which is the source of the soul's moral obligation. Moreover, More expounds moral choice in the metaphorical language of spiritual "touch" or "embrace", which is a key tenet of the Cambridge Platonists' ethical mysticism: "As a consequence, therefore, a certain choice of this kind (like a certain singular operation in special arithmetic) leads to a general theory or a kind of unchanging and eternal idea of that which must be done under the given circumstances. We are as much obliged to embrace it (however unpleasant it may be to our animal appetite) as we are obliged to acknowledge a truth, even though it may be contrary to our external sense."
19 More's original diction is more nuanced and includes another important reference to spiritual "touch". Thus, it is a volitional failure to be "carried away or blinded" by one's animal impulses instead of "embracing" the absolute good.
20 Southwell's translation altogether fails to do justice to the philosophical and metaphorical richness of More's detailed exposition of the soul's divine moral sensation: "For it is the will's own fault and defect if it [i.e. the good] is not so pleasant to it at present. It has not yet awakened that supreme and most divine faculty by which we savour the most that which is absolutely the best and are delighted and filled with the greatest joy and passion. We, then, begin to love and admire it so much that we would rather die a thousand deaths than allow ourselves to be deprived of such great sweetness or offend, hurt and violate such a lovable flower of life or the integrity of the divine sense by committing a vile or dishonest deed."
21 Southwell slightly shortens More's *reductio* argument of the madmen who "pursue what is pleasing to them, however vile and ridiculous, in every single action."
22 The reference to the "imagination" is Southwell's, not More's.
23 In More, it is the "norm and measure of all the rest".
24 More again uses the two-part expression "norm and measure".
25 In More, this love "is stirred in the boniform faculty".
26 In the mystical tradition of the spiritual senses, More has the soul "embrace" God.
27 Southwell has added the very apposite "and beneficence", which stresses the Morean notion of God sharing with his creation the riches of his own perfect being.

28 More's original two-part expression *licitum & decorum*, characteristically expanded upon by Southwell into a three-word one, is probably not a hendiadys, but carries philosophical meaning. Whatever is approved of by the boniform faculty is "permissible and decorous".
29 More is more precise, charging his opponents with not acknowledging the soul's higher power beyond its intellect: "than which those people consider nothing either older or more divine".
30 Throughout, More makes use of the hylomorphist language of Aristotelian psychology. Hence, Southwell's "*Effort*" fails to capture the technical meaning of the Greek term ἐνέργεια, as does his earlier "action". Instead, both *hic actus* at the beginning and *divinissima* ἐνέργεια at the end of this important sentence designate the fulfilment of the soul's innermost potency or essence in the vision of divine goodness.
31 Southwell once again seems at pains to diminish the force of More's ὁμοίωσις-doctrine, replacing his "divinity" with the more innocuous and orthodox "dignity".

Chapter 20

Libertarian Freedom

A More, *Enchiridion Ethicum*, III,1,8–13

Chap. I. Of Free-Will

VIII. BUT to make the truth of this Opinion more manifest; Let us take Notice what this *Liberum Arbitrium* or *Free-Will* is; and then Demonstrate that there is really such a Principle within us. First, Liberty of the Will, which the *Greeks* call *Autexousion*, seems almost to imply, The *having a power to Act or not Act within our selves.*[1] Now in that *Free-Will* is a Principle of Acting within one's self, it so far agrees with what the Greeks call *Hecousion*, which is the same as Spontaneous: And which (as *Andronicus* defines it) is that, *Whose Principle of Acting is wholly in the Agent.* Yet what he straight subjoins in the same Chapter, saying, *That in what a Man Acts, as mov'd thereunto by himself, he is Lord and Master of Doing it, or letting it alone* (Lib. 3. Cap. 1). This I think is not altogether so exact.

For a Man may Act out of his own mere Motion; that is to say, from such inbred Principles of Virtue,[2] and by so strong and efficacious a sense of Honesty, as not to be able to act otherwise, or to draw his Will to any different Thing. For instance, an Honest Man has Power indeed, by his Wit and bodily Force, treacherously to destroy and Innocent Man, and even one that has well deserved of him. But can that Honest Man do this Thing? No, God forbid! He dare not let himself do it. For that vigorous and lively sense of what is Honest, and with which his Mind is tinctur'd and possess'd, can by no means permit him to execute so horrid a Villany. Now as such a Person, tho never so much solicited by Promises and Rewards, starts back, and (in the sense of *Antonine*) stops all his Faculties of Motion,[3] and does not resign himself to so base a Fact; this doubles is entirely *from himself*, and none else is the Cause, why that Advantage is not taken. However, I say, he is not, in this Case, so much Master of his Forbearance, as that it is in his power not to forbear. I grant (indeed) that if we would, he were able to commit so wicked a Thing; but that he is able to Will it, or bring his Will unto it, is what I utterly deny.

IX. WE say therefore there is some Difference between having *Free-Will*, and being a *Voluntary* or *Spontaneous Agent*. The former is more restrain'd and particular, and obtains in fewer Cases; the latter is more large and general. When we say that a Man has *Liberum Arbitrium* or *Free-will*, we add a particular Difference to the general Notion of *Voluntariness*, that is to say, We suppose he is such a voluntary Agent, as can Act and not Act as he pleases[4]: Whereas to the being a voluntary Agent, simply or generally speaking, there is no such Difference required. It is sufficient to denominate any Agent to be such, whose Principle of Action is in himself, and who understands and takes cognizance of his own Actions and the Circumstances that relate to them (Andronicus, *Lib. 3. Cap. 2*): Tho, in the mean time, it may not be in his Power, every time he Acts, to Act otherwise than he does.[5]

This now being the Notion of *Spontaneous* or *Voluntary*; we see plainly what is the Opposite to it; namely, every thing that proceeds either from *Ignorance*, or *Outward Force*. Whatever Action is done from either of these Principles, must needs be inspontaneous and involuntary. For in the one Case (that of *Force*) the Agent does not act from his own Principles, but is compelled from without: In the other Case (that of *Ignorance*) tho he act from his own Principle, yet he has no Notice of the Moral Circumstances of the Action, which if he had known, he would not have done that Action.[6]

X. BUT now as to *Liberum Arbitrium*, or *Freedom of the Will*; what we call by that Name is only that sort of Spontaneity or Voluntariness in us; which is so free and undetermin'd,[7] that it is in our Power, to Will or Act this way or the other way, as we please. This (I say) is properly Free-Will; and it supposeth a free Election or Choice in our selves: And accordingly *Andronicus* (from *Aristotle*) defines it to be, *A deliberate Wishing or Appetition of those Things, which are within our Power* (Lib. 3. Cap. 4). For those things (says he) are the subjects of Deliberation, whereof every one is Master to do them, or to leave them undone: and these are those very Things, which he declares to be within our Power.[8]

Now this Power of not Acting, when it regards those things which are Base and Dishonest, is a great Perfection; But when it has respect of things that are Noble and Honest, 'tis a great Imperfection[9]: For 'tis in the very next Degree to Acting dishonestly, to be able to incline the Will towards an Action that is vile.

However, to know we are able, and possess'd with a Power to abstain from a vile Thing (tho possibly we do not abstain) this is a sort of Perfective State, and of high Consequence for a Man to discover in himself whether he have it or no.[10]

Now that such a real Power is planted in Man, of being able to abstain from doing ill, tho he fails at some times to exert that Power, is very plain from the Instances that follow.

XI. WE need not bring hereunto any other Help, than what was noted before, in the Chapter about the Interpretation of the Passions. For as we feel the Checks of Conscience after doing some things which were doubtingly Acted, and without mature Deliberation[11]: Even from hence it is manifest, that we sometimes Act so, as that to have Will'd and Acted otherwise, was in our Power. And This Power, of abstaining from Ill, is that very Thing, which is truly called *Free-Will*.

XII. THE Reason also of Repentance, is close of Relation hereunto. For when we are captivated by some Appetite, and commit what we know, and are very sensible, is against the Dictates of Honesty; 'tis of these things we are afterwards said to Repent. 'Tis not said, We lament such things as *Misfortunes*; which they ought in reason to pass for, if either by Fate, or a necessary Chain of Causes, we were always destined or irresistibly determin'd to them, and that it had never been within our Power or Capacity to have avoided them (*Lib. 2. Cap. 3*). For no Man Repents himself of his *Misfortunes*, but of his *Sins*; because these are committed by his own Crime, when he might have abstain'd, and done otherwise. But to Repent of Sins, which were never in our Power to withstand; is as if a Man should greatly lament his Improbity and Malice, or undertake some sharp Penance, for not having been Created an Angel, or else born a Prince (L. 2. c. 1. § 15). As to the like Effect we have hinted before.

XIII. BUT, in the last place, To what purpose do we reprehend some Men for what they act, pardon others, and have pity on the rest; if Mankind be destitute of *Free-Will*; If it be not given him, to turn away from what is Vile, and to embrace what is Laudable and Just: For we might, in point of Justice, insist upon it, that if Men are ty'd to Sin, and do it by *Necessity*, and cannot otherwise act; there is both Pardon and Commiseration due unto them: Also by how much a Man's Sins were crying and flagitious, by so much would they become the more worthy of such Pardon and Moral Pity. But since these things are repugnant to common Sense, and the inbred Characters of our Mind[12]; it follows of Necessity, that we must acknowledge some Actions, at least, of Man to be *Free*: that is to say, that they spring from such a Principle, as we have out of Aristotle describ'd, and which we call *Free-Will*. And we hope no Man will doubt hereof, when we shall have satisfi'd the Two Principal Objections, wherewith the Champions of the other side do so loudly, and with such Clamours contend.

B More, *Enchiridion Ethicum*, III,2,7–14

Chap. II. Two Principal Objections against Free-Will are Propos'd and Answer'd.

VII. HOWEVER, as to those, who are so endow'd as to have some Native Fortast of this high and Excellent Good; it seems to be plac'd within their Power, either to acquire to themselves a clearer and more extended Knowledg therein, or else to let that by degrees extinguish which already they have. Into which Error, if they shall unhappily run; 'tis with the same reason they may be said to be *Willingly wicked*, as of the Intemperate man, that he throws himself *Wilfully into a Distemper*. And of whom Andronicus speaks in this sort, *Before the Man fell sick, it was in his own Power to have preserv'd his Health: But when Health is lost by Incontinence and Debauch, it is not in his Power to Recover it. So any Man may throw a Stone to the Bottom of the Sea, but being cast thither he cannot recover it: However the Stone was willingly cast by him, for it was in his Power, either to Cast, or to have with-held it* (L: 3. c. 6).[13]

VIII. AS for those Men, who throw off all Distinction of Things Honest and Vile[14]; who have no other Sense than of the *Animal Life*, who consider only for themselves, be it Right or Wrong; who think that *Good* is but of one Sort, and this only referable to Animal Content (or if, perchance, they think Good to be various, yet still they fix and appropriate all to themselves;) In such Men as these, I do confess, their Will is perpetually determin'd to what is the most apparent Good. They enjoy no more Liberty than Brutes, whose Appetite is necessarily ty'ed down to the greater Good: For they have but one single Principle of Acting, and 'tis but one sort of Object that is before their Senses. And in this single Case 'tis confessed, that the Second Objection has its Force.

IX. BUT when we consider, how there is a double Principle in the greatest Part of Mankind; the one *Divine*, and the other *Animal*. How that the Voice and Dictate of the *Divine Principle* (L. 1. c. 6. § 4), is ever for that which is simply and absolutely the Best; and Virtue proposeth, in every of our Thoughts or Actions, that which is most conforming to the Eternal and immutable Law of Reason: Which (in *Tully*'s Opinion before mention'd) is the common Standard both to God and to our selves. When also, on the other side, we consider that the *Animal* Principle dictates nothing to Man, but what to himself is either good, pleasing, or advantageous; that is, what may be grateful to himself alone, tho it never so much violate that Law, or Universal Reason of things, before spoken of (L. 1. c. 6. § 4). I say, that from the Conflict and Opposition of these two Principles, we have a clear Prospect what is the Condition, and what the Nature of that Free-Will whereof we treat.

X. THIS is a thing, which all Men have experience of, that at some times, and even then when we behold clearly what were best[15] and consonant to the Divine Law; yet we do not excite our Minds to it; or put on that Courage, which we know we have, to pursue so fair and so fit an Object; but yield and go on[16] where-ever the Stream[17] of Pleasure, or of our own Utility, will carry us. But certainly we have the more to answer for herein; as at the same time we are inwardly conscious, it is in our Power to over-rule all external Motions of the Body. And that, if we would obey such Power, and abstain from acting, there would nothing of that Guilt ensue, which for Self-Interest or Concupiscence we too frequently incur.

XI IN the mean time, while such Men as these do still go on, and still delude themselves with Apologies for their Sloth and Immorality (as either trusting to the Divine Goodness for Pardon, or else putting off their Amendments to a further Day) 'tis manifest, that altho they do persist to satisfie their ill Desires, and postpone their Repentance to future time: yet are they convinc'd, it were far better, if already done; and that 'tis equally now, as well as hereafter, within their Power to do it. And this is enough to shew, how plainly, even these confess the *Liberty of Man's Will*.

XII. AND thus is it made evident, that 'tis not necessary, that Man's Will should still be carried on to the greater (that is, to the more excellent) Good. For it may, according to the Liberty it hath, desert what is absolutely the best[18]; and either close with what is most grateful to the Animal Life, or suffer it self to be captiv'd by it, for want of exerting the Power and Faculties it hath.

XIII. AND here I do as freely confess, that were there no other Life or Law in us, than to relish and pursue what were most for our particular Pleasure, and not that which is the most simple and most absolute Good (which assuredly is some Divine Thing, and by Nature congruous and consonant to that Eternal Wisdom, which has fram'd and does preserve the Universe) it would be hard to prove, that we had any Free-Will; or that our Will was not necessarily determin'd to some one thing, which, in all Deliberations, appear'd to us for the best.

XIV. BUT, on the other side, it is plain and manifest to me, that this Divine Law is as perfectly in us, as the Animal; and that Right Reason is that Law (and it is a high Gift and Blessing of God unto morals)[19] by which we are taught, and stand bound, to prefer publick Good before our private, and never to make our own Pleasure or Utility to be the Measure of human Actions. And whoever he be, thank thinks himself justly discharged from the Obligation of this Heavenly Law; I am bold to affirm, he deserves to pass for the most vile, as well as most contemptible, Creature upon Earth.

XV. THUS much of *Free-Will*, and with what Brevity and Perspicuity we are able. For what concerns the chief Arguments, or rather Sophisms of Mr. *Hobbs*; we have sufficiently refuted them in our Treatise Of the Immortality of the Soul (Lib. 2. c. 3): Whereunto the Reader is already refer'd. So that we now pass to those Theorems or Precepts, which are useful in the acquiring of Virtue.

C Ralph Cudworth, *Treatise of Freewill*, Chapter 1 (ed. Hutton, 155–156)

We seem clearly to be led by the instincts of nature to think that there is something ἐφ' ἡμῖν', *in nostra potestate*, in our own power (though dependently upon God Almighty), and that we are not altogether passive in our actings, nor determined by inevitable necessity in whatsoever we do. Because we praise and dispraise, commend and blame men for their actings, much otherwise than we do inanimate beings or brute animals. When we blame or commend a clock or automaton, we do it so as not imputing to that automaton its being the cause of its own moving well or ill, agreeably or disagreeably to the end it was designed for, this being ascribed by us only to the artificer. But when we blame a man for any wicked actions, as for taking away another man's life, either by perjury or by wilful murder, we blame him not only as doing otherwise than ought to have been done, but also than he might have done, and that it was possible for him to have avoided it, so that he was himself the cause of the evil thereof. We do not impute the evil of all men's wicked actions to God the creator and maker of them, after the same manner as we do the faults of a block or watch wholly to the watchmaker. All men's words at least free God from the blame of wicked actions, pronouncing ὁ θὲς ἀναίτιος, God is causeless and guiltless of them, and we cast the blame of them wholly on the men themselves, as principles of action; and the true causes of the moral defects of them. So also do we blame men's acting viciously and immorally in another sense than we blame a halting or a stumbling horse; or than we blame the natural and necessary infirmities, of men themselves when uncontracted by vice. For in this case we so blame the infirmities as to pity the men themselves, looking upon them as unfortunate but not as faulty.

D Cudworth, *Freewill*, 7

But this scholastic philosophy is manifestly absurd, and mere scholastic jargon. For to attribute the act of intellection and perception to the faculty of understanding, and acts of volition to the faculty of will, or to say that it is the understanding that understandeth, and the will that willeth—this is all one as if one should say that the faculty of walking walketh, and the faculty of speaking speaketh, or that the musical faculty playeth a lesson upon the lute, or sings this or that tune.

Moreover, since it is generally agreed upon by all philosophers, that *actiones sunt suppositorum*, whatsoever acts is a subsistent thing, therefore by this kind of language are those two faculties of understanding and will be made to be two *supposita*, two subsistent things, two agents, and two persons, in the soul. Agreeable to which are these forms of speech commonly used by scholastics, that the understanding propounds to the will, represents to the will, allures and invites the will, and the will either follows the understanding, or else refuses to comply with its dictates, exercising its own liberty. Whence is that inextricable confusion and unintelligible nonsense, of the will's both first moving the understanding, and also the understanding first moving the will, and this in an infinite and endless circuit. So that this faculty of will must needs be supposed to move understandingly, or knowingly of what it doth, and the faculty of understanding to move willingly, nor not without will. Whereas to intellect as such, or as a faculty, belongs nothing but mere intellection or perception, without anything will; and to will as such, or as a faculty, nothing but mere volition, without anything of intellection.

But all this while it is really the man or soul that understands, and the man or soul that wills, as it is the man that walks and the man that speaks or talks, and the musician that plays a lesson on the lute. So that it is one and the same subsistent thing, one and the same soul that both understandeth and willeth, and the same agent only that acteth diversely. And thus may it well be conceived that one and the same reasonable soul in us may both will understandingly, or knowingly of what it wills; and understand or think of this or that object willingly.

E Cudworth, *Treatise of Freewill*, 8

It is a very material question which Aristotle starteth, τί τὸ πρώτως κινοῦν—what is that that first moveth in the soul and setteth all the other wheels on work? That is, what is that vital power, and energy which the soul first displayeth itself in, and which in order of nature precedes all its other powers, it implying them, or setting them on work? [. . .] Wherefore, we conclude that the τὸ πρώτως κινοῦν, that which first moveth in us, and is the spring and principle of all deliberative action, can be no other than a constant, restless, uninterrupted desire, or love of good as such, and happiness. This is an ever bubbling fountain in the centre of the soul, an elater or spring of motion, both a primum and perpetuum mobile in us, the first wheel that sets all the other wheels in motion, and an everlasting and incessant mover. God, an absolutely perfect being, is not this love of indigent desire, but a love of overflowing fulness and redundancy, communicating itself.

F Cudworth, *Treatise of Freewill*, 10

I say, therefore, that the τὸ ἡγεμονικόν in every man and indeed that which is properly we ourselves (we rather having those other things of necessary nature than being them), is the soul as comprehending itself, all its concerns and interests, its abilities and capacities, and holding itself, as it were, in its own hand, as it were, redoubled upon itself, having a power of intending or exerting itself more or less in consideration and deliberation, in resisting the lower appetites that oppose it, both of utility, reason, and honesty; in self-recollection and attention, and vigilant circumspection, or standing upon our guard; in purposes and resolutions, in diligency in carrying on steady designs and active endeavours—this in order, to self-improvement and the self-promoting of its own good, the fixing and conserving itself in the same. Though by accident and by abuse, it often proves a self-impairing power, the original of sin, vice, and wickedness, whereby men become to themselves the causes of their own evil, blame, punishment, and misery. Wherefore this hegemonicon always determines the passive capability of men's nature one way or other, either for better or for worse. And it has a self-forming and self-framing power, by which every man is self-made, into what he is. And accordingly deserves either praise or dispraise, reward or punishment.

Now I say, in the first place, that a man's soul as hegemonical over itself, having a power intending and exerting itself more or less in consideration and deliberation, when different objects, or ends, or mediums, are propounded to his choice, that are in themselves really better and worse, may, upon slight considerations and immature deliberations (he attending to some appearance of good in one of them without taking notice of the evils attending it), choose and prefer that which is really worse before the better, so as to deserve blame thereby. But this is not because it had by nature and equal indifferency and freedom to a greater or lesser good, which is absurd, or because it had a natural liberty of will either to follow or not follow, its own last practical judgement, which is all one as to say a liberty to follow or not follow its own volition. For upon both these suppositions there would have been no such thing as fault or blame. But here also the person being supposed to follow the greater apparent good at this time and not altogether to clash with his last practical judgement neither. But because he might have made a better judgement than now he did, had he more intensely considered, and more maturely deliberated, which, that it did not, was its own fault. Now to say that a man hath not this power over himself to consider and deliberate more or less, is to contradict common experience and inward sense. And to deny that a man is blameworthy for inward temerity in acting in any thing of moment without due and full deliberation, and so choosing the worser is absurd. But if a man have this power over himself to consider and deliberate more or less; then is he not always determined thereunto by any antecedent necessary causes. These two things being inconsistent and contradictious. And consequently there was something of contingency in the choice.

Notes

1 More rather lists two largely synonymous terms, subsequently providing a first definition: "However, 'free will' apparently means largely the same as the Greeks' αὐτεξούσιον, which is the same as 'having in oneself the power to act or not to act'."
2 Southwell wrongly renders the singular *principio* as "principles". However, on More's scheme, there is but one single principle of virtuous action, i.e. the boniform faculty and the intellectual love it stirs in the soul.
3 Marcus Aurelius' expression is more graphic: "He stops the attraction caused by his nerves and members".
4 Southwell clearly tries to render more intelligible a somewhat difficult bit of Morean definition, which, in a more literal rendering, reads: "'Free will' is less wide than 'voluntary' and 'spontaneous', as it includes in itself as its [specific] difference 'power to act or not to act'. 'Spontaneous, by contrast, is simply defined as 'that whose principle is in the one knowing the details of the situation of his action'."
5 This final sentence is an explanatory note added by Southwell. An action may be classified as "voluntary" or "spontaneous", even though the agent lacks the power to act otherwise. However, it is not an action of "free will", which presupposes this capacity.
6 Southwell has added these last two phrases so as to clarify More's rather terse definitions.
7 This relative clause has been added by Southwell.
8 Like "freedom" and "voluntary", "within our Power" or τὰ ἐφ' ἡμῖν (more frequently used in the singular) is another technical expression of the ancient debate about determinism.

9 Southwell adds "of not acting" to remedy what appears to be an oversight on the part of the author who, in the original, says: "This power, when it refers to that which is base, is a kind of perfect, whereas, when it refers to that which is beautiful and honest, is the worst imperfection."
10 More's original Latin is more precise. Moreover, Southwell has omitted More's announcement that he is about to provide evidence for the existence of the power defined: "However, it is a certain perfectible power that we were able to abstain from base deeds, even though in actual fact we failed to do so, and it is indeed quite important to acknowledge that we possess this power."
11 More's exact wording is of philosophical importance here. We feel remorse on doing things "resolved upon prior to the required deliberation and without any uncertainty of the mind".
12 More again uses technical Stoic vocabulary here, referring to the "common notions of our mind".
13 Southwell has left out More's reference: "as we are rightly taught on the basis of Aristotle by the most learned of his commentators."
14 More's thought experiment is more radical. It revolves around those "whose sense of distinguishing between good and bad has been extinguished altogether."
15 Two aspects of terminological subtlety, namely the criterion of "sufficient" clarity and the notion of moral duty or value as something that "is better in a simple and absolute sense" are lost in Southwell's rendering: "that sometimes even when they perceive with sufficient clarity what would be better in an absolute and simple sense".
16 Southwell's two-part expression "yield and go on" is a particularly apt translation of the ambiguous Latin *ferri se sinunt*. The soul allows itself to be carried away by its animal life and acts accordingly.
17 The metaphorical "Stream" is an addition of Southwell's meant to stress the notion of a soul being carried away by its passions of its own accord.
18 More again uses the comparative *absolutè melius*: "what is better in an absolute sense".
19 More's praise is more philosophical in character: "than which nothing either more perfect or more divine has been given, or could be given."

Chapter 21

Theoretical Reason and Knowledge

A Cudwort, *A Treatise Concerning Eternal and Immutable Morality* (1731), Book III Chapter 1, Sections 3

3. But foreasmuch as sense is not mere local motion impressed from one body upon another, or a body's bare reaction or resistance to that motion of another body, as some have fondly conceited, but a cogitation, recognition, or vital perception and consciousness of these motions or passions of the body, therefore, there must of necessity be another kind of passion also in the soul or principle of life, which is vitally united to the body, to make up sensation. Which passion notwithstanding is of a different kind or species from the former. For the soul, that is a cogitative being, is supposed to be such a thing as can penetrate a body, and therefore cannot be conceived to be moved by the local motion of the body. For we see that light which pervades the air, though it be a corporeal motion, yet it is not moved or shaken by the agitations of the air, because it is not a body far more subtle than the air, that runs through the spongy pores of it. Wherefore the soul, though it be conceived to be an extended substance, yet being penetrative of body not by filling up the pores of it, but co-existing in the same place with it, cannot be locally moved by the motions of it.

Neither is this passion of the soul in sensation a mere naked passion or suffering, because it is a cogitation or perception which hath something of active vigour in it. For those ideas of heat, light, and colours, and other sensible things, being not qualities really existing in the bodies without us, as the atomical philosophy instructs us, and therefore not passively stamped or imprinted upon the soul from without in the same manner that a signature is upon a piece of wax, must needs arise partly from some inward vital energy of the soul itself, being phantasms of the soul, or several modes of cogitation or perception in it. For which cause some of the Platonists would not allow sensations to be passions in the soul, but only active knowledges of the passions of the body (παθῶν γνώσεις).

B Cudworth, *Eternal and Immutable Morality*, 4,1,2

2. A thing which is merely passive from without, and which doth only receive foreign and adventitious forms, cannot possibly know, understand, or judge of that which it receives but must needs be a stranger to it, having nothing within itself to know it by. The mind cannot know anything, but by something of its own, that is native, domestic, and familiar to it. When it in a great throng or crowd of people, a man looking round about, meets with innumerable strange faces that he never saw before in all his life and at last chances to espy the face of one old friend or acquaintance, which he had not seen or thought of many years before, he would be said in this case to have known that one, and only that one face in all that company, because he had no inward previous or anticipated form of any other face, that he looked upon in his mind. But as soon as ever he beheld that one face,

immediately there reived and started forth a former anticipated form or idea of it treasured up in his mind, that, as it were taking acquaintance with that newly received form, made him know it or remember it. So when foreign, strange and adventitious forms are exhibited to the mind by sense, the soul cannot otherwise know or understand them, but by something domestic of its own, some active anticipation or prolepsis within itself, that occasionally reviving and meeting with it, makes it know it or take acquaintance with it. And this is the only true and allowable sense of that old assertion, that knowledge is reminiscence, not that it is the remembrance of something which the soul had some time before actually known in a pre-existent state, but because it is the mind's comprehending of things by some inward anticipations of its own, something native and domestic to it, or something actively exerted from within itself.

C Cudworth, *Eternal and Immutable Morality*, 4,2,13

But the intellect doth not rest here, but upon occasion of those corporeal things thus comprehended in themselves, naturally rises higher to the framing and exciting of certain ideas from within itself, of other things not existing in those sensible objects, but absolutely incorporeal. For being ravished with the contemplation of this admirable mechanism and artificial contrivance of the material universe, forthwith it naturally conceives it to be nothing else but the passive stamp, print, and signature of some living art and wisdom, as the pattern, archetype, and seal of it, and so excites from within itself an idea of that divine art and wisdom. Nay, considering further, how all things in this great mundane machine or animal (as the ancients would have it) are contrived, not only for the beauty of the whole, but also for the good of every part in it, that is endued with life and sense, it exerts another idea, viz. of goodness and benignity from within itself, besides that of art and wisdom, as the queen regent and empress of art, whereby art is employed, regulated, and determined.

Chapter 22

Practical Reason and Virtue

A More, *Enchiridion Ethicum*, I,3, 1–2

Chap. III. Of Virtue in general: and of Right Reason

I. VIRTUE *is an intellectual Power of the Soul, by which it over-rules the animal Impressions or bodily Passions; so as in every Action it easily pursues what is absolutely and simply the best.*

Here it seems fit, in the Definition, to call Virtue rather a *Power* than a *Habit*.[1] First, because the word *Virtue* implies as much, and signifies the same thing as Fortitude.[2] And next because an *Habit* is not essential to Virtue. For if a Man had this *intellectual Power* born in him, he would doubtless be virtuous, tho it came not to him in the way of repeated Actions, such as constitute a Habit. For it is not the external Causes, but the internal,[3] which make the essence of a thing. Besides it is this Idea of Virtue which elevates and inclines the mind to love her, and tread in her ways, and which argues Virtue to be quick and vigorous heat,[4] by which the mind is easily and irresistibly moved to do things which are good and honorable. So that we esteem this very notion of Virtue able to rowze up men from Sloth and Lethargy,[5] and make those ashamed, who on a few moderate Performances think to set up for Men of Virtue.

II. WE term this a *Power intellectual*, not only because of its situation,[6] which is in the *intellectual* part of the Soul (★ and not in the *animal* part of it, where that Power resides which governs the Members) but also because it is always excited by some Principle which is *intellectual* or rational. By animal *Impressions* we understand every motion of the Body, which being obtruded with any sort of Violence on the Soul, brings danger of Sin and Error, if not carefully watched.

Therefore all such Delusions and Imaginations, as strongly[7] assault the Mind, may fitly be referred to this Head. By *Actions*, I mean all Motions made by the Soul upon deliberation, which is to say, all such as may properly be termed human Actions; whether they be such as the School-men call *Elicitae* or *Imperatae*: that is, whether they do immediately proceed from the Soul it self; or whether they are occasioned from any outward Impressions made upon the Soul. Under which Heads we may rightly comprehend the accepting or refusing any Philosophical Opinion, whether Physical or Metaphysical. And so of any thing else.

III. AS to the *Pursuit of the Soul*, we spake of, this was to set off, and more openly express the *intellectual Power*.[8] for if it had not that force to pursue,[9] it would not be Virtue, but only a Disposition towards it. So *Theages* the *Pythagorean* hath it: *That Reason doth not beget in us a Continency and Forbearance, but by putting a forcible Restraint upon Lust and Anger. And that when the Passions do overcome, and put the same forcible restraint upon Reason, she then gives place to Incontinency and a softness of mind which receives all Impressions;*[10] *when as bare Dispositions without such a forcible restraint, can only produce imperfect Virtues, and imperfect Vices.*[11]

Wherefore the Philosopher makes these interchangeable Conflicts, and Dispositions of the Soul, to be but Virtues half perfect, as also the Vices but half inveterate.[12]

And whereas we say, the Soul pursues what was *absolutely and simply the best*, this was to manifest that famous distinction of a twofold Good; one *General*, which *was absolutely good*, or *absolutely better*. The other *Particular*, and which in respect of some *single Inclination of any particular person, was good or better*: that is to say, either grateful, or more grateful.[13] But what we hold to be the *absolute Good*, or *better thing*, is that which proves grateful, or more grateful, to the *Boniform Faculty of the Soul*, which we have already pronounced to be a *Thing Divine*.[14]

IV. ARISTOTLE seems to me, in his Ethicks to *Nicomachus*, to point at this very Faculty, saying, *That what is best, in whatever Subject it be, is not apparent, but to a good Man* (*Moral. Nicom.* l. 6 c. 13). By which he means, that men do discover that which is best in every Subject (I mean really and simply best) not as they are *knowing*, but as they are *Good*. So that methinks he had spoken more correctly had he styled this Faculty, *The very Eye of the Soul*, than to call it that sort of Natural *Industry*, which seems too much bordering upon *Craft*. But forasmuch as no man can feel the Motives and Dictates of this Divine Faculty, but one who hath attained to it by diligent application,[15] we must have recourse to some middle Principle to serve as *Mercury* did of old, and be an Interpreter between God and Man. And for this we shall constitute that which we call *Right Reason*.[16] Wherefore that certainly is *absolutely and simply the best*, which according to the Circumstances of the Case in question,[17] comes up closest to *Right Reason*, or is rather consentaneous with it.[18]

Chap. IV Certain Axioms or Intellectual Principles into Which Almost all the Reasons of Morality[19] may be Reduced

I. BUT since there is a Race of Men in the World, who are quite seared up as to God, and all that is Divine;[20] who allow no such thing as Superiority in the Faculties,[21] but assert Obedience to that Passion in particular, which shall happen to usurp above the rest, and make it the top of human Felicity[22] to fullfill the desires thereof. To such as these, who would injuriously pass for men, which they are not;[23] we must proceed by other steps than what are already set down.[24] For we must not talk of our *Boniform Faculty*, as the measure of Right Reason, and flowing from the Divine part of the Soul, but meetly insist with them upon what refers to the Intellect:[25] since, as *Aristotle* notes, *some things are intelligible, tho men know not the reason why* (*Moral. Eudem. lib.* 5. c. 8).

II. FROM this Magazine therefore let us draw forth a stock of such Principles as being immediately and irresistibly[26] true, need no proof; such, I mean, as all Moral Reason may in a sort have reference unto; even as all Mathematical Demonstrations are found in *some first undeniable Axioms*.[27] And because these Principles arise out of that Faculty, which the *Greeks* call Νοῦς,[28] that signifies the Mind or intellect; and that the Words *Noema* and *Noemata* derive therefrom, and properly signifie Rules intellectual: we do not therefore improperly stile the Rules that hereafter follow, *Moral Noema's*. But, lest any should fansie them to be morose and unpracticable, I must here affirm, they propose nothing for good, which at the same time is not grateful also, and attended with delight.[29]

NOEMA I.

Good is that which is grateful, pleasant, and congruous to any Being, which hath Life and Perception,[30] *or that contributes in any degree to the preservation of it.*

NOEMA II.

But, on the other side, whatever is ungrateful, unpleasant, or any ways incongruous to any being which hath Life and Perception,[31] is evil. And if it finally tend to the destruction of being, it is the worst of evils.

As for example sake, if any thing should not only offend your Eyes or Ears, but bring also blindness and deafness upon you; this were the worst that could happen. But if the sight and hearing were but only impaired thereby, this were but an inferior Evil. And the Reason holds the same in the other Faculties.

NOEMA III.

Among the several kinds or degrees of sensible Beings[32] which are in the world, some are better and more excellent than others.

NOEMA IV.

One Good may excel another in Quality, or Duration, or in both.

This is self-evident: yet it may be illustrated from this absurdity, that otherwise one Life would not be better, nor one sort of Happiness greater than another: so as Gods, Angels, Men, Horses, and the vilest Worm, would be happy alike; which none but a mad man can fancy. And as to duration there is no scruple thereof.[33]

NOEMA V.

What is good is to be chosen; what is evil to be avoided, but the more excellent Good is preferable to the less excellent: and less Evil is to be born, that we may avoid a greater.

NOEMA VI.

In things of which we have no experience,[34] we must believe those who profess themselves to have experience. Provided always that there be no suspicion of fraud or worldly contrivance,[35] but that there be a Conformity between their Professions and their Lives.

NOEMA VII.

'Tis more eligible to want a Good, which for weight and duration is very great, than to bear an Evil of the same proportion.[36] And by how much any Evil shall in weight and duration exceed the Good, by so much the more willingly can we be without such Good.

NOEMA VIII.

That which must certainly come to pass, ought to be reputed as present; inasmuch as the future will one day come upon us.[37] And herein some proportion of Reason holds in things future, which are very probable.[38]

NOEMA IX.

Good things, which excel less, are distinguished[39] by Weight and Duration, from those things which excel more.

NOEMA X.

A present Good is to be rejected or moderated,[40] *if there be a future Good of infinite more value, as to weight and duration to be but probably expected: and much more therefore if such expectation be certain.*

NOEMA XI.

A present Evil is to be born, if there be a probable future Evil infinitely more dangerous, as to weight and duration, to be avoided thereby: and this is much more strongly incumbent, if the future evil be certain.

NOEMA XII.

A mind which is free from prejudices that attend passion,[41] *judges more uprightly*[42] *than a mind which by such passions, or any other corporeal Impressions is solicited*[43] *or disturbed. For even as a cloudy Sky, and turbulent Sea will neither transmit or reflect any Light; so a disturbed mind admits no Reason, tho it come never so plain and clear.*

Boethius[44] sets this forth in very elegant Verse,[45] which thus begins,

Nubibus atris   *Fundere possunt*
Condita nullum   *Sydera Lumen, etc.*

The Stars, tho of themselves so bright,
When hid in Clouds can give no light.[46]

III. AND these are those Rules or *Noemata*, which almost suffice to engender in the Soul that *Prudence, Temperance*, and *Fortitude* which regard the Duties *we owe our selves*.[47] Those which follow regard we owe *unto others*; as to *God*, to *Man*, and to *Virtue* it self. And therefore they are the Rules and Principles[48] of *Sincerity, Justice, Gratitude, Mercy* and *Piety*. For I account *Piety* among the Moral Virtues, inasmuch as God may by the Light of Nature be known.

Notes

1 While not wrong, Southwell's translation is misleading for a modern reader, since "habit" is supposed to express its original etymological meaning of "character", rather than a "custom".
2 Here, the Greek cited is of the essence, as More traces ἀρετή back to the proper name Ἄρης, the Greek god of war, hence concluding that "virtue and ἀρετή are military terms".
3 The translator has omitted More's *solummodo* added for the purpose of additional emphasis: "but solely internal ones".
4 Not only does Southwell's early modern English rendering fall short of More's careful Latin wording, but it also falsely intrudes ideas like the soul's being "elevated" by an inner "heat" that invites materialist associations alien to More's moral idealism: "Lastly, it is this notion of virtue which affects the mind quite strongly, impelling it to love and exercise virtue. Moreover, it reveals virtue to be a certain swift and ready power whereby the mind is easily and irresistibly moved to do that which is honest and beautiful."
5 Southwell's translation is a free paraphrase doing scant justice to the argument: "Hence, it contributes to the overcoming of that sloth and weariness in which some may have allowed themselves to indulge, while nevertheless fancying that they had truly acquired virtue through a few acts of honesty."
6 Again, the usage is archaic, "situation" here having its original Latin meaning of "being situated".
7 In the original, it is a comparative: "more strongly".
8 Southwell provides an imprecise and barely intelligible translation of an overly-terse elliptic expression in More's original Latin. Quoting his original definition of virtue given in the first lines of this chapter, More

goes on to explain it in the light of his notion of the soul's "intellectual power": "Moreover, I say that "the soul 'easily pursues' it [i.e. that which is absolutely and simply the best]. For a fuller explanation, [we need] the soul's intellectual power."

9   More does not refer to any special "force" here, but puts forward a conceptual *reductio* argument for his claim: "For, if that did not happen, . . . ".
10 Again, Southwell extensively rephrases a quotation. In a more literal rendering, it reads: "On the other hand, however, if by that self-same power it allows itself to be led astray by irrational passions, it produces inconstancy and softness of mind." Southwell's addition of the relative clause "which receives all impressions" may be read as a comment on the "softness of mind" which accepts all sorts of erroneous ethical and metaphysical teachings.
11 The final sentence is not a translation either: "However, the dispositions of such souls are semiperfect virtues and equally semiperfect vices."
12 There is no Latin sentence corresponding to this English one which appears to be a brief gloss on the earlier quotation.
13 More's Latin is more succinct than Southwell's English: "Finally, the fact that 'the soul', as I say, 'pursues easily' that which is absolutely and simply the best reveals that noble distinction of the good into what is simply good or simply better and into that which is good or better, i.e., which is pleasant or more pleasant to some person or some particular affect of some person."
14 In the Latin, More is less wary of pointing out the godlike quality of the "boniform faculty of the soul, which is clearly divine".
15 "By diligent application" has been added by Southwell.
16 By *vulgo*, which the translator omits, More aligns himself with the long Greek tradition of ethical rationalism: "Which we generally call 'right reason'."
17 Southwell' rendering of More's concise *in datis circumstantiis*, which simply denotes "under the circumstances given", is overly long.
18 Once again, an unnecessarily complex rendering threatens to obscure More's clear moral criterion by which 'what accords best with right reason" is to be judged to be coming close to that which is "simply and absolutely the best".
19 "*Reasons of Morality*" is a somewhat misleading translation of *Ratio moralis*, which rather means "moral reasoning" in general.
20 Rather they are "people from whose minds the sense of God and things divine has faded away".
21 The English is slightly misleading here again. "Superiority" lacks the active dimension of the political metaphor of the Latin original. The atheists criticized "do not recognize any kind of stabile rule exercised by the faculties [i.e. of the soul]". Instead, as More goes on to explain, they have an agent yield to the allure of any random passion most powerful at a given moment.
22 Again, *summa* rather means the "sum". The said atheists, in other words, are hedonists who identify human happiness with the satisfaction of sensual lust entirely.
23 Though polemical in tone as well, the Latin parenthesis leaves open whether these hedonists still qualify as human beings: "provided they are still human being, not the worst of beasts".
24 The somewhat redundant phrase "than what are already set down" is Southwell's, not More's own.
25 Southwell has mistranslated this passage, thereby adding a hierarchical scheme of the soul's primary powers which, though certainly Morean in character, is not to be found in the passage at hand: "and we must discuss the measure of right reason, which we must enquire about not from that divinest part of the soul which we call *boniform*, but from its intellectual part in the proper sense of the word."
26 "And irresistibly" has been added for the purpose of additional emphasis.
27 Southwell mistranslates the predicate *resolvitur*, already used in the title: All of morality and mathematics can be "reduced" to a few axioms which More, in the original's Stoic parlance, calls κοιναὶ ἔννοιαι. Moreover, *perspicuè facilèque* refers not to the principles as such, but to the rationalistic reduction, which can be done "with great clarity and ease".
28 The *proprie*, which Southwell translates as "properly" in the subsequent part of the sentences, refers to the Greek term given here.
29 More's Latin, couched in the vocabulary of the mystical tradition of spiritual sensation, is more graphic than Southwell's comparatively sober English. It also includes an important reference to an intellectual perception not unlike that of the higher boniform faculty: "Of such kind are the following ones [i.e. principles] whose taste, lest anyone fear they may do them harm, I assure you is neither sour nor bitter, but one of great sweetness, as they propose no other good but such a one as is nice and joyful to the one who perceives it."

30 Southwell's translation is overly free here and misses the reference to More's *scala naturae* of different levels of life: "A good is that which is pleasing, delightful and congruous to a kind of perceptive life or any degree of that life".
31 See the preceding note.
32 Again, the reference is to "various kinds and levels of life".
33 More's Latin is stronger: "As to duration, there cannot even be the slightest doubt or difficulty."
34 Southwell leaves out *nondum* and *ipsi*: "In things of which we do not have any experience ourselves yet".
35 The metaphorical *mundaníque commodi aucipium* designates "a longing for worldly advantage" which renders the expert consulted untrustworthy.
36 The archaic "want", which means "lack" in Southwell's early modern English, may be misleading here. Moreover, More himself advances a concrete numerical example, which the translator renders by the more natural abstract noun "proportion": "The absence of a good which is like an eight is preferable over the presence of an evil that is likewise an eight in weight and duration".
37 A more literal translation of the somewhat convoluted second half of this sentence reads: "inasmuch as it will in reality happen to us one day as a present event in our present."
38 While not wrong grammatically, the intended meaning is that of probable, rather than future events: "And we must repute those things that are very likely to happen in a very similar fashion." The contrast is between *certo futurum* and *valdè probabiliter . . . futurum*. The neuter *quod* refers back to the good and the bad of Noema VII. We are called on to treat as present goods and evils those future ones that we are certain or very likely to enjoy or suffer from in the future.
39 Rather, they are to be "measured with regard to".
40 "Moderated" is a barely intelligible rendering of the Latin *minuendum* which designates a smaller degree of enjoyment of a good received. Moreover, the syntax is overly complex and threatens to obscure the overall meaning. A paraphrase might be preferable here: "We must forgo or lessen the enjoyment of a present good whenever we expect as probable a future good of infinite more value than the present one."
41 While the paraphrase of More's *affectuum praejudicio* is correct, it may lose some of the intended philosophical meaning within his largely Stoic theory of action on which "the prejudice of affects" is both intellectual and affective in character.
42 It is likely to judge "more correctly".
43 Rather, the mind is "entangled" by prejudice and passion which are likened to a "net" through the word *irretire*.
44 *Consolation of Philosophy* I (final poem).
45 More is more precise here, calling Boethius' comparison a "simile".
46 In the original, More apologizes to the reader for the brevity of the excerpt from Boethius' poem: "However, it is too long for us to transcribe it here."
47 The *fere* does not refer to the formation of a moral character, but to the list of *noemata* provided which More deems "fairly" complete. Moreover, the latter are said to "help engender in the soul" the virtues enumerated which, significantly, the author views as "referring to the duty that we owe to ourselves". Strictly speaking, there is but one duty which takes on several forms designated by the different virtues mentioned.
48 The two words "Rules and Principles" render the one Latin noun *fundamenta*, i.e. "foundations".

Chapter 23

The Sources of Political Power

A Ralph Cudworth, *The True Intellectual System of the Universe*, Chapter 5 (pp. 895–898)

Wherefore since it is plain, that *Sovereignty* and *Bodies Politick* can neither be meerly *Artificial*, nor yet *Violent* things, there must of necessity be some *Natural* Bond or *Vinculum* to hold them together, such as may both really *Oblige Subjects* to *Obey* the Lawful Commands of *Sovereigns*, and *Sovereigns in Commanding*, to seek the *Good* and [896] *Welfare* of their *Subjects*; whom these *Atheistick Politicians*, (by their *Infinite* and *Belluine Right*) quite discharge from any such thing. Which Bond or *Vinculum* can be no other, than *Natural Justice*; and something of a *Common* and *Publick*, of a *Cementing* and *Conglutinating Nature*, in all Rational Beings; the Original of both which, is from the Deity. The *Right* and *Authority* of God himself is Founded in *Justice*; and of this is the Civil Sovereignty also a certain *Participation*. It is not the meer *Creature* of the People, and of mens *Wills*, and therefore *Annihilate* again by their *Wills* at pleasure; but hath a *Stamp* of Divinity upon it, as may partly appear from hence, because that *Jus Vitae & Necis*,[1] that *Power of Life and Death*, which *Civil Sovereigns* have, was never lodged in *Singulars*, before *Civil Society*; and therefore could not be Conferred by them. Had not God and Nature made *a City*; were there not a *Natural Conciliation* of all *Rational Creatures*, and *Subjection* of them to the *Deity*, as their Head (which is Cicero's,[2] *Una Civitas Deorum atque Hominum, One City of Gods and Men*), had not God made ἄρχειν καὶ ἄρχεσθαι,[3] *Ruling and being Ruled*, *Superiority* and *Subjection*, with their respective *Duty* and *Obligation*; men could neither by *Art*, or *Political Enchantment*, nor yet by *Force*, have made any firm *Cities* or *Polities*. The Civil *Sovereign* is no *Leviathan*, no *Beast*, but a *God* (*I have said, ye are Gods*:)[4] he reigns not in mere *Brutish Force* and *Fear*, but in *Natural Justice* and *Conscience*, and in the *Right* and *Authority* of God himself. Nevertheless we deny not, but that there is need of *Force* and *Fear* too, to Constrain those to Obedience, to whom the *Conscience* of *Duty* proveth ineffectual. Nor is the *Fear* of the *Civil Sovereigns* own *Sword*, alone sufficient for this neither, Unassisted by *Religion*, and the *Fear* of an *Invisible Being Omnipotent*, who seeth all things, and can Punish Secret, as well as Open Transgressors, both in this Life, and after Death. Which is a thing so confessedly true, that Atheists have therefore Pretended, *Religion* to have been at first a mere *Political Figment*. We conclude therefore, that the Civil Sovereign reigneth not, meerly in the *Fear* of his own *Power* and *Sword*; but first in the *Justice* and *Authority*, and then in the *Power* and *Fear* also, of *God Almighty*. And thus much for the *First Atheistic Pretence*, from the *Interest* of Civil Sovereigns.

To their *Second*, that *Sovereignty is Essentially Infinite*, and therefore altogether *Inconsistent*, with *Religion*, that would Limit and Confine it, We Reply; That the *Right* and *Authority* of Civil Sovereigns, is not as these our *Atheistick Politicians* ignorantly suppose, a meer *Belluine Liberty*, but it is a *Right* essentially *Founded* in the Being of *Natural Justice*, as hath been declared. For *Authority of Commanding* is such a *Right* as supposes *Obligation* in others to *Obey*, without which it could be nothing but meer

Will and *Force*. But none can be *Obliged* in *Duty* to *Obey*, but by *Natural Justice*; *Commands* as such, not *Creating Obligation*, but *Presupposing* it. For if Persons were not before *Obliged* to *Obey*, no Commands would signifie any thing to them. Wherefore the First *Original Obligation* is not from *Will* but *Nature*. Did Obligation to the things of *Natural Justice*, as many suppose, arise from the *Will* and *Positive Command* of God, [897] only by reason of Punishments Threatened, and *Rewards* Promised; the Consequence of this would be, that no man was *Good* and *Just*, but only *By Accident*, and for the *Sake of Something else*; Whereas the *Goodness* of *Justice* or *Righteousness* Is *Intrinsical* to the thing it self, and this is that which Obligeth, (and not any thing *Foreign* to it) it being a different *Species of Good* from that of *Appetite*, and *Private Utility*, which every man may Dispense withal. Now there can be no more *Infinite Justice*, than there can be an *Infinite Rule*, or an *Infinite Measure*. *Justice* is Essentially a Determinate thing; and therefore can there not be an *Infinite Jus, Right* or *Authority*. If there be any thing in its own Nature *Just*, and *Obliging*, or such as *Ought to be done*; then must there of necessity be something *Unjust*, or *Unlawful*, which therefore cannot be *Obligingly Commanded* by any *Authority* whatsoever. Neither ought this to be thought any *Impeachment* of Civil Authority, it extending Universally to all, even to that of the Deity it self. The *Right* and *Authority* of *God* himself, who is the *Supreme Sovereign* of the *Universe*, is also in like manner *Bounded* and *Circumscribed* by *Justice*. God's *Will* is *Ruled* by his *Justice*, and not his *Justice Ruled* by his *Will*; and therefore God himself cannot *Command*, what is in its own nature *Unjust*. And thus have we made it Evident, that *Infinite Right* and *Authority*, of Doing and Commanding any thing without Exception, so that the *Arbitrary* will of the Commander, should be the very Rule of *Justice* it self to others, and consequently might *Oblige* to any thing, is an *Absolute Contradiction*, and a *Non Entity*; it supposing nothing to be in its own *Nature, Just* or *Unjust*, which if there were not, there could be no *Obligation* nor *Authority* at all. Wherefore the *Atheists* who would flatter *Civil Sovereigns*, with this *Infinite Right*, as if their *Will* ought to be the very *Rule* of *Justice* and *Conscience*, and upon that Pretence Prejudice them against *Religion*, do as ill deserve of them as of Religion hereby, they indeed Absolutely Devesting them of all *Right* and *Authority*, and leaving them nothing but meer *Brutish Force* and *Belluine Liberty*. And could Civil Sovereigns utterly Demolish and Destroy, Conscience and Religion in the Minds of Men, (which yet is an *Absolute Impossibility*) they thinking thereby to make *Elbow*-room for themselves, they would certainly *Bury* themselves also, in the *Ruins* of them. Nevertheless thus much is true; That they in whom the *Sovereign Legislative Power* of every *Polity* is lodged, (whether *Single Persons* or *Assemblies*;) they who Make *Civil Laws* and can Reverse them at pleasure, though they may Unquestionably *Sin* against God, in making *Unjust Laws*, yet can they not *Sin Politically* or *Civilly*, as *Violators* or Transgressors of those Laws Cancelled and Reversed by them, they being Superiour to them. Nor is this all, But these *Sovereign Legislative Powers*, may be said to be *Absolute* also, in another Sense, as being ἀνυπεύθυνοι, *Un Judicable* or *Un Censurable* by any *Humane Court*; because if they were so obnoxious, then would that *Court* or *Power* which had a *Right* to *Judge* and Censure them, be Superiour to them; which is contrary to the *Hypothesis*. And then if this *Power* were again *Judicable* by some other, there must either be, an *Infinite Progress* or *Endless Circulation* (a thing not only *Absurd*, but [898] also utterly Inconsistent with *Government* and *Property*; because there being no *Ultimate Judgment* Unappealable from, there could never be any *Final Determination* of Controversies;) or else at last, all must be devolved, to the *Multitude* of *Singulars*, which would be a *Dissolution* of the *Body Politick*, and a *State of Anarchy*. And thus have we Fully *Confuted*, the Second *Atheistick Pretence* also, for the *Inconsistency of Religion with Civil Sovereignty*.

Commentary

The "boniform faculty" or "natural sagacity" in which all the categories of practical and theoretical reason originate is the power "to distinguish not only what is simply and absolutely the best, but to relish it, and to have pleasure in that alone". It instils in man a sensation of the good which More and Cudworth concur in calling "intellectual love" (*amor intellectualis*). The soul's love for God's supreme goodness is twofold. It is directed towards him both as the transcendent principle of all of reality and as its immanent form or soul. More draws upon both the vocabulary of the ancient Platonic metaphysics of love and spiritual sensation and that of the early modern Cartesian physics of the world as a "mass" of atoms engaged in motion to describe the soul's vision in which it "relishes" and takes "pleasure" in a God both transcendent to and ubiquitously active in the world. Likewise, Cudworth follows the "Holy Scripture", which he commends for its general lack of "Metaphysical Pomp and Obscurity", in viewing "*Love or Charity*" as the "Source, Life and Soul of all Morality", which, as such, cannot itself be "Better than Reason and Knowledge". Hence, it must be "vital and not notional" in nature (Cudworth, *True Intellectual System*, 315). The whole intuited in "vital" sensation, rather than "notional" reflection is that of God's own infinity and eternity alike. Cudworth's depiction of the soul's mystical union with God, for one, bears the imprint of the Cambridge Enlightenment's profound debt to Descartes. As well as describing knowledge of the Divine in tactile metaphors along the lines of the Cartesian *cogitatione contingere*, Cudworth invokes the notion of divine infinity as the object of the soul's superintellectual intuition. For another, however, the God touched is not infinity *per se*, but "boundless love". Savouring God's "boundless sweetness" in superintellectual vision, man transcends all spatial and temporal boundaries whatsoever. Instead, "he enclasps the whole world within his outstretched arms" with his soul, in this process, becoming "as wide as the whole universe, as big as yesterday, today and forever". However, while the intuitive vision and "intellectual" or "Orphic-Platonic love" of divine goodness is above reason, of which it is the principle, it is not contrary to it. The assent given to it is "vital" or above reason. It denotes the soul's existential commitment to absolute moral value. The insight into goodness itself, however, is "notional" and reasonable. Thus, More is careful to distinguish between the two defining aspects of the soul's foremost epistemic power. In contradistinction to the sectarian enthusiasm of the Interregnum era, Cambridge Platonist mysticism is one of practical reason. In his critique of the irrational enthusiasm of his day, More espouses the vision of a transformative practical vision of God whom the soul imitates in its own love for all of his creation: "But I say that a free divine universalized spirit is worth all. How lovely, how magnificent a state is the soul of man in, when the life of God inactuating her, shoots her along with himself through Heaven and Earth, make her unite with, and after a sort feel herself animate the whole world, as if she had become God and all things? This the precious clothing and rich ornament of the mind, farre above reason or any other experiment." The boundlessness of God's creative goodness in space and time, intuited and embraced in the soul's original vision, provides the "open Champain" or the "Plain of Truth" (πέδιον τῆς ἀληθείας) of Plato's *Phaedrus* upon which the soul exercises its reasoning powers, both theoretical and practical. In theoretical speculation, the rational belief in "creation" as a meaningful whole provides "the first Rise of successful Reason", as it sets out to understand all of reality as one comprehensive and coherent image of archetypal divine perfection from which it proceeds and to which it returns. The boniform faculty provides the soul with a first original intuition of the comprehensive unity of all reality in God's love. It goes on to serve as the "measure" or yardstick of all subsequent cognition: "Therefore, I say, this most simple and Divine Sense and feeling in the boniform faculty of the soul is that rule or boundary whereby reason is examined and approves itself." As the "rule or boundary" of theoretical and practical reason alike, the boniform faculty is situated on the threshold between God and the soul. They act in unison in theoretical intellection and moral action as the all-encompassing vision of divine goodness and love informs human reasoning not from without, but from within. God, as More expounds the etymology of his newly-coined neologism of the "boniform faculty", is "the form of the good" that "moves" or "inactuates" the soul. It is he himself who becomes "the precious clothing and rich ornament of the mind", i.e. the formative principle of all the latter's agency in cognition and action alike. Still, although it is God who moves the soul both as its formal and final cause, the latter's boniform vision is throughout qualified as "freedome", since the soul acts in accordance with the formative principle of its own essence. Paradoxically, its vision is at once active intellection and passive perception as the soul, while engaged in the highest form of active reasoning, finds its every cognitive act to be passively informed by the principle of God's universal goodness. The intellectual love aroused by the boniform faculty is equally divine and human with the one universal love and the many passions corresponding to God himself and the soul respectively.

It is the soul's boniform vision of God's universal goodness and the imperative to act accordingly and "restore every thing to the state of Felicity, which God and Nature intended for it" which disclose to it its ability to break free from the constraints of its inferior animal nature. The obligation to follow the bidding of the "universalized spirit" which "inactuates" the soul in the boniform vision is evidence for its freedom of will. If it were not for its sublime *a priori* vision of God's own perfect intelligible reality which it is called upon to realize in its every moral choice and action, the soul might erroneously consider its inferior animal life to be its sole mode of existence. The soul's freedom is not one of arbitrary indifferent choice, which is as anathema to More in his theory of action as it is in his doctrine of God, but the soul's innate capacity to "mount aloft" and "shake off, or gradually destroy those ill Desires" by which it tied to an inferior earthly existence. Accordingly, drawing upon the treatises on freedom in Aristotelianism and pagan and patristic Platonism, More defines "that Faculty which the Greeks call αὐτεξούσιον" as the "Power in our selves, notwithstanding any outward assaults or importunate temptations, *to cleave to that which is virtuous and honest, or to yield to pleasures or other vile advantages*". Cudworth's theory of free will, while close to More's in general intention and outlook, is the more polished libertarian theory. At the beginning of the *Treatise of Freewill*, Cudworth restates the classic argument that human freedom is the *sine qua non* of human praise and blame as well as divine reward and punishment. We generally assume that the perpetrator whom we blame and punish for his misdeed would have been able to choose and act otherwise had he wanted to. While we blame the "artificer" if an "automaton" fails to function properly, rather than the "automaton" itself, we ascribe the responsibility for an immoral action to the agent himself, not to his creator, assuming that he, contrary to the inanimate object, could have acted differently. However, not only do praise and blame require freedom of choice, but also a personal subject or agent whom we hold responsible for his deeds and misdeeds. Every moral speech act is not directed against a crime alone, but against the agents "as principles of action, and the true causes of the moral defects of them" as well: "But we blame men's vices", Cudworth states in his introductory analysis of this speech act, "with a displeasure *against the persons themselves.*" It is this holistic aspect of moral blame that informs Cudworth's rejection of scholastic psychology and theory of action revolving around the soul's allegedly separated faculties of will and intellect. Repudiating the traditional voluntarist and intellectualist options of libertarianism as a fallacious *bivium*, Cudworth subjects the notion of distinct faculties of the soul to detailed criticism. The "principle" or "cause" of action postulated cannot be identified either with man's understanding or will. Not only would both an intellectualist and voluntarist account of moral agency fall short of its holistic nature with the one responsible person required for praise and blame inevitably being replaced with "two *supposita*, two subsistent things, two agents, and two persons, in the soul", but they are both proven to be conceptually empty at best and destructive of all moral agency at worst. Thus, for one thing, it amounts to an inane tautology "to attribute the act of intellection and perception to the faculty of understanding, and acts of volition to the faculty of will, or to say that it is the understanding that understandeth, and the will that willeth". For another, either faculty, being, by definition, devoid of the attributes of the other, cannot but be and remain entirely independent of it with all interaction rendered impossible on conceptual grounds. Hence, if, as his held by the proponents of the "intellectualist way", the intellect is the sole cause of man's action, intellect would be deprived of all intentionality, passing judgement on all objects alike and directing the will according to the logic and necessity of its inferences alone. Taking issue with a key problem of Cartesian libertarianism, as delineated, above all, in the fourth *Meditation*, Cudworth views the necessity of infallible clear and distinct understanding as undermining free action altogether, as an agent could not but follow the commandment of infallible reason. If, on the other hand, as is assumed by the "voluntarist way", it is the will that sets in motion man's understanding, afterwards choosing either to obey or disobey its final judgement, there can be no sensible and responsible agency either. As well as being circular, since the will is dependent upon the objects presented to it by the very intellect which is supposed to direct, the voluntarist position, even worse, is shown to sacrifice rational agency to irrational randomness. Being devoid of reason and, hence, impervious to its commands, the will, on the voluntarist's principles, is neither able to *move* the understanding to initiate moral reasoning in the beginning nor to *be moved* by it in implementing it in accountable action in the end. Hence, despite a final judgement which it may or may not choose to follow, the will continues to retain its independence *vis-à-vis* intellect, being, by the voluntarists' definition, both prior to and devoid of all reason. Not only would libertarian choice, therefore, be entirely arbitrary, but character development of any kind would be rendered impossible *tout court*. Instead, virtuous and vicious persons would literally be free to change entirely from one moment to the next at will. As the ἀρχὴ πράξεων, Origen's ἡγεμονικόν is instead the sum total of all of an agent's manifold cogitations and volitions upon which the latter can reflect and which he can either move towards "moral evil" or "vice, or wickedness, which is truly evil". Moral action, therefore, does not originate in a single power of the soul, either in its understanding or its will, but in all of them combined. In metaphorical language indicated by the repeated "as it were", the ἡγεμονικόν or the "we ourselves" is defined as the soul's subjectivity by which it is able to review the whole of its personality in a stance of reflective detachment. Moreover, Cudworth's is a thoroughly practical concept of subjectivity linked to the Origenist key category of self-motion conceived of as ethical self-creation in which the rational self constructs itself in more or less careful moral reasoning. Thus, the ἡγεμονικόν effects a self-fashioning in which the agent chooses not only a course of action, but his own being as well, hence being fully responsible for all future action caused by the moral character chosen. The self-creation effected by the Origenist ἡγεμονικόν is that of the Cartesian *cogito* which chooses to engage in contemplation to a lesser or greater degree before initiating moral action. While outspoken in the rejection of the French philosopher's distinction between understanding and will, also criticizing him sharply both for his voluntarism of a will endowed with greater scope than the understanding and his intellectualism of clear and distinct ideas, Cudworth endorses Descartes' notion that immoral action results not from understanding per *se*, but from premature assent to insufficient reasoning. The extension beyond the boundaries of corporeal reality of which the soul qua incorporeal substance is capable in Cudworth's ontology of action is thereby shown to be that of thought in which it may engage to a higher or lesser degree. Following both Origen and Descartes, Cudworth identifies the ἐφ' ἡμῖν proper with the soul's care in reflection on its future course of action. However, if the ἡγεμονικόν, defined as the sum total of an agent's cogitations, volitions and passions, is viewed as the cause of his libertarian action, what causes the ἡγεμονικόν to direct the soul towards good or evil in the first place? Cudworth himself is aware that the ἡγεμονικόν of his Origenist notion of freewill might be subject to the same aporiae as will and understanding in more traditional voluntarist and intellectualist accounts of libertarian freedom, crediting Aristotle with first raising the question of the ἡγεμονικόν's "first mover". Cudworth's complex answer to the chief conundrum of libertarian choice is twofold, and revolves around his rational psychology and theology. In rational psychology, the English philosopher subscribes to Origen's Platonist definition of the soul as self-motion, arguing at length that the latter is not a static, but a thoroughly dynamic entity or "reduplicate Self-activity". (BL Ms. Add. 4981,4). Nor can the ἡγεμονικόν, which has been proven to be an entity endowed with intellectual and volitional attributes, be moved by arbitrary will or necessary intellect. Instead, it is divine goodness itself which sets in motion the soul, viewed as a composite of lower corporeal plastic vitality, the middle life of sensuality and higher hegemonic subjectivity. In response to the impending conceptual impasse of a moving principle that is itself unable to move itself, Cudworth, therefore, posits the good itself as first mover of the ἡγεμονικόν. Just as the ἡγεμονικόν moves the whole of the soul, so does God or goodness, its archetype, move the ἡγεμονικόν as its primordial "vital power and energy" constantly impelling and informing its every cogitation and volition towards the fulness of his own essence of which he is the first principle and final cause. This "thread of life always spinning out, and living spring or fountain of cogitation in the soul itself" originates in God's own overflowing goodness. Hence, the last of the three doctrines of the true "philosophy of religion", man's ἐφ᾽ ἡμῖν, as outlined in the manuscript drafts of the third part of the unfinished *True Intellectual System of the Universe*, is intimately linked to the first and second, as Cudworth invokes the Cambridge Platonists' key conviction of a God or τὸ θεῖον whose every action is determined by and whose very essence is identical to an immutable φύσει καλὸν καὶ δίκαιον, i.e. an objective universal creative and salvific benignity, as a solution to the key aporia of libertarian agency. The ἡγεμονικόν possesses an intuitional awareness of the good.

It is through its own autonomous discursive activity that the soul gains an ever-growing participation in the one and coherent divine whole of reality of which it acquires a first intuitive grasp. In their sharp critique of nascent contemporary empiricism, as put forth, above all, in their philosophical archfoe Hobbes' *Elements of Philosophy* and *Leviathan*, both More and Cudworth go to great lengths to prove that human perception and intellection must not be understood along the lines of the celebrated empiricist metaphor of a *tabula rasa* gradually filled with external sense impressions beyond the subject's control. Instead, they argue, not even sensation can be understood as entirely passive. It requires an "active vigour" on the part of an incorporeal soul without which no sense impression can be explained. Cudworth's argument hinges upon the atomistic cosmology of Descartes' *Principles of Philosophy* and the concomitant epistemological distinction between primary and secondary qualities. If body, as has been established beyond doubt by the atomism of the ancient theology and early modern cosmology alike, in reality consists of nothing but the primary qualities of size, shape, place and locomotion, its secondary qualities such as the "ideas of heat, light and colours and other sensible things", which Cudworth, endorsing the usage of Descartes' *Meditations*, views as "several modes of cogitation", cannot be accounted for without "some inward vital energy of the soul itself" giving rise to them. However, despite the vital active contribution whereby a subject turns the senseless locomotion of atoms into sensual impressions, sense is subject to physical stimuli from without and physiological responses from within and as such predominantly passive. While emerging from the ἡγεμονικόν as the source and principle of intentionality by which a subject may choose to perceive any given object, the process of perception itself occurs in accordance with a necessity beyond the latter's voluntary conscious control. Conceptual reasoning, by contrast, is pure "active vigour". It brings to bear upon reality without its own categories and concepts within. Whereas in sense the rational mind bows to the ineluctable laws governing the physico-biological interaction of the world's void and atoms and the body and its sense organs, in knowledge, the soul, as Cudworth sets out to prove in his in-depth rebuttal of empiricist sensualism, "conquers" the reality outside itself, subjecting it to its own categories. The object known is merely the "occasion" for the rational soul to exercise the pure "active vigour" of its own innate *a priori* concepts and categories. According to the two chief Cambridge Platonists' epistemological occasionalism, therefore, the occurrence of a possible object of cognition acts as a catalyst for the soul to make use of its own rich conceptuality to acquire and create knowledge, thereby exercising its highest capacity of participating in God's own creative power. But for its own categorical and conceptual resources, the soul would be as unable even to engage in cognition in the first place as a person would be to identify an unknown person amidst a crowd of people. Cudworth, therefore, subscribes to the time-honoured concept of knowledge and learning as recollection delineated in Plato's *Meno* and the *Phaedo*. Knowledge, on his account, is not imposed upon a passive subject from without, but acquired by the latter's own conscious activity from within. The Cartesian "adventitious ideas" are likewise revealed to be "innate" ones instead. Instead, the *a priori* of the soul's "inward anticipations" by which it knows external objects as "something native and domestic to it" is strictly formal in character. The "inward anticipations" upon which the soul, whenever "occasioned" to do so by sense and perception, draws are several kinds of abstract concepts and categories, notably those that define its own practical and theoretical cogitation and those that constitute an object qua object such as "cause and effect" or "means and end". The discursive knowledge emerging from the soul's "recollection" throughout bears the imprint of its original intuition of the all-oneness of divine goodness as its intellect exercises its "unitive, active and comprehensive power" upon the manifold contents of sensual perception. Hence, it views each particular object as a structured whole (*totum*) defined by its form and function (*ratio*) to which its every single part is actively judged to be subservient in purposeful cooperation with all the others. The soul's innate power of acquiring knowledge by actively making use of abstract concepts to transform *prima facie* chaotic multiplicity into unified objects of rational functionality finds its logical upshot in the holistic vision of the cosmos at large. In its most comprehensive of insights, iconic intellection can be seen to approximate its original boniform intuition which throughout acts as its first moving principle, its chief criterion and its final objective. More's definition of "reason" reveals the close tie between the soul's initial universal boniform vision and its subsequent particular iconic intellection. Drawing upon the formal *a priori* of its concepts and the *a posteriori* of sense perception and secular and religious tradition, the mind acquires knowledge by placing a part into a coherent whole for the sake of rational scientific enquiry into and ethical and political action in the world. The intellect, as Cudworth puts it with another neologism of Cambridge Platonist epistemology, possesses "a potential omniformity". It is "all things intellectually" or "in a manner all things", as Plato and Aristotle concur. Man's intellect is a universal icon potentially encompassing in itself the representations or images of the whole of the outer world which it, as it were, gradually paints and recreates upon the canvass provided in its original vision of God's all-encompassing creative goodness. In so doing, it throughout re-enacts God's primordial act of creative and self-diffusive kenotic goodness of which its every cognition and action is an imperfect image. The human soul, for one thing, participates in the divine intellect in all subjectivity and self-knowledge. For another, the soul's metaphysical vision driving its every conscious act is both aesthetic and ethical in character. It is this universal vision which the soul is called upon to bring about in moral action. In practical reasoning, the boniform faculty is the source of the first general imperative "to restore every thing to the state of Felicity, which God and Nature intended for it," thereby enabling it to share in the fullness of divine perfection envisaged in the faculty's original vision: "In short, it turns all its Faculties to make good Men happy; and all its Care and Discipline is to make bad Men good." At the same time the vision is political. The universal obligation which is tied to the vision of God's infinite benignity is the source of all normative power by which a sovereign is obliged to take care of the welfare of those entrusted to him.

Notes

1 In Roman Law, the *ius vitae necisque* was part of the legal right of Roman fathers.
2 Cicero, *De natura deorum* II 62.
3 Plato, *Protagoras* 326d7.
4 *Psalm* 82:6.

Part VI

Rational Theology

Introduction

Participation

The eminent Scottish Divine John Tulloch (1823–1886), principal of St Mary's College, St Andrews and sometime moderator of the General Assembly of the Church of Scotland, in his magisterial work *Rational Theology and Christian Philosophy* (Edinburgh: William Blackwood and Sons, 1872) defined the Cambridge Platonists in terms of their rational and liberal theology. The Cambridge Platonists were united in rejecting the dogmatic spirit and much of the doctrinal content of the Westminster Confession of Faith, the Calvinist document produced in 1646 by divines summoned at the behest of the English Parliament. Led in many ways by Whichcote, who had been appointed as Provost of King's College in 1644, they took a broader and more speculative turn in theology. Whichcote's powerful and popular preaching in Trinity Church in Cambridge on Sunday afternoons for almost two decades formed the basis for the movement that was emerging as a critique of the rigid doctrinal Calvinism of the Westminster divines.

Fideism is the theory that faith is independent of, and superior to, rationality. Many philosophers have supported some version of fideism, and it has been an attractive theory to many thinkers in the Christian tradition from Tertullian to Kierkegaard. It is quite explicitly rejected by the Cambridge Platonists. One of the key texts is the debate between Anthony Tuckney and Benjamin Whichcote over the proper interpretation the Proverbs 20:23, "The spirit of man is the candle of the Lord." Tuckney accused Whichcote of placing too much stress on reason and not enough upon faith, and Tuckney accused Whichcote of relying too much upon liberal divines and Plato. Whichcote admitted his reliance upon Platonism, while (somewhat disingenuously) minimising the influence of Arminian divines. For Tuckney, the 'Candle of the Lord' is scripture, inspired by the Holy Spirit; Whichcote meanwhile views the candle as a reference to the innate awareness of the divine in the human mind, whether the human in question be Christian or heathen. At the heart of the theology of the Cambridge Platonists lies a critique of fideistic and forensic theological norms. The most extensive work of theology is Henry More's *Grand Mystery of Godliness*, but the theology of the group can be found succinctly expressed across sermons, aphorisms and letters.

The stress upon reason in the Cambridge Platonists should not be confused with a narrow rationalism. Their conviction is that love reveals the mystery of life, and their theology is one of divine goodness. Participation in that divine goodness is the centre of their spirituality; this provides the basis for mysticism and yet for a full of respect for science and reason in the created world. Their God is a loving one, rather than an almighty wrathful deity who requires satisfaction for mankind's sin. The Alexandrian, as opposed to the Augustinian, side of Cudworth emerges when he says: "There is a nature of goodness and a nature of wisdom antecedent to the will of God, which is the rule and measure of it".[1] That is, Cudworth would likely agree with the sentiment of the Victorian agnostic John Stuart Mill, who stated "I will call no being good, who is not what I mean when I apply that epithet to my fellow-creatures; and if such a being can sentence me to hell for not so calling him, to hell I will go".[2]

Of course, this insistence upon the univocity of Divine and human goodness generates severe problems for Cudworth's theodicy. In general, sin is not emphasised in the theology of the Cambridge Platonists. They do not deny the tenet, but it does not play a prominent role in their thought. One of the striking aspects of their thought is a stress upon liberty of conscience, and linked to this principle is their comprehension of a variety of doctrinal standpoints and even pagan or non-Christian religions. Whichcote insisted that "the Good Nature of an Heathen is more God-like, than the furious Zeal of a Christian." The goodness of God leads to not only to an accommodating approach toward non-Christians but also speculation about protology and eschatology, in particular the pre-existence of souls and salvation of all, though only Anne Conway subscribes explicitly to universal salvation, whereas the other figures tend to wrestle with the question—indeed, Henry More tries to justify eternal punishment.

With regard to miracles, the Cambridge Platonists, like the Alexandrian church fathers before them, often allegorise miraculous narratives to uncover a more profound spiritual meaning. But unlike the deists or Spinoza they do not express overt disbelief in miracles. Cudworth critiques the "high flown spiritualists" who effectively deny the historical death and resurrection of Christ.[3]

Mysticism

The term 'mysticism' is highly contested, but nevertheless helpful in this context. Henry More was quite candid about his dependence upon the *Theologia Germanica*, and his work is grounded in the medieval German mystical tradition, in particular the school of Eckhart. One should note Henry More's usage of the term 'mystery', of which *The Grand Mystery of Godliness* contains an extended discussion:

> Nor indeed could it be at all if it were *utterly Unintelligible*. Wherefore *Intelligibleness* adds this further requisite also to a *Mystery*, that it thereby becomes *Communicable* to such as are fitly prepared to be instructed therein. For which reason the Etymologists give also this Notation of Μυστήριον, that it is from μυέειν, which is to *teach* and *instruct* a man *in Divine matters* so far forth as the party is fit to receive. Hence is also Μύστης, Mysta, a Scholar or Commencer in Divine Mysteries, one that is more slightly imbued in the knowledge of such Holy things.[4]

The term 'mystery' plays a central role in Henry More's thought. This term is of Neoplatonic provenance and More's discussion reveals his links to the Alexandrian tradition of Origen. More's 'mysticism' is derived from the Greek *mysteria*, a term which refers to the mystery cults, the word *mystes* meaning 'initiate'. Plato himself uses the languages of the mysteries in his dialogues, not least in the *Phaedrus*. For More, the Pythagorean-Orphic dimension of Plato, with the experience of mystic initiation at its core, needs no justification: Platonism, for More, is a breach or rupture in 'ordinary life', a change or renewal of life grounded in the revelation of what was previously secret. The enigmatic nature of the mysteries serves both to enhance the sense of the numinous to the pious but also to form a veil to the undeserving, a wonderful secret.

However, the enigmatic should not be confused with brute paradox. Mysteries must be sufficiently intelligible to be communicated, and one should recall that the world itself is an enigma of the divine, a viewpoint with biblical warrant in I Cor. 13:12: "For now we see through a glasse darkly: but then face to face". But further, for More, these revelatory and theophanic mysteries have a soteriological meaning and purpose:

> The scope or aim of all Religious Mysteries is the bringing back faln man into his pristine condition of Happiness, and to lead him again to that high station which he then first forsook when he preferr'd his own Will and the pleasure of the Animal life before the Will of God and that Life and Sense which is truly Divine.[5]

Sin is voluntary alienation from God and salvation, the grand mystery itself, is deification—the soul's transformation as it enters into the divine life.

The Fall of the Soul and the Resurrection of the Body

Henry More, George Rust, Joseph Glanvill and Henry Hallywell held the Origenian doctrine of the pre-existence of the soul. Their stress on the absolute goodness of God required them to attempt to protect him from any accusation of causing human sin and misery. Human souls were created in the image of God but had, through free will, turned away from him and fallen into disobedience. The journey of pre-existent souls into terrestrial bodies resulted from transgressions in their prior ethereal state, and life on earth was potentially a period of purgation in which a combination of free human choices and divine grace might fit the soul to assume an aerial body upon the death of the body of flesh. After a further period of testing and free response, the soul might permanently return to its original ethereal state and communion with God. From their own time to the present, this has been viewed as an eccentric, even absurd, belief. Yet a series of writers have shown how pre-existence formed an integral and necessary part of More's doctrine of the immortality of the soul and the final purpose of man's creation.

Our group's sequence of writings on pre-existence began with More's poem *The Præexistency of the Soul* (1642) and then rumbled on through his writings during the 1650s until it was fully presented in *The Immortality of the Soul* (1659) **(A)**. The book forms a pair with his *Grand Mystery of Godliness* (1660), the first based on natural reason ("*so farre forth as it is demonstrable from the knowledge of nature and the light of reason*") and the second on revelation. *The Immortality of the Soul* is a deeply Origenian account of the soul's journey from its celestial home, through its fall into a terrestrial body to its eventual reunion with God in an ethereal vehicle. It was dedicated to Lord Conway, at whose country retreat, Ragley Hall, More was spending his summer long vacations, surrounded by stimulating conversation and relaxing on long woodland walks during which he contemplated the ideas he would set forth in the book.

In 1661, *A Letter of Resolution concerning Origen* **(B)**, probably written by Rust, set out the doctrine of pre-existence, perhaps giving it greater prominence than Origen himself had done. Rust is unaccounted for between the resignation of his Christ's College fellowship in March 1659 and his embarkation for Ireland with Lord and Lady Conway in early 1661. We might suppose that he was writing *A Letter of Resolution* during this time. It was then that he met Joseph Glanvill, who became very fond of him, and the two apparently discussed the pre-existence of the soul. *A Letter of Resolution* was "Written to the Learned and most Ingenious C. L. Esquire and by him published". While this may be an entirely fictional construction, it seems possible that it was written with Lord or Lady Conway in mind. Against this ascription is the possibility that Rust met them for the first time as they all prepared to travel to Ireland, although the address to C.L. could have been added to a finished work immediately before it went to the press. *A Letter of Resolution* was thought to be a dangerous book and was censured by Theophilus Dillingham, vice-chancellor of the University of Cambridge. More sent a copy to Lady Conway but declared, perhaps disingenuously, that he had no idea who the author might be.

Early in 1662, Glanvill wrote to an unnamed correspondent, who has been assumed to be Rust, posing questions about the pre-existence and future state of the soul, which he thought the expertise of his addressee would satisfy. Later that year, Glanvill's *Lux Orientalis* **(C)** was published anonymously. The book is a very full statement of the Cambridge Platonists' arguments for the pre-existence of the soul, and it acknowledges a debt to both Henry More and the author of *A Letter of Resolution concerning Origen*. More recommended the newly published book to Anne Conway. It is dedicated to Sir Francis Willoughby, the friend and supporter of the botanist John Ray, whom Glanvill will have met at the Royal Society. Glanvill thanks Willoughby for many conversations they have had concerning pre-existence, even though Willoughby is not convinced of the truth of the theory. This dedication was perhaps intended to place the arguments for pre-existence within the up-to-date scientific discussions of the London intelligentsia.

This flurry of works on pre-existence provoked Samuel Parker's highly critical *Account of the Nature and Extent of the Divine Dominion and Goodnesse, especially as they Refer to the Origenian Hypothesis concerning the Preexistence of Souls* (1666). Parker had already attacked the Platonism of the Cambridge circle and stressed the primacy of God's will over his essential goodness. Now, he posed two major objections to pre-existence: the injustice of punishing a soul for sins in a prior life of which it retained no memory; and the further injustice of placing an erring soul into the perilous situation of life on earth and then expecting it to have the strength to improve itself. Edward Warren's *No Præexistence* followed in 1667, advancing God's will above his goodness and denying the Origenian doctrine of remedial punishment. More waited fifteen years before responding to these two critics, but, in 1682, he would bring out (anonymously) a heavily annotated edition of Glanvill's *Lux Orientalis*, which answered Parker and Warren point by point. The volume also included a new edition of Rust's *Discourse of Truth*, originally published by Glanvill in 1677. While Rust had not discussed pre-existence in this discourse, its placement by More in proximity with Glanvill's full statement of the doctrine definitely associated Rust with it.

Henry Hallywell, a pupil of Rust's at Christ's College from 1657 to 1659 and a fellow there from 1662 to 1667, replied to Parker in 1668 in *Some Reflections on a late Discourse of Mr. Parkers, concerning the Divine Dominion and Goodness* **(D)**, appended to his refutation of Calvinist predestination, *Deus Justificatus*. Hallywell gives only the smallest hint of his belief in pre-existence, and he does not refute Parker on this subject. Rather, he goes straight to the heart of the matter: the primacy of God's goodness over his will. Although Hallywell published his comments anonymously, he sent a copy to Parker "with the Author's reall respects".

The doctrine of pre-existence formed part of a wider argument concerning the immortality of the soul, which included controversy over the nature of the resurrection body. Like all our Platonist authors in this section, Rust held an Origenian understanding of the resurrection body as distinct from the numerical terrestrial body which had died. The soul would assume an aerial vehicle and eventually hope to advance to a resumption of its original ethereal vehicle and communion with God. Rust discoursed on the resurrection body at the Cambridge University annual Commencement of 1658, apparently after discussing the matter with More and seeing his *Immortality of the Soul* and *Grand Mystery of Godliness* in manuscript. Rust's *The Holy Scripture tells of the Resurrection of the Dead, nor does Reason oppose it* **(E)** was presented as a Latin position in a formal disputation for the degree of Bachelor of Divinity. With the Cambridge Platonist John Worthington, vice-chancellor for the year, in the chair and Nathaniel Ingelo presenting a highly Origenian discourse for the degree of Doctor of Divinity, this was the Cambridge Platonists' most high-profile public occasion in Interregnum Cambridge. The manuscript of Rust's discourse was archived with the papers of the London intelligencer Samuel Hartlib at the University of Sheffield. Worthington had sent it to Hartlib, who had promised to return it but had never done so. In his edition of Rust's *Remains* in 1686, Hallywell had appealed for a copy of it, to no avail. In 2017, a team headed by Marilyn Lewis and including Davide Secci and Christian Hengstermann, published an annotated English translation in the Oxford University Press journal, *History of Universities*.

In both *The Immortality of the Soul* and *The Grand Mystery of Godliness*, More presented Origenian ideas concerning the resurrection body, but these were challenged by two Restoration heads of Cambridge Colleges, Joseph Beaumont of Peterhouse and John Pearson of Trinity, who insisted on the necessity of the resurrection of the same numerical body which had died. Beaumont privately circulated an anonymous list of accusations of heresy against More, which included his beliefs about the nature of the resurrection body. When More published Beaumont's list without permission and defended himself in his *Apology* (1664) **(F)**, Beaumont responded by publishing further criticisms, which were commended by Anthony Sparrow, as vice-chancellor, for rebutting More's "pernicious teachings", but More decided to let the matter rest and did not reply. It was within this context that More reported to Anne Conway that Ralph Widdrington had accused him and Cudworth of being "latitude-men" and had petitioned Archbishop Gilbert Sheldon "against the Colledge as a seminary of Heretics".

Hallywell's *Private Letter of Satisfaction to a Friend* (1667) **(G)** was heavily dependent on More's *Immortality of the Soul*. The little book assumes the pre-existence of the soul and discusses its post-terrestrial afterlife in Origenian terms. It was written in 1665 and published anonymously two years later. Although the *Letter* purports to be written to a friend whose wife had died, it is worth noting that Hallywell's parents had both died, probably of plague as it radiated out from London, in early 1667. Hallywell's immediate response, within weeks of his parents' death, was to secure his father's parochial living of Ifield in Sussex for himself and to marry his long-term sweetheart: he chose and affirmed life on earth while contemplating the afterlife.

Soul-Making Theodicy

Several of the Cambridge Platonists' works of rational theology revolve around the vexed question of the whys and wherefores of human hardship and suffering or the theodicy question. It had to be a particularly urgent question for the Cambridge Platonists given the emphasis they consistently placed upon an infinitely benign Deity. However, if the creator is indeed a God of supreme goodness, intellect and power, why is the human condition conspicuously marred by rampant sin and misery? Among the Cambridge Platonists' exercises in rational theodicy, More's early 1647 *Prae-existency of the Soul* **(A)** and his mature 1668 *Divine Dialogues* **(C–D)** and Rust's 1661 *Letter of Resolution Concerning Origen and the Chief of His Opinions* **(B)** take pride of place. Not coincidentally, they date from the civil war and early and later Restoration eras. For all their speculative effort, the Cambridge Platonists clearly responded to what they, like many of their contemporaries, felt to be a world turned upside down. Not only did they witness the enormous death toll inflicted by the political and religious factions of a brutal civil war, but also the 1666 Great Fire of London, catastrophes which could not but make even more pressing the twin problems of moral and natural evil which apparently belied their lofty notion of a God of infinite moral and intellectual perfection. Both More and Rust subscribed to an emphatically Origenist account of moral evil which, they averred, originated not in God's eternal and immutable goodness, but in man's changeable free will alone. A chief text of reference for all of the Cambridge Platonists' rational theology in general and their theodicy in particular is Origen's *Contra Celsum* of which their fellow Cambridge scholar William Spencer produced a landmark new edition in 1658. Besides the Alexandrian theologian's late principal work against Celsus, an otherwise unidentifiable 2nd century Middle Platonist critic of Christianity, Spencer reproduced Origen's *Philocalia*, a late antique anthology of texts about scriptural hermeneutics and free will, largely drawn from the Alexandrian Christian Platonist's early *On First Principles*. It is from this latter work in particular that More and his friend and follower Rust draw inspiration for their view of man as a being endowed with free will and responsible for the woes in the world. However, their free will defence is supplemented by a soul-making approach indebted to Origen's in the *Contra Celsum* in which man is tested in his dire earthly existence, maturing and regaining the moral and intellectual perfection forfeited in his pre-existent soul's fall. While there is very little systematic disagreement between More and Rust, the two foremost representatives of Cambridge Platonist rational theodicy, the differences in detail are telling. Rust clearly draws on More's early poetry, building upon it in a detailed summary of Origen's argument in the *Contra Celsum*. His argument revolves around the social conditioning that inevitably determines a soul's choices prior to and, perhaps, independently of any conscious effort on its part. While seemingly detached from any political context, Rust's patristic study that is his *Letter of Resolution* shows the Cambridge Platonists struggling with a world characterized by political chaos and human suffering. Their debates are documented in More's 1668 *Divine Dialogues* in which he carries to their logical conclusion the arguments of the group's free will and soul-making theodicy. It encapsulates Cambridge Platonist rational theology with its stress upon divine goodness defined in terms of God's ungrudging self-communication in creation and salvation and upon human freedom conceived of as the ability to participate in this process to an ever-growing extent.

The Conflagration and Restitution of All Things

While unequivocally subscribing to the Origenian doctrine of the soul's pre-existence from first to last, More, despite his express design of a universal soteriology becoming of God's all-encompassing goodness, remained wary of the twin tenet of the restitution of all things throughout his intellectual career. It is particularly telling evidence of More's life-long commitment to Origenism that at no stage did he cease to wrestle with universal salvation. As early as his metaphysical poetry of the 1640s, he explicitly raised the question of universal salvation: "Why will not God save/All mankind"? (*Psychathanasia*, III 4,28 [ed. Jacob 395]). However, instead of the redemption of all creation, More opted for a cyclic eschatology of periodic conflagrations and renewals by which the spirit of nature, despite the permanence of apparently insurmountable human wickedness, continues to display the riches of God's goodness. Throughout the 1650s, he discussed this controversial subject with his students, notably Anne Conway and George Rust. The former in particular early on found fault with his soteriological particularism which she believed to fall short of the infinite benignity and generosity of the divine first principle. In two of his principal works published shortly before the Restoration, the 1659 *Immortality of the Soul* and the 1660 *Grand Mystery of Godliness*, More can once again be seen to wrestle with this particularly vexing question of the Cambridge Platonists' and his own rational theology of divine goodness. The latter work paints a particularly gruesome picture of God's vengeance, evoking in graphic detail the mayhem unleashed upon the recalcitrant atheists. In the account of the *Grand Mystery of Godliness*, More conjures up a dire vision of Judgement Day called "*a Day of Wrath*", "*a Day of Devastation and Desolateness*" or "*a Day of Darkness of Gloominess*" (*Grand Mystery*, 8,18,4 [*Theological Works*, 312])" on which Christ returns and wreaks havoc upon those still obstinate in their sinfulness. The concepts used in More's vivid retelling of the Old and New Testament apocalypses are not metaphorical, but literal in meaning. It is in a series of devastating natural catastrophes that God unleashes his "*Final Vengeance*" upon the sinners on earth and in the air. At the same time, however, Christ finally saves the church whose members join his angelic host. The angels themselves will rejoice at the incorporation of the faithful into ethereal vehicles on that *"greatest Day of Solemnity"*, celebrating *"the highest Festival that can be celebrated in the Heavens"*. Those redeemed will be restored into "the ancient Liberties of the Sons of God", being made "Fellow citizens with the pure and unpolluted Angels, and free Partakers of all the Rights and Immunities of the Celestial Kingdom". The "Celestial Kingdom" is situated in the ether, the highest of the three strata of More's Cartesian cosmos, which will be exempt from the dreadful "Scene of the Earth and Air", the apocalyptic mayhem unfolding below it. More's account in the Immortality of the Soul **(A)** is remarkable for applying the key convictions of Cambridge Platonism, notably God's infinite benignity and the soul's immortality, to a variety of philosophical interpretations of the Stoic ἀποκατάστασις, none of which he felt confident to embrace in the end. Not surprisingly, More's aporetic account invited further debate, involving his two aforementioned students as well as Joseph Glanvill. A chief document of their controversial discussions is the 1661 *Letter of Resolution Concerning Origen and the Chief of His Opinions*. Not surprisingly considering their debates on pre-existence and universal salvation, More repeatedly recommended to Conway a book that went into print in May 1661. The anonymous *Letter of Resolution Concerning Origen and the Chief of His Opinions*, he pointed out to her time and again, was "a book that has witt and learning in it" (*Conway Letters*, 194). When Conway received More's final letter on the subject in July 1662, she dwelt on her family's Irish estate in Portmore. Alongside her husband, she had been accompanied there by George Rust, the *Letter*'s author, who had just been made Dean of Connor. Rust had expressed his Origenist concerns in public in his 1658 "God is Love" sermon in which he had not only expounded several shortcomings of classical Christian theism, but also in no uncertain terms hinted at an Origenist solution. His exposition of Origen's doctrine of universal salvation, the fifth of the six chief doctrines outlined in the *Letter of Resolution* is close to More's own in the *Immortality*. While eventually embracing More's fifth option, that of an endless cycle of birth, trespass and death, Rust **(B–C)** entertains the option that sinners, tormented in hellfire, may repent and, consequently, be saved by God. In concise argument, his account discusses the cyclical and the linear reading of Origenian apokatastasis in the light of the Cambridge Platonists' definition of punishment which, on the first principles of their rational theology, must serve no other purpose than the moral improvement of the culprit. It is a means by which God promotes the designs of his justice. God's justice, in turn, serves his goodness in enabling the sinner to mend his ways and share in his goodness. More reacted to Rust's account in print, defending the possibility of God inflicting punishment on the sinner without any view to his moral improvement **(D)**. Such may be the trespass that God is entitled to inflict eternal punishment upon him.

Chapter 24

Faith and Reason

Douglas Hedley

A Benjamin Whichcote, *The Glorious Evidence, and Power of Divine Truth* (Complete Works [1751] Volume III, 20–22, 28)

[20] Truth is of a different emanation, for I cannot distinguish truth in itself; but in way of descent to us; *truth either of first inscription, or of after-revelation from God.*

Concerning the *former*; nothing is more knowable than the great instances of natural truth, *viz. to do justly, to love mercy and walk humbly with God*; Mic. Vi. 8. *To live godly, righteously and soberly in this present world*, Tit. Ii. 12. The truth of first inscription is connatural to man, it is the light of God's creation, and it flows from the principles of which man doth consist, in his very first make. This is the soul's complexion.

Concerning the *latter*: nothing more credible and worthy of belief than the great matters of faith; *viz.* pardon of sin in and thro' Christ, upon our repentance and faith in him. The truth of after-revelation is the soul's cure, the remedy for the mind's ease and relief. The great expectation of souls, is the promise of God's *Messiah*. They *wait for the consolation of Israel*. For this hath been the state of the world: man in degeneracy and apostasy disabled himself, prejudiced his interest in God: losing his interest by his degeneracy and apostasy, he is in hope and expectation of some revelation from God, concerning terms of reconciliation and recovery; and when these did appear, then was it said; *Lord, now lettest thou thy servant depart in peace.* [21] Here comes truth of *after-revelation* for the recovery of man, when he was apostatiz'd from the truth of *first inscription*.

The former of these, is of things necessary in themselves, in their nature and quality; so, immutable and indispensable. The latter is the voluntary results and determinations of the divine will. Things that are of an immutable and indispensable nature, we have knowledge of them by the light of first impression. The voluntary results of the divine will we have by revelation from God. Man's observance of God in all instances of morality; these are truths of *first inscription*. Now these are abundantly knowable if we consider ourselves; these have a deeper foundation, greater ground for them, than that God gave the law on mount *Sinai*; that he did after engrave it 'n tables of stone that we find the ten commandments in the bible. For God made man to them, and did write them upon the heart of man before he did declare them upon mount Sinai, before he engraved them upon the tables of stone, or before they were writ in our bibles; God made man to them, and wrought his law upon mens hearts ; and as it were, interwove it into the principles of our reason; and the things thereof are the very sense of man's soul, and the image of his mind: so that a man doth undo his own being, departs from himself, and unmakes himself, confounds his own principles, when he is disobedient and unconformable to them ; and must necessarily be self-condemned.—The law externally given was to revive, awaken man, after his [22] apostacy and sin, and to call him to remembrance, advertency and consideration. And, indeed, had there not been a law written in the heart of man; a law without him could be to no purpose. For had we not principles that *concreated*; did we not know something, no man could prove anything. For he that knows nothing, grants nothing. Whosoever finds not within himself principles suitable to the moral law, whence with choice he doth comply with it; he hath departed from himself, and lost the natural perfection of his being: and to be conformable to this is the restitution to his state. [. . .]

[28] This is the sum. All divine truth is of one of these two emanations: either it flows from God, in the first instant and moment of God's creation, and then it is the light of that candle which God set up in man to light him; and that which by this light he may discover, are all the instances of morality; of good affection, and submission towards God; the instances of justice and righteousness to men, and temperance to himself: *or else* it is of an after revelation and discovery. Man being out of the way of his creation, by his defection from God, is recovered by this revelation. Upon this consideration, that a man was never better than finite and fallible, and considering that we have given an offence, and considering the relation that God stands in to his creatures; and that he is the first and chiefest goodness; it is what may be fairly supposed, that God will recover his creation, one way or other, wherefore, that which the new testament doth discover, is that which was in general expectation.

B Benjamin Whichcote, *The Glorious Evidence, and Power of Divine Truth* (Complete Works [1751], Volume III, 37)

[37] II. I now pass to *intrinsick arguments*: for this is an argument very foreign: but yet proper for those that pretend to wit and parts. Now I shall give you some *intrinsick arguments*, by which I shall convince those of their wickedness and folly, that affect either atheism, or infidelity. The first is this (which is the second assurance we have of divine truth.) The representation that religion makes to the mind of man concerning God, even such a representation as the mind of man if duely used, and well informed, would conceive concerning him. And this is a great argument. Concerning God; both natural and revealed truth represent him lovely, amiable and beautiful, in the eyes of Whatsoever is said of God either acknowledged in scripture, or declared; whatsoever you have contained in these books concerning God, is worthy of him, and is consistent with what man is made to think, or know concerning him. This is as demonstrable as any thing that was ever held forth in the world. For this is truly divine, and godlike, to do good, to compassionate, to relieve, and gratify, and to pardon sin upon fitting terms. *Divinum est condonare, gratificare, benefacere.* And on the contrary it is diabolical and most opposite to the divine nature to destroy, to worry, to grieve, to wrong, to oppress where: and [38] where is the beastly and devilish nature, there is cruelty, and a readiness to destroy. And what a relation doth the bible make of God? *Gracious, merciful, slow to anger, of great kindness*, Neh. ix 17. So, on the other side; how is the devilish nature described and represented to us? The devilish nature is hurtful, given to malice, hatred, and revenge; but the divine nature is placable, and reconcileable; ready to forgive, full of compassion, and of great goodness and kindness.

C Benjamin Whichcote, *The Venerable Nature, and Transcendent Benefit of Christian Religion* (Complete Works [1751], Volume III, 98–99, 104)

[98] Against sensuality and worldliness, I propose for remedy, the application of the principles of reason and virtue, and the applying of our highest faculties to their end and object. For while the mind is employed in heavenly meditation, or in extracting spiritual notions from material things, it is employed worthy of intellectual nature: and our proper business is to be thus employed: by which the concerns of the body will be either laid aside, or moderately engaged in, and rewarded. Whereas

this power of our souls is, as it were, lost, where men use themselves as if they had no spirits, but were altogether body, or as if the body were the principle or governing part. And in such a condition are they, who cannot understand what me mean, when we big them *lift up their hearts to God*. For the candle of God's lighting within them, whereby they are qualified to find God out in his works, and to follow him in his ways, either it burns so dim that they cannot see by it, or it is quite put out. [99] For it is found by experience, that the malignity of the heart doth bling the understanding: and true wisdom will never abide in a malicious and wicked soul.—There are indeed souls that are so active and so well acquainted with the heavenly meditation; that very well know what is the food od souls, ad have the foretaste of the delight and pleasure of the other world. [. . .]

[104] Religion puts the soul in a right posture towards God; for we are thereby *renewed in the spirit of our minds*. The soul of man to God is as the flower of the sun; it opens at its approach, and shuts when it withdraws. Religion in the mind is as a byas upon the spirit, inclines it in all its motions; tho' sometimes it be jogged and interrupted, yet it comes to itself. It is a rule within, a law written in man's heart; it is the government of his spirit. We say men shew their spirit by their carriage, behaviour and words; and it is true.

D Benjamin Whichcote, *Think on these things* (Complete Works [1751], Volume IV, 144, 146)

[144] Man is not at all settled or confirmed in his religion, until his religion is the self-same with the reason of his mind; that when he thinks he speaks reason, he speaks religion; or when he speaks religiously, he speaks reasonably; and his religion and reason is mingled together; they pass into one principle; they are no more two, but one: just as the light in the air makes one illuminated sphere; so reason and religion in the subject, are one principle. [. . .]

[146] The seat of religion is the inward man; it is first the sense of a man's soul, the temper of his mind, the *pulse* of his heart. You have always in intellectual nature, the elicit acts, as we call them; that is, mental and internal acts; and they always precede and go before imperate *acts*, that is, external acts. The elicit acts of the mind, they are first. It lies first *within the mind*; after that, it doth appear externally, in speeches, gestures, actions, and the effects of all good self-government.

E Benjamin Whichcote, *Moral and Religious Aphorisms* (1753)

114. Nothing spoils human Nature more, than false Zeal. The *Good nature* of an Heathen is more God-like, than the furious *Zeal* of a Christian.
294. *Good men*, under the Power of Reason and Religion, are *Free*; in the worst Condition: *Bad men*, under the Power of Lust and Vice, are *Slaves*; in the best Condition.
295. He, that useth his *Reason*, doth acknowledge God.
297. *Heavenly Things* are the greatest Truths and Realities in the World; and our Life is them.
298. In *Morality*, we are sure as in Mathematics.
299. Religion Teaches less, than we desire to *Know*; and *Requires* more, than we are willing to *Practice*.
300. *Truth* in practice, proves Goodness.
562. Truth is first in *Things*, and then the Truth is in our *Understanding*. Things give *Law* to Notion, and Apprehension.
587. Morals are inforced *by* Scripture; but were *before* Scripture: they were according to the Nature of God.
798. Reverence God in *thyself*: for God is *more* in the *Mind* of Man, than in any part of this world besides; for we (and we *only* here) are made after the Image of God.

880. Nothing *without* Reason is to be *proposed*; nothing *against* Reason is to be *believed*: Scripture is to be taken in a rational sense.

916. The *Spirit of a Man is the Candle of the Lord*; Lighted *by* God, and Lighting us *to* God. *Res illuminata, illuminans.*

F Benjamin Whichcote, *Eight Letters of Dr. Antony Tuckney and Dr. Benjamin Whichcote* (1650), First Letter in Answer (ed. Salter, 72–73, 107–109, 112–113)

Dr Tuckney's Third Letter

[72] ᵖ For what you say, to that of Prov. xx. 27; that, "I instance in the *use* of the principle; and You instiste-on the qualitie fittness and sufficiencie of itt, as from God and in His hand; as *res illuminata illuminans:* and so you persuade yourself; that is in the wordes, which you have alledged them for:"— I answer; 1. that I indeed instance in the use of the principle: and that use to which by interpreters, and by both the sense and context of the wordes, they are there applied: and itt is *rimari res hominum, non Dei*⁶: and no more can from the place bee inforced. And when hee saith, it is "the candle of the Lord", for this use; we can no more inferre thence, that itt is so for farther use; in the things of God and mysteries of faith: than hee, that saith [73] such a man is the King's searcher in the Custom-house, to finde-out merchants' conceled goods; can thence inferre, that hee is so to search-out the King's Council: or, because a candle can helpe to search-out a dark corner in the house; that therfore itt can in a dark night help mee to see the heavens. 2. Though some interpreters adde; not onlie man's secrets, but God's councils; yett they explaine themselves to meane that Grace, which out of his love hee reveleth by his worde; and infuseth by his spirit: and so "the spirit of a man" is, as itt were, *naturaliter capax divinae illuminationis*; so being by the spirit illuminated, wee denie not but it can perceeve the things of God; which otherwise it cannot⁷: In these things especiallie, however there is a spirit in a man; yett the inspiration of the Almightie giveth understanding.

Dr Whichcote's Third Letter

[107] ᵐ For the present, I confesse, I do extreamlie wonder att your advice; upon divers grounds: and att several things, which you say in this paragraph. But I do so reverence your person; that I shall dulie weigh and consider what you here offer.—"Not so much nor so often to handle such texts, as are examinable by *ratio rei.*" Are not such truths of high importance, of clearest evidence and assurance, knowable *lumine innato et naturali, quorum non potest esse ignorantia invincibilis?* whereas *de Christo* there easilie may bee *ignorantia invincibilis*; which, as necessarie as the knowledge of Christ is to Salvation, *neminem damnat:* the neglect and contradiction whereof damnes, where Christ doth not—the knowledge and observance whereof necessarie, where Christ comes to save. I mean, the neglect and contradiction *veritatum, quarum non est invincibilis ignorantia*, damnes; whereas *ignorantia in* [108] *vincibilis de Christo* doth not damne. Such points are, the creature's due observance of God, complyance with His will, surrender of self up to Him, dependence upon Him, acknowledgement of Him, affection settled on Him, reference to Him: good self-government and moderation in worldlie desires and affections; and composure in a still, quiet, calm, serene apprehension of God: the minde discharged of passion undue affection and molestation from sense: justice, righteousness, equall and fair dealing with men; no insolencie, usurpation, arrogancie, oppression: and a mulititude of such excellent doctrines; which, if settled in the heartes and lives of men, wou'd make this worlde resemble Heaven; whereas nowe the contrarie speak Hell broken loose. And *too much* and *too often* on these poyntes! The scriptures full of

such truths: and I handle them too much and too often! and not discourse of them, rationallie!—Sir, I oppose not rational to spiritual; for spiritual is most rational: But I contradistinguish rational to conceited, impotent, affected CANTING; (as I may call it; when the Ear receeves wordes, which offer no matter to the Understanding; make no impression on the inward sense.) And I think, where the demonstration of the spirit is, there is the highest purest reason; so as to satisfie, convince, command, the minde: things are most thorowlie seen-into, most cleerlie understood; the minde not so much amused with forms of Wordes, as made acquainted with the inwards of things; the reason of them and the necessarie connexion [109] of termes cleerlie layde-open to the mind and discovered. I have no skill at all in the Bible; if the Prophets, and Apostles, and our Saviour himselfe are not frequente in rationall arguments and argumentations. I acknowledge; that, in matters merelie arbitrarie, and of pure revelation; as manie matters they are engaged in are; [as matters of faith, matters *divinæ voluntatis et beneplaciti*; for which no rule but pleasure: for *in gratuitis non fit injuria:* as Matt. xx. 15.] they say, *Deus dixit*; and that is enough and most proper, in that case: but they carefullie make appear, that *ratio rei* is not to the contrarie. They do prove, *per rationes rerum, in necessariis ex se*; *per authorinatem Dei, quoad ea quae determinantur a libera Dei voluntate.* And this I dare undertake to make-out, by a thousand scriptures.

[112] ᵖ I receeve no satisfaction att all, in your scant and narrow interpretation of Prov. xx. 27. whereby you prejudice God's talent, committed to our trust; and so lessen both our charge and work. The use, as you express itt, is inadæquate to the principle: [so farre as you weaken the principle in man, you also lessen man's sinne and guilt; and so make man less accountable to God, and less obnoxious:] "The candle of the Lord" signifies no shallow thing: itt is a principle, which speakes much of God in the worlde; and is of great pregnancie: and, under the super-intendencie of God's spirit, is of great sufficiencie and efficiencie. And, I am sure, itt hath verie manie parallel and consignificant scriptures; in the sense given by mee. For the purpose, for which you quote Job. xxxij. 8. and 1 or. ij. 14. I refer you back agen to ᵈ: I will as freelie and fullie acknowledge God, as I can possiblie; and will thankfullie learne of you to do itt more. I count itt true sacriledge, to take from God; to give to the Creature: yett I look att itt, as a dishonouring God, to nullify and make base his workes; and to think Hee made a sorrie worthless peece, fitt for no use; [113] when hee made man. I cannot but think of a noble able creature; when I reade *ad imaginem et in similitudinem Dei*: or if, *in statu lapso*, itt bee as nothing; then you vilifie the restitution by Christ: as more hereafter.

G Henry More, *Grand Mystery of Godliness* (1660), Chapter 1 (pp. 1–3)

[1] 1. EVery legitimate *Mystery* comprehends in it at least these Four *Properties*. *It is a piece of Knowledge*, First, *competently Obscure, Recondite and Abstruse:* That is, It is not so utterly hid and intricate, but that, in the Second place, *It is in a due measure Intelligible.* Thirdly, *It is not only Intelligible, what is meant by it;* but it is evidently and certainly True. Fourthly and lastly, *It is no impertinent or idle Speculation, but a Truth very Usefull and Profitable*: We may well add also, *for some Religious End.*

2. This *Obscuritie* and *Abstruseness* makes not only the *Mystery* more *solemn* and *venerable* to those to whom it is communicated, but *hides* it also from their eyes that are *not worthy* to partake thereof. From whence some Criticks have derived *Mysterium* from the Hebrew word מסתר, which is from סתר *to hide:* Which is well aimed at as to the sense. But others, with more judgment in Grammar, acknowledge μυστήριον to be a proper Greek word, and fetch the Derivation of it from μύειν, παρὰ τὸ μίειν τὸ στόμα, because they to whom it is communicated are *to keep silence*, and not to impart it to *unmeet* persons. And in this sense *Chrysostome* expounds *Mysterium*, Τὸ ἀπόρρητον καὶ θαυμαστὸν [2] καὶ ἀγνοούμενον, *A matter wonderfull, unknown, and not to be easily or rashly communicated to others.*

3. Nor indeed could it be at all if it were *utterly Unintelligible*. Wherefore *Intelligibleness* adds this further requisite also to a *Mystery*, that it thereby becomes *Communicable* to such as are fitly prepared to be instructed therein. For which reason the Etymologists give also this Notation of Μυστήριον, that it is from μυέειν, which is to *teach* and *instruct* a man *in Divine matters* so far forth as the party is fit to receive. Hence is also Μύστης, *Mysta*, a Scholar or Commencer in Divine Mysteries, one that is more slightly imbued in the knowledge of such Holy things.

4. But there is afterward a clearer manifestation and a fuller satisfaction, and the μύστης then becomes ἐπόπτης or ἔφορος, being now more firmly ascertained of the *Truth* which he did but obscurely apprehend before. From which *Clearness* and *Certainty* of the thing represented there necessarily arises *a full and free assent* of his Understanding without any further doubt or hesitancy; the Proverb being made good in this case, That *Seeing is Believing*.

5. But that there may not be a mere dry *Belief* without any love or liking of the Object thereof, we added also that this *Mystery* is not only *certainly True*, but very concerningly *Usefull* and *Profitable*; which though the word Μυστήριον it self does not implie, yet another in the same language and of the like sense does, which is *Τελεταὶ*, i. e. *Initiations into sacred Mysteries*. The *Usefulness* whereof a *Platonist* admirably well describes, not without a verbal allusion, in this manner, Σκοπὸς τῶν τελετῶν ἐστιν εἰς τέλος ἀναγαγεῖν τὰς ψυχὰς ὀφ' οὑτὴν πρώτην ἐποιήσαντο κάθοδν, ὡς ἀρχῆς.,[8] Which, if we would render it in our more familiar language, sounds thus; The scope or aim of all Religious Mysteries is the bringing back faln man into his pristine condition of Happiness, and to lead him again to that high station which he then first forsook when he preferr'd his own Will and the pleasure of the Animal life before the Will of God and that Life and Sense which is truly Divine.

6. Wherefore not to dwell too long on the threshold, we conclude briefly and in general, that a *Mystery* is a piece of Divine knowledge *measurably Abstruse*, whereby it becomes *more Venerable*, but yet *Intelligible* that it may be *Communicable*, and *True* and *Certain* that it may win *firm Assent*, and lastly *very Usefull* and *Effectual* for the *perfecting* of the Souls of men, and restoring them to that *Happiness* which they anciently had faln from; that so near a Concernment may as well gain upon their *Affections* as the Evidence of *Truth* engage their *Understandings*; and so the whole man may be carried on to a devout embracement of what is exhibited unto him by the knowledge of his Religion.

7. What we have thus Generally proposed we shall now applie more Particularly, and more fully prosecute those *Four primary Properties* in that *Grand Mystery of Godliness* which we call *Christianity*: distributing our Discourse into these *Four main Parts*; The First whereof shall insist somewhat upon the *Abstruseness* and *Obscurity* of our Religion, the Second upon the *Intelligibleness* of it, the Third upon the [3] *Certainty* of it; and the Fourth on the *great concerning Usefulness* thereof. To which we shall add what Considerations we think fittest concerning the *Secondary Properties* which emerge out of these *Primary* ones.

H John Smith, *Of Prophesie*, Chapter 1 (*Select Discourses* [1660], 169–175)

[169] Chap. I.

That Prophesie *is the way whereby Revealed Truth is dispensed and conveighed to us. Man's Mind capable of conversing and being acquainted as well with Revealed or Positive Truth, as with Naturall Truth. Truths of Naturall inscription may be excited in us and cleared to us by means of Propheticall Influence. That the Scripture frequently accommodates it self to vulgar apprehension, and speaks of things in the greatest way of condescension.*

HAving spoken to those *Principles of Naturall Theologie* which have the most proper and necessary *influence* into *Life* and *Practise*, and are most pregnant with morall goodness; we come now to consider *Those pieces of Revealed Truth* which tend most of all to foment and cherish true and reall Piety.

But before we fall pressly into any strict Enquiry concerning them, it may not be amiss to examine *How and in what manner This kind of Truth, which depends solely upon the Free will of God, is manifested unto mankind*; and so treat a little concerning *Prophesie*, which indeed is the *onely way* whereby *This kind of Truth* can be dispensed to us. For though our own Reason and [170] Understanding carry all *Natural Truth* necessary for *Practice* in any sort, engraven upon themselves, and folded up in their own Essences more immediatly, as being the first participations of the Divine Minde considered in its own Eternal nature: yet *Positive Truth* can only be made known to us by a free influx of the Divine Mind upon our Minds and Understandings. And as it ariseth out of nothing else but the free pleasure of the Divinity, so without any natural determination it freely shines upon the Souls of men where and when it lifteth, hiding its light from them or displaying it forth upon them, as it pleaseth.

Yet the souls of men are as capable of conversing with it, though it doe not naturally arise out of the fecundity of their own Understandings, as they are with any Sensible and External Objects. And as our Sensations carry the notions of Material things to our Understandings which before were unacquainted with them; so there is some Analogical way whereby the knowledge of Divine Truth may also be revealed to us. For so we may call as well that Historical Truth of Corporeal and Material things, which we are informed of by our Senses, *Truth of Revelation*, as that Divine Truth which we now speak of: and therefore we may have as certain and infallible a way of being acquainted with the one, as with the other. And God having so contrived the nature of our Souls, that we may converse one with another, and inform one another of things we knew not before, would not make us so deaf to his Divine voice that breaks the rocks, and rends the mountains asunder; He would not make us so undisciplinable in Divine things, as that we should not be capable of receiving any Impressions from himself of those things which we were before [171] unacquainted with. And *this way* of communicating Truth to the Souls of men is originally nothing else but *Prophetical* or Enthusiastical; and so we may take notice of *the General nature of Prophesie*.

Though I would not all this while be mistaken, as if I thought no *Natural Truth* might be by the means of Prophetical influence awakened within us, and cleared up to us, or that we could not *lumine prophetico* behold the *Truths of Naturall inscription*; for indeed one main end and scope of the *Prophetical Spirit* seems to be the *quickning up* of our Minds to a more lively converse with those *Eternal Truths* of Reason, which commonly lie buried in so much fleshly obscurity within us, that we discern them not. And therefore the Scripture treats not only of those Pieces of Truth which are the Results of God's free Counsells, but also of those which are most a-kin and allied to our own Understandings, and that in the greatest way of Condescention that may be, speaking to the weakest sort of men in the most vulgar sort of dialect: which it may not be amiss to take a little notice of.

Divine Truth hath its *Humiliation* and *Exinanition*, as well as its *Exaltation*. *Divine Truth* becomes many times in Scripture *incarnate*, debasing it self to assume our rude conceptions, that so it might converse more freely with us, and infuse its own Divinity into us. God having been pleased herein to manifest himself not more jealous of his own Glory, then he is (as I may say) zealous of our good. *Nos non habemus aures, sicut Deus habet linguam*. If he should speak in the language of *Eternity*, who could understand him, or interpret his meaning? or if he should have declared his Truth to us only in a way of the *purest abstraction* that Humane Souls are capable of, how should then [172] the more rude and illiterate sort of men have been able to apprehend it? *Truth* is content, when it comes into the world, to wear our mantles, to learn our language, to conform it self as it were to our dress and fashions: it affects not that State or *Fastus* which the disdainfull Rhetorician sets out his style withall, *Non Tarentinis aut Siculis hæc scribimus*; but it speaks with the most *Idiotical* sort of men in the most *Idiotical* way, and becomes all things to all men, as every sonne of Truth should doe, for their good. Which was well observed in that old Cabbalistical Axiome among the Jewes, *Lumen supernum nunquam descendit sine indumento*. And therefore (it may be) the best way to understand the true sense and meaning of the Scripture is not rigidly to examine it upon Philosophical Interrogatories, or to bring it under the scrutiny of School-Definitions and Distinctions. It speaks not to us so much in the tongue of the learned *Sophies* of the world, as in the plainest and most vulgar dialect that may be. Which the Jews constantly observed and took notice of, and therefore it was one common Rule among them for a true understanding of the Scripture, הרותה הרבד וושלב ינב םדא, *Lex loquitur linguâ filorum hominum.* Which *Maimonides* expounds thus, in *More Nevoch.* Par. 1. C. 26. *Quicquid homines ab initio cogitationis suæ intelligentiâ & imaginatione suâ possunt assequi, id in Scriptura attribuitur Creatori.* And therefore we find almost all *Corporeal properties* attributed to God in Scripture, *quia vulgus hominum ab initio cogitationis Entitatem non apprehendunt, nisi in rebus corporeis,* as the same Author observes. But such of them as sound *Imperfection* in vulgar eares, as *Eating* and *Drinking,* & the like, these (saith he) the Scripture no where attributes to him. The reason of this plain and Idiotical [173] style of Scripture it may be worth our farther taking notice of, as it is laid down by the forenamed Author C. 33. *Hæc causa est propter quam Lex loquitur linguâ filiorum hominum,* &c. For this reason the Law speaks according to the language of the sons of men, because it is the most commodious and easie way of initiating and teaching Children, Women, and the Common people, who have not ability to apprehend things according to the very nature and essence of them. And in C. 34. *Et si per Exempla & Similitudines non deduceremur,* &c. *And if we were not led to the knowledge of things by Examples and Similitudes, but were put to learn and understand all things in their Formal notions and Essential definitions, and were to believe nothing but upon preceding Demonstrations; then we may well think that (seeing this cannot be done but after long preparations) the greater part of men would be at the conclusion of their daies, before they could know whether there be a God or no,* &c. Hence is that Axiome so frequent among the Jewish Doctors, *Magna est virtus vel fortitudo Prophetarum, qui assimilant formam cum formante eam,* i. e. Great is the power of the *Prophets,* who while they looked down upon these Sensible and Conspicable things, were able to furnish out the notion of Intelligible and Inconspicable Beings thereby to the rude Senses of Illiterate people.

The Scripture was not writ only for Sagacious and Abstracted minds, or Philosophical heads; for then how few are there that should have been taught the true Knowledge of God thereby? *Vidi filios cœnaculi, & erant pauci,* was an antient Jewish proverb. We are not alwaies rigidly to adhere to the very Letter of the Text. There is a הלגנ and a רתסנ in the Scripture, as the Jewish interpreters observe. We must not think [174] that it alwaies gives us Formal Definitions of things, for it speaks commonly according to Vulgar apprehension[9]: as when it tells of *the Ends of the heaven,* which now almost every Idiot knows hath *no ends* at all. So when it tells us Gen. 2. 7. that *God breathed into man the breath of life, and man became a living soul;* the expression is very Idiotical as may be, and seems to comply with that vulgar conceit, that the Soul of Man is nothing else but a kind of *Vital breath* or *Aire*: and yet the *Immortality* thereof is evidently insinuated in setting forth a double Original of the two parts of Man, his Body and his Soul; the one of which is brought in as arising up out of the *Dust* of the earth, the other as proceeding from the *Breath* of God himself.

So we find very Vulgar expressions concerning God himself, besides those which attribute *Sensation* and *Motion* to him, as when he is set forth as *riding upon the wings of the Wind, riding upon the Clouds, sitting in Heaven,* and the like, which seem to determine his indifferent Omnipresence to some peculiar place: whereas indeed such passages as these are can be fetch'd from nothing else but those crass apprehensions which the generalitie of men have of God, as being most there, from whence the objects of dread and admiration most of all smite and insinuate themselves into their Senses, as they doe from the *Aire, Clouds, Winds* or *Heaven.* So the state of *Hell* and Miserie is set forth by such denominations as were most apt to strike a terror into the minds of men, and accordingly it is called *Cœtus Gigantum,* the place where all those old *Giants,* whom divine vengeance pursued in the general Deluge, were assembled together, as it is well observed by a late Author of our own upon *Proverbs* 21. 16.[10] *The* [175] *man that wandreth out of the way of understanding, in cœtu Gigantum commorabitur.* And accordingly we find the state and condition of these expressed *Job* 26. 5. *Gigantes gemunt sub aquis; & qui habitant cum iis. Nudus est infernus coram illo, & nullum est operimentum perditioni*, as the *Vulgar Latin* renders it, *The Giants groan under the waters, and they that dwell with them. Hell is naked before him*, (that is, God,) *and destruction hath no covering.* In like manner our Saviour sets forth *Hell* as a great valley of fire like that of *Hinnom*, which was prepared with a great deal of skill, to torture and torment the Devils in. Again we find *Heaven* set forth sometimes as a place of continual *banqueting*, where, according to the Jewish customes, they should lye down in one anothers bosomes at a perpetuall Feast: Sometimes as a *Paradise* furnished with all kinds of delight and pleasure. Again, when the Scripture would infinuate God's seriousness and realitie in any thing, it brings him in as ordering it a great while agoe before the foundation of the world was laid, as if he more regarded that then the building of the world.

I might instance in many more things of this nature, wherein the *Philosophical* or *Physical* nature and Literal veritie of things cannot so reasonably be supposed to be set forth to us, as the *Moral* and *Theological*. But I shall leave this Argument, and now come more precisely to consider of *the nature of Prophesie*, by which God flows in upon the Minds of men extrinsecally to their own proper operations, and conveighs truth immediately from himself into them.

I Henry More, *Discourses on Several Texts of Scripture* (1692) (p. 315)

[315] So then he that is thus affected; whose bowels are enlarged to his fellow-creatures, to every one as they are capable: He that is merciful to the beast, loving to men; feeds the hungry; clothes the naked; visits the sick; directs the traveller; is courteous to the stranger; informs the ignorant; heartens the poor-spirited; sheweth the proud his folly; comforts him that is in sorrow; ballasts him that floats in vain joy; soders up enmities, and stints strife; flies envy, and exerciseth an universal amity to all: This man is like his Heavenly Father, who *makes his Sun to rise on the evil and the good, and sendeth rain on the just and the unjust*. This man will neither persecute his enemy out of hatred, nor acquit his friend in his fault, out of fond love: But deals his doals of all kinds to every one as he is fitted for receiving; slips no opportunity of doing any manner of good; loseth no occasion of hindering of evil. His Soul is nothing but the inward Life of Charity; his Life nothing but the passing from munificency to munificency, from one good deed to another.

Notes

1 Cudworth, *Eternal and Immutable Morality*, 187.
2 John Stuart Mill, *An Examination of Sir William Hamilton's Philosophy* (London: Longman, Green, Longman, Roberts and Green, 1865), 131.
3 Cudworth, *Sermon before Lincolnes Inn*, 10.
4 More, *Grand Mystery of Godliness*, 2.
5 More, *Grand Mystery of Godliness*, 2.
6 Zeph. i. 12.
7 I Cor. ii. 4.
8 This seems to be from Olympiadorus. See Scholia in Platonis Phaedonem; ed. Christophorus-Eberhardus Finckh.—Heilbronnae, Landherr 1847 p. 95, beginning at line 14.
9 Psal. 19. Mat. 24.
10 Mr. *Mede* in Diatrib. first part.

Chapter 25

The Fall of the Soul and the Resurrection of the Body

Marilyn A. Lewis

A Henry More, *The Immortality of the Soul*, Book 2, Chapter 12, Sections 4–5, 7 (*Collection of Several Philosophical Writings*, 111, 112 = ed. Jacob pp. 147, 148)

4. The second is this, That if the sequel were granted, that no Absurdity can be detected from thence in Reason, if the prejudices of Education, and the blinde suggestion of unconcerned Faculties, that have no right to vote here, be laid aside. To speak more explicitely, I say, This consequence of our Souls *Praeexistence* is more agreeable to Reason then any other Hypothesis whatever; has been received by the most learned Philosophers of all Ages, there being scarce any of them that held the Soul of man *immortal* upon the meer light of Nature and Reason, but asserted also her *Praeexistence;* That *Memory* is no fit Judge to appeal to in this Controversy; and lastly, That *Traduction* and *Creation* are as intricate and unconceivable as this opposed Opinion.

5. I shall make all these four parts of my Answer good in order. The truth of the first we shall understand, if we compare it with those Opinions that stand in competition with it, which are but two that are considerable. The one is of those that say, the Soule is *ex traduce;* the other of those [241] that say it is *created,* upon occasion. The first Opinion is a plain contradiction to the *notion* of a Soul, which is a *Spirit,* and therefore of an *Indivisible,* that is of an *Indiscerpible,* Essence. The second Opinion implies both an Indignity to the Majesty of God, (in making Him the chief assistant and actour in the highest, freest, and most particular way that the Divinity can be conceived to act, in those abominable crimes of Whoredome, Adultery, Incest, nay Buggery it self, by supplying those foul coitions with new created Souls for the purpose:) and also an injury to the Souls themselves; that they being ever thus created by the immediate hand of God, and therefore pure, innocent and immaculate, should be imprisoned in unclean, diseased and disordered Bodies, where very many of them seem to be so fatally over-mastered, and in such an utter incapacity of closing with what is good and vertuous, that they must needs be adjudged to that extreme calamity which attends all those that forget God. Wherefore these two opinions being so incongruous, what is there left that can seem probable, but the *Praeexistency* of the Soul?

[242] 7. But this is not all. Both the *Attributes* of God, and Face of things in the world, out of which his *Providence* is not to be excluded, are very strong Demonstrations thereof to Reason unprejudiced. For first, if it be good for the Souls of men to be at all, the *sooner* they are the *better*. But [243] we are most certain that the *Wisdome* and *Goodness* of God will doe that which is the *best;* and therefore if they can enjoy themselves before they come into these terrestrial Bodies (it being better for them to enjoy themselves then not) they must *be* before they come into these Bodies; that is, they must be in a capacity of enjoying themselves without them for long periods of time, before they appeared here in this Age of the World. For nothing hinders but that they may live before they come into the

Body, as well as they may after their going out of it: the latter whereof is acknowledged even by them that deny the *Praeexistence*. Wherefore the *Praeexistence* of Souls is a necessary result of the Wisdome and Goodness of God, who can no more fail to *doe* that which is *best*, then he can to *understand* it: for otherwise his *Wisdome* would *exceed* his *Benignity;* nay there would be less hold to be taken of his Goodness, then of the Bounty of a very benign and good man, who, we may be well assured, will slip no opportunity of doing good that lies in his power, especially if it be neither *damage* nor *trouble* to him; both which hinderances are incompetible to the Deity.

B [George Rust], *A Letter of resolution concerning Origen* (1661), 46–47, 48–49

His *Third* [opinion] is this, That those *præxsisting Souls* through their Fault and negligence became inhabitants of the Earth in *terrestrial* bodies.

Which Opinion he grounds upon these considerations.

1. That that infinitely full *goodness*, the first blessed *Spring* and *original* of all things, communicated of himself in their production to all possible varieties and degrees of life, which his *essential* and *eternally assistant wisdom* judged best for the things produced, and most fitting and decorous in it self, so as they might neither incommodate one another, nor yet be unhandsomely crowded together without due distance and discrimination of their Natures. In which long chain of life and Being propagated from the highest to the lowest of all, from the most *Incorporeal* Deity to *Matter* itself, 'tis not to be wondered at, nay 'tis necessary, that many of the *intermediate* Essences should partake of the *extremes*, and so there be brought into light *spirits incorporate*. But [47] since few Spirits after the *First* and *Best* are of immutable purity, and since every different degree of their changeable purity is proportion'd to a correspondent degree of purity in matter, and since matter is actually existent in the world according to all degrees of purity, 'tis not to be wondered at neither that the same individual Spirit or same order of Spirits should be sometimes united with one sort of matter and sometimes with another. [. . .] Who then should turn them out of that better condition in which the order and course of Nature and the internal congruity of their own Essence had placed them? Certainly not *he* whose overflowing goodness first brought them into Life and Being, and who no doubt in the first moment of their existence set them to exercise those powers of [48] life he had given them, in those parts of the world as were most advantageous for the happiness they were capable of. [. . .] What then remains but that through the faulty and negligent use of themselves, whilst they were in some better condition of life, they rendred themselves less pure in the whole extent of their powers both *Intellectual* and *animal*, and so by degrees became disposed for the susception of such a degree of corporeal life as was less pure indeed then the former, but exactly answerable to their present disposition of spirit; so that after certain periods of time they might become farre less fit to actuate any sort of matter then the [49] *terrestrial*; and being originally made with a capacity to joyn with this too, and in it exercise the powers and functions of life, it seems necessary according to the course of nature that they should sink into, and so appear *terrestrial men*?

C [Joseph Glanvill], *Lux Orientalis* (1662), 66–70

2) Then, whoever conceives rightly of *God*, apprehends him to be *infinite* and *immense Goodness*, who is always shedding abroad of his own *exuberant fulness:* There is no *straitness* in the *Deity*, no *bounds* to the *ocean* of *Love*. Now the *divine Goodness* referrs not to himself, as ours *extends not unto him*. He acts nothing for any *self-accomplishment*, being *essentially* and *absolutely compleat* and *perfect*. But the object and term of his *goodness* is his creatures *good* and *happinesse*, in their respective capacities. He is that

infinite *fountain* that is continually *overflowing;* and can no more cease to shed his *influences* upon his *indigent dependents* than the *sun* to shine at *noon.* Now as the *infinite Goodness* of the deity, obligeth him always to do *good*, so by the same reason to do that which is *best;* since to omit any degrees of *good* would argue a *defect* in *goodness*, supposing *wisdom* to *order*, and *power* to *execute.* He therefore that supposeth *God* not always to do what is *best*, and *best* for his *Creatures* (for he cannot act for his own *Good*) apprehends him to be less *good* than can be *conceived*, and consequently not *infinitely* so. For what is *infinite*, is beyond *measure and apprehension.*

Therefore to direct this to our purpose, *God* being *infinitely good*, and that to his *Creatures*, and therefore doing always what is *best* for them, methinks it roundly follows that our *souls lived* and injoy'd themselves of *old* before they came into these *bodies.* For since they were *capable* of *living*, and that in a much *better* and *happier* state long before they [67] descended into this *region of death* and *misery;* and since that condition of *life* and *self-enjoyment* would have been *better*, than *absolute not-being;* may we not safely conclude from a due consideration of the *divine goodness*, that it was *so*? What was it that gave us our *being*, but the *immense goodness* of our *Maker*? And why were we drawn out of our *nothings*, but because it was *better* for us to *be*, than *not to be*? Why were our *souls* put into *these bodies*, and not into some more *squalid* and *ugly;* but because we are capable of *such*, and 'tis *better* for us to *live* in *these*, than in those that are less sutable to our natures? And had it not been *better* for us, to have injoy'd our selves and the bounty and favours of our *Maker* of old, as did the other order of *intellectual* creatures, than to have layn in the comfortless *night* of *nothing* till 'tother day? Had we not been *better* on't to have lived and acted in the joyful regions of light and blessedness with those Spirits that at first had being, than just now to jump into this sad plight, [69] and state of *sin* and *wretchedness*?

Infinite Power could as well have made us all at once, as the *Angels;* and with as good *congruity* to our *natures* we might have *liv'd* and been happy without these bodies, as we shall be in the *state* of *separation:* since therefore it was *best* for us, and as easie for our *Creator* so to have effected it, where was the *defect*, if it was not so? Is not this to slurr his *goodness*! and to *strait-lace* the *divine beneficence*? And doth not the contrary *Hypothesis* to what I am pleading for, represent the *God of Love* as less *good* and *bountiful*, than a *charitable* mortall, who would neglect no opportunity within his reach of doing what good he could to those that want his help and assistance?

I confess, the world generally have such *Narrow* and *unbecoming apprehensions* of *God*, and draw his *picture* in their *imaginations* so like themselves, that few I doubt will feel the *force* of this *Argument;* and mine own observation makes me enter the same suspicion of [70] its success that some others have who have used it. 'Tis only a *very deep sense* of the *divine goodness* can give it any *perswasive energy*. And this noble sentiment there are very few that are possest of. However to lend it what strength I can, I shall endeavour to remove some *prejudices* that hinder it's force and efficacy; And when those *spots* and *scum* are *wiped* away, that *mistake* and *inadvertency* have fastned on it, 'twill be *illustrious* by its own brightness.

D [Henry Hallywell], *Some Reflections on a late Discourse of Mr. Parkers* (1668), 275–276

Let us see now how he confutes the *Platonists*, with whom he is very angry for asserting, *That God being Infinite Goodness, will necessarily do that which is best, page* 27. His first Argument to prove the falsity of this Position he sets down *page* 29, 30. *&c.* the sum of which in brief is this, *That the necessity of Infinite Wisdom doing that which is best, takes away the liberty and freedom of the Divine Will.* To which I answer, That the liberty of the Divine Will consists not in an Arbitrary Indifferency of acting or not acting; but in acting always sutably and conformablely to his own Infinite Rectitude and Perfection: As the true Excellency and Freedom of our wills consists not in an indifferency or dubious suspension between Good and Evil (for this is a debility and imperfection in us) but in a constant Election of that which Right Reason and Intellect propound to them as Best: So that when once that Eternal Providence which sent us down upon Earth, shall reinstate us in the Possession of our Native Glory, our Wills which shall then obtain their freedom in it's greatest latitude and dimensions, yet shall not be left to a bare Indifferency: but will as certainly adhere to that which is Good, as a wise and [276] prudent man will alwayes give the same judgment of the same thing in the same circumstances. Wherefore to answer in short, I say, that Gods actions are not so fatal and necessary as the motions of an *Automaton* or *Engine*, because he is endued with an Energetical Power of Reason and Intellect; but are free and unconstrained by any external Principle: but because his Nature is infinitely Good, it will always do that which is Best, because Goodness is the chief and first active Principle in it.

E George Rust, *The Holy Scripture tells of the Resurrection of the Dead* (1658) (Marilyn A. Lewis, et al., trans and eds, "Origenian Platonism in Interregnum Cambridge", (*History of Universities*, vol. 30, nos 1–2, 2017), 120–121

Besides, the vastly different properties that the Apostle attributes to these bodies and the future ones abundantly demonstrate the difference between them. Hence, it should be understood that the identity of the [121] body cannot be derived only from bare and naked matter, but in the first place from its modifications. In fact, if the numerically identical matter that at some point had constituted a human body, remaining the same in quantity, afterwards were transferred to a plant, none could be so insane or so disregard the common use of language as to believe and say that the body of the man and of the plant are the same. Wherefore anyone who imagines that our bodies will be so pure and luminous that they will imitate the shining of the sun, and so fine, agile, and subtle as to become spiritual, aerial or, even more, ethereal, and nevertheless remain flesh, blood and bones, etc., will inevitably create contradictions and shape chimeras. Likewise, if we supposed a stone to be divided in parts so minuscule that they were as fine as air or celestial matter, but remaining stone at the same time, this would be what they call a *contradictio in adjecto*. In fact, the nature of stone is to be hard, solid, opaque, heavy, etc. If you remove these properties, of course the matter remains, but the stone is lost. At the resurrection, we are going to be made either of different matter or the same. It will definitely be impossible to have the same bodies. Therefore the Apostle, as if summing up the arguments at verse 50, says: "Now this I say, brethren, (these things up to this point have been said by me) that flesh and blood cannot inherit the kingdom of God; (as though adding the principle on which this assertion is founded), neither doth corruption inherit incorruption."

F Henry More, *The Apology of Dr. Henry More* (1664) (issued with *A Modest Enquiry into the Mystery of Iniquity*), 495–496

But this is a point of so great importance, that it must not be so slightly passed over before a more narrow search into the true nature of a *Glorified Body*, according to the genuine and natural inclinations of the Holy Scripture. Whence it will appear, whether I have rightly asserted the *Glorified Body* of Christ to be *Organised Light*, or no.

According to testimony of Scripture we shall find that a *Glorified Body*, or that Body wherewith they shall be rewarded who shall attain to the blessed Resurrection which is the most precious hope of all true Christians, may be dignified with these three titles, *Angelical*, *Spiritual* and *Celestial*. It is an *Angelical Body*, because the *Sons of the Resurrection* are said to be ἰσάγγελοι, that is, in every actual respect that tends to any real perfection or happiness *equal unto Angels*. For Christ argues thus, *Luk.*

20. 36. They cannot die, ἰσάγγελοι γὰρ εἰσιν, *For they are equal to the Angels.* Which would be scarce an illustration, much less a proof and convincing illation, unless it be understood in that sense I above intimated. For it would be but a languid kind of reasoning and of small satisfaction, to conclude the *Sons of Resurrection* immortal, because they are immortal as the Angels are immortal. That looks like the proving *Idem per Idem.* And yet this would be all, if they were equal to the Angels onely in that thing. Nor would they be so properly said to be *equal* to them, especially in so general terms, if they did but *equalize* them in this one particular. [. . .]. But taking ἰσάγγελοι in the same latitude that it most naturally sounds, that the *Sons of the Resurrection* are absolutely in all such actual respects as I have above intimate *equal to the Angels,* this of *Immortality* will necessarily be included as part in the whole summe. Nor can the condition of their *Bodies* be left out, as touching the nature and glory of them, but a *Son of the Resurrection* and an *Angel* must be in every such regard all one. For they were *Sons of God* in a *Moral* or *Spiritual* sense before the Resurrection.

G [Henry Hallywell], *A Private Letter of Satisfaction to a Friend* (1667), 19–20

[I shall] withall consider that the great Crown of our Faith and Patience, the happiness and reward of glorified Spirits, to purchase which for mankind the ever blessed Son of God left the sacred mansions of Heaven, the bosome of blessedness, and veiled his glory under the clouds of flesh and blood, shall be an ethereall and heavenly body, which Plato calls [Greek words] a *resplendent vehicle,* and St. Paul [Greek words] a *spiritual body*: he, I say that attentively perpends this, that the instruments of the Souls operations both in this life and the next are corporeal, will likewise think it probable, that she is not wholly denudated of Matter in the intermediate space between death and the resurrection, at what time she shall be possessed of her long expected joy, and her vile body shall be transformed into the similitude of the glorious body of the Son of [20] God.

Chapter 26

Soul-Making Theodicy

Christian Hengstermann

A Henry More, *The Praeexistency of the Soul* (1647), Cantos 7–10 (ed. Jacob, 493–494)

7

But *Pan* nor *Rhea* be our Parentage
We been the Of-spring of all-seeing *Jove*
Though now, whether through our own miscarriage
Or secret force of fate, that all doth move
We be cast low, for why? The sportfull love
Of our great Maker (like as mothers dear
In Pleasance from them do their children shove
That back again they may recoil more near)
Shoves off our souls a while, the more them to endear.

8

Or whether Justice and due Equity
Expects the truth of our affection,
And therefore sets us 'twixt the Deitie
And the created world, that thereupon
We may with a free resignation
Give up our selves to him deserves us best.
That love is none that's by coaction.
Hence he our souls from his own self releast
And left us free to follow what the most us pleas'd.

9

And for this purpose did enrich our choice
By framing of the outward Universe.
The framing of this world a meet devise
Whereby Gods wisedom thorough all may pierce,
From hight to depth. In depth is vengeance fierce,
Whereby transgressing souls are sorely scourged

And back again are forced to reverse
By *Nemesis* deep-biting whips well urged.

10

Thus nothing's lost of God fecundity.
But stretching out himself in all degrees
His wisedom, goodnesse and due equity
Are rightly rank'd, in all the soul them sees.
O holy lamps of God! O sacred eyes
Filled with love and wonder every where!
Ye wandring tapers to whom God descries
His secret paths, great Psyches darlings dear!
Behold her works, but see your hearts close not too near.

B [George Rust], *A Letter of Resolution Concerning Origen and the Chief of His Opinions* (pp. 35–38)

The second part of the Father's argument from providence is much-what the same with the first, *mutatis mutandis*. For the experience of most men can bear witness that there are not stronger allurements from without to all manner of viciousness than we find incitations to the same from our own intrinsic constitution, which, according to the common hypothesis, is not properly our fault nor any fruit of it, nor was it in our power to prevent it. Yet we are so fatally entangled in it that it is next to a miracle to rid ourselves in any good measure of its chains. Is not the world disordered, and Society poisoned, and men's own particular peace and honour miserably violated with the baleful effects of the four elements of our terrestrial composition, whiles some live even in this world in a perpetual fire and are tormented before their time through wrathfulness and strives, contentiousness and injurious zeal which their choler kindles in them? Others, on the contrary, are drowned in sottishness and stupidity and an utter ineptness of all things worthy of a man by the overflowing of stupifying phlegm, a third sort tossed about like feathers with light-mindeness and admiration of trifles or wafted into the foul lake of bodily pleasures by the gusts of reeking blood, a fourth consumed by that flow-devouring Demogorgon in the earthy melancholy in which lodge anxious fear, dark suspicion and fretting envy. And though you possibly may [35] have heard some men talk of liberty and freewill and a sovereign power in us to keep all these rebellious humours in good order and that, with much ease, if we would but give our minds to it, yet if you but consider whence it is that they talk in that high strain, you will begin to think they reckon without their host and against experience. Such men have a sort of adversaries who from the assurance of their very senses that there is a great lapse and degeneracy in universal mankind, do, without all ceremony, bluntly cast the cause upon God, or at best assign such a reason of it as their antagonists think comes to the fame, who, therefore, out of an abhorrency to such blasphemy, as they call it, think it better and more pious to deny the truth of a manifest observation than to make God the author of so calamitous a phenomenon. Where, by the way, you may observe that both sides, by their earnest contention making good half of their respective opinions, have, to the free enquirer and lover of truth, facilitated his finding out the true cause which neither contradicts experience nor is injurious to the glory of the almighty. But granting to these contenders for freewill that something of what they plead for is true, as indeed it cannot be denied, I yet would ask them whether or no, the condition of our nature considered, the strong inclinations in us naturally to that which is evil and these strengthened and further confirmed for several years before we can come to have any considerable use of our reason or arrive to any command over ourselves, lastly, the way and manner how the elections of our will are performed, which we never find free [36] where there is a custom or passion against it and how corporeal motions determine the thoughts and passions of our mind, I ask them whether, these things being considered, it be not hundreds to one odd that we shall choose the ways of vice rather than virtue. Or let the disproportion be as little as they can with any colour pretend, they cannot clear the goodness and rectitude of divine providence by their hypothesis which thrusts pure and immaculate and most innocent spirits into so great danger of being defiled and corrupted by the passions of the body and of soundly smarting for it hereafter.

But for my own part, I think the observation of their adversaries is much the truer, that the disproportion is exceeding great. For since the ways of holiness and virtue are so full of peace and unspeakable contentment and shine with so enravishing and irresistible pulchritude to prepared minds and do so perfectly correspond to all the senses of so happy a temper that we are fully assured our soul is then as she should be and it connection with her most proper good I cannot see why men should universally take the contrary course and that with so much passion as they do, jeering at those who have made the better choice as mad-men or fools, if there was any liberty in them worth speaking of to virtue or piety. 'Tis true indeed there is great variety as to degree in the backwardness of men to goodness and virtue and proneness to that which is evil. Yet those who have the care and nurture of youth, fathers, schoolmasters and tutors, do with one consent affirm that they not seldom have some in their charge who from their earliest [37] years are of so inexpugnable a propension to that which is naught, so wretchless and insensible of all wholesome counsels and have their eyes so perfectly sealed up and their hearts so frozen to all impressions of virtue and sobriety that you may as well read lectures of temperance to a goat or a boar and as successfully teach goodness, pity and kindness to a bear robbed of her whelps or a tiger enraged with hunger as think to fasten any such things upon their blind and obdurate minds. Whence is this strange phenomenon? If the soul was not in the world before she was born upon Earth, it is not conceivable how she should in so little a time contract so peremptory an affection to vice amidst those continual chidings and reproofs, those sharp and painful corrections, those several ways of ignominious punishments she meets with, those advantageous representations made to her of that which is good and laudable, those many and earnest invitations and allurements of her to embrace it, with all other methods of a good and prudent institution. That she comes pure and undefiled out of the hands of her creator all grant and, be this pureness what it will, whether with or without those natural notions of what is good and honest, the business will be much-what the same as to our present purpose. For if the latter way be the truth, even this negative purity will leave her in an indifference to virtue of vice and, therefore, if her first precepts and earliest inculcations be good and virtuous, she would be formed unto virtue, which yet we see is so far from happening to some, though the very same instruction to others proves successful, that [38] they, on the contrary, impatient of every curb and rein and deaf to all calls and charms, run headlong into all iniquity. If the former way be true, it would be still more wonderful how her first-appearing inclinations should so eagerly carry her to that which is vicious, contrary to the positive restraint of her inward light. But if they say, as they generally do, that the soul herself is pure and immaculate, but that she contracts this unreclaimable proclivity of vice from the body she is put into, beside the ignorance they discover by so saying in the speculation of things in joining such ill-agreeing mates together into one vital composition where Sympathy and congruity is the only *vinculum*, the Father asks them how it is consistent with the goodness and righteousness of God, the blessed spring of all virtue and holiness and tender lover of all his creatures, to put such innocent souls into such foul and untamed bodies which so fatally and necessarily hurry them to that which alone of all things in the world he disapproves of and which, he knows, will be their utter bane and miserable ruin. And therefore, upon the whole of this second part of his argument from providence, he concludes that since so great a part of our pitiable bondage to vice and passion in the judgement of all sides proceeds from these bodies of ours, if the soul was merely passive in being born into this world and was not before she was born here, much of the calamity she suffers from vice, for which she must suffer more hereafter, must in his judgement be cast upon God, which, he thinks, is impious to affirm and utterly contradictious to his holy attributes.

C Henry More, *Divine Dialogues* (1668), Book II, Chapter 5 (Second edition, 98–102)

Philoth. No, by no means, *Hylobares.* For the Scene of the World then would be such a languid flat thing, that it would disgrace the great *Dramatist* that contrived it. For there would be no compass or circuit of any Plot or Intrigue, but every thing so shallow or sudden, so simple and obvious, that no man's Wit or Vertue would finde any Game to exercise themselves in. And assure [99] your self, it is one fundamental point of the Divine Counsel, and that laid deep in his Wisedome and Goodness, *that at least on this terrestrial Stage there should be sufficient difficulty and hardship for all Sensible and Intellectual Creatures to grapple and contest with*, that an ignoble and corruptive torpour may not seize their bodies and spirits, and make their life languid and their Faculties useless, and finde nothing to doe in the world but to eat and drink and sleep. For there are very few men given to *Contemplation*, and yet fewer successfull in it. That therefore that I contend for is this, That in these general, but constant and peremptory, strokes of Nature there is an exact Providence of God; and that which you account a Defect is indeed a Perfection and a surer pledge of a Divine Foresight, that does thus manifestly in the compute of things defalcate either useless or hurtfull supefluities; as this guidance of the *Rain* from the High-ways in Winter. For has he not given man wit and art to make a supply by good wax'd Boots, oil'd Coats and Hoods, and eyes in his head to chuse his way, if one be better then another; or if all be intolerable, politicall wit to make Laws and Orders for the mending of the High-ways? For thus are men honestly employed for their own and the common good. And judge you what a ridiculous thing it were, that the *Sun* should so miraculously turn off his beams from every fair Face, whenas the same End is so easily served by the invention of Masks; or that the continued Shadow of the Earth should be broken by sudden miraculous eruptions or disclusions of light, to prevent the Art and officiousness of the Lantern-maker and the Link-boy; or lastly, that the Aire should not resound a Lie, nor the point of a Sword pierce the skin of the innocent. For this were an exprobration to the Wisedom of God, as if he had mistook himself in creating of free Agents, and [100] by an After-device thus forcibly ever defeated their free Actings, by denying them the ordinary assistences of Nature. This would be such a force and stop upon the first spring of Motion, that the greatest trialls of mens spirits and the most pompous externall solemnities would be stifled thereby, or utterly prevented; and all Politicall Prudence, Sagacity, Justice and Courage would want their Objects. Wherefore this indifferent and indiscriminating constancy of Nature ought to be; it being reckoned upon in those Faculties God has endow'd both men and other Animals with, whereby they are able to close with the more usual advantages of these standing Laws of Nature, and have sense and foresight to decline or provide against any dangerous circumstances of them; and that with at least as much certainty as is proportionable to the considerableness of the safety of such an individual Creature as cannot live always, nor was ever intended to live long upon Earth.

Hyl. I partly understand what you would be at, *Philotheus*, and indeed so far, that I am almost disheartned from propounding the remainder of the Meditations that met me on the Rode touching the *Hail* also and the *Thunder*. For methought Nature seem'd very unkinde to pelt a young Foal so rudely with so big Hail-stones, and give him so harsh a welcome into the world.

Philoth. Tush, *Hylobares*, that was but a sportfull passage of Nature, to try how tight and tinnient her new workmanship was; which if it were not able to bear such small Fillips, it would be a sign that things hung very crazily and unsoundly together. Wherefore Nature does but justifie the accuracy of her own Artifice, in exposing her works to a number of such trialls and hardships. This is but a slight Scruple, *Hylobares;* but surely some profound conceit surprized your minde in your meditations touching the *Thunder.*

[101] *Hyl.* The main thing was this, That if Providence were so exact as some pretend, those Thunder-claps that doe any execution should ever pick out some notoriously-wicked fellow to make him an example, and not strike an heedless Goat brouzing on the side of a Rock, or rend some old Oak in a Forest.

Philoth. This indeed is more shrewdly urged. But are you sure, *Hylobares*, that this were the most perfect way that Nature could pitch upon?

Hyl. So it seems to me.

Philoth. I suppose then it is because you take this to be the most effectuall way to make men good.

Hyl. Why not, *Philotheus?*

Philoth. But suppose a mighty, if not an almighty, Arm out of the Clouds should pull men by the ears as often as they offered to offend, would not that be more effectuall?

Hyl. One would think so.

Philoth. Wherefore upon this ground you should require that also, *Hylobares.*

Hyl. But that would be too great a force upon free Agents, O *Philotheus.*

Philoth. And how do you know, *Hylobares*, but that other would be so likewise?

Hyl. I must confess, *Philotheus*, it is an hard matter to define what measure of force is to be used by Providence to keep men from Sin.

Philoth. And therefore a rash thing to prescribe laws or ways to Providence in so obscure a matter. Besides, there are so many notoriously wicked, that there would be such thundring and rattling, especially over great Cities, that we should be never quiet night nor day. And those that escaped would be forward to phansie themselves Thunder-proof; and others, that there was no Judgement to come, because Vengeance was taken so exactly in this life. Besides that you seem to forget that the strokes of Na[102]ture levell not at particulars. For she is an unperceptive Principle, and cannot act *pro re nata*, or suspend her self from acting; and that the end of *Thunder* is not to forestall the last Day of Judgement, but for clearing the Air, and sending more fattening showrs into the bosome of the Earth.

Hyl. But do *Thunderbolts* conduce any thing to that, *Philotheus?*

Philoth. Those are very seldome, *Hylobares*; and I deny not but they may have their moral use: but best so moderated as they are, not so constantly vibrated as your Curiosity would have them. For if every perjured or notoriously-wicked person is to be pelted from Heaven with *Thunderbolts*, people will presume them innocent when-ever they die without this solemn Vengeance done upon them.

Hyl. Well, I perceive I must produce new Objections, and such as I have thought on more deliberately. For these *Philotheus* easily blows away.

D More, *Divine Dialogues*, 2,22 (Second edition, 158–161)

Philoth. But lastly, *Hylobares*, though we should admit that the whole design of Divine Providence is nothing else but the mere disburthening of his overflowing Goodness upon the whole Creation, and that he does not stand upon the terms of Justice and Congruity, or any such punctilio's, (as some may be ready here to call them) but makes his *pure* Goodness the measure of his dealing with both Men and Angels; yet I say that it does not at all contradict, but that God may permit Sin in the World, he having the privilege of bringing Light out of Darkness, and the nature of things being such, that the lessening of Happiness in one is the advancement of it in another: As it is in the Motion of Bodies, what agitation one loses, is transferred upon another; or like the Beams of the Sun, that retunded from this Body are received by another, and nothing is lost. So that in gross the Goodness of God may be as fully derived upon the Creation, though not so equally distributed [159] to particular Creatures, upon his permitting Sin in the World, as if he did forcibly, and against the nature of free Creatures, perpetually keep it out. This is that therefore that I would say, that the Vices of the wicked intend and exercise the Vertues of the just. What would become of that noble Indignation of minde that holy men conceive against wicked and blasphemous people, if there were neither Wickedness nor Blasphemy in the world? What would become of those enravishing Vertues of Humility, Meekness, Patience and Forbearance, if there were [160] no Injuries amongst men? What had the Godly whereupon to employ their Wit and Abilities, if they had no enemies to grapple with? How would their Faith be tried, if all things here below had been carried on in Peace and Righteousness and in the Fear of God? How would their Charity and Sedulity be discovered in endeavouring to gain men to the true Knowledge of God, if they were alwaies found so to their hands? Terrestriall Goodness would even grow sluggish and lethargicall, if it were not sharpened and quickned by the *Antiperistasis* of the general Malignity of the World. There are no generous Spirits but would even desire to encounter with Dangers and Difficulties, to testifie their love to the parties they are much endeared to; and it is an exceeding great accession to their enjoyments, that they have suffered so much for them. But if the World were not generally wicked for a time, no Soul of man could meet with any such adventure, and the History of Ages would be but a flat Story. Day it self upon this Earth would be tiresome, if it were alwaies Day, and we should lose those chearfull Salutes of the emerging Light, the cool breathings and the pleasing aspects of the Rosie Morning. The Joys and Solemnities of Victories and Triumphs could never be, if there were no Enemies to conflict with, to conquer and triumph over. And the stupendious undertakings of the Saviour of Mankinde, and the admirable windings of Providence in her Dramatick Plot which has been acting on this Stage of the Earth from the beginning of the World, had been all of them stopped and prevented, if the Souls of men had not been lapsed into Sin. And the sweetest and most enravishing Musicall touches upon the melancholized Passions (so far as I know) of both men and Angels had never sounded in the consort of the Universe, if the Orders of free Agents had never played out of tune.

Nothing therefore of the Divine Goodness seems to be lost, whenas the very Corruption of it, as in a grain of Corn cast into the ground, makes for its encrease; and what of it is rejected by some, is by the Wisedome of God so unavoidably conveyed upon others. But that it is best that all should partake alike of the Overflowings of God, will, I think, be no less difficult to prove, then that all Subordination of estates and conditions in the world should be taken away, and that God should not have created any of the more vile and contemptible kinde of Creatures, such as the Worm, the Fly, the Frog, and the Mouse. Wherefore it being so disputable a Point, whether it be not in it self as good that there should be those that are rightly called evil and wicked in the World, as that there should be such and such viler or more mischievous Creatures on the face of the Earth, it is an unexcusable piece of Rashness to conclude, that the Permission of Sin is any such Argument against the

          Goodness of that Providence that guideth all things. For why should she *generally* force or certainly determine the Faculties of men that are naturally free, and so perpetually keep them off from acting of Sin, whenas Sin it self is so pompously led captive by the power of Righteous[161]ness, and by the admirable Wisedome of God serves for the equal advancement of his intended Goodness?

Hyl.   Your Reason, or your zealous Eloquence, or both of them jointly, strike so strongly upon my minde, O *Philotheus*, that I am, whether I will or no, constrained to look upon it as a desperate Doubt or Difficulty, and such as I never hope to be resolved of, Whether, considering the comprehension of all, God's permission of Sin be more becoming his Goodness, or his perpetuall forcible hindering thereof. And therefore the Goodness of Divine Providence being so conspicuous in other things, I think I ought not to call it into question from matters that be so obscure, but to surmize the best.

Sophr. Excellently well inferred, *Hylobares*.

Chapter 27

Christ's Sacrifice

Douglas Hedley

Ralph Cudworth, *The true Notion of the Lords Supper* (1642) Chapters IV and V *(pp. 52–56)*

[52] Chap. IV.

BUT lest we should seeme all this while, to Set up Fancies of our owne, and then Sport with them; We come now to Demonstrate and Evince that the *Lords Supper* in the proper *Notion* of it, is Epulum Ex Oblatis, or, A Feast Upon Sacrifice; in the same manner with the *Feasts* upon the Jewish *Sacrifices* under the Law; and the *Feasts* upon ΕΙΔΩΛΟΘΥΤΑ (*things offered up to Idols*) among the Heathens: And that from a place of Scripture where all these three shall be compared together, and made exact *Parallels* to one another.

1 CORIN. 10.
14. *Wherefore my dearely beloved, flee from Idolatry.*
15. *I speake as to wise men, judge you what I say.*
16. *The Cup of Blessing which we blesse, is it not the Communion of the Blood of Christ? The Bread which we breake, is it not the Communion of the Body of Christ?*
18. *Behold Israel after the flesh, are not they which eate of the Sacrifices partakers of the Altar?*
20. *Now I say the things which the Gentiles Sacrifice, they Sacrifice to Devils and not to God; and I would not that you should have Fellowship with Devils.*
21. *Ye cannot drinke the Cup of the Lord, and the cup of Devils: ye cannot be partakers of the Lords Table, and the Table of Devils.*
[53]

Where the Apostles Scope being to convince the *Corinthians* of the unlawfulnesse of Eating things Sacrificed to Idols; He doth it in this manner: Shewing, that though an Idoll were truely Nothing, and things Sacrificed to Idols were Physically, Nothing, as different from other Meates; [as it seemes they argued, and Saint *Paul* confesses, ver. 19.] Yet Morally and Circumstantially, to Eate of things Sacrificed to Idols, in the Idols Temple, was to consent with the Sacrifices, and to be guilty of them: Which he doth illustrate, First, from a *Parallel Rite*, in Christian Religion. Where the Eating and Drinking of the Body and Blood of Christ, offered up to God upon the Crosse for us, in the *Lords Supper*, is a Reall Communication in his Death and Sacrifice, ver. 16. *The Cup of blessing which we blesse, is it not the Communion of the blood of Christ? &c.*

Secondly, From another *Parallel* of the same Rite among the Jewes. Where, always they that Eate of the Sacrifices, were accounted partakers of the Altar, that is, Of the Sacrifice offered up upon the

Altar, ver. 18. *Behold Israel after the flesh, are not they which Eate of the Sacrifices partakers of the Altar?* In *veteri Lege quicunque admittebantur ad Edendum de Hostiis Oblatis, censebantur ipsius Sacrificii tanquam pro ipsis Oblati, fieri Participes, & per illud Sanctificari*: As a Late Commentator fully expresses it.

Therefore, as to Eate the Body and Blood of Christ in the *Lords Supper*, is to be made partaker of his Sacrifice offered up to God for us; as to Eate [54] of the Jewish Sacrifices under the Law, was to partake in the Legall Sacrifices themselves: So to Eate of things offered up in Sacrifice to Idols, was to be made partakers of the Idoll-Sacrifices: And therefore was unlawfull.

For, the things which the Gentiles Sacrifice, they Sacrifice to Devils, but Christs Body and Blood was offered up in Sacrifice unto God, and therefore they could not partake of both together; the Sacrifice of the true God, and the Sacrifice of Devils. *Ye cannot drinke the Cup of the Lord, and the Cup of Devils; ye cannot be partakers of the Lords Table, and the table of Devils.* S. *Pauls* Argument here, must needs suppose a perfect *Analogy* between these three, and that they are all *Parallels* to one another, or else it hath no strength. Wherefore I conclude from hence, that the LORDS SUPPER is the same among Christians, in respect of the *Christian Sacrifice*, that among the Jewes the *Feasts* upon the *Legall Sacrifices* were, and among the Gentiles, the *Feasts* upon the *Idoll-Sacrifices*: and therefore EPULUM SACRIFICIALE, *or*, EPULUM EX OBLATIS: ΟΠΕΡ ΕΔΕΙΔΕΙΞΑΙ.

Chap. V.

THUS having Declared and Demonstrated *The True Notion of The Lords Supper.* We see then, How that Theologicall Controversie, which hath cost so many Disputes, *Whether the Lords* [55] *Supper be a Sacrifice*, is already decided; for it is not Sacrificium, but Epulum ΕΚ ΤΗΣ ΘΥΣΙΑΣ: Not A Sacrifice, but *A Feast upon Sacrifice*: or else in other Words, Not Oblatio Sacrificii, but as *Tertullian* excellently speakes, Participatio Sacrificii: Not the *Offering of something up to God upon an Altar*, but the *Eating of something which comes from Gods Altar*, and is set upon Our Tables. Neither was it ever knowne amongst the Jewes or Heathens, that those Tables upon which they did eate Their Sacrifices, should be called by the Name of Altars. Saint *Paul* speaking of the Feasts upon the Idoll-Sacrifices, calls the places upon which they were eaten, *The Tables of Devils*, because the Devils meate was eaten on them, not the Altars of Devils: and yet doubtlesse he spake according to the true Propriety of speech, and in those Technicall Words that were then in use amongst them. And therefore keeping the same Analogy, he must needes call the *Communion Table*, by the name of the *Lords Table*: *i. e.* The Table upon which *Gods Meate* is eaten, not his Altar, upon which it is offered. It is true, an *Altar* is nothing but a *Table*, but it is *A Table upon which* GOD *himselfe eates*, consuming the Sacrifices by his *Holy Fire*: but when the same Meate is given from God unto Us to Eate of, the relation being changed, the place on which We Eate, is nothing but a *Table*.

And because it is not enough in any Discourse, as *Aristotle* well observeth in his *Ethicks*, to confute [56] an Error, unlesse we can also shew τὸ ἄιτιον τοῦς ψεύδους, *The Cause of that Error*; Having thus Discovered *The True Notion of the Lords Supper*, we may easily from hence discerne also, How that mistake grew up, and that by the Degeneration of this Truth. There is a Sacrifice in the Lords Supper Symbolically, but not there as Offered up to God, but Feasted on by us; and so not a Sacrifice, but a Sacrificiall Feast: Which beganne too soone to be misunderstood.

John Smith, *Of the Existence and Nature of God* (1660), Chapter 8 (*Select Discourses*, 155–158)

[155] We cannot say indeed that God was absolutely determin'd from some Law within himself to make us; but I think we may safely say, when he had once determin'd to make us, he could neither

make us *sinfull*, seeing he had no *Idea* nor shadow of Evil within himself, nor lap us those dreadfull fates within our Natures, or set them over us, that might *arcanâ inspiratione* (as some are pleas'd to phrase it) secretly work our ruine, and silently carry us on, making use of our own naturall infirmity, to eternall misery. Neither could he design to make his creatures *miserable*, that so he might shew himself *Just*. These are rather the by-waies of *Cruell* and *Ambitious* men, that seek their own advantage in the mischiefs of other men, and contrive their own Rise by their Ruines: this is not Divine *Justice*, but the *Cruelty* of degenerated men.

But as the Divinity could propound nothing to it self in the making of the World but the *Communication* of its own *Love* and *Goodness*; so it can never swerve from the same Scope and End in the dispensation of it self to it. Neither did God so boundlesly enlarge the appetite of Souls after some All-sufficient Good, that so they might be the more unspeakably tortur'd in the missing of it; but that they might more certainly return to the Originall of their Beings. And such busie-working Essences as the Souls of men are, could neither be made as dull and sensless of true Happiness as Stocks and Stones are, neither could they contain the whole summe and perfection of it within themselves: therefore they must also be inform'd with such Principles as might conduct them back again to Him from whom they first came. God does not make Creatures for the meer sport of his Almighty arm, to raise and ruine and toss up and down at meer pleasure. [156] No, that εὐδοκία or good pleasure of that Will that made them is the same still, it changes not, though we may change, and make our selves uncapable of partaking the blissfull fruits and effects of it.

And so we come to consider that Law embosom'd in the Souls of men which ties them again to their Creatour, and this is called *The Law of Nature*; which indeed is nothing else but a Paraphrase or Comment upon the Nature of God as it copies forth it self in the Soul of Man.

Because God is the *First Mind* and the *First Good*, propagating an *Imitation* of himself in such Immortall Natures as the Souls of Men are, therefore ought the Soul to renounce all mortall and mundane things, and preserve its Affections chast and pure for God himself; to love him with a most Universall and Unbounded Love; to trust in him and reverence him; to converse with him in a free & chearful manner, as One *in whom we live and move and have our Beings*, being perpetually encompassed by him, and never moving out of him; to resign all our Waies and Wills up to him with an equall and indifferent mind, as knowing that he guides and governs all things in the Best way; to sink our selves as low in *Humility*, as we are in *Self-nothingness*.

And because all those scatter'd *Raies* of *Beauty* and Loveliness which we behold spread up and down all the World over, are onely the *Emanations* of that inexhausted *Light* which is above; therefore should we *love* them all in that, and climb up alwaies by those Sun-beams unto the Eternall Father of Lights: we should look upon him and take from him the pattern of our lives, and alwaies eying of him should ἀγάλματα θεῖα τεκταίνειν, &c. (as *Hierocles* speaks) polish and [157] shape our Souls into the clearest resemblance of him; and in all our behaviour in this World (that Great Temple of his) deport our selves decently and reverently, with that humility, meekness and modesty that becomes his house. We should endeavour more and more to be perfect, as he is; in all our dealing with men, doing good, shewing mercy and compassion, advancing justice and righteousness, being alwaies full of charity and good works; and look upon our selves as having nothing to doe here but to display & blazon the glory of our heavenly Father, and frame our hearts and lives according to that Pattern which we behold in the Mount of a holy Contemplation of him. Thus we should endeavour to preserve that Heavenly fire of the Divine Love and Goodness (which issuing forth from God centres it self within us, and is the Protoplastick virtue of our Beings) alwaies alive and burning in the Temple of our Souls, and to sacrifice our selves back again to him. And when we fulfill this *Royall Law* arising out of the heart of Eternity, then shall we here appear to be *the Children of God*, when he thus lives in us, as our Saviour speaks *Matth.* 5. And so we shall close up this Particular with that *High privilege* which Immortall Souls are invested with: they are all *the Off-spring of God*, for so S. *Paul* allows the Heathen Poet to call them: they are all royally descended, and have no Father but God himself, being originally formed into his image and likeness; and when they express the purity and holiness of the Divine Life in being perfect as God is perfect, then they *manifest themselves* to be his *Children, Matth.* 5. And in *Matth.* 7. Christ encourageth men to seek and pray for the *Spirit*, (which is the best gift that God can give to men) because he is their Heavenly Father, much more boun [158] tifull and tender to all helpless Souls that seek to him, then any earthly parent, whose Nature is degenerated from that primitive goodness, can be to his children. But those Apostate Spirits that know not to return to the Originall of their Beings, but implant themselves into some other stock, and seek to incorporate and unite themselves to another line by sin and wickedness, cut themselves off from this divine priviledge, and lose their own birth-right; they doe μεταβαίνειν εἰς ἄλλο γένος (if I may borrow that phrase) and lapse into another nature. All this was well express'd by *Proclus*,[1] πᾶσαι ψυχαῖ θεῶν παῖδες, ἀλλ' οὐ πᾶσαι τὸν ἑαυτῶν ἐπέγνωσαν θεόν. αἱ δὲ ἐπιγνοῦσαι καὶ τὴν ὁμοίαν ἑλόμεναι ζωὴν, καλοῦνται θεῶν παῖδες, *All Souls are the Children of God, but all of them know not their God; but such as know him and live like to him, are called the Children of God.*

Benjamin Whichcote, *Moral and Religious Aphorisms* (1753)

235. If a man will either enjoy God or Himself; let a Man *simplify* himself; think and do *Uniformly*; let him have but *One* governor within himself, and always observe it's commands: (that is the government of Reason and Understanding; not Passion, Interest, Humour, Fashion or Custom of the World:) else a man can have no Peace.
236. Truth is *connatural* to a man's Soul; and in Conjunction with it, becomes the mind's Temper, and Complexion, and Constitution.
247. A man hath his Religion to little purpose; if he doth not Mend his *Nature*, and Refine his Spirit, by it.
248. We *Worship* God best; when we Resemble Him most.

Note

1 *Lib. 4. in Timæum.*

Chapter 28

The Conflagration and Restitution of All Things

Christian Hengstermann

A Henry More, *The Immortality of the Soul*, Book III, Chapter 18, Sections 7–11 (Collection of Several Philosophical Writings, 248–250 = ed. Jacob 298–300).

7. But to leave these Poetical Riddles, and take a more serious and distinct view of the condition of the Soul after the *Conflagration* of the Earth; we shall finde five several sorts of Opinions concerning it. The first hold, *That this unmerciful heat and fire will at last destroy and consume the Soul as well as the Body*. But this seems to me impossible, that any created Substance should utterly destroy another Substance, so as to reduce it to nothing. For no part of Matter, acting the most furiously upon another part thereof, does effect that. It can onely attenuate, dissipate and disperse the parts, and make them invisible. But the Substance of the Soul is *indissipable* and *indiscerpible*, and therefore remains entire, whatever becomes of the Body or Vehicle.

8. The second Opinion is, *That after long and tedious torture in these flames, the Soul by a special act of Omnipotency is annihilated*. But, me thinks, this is to put Providence too much to her shifts, as if God were so brought to a plunge in his creating a Creature of it self immortal, that he must be fain to uncreate it again, that is to say to annihilate it. Besides that that divine *Nemesis* that lies within the compass of Philosophy, never supposes any such forcible eruptions of the Deity into extraordinary effects, but that all things are brought about by a wise and infallible or inevitable train of secondary Causes, whether natural or free Agents.

9. The third therefore to avoid these absurdities, denies both *absumption by Fire* and *annihilation*; but conceives, *That tediousness and extremity of pain makes the Soul at last, of her self, shrink* [249] *from all commerce with Matter*; the *immediate* Principle of Union, which we call *Vital Congruity*, consisting of a certain modification of the Body or Vehicle as well as of the Soul, which being spoiled and lost, and the Soul thereby quite loosned from all sympathy with Body or Matter, *she becomes perfectly dead, and sensless to all things*, by Axiome 36. and, as they say, *will so remain for ever*. But this seems not so rational; for, as *Aristotle* somewhere has it, ἕκαστον, οὗ ἐστιν ἐνέργεια, ἔστιν ἕνεκα τοῦ ἔργου. Wherefore so many entire immaterial Substances would be continued in being to all Eternity to no end nor purpose, notwithstanding they may be made use of, and actuate Matter again as well as ever.

10. A fourth sort therefore of Speculators there is, who conceive that after this solution of the Souls or Spirits of Wicked Men and *Daemons* from their Vehicles, *That their pain is continued to them even in that separate state, they falling into an unquiet sleep, full of furious tormenting Dreams, that act as fiercely upon their Spirits, as the external Fire did upon their Bodies*. But others except against this Opinion as a very uncertain Conjecture, it supposing that which to them seems not so sound, *viz*. That the Soul can act when it has lost all vital Union with the Matter; which seems repugnant with that so intimate and essential aptitude it has to be united therewith. And the Dreams of the Soul in the Body are not

transacted without the help of the Animal Spirits in the Brain, they usually symbolizing with their temper. Whence they conclude, that there is no certain ground to establish this Opinion upon.

11. The last therefore, to make all sure, that there may be no inconvenience in admitting that the Souls or Spirits as well of evil *Daemons* as wicked *Men*, disjoyned from their Vehicles by the force of that fatal *Conflagration*, may subsist, have excogitated an odde and unexpected Hypothesis, *That when this firing of the World has done due execution upon that unfortunate Crue, and tedious and direful torture has we aried their affected Ghosts into an utter recess from all Matter, and thereby into a profound sleep or death; that after a long Series of years, when not onely the fury of the Fire is utterly slaked, but that vast Atmosphere of smoak and vapours, which was sent up during the time of the Earths Conflagration, has returned back in copious showres of rain* (which will again make Seas and Rivers, will binde and consolidate the ground, and, falling exceeding plentifully all over, make the soil pleasant and fruitful, and the Aire cool and wholsome) *that Nature recovering thus to her advantage, and becoming youthful again, and full of genital salt and moisture, the Souls of all living Creatures belonging to these lower Regions of the Earth and Aire will awaken orderly in their proper places.* The Seas and Rivers will be again replenished with Fish; the Earth will send forth all manner of Fowls, four-footed Beasts, and creeping things; and the Souls of Men also shall then catch life from the more pure and balsamick parts of the Earth, and be clothed again in terrestrial Bodies; and lastly, the Aerial *Genii*, that Element becoming again wholsome and vital, shall, in due order and time, awaken and revive in the cool rorid Aire. Which Expergeraction into life is accompanied, say they, with propensions answerable to those [250] resolutions they made with themselves in those fiery torments, and with which they fell into their long sleep.

B [George Rust], *A Letter of Resolution Concerning Origen and the Chief of His Opinions* (1661) (pp. 74–77)

For beside her ordinary and natural ways of nature and correction, she [i.e. divine providence] can and will, when it seems fit or necessary, with a severer hand scourge these rebels to her gentler laws and contemners of her milder rebukes. And such will be that day of fiery vengeance, when the inferior elements of nature shall melt with fervent heat the earth and all the works thereon be burnt up and the air be filled with suffocating smoke which she shall send up from her inflamed entrails. Into which far-spreading lake of slow-consuming fire and sulphurous stench the unreclaimable devils and obstinately-wicked men shall be by the righteous hand of God precipitated. A sad pitiable Fate and torture unsufferable, but no doubt as just as great! Just, I say, not only according to the estimation of modern theology, which from an excess of complement to the justice of God becomes almost as rude and troublesome as the ass in the fable who did not fawn upon, but invade his master and which tragically pronounces that the least *peccadillo* highly deserves the greatest punishment conceivable, but [75] also in the compute and judgement of that all-righteous mind which judges and orders all things by the living law of equity. But what, though it be so great and just, is it, therefore, so quite different from the reason of all other punishments inflicted by God or man that there is nothing in it of that end for which they are inflicted? They are curative and for the emendation of the party suffering, but this, if it be eternal in the scholastic sense of the word, leaves no place for the bettering of the sufferers who are never to get out of this inexplicable labyrinth of woe and misery. Or because this exceeds all other punishments imaginable, must it also so infinitely transcend the very measures and proportions of this kind of distributive justice? If not, why should we think that the pain and smart of it shall be infinitely great and long when the pleasure reaped by the transgression which brought the punishment is not in any degree equal and when a shorter torture may make the punished change their mind or leave it very probable they would do so were they out of their torture and in an opportunity to shew it? And to imagine that God suffers any real injury and detriment from the transgressions of a peccable creature, which must, say they, be infinite, because he is so, and, therefore, deserve a punishment in all respects infinite is to talk of God very meanly and too much after the manner of men. And to set such a rule for the measuring the demerit of a fault by as will make all sins equal and which, they themselves confess, will not universally hold good towards any person beside God and, therefore, may be justly suspected to be a false one. Now to think these mise[76]rable souls are so far amiss as to be beyond the power of all redress and restitution is to suppose God made some of his creatures very untowardly and that when he pronounced they were all very good, he looked only upon the primitive state they were in when they came fresh out of his gracious hands and was so taken with that that he omitted to cast his all-comprehensive eyes to all possible conditions they might afterward fall into. For certainly, if he had done so and seen this never-to-be-ended doom of intolerable pain and anguish of body and mind, the infinite compassionateness of his blessed nature would scarcely have given so cheerful an approbation to the works of his hands. For none of them are good to him as advantaging him aught and those of them he foresaw would be so remedilessly calamitous as this hypothesis supposes would have been so far from being good as to themselves that it would have been the greatest favour God could do them never to have brought them into being. But then to think they are not beyond the power of redress and recovery and that that great punishment they shall undergo in the end of this world may contribute much thereto and yet to imagine they shall, for all this their better disposition, be still kept in it for ever and ever is to fix so harsh a note upon the mercy and equity of the righteous judge of all the world that the same temper in a man we should for ever execrate and abominate. And that they are in the possibility of being better, if God so please and do not purposely hinder it, is not improbably concluded by the Father from hence, that sin wherein they are so obdurately settled, though it hath [77] extinguished or silenced the divine life in them and, for the present, subjected them only to the sense, relish and exercise of the natural or animal, yet it hath left them their reason and understanding, such as it is, consideration and memory, which, like mercenary soldiers, will fight on either side and incline to and serve that life which is most powerful.

C [George Rust], *A Letter of Resolution Concerning Origen and the Chief of His Opinions* (1661) (pp. 78–81)

If, therefore, the vigorous alliciency of the brutish nature be abated, those powers will listen to better counsels and resume the seeds and inchoation of a better life and nature. And certainly, a searching ceaseless pain spreading through soul and body will so abate and consume all that joy they formerly took in their brutish rebellion that any offer of release will be welcome to them now the tumult and hurry of their former lusts and eager affections is flaked, which alone before made them uncapable of better advice, and their close-adhering pain, which sticks to them and scorches them worse than Hercules his shirt, should, methinks, necessarily force them to take up strong and peremptory resolutions and indignation against those courses whose fruits they now feel so direful to them. What is it, then, that should make the merciful governor of heaven and earth and hell, too, the compassionate "father of spirits" either forcibly to keep off and prevent this natural course of things or, which is worse, suffer those offers and preparations which it induces for the bettering the present condition of so great and so considerable a part of his creation and for the putting of them in a way of return to what he at first made them to come to naught?

If we look but into the natural world, we shall find that disposition of matter to the susception of life is rendered void and frustrate, but that there is always ready at hand so fruitful a principle as perfects and completes whatever is presented to its further vivification. And yet, this principle is but the brute, obscure shadow of that almighty goodness and exuberant life which actuates and manages the moral and intellectual world. Surely, then, no preparation happens here which is not carried onwards as far as it is capable, especially since this may be done, and yet these miserable souls we are speaking of pay fondly for their rebellious transgressions by a very long exceedingly great and intolerable torture both of body and mind. And indeed, by how much greater it is, by so much surer may we be that it will sometimes have an end by the necessity of nature. *Si gravis, brevis* takes place here too. For, it being unconceiveable how the soul should suffer any pain or torture but by the harsh and discordant motions of the body wherewith she is vitally united, if this union ever cease, she will become senseless. And this union being conditional upon certain terms on both sides and the conditions being such as are not necessarily at all times present to either of them, it may very well be thought that it may be dissolved. For if the induction of an unnatural foulness and impurity or an over-vehement agitation into the blood and spirits and other fluid parts of the body, if old age itself can make the soul quit her unfit tenement, what shall we think she will do when it is all on fire, when all the motions of it are but one continued great pain? Which disposition of body, when come to its height by long [79] continuance, is certainly far more contrary to that vital temper the soul requires in the body she will livingly join with than either coarseness of blood or consumption of animal moisture. For as, if an actually perceived pleasure was that which tempted and drew out the Soul to join with her body, no man would say she would ever unite with that body from whose cross constitution she should be affected with naught but pain, so where that congruity in her which disposes her to that union is more deeply pitched in her imperceptive powers, a man would be apt to think nevertheless that she could not vitally take hold of any body from conjunction with which she should after feel not motions but such as would torture her. And we may easily persuade ourselves that that disposition of body which will not prolicite the soul to join with it when she is free and her unfelt appetite catching, cannot forever tie her to it when forced upon her by her sad fate. And the matter she is then surrounded with being all of that unvital temper, it seems necessary that she should cease from all life and sense so that, whithersoever we look, whether to the gracious providence of God or the necessity of the nature of things, we find some probable hope that the punishment of the damned, as it implies the sense of pain, shall not be eternal in the highest sense of the world. And the Scripture, too, may seem to favour us in that it calls this dreadful doom by the name of "eternal death", which, one would think, did very strangely set out that state and condition wherein is the highest and most pungent sense, but it does very appositely express the sense of Origen's hypo[80]thesis explained after the latter and more probable way. But whether their release be by any change wrought in the disposition of their spirits but without death or whether by an escape, as it were, by dying to the body so tortured, there is no doubt to be made but that both ways they may come into play again and try their fortunes once more in such regions of the world as providence judges fit for them. For all things were made that they might have their being, and such of them as are capable of life and sense and yet never exercise it had as good not be at all, for they would be useless both to themselves and others, but certainly, there never were nor ever will be such things in the world, which was created and is governed by the eternal mind which does nothing foolishly and in vain. And though that raging fire which will in the consummation of all things seize upon the earth will render it and the adjoining atmosphere unhabitable for the present, yet that this ruinous defacement of things will extend through the whole compass of nature is neither the belief of Christians nor the assertion of such philosophers as were through their skill in the constitution of the world fit to judge of such theories. And therefore, if any man can conceive any of these souls which shall be punished in that sulphurous lake fit to emerge out of it, he need not be at a loss for habitations for them elsewhere. But if the other way be more probable, that there is no getting out but by death, which is rather a dying in it, yet, since they, therefore, only die because the matter all about them is then such as they cannot livingly unite with it, though their radical principles [81] of vitality are still safe and unperishable, and since that matter which for the present is so deadly is as capable as ever of such modifications as are vital and healthful and will even, by the course of nature, after long periods of time settle again into such a wholesome temper, what should hinder but that these punished souls, whom long-vexing pain drove from all commerce with matter and cast them into a senseless sleep, will after their long inactivity awake again into life and action when all things are become to fresh and fit to receive them? For if providence hath been so favourable as to establish so gracious an order in the nature and course of things as will lead those miserable spirits to a release at last, she certainly will not be unwilling that they should live again when all things conspire to give them life and they continue capable of receiving it.

D More, *Divine Dialogues*, Book 2, Chapter 21 (Second edition, 153–158)

Philoth. But now in the second place, *Hylobares*, supposing mankind of a vincible Freeness or Liberty of Will; what, would you have God administer some such powerfull *Philtrum* to all of them, that he might even force their Affections towards those more precious emanations of himself which are more properly called Divine?

Hyl. Yes, *Philotheus*, I would.

Philoth. But I much question how this will always consist with the Divine Justice. For I think it as incongruous that the *Divine Goodness* should [154] always act according to the *Simplicity* of its own nature; as it is unnatural for the Beams of the Sun to be reverberated to our eyes from several Bodies variously surfaced in the same form of Light, and not to put on the face of divers Colours, such as yellow, green, red, purple, and the like. For as the various Superficies of Bodies naturally causes such a diversification of pure Light, and changes it into the form of this or that Colour; so the variety of Objects the Divine Goodness looks upon does rightfully require a certain modification and figuration of her self into sundry forms and shapes, (as I may so call them) of Vengeance, of Severity, of Justice, of Mercy, and the like. This therefore is the thing I contend for, That free Agents, such as Men and Angels, may so behave themselves in the sight of God, that they will become such Objects of his Goodness, that it cannot be duly and rightfully expected that it should act according to its pure and proper benign form, dealing gently and kindly with all the Tenderness that may be with the party it acts upon; but it must step forth in some of those more fierce and grim forms, (I speak after the manner of men) such as *Vengeance* and *Justice*. And I will now put a Case very accommodately to our own Faculties. Suppose some Vertuous and Beautifull Virgin, royally descended and Princely attired, who, venturing too far into the solitary Fields or Woods, should be light upon by some rude Wretch, who, first having satisfied his Lustfull desires upon her by a beastly Rape, should afterwards most barbarously and despightfully use her, haling her up and down by the Hair of the head, soiling her sacred Body by dragging her through miry Ditches and dirty Plashes of water, and tearing her tender Skin upon Briars and Brambles, whiles in the mean time some Knight-Errant or Man of Honour and Ver[155]tue (but of as much Benignity of spirit as God can communicate to humane nature without Hypostaticall Union) is passing by that way, and discerneth with his astonished eyes this abhorred Spectacle: I now appeal to your own sense and reason, *Hylobares*, whether it be enough for that *Heros* to rescue this distressed Virgin from the abominable injury of this Villain, and to secure her from any farther harm; or whether there ought not to be added also some exquisite Torture and shamefull Punishment worthy so hainous a fact, and proportionable to the just indignation any noble spirit would conceive against so villainous a Crime, though neither the wronged person nor punished party were at all bettered by it.

Hyl. For my part, *Philotheus*, I should be in so high a rage against the Villain, if I were on the spot, that I should scarce have the discretion how to deliberate to punish him so exquisitely

	as he deserved; but in my present fury should hew him a-pieces as small as Herbs to the pot. I should cut him all into mammocks, *Philotheus*.
Philoth.	Wherefore, *Hylobares*, you cannot but confess that *Goodness* it self in some circumstances may very justly and becomingly be sharpened into *Revenge:* Which must be still the less incongruous, in that the *Revenge* is in the behalf of *injured Goodness*, though she get nothing thereby but that she is revenged. To this case that Notion of *Punishment* appertains which the *Greeks* call τιμωρία,[1] as *Gellius* (*Noct. Att. I 6. c 14*) observes; which nothing concerns the Reformation or amendment of the punished, but onely the Honour of the injured or offended.
Philoth.	Right, *Euistor*. But in the mean time it is manifest from hence, as I was making inference to *Hylobares*, That the Divine Goodness may step forth into Anger and Revenge, and yet the Principle of such Actions may be the very [156] Goodness it self. Which therefore we contend is still (notwithstanding that evil which may seem to be in the World) the measure of all God's works of Providence, even when *Sin is punished with Sin*, and Men are suffered to degenerate into Baboons and Beasts.
	[. . .]
Philoth.	That is, *Hylobares*, you may give the Clown a *Philtrum* or *Love-potion*. But is not this still a great disparagement to the Bride? Wherefore for the general it is fit, that God should deal with free Creatures according to the freedom of their nature: But yet, rather then all should go to ruin, I do not see any incongruity but that God may as it were lay violent hands upon some, and pull them out of the fire, and make them potent, though not irresistible, Instruments of pulling others out also. This is that Election of God for whom it was impossible for others that have arrived to a due pitch of the Divine Life. But for those that still voluntarily persist to run on in a rebellious way against God and the Light that is set before them, and at last grow so crusted in their Wickedness, that they turn professed enemies of God and Goodness, scoff at Divine Providence, riot and Lord it in the world, with the contempt of Religion and the abuse and persecution of them that profess it; that out of the stubborn Blindness of their own hearts, being given up to Covetousness, Pride and Sensuality, vex and afflict the conscientious with abominable Tyranny and Cruelty; I think it is plain that these are a very suitable Object for *Divine Fury* and *Vengeance*, that sharp and severe Modification of the *Divine Goodness*, to act upon.
Hyl.	Truly this is very handsome, *Philotheus*, and pertinent, if not cogent.

Commentary

The first of several selections from Whichcote in our chapter on faith and reason **(23 A)** concerns the two forms of moral law: the natural law which is "wraught upon men's hearts" and the revealed law, given to Moses on Mount Sinai. These two forms of law are naturally interwoven with the Cambridge Platonist's commitment to both with the principles of reason innate to humanity and the truths of the Christian religion known only though divine revelation. The second, revealed, law, is intended to call humanity to repentance and renewal; and in this way it presupposes the first, for if there had not been a law written in the heart, the external law given from without, though it comes from God, would have been ineffective. Whichcote's thinking here and in our other extracts is in line with the theological principle that grace does not abolish nature but fulfils it; and this fulfilment of human nature through divine grace brings the doctrine of divinisation in to view as the final destiny of faithful human beings.

In our second extract, from Whichcote's sermon on *The Glorious Evidence, and Power of Divine Truth* **(23 B)** he defends the reasonableness of the account of the divine found in human scripture. For

Whichcote, reason and revelation concur in pointing us towards the radical goodness of God. His is a thoroughly axiological theology.

In our third extract **(23 C)**, Whichcote's preaching on *The Venerable Nature, and Transcendent Benefit of Christian Religion* introduces the beautiful image of the flower in the sun. By means of this Whichcote presents an illuminationist theory of the relationship between the human soul and the divine spirit. This relationship—for Whichcote the point of religion—is one in which the soul is continually redirected toward its source, and the intellect illuminated by its transcendent ground, so that through the process of conversion the finite mind comes to understand itself. Its reorientation within should finds expression in outward renewal "in courage, behaviour and words". Thus for Whichcote inner conversion brings about an enhancement of the ethical. Our next extract **(23 D)**, from Whichcote's *Think on these things*, continues with these themes.

We turn next to Whichcote's aphorisms **(23 E)**, for which he is most famous. Emerging from them we find once again an illuminationist metaphysic according to which the soul by turning away from material phenomena and turning within encounters an inner divine principle—"for God is more in the mind than in any part of the world". The scriptural justification for this inner divinity is the teaching that humanity is made in the image of God. Whichcote further stresses the inextricable connection between divine contemplation and ethical practice.

Our extract **(23 F)** from the Tuckney-Whichcote correspondence has been chosen to feature their contrasting interpretations of Proverbs 20.23 is striking. Tuckney interprets the "Candle of the Lord" to refer to scripture, divine revelation inspired by the Holy Spirit. But for Whichcote it refers to natural reason, to the innate wisdom within that is shared by heathens as well as Christians, indeed by people of all religions.

In our passage from More's *Grand Mystery of Godliness* **(23 G)**, discussed in part in the introduction to this chapter, sees the philosopher reflecting on the meaning of the religious mysteries. More is following the Alexandrian fathers in his appropriation of the Greek pagan notion of the mysteries. In this passage we find a characteristic emphasis upon the intelligibility of religious truths, and at the same time an insistence that there are quite properly elements of Christian belief that elude any narrow rational analysis.

In the following passage on the nature of prophesy **(23 H)**, John Smith explores the manner in which knowledge of divine truth can be both revealed and understood. The key claim is that, while divine truth raises the human mind to God, in revelation God also condescends to meet the measure of the human mind. We should not be surprised, therefore, given that scripture was written not only for philosophers but for fishermen—"the vulgar"—that truths of scripture should be conveyed in images and symbols, and prophecy is a prime instance of this manner of communicating divine truths to the souls of men.

In the final extract selected for this section **(23 I)**, More is expounding his conception of the boniform life, according to which renewal in the spirit is inseparable from the imitation of the divine goodness.

Chapter 24 turns to the questions of the fall of the soul and the resurrection of the body in the theology of the Cambridge Platonists. In *The Immortality of the Soul* (1659) **(24 A)**, Henry More contrasts the doctrine of pre-existence with its two philosophical competitors, which he quickly dismisses. Traductionism, the doctrine that the soul is passed on to the child through the parents' sexual intercourse, would mean that the soul is material, which More will not allow: it is spiritual and indivisible. Creationism, which, incidentally, was held by Ralph Cudworth, the doctrine that a new soul is created at the conception of each child, would mean that God participated in immoral unions, at which More is shocked. This leaves the field clear for pre-existence, which More thinks he can prove by "the light of nature" without the Christian revelation. It demonstrates God's essential goodness, since to be is better than not to be and God always acts for the best. Further, it is an essential component of the life of an immortal soul, which extends not only forwards but backwards from its terrestrial life.

The section on the pre-existence of the soul in *A Letter of Resolution concerning Origen* (1661) **(24 B)** acknowledges a great debt to More's *Immortality of the Soul*. The passage selected attempts to explain how pre-existent souls could fall from their previous celestial bliss and find themselves embodied as human beings. It is the exercise of free will, with which they are endowed by God, which enables them to turn away from him through negligence. God is entirely without fault here, and human beings must bear the culpability. Even so, God in his infinite goodness has prepared appropriate material bodies for them, in which they will be able to attempt to begin the return journey to their former glory. This passage also contains a brief reference to the Platonic emanation theory of creation, in which all that is emanates from God's supreme goodness, beginning with the most intellectual natures and ending with matter.

The acknowledged dependence of Glanvill's *Lux Orientalis* (1662) **(24 C)** on More and Rust results from the fact that they were all close friends, forming a circle which advocated pre-existence. Glanvill, in the passage selected, expands on More's justification of pre-existence because of the goodness of God. This is a constant theme with all the Cambridge Platonists, not only in its application to pre-existence. God's three primary attributes are his goodness, wisdom and power, but the latter two are always controlled by his goodness. Indeed, his essential nature constrains God always to act in accordance with eternal and immutable goodness. This does not mean that there is some higher power above or outside God but only that he cannot act in a way which contradicts that which he is. God's goodness entails love and mercy to all creation, and he desires that every human being should be saved. It was this stress on God's preeminent goodness, rather than his will, that evoked the harsh critiques of Samuel Parker and Edward Warren. Hallywell's *Some Reflections on a late Discourse of Mr. Parkers* **(24 D)**, states this point very clearly, only briefly referring it to pre-existence.

Rust's *The Holy Scripture tells of the Resurrection of the Dead* (1658) **(24 E)** presents an Origenian version of the journey of the soul from its terrestrial vehicle to its aerial vehicle and finally to its celestial vehicle and reunion with God. He also draws heavily on the Oxford Platonist Thomas Jackson's (1579–1640) writing on the clause in the Apostles' Creed on "the resurrection of the body". In the passage selected here, Rust discusses the impossibility of the resurrection body being composed of flesh and blood. Thus, he refutes those who argue for the resurrection of the same numerical body of the person who died, but he will go on to conclude that the resurrection body will have the same shape as our present bodies, that it will be connected to the same soul and that the soul will carry with it some kind of seed from which the resurrection body will sprout and grow. At the end of his discourse, he hints at the coming publication of More's *Immortality of the Soul* and *Grand Mystery of Godliness*, texts with which he was already familiar and on which he had drawn heavily in composing his discourse.

The selected passage from Henry More's *Apology* (1664) **(24 F)** immediately follows his own quotation of 1 Corinthians 15:50, with which the Rust passage above ended: "Flesh and blood cannot inherit the kingdom of God". More goes on to describe the resurrection body of Christ as "*Organized Light*". Our own risen bodies will be "*Angelical, Spiritual* and *Celestial*", not material. To be angelical is not just to be immortal but to have a body like that of an angel. In the pages following our selection, he will go on to explain that that means a body of fire, or more properly, of light. This body will not be possessed of a spirit but will be spiritual itself, and it will be morally celestial. It will, in every respect, be like the body of the Risen Christ, yet we will know ourselves and others will know us to be the same persons that we were on earth. More's opponents saw this as clearly heretical, although they were mistaken in claiming that the entire doctrinal history of the resurrection body had favoured the resurrection of the same numerical body with which the human soul had been clothed on earth. They were unable to say at what age or state of health a person would rise, but More, like Rust, found these to be pointless questions.

In *A Private Letter of Satisfaction to a Friend* (1667) **(24 G)**, Henry Hallywell's main concern is a "morally dynamic" afterlife, in which the soul can progress from an aerial to an ethereal body, journeying towards its original celestial state. Hallywell refutes psychopannychism, the doctrine of the sleep of souls between the death of the terrestrial body and the final judgement, which Origen had also dismissed. He had been much troubled by local General Baptist preacher, Matthew Caffyn, who had taught this doctrine. Hallywell argued for a more vigorous life of the soul when it was freed from the prison of the earthly body as it journeyed towards its Platonic *"resplendent vehicle"*, which was the same thing as the Pauline *"spiritual body"*.

Our next chapter considers Cambridge Platonist responses to the perennial issue of theodicy. From his earliest poetical works **(25 A)**, More subscribed to a thoroughly Origenist soul-making theodicy, viewing the flourishing of autonomous human agency as the very *raison d'être* of a world suffused by God's own creative and salvific omnipresence. In accordance with the principles of his Origenist metaphysics of freedom, the ways of God's providential designs are inevitably such as both respect and reform free human agency. It is with a view to providing free agents with opportunities to reacquire the virtues of their original "life" or "centre", i.e. the fullness of their boniform vision, that God places them in bodies endowed with violent passions. It is up to them to exercise the power of their free will to master their passions in autonomous moral agency. God's decision "to enrich our choice/ By framing of the outward Universe" is expressed in the latter's overall moral structure, its heights and depths corresponding, quite literally, to the ascents and descents of its inhabitants who, as agents endowed with libertarian freedom, move up and down the chain of being in accordance solely with the moral and intellectual effort undergone in the providential pedagogy governing each and every stratum of reality. Whereas God punishes souls at the terrestrial bottom of the multi-level cosmos, inflicting upon them physical hardship, he can be seen to reward those at its aerial and ethereal top. As the creature engages in a life-long enterprise of purification, it deepens its relationship to the creator who benignly and caringly watches over it. In heartfelt verse, the metaphysical poet More likens man's sojourn in the foreign country of the terrestrial world in which his soul must undergo a process of soul-making to a child being temporarily pushed away by its mother so as to develop an even closer bond with her than before. While More's students and admirers, notably George Rust, Anne Conway and Joseph Glanvill, are indebted to his Origenist concept of soul-making, they greatly modify its overall theodicy strategy. In his *Letter of Resolution* **(25 B)**, Rust provides a remarkably pessimistic view of man's freedom. Not only is it fatefully clouded by his earthly body with which he is clothed in his present existence, but it is also frequently led astray by the social circumstances into which his soul, ostensibly without any prior fault on its part, is born. Rust shares with Origen and the ancient Greek fathers the concern with education, which the Cambridge Origenist believes the *sine qua non* for man to realize the moral potential inherent in his soul. He goes so far as to propose a general social determinism of sin, arguing that a soul, sent into an environment indifferent or even hostile to morality, is well-nigh bound to succumb to the prevalent immoral customs "when or where either these are wanting or of little credit and esteem, or the contrary more in use and practice, there seems little less than a *necessity* of our running into all wickedness and vice" (*Letter of Resolution*, 27). At the same time, the contrast between the dire *a posteriori* of the terrestrial world and the resplendent *a priori* of moral obligation allows the soul to prosper in a divinely instituted soul-making process in which God enables it to reacquire the practical and theoretical virtues lost in the fall. Significantly, the very depth of man's fall and depravity, invoked in graphic detail in Rust's retelling of the Origenian narrative of the soul's fall and restitution in the *Contra Celsum*, establishes both his sublime vocation and his origin in God to whose fullness he cannot but aspire in action and contemplation alike. Moreover, what with the chasm between the soul's imperfect *de facto* state and its inborn potential for infinite moral and intellectual perfection, there can be doubt that God, given the infinity of his goodness, intellect and power, cannot but come to its aid and perfect its painful imperfections in future lives. The most exhaustive Cambridge Platonist soul-making theodicy is provided in the second book of More's most popular work. Throughout his *Divine Dialogues*, which is at once the most Platonist and most Origenist of his works, More has his mouthpiece Bathynous impress upon his interlocutors the significance of free agency to the designs of benign divine providence whose existence seems doubtful only *prima facie* on the two chief grounds of "moral evils" and, above all, "*Natural Evils*" (*Divine Dialogues*, II,5 [second edition, 96]). Contrary to the former, which manifestly spring from culpable human agency, the latter pose a particularly formidable problem by the group of speakers. For one thing, they do not originate in God's own, but in nature's autonomous agency. For another, they provide an incentive for humankind's ingenuity and freedom in conquering them. If God instead were to intervene whenever man faces an adversity apparently beyond his skills, his moral agency, which is the chief end of all reality, would be undermined by an intolerable divine "After-device". The aporia would be exacerbated by a divine intervention whenever a trespassing is about to be committed, effectively annulling human freedom and agency altogether. Philotheus' suggestion that "a mighty, if not an almighty Arm out of the Clouds should pull Men by the Ears as they offered to offend", is rejected even by the materialist Hylobares as exerting "too great a force upon free agents". "Liberty of Will" is viewed as "an essential Property of the Soul of Man" so that its interventionist removal at the hands of God would indeed rob him of his very being, inevitably transforming him into an entirely different kind of being in the process: "Wherefore if you take away this vertible Principle in Man, you would make him therewithal of another Species, either a perfect Beast or a pure Intellect" (*ibid.*, II 20 [151]). Any theological interventionism, in other words, comes at the inevitable price of a contradiction in terms by which God would for salvific reasons have to undo the very being of a part of his original creative work. Instead of imposing upon the middle creature man whose essence is such that he can move freely between animal sense and angelic intellect, God's wisdom imparts itself to him in a great variety of forms and shapes. Just as man, reacting in responsible freedom to the challenges of the soul-making process, is compelled to exercise all his virtues, so is the light of God's simple goodness, the measure of his every providential action, reflected differently in the many agents to whom he imparts it in ungrudging self-communication. In many ways, man's fall may be seen along the *felix culpa* trope in that God, exercising different virtues to redeem him, is enabled to express his simple goodness in a great variety of fashions. In yet another example of the Morean synthesis of ancient theology and modern cosmology, divine goodness is viewed as the unchanging amount of energy communicated from one agent to another without any loss to its substance. It is the metaphorical fire of the boniform vision by which all of the souls are inevitably "inactuated" in the redemptive soul-making process, also "inactuating" others. In a particularly memorable metaphor of biblical origin, More stresses the key insight that "nothing is lost" by likening divine agency to the planting of a seed. To its growth corresponds the moral development of human beings who either reject or embrace of their own accord the gift of God's "self-communication": "Nothing therefore of the Divine Goodness seems to be lost, when as the very Corruption of it, as in a grain of Corn cast into the ground, makes for its encrease; and what of it is rejected by some, is by the Wisdom of God so unavoidably conveyed upon others." God's self-communication or the "disburthening of his overflowing Goodness" in the interactions between him and man occurs in historical stages. God's overflowing divine goodness in creation and salvation is such that the redemption of the whole in the renewed participation in it is wrought by the parts themselves imparting to others the "motion" or "light" received from God as the first mover and sun of their freedom. Despite apparent evidence to the contrary, it is always with a view to the moral good and welfare of the whole, i.e. humanity, that God gradually furnishes the parts, i.e. individual human beings, with his gifts, both moral and intellectual.

Chapter 26 begins with an extract from an early sermon **(25 A)** in which Cudworth treats the contentious issue of the nature of the sacrifice in Christian eucharistic theology. He comes to the conclusion that the eucharist should be understood as a feast *on* a sacrifice, that is to say, as communion or participation in the divine, rather than a sacrifice itself, a repetition of Christ's sacrifice. This high point of Christian ritual is not an offering to God on an altar, but rather the consumption of that which comes from God's altar.

For Smith **(25 B)**, as for Cudworth, it is participation in God that is key to soteriology. The Christian should try to preserve what he calls the "heavenly fire" of divine love and goodness, and here he explicitly uses the imagery of the temple of our souls and refers to the Christian life as a sacrifice of ourselves, albeit a sacrifice which is in fact a renewal, sanctification and fulfilment of the yearning of the heart.[2] This is, as he says "the return to the original of our beings."

These further aphorisms from Whichcote **(25 C)** reflect his theology of sanctification. His soteriology is mystical rather than forensic: indeed, sanctification is swallowed up in deification, the ultimate goal of the religious life being unification with the divine. And since truth is "connatural" to a man's soul, the renewal that emerges from the indwelling spirit of Christ is not the repudiation of human nature but its fulfilment. The perfection of worship is the imitation of God.

Our final chapter of this section considers eschatological matters. More built upon his early cosmology of periodic cycles of world conflagrations and renewals in his 1659 principal philosophical work *The Immortality of the Soul* **(26 A–)** and his 1660 principal theological work *The Grand Mystery of Godliness* In the longer former exposition,[3] More discussed at length five possible scenarios of the world conflagration:

1. an annihilation of the soul alongside its body in the cataclysmic fire of the Apocalypse
2. the soul's deliberate destruction at the hands of God himself
3. its permanent disembodiment in a state of aloofness which inevitably causes any vital congruity on its part to wither and decay
4. the soul's punishment in nightmares experienced in its disembodied state
5. a renewal in which the souls eventually come to re-inhabit suitable bodies once the spirit of nature has recreated the world devastated by the original conflagration.

While the last of the five models outlined comes close to that embraced in his early metaphysical poetry, More now seems unwilling to countenance any of them. All of them are rejected as incompatible with his rational psychology which admits neither of the soul's annihilation by fire or by God nor any tormenting dreamlike states in a state of disembodiment in which it lacks the imagination required. Still, despite the apparent aporia, More nevertheless holds to key tenets of his earlier Origenist eschatology. Above all, his emphasis throughout lies upon living natural and free human agency alone which forbid God to take any interventionist action to bring about a future state of the soul or the world at large. Instead, the fate of the world at large is determined solely by the moral choices of its inhabitants and the natural consequences which follow according to the "Divine *Nemesis*" incorporated into the very framework of the things themselves: "Besides that that Divine Nemesis that lies within the compass of Philosophy never supposes any such forcible eruptions of the Deity into extraordinary effects, but that all things are brought about by a wise and infallible or inevitable train of secondary Causes, whether natural or free Agents." The graphic exposition of Judgement Day in the two principal philosophical and theological works of the late 1650s and early 1660s could not fail to constitute a major challenge to the two twin principles of More's Origenist rationalism, i.e. divine goodness and human freedom. Rust responded to that challenge and provided his own account of the *"day of fiery vengeance"* (*Letter*, 74). No finite creature, Rust argues, can ever commit an infinite crime, which alone could warrant the infinite punishment of traditional Christian theology. In the *Letter*'s Origenian metaphysics of salvation, there are two eschatological options connected to divine goodness and justice. It wholly depends upon man's freedom whether God's goodness or justice will prevail. According to the optimistic first reading of the Origenian restitution of all things, the sinner, punished and cleansed by God's "consuming fire" ('God is Love', 2), eventually repents of his crimes. Divine goodness cannot but step in and come to the contrite sinner's aid. However, according to the pessimistic second reading, in which Rust endorses the fifth of More's five possible Christian accounts of the Stoic conflagration in his *Immortality of the Soul* two years earlier, the sinner, despite God's fiery pedagogy, remains obdurate till the end. To substantiate the position which More himself turns down as a product of the Stoics' misguided materialist metaphysics, Rust makes use of his teacher's concept of "vital congruity" again, arguing that the pain suffered in the apocalyptic fire is such that it eventually severs the bond linking the sinner's soul to its body. By dying a violent death at the hands of the vengeful Deity, however, the soul has paid for the crimes of its prior life in the earthly element, however heinous. The soul subsequently leaves its body behind, losing all feeling whatsoever in the process. However, divine justice served, its physical immortality, which it shares with its divine archetype, prevents the soul from being completely annihilated. Once the spirit of nature, another of the key entities of More and Rust's spiritual cosmology, has restored the earth after its conflagration and in due time refurnished it with its original corporeal entities, the soul, awakening from its deep slumber, will once again come to actuate an earthly body. Either way, Rust argues at the end of his thorough analysis of the eschatological interaction between divine goodness and justice and human freedom, Origen is proven right. The souls will indeed "try their fortunes again in such regions of the world as their Nature fits them for", which, he adds in the final sixth question, will happen "in eternal vicissitudes" (*Letter*, 81). While God's goodness and justice are conspicuously absent from the rational eschatology of *The Immortality of the Soul* and *The Grand Mystery of Godliness*, More went on to tie the question of eternal hell punishment to that of God's two foremost attributes in the deeply Origenist *Divine Dialogues* of 1668. Not only is the *"final vengeance"* inflicted by God upon the sinners shown to be compatible with, but indeed required by his goodness and justice. More's argument is put forward in a thought experiment couched in an allegorical narrative. Like a knight errant slaying in commendable wrath "some rude Wretch" who ravaged "some Vertuous and Beautiful Virgin", a good God is entitled to inflict capital punishment upon an unreformed sinner, "though neither the wronged Person nor punished Party were at all bettered by it". More's line of argumentation hinges upon the virtuous agent's boniform vision or practical "sense and reason" of univocal goodness shared by God and man alike. If an agent "of Honour and Vertue (but of as much Benignity of Spirit as God can communicate to humane nature without Hypostatical Union)" may kill a vile offender, God's "final vengeance" or vindictive justice envisioned in such gruesome detail in the earlier *Grand Mystery of Godliness* is compatible with his archetypal goodness. The example proves that eternal punishment may well be seen as a "sharp and severe Modification of the *Divine Goodness*", acting upon free agents through the mediation of the spirit of nature and the laws by which God implements his punitive measure in the world conflagration.

Notes

1 Punishment.
2 On these themes in relation to sacrifice, see Douglas Hedley, *Sacrifice Imagined* (New York: Continuum, 2011).
3 *Immortality of the Soul* III 18,7–10 (p. 298–300 JACOB).

Part VII

Epilogue

Douglas Hedley

Chapter 29

The Reception History of the Cambridge Platonists

The eminent German philosopher Ernst Cassirer viewed the Cambridge Platonists as anti-moderns, and came to the conclusion that their legacy was limited to aesthetics, especially through the influence of Shaftesbury. This is an intriguing instance of a flawed but influential assessment. As we shall note, Cassirer is correct in what he affirms, but incorrect in what he denies. The influence upon aesthetics via Shaftesbury is indeed part of the bequeathal of the Cambridge Platonists, especially through the reception of Shaftesbury in Germany. But this is just one of many areas in which their influence has been felt. The influence can also be noted in ethics and the view of nature. We will consider the impact of the Cambridge Platonists on 'British Empiricism' and the literary legacy of the Platonists, before considering the links with German Idealism and subsequent philosophical movements.

Ethics

The illustrious Victorian Unitarian James Martineau's *Types of Ethical Theory*, contains a fine chapter on Cudworth. It begins in a most memorable fashion:

> There is a singular contrast between the calm, contemplative philosophy of Cudworth and the fierce contentions of his time. Born at a country Rectory (Aller, Somerset) in 1617, the year of Raleigh's execution, and dying in 1688, the year of James the Second's abdication, he spans, by his term of life, the whole period of the Stuart troubles and the Commonwealth: yet his writings might have been produced in a lonely and silent monastery, instead of amid the rage of factions and the reverberation of the Naseby guns.[1]

It is thoroughly misleading to overlook the profound influence of the Cambridge Platonists on the development of ethics in Britain. One obvious impact of their thought is over the key problem of moral certainty. The Scottish sentimentalists Francis Hutcheson, David Hume, and Adam Smith were familiar with the Cambridge Platonists, even if explicit references to the Platonists in their work are rather fleeting.[2] It is clear, however, that the influence of the Cambridge figures on these North Britons was marked. Ralph Cudworth is explicitly mentioned by Hume in his *Enquiry Concerning the Principles of Morals* of 1764 in relation to the "abstract theory of morals".[3] The radical Richard Price's *A Review of the Principal Questions in Morals* exhibits the influence of Cudworth's *Eternal and Immutable Morality*, posthumously published in 1731.[4]

Nor was the legacy limited to the eighteenth-century debates about moral certainty: the Cambridge Platonists also informed the discussions of reasons and sentiment in ethics. At the end of the nineteenth century, Selby-Bigge published his influential anthology *The British Moralists* (Oxford: Clarendon Press, 1897), which quite rightly included Cudworth as one of the pivotal ethicists of the early modern period. Since then, historians of philosophy have disputed whether Selby-Bigge was correct to place Cudworth amongst the moral rationalists rather than with the sentimentalists. More recently, Stephen Darwall in his work *The British Moralists and the Internal Ought 1640–1740* (Cambridge, UK: Cambridge University Press, 1995) has argued that Cudworth represents an important stage in the development of modern ethics culminating in Kant's theory of autonomy.

Nature

> Look round our world; behold the chain of love
> Combining all below and all above.
> See plastic nature working to this end,
> The single atoms each to other tend,
> Attract, attracted to, the next in place
> Form'd and impell'd its neighbour to embrace.
> See matter next, with various life endu'd,
> Press to one centre still, the gen'ral good.
> See dying vegetables life sustain,
> See life dissolving vegetate again:
> All forms that perish other forms supply,
> (By turns we catch the vital breath, and die)
> Like bubbles on the sea of matter born,
> They rise, they break, and to that sea return.
> Alexander Pope[5]

Pope's lines are a fine exhibit of the influence of the Cambridge Platonists on the eighteenth century's view of nature. The Cambridge Platonists opposed both the mechanists and certain vitalists—Cudworth clearly viewed particular philosophers and natural philosophers, such as Francis Glisson in his *Tractatus de natura substantiae energetica*, as confederates of Spinoza—and in Pope's lines we find a statement of Cudworth's preferred alternative: a Platonic atomism, with a teleological conception of the universe that is bound by the chain of love. The presence of this notion here, and Cudworth's idea of plastic nature, is not an example of an arcane interest in Platonism but of ideas firmly entrenched in eighteenth century thought.

John Ray (1627–1705), perhaps the most important biologist before Linnaeus and the first to produce a biological definition of a species, was a student of Whichcote, Cudworth and More. In 1691 Ray produced his work the *Wisdom of God Manifested in the Works of Creation*, which attempted to follow Cudworth and More in opting for middle way between a crudely anthropomorphic model of creation as a unique divine initiative, and the reductionistic mechanistic model of the Cartesians.[6] Nehemiah Grew (1641–1712), sometimes dubbed the 'father of plant anatomy', was less clearly dependent upon Cudworth but the distinguished author of the *Catalogue of the Museum of the Royal Society* and of *Cosmologia Sacra* was very much in the wake of Cambridge Platonists.[7]

Anthony Ashley Cooper, 3rd Earl of Shaftesbury (1671–1713), Lord Ashley from January of 1683, was close to Cudworth's daughter, Lady Masham, and John Locke. Shaftesbury's major work, *Characteristicks of Men, Manners, Opinions, Times* was one of the most influential English works in the eighteenth century and was frequently reprinted, but he was also the main conduit of the intellectual inheritance of the Cambridge Platonists.[8] In 1698 he published the first edition of the *Sermons of*

Dr. Whichcote, to which he himself wrote the preface. In *The Moralists: A Philosophical Rhapsody*, published in 1709, he writes of Cudworth as "that Pious and Learned man".[9] *The Moralists* is a dialogue, narrated from the perspective of Philocles, a sceptic who engages with the rhapsodic Theocles about the search of happiness and the good.[10] Theocles repeatedly uses the word 'System'—a distinctively Cudworthian term—and stresses the world ought to be viewed as such, i.e., that "All things in this World are united".[11] Careful observation of nature reveals that all is "fitted and join'd' together", each thing contributing to the "Order, Union, and Coherence of the Whole".[12] Shaftesbury's Platonic-Stoic insistence upon the order and beauty of the cosmos is a striking instance of his proximity to Cudworth, and indeed his debt.[13]

On the continent, Cudworth thought was influentially received by Amsterdam theologian, philosopher and editor Jean Le Clerk (1657–1736). A cosmopolitan figure of Huguenot extraction, Le Clerk corresponded with Cudworth in his lifetime, as well as Leibniz, Shaftesbury, and Locke. Le Clerk's great legacy were his *Bibliothèque universelle et historique*, which he began with J. C. de la Croze; *Bibliothèque choisie*, and *Bibliothèque ancienne et moderne*. Volumes 6 and 7 of *Bibliothèque choisie* contain a positive account of Cudworth's thought, which includes the Cambridge Platonist's categorisation of Spinoza's philosophy, especially in his *Tractatus Theologico-Politicus*, as revival of 'Hylozoic' or 'Stratonical' atheism (for Cudworth, 'Stratonism' is the view that matter is the sole substance of an animated cosmos lacking any transcendent rational principle).

In his *Bibliothèque Choisie* Le Clerk also presented parts of Cudworth's theory of plastic nature. Cudworth, like More, admired the theism of Descartes and his emphasis upon the centrality and irreducibility of mind or spirit; yet Cudworth worried about the radical dualism of mind and matter in Descartes. Cudworth, like More (and other contemporaries, such as Baxter and Casaubon), began to turn metaphysically against Cartesianism and the anti-teleology of the Galilean programme more generally as de facto atheism that colluded with Epicurean materialism. 'Plastic nature' was the term that Cudworth used for the intermediary between the divine mind and the world of nature, an unconscious spirit that is responsible for and explains order and purpose in the physical world—in essence a version of the Platonic *anima mundi*. Le Clerk's propagation of the idea generated a celebrated dispute between Le Clerk and Pierre Bayle, who replied to Le Clerk with his "Continuation des Pensées diverses sur les Comètes", averring that this vision of an animated nature unwittingly supported the atheist position. The debate continued with Le Clerk replying again in the *Bibliothèque Choisie*, and Bayle in the "Ouvrages des Sçavants".[14]

The British Empiricists: From Locke to Hume and Reid

Unlike a textbook contrast between Cartesian rationalism and British empiricism, Cudworth viewed the key debate in his age in rather different terms:

> Wherefore the same Plato tells us, that there had been always, as well as then there was, a perpetual War and Controversie in the World, and as he calls it, a kind of Gigantomachy betwixt these two Parties or Sects of men; The one that held there was no other Substance in the World besides Body; The Other that asserted Incorporeal Substance.[15]

The tradition of identifying *the* British empiricists as Locke, Berkeley and Hume tends to occlude or diminish the strong links between all three figures and the Cambridge Platonists. Cudworth's passage about Plato might well be employed to describe seventeenth and early eighteenth-century British philosophy. Hobbes constitutes the materialist rage for reduction to "Body", whereas Cudworth and More stand for the critique of the naturalist and atheist vision and in favour of "Incorporeal

Substance". From this perspective, Locke and Berkeley are successors of the Cambridge Platonists while Hume is the follower of Hobbes.

The seventeenth century was particularly fertile for the philosophy of religion. Descartes constructed his so-called trademark argument in the third meditation and fashions a version of the infamous ontological argument in the fifth. But Henry More's *Enchiridion Metaphysicum* argued that Descartes blocks the traditional arguments for God, emphasising the rejection of final causes, and pointing out the French thinker's excessive reliance on the ontological argument. Cudworth's *True Intellectual System* provided a monumental taxonomy and critique of atheism and fatalism. The interest of More and Cudworth in natural philosophy was closely linked to a concern with the question of freedom and responsibility. The radical empiricism and materialism of Hobbes was combined with a doctrine of the state that the Platonists found deeply uncongenial: metaphysical and ethical questions assumed enormous political importance during the turbulent civil war period.

Again, Cudworth's contribution is of great import in this respect. Sarah Hutton makes a convincing case for the influence of Cudworth upon Hume in the wording of the *Dialogues Concerning Natural Religion* and certainly the *Natural History of Religion*.[16] In Hume's classic dialogues there are various reverberations of Cudworth, not least in language, when for example Hume refers to 'archetypes' and 'ectypes'. Most of chapter IV of *The True Intellectual System* is devoted to the priority of monotheism. Drawing upon Vossius' *Origins of Gentile Theology* and his own extensive knowledge of antique sources, Cudworth endeavours to show that monotheism was generally accepted among the "pagan theologers", insisting that "It was Universally agreed upon amongst them, that the World and the Inferior Gods, however supposed by some to have existed from Eternity, yet were nevertheless all derived from one Sole-Self-existent Deity as their Cause".[17] This thesis, that the pagans agreed upon one supreme Deity is precisely the target of Hume's *Natural History of Religion* and his claim that there was an oscillation between pagan monotheism and polytheism.[18]

Cudworth also provided the structure for an argument that would be rehearsed well into the eighteenth century, when it was decisively attacked by David Hume. The argument, which can be found in part IV, chapter 15 of the present volume, aims to show that the presence of mind in the cosmos has to be explained by a kindred but higher principle, an eternal mind senior to the world. Hume ridiculed the argument, wondering, "What peculiar privilege has this little agitation of the brain which we call thought that we must thus make it the model of the whole universe."[19]

Cudworth's argument is based upon what he, after Lucretius,[20] took to be the basic principle of atheism: *ex nihilo nihil fit*, out of nothing, nothing comes. For Cudworth, this principle is in fact the

> Achilles of the Atheists; their Invincible Argument, against a Divine Creation and Omnipotence; because Nothing could come from Nothing. It being concluded from hence, that whatsoever Substantially or Really Is, was from all Eternity Of It Self, Unmade or Uncreated by any Deity.[21]

If nothing comes of nothing then there must be something eternal, something that is ultimately the cause of all other things. Yet for Cudworth here lies atheism's fatal flaw. The first cause cannot be dead and mindless eternal matter, because if effects require causes then causes must account for their effects in every aspect. The effects of the first cause include living intelligent creatures, rational minds, and dead and mindless matter does not possess the explanatory resources to account for these as cause. If nothing comes from nothing and we must explain intelligence, what we require is something which itself possesses intelligence essentially and at a higher level such that it can be the cause of it in other things.

Thus, Cudworth believes that from this postulate of atheism he can furnish an argument for an eternal intelligence—for God. Hume took a dim view of this, referring to the *ex nihilo nihil fit* principle as

> THAT impious maxim of the ancient philosophy, Ex nihilo, nihil fit, by which the creation of matter was excluded, ceases to be a maxim, according to this philosophy. Not only the will of the supreme Being may create matter; but, for aught we know a priori, the will of any other being might create it, or any other cause, that the most whimsical imagination can assign.[22]

Hume pours scorn on the principle as he casts doubt on the laws of causality in general, and, by questioning whether the theist who employs Cudworth's argument has fairly accounted for the cause of matter by appealing to an immaterial deity, he places himself with the first side in the "perpetual War and Controversie" recounted by Cudworth in the quotation at the beginning of this section, the conflict between the partisans of corporeal and of incorporeal substance—the conflict between empiricists and rationalists that was so important in early modern philosophy.

The Literary Legacy of the Platonists

> I declare that to recommend goodness and innocence hath been my sincere endeavour in this history. This honest purpose you have been pleased to think I have attained; and to say the truth, it is likeliest to be attained in books of this kind; for an example is a kind of picture, in which virtue becomes as it were an object of sight, and strikes us with an idea of loveliness, which Plato asserts there is in her naked charms ... Besides displaying that beauty of virtue which may attract the admiration of mankind, I have attempted to engage a stronger motive to human action in her favour, by convincing men, that their true interests directs them to a pursuit of her.
>
> Henry Fielding[23]

Fielding's reference to Plato might seem puzzling, but the influence of the Cambridge Platonists upon eighteenth century literature up to Wordsworth and Coleridge is complex but pervasive. More's *Divine Dialogues* of 1674 could readily be seen as the blueprint for eighteenth century dialogues on religion in authors such as Shaftesbury or Berkeley. Themes such as rational theology and scepticism, or innatism versus empiricism run through the great works of the eighteenth century in authors such as Henry Fielding or Laurence Sterne. And indeed, there is much evidence for the presence of the Cambridge Platonists in the great literary figures of the Augustan Age in Britain.[24] The literary scholar Battestin notably cites Cudworth on the divine exemplar of art:

> The Evolution of the World, as *Plotinus* calls it,[25] is ἀλητέστερον ποίημα, a *Truer Poem*, and we men Histrionical Acters upon the Stage, who notwithstanding insert something of our *Own* into the *Poem* too; but God *Almighty*, is that *Skilful Dramatist*, who always connecteth that of ours which went before, with what of his follows after, into good *Coherent Sense*; and will at last make it appear, that a *Thred* of exact *Justice* did run through all, and that *Rewards* and *Punishments* are measured out in *Geometrical Proportion*.[26]

Thomas Burnet (1635?–1715) was a pupil of Cudworth, following him from Clare Hall to Christ's College in 1654, and a friend of Henry More. Burnet was the author of *The Sacred Theory of the Earth* of 1684 (a corrected version appeared in subsequent years, and a Latin version, *Telluris Theoria Sacra* was also published in 1684). The work was read and admired by literary notables such as Addison, Steele, Warton, Young and read by Blake.[27] Burnet was regarded as a great stylist and is quoted by Coleridge in the 1817 version of *The Rime of the Ancient Mariner*. Thomas Burnet's anonymous 1697 critique of Locke is less renowned than his speculative cosmogony, yet it also addresses one of the great themes of eighteenth century literature—an innate moral sensibility. In his first remarks of that work, Burnet attacks Locke's empiricism:

> Your general principle of picking up all our knowledge from our five senses I confess does not sit easily in my thoughts . . .
>
> As to morality, we think the great foundation of it is the distinction of good and evil, virtue and vice- *turpis et honesti*, as they are usually called ; and I do not find that my eyes, ears, nostrils or any other outward sense make any distinction of these things, as they do of sounds, colours, scents or other outward objects; nor from any ideas taken in from them, or from their reports, am I conscious that I do conclude, or can conclude, that there is such a distinction in the nature of things; or that it consists only in pleasure or pain, conveniency or inconveniency. This I am sure of: that the distinction, suppose of gratitude and ingratitutude, fidelity and infidelity, justice and injustice and such other, is as sudden without ratiocination, and a s sensible and piercing, as the difference I feel from the scent of a rose of assafoètida.'Tis not like a theorem which we come to know by the help of precedent demonstrations and postulatums, but it rises as quick as any of our passions, or as laughter at the sight of a ridiculous accident or object.[28]

That is to say that, just as the delicious scent of the rose is as immediate as the stench of the asafoetida, so too the sense of right and wrong is immediate and innate. It is not, Burnet insists, reliant upon some form of 'ratiocination' or even appeal to Divine will. Empiricism simply cannot, according to him, account for moral knowledge. In this, Burnet was followed by thinkers and writers as diverse in their views as Lord Shaftesbury and Bishop Butler.

Leibniz, the Ragley Circle, and Jacob Böhme

Leibniz, one of the most potent critics of empiricism, described his own philosophical position in relation to both Lady Anne Conway and Henry More in the following terms:

> My feelings in philosophy are somewhat close to those of the Countess Conway and hold a mean between Plato and Democritus. For I think that every happens mechanically, as is held by Democritus and Descartes, against the view of Mr More and others like him. And nevertheless, everything also happens vitally and in accordance with final causes, everything being of life and perception, against the view of the Democriteans.[29]

Leibniz's self-assessment in relation to Henry More and Lady Anne Conway certainly deserves some attention. It should be viewed in relation to the astonishing and brilliant milieu at Ragley,[30] a house which contained one of the largest private early modern libraries in England. Francis Mercury van Helmont (1614–1699), the son of the Flemish natural philosopher Jan Baptist van Helmont (1580–1644), also stayed at Ragley. Van Helmont supported Lady Conway's study of the Jewish Cabbala, and introduced Conway to Quakers such as George Fox, Robert Barclay, George Keith, and William Penn, whose religion she would finally adopt. Van Helmont also introduced Christian Knorr von Rosenroth, the foremost Christian expert on the Cabbala in the late seventeenth century.[31]

The collaboration of van Helmont and von Rosenroth culminated in the publication of the hugely influential Latin *Kabbalah Denudata* in 1677.[32] It was also through van Helmont that Leibniz became familiar with Conway's thought.[33] Anne Conway's monistic vitalism, expressed in her *The Principles of the Most Ancient and Modern Philosophy*, is the product of her own considerable intellect and learning and an enduring testimony to the remarkable milieu at Ragley.

Leibniz's theodicy would go on to inspire Pierre Bayle, and Leibniz was the principal source lying behind Lessing's philosophical position. Leibniz corresponded with Lady Damaris Masham, Cudworth's daughter and close friend of John Locke. As has been argued by Catherine Wilson, the use of the term 'monad' is probably derived from More or Cudworth. Wilson writes:

> It is impossible to talk about Leibniz's ideas concerning vital principles in nature without discussing his reception of the work of Ralph Cudworth, defender of the theory of "plastic natures". . . . For Cudworth was, quite simply, the most able critic of Cartesianism in the realm of a general theory nature. Despite the proliferation there of controversies about Cartesian physics and epistemology, no one in France could claim to have mounted an attack comparable in breadth and depth to his own. Moreover, Cudworth was the single most important medium for the transmission of Plotinian and Platonic intellectualism in the period, a fact of particular significance to Leibniz, who was himself one of the rare appreciators of Plato in the late seventeenth century.[34]

Let us turn to Böhme. Hegel named Jacob Böhme as the *philosophus teutonicus*, yet his reception within Germany was erratic. Böhme, however, enjoyed considerable popularity in England and the Netherlands, particularly among radical Protestant groups such as the Quakers and the Philadelphians.[35] Rufus Jones, in his magisterial work, *Spiritual Reformers in the 16th and 17th Centuries* (Eugene, OR: Wipf and Stock, 2005) concentrates upon Sterry, Whichote and John Smith. Yet he fails to discuss Henry More, and the Ragley circle of Anne Conway which was pivotal for the for the Quakers, who had and their strong links with continental pietism and Behmenism that were often mediated through van Helmont.

In England, the Böhme influence was sustained throughout the eighteenth century by William Law, a writer of uncommon genius bound to the Cambridge Platonists through his alma mater Emmanuel College, as well as in many of his theological and philosophical tenets. Law was greatly admired by both S.T. Coleridge and William Blake. One might even say that Böhme, whose influence upon German Romanticism was so profound, came back to Germany via England and the Netherlands. Here the part played by More, and his reception on the continent, is key. To the 'Republic of Letters' in the seventeenth century—the age of 'nice and hot disputes'—national boundaries were porous. Rosalie Colie's 1957 book, *Light and Enlightenment: A Study of the Cambridge Platonists and the Dutch Arminians* (Cambridge, UK: Cambridge University Press, 1957) remains an important work. Collie explores the links between the pre-eminent Protestant powers of the age, and concentrates upon the Cambridge Platonists and the Dutch Arminians, and their shared disputes with Orthodox Calvinism, whether of the Dutch Reformed version or the Westminster Confession. The links between the Dutch Remonstrants and the Cambridge Platonists were mediated through common friends, interests and controversies. The Dutch Arminian Philippus van Limborch, while best known for his close connection with Locke, also corresponded with both More and Cudworth. The Low Countries were at the heart of controversies emanating from Descartes and Spinoza, and More in particular played a prominent role in the Dutch context among warring Arminians as a notable anti-Spinozist. In this way, More became highly significant to the wider reception of Spinoza's philosophy on the European continent.[36] More also offered a critique of Böhme, and, crucially, identified Spinoza as a Behmenist and a Kabbalist—an idea which enjoyed a long afterlife in the eighteenth century. Leibniz, Herder and Goethe were all deeply influenced by mystical pietism, and full the role of the Cambridge Platonists and Anne Conway in this trajectory has yet to be explored.[37]

German Idealism and Romanticism

> The feeling of gratitude, which I cherish toward these men, has caused me to digress further than I had foreseen or proposed; but to have passed them over in an historical sketch of my literary life and opinions, would have seemed to me like the denial of a debt, the concealment of a boon. For the writings of these mystics acted in no slight degree to prevent my mind from being imprisoned within the outline of any single dogmatic system. They contributed to keep alive the *heart* in the *head*; gave me an indistinct, yet stirring and working presentment, that all the products of the mere *reflective faculty* partook of DEATH, and were as the rattling twigs and sprays in winter, into which a sap was yet to be propelled from some root to which I had not penetrated, if they were to afford my soul either food or shelter. If they were too often a moving cloud of smoke to me by day, yet they were always a pillar of fire throughout the night, during my wanderings through the wilderness of doubt, and enabled me to skirt, without crossing, the sandy deserts of utter unbelief. That the system is capable of being converted into an irreligious PANTHEISM, I well know. The ETHICS of SPINOZA, may, or may not, be an instance. But at no time could I believe, that *in itself* and *essentially* it is incompatible with religion, natural or revealed: and now I am most thoroughly persuaded of the contrary.
>
> Samuel Taylor Coleridge[38]

Samuel Taylor Coleridge's memorable encomium on the mystics who managed to "keep alive the heart in the head" in his *Biographia Literaria* is notable for its beauty, with the reference to Exodus 13 and the pillar of cloud that went ahead of the Israelites by day to guide their way and the pillar of fire that by night gave them illumination, and the image of the "sandy deserts of utter unbelief": culminating by broaching the name of Spinoza and the problem of pantheism.

The *Pantheismusstreit*, or Pantheism Controversy, began in 1785, when F.H. Jacobi reported a meeting with Lessing five years prior at which Lessing had confessed his Spinozism. Jacobi writes:

> Lessing once said, with half a smile, that perhaps he was himself the supreme Being, and he was now in the state of extreme contraction. – I beseeched him for my existence. – He replied that that was not at all how it intended was intended to be, and explained himself in a way that reminded me of Henry More and von Helmont Lessing became ever more explicit, to the point that, when pressed, I could again raise the suspicion of cabbalism against him. That delighted him not a little, and I took the occasion to speak in favour of the Kibbel, or the cabbala in the strict sense – that is, taking as starting point the view that it is impossible, in and for itself, to derive the infinite from a given finite, or to define the transition from the one to the other or their proportion, through any formula whatever. Hence if anyone wants to say anything on the subject, one must speak on the basis of revelation Lessing insisted on having everything "addressed to him in natural terms," and I, that there cannot be any natural philosophy of the supernatural, yet the two (the natural and the supernatural) obviously exist.[39]

It is well known that German Idealism emerged out of the *Pantheismusstreit*; less well known is the role of Henry More in uniting the Cartesian Spinoza with Jacob Böhme and indeed with the mysticism of the Jewish Cabbala through the circle discussed above. Both Lessing and Jacobi would have encountered More and van Helmont through the publication of von Rosenroth's *Kabbala Denudata*.

The Pantheism Controversy would initiate a remarkable revival of Spinozism that influenced German thought from Hegel to at least Nietzsche, if not to Heidegger and Benjamin. In fact, one could say that the soi-disant classical German philosophy of Fichte, Schelling, and Hegel is inconceivable without this Spinozan renaissance. On July 6th 1780, Jacobi reports Lessing's rejection of the orthodox concept of the Godhead: "I can no longer relish it. Ἕν καὶ πᾶν! I know no other." This Greek tag, *hen kai pan*, became the rallying call of the Pantheism Controversy. It was taken from the 1733 Latin translation of Ralph Cudworth's *The True Intellectual System of the Universe*, in which we find the precise wording used by Jacobi in the controversy: "τὸ ἕν καὶ πᾶν, unum & omnem"; in *The True Intellectual System* of 1678, one discovers *hen to pan*, "ἕν τὸ πᾶν, One-All".[40] Thus, via Johann Lorenz Mosheim's paraphrase of Cudworth, *hen kai pan* became the call to arms of the German Idealists.[41]

Mosheim (1693–1755), the so called 'Erasmus of the eighteenth century', played a salient role in the transmission of the Cambridge Platonists on the European continent, especially in Germany. Mosheim's translation of Cudworth with extensive critical notes became a textbook in German universities, especially in Tübingen and Jena, which were key in the emergence of German Idealism and Romanticism. Cudworth's *Systema Intellectuale hujus Universi* in two large volumes. In 1773 there was a second edition, and this was reviewed by Friedrich Nicolai (1733–1811) in the influential *Allgemeine deutsche Bibliothek*. It is worth remembering that the German Idealists were trained as theologians and classicists, and the Mosheim-Cudworth edition of the *True Intellectual System* assumes much greater significance once one realises the importance of the patristic-theological legacy in eighteenth century German thought. Lessing, for example, the man posthumously at the heart of the *Pantheismustreit*, as well as a poet, philosopher, and general man of letters, was a particularly learned theologian.

The New England Legacy

The links between Cambridge in England and the colonial settlement in New England were considerable. Cudworth's older brother James was a prominent figure in Massachusetts. It is unsurprising that the influence in the New World was swift and profound, though there was much controversy arising from the relation between the more liberal tenets of the Cambridge Platonists and the stringent Calvinism of the New England puritan ascendency. While tracing the influence is therefore often thorny, the legacy of the Cambridge Platonists upon thinkers from Edwards to Emerson is well attested.[42] Jonathan Edwards certainly read Henry More, whose *Enchiridion Ethicum* was a textbook at Yale (as it was also at Harvard); he also studied More's *Immortality of the Soul*.

Much later, the great sage of Concord, the eloquent and visionary Ralph Waldo Emerson (1803–1882), was perhaps the leading figure of the movement known as Transcendentalism, which had a significant Neoplatonic provenance.[43] Cudworth was perhaps the chief source for Emerson's knowledge of Neoplatonic thought, together with S.T. Coleridge and Thomas Taylor. Emerson's knowledge of Proclus came through Taylor's *Commentaries of Proclus on the Timaeus of Plato* and *Six books of Proclus*, but Emerson seems to pursue themes and ideas in the Neoplatonists that he first found adumbrated by Cudworth, and he continued to use Cudworth as a handbook even after acquiring works of Plotinus, Proclus and Iamblichus, in one place accounting his own thought as 'Nothing but old Plotinus, Iamblichus, Mores, Cudworths and Browns'.[44]

The Bengal Renaissance and the Cambridge Platonists

The great linguist and Indologist Sir William Jones saw analogies between Vedanta and Parmenides, Plato and Berkeley. Possibly through the influence of fellow Welshman Richard Price, Jones was drawing on the tradition of ancient theology, of which Cudworth was such a distinguished exponent. But whereas the Cambridge Platonists, like many before them, saw Egypt as the font of this theology, India rather than Egypt was the object of Jones's ruminations. Jones saw Vedanta as in harmony with Neoplatonism in presenting the created realm as divine energy rather than as a finished work, a theophany rather than an artefact.[45]

Calcutta was, of course, the capital of British India, and the Bengal Renaissance saw a remarkable flowering of thought there in the nineteenth and twentieth centuries. The *Tattvabodhini Patrika*—'The Truth-Enlightening Journal'—was one of the most influential organs of that renaissance. Its purpose was to expressed of the ideas of a group around Debendranath Tagore called the *Tattvaranjini Sabha* or 'The Society of Those Who Delight in Truth'. The context was one of intense Christian proselytising in colonial Calcutta, and the Society was pursuing the soi-disant father of modern India, Rammohan Roy. Theirs was a vision of a renewed Vedantic theism, the theistic reform movement in Bengal known as the *Brahmo Samaj* having been disrupted by the death of Rammohan Roy in Bristol in 1833. Faced with the prospect of answering the challenge of evangelists like Alexander Duff, whose combination of educational institutional activity and Christian zeal ignited a vigorous response from the Hindu reformers, *Tattvabodhini Patrika* published Debendranath's own interpretations of the Upanishads alongside extracts from Rammohun's translations of the Upanishads. Among the critiques of the attacks of Christian missionaries upon Hinduism as a pantheistic, monistic, and idolatrous religion, we find in the following passage from 1864:

> Our reverend friends maintain that it was Christ who first revealed correct notions of religion to mankind, and that they did not possess them before his appearance. Now this is a statement contradicted by all history.
> I would recommend Gentleman to your attentive perusal the 'Intellectual System of the Universe' by old Dr Cudworth, whose liberal Christianity the revered gentlemen in question would do well to imitate. This book contains innumerable proofs of the existence of correct notions of the godhead prevailing among the ancient Greeks and Romans.[46]

Why do we find a reference to the Cambridge Platonists, "old Dr Cudworth" and his "liberal Christianity"?[47] These figures of the Bengal elite do not want to fall into the arms of the Enlightenment agnosticism of Hume and Gibbon. Cudworth represents that Alexandrian strand of Christianity that happily drew upon pagan Hellenic thought, and what might be called a more 'fluid' or 'mystical' monotheism as opposed to the exclusive monarchical theism of high Protestant or Catholic orthodoxy. To use the language of John Kenney, 'exclusive theism' concentrates on the numerical singularity of deity, while the more 'inclusive theism' of Hellenic monotheism laid stress upon the ultimacy and unity of the supreme principle.[48] Much of Cudworth's *The True Intellectual System of the Universe*, in particular the enormous fourth book, is devoted to showing that monotheism was the foundational religion of the ancient world through the Egyptians, this primordial monotheism having only later lapsed into polytheism and pantheism.[49] It is no accident that one of Cudworth's liberal Christian successors, B.F. Westcott (1825–1901), should have been a driving force behind the foundation of St Stephen's College in Delhi. Westcott was a great admirer of Plotinus and Origen and the Cambridge Platonists as their successors in the modern world.

The Romantic and Nineteenth Century Legacy

The Cambridge Platonists had scant sympathy for the attitude which Richard Rorty would later take to be the characteristically (and fatally) Platonic—the idea of the mind as simply "a mirror of nature". It was rather the empiricists who saw the mind as a passive mirror! The idealists and Platonists insisted otherwise: they celebrated the human mind as a divine creative spark.[50]

This creative aspect of the mind was immensely significant for the English Romantics, who were deeply indebted to the Cambridge Platonists.[51] When Coleridge presents poetic and philosophical intelligence as the capacity to see the infinite in the finite, to 'counterfeit eternity', he is at the same time alluding to Ralph Cudworth[52]:

And what if all of animated nature
Be but organic Harps diversly fram'd,
That tremble into thought, as o'er them sweeps
Plastic and vast, one intellectual Breeze,
At once the Soul of each and God of all?[53]

The image of the Aeolian Harp is often presented as a pantheistic enthusiasm of the young Coleridge. The Aeolian harp was a fashionable piece of garden furniture that produced sounds through the blowing of the wind. It becomes an image of poetic inspiration when tied to the ancient idea of poetic afflatus and the Romantic notion of genius. On such a model, the poet is one breathed upon by the divine. It is quite clear that the use of Cudworthian language does not necessarily imply pantheism; the Platonism, however, is undeniable.

Coleridge's late work, *Aids to Reflection*, was inspired by the works of the Scottish Episcopalian Robert Leighton. Knox, Leighton's biographer, claimed that "the Cambridge of the Cambridge Platonists was his spiritual and intellectual home".[54] Whether or not Knox is correct in this judgement, Henry Scougal (1650–1678) was influenced by both Leighton and Henry More, and his classic text *The Life of God in the Soul of Man* was witness to the links between these Scottish mystical divines and the Cambridge Platonists. *Aids to Reflection* was itself a homage to 'Spiritual Old England' and included selections from Henry More.[55]

Brooke Foss Westcott (1825–1901), who we mentioned above, in 1885 gave a beautiful address at King's College on Benjamin Whichcote. Whilst Westcott noted the limitations of Whichcote's theology, especially the lack of an adequate ecclesiology or much sense of the sacraments, Westcott welcomed and relished the nobility of Whichcote's ideas, expressed vividly as they were in an age of "unparalleled distress and anxiety".[56] F.J.A. Hort was, like Westcott, a great admirer of the Cambridge Platonists, and saw them as belonging to a longer 'Alexandrian' Christian tradition. Hort was a fellow of Emmanuel College Cambridge from 1872 to 1892, and the visitor to the college today can find Hort's philosophical-theological affinities displayed in the windows of the college chapel. In accordance with a plan devised by Hort and executed in 1884, the originally plain windows now bear images of Benjamin Whichcote, John Smith and Peter Sterry, as well as Origen and Eriugena, the seventeenth century figures being presented as their intellectual and spiritual heirs.[57]

W.R. Inge (1860–1954) studied under Westcott, and was in many ways, along with Emile Brehier, the source of a revival of Neoplatonic studies in the twentieth century. An admirer of the Cambridge Platonists, Inge succeeded Westcott as a Lady Margaret Professor of Divinity, subsequently becoming the White's Professor of Moral Philosophy at Oxford from 1897 to his retirement in 1927. His pupils included the classicist E.R. Dodds and the poet and critic T.S. Eliot. A.E. Taylor started his career with a prize fellowship at Merton College, Oxford in 1891. He then taught at the Universities of Manchester (1896–1903), as Frothingham Professor of at McGill University, Montreal (1903–1908) and then the University of St Andrews (1908–1924). He ended his career as professor of moral philosophy at the University of Edinburgh, from which he retired in 1941. Taylor made no secret of his admiration of, and sympathy for, Cudworth and More. Finally, John Muirhead, William Temple and Stephen R.L. Clark might be mentioned as eminent philosophers in the tradition of the Cambridge Platonists.[58]

Conclusion

> La Nature est un temple où de vivants piliers
> Laissant parfois sortir de confuses paroles;
> L'homme y passé a travers des forêts de symbols
> Qui l'observent avec des regards familiers
> Baudelaire[59]

The literature, philosophy, and art of the twentieth century bears the deep imprint of Neoplatonic thought. Poets like T.S. Eliot or W.B. Yeats, or painters like Kandinsky, Mondrian or Kiefer were profoundly influenced by Neoplatonic ideas. Many of these elements were derived from the European Romantic period, yet the Romantic age itself was a period of Neoplatonic revivals. As has been conclusively established by the work of writers like Kathleen Raine, Werner Beierwaltes or Veillard-Baron, many of the great thinkers, painters and poets of the nineteenth century—e.g., Friedrich, Creuzer, Schelling, Novalis, Cousin, or Blake—were deeply shaped by Neoplatonic ideas. Far less familiar, however, is the decisive role of the Cambridge Platonists in this process. Between the Florentine Platonists and European High Romantic Platonism, the Cambridge Platonists form a decisive link. We have cited Baudelaire, one of the seminal poets of the European traditions, as an example. Baudelaire drew upon Joseph de Maistre, one the great admirers of Cudworth among continental philosophers of the nineteenth century.

One of the most striking instances of the abiding influence of the Cambridge Platonists in recent literature outside the parameters of academic philosophy but nevertheless philosophical in spirit is within the literary set known as the Inklings.[60] C.S. Lewis intended to write a doctoral thesis on Henry More, and his first book, *The Allegory of Love*, was an encomium on his great favourite Edmund Spenser, the initial Platonic inspiration for Henry More.[61] Lewis's close friend Owen Barfield was an admirer of Coleridge and the Cambridge Platonists, and Barfield's thought could be seen as an extended meditation on the idea of reason as the *Lumen intellectus* (Light of the Divine Intellect). Barfield wrote:

> There has perhaps been no better characterisation of the distinction between Platonism *tout simple* and Neoplatonism than was made by whoever defined the latter as "Platonism plus the concept of genius". At all events it seems to me to be in this sense that the stream of though to which I referred may properly be termed "Neo-platonic". Plotinus, Plutarch, Iamblichus, Synesius, Augustine, Ficino, Bruno, Boehme, Henry More, Shaftesbury, Blake, Goethe, Coleridge, Emerson and Yeats were no doubt very unlike each other in many respects; but they were all aware, in a way that Pythagoras and Plato were not yet aware, of the active role of the individual human spirit.'
> (*Poetic Diction*, 221)

Barfield was clearly thinking of ideas like the 'vital efflux' of John Smith, or the 'Divine Sagacity' of More, or Cudworth's "all created beings are themselves in some sense, but the rays of the Deity"—he was thinking, that is, of the divine creative spark that constituted such a pivotal moment in Romantic aesthetics. Barfield's claim is that the Platonic doctrine of anamnesis could serve in the modern period as an impetus to theories of subjectivity; just as the ancient notion of the tutelary spirit or guardian angel could be transformed into the modern notion of genius.

Far from being an isolated and anachronistic group in seventeenth century England, the Cambridge Platonists were a band of erudite and ingenious philosopher-Divines, grappling with the great controversies of their age, who enjoyed a network and an influence throughout the British Isles and helped to forge some of the seminal debates in early modern and Romantic continental Europe.

Amid the ruins of positivism and the foundering of the 'linguistic turn', these pressing questions remain unresolved in the twenty-first century: the relationship between consciousness and matter; mechanism and teleology; fact and value; theism, pantheism and atheism. The Cambridge Platonists coined the terminology of much modern philosophy in the English language: when these problems are being addressed today, the candle of their spirit is still flickering.

Notes

1. James Martineau, *Types of Ethical Theory* Volume II (Oxford: Clarendon Press, 1886), 427.
2. See further on this M. Gill, "From Cambridge Platonism to Scottish Sentimentalism", *Journal of Scottish Philosophy* 8, no.1 (2010): 13–31.
3. David Hume, *An Enquiry Concerning Human Understanding*, ed. L.A. Selby-Bigge, Third Edition, ed. P.H. Nidditch (Oxford: Oxford University Press, 1979), 158n.
4. Louise Hickman, *Eighteenth-Century Dissent and Cambridge Platonism: Reconceiving the Philosophy of Religion* (Abingdon: Routledge, 2017), 43ff.
5. Essay on Man III, 7–15.
6. Charles E. Raven, *Natural Religion and Christian Theology* (Cambridge, UK: Cambridge University Press, 1952), 117ff.
7. Conrad Bonifazi, *The Soul of the World: An Account of the Inwardness of Things* (Lanham, MD: University Press of America, 1978), 64–79.
8. On the one facet of the Cambridge Platonist legacy through Shaftesbury, see Seth Lobis, *The Virtue of Sympathy* (New Haven, CT: Yale University Press, 2014) 198–255.
9. *The Moralists*, 2.3.
10. On *The Moralists* see Michael Prince, *Philosophical Dialogue in the British Enlightenment: Theology, Aesthetics, and the Novel* (Cambridge, UK: Cambridge University Press, 1997), esp. 47ff.
11. *The Moralists*, 2.162.
12. See further *The Moralists*, 2.10–12.
13. On this debt see Dirk Großklaus, *Natürliche Religion und aufgeklärte Gesellschaft. Shaftesburys Verhältnis zu den Cambridge Platonists* (Heidelberg: Universitätsverlag C. Winter, 2000).
14. See Bayle, *Œuvres Diverses*, iii. 216, 285, 886, iv. 181, 853, 861, &c. For more on this element of the Cambridge Platonist legacy see Alan Charles Kors, *Naturalism and Unbelief in France, 1650–1729* (Cambridge, UK: Cambridge University Press, 2016), 269ff.
15. Cudworth, *True Intellectual System*, 18.
16. Sarah Hutton, "From Cudworth to Hume: Cambridge Platonism and the Scottish Enlightenment", *Canadian Journal of Philosophy* 42, no.1 (2012): 8–26.
17. Cudworth, *True Intellectual System*, 253.
18. On this see Richard Popkin, *The Third Force in Seventeenth Century Thought* (Leiden: Brill, 1992), 333–350.
19. David Hume, *Dialogues Concerning Natural Religion and The Natural History of Religion*, ed. J.C.A. Gaskin (Oxford: Oxford University Press), 50.
20. See *De Rerum Natura* 1.44 and 11.155–158.
21. Cudworth, *True Intellectual System*, 738.
22. Hume, *An Enquiry Concerning Human Understanding*, 164n.
23. *The History of Tom Jones*, (London: Penguin Books, 2005), Dedication.
24. On Fielding and the Cambridge Platonists see Ralph W. Rader, "Ralph Cudworth and Fielding's Amelia", *Modern Language Notes* 71, no. 5 (1956), 336–338; Martin C. Battestin, *The Moral Basis of Fielding's Art: A Study of Joseph Andrews* (Middletown, CT: Wesleyan University Press, 1967); and James Bryson, "The Cambridge Platonists in Henry Fielding's Christian Platonic History of Tom Jones", *The Cambridge Platonist Research Group*, accessed November 6, 2022, https://cprg.hypotheses.org/837.
25. Plotinus, *Enneads* III 2.16.
26. Cudworth, *True Intellectual System*, 879–880.
27. On these literary influences see Marjorie Hope Nicholson, *Mountain Gloom and Mountain Glory: The Development of the Aesthetics of the Infinite* (Seattle, WA: University of Washington Press, 1997).
28. George Watson (ed.), *Remarks on John Locke by Thomas Burnet with Locke's Replies* (Brynmill Press, 1989), 24.
29. Leibniz, Letter to Burnett, 24th August 1697.

30 On several of the figures discussed here see Marjorie Hope Nicholson, rev. Sarah Hutton, *The Conway Letters: The Correspondence of Anne, Viscountess Conway, Henry More, and their Friends* (Oxford: Clarendon Press, 1992).
31 See further Mogens Laerke, *Les Lumières de Leibniz: Controverses Avec Huet, Bayle, Regis Et More* (Paris: Classiques Garnier, 2015), 335–386.
32 David Byrne, "Ragley Hall and The Decline and Fall of Cartesianism", *Restoration: Studies in English Literary Culture, 1660–1700* 40, no.2 (2016): 43–58.
33 Popkin, *The Third Force*, 117.
34 Catherine Wilson, *Leibniz's Metaphysics* (Princeton, NJ: Princeton University Press, 2016), 181.
35 See Liam Peter Temple, *Mysticism in Early Modern England* (Woodbridge: Boydell Press, 2019), 155ff.
36 See Tristran Dagron, *Toland Et Leibniz: L'Invention Du Neo*-Spinozisme (Paris: Vrin, 2009), esp. 261–307.
37 Though a good study is Andrew Weeks, *German Mysticism: From Hildegaard of Bingen to Ludwig Wittgenstein. A Literary and Intellectual History* (Albany, NY: State University of New York Press, 1993).
38 *Bibliographia Literaria* vol. I, eds. James Engell, and W. Jackson Bate, (Princeton, NJ: Princeton University Press), 152.
39 George Di Giovanni, Friedrich Heinrich Jacobi, *The Main Philosophical Writings and the Novel Allwill* (Montreal: McGill-Queen's UP, 1994), 195–196.
40 Adrian Mihai, "The Reception of Ralph Cudworth", *The Cambridge Platonist Sourcebook*, accessed November 6, 2022, www.cambridge-platonism.divinity.cam.ac.uk/view/texts/normalised/about-the-cambridge-platonists/reception/cudworth-ralph.
41 On the place of Platonism in German Idealism see Jens Halfwassen, "No Idealism Without Platonism: On the Origins of German Idealism at the Tübinger Stift", in *Mystik und Idealismus: Eine Lichtung des deutschen Waldes*, eds. Andrés Quero-Sánchez and Ben Morgan (Leiden: Brill, 2019), 144–159.
42 See Willie T. Weathers, "Edward Taylor and the Cambridge Platonists", *American Literature* 26, no. 1 (1954): 1–31; and D.W. Howe "The Cambridge Platonists of Old England and the Cambridge Platonists of New England", *Church History* 57, no.4 (1988): 470–485.
43 J. Bregman, "The Neoplatonic Revival in North America", *Hermathena* 149 (1990): 99–119.
44 R.W. Emerson, *The Letters of Ralph Waldo Emerson*, eds. Ralph L. Rusk, and Eleanor M. Tilton (New York: Columbia University Press, 1939–1995) vol. 2, 451. See further Edwin Cady, *On Emerson: The Best from American Literature* (Durham, NC: Duke University Press, 1988).
45 Michael J. Franklin, *Orientalist Jones: Sir William Jones, Poet, Lawyer, and Linguist, 1746–1794* (Oxford: Oxford University Press, 2011), 228ff; Jessica Patterson, *Religion, Enlightenment, Empire* (Cambridge, UK: Cambridge University Press, 2021), 288.
46 *Tattva-bodhini Patrika*, 78.
47 I am grateful to my colleague Ankur Barua for this reference.
48 John Peter Kenney, *Mystical Monotheism: A Study in Platonic Theology* (Eugene, OR: Wipf and Stock, 1991), 91.
49 See further Douglas Hedley, "Gods and giants: Cudworth's platonic metaphysics and his ancient theology", *British Journal for the History of Philosophy*, 25, no.5 (2017): 932–953.
50 See Melissa Lane, *Plato's Progeny: How Plato and Socrates still Captivate the Modern Mind* (London: Bristol Classical Press, 2001).
51 On this aspect see James Vigus, "'This Is Not Quite Fair, Master More!': Coleridge and the Cambridge Platonists", in *Revisioning Cambridge Platonism: Sources and Legacy*, eds. Douglas Hedley, and David Leech (Springer, 2019), 191–214.
52 S.T. Coleridge, *Collected Letters of Samuel Taylor Coleridge, Vol. 1: 1785–1800*, ed. Earl Lesley Griggs (Oxford: Oxford University Press, 1956), I 349, §209.
53 Coleridge, *The Eolian Harp*, cited in: *Coleridge, Poems*, ed. by John Beer, London 1986, 53.
54 E.A. Knox, *Robert Leighton, Archbishop of Glasgow: A Study of his Life, Times, and Writings* (London: James Clarke, 1930), 70–71.
55 See Douglas Hedley, *Coleridge, Philosophy and Religion: Aids to Reflection and the Mirror of the Spirit* (Cambridge, UK: Cambridge University Press, 2000).
56 David Newsome, *Bishop Westcott and the Platonic Tradition* (Cambridge, UK: Cambridge University Press, 2009).
57 Information about these chapel widows can be found at: www.emma.cam.ac.uk/chapel/windows/ (accessed November 6, 2022).
58 See Steven R.L. Clark's article "Patrides, Plotinus and the *Cambridge Platonists*", *British Journal for the History of Philosophy* 25, no.5 (2017): 858–877.

59 "Correspondances" in *Les Fleurs du Mal* (Munich: Maison Kurt Wolff, 1922).
60 On this connection see Mary Carman Rose, "The Christian Platonism of C.S. Lewis, J.R.R. Tolkien, and Charles Williams" in *Neoplatonism and Christian Thought*, ed. Dominic J. O'Meara (Albany, NY: State University of New York Press, 1981).
61 James Bryson, "'It's all in Plato': Platonism, Cambridge Platonism, and C.S. Lewis", *Journal of Inklings Studies* 11, no.1 (2021): 1–34.

Suggested Further Reading

Previous Anthologies

Campagnac, Ernst T. (ed.), *The Cambridge Platonists. Being Selections from the Writings of Benjamin Whichcote, John Smith and Nathanael Culverwell*, Oxford: Clarendon Press, 1901.
Cragg, Gerald R., *The Cambridge Platonists*, New York: Oxford University Press, 1968.
Hedley, Douglas/Hutton, Sarah/Leech, David, The Cambridge Platonism Sourcebook.
Patrides, Constantinos A. (ed.),*The Cambridge Platonists*, Cambridge, UK: Cambridge University Press, 1969.
Taliaferro, Charles/Teply, Alison J. (eds.), *Cambridge Platonist Spirituality*, New York: Paulist Press, 2004.

Part I: Cambridge Platonism at the Origins of the Enlightenment

Crocker, Robert, *Henry More, 1614–1687. A Biography of the Cambridge Platonist*, Dordrecht: Springer, 2003.
Darwall, Stephen, *The British Moralists and the Internal "Ought": 1640–1740*, Cambridge, UK: Cambridge University Press, 1995.
Deznan, Bogdan-Antoniu, "The Eternal Truths in Henry More and Ralph Cudworth", *Journal of Early Modern Studies* 11, no.1 (2022): 93–114.
Hedley, Douglas, "Gods and giants: Cudworth's platonic metaphysics and his ancient theology", *British Journal for the History of Philosophy* 25, no.5 (2017): 932–953.
___, "Samuel Parker's Free and Impartial Censure of the Platonick Philosophie", in: Corrias, Anna/Soldato, Eva Del (eds.), *Harmony and Contrast: Plato and Aristotle in the Early Modern Period*, London: Cambridge University Press, 2022, 122–146.
Leech, David, *The Hammer of the Cartesians: Henry More's Philosophy of Spirit and the Origins of Modern Atheism*, Leuven: Peeters, 2015.
Lotti, Brunello, "Universals in English Platonism: More, Cudworth, Norris", in: Di Bella, Stefano/Schmaltz, Tad M. (eds.), *The Problem of Universals in Early Modern Philosophy*, New York: Oxford University Press, 2017, 166–197.
Muirhead, John H., *The Platonic Tradition in Anglo-Saxon Philosophy: Studies in the History of Idealism in England and America*, London: George Allen & Unwin, 1931.
Reid, Jasper, *The Metaphysics of Henry More*, Dordrecht: Springer, 2012.
Rogers, Alan John/Vienne, Jean-Michel/Zarka, Yves Charles (eds.), *The Cambridge Platonists in Philosophical Context. Politics, Metaphysics and Religion*, Dordrecht: Springer, 1997.
Taliaferro, Charles, *Evidence and Faith. Philosophy and Religion since the Seventeenth Century*, Cambridge, UK: Cambridge University Press, 2005, 11–56.

Part II: Historical Context and Philosophical Programme

Davenport, Paul Miles, *Moral Divinity With a Tincture of Christ? An interpretation of the theology of Benjamin Whichcote, founder of Cambridge Platonism*, Nijmegen: Peeters, 1992.
Fisher, Nicholas, *Symon Patrick (1626–1707) and his Contribution to the Post-1660 Restored Church of England*, Newcastle upon Tyne: Cambridge Scholars Publishing, 2019.

Griffin, Martin I. J., *Latitudinarianism in the Seventeenth-Century Church of England*, Leiden: Brill, 1992.
Hickman, Louise, *Eighteenth-Century Dissent and Cambridge Platonism*. London/New York: Routledge, 2017.
Leedham-Green, Elisabeth, *A Concise History of the University of Cambridge*, Cambridge: CUP, 1996.
Lewis, Marilyn A., "'Christ's College and the Latitude-Men' Revisited: A Seminary of Heretics?", *History of Universities*, vol. 33, no. 1 (2020), 17–68.
Nicolson, Marjorie H., "Christ's College and the Latitude-Men", *Modern Philology*, vol. 27, no. 1 (1929), 35–53.
Powicke, Frederick J., *The Cambridge Platonists. A Study*, London/Toronto: J.M. Dent and Sons LTD., 1926.
Roberts, James D., *From Puritanism to Platonism in Seventeenth Century England*, The Hague: Martinus Nijhoff, 1968.
Spellman, W. M., *The Latitudinarians and the Church of England, 1660-1700*, Athens, GA/London: University of Georgia Press, 1993.
Twigg, John, *The University of Cambridge and the English Revolution, 1625–1688*, Woodbridge: Cambridge University Library, 1990.
Tyacke, Nicholas, "From Laudians to Latitudinarians: A Shifting Balance of Theological Forces", in: Grant Tapsell, ed., *The Later Stuart Church, 1660-1714*, Manchester: Manchester University Press, 2012, 46–67.

Part III: Cambridge Platonism in Early Modern Thought

Achermann, Eric, "Fromme Irrlehren. Zur Böhme-Rezeption bei More, Newton und Leibniz", in: Kühlmann, Wilhelm/Vollhardt, Friedrich (eds.), *Offenbarung und Episteme. Zur europäischen Wirkung Jakob Böhmes im 17. und 18. Jahrhundert*, Berlin/Boston: de Gruyter, 2012, 313–361.
Becco, Anne, "La substance unique face aux substances simples. D'H. Morus à G.W. Leibniz," in: Marco M. Olivetti (ed.), *Lo Spinozismo Ieri e Oggi*. Padua: Cedam, 1978, 103–119, and Hans-Petter Schütt, "Zu Henry Mores Widerlegung des Spinozismus." In: Konrad Cramer et al. (eds.), *Spinozas Ethik und ihre frühe Wirkung*, Wolfenbüttel: Herzog August Bibliothek, 1981, 19–50.
Bailey, Margaret Lewis, *Milton and Jakob Boehme. A Study of German Mysticism in Seventeenth-Century England*, New York: Oxford University Press, 1914.
Bonheim, Günther/Regehly, Thomas (eds.), *Mystik aus Frankfurt. Die Theologia Deutsch*, Berlin: WeißenseeVerlag, 2000.
Colie, Rosalie L., *Light and Enlightenment. A Study of the Cambridge Platonists and the Dutch Arminians*, Cambridge, UK: Cambridge University Press, 1957.
Coudert, Allison P., *The Impact of the Kabbalah in the Seventeenth Century. The Life and Thought of Francis Mercury van Helmont (1614–1698)*, Leiden/Boston/Cologne: Brill, 1999.
Crocker, Robert, "Mysticism and enthusiasm in Henry More", in: Hutton, *Henry More*, 137–155.
___, "The Role of Illuminism in the Thought of Henry More", in: Graham A.J. Rogers/Jean-Michel Vienne/Yves Charles Zarka (eds.), *The Cambridge Platonists in Philosophical Context. Politics, Metaphysics and Religion*, Dordrecht/Boston/London: Kluwer Academic Publishers, 1997, 129–144.
Hedley, Douglas, "Censuring the Teutonic Philosophy? Henry More's Ambivalent Appraisal of Jacob Böhme, in: *Aries* 18 (2018), 54–74.
Hutton, Sarah, "Henry More and Jacob Boehme", *Henry More (1614–1687). Tercentenary Studies*, Dordrecht/Boston/London: Springer, 1990, 157–171.
Muratori, Cecilia, "'A Philosopher at Randome': Translating Jacob Böhme in Seventeenth-Century Cambridge", in: Hedley/Leech, *Revisioning Cambridge Platonism*, 47–64.
Reid, Jasper, "Henry More and Nicolas Malebranche's Critiques of Spinoza", in: *European Journal of Philosophy* 23 (2013), 764–792.

Part IV: Ontology and Metaphysics

Bergemann, Lutz, *Ralph Cudworth, System aus Transformation: Zur Naturphilosophie der Cambridge Platonists und ihrer Methode*, Berlin: De Gruyter, 2017.
Burtt, A.E., *The Metaphysical Foundations of Modern Science*, London: Kegan Paul, 1925.
Dolezal, James E., *God without Parts*, Eugene, OR: Wipf and Stock, 2011.

Hedley, Douglas, "Ralph Cudworth as Interpreter of Plotinus", in: Gersh, Steven L. (ed.), *Plotinus' Legacy: The Transformation of Platonism from the Renaissance to the Modern Era*, Cambridge, UK: Cambridge University Press, 2019, 146–159.
Joost-Gaugier, Christiane L., *Measuring Heaven: Pythagoras and His Influence on Thought and Art in Antiquity and the Middle Ages*, Ithaca, NY: Cornell University Press, 2007.
Reid, Jasper, *The Metaphysics of Henry More*, Dordrecht: Springer, 2012.
Yolton, John, *Thinking Matter: Materialism in Eighteenth Century Britain*, Minneapolis, MN: University of Minnesota Press, 1983.

Part V: Epistemology and Ethics

Breteau, Jean-Louis, "'Un grand espace pour la liberté?' Le dilemme du libre arbitre dans la pensée de Ralph Cudworth", in: *Archives de Philosophie* 58 (1995), 421–441.
Crocker, Robert, "The Role of Illuminism in the Thought of Henry More", in: Graham A.J. Rogers/Jean-Michel Vienne/Yves Charles Zarka (eds.), *The Cambridge Platonists in Philosophical Context. Politics, Metaphysics and Religion*, Dordrecht/Boston/London: Kluwer Academic Publishers, 1997, 129–144.
Darwall, Stephen, *The British Moralists and the Internal "Ought": 1640–1740*, Cambridge, UK: Cambridge University Press, 1995.
Dolson, Grace N.I., "The Ethical System of Henry More", in: *The Philosophical Review* 6 (1897), 593–607.
Esquisabel, Oscar M./Gaiada, María Griselda, "Le libre arbitre et 'le paradoxe des facultés'. Suárez, Hobbes et Leibniz selon le jugement de Cudworth", in: *Studia Leibnitiana* 47 (2015), 162–185.
Gill, Michael B., *The British Moralists and the Birth of Secular Ethics*, Cambridge, UK: Cambridge University Press, 7–74.
Hedley, Douglas, "Seeing is Believing. Henry More and the Transformation of Mystery into Revelation", in: Hengstermann, *"Miracle of the Christian World"*, 187–202.
Leech, David, "Cudworth on Superintellectual Instinct as Inclination to the Good", in: *British Journal for the History of Philosophy* 25 (2017), 954–970.
___, "Does Henry More's Conception of a 'Divine Life' Bear Traces of Origen's influence?", in: Hengstermann, *"Miracle of the Christian World"*, 125–139.
Leisinger, Matthew, "Cudworth on Freewill", in: *Philosophers' Imprint* 21 (2021), 1–25.
Michaud, Derek, *Reason Turned into Sense. John Smith on Spiritual Sensation,* Leuven: Peeters, 2017.

Part VI: Rational Theology

Hedley, Douglas, *Sacrifice Imagined*, New York: Continuum, 2011.
Hengstermann, Christian (ed.), *"That Miracle of the Christian World": Origenism and Christian Platonism in Henry More*, Münster: Aschendorff, 2020.
Inge, William Ralph, *Christian Mysticism*, London: Methuen & Co., 1899.
Taliaferro, Charles/Teply, Alison J. (eds.) *Cambridge Platonist Spirituality*, Mahwah, NJ: Paulist Press, 2004.
Westcott, Brooke Foss, *History of Religious Thought in the West*, London: Macmillan & Co., 1891.

Part VII: Epilogue

Cassirer, Ernst, *Die Platonische Renaissance in England und die Schule von Cambridge* (1932), in: *Gesammelte Werke*, vol. 14, edited by Friederike Plage/Claus Rosenkranz, Darmstadt: Wissenschaftliche Buchgesellschaft, 2002, 223–380 (English translation: *The Platonic Renaissance in England*. Translated by James P. Pettegrove, Edinburgh: Nelson, 1953).
Dagron, Tristran, *Toland Et Leibniz: L'Invention Du Neo-Spinozisme*, Paris: Vrin, 2009.
Hedley, Douglas, *Coleridge, Philosophy and Religion: Aids to Reflection and the Mirror of the Spirit*, Cambridge, UK: Cambridge University Press, 2000.
___/Leech, David (eds.), *Revisioning Cambridge Platonism: Sources and Legacy*, Dordrecht: Springer, 2019.

Lobis, Seth, *The Virtue of Sympathy*, New Haven, CT: Yale University Press, 2014.
Nicholson, Marjorie Hope, *Mountain Gloom and Mountain Glory: The Development of the Aesthetics of the Infinite*, Seattle, WA: University of Washington Press, 1997.
Popkin, Richard, *The Third Force in Seventeenth Century Thought*, Leiden: Brill, 1992.
Prince, Michael, *Philosophical Dialogue in the British Enlightenment: Theology, Aesthetics, and the Novel*, Cambridge, UK: Cambridge University Press, 1997.
Temple, Liam Peter, *Mysticism in Early Modern England*, Woodbridge: Boydell Press, 2019.

A Brief Cambridge Platonist Prosopography

Marilyn A. Lewis

Anne Conway (1631–1679)

Anne Finch married Edward Conway, who would later become Viscount Conway and Killultugh, in 1651 and spent her married life first in London, then on his Irish estates from 1661–1664 and finally at his country seat, Ragley Hall in Warwickshire. Her beloved half-brother, John Finch, had been a pupil of Henry More at Christ's College, Cambridge, and More was persuaded to take her through a course of Cartesian philosophy by correspondence. She became his 'heroine pupil' and dear friend, with whom he spent a number of summers. At Ragley, More was able to participate in an informal discussion group which included the Kabbalist Francis Mercury Van Helmont, the Quaker George Keith, Benjamin Whichcote's sister Elizabeth Foxcroft and other members of the Cambridge Platonist circle. An invalid who suffered from crippling headaches all her adult life, Anne Conway eventually sought comfort in Quakerism. At her death, a short treatise in English was found among her effects and anonymously published in Latin translation in 1690 as *Principia philosophiae antiquissimae et recentissimae*. An English re-translation, entitled *The Principles of the most Ancient and Modern Philosophy*, was published in 1692, but the original English manuscript is no longer extant. This important treatise is directed against the contemporary philosophers Descartes, Hobbes and Spinoza, but it also shows that she had in some ways moved in opposition to her mentor More.

Ralph Cudworth (1617–1688)

Cudworth was a pupil of Benjamin Whichcote at Emmanuel College, Cambridge, and later became a popular tutor there. In 1645, he became regius professor of Hebrew in the University of Cambridge and was also appointed master of Clare Hall, although he seems not to have taken up the post until 1650. In 1654, he became master of Christ's College where his friendship with Henry More flourished. In 1647, he preached before the House of Commons, and this sermon is considered to be a seminal document of Cambridge Platonism. Three more published sermons followed, and in 1678 the first part of *The True Intellectual System of the Universe* was published. This massive work was intended to refute all philosophical forms of atheism, but it has often been used as a handbook of historical philosophy. A large deposit of manuscripts in the British Library, London, gives witness to his intention to publish further parts of *The True Intellectual System*, but this never came to fruition. In 1731, *A Treatise concerning Eternal and Immutable Morality* was published for the first time, followed by *A Treatise of Freewill* in 1838. Together with More, Cudworth established at Christ's College a place where Christian Platonist scholarship could be freely pursued, despite bitter opposition from another fellow of the college, Ralph Widdrington, and a group of high church Anglican heads of other colleges at the Restoration.

Joseph Glanvill (1636–1680)

Glanvill was educated at Lincoln College, Oxford, and was then a fellow of Exeter College before becoming rector of Bath Abbey. After reading Henry More's *Enthusiasmus Triumphatus* (1656) and *The Immortality of the Soul* (1659), Glanvill sought his friendship and warmly complimented More in his own first book, *The Vanity of Dogmatizing* (1661). Glanvill also became friends with George Rust about that time and wrote a glowing introduction to a posthumous edition of Rust's *Discourse of Truth* (1677). In an unpublished manuscript now kept at the University of Chicago, Glanvill created a fictional portrait gallery of divines whom he called 'Cupri-Cosmits' but later historians would designate 'Latitudinarians', including Cudworth, Whichcote, Rust, Smith and More. Glanvill cooperated with More in supporting the pre-existence of the soul and the existence and malevolent power of witches. Despite the latter belief, he was an ardent supporter of the newly formed Royal Society. He was also a strong advocate of the established Church of England, notwithstanding his frequent latter classification as a Latitudinarian.

Henry Hallywell (1641–1703)

Hallywell was George Rust's pupil at Christ's College and became well acquainted with More and Cudworth during his five-year fellowship there in 1662–1667. For the remainder of his career, he was the incumbent of several parishes in Sussex, in the diocese of Chichester. He seems to have visited London regularly, and most of his books were published by Walter Kettilby, More's London publisher and bookseller. He was almost certainly an auditor of Benjamin Whichcote at St Lawrence Jewry on these visits to the capital. His special contribution to the Cambridge Platonists' writings was a series of short books which presented their essential message simply but eloquently for the non-academic reader. Our knowledge of Rust's writings is almost entirely dependent on Hallywell's editions of them, published during the 1680s.

Henry More (1614–1687)

More spent his entire academic career at Christ's College, Cambridge, being elected to a fellowship in 1641 and retaining it until his death in 1687. He was the most prolific of the Cambridge Platonist writers. A full, annotated bibliography of More's published works can be found in: Robert Crocker, *Henry More, 1614–1687: A Biography of the Cambridge Platonist* (Dordrecht: Kluwer Academic Publishers, 2003). More was a controversial writer, composing early poetry strongly influenced by Plotinus, combatting enthusiasm and atheism, introducing Cartesian studies at Christ's but eventually turning against the French philosopher, perpetually hostile to the materialism of Hobbes and finally combatting Spinoza's pantheism and atheism. Most importantly, he espoused the Christian Platonism of Origen of Alexandria, allowing it to inform his soteriology and his firm belief in human free will. More has perhaps been best known for *An Explanation of the Grand Mystery of Godliness* (1660), his *Divine Dialogues* (1668), and his *Enchiridion Ethicum* (1667, with an English translation in 1690). He published two collections of his writings during his own lifetime: *A Collection of Several Philosophical Writings* (1662) and a three-volume Latin *Opera Omnia* (1675–1679). During the years of his fellowship, he and Ralph Cudworth were close friends, together influencing a number of pupils and younger colleagues to study Christian Platonism and write their own books and sermons conveying its message. Especially notable among their protégés were George Rust, Henry Hallywell, a little-known parish priest called Henry Maurice and a dissenting minister, Thomas Wadsworth, and Joseph Glanvill, an Oxford man who sought More's acquaintance and became a close friend. As noted above, his long friendship with Anne Conway was an essential component of his intellectual development.

John Smith (1618–1652)

Smith was a pupil of Benjamin Whichcote at Emmanuel College, Cambridge, and then a fellow of Queens' College from 1644 until his early death in 1652. Some of the sermons he preached in the chapel there were published as Smith's *Select Discourses* in 1660 by John Worthington, the Interregnum master of Jesus College, Cambridge. Worthington was a member of the Cambridge Platonist circle, a close friend of More and Cudworth and Whichcote's uncle by marriage. Smith's writing is considered to be the most beautiful among the works of the Cambridge Platonists. At Queens', he influenced a number of younger men, especially the Latitudinarian Symon Patrick.

George Rust (c.1628–1670)

Rust took his Bachelor of Arts degree at St Katharine's College, Cambridge, but then held a fellowship at Christ's College from 1649–1659. He read for his Bachelor of Divinity degree there, under the supervision of More and Cudworth. Of the five extant discourses from his Cambridge years, four were published by his pupil Henry Hallywell during the 1680s. The remaining discourse was published in 2017 in *History of Universities*, vol. 30, by an editorial team headed by Marilyn Lewis. He was most likely the anonymous author of the highly controversial *A Letter of Resolution concerning Origen* of 1661, and all of his writings present an Origenian Platonist view of Christian theology. From 1661, he pursued a clerical career in Ireland under the patronage of the Conway family. He succeeded Jeremy Taylor as bishop of Dromore in 1667 but died only three years later. Only two of his Irish sermons are extant and they were the sole works published in his lifetime, the second one being a funeral sermon for Taylor.

Benjamin Whichcote (1609–1683)

Often called "the Father of Cambridge Platonism", Whichcote was a fellow of Emmanuel College, Cambridge, where he tutored a number of young men who would become associated with the Cambridge Platonist circle, including Ralph Cudworth, John Smith and John Worthington. In 1645, he was appointed provost of King's College, and he served as vice-chancellor of the University of Cambridge in 1650–1651. He preached for nearly twenty years, probably from c.1636 to c.1656, on Sunday afternoons to a large auditory at Holy Trinity Church in Cambridge. His correspondence with his friend and critic Anthony Tuckney tells us that his sermons were considered controversial by his Calvinist auditors. After the Restoration, his most important appointment was in 1668 to the vicarage of St Lawrence Jewry in the City of London, which became a centre of liberal preaching in the capital. He preached very regularly there, but none of his sermons were published in his lifetime. He seems never to have written his sermons out in full, preferring to speak extempore from notes. Our knowledge of his sermons is dependent on his own manuscript notes and on shorthand notes taken down by his auditors. There are three main published versions of his sermons. A collection of twelve sermons, partially based on manuscript transcriptions in two unidentified hands, was published by the Earl of Shaftesbury in 1698. A somewhat different collection of thirty sermons was published by John Jeffrey in 1701–1703, based on Whichcote's own manuscript notes. A fourth volume containing a further twenty-six sermons was edited by Samuel Clarke in 1707, based on transcriptions by one 'Smith'. An edition combining all three strands of the Whichcote tradition in ninety-seven sermons was published anonymously in Aberdeen in 1751. Finally, a collection of 1,200 Aphorisms, drawn from Whichcote's own notes, was published by Samuel Salter in 1753, together with his correspondence with Anthony Tuckney.

Name Index

Anaxagoras 138, 219, 221, 222, 223, 238
Andronicus of Rhodes 241, 247, 248, 251, 252, 253
Apelles 212
Aquinas, Thomas 236
Aristotle 3, 5, 6, 18, 19, 46, 88, 112, 119, 134, 141, 142, 144, 145, 154, 155, 189, 199, 200, 204, 206, 209, 210, 214, 217, 220, 221, 222, 223, 230, 234, 238, 239, 241, 248, 252, 253, 255, 257, 261, 270, 272, 303, 306, 336
Augustine 3, 4, 7, 15, 72, 234, 239, 332
Aurelius, Marcus 221, 241, 256

Barfield, Owen 332
Baudelaire, Charles 332
Bayle, Pierre 4, 323, 327, 333, 334
Beaumont, Joseph 25, 277
Beierwaltes, Werner 7, 19, 332
Berkeley, George 1, 3, 4, 323, 324, 325, 329
Boethius 7, 155, 209, 263, 265
Böhme, Jacob 36, 84, 85, 86, 87, 89, 90, 156, 157, 159, 161, 162, 165, 166, 177, 188, 189, 190, 191, 326, 327, 328, 337
Burnet, Gilbert 43
Burnet, Thomas viii, 26, 325, 326, 333

Calvin, John v, 13, 18, 21, 22, 25, 26, 29, 30, 33, 34, 35, 39, 40, 41
Cassirer, Ernst 4, 8, 16, 29, 30, 35, 36, 321, 338
Chillingworth, Edward 155
Cicero, Marcus Tullius 3, 4, 96, 119, 138, 266, 272
Clark, S.R.L. vii, 20, 332, 334, 343
Clement, of Alexandrinus 6–7
Coleridge, S.T. i, 3, 4, 325, 326, 327, 328, 329, 331, 332, 334, 338
Conway, Lady Anne, nee Finch 25, 26, 27, 35, 42, 43, 61, 69, 76, 78, 80, 81, 83, 85, 86, 87, 88, 89, 119, 129, 130, 147, 149, 185, 186, 188, 197, 230, 239, 240, 274–279, 314, 326–328, 334, 340, 342
Craig, Edward 7, 16, 20

Darwin, Charles 8
Democritus 19, 79, 112, 113, 121, 125, 183, 210, 220, 239, 326
Denys the Areopagite (Pseudo-Dionysius) 7, 9, 10, 14, 19
Descartes vi, 3, 4, 7, 8, 12, 13, 18, 19, 23, 36, 76, 79, 80, 81, 83, 84, 90, 91, 92, 121, 123, 124–129, 131, 133, 134, 135, 137, 138, 139, 141, 143, 145, 147, 149, 151, 152, 153, 154, 155, 178, 180, 181, 185, 186, 187, 188, 189, 191, 195, 210, 236, 238, 241, 268, 270, 271, 323, 324, 326, 327, 340
Diogenes Laertius 210
Dodds, E.R. 240, 331

Edwards, Jonathan 329
Eliot, T.S. 331, 332
Emerson, Ralph Waldo i, 14, 329, 332, 334
Empedocles 209
Epictetus 241
Epicurus 51, 65, 125, 207, 210, 224
Erasmus, Desiderius 4, 7, 8, 9, 36, 39, 329
Eriugena, John the Scot 7, 9, 19, 331

Feuerbach, Ludwig 20
Ficino, Marsilio 4, 5, 7, 8, 9, 19, 22, 30, 34, 36, 39, 332
Findlay, John Niemeyer 6, 18
Fowler, Edward 26, 43, 63, 69
Freud, Sigmund 12

Gadamer, Hans Georg 5, 18
Gassendi, Pierre 216, 217
Glanvill, Joseph i, 24, 25, 27, 40, 41, 44, 58, 63, 68, 69, 73, 86, 224, 238, 275
Glisson, Frances 88, 91, 174, 175, 193, 194, 322
Goethe, Johann Wolfgang v, 328, 332

Hallywell, Henry 23, 25–28, 36, 37, 40–42, 57–58, 68, 75, 102–103
Hegel, Georg Wilhelm Friedrich 17, 327–329
Heidegger, Martin 5, 328

Helmont, van, Franciscus Mercurius 23, 24, 27, 88, 89, 119, 147, 326–328, 337, 340
Herder, Johann Gottfried 328
Hermes, Tristmegistus 105
Hierocles, of Alexandria 304
Hobbes, Thomas v, 4, 7, 8, 10, 13, 16, 19, 30, 31, 36, 69, 75, 76–79, 88, 90, 107, 109, 111, 113, 115, 117–120, 182–185, 189, 197, 271, 323, 324, 338, 340, 341
Hooker, Richard 21
Hort, F.J.A. 331
Hotham, Durand 84–85, 191; *see also* Böhme, Jacob
Hume, David 3, 16, 321, 323–325, 330, 333
Hutton, Sarah vii, 3, 30, 31, 36, 43, 77, 240, 254, 324, 334, 336, 337

Iamblichus 34, 240, 329, 332
Inge, W.R. vii, 331
Ingelo, Nathaniel 24, 276

Jacobi, Friedrich Heinrich 328, 329, 334
Jones, Sir William 327, 329, 330, 333–334
Jowett, Benjamin 3–5
Justinian, Emperor 7

Kant, Immanuel 17, 30, 322
Keith, George 23, 27, 326, 340
Kierkegaard, Søren 18, 273

Law, William 327
Le Clerk, Jean 4, 323
Leibniz, Gottfried Wilhelm i, 8, 30, 323, 326–328, 333, 334, 337, 338
Lewis, C.S. 332, 334, 335, 337, 338
Limborch, Philippus van, 39, 49, 88, 89, 90, 327
Locke, John 3, 4, 8, 15, 30, 49, 95, 155, 197, 234, 322, 323, 324, 326, 327, 333
Lucretius 124, 125, 154, 204, 224, 324
Luria, Isaac 27, 89

Maistre, de, Joseph i, 332, 333
Martineau, James 321
Moses 7, 77, 173, 177, 193, 311; Attic 6
Mosheim, Johann Lorenz 329
Muirhead, John 331, 336

Nagel, Thomas 17, 18, 20
Niclaes, H. 189
Norris, John i, 19, 33, 34, 211, 212, 237, 336

Origen i, vii, 4, 6, 7, 8, 9, 10, 13, 19, 23, 24, 25, 27, 29, 30, 34, 35, 36, 41, 42, 72, 75, 82, 87, 143, 191, 242, 270, 274, 275, 276, 277, 278, 279, 291, 293, 296, 307, 308, 309, 313, 314, 315, 316, 317, 330, 331, 338, 341, 342

Parker, Samuel 7, 19, 27, 74, 75, 182, 276, 292, 313, 336
Patrick, Symon 25, 26, 42, 44, 68, 69, 336, 342
Philo 7
Pico della Mirandola 7, 34, 36
Plato 3, 5, 6, 14, 16, 17, 19, 41, 72, 73, 105, 106, 109, 113, 170, 183, 186, 195, 201, 208, 209, 214, 222, 236, 238, 272, 294, 332, 334, 335
Plotinus 4, 9, 11, 12, 14, 19, 22, 34, 35, 39, 41, 47, 68, 144, 145, 155, 158, 162, 165, 166, 189, 190, 191, 201, 203, 209, 214, 217, 221, 223, 229, 235, 237, 238, 239, 246, 249, 325, 329, 330, 332, 333, 334, 336, 337, 338
Pope, Alexander 322
Porphyry 7, 34, 155, 217
Price, Richard 321, 329
Proclus 7, 9, 34, 161, 195, 240, 305, 329
Protagoras 113, 120, 272
Pythagoras 5, 235, 239, 332

Reuchlin 5, 325
Rosenroth, Christian Knorr v, 24, 27, 89, 326, 327, 328
Roy, Rommohan 330
Rust, George i, 12, 21, 23, 24, 26, 27, 30, 33, 36, 37, 40, 41, 42, 49, 51, 57, 60, 61, 64, 68, 69, 73, 74, 75, 79, 83, 86, 93, 97, 98, 105, 115, 131, 132, 165, 185, 186, 216, 218, 243, 253, 265, 272, 275–279, 285, 291, 293, 296, 297, 304, 307, 308, 311, 313, 314, 317, 341, 342

St Paul 9, 14, 19, 27, 42, 201, 239, 294, 302, 303, 305, 314
Schelling, Friedrich Wilhelm Joseph v, 17, 329, 332
Scougal, Henry 331
Smith, John i, 8, 9, 10, 13, 14, 17, 19, 22, 24, 25, 29, 33, 34, 41, 42, 54, 68, 72, 73, 96, 201–202, 234–235, 237, 286, 303, 312, 316, 321, 327, 331, 332, 336, 338, 341, 342, 343
Southwell, Edward 26, 36, 241, 242, 248, 249, 250, 256, 257, 263, 264, 265
Spencer, William 24, 227, 278
Spinoza, Baruch vi, 4, 10, 17, 19, 26, 30, 36, 40, 87–91, 167, 171–179, 183, 185, 187, 189, 191–195, 197, 274, 322, 323, 327, 328, 329, 337, 340–341
Sterry, Peter 35, 327, 331
Stillingfleet, Edward 15, 26, 43

Tagore, Debendranath 330
Taliaferro, Charles v, 3, 33, 35, 37, 336, 338
Temple, William 331
Tillotson, John viii, 26, 27, 43

Tuckney, Anthony 5, 7, 15, 18, 19, 20, 21, 23, 28, 73, 95, 273, 284, 312, 342, 343
Tulloch, John 18, 20, 29, 273

Virgil 124, 154
Vossius, Gerardus 324

Ward, Richard 77, 200
Westcott, B.F. vii, 130, 331, 334, 338
Whichcote, Benjamin i, 4, 5, 8, 10, 12, 18–29, 33, 34, 41, 43, 53, 68, 72, 73, 79, 95, 273, 274, 281–284, 305, 311, 312, 316, 322, 323, 331, 336, 340, 341, 343
Widdrington, Ralph 22, 25, 26, 43, 61, 62, 69, 277, 340
Wilkins, John 26, 43
Worthington, John 22, 24–26, 33, 41, 72, 73, 79, 85–87, 276, 277, 342

Xenophanes 12, 72

Yolton, John 197, 338

Subject Index

Note: The 'f' and 'ff' means 'and the following page/pages'.

actus purus 187, 250; *see also* God
alchemy vi, 85, 87, 156
allegory 22, 163, 236, 332
analogy 12, 117, 134, 135, 161, 188, 232, 249, 303
anarchy 13, 267
angels 53, 67, 81, 84, 97, 123, 159, 163, 165, 167, 173, 176, 181, 194, 219, 229, 230, 262, 278, 279, 292, 293, 294, 300, 310; dancing on a needle 155
animals 67, 118, 138, 146, 168, 169, 170, 171, 175, 176, 179, 215, 219, 220, 221, 222, 223, 225, 231, 254
anima mundi *see* soul, world-
anthropomorphism 12, 40, 72, 73, 75, 143, 182, 190, 194, 322
apokatastasis 278–279; *see also* salvation, universal
appetite 97, 109, 114, 116, 168, 173, 174, 202, 203, 205, 245, 246, 248
archetypes 10, 15, 17, 74, 146, 185, 190, 191, 193, 212, 224, 235, 249, 259; *see also* ideas
Arminianism 21, 25, 29, 39, 41, 42, 60, 69, 75, 273, 327, 337
Articles, of Church of England 24, 25, 60, 68, 77, 78
atheism vi, 3, 10, 16, 17, 24, 59, 61, 65, 66, 68, 81, 82, 83, 87–91, 108, 112, 114, 133, 141, 167, 171, 173, 177, 179, 186, 188, 192, 194, 197, 205, 222, 227, 238, 239, 282, 323, 324, 325, 333, 336, 340, 341; ignorance of 57, 64, 199; vile and sordid 177
atoms 74, 79, 86, 91, 121, 123, 125, 171, 174, 175, 183, 187, 190, 192, 194, 204, 206, 210, 224, 225, 238, 268, 271, 322
attributes, divine 67, 77, 80, 90, 95, 114, 115, 120, 147, 149, 152, 153, 164, 170, 173, 176, 177, 180, 182, 184, 189, 194, 203, 206, 207, 211, 226, 231, 232, 233, 236, 237, 269, 271

beauty 11, 18, 49, 50, 100, 174, 183, 203, 235, 247, 259, 304, 323, 325; *see also* goodness, divine; truth, divine
Behmenism 84–87, 157, 158, 159, 177, 189, 191, 327
being (perfect) 7, 9–15, 17, 21, 24, 45–47, 49–52, 54–56, 58–60, 65–69, 72, 76–78, 80, 82, 83, 85, 89, 96, 97, 98, 105, 118, 119, 121, 122, 123, 130, 132, 134, 142, 143, 151, 171, 172, 173–180, 193, 204, 206, 208, 215, 218, 222, 237, 255, 291, 292, 328; chain of 239
Bible 281, 282, 285
body: discerpible 109ff, 117ff, 224ff; impenetrable 108, 123, 124, 127, 131, 148, 216, 225, 232, 233, 234; resurrection 290; terrestrial, aerial, celestial 290ff

Calvinism 13, 29, 35, 39, 40, 41, 46, 71, 72, 74, 75, 181, 273, 327, 329
Cartesianism 4, 13, 76, 82, 83, 186, 323, 327, 334
causality 78, 81, 91, 187, 188, 191, 197, 220, 325
Christology 6, 86
cognition 8, 185, 186, 242, 268, 269, 271, 272; *see also* faculty, boniform
communion, with God 21, 61, 97, 275, 276, 302, 303
congruity (vital) 116, 206, 230, 239, 247, 291, 292, 297, 299, 306, 309, 311, 316, 317
conscience, liberty of 63, 266, 267, 272
consciousness 48, 169, 170, 188, 191, 219, 239, 258, 333
conspissation 123
contemplation 8, 18, 68, 84, 181, 200, 234, 244, 259, 270, 298, 304, 312, 315
corpuscularianism 197; *see also* atoms
creation 9, 13, 14, 31, 35, 58, 72, 73, 232, 235, 240, 247, 249, 268, 270, 275, 278, 281, 282, 290, 299, 300, 308, 312, 313, 315, 322, 324, 325

death 11, 13, 22, 23, 26, 27, 41, 51, 56, 58, 73, 74, 79, 80, 81, 99, 103, 104, 105, 143, 156, 157, 163, 165, 168, 185, 216, 227, 229, 230, 243, 246, 249, 266, 274, 275, 277, 279, 292, 294, 302, 307, 309, 314, 317, 328, 330
deification 14, 15, 275, 316
deiformity 21, 33, 41, 42, 68, 244; partakers of the divine 55, 231, 279, 302, 303
desire: vain or worldly 56, 162, 165, 204, 254, 261, 269, 284, 310, 313; spiritual 61, 114, 203, 235, 243, 255, 300
determinism 40, 69, 77, 78, 91, 182, 184, 256, 314
divinisation 311
divinity 5, 14, 15, 56, 61, 74, 87; of Christ 25

ecstasy 14, 165; *see also* experience, religious
emanation, divine 97, 133, 134, 150, 151, 152, 174, 194, 281, 282, 304, 310, 313; *see also* creation
empiricism, error thereof 30, 271, 321, 323, 324–326
enthusiasm 9, 14, 23, 24, 61, 68, 69, 78, 85, 86, 156, 158, 188, 189, 238, 246, 268, 331, 337, 341
eschatology *see* salvation, universal
eternity 50, 93, 119, 126, 127, 141, 143, 148, 149, 163, 177, 179, 180, 185, 190, 200, 204, 205, 211, 212, 214, 268, 287, 304, 306, 324, 331
eucharist 316; *see also* Lord's Supper
evil 7, 11, 13, 50, 63, 65–67, 69, 95, 98, 103–106, 117, 132, 142, 191, 193, 263, 265, 277, 289, 297, 300, 304, 316, 326; daemons 307; moral 52, 58, 97, 116, 231, 254, 256, 270, 311; natural 51, 262
experience, religious 14, 190, 202, 274, 316; of freedom 110, 128, 135, 256
extension (spiritual) 12, 14, 77, 79, 81, 82, 83, 90–92, 111, 120–126, 138, 140, 146–148, 151, 153, 155, 176, 177–179, 181, 183, 186, 187, 188, 194, 195, 210–216, 218, 227, 232, 233, 237, 238, 270

faculty, boniform 86, 87, 90, 164, 166, 191, 241, 242
faith: in Christ 52, 75, 100, 165; and reason vi, 3, 5, 7, 15, 18, 25, 30, 35, 59, 61, 69, 71, 99, 133, 181, 273, 275ff
familism 27, 158
fatalism 65, 66, 67, 324
fideism 89, 90, 273
force: divine 95, 135, 204, 219, 266, 267, 299, 301; natural 83, 111, 115, 116, 146, 185, 188, 202, 215, 251, 252, 260, 264, 315
forms: angel 51; divine 74, 77, 185, 190, 191, 193, 258, 315, 322; substantial 4
foundationalism 79, 80, 185

God: existence of 167, 170, 173, 175, 177, 179, 181, 183, 185, 193, 194, 202–205, 236; idea of 129f, 133–135, 143, 149, 172, 203–209, 236; self-communication 278, 315; *see also* voluntarism, divine
godliness 24, 25, 27, 35, 273, 274, 275, 276, 277, 278, 285, 286, 289, 312, 313, 316, 317, 341
goodness, divine 9, 10, 11, 13, 14, 18, 21, 27, 35, 39, 40, 45, 48, 50, 53, 54, 55, 58, 65, 66, 67, 69, 71, 72–80, 83, 94, 95, 98, 101, 102, 104, 105, 120, 121, 132, 147, 148, 162, 181, 182, 185, 186, 189–194, 203, 204, 218, 222, 231, 232, 235, 241–243, 245, 247, 249, 250, 253, 259, 267–269, 271, 273–279, 282, 283, 286, 290–293, 296–301, 304, 305, 308, 310–313, 315–317, 325
government 3, 43, 60, 68, 173, 267, 283, 284
grace 21, 34, 39, 49, 50, 63, 68, 72, 73, 95, 97, 99, 101, 121, 165, 225, 227, 275, 284, 298, 311, 338

happiness 8, 14, 24, 46, 53, 54, 83, 93, 94, 97, 99, 100, 104, 105, 131, 202, 203, 207, 234, 241, 245, 248, 255, 262, 264, 275, 286, 291, 293, 294, 300, 304, 323
hell 39, 45, 58, 74, 94, 95, 96, 100, 102, 120, 158, 162, 163, 189, 191, 241, 274, 279, 284, 288, 289, 308, 317, 329, 330, 332
holenmerism 82, 111, 187
hylozoism vi, 77, 88, 89, 91, 92, 167–169, 190, 193, 194
hypostasis 86, 166, 218

idea: Cartesian 13, 179, 226, 227, 270, 272; innate 76, 113, 184, 188, 259, 272, 288, 290, 294, 306, 312; Platonic i, 3, 5, 10, 50, 54, 55, 57, 117, 149, 180, 181, 222, 230, 234, 238, 248, 325; *see also* wisdom, divine
idealism 20, 36, 190, 263, 321, 328, 334, 336; *see also* Platonism
ignorance 57, 64, 119, 139, 142, 166, 208, 212, 224, 230, 252, 297; *see also* atheism
image, of God 101, 105, 129, 178, 181, 188, 190, 191, 193, 201, 203, 205, 238, 268, 272, 275, 281, 283, 305, 312, 316
immortality 19, 24, 27, 67, 69, 74, 76, 77, 81, 91, 107, 108, 109, 110, 154, 155, 223, 229, 239, 254, 276–279, 294, 306, 312, 313, 316, 317, 329, 341
infinity 8, 10, 11, 14, 18, 31, 46, 50, 52, 55, 58, 72, 75, 79, 80, 82, 83, 85, 90, 91, 95, 97, 100, 101, 103, 104, 111–113, 115, 118, 121, 125–127, 130–132, 141–149, 153, 163, 169, 172–180, 185–188, 190, 193, 200, 202–207, 211–220, 232–237, 244, 255, 263, 265–267, 272, 277–279, 291–293, 307, 308, 313, 315, 317, 328, 331, 333, 339
iniquity 96, 103, 293, 297
instinct: selfish 13; superintellectual 47, 231, 254, 338; *see also* faculty, boniform

intellect: divine 10, 12, 57, 73, 74, 80, 83, 87, 104, 118, 154, 161, 162, 164, 172–174, 179, 222, 245, 246, 248; human 69, 104, 147, 164, 232, 237, 250, 259, 270, 272, 277, 291, 293, 312–316
intelligibility 17, 83, 147, 185, 186, 191, 236, 249, 312

judgement 64, 78, 121, 130, 136, 154, 175, 179, 210, 226, 256, 270; divine 278, 298, 299, 307, 314, 316
justice 66, 78, 105, 185, 245, 288, 326; divine 11, 39, 45, 58, 65, 66–69, 75, 95, 97, 98, 101–103, 105, 106, 114–117, 165, 173, 184, 185, 204, 242, 244, 247, 249, 252, 263, 266, 267, 276, 279, 282, 284, 295, 299, 304, 307, 310, 317, 325

kabbalah 27, 89, 90, 164, 229, 235, 326–327, 337
knowledge 10–13, 147, 150ff, 168f, 170, 175, 185ff, 189, 199ff, 225ff, 243ff, 258–259, 281–289

latitudinarianism 26, 35, 42, 43, 87, 182, 337
life: plastic 31, 88, 153, 161, 168, 169, 170, 171, 192, 219, 220, 221, 237, 271, 322, 323, 327, 331
likeness 26, 53, 63, 69, 86, 193, 231, 305; *see also* image, of God
logos 7, 15, 20; *see* Trinity
Lord's Supper 23, 302, 303; *see also* communion, with God; eucharist
love 13, 39, 40, 47–50, 52, 55, 56, 58, 62–64, 72, 80, 84, 90, 93, 94, 97, 100, 101, 102, 105, 120, 132, 133, 139, 158, 159–163, 165, 167, 189, 191, 193, 201, 202–204, 211, 229, 230–232, 239, 243, 244, 248, 249, 255, 256, 260, 263, 268, 269, 273, 279, 281, 282, 284, 286, 289, 291, 292, 295–297, 300, 302, 304, 311, 313, 316, 317, 322, 325, 332, 340

magic: black 51, 167, 228; philosophical and sublime 138, 158, 220–222, 238
mankind 48, 59, 207, 330; belief in God 207, 208; destiny 55, 56, 105, 253, 294; fallen 58, 64, 71, 85, 98, 101–103, 273, 296; free 310, 315; Hobbes on 13, 15, 119
materialism 4, 10, 13, 17, 18, 36, 69, 75–79, 86, 88, 182, 185, 188, 190, 192, 197, 238, 323, 324, 341
mathematics 81, 137, 178; and morality 264, 283
measure 12, 46, 53, 97, 103, 105, 121, 123, 125, 142–148, 205, 212, 215, 216
mechanism 10, 51, 76, 149, 205, 220, 221, 238, 259, 333
melancholy 34, 47, 86, 156, 157, 158, 188, 189, 190, 296
metaphysics vi, vii, 3, 4, 5, 6, 10, 11, 12, 18, 30, 31, 34, 36, 39, 40, 75, 76, 79, 81, 85, 86, 111, 139, 155, 183, 185, 187, 190, 191, 197, 199, 200, 202, 204–240, 268, 314, 317, 334, 336, 337, 338
mind (almighty) 55, 202, 203, 214
miracles 87, 90, 167, 168, 171, 172, 173, 192, 274
monads 83, 139, 161, 178, 186, 188, 190, 191, 192, 225
monism 78, 79, 81, 185, 194, 197
mysteries 11, 158, 168, 201, 230, 274, 275, 284, 286, 312
mysticism vii, 4, 15, 248, 249, 268, 273, 274, 334, 337, 338, 339

nature 121–123, 124, 127, 156, 162, 163, 167, 168, 218–240, 266, 281, 298, 299, 307, 309, 310, 315, 322–323, 332; of the Deity 144, 149, 159, 160, 175, 181, 182, 202–209, 276, 287, 293, 303–304, 308, 313; fallen 282; hylozoist 169; laws of 117, 118, 119, 172, 173; light of 263, 290; mirror of 330; (plastic) spirit of 87, 90, 91, 100, 153, 154, 158, 161, 163, 170, 172, 176, 192, 278, 327, 331; scale of 183, 255; Spinozist 177, 179, 180
necessity 48, 65, 66, 67, 69, 75, 76, 78, 80, 83, 91, 99, 104, 106, 109, 113, 114, 115, 118, 119, 120, 124, 125, 134, 143, 147, 153, 168, 170, 172, 173, 174, 178, 179, 182, 183, 184, 185, 188, 193, 205, 207, 209, 212, 215, 216, 218, 220, 243, 249, 252, 254, 258, 266, 267, 270, 271, 277, 292, 309, 314
neoplatonism 4, 5, 6, 9, 14, 17, 238, 240, 330, 332, 335
nullibism vi, 77, 82, 83
number 55, 141, 143, 144, 146, 147, 148, 212, 213, 215, 247, 249
numen 6, 138, 170, 200, 205, 211, 222, 324

omnipotence 12, 40, 71–73, 75, 115, 141, 142, 147, 152, 175, 179, 186, 194
omnipresence 31, 124, 187, 214, 288, 314
omniscience 169
Origenism i, 9, 25, 30, 36, 72, 75, 76, 191, 242, 270, 277, 278, 279, 314, 315, 316, 317, 338

pantheism vi, 4, 20, 85, 156, 190, 191, 328, 329, 330, 333, 334, 341
participation: Platonic 21, 26, 35, 53, 54, 56, 58, 63, 66, 69, 74, 84, 118, 182, 190, 235, 266, 273, 287, 315, 316; in Christ 56, 316
passion 50, 56, 62, 103, 109, 113, 184, 203, 241, 242, 247–249, 252, 257, 258, 260–265, 269, 270, 282, 284, 297, 298, 300, 304–305, 314, 326
perception 57, 91, 110, 150, 168–170, 174, 183, 184, 188, 189, 204, 205, 225, 247, 248, 255, 258, 261, 262, 269, 271, 272, 326

perfection 16, 31, 53–55, 73, 76, 78, 79, 80, 82, 87, 91, 97, 98, 100, 103, 104, 120, 132, 142, 143, 150, 152, 155, 164, 172, 173, 175, 180–182, 185, 188, 191, 194, 201, 203, 204, 206–208, 218, 219, 223, 231, 232, 236, 237, 243, 247, 252, 257, 268, 272, 277, 278, 282, 288, 293, 298, 304, 315, 316
phenomena 16, 17, 77, 92, 138, 139, 179, 192, 219, 312
philosophy: experimental 25, 30, 44; true, i, viii, 4–8, 10, 13, 15, 16, 19, 25, 29, 34, 35, 61, 69, 71, 197, 222, 234, 236, 239, 322, 323, 327, 329
piety 62, 83, 90, 114, 137–139, 157, 173, 189, 263, 286, 297
Platonism: Alexandrian 4–7, 15, 35, 72, 143, 182, 272, 274, 278, 312; Cambridge i, v, vii, 1–28
predestination 13, 21, 25, 41, 42, 45, 68, 71, 73, 75, 104, 181, 276
prophecy 6, 165, 312
providence 10, 11, 84, 90, 104, 105, 121, 132, 163, 164, 167, 172–174, 193, 219, 247, 290, 293, 296–301, 306, 307, 309, 310, 311
punishment, divine 11, 13, 65–67, 96, 104, 231, 256, 267, 269, 274, 276, 279, 297, 307–311, 316, 317
Puritanism 5, 21, 22, 25, 29, 34, 41, 43, 52, 71–73, 329, 337

Quakerism 27, 189, 340

reason, right 258–259
reflection: of consciousness 234, 270; image 5, 13, 235, 239, 268
regeneration 56, 100, 163
religion 11, 16, 17, 20, 25–31, 48, 53, 54, 56–59, 61–63, 68, 69, 71–78, 82, 85–89, 94, 100–102, 114, 115, 139, 155, 157–159, 173, 189, 201, 207, 224, 236, 266, 267, 271, 274, 282, 283, 286, 302, 305, 311, 312, 324–328, 330, 333, 334, 336–338
resurrection vi, 25, 56, 239, 240, 255, 274–277, 290–294, 312, 313
revelation 8, 15, 31, 33, 34, 52, 57, 58, 61, 73, 90, 189, 200, 235, 274, 275, 281, 282, 285, 287, 311, 312, 328, 338
righteousness, imputed 15, 46, 53, 54, 56, 63, 71, 93, 96, 99–101, 181, 182, 267, 282, 284, 297, 300, 304

sacrifice vi, 15, 31, 58, 68, 75, 95, 99, 101, 102, 270, 302–305, 316–317, 338
Sadducism 27
sagacity, divine 90, 112, 157, 244, 267, 298, 332
salvation, universal 15, 24, 41, 42, 68, 69, 72–74, 87, 96, 173, 181, 182, 274, 275, 278, 279, 284, 315, 317

scepticism 10, 11, 47, 117, 131, 132, 185, 325
scholasticism 4, 8, 13, 34, 77, 82, 105, 109, 143, 154, 182, 183, 238, 255, 269, 307
scripture 5, 6, 8, 25, 52, 55, 59, 61, 63, 64, 68, 73, 93, 95, 99, 101, 105, 172, 234, 268, 273, 276, 282, 283–289, 293, 302, 309, 311, 312, 313
sensation, spiritual 77, 91, 188, 189, 249, 264, 268, 338
senses 78, 110, 122, 124, 126, 132, 150, 210, 233, 245, 249, 253, 287, 288, 296, 297, 326
sensualism 76, 78, 182, 271
sentimentalism 31, 333
simplicity 49, 60, 106, 236, 310
sin 101, 104, 105, 132, 149, 152, 243, 252, 256, 260, 273–276, 277–279, 281, 282, 285, 300–306, 308, 311
soteriology 71–74, 182, 278, 316, 341
soul: fall of 290ff; (plastic) vegetative 171; preexistent 24, 27, 29, 36, 74, 75, 163, 164, 165, 183, 191, 208, 235, 242, 259, 274–279, 312, 313, 341; self-motion 80, 84, 91, 184, 194, 205, 270; world- 10, 11, 236ff
sovereignty 12, 13, 35, 76, 117, 181, 266, 267
space 14, 31, 51, 80, 82, 85, 108, 109, 112, 121, 123, 125, 126, 130, 131, 141, 145, 146, 148, 149, 150, 153, 179, 182, 186, 193, 197, 210–217, 232, 233, 236, 237, 239, 268
species 4, 48, 51, 67, 78, 106, 152, 166, 179, 186, 212, 213, 226, 231, 258, 267, 315, 322
spirit: extended 83, 92, 108, 111–115, 183; Holy Spirit 15, 49, 51, 52, 56, 61, 72, 73, 84, 86, 89, 100, 103, 156, 157–160, 165, 173, 188–190, 229, 268, 273, 274, 293, 298, 300, 312, 313; metaphysics of 3, 4, 11, 14, 15, 18, 31, 35–37, 54–61, 77–79, 81–87, 224–240; see also Trinity
spissitude 12, 213, 237, 239
substance, incorporeal 50, 76, 77, 82, 107–109, 112, 114, 117, 119, 128, 135, 138, 140, 143–145, 168, 169, 171, 180–183, 190, 199, 200, 210, 211, 213–216, 220, 234, 237, 270, 323, 325
symbol 31, 52, 74, 160, 303, 307, 312, 332
system vi, 3–6, 8–10, 13, 16, 17–19, 26, 28, 30, 31, 34–36, 39, 65–68, 71, 75, 77, 79–91, 113–115, 118, 140–145, 167–170, 174, 183, 186, 192, 197, 203–208, 214, 216, 218, 219, 235, 239, 240–242, 249, 266, 268, 271, 278, 323, 324, 328–330

teleology 17, 197, 323, 333
theism v, vi, 16, 65–69, 71, 141, 186, 207, 236, 279, 324, 330, 331, 333
theodicy 30, 31, 274, 295–301, 314, 315, 327
theogony 84, 188, 190; see also Böhme
theology: ancient 183, 189, 315; apophatic 9, 10; natural 16, 24, 29, 76, 199, 200, 234, 236, 238; rational 30, 59, 78, 90, 273–318

Trinity: Holy 15, 72, 143, 190; Platonic 10, 15, 16, 19, 25, 85, 190, 235, 237
truth, divine 13, 51, 53, 55, 71, 80, 82, 83, 125–126, 132, 135, 142, 147, 181, 184, 185, 186, 189, 229, 234, 235, 237, 245, 246, 249, 268, 276, 281, 282, 286, 287, 305, 311, 312, 316, 325, 330, 341

understanding 53, 58, 102, 113, 143, 205, 207, 287
union: spiritual 14, 55, 84, 162, 244, 245, 248, 268, 313; Vital 132, 229, 230, 233, 268, 306, 309, 317; *see also* congruity
unity, absolute 7, 11, 15, 16, 19, 20, 55, 91, 135, 174, 194, 231, 232, 247, 268, 330; *see also* Trinity

vice 47, 105, 115, 173, 254, 256, 260, 261, 269, 270, 277, 283, 297, 298, 300, 314, 326
virtue vi, 15, 36, 39, 41, 48, 50, 53, 54, 120, 151, 163, 172, 173, 175, 181–183, 187, 214, 223, 237, 242, 247, 248, 260–265, 297, 304, 314, 315, 325, 326, 333

vision, divine 15, 16, 34, 43, 84–87, 90, 114, 188–192, 215, 238, 241, 242, 243–250, 268, 269, 272, 278, 315, 317, 323, 330
voluntarism, divine 12, 13, 69, 71, 75, 82, 181, 270

will, free-will 11, 28, 30, 39, 40, 42, 43, 48, 49–51, 55, 60, 61–63, 67, 69, 71–73, 75, 77, 78, 96, 99, 104, 110, 118, 121, 127, 132, 135, 139, 140, 149, 152, 154, 173, 179, 181, 182, 184, 187, 191, 193, 210, 221, 234, 235, 239, 243–245, 249, 251–256, 263, 269, 270, 275, 277, 279, 283, 287, 290, 292, 293, 296, 297, 299, 300, 301, 306, 309, 310, 314–317; self-will 72
wisdom, divine 5, 6, 10, 11, 13, 46, 50, 57, 58, 75, 97, 104, 107, 114, 118, 120, 142, 149, 162, 164, 165, 177, 181, 184, 186, 193, 199, 200, 203, 204, 207, 212, 219, 220, 228, 235, 244, 245, 248, 254, 259, 274, 283, 290, 291, 292, 312, 313, 315, 322
witches 24, 100, 127, 248, 341

Printed in Dunstable, United Kingdom